Praise for the previous edition:

'I whole-heartedly recommend this scholarly book. The authors provide a vibrant and enquiring overview of contemporary debates in developmental psychology, with inspirational coverage of such topics as the voice of the child and the families and communities in which children grow. The book is grounded in the authors' deep understanding of fundamental theories and their willingness to relate these to practice. This book will give generations of students the opportunity to reflect on the meaning of child development in a multi-ethnic, ever-changing social context.'

Helen Cowie, *Faculty of Health and Medical Sciences, University of Surrey, UK*

'The text is strikingly comprehensive – from historical approaches to post-modern interpretations, and with frequent citations from non-Western writing. Adept at linking various theoretical approaches, the authors include a very useful chapter on theoretical integration. A refreshing combination of theory and practice, the authors take a holistic approach, with theory serving as the underpinning for research, teaching and practice. Sophisticated and up-to-date – and highly recommended!'

John D. Hogan, *Department of Psychology, St. John's University, USA*

'I was pleased to hear that this book, one that I have used for a number of years in my graduate introductory child development course, has been updated and revised. The new edition accurately reflects advances in the integration and inseparability of heredity/environment, brain/behavior, and self/other. I am very much looking forward to using and learning more from it in the coming years.'

Richard Volpe, *Department of Applied Psychology & Human Development, University of Toronto, Canada*

'I enjoyed reading this book. Abstract and complex ideas are described in a clear and uncomplicated style, which makes it a very readable book that is detailed but not burdensome. I particularly liked the short stories, anecdotes, and poems, which clarified some of the more abstract ideas and issues. I wholeheartedly recommend this scholarly book to anyone who wants to have a comprehensive overview and critical discussion of the main theories that have been developed and an accurate picture of contemporary debates in child and adolescent psychology. As such, the book is a very good choice for a (graduate) introductory child development course.'

Freek Bucx, *The Netherlands Institute for Social Research, Journal of Family Theory & Review*

Child Development

Child Development: Theories and Critical Perspectives provides a perceptive and engaging overview of theories in child and adolescent psychology, uniquely combining traditional scientific perspectives with critical (postmodern) approaches. This new edition has been extensively revised to incorporate recent advances in the field, featuring a new chapter, 'Theorizing about children's digital worlds', that explores contemporary issues including social media, artificial intelligence, internet addiction and the banning of mobile phones in schools.

The authors skilfully place developmental theories within philosophical and cultural contexts, tracing historical developments across different schools of thought while exploring their interconnections and practical implications. Early chapters cover mainstream theorists such as Piaget, Skinner, Freud and Vygotsky. Other influential theorists include Maccoby and Thelen, and contemporary thinkers such as Overton and Stetsenko. Significant figures less well-known today, like Dewey and Rubinstein, are also introduced. The text also addresses broader frameworks including lifespan perspectives, systems theory, evolutionary theory, epigenetics, feminist approaches, children's voices and Indigenous theories. Current controversies such as 'decolonizing' developmental psychology and the role of universities in knowledge production are also discussed.

Written with students in mind, the book includes valuable pedagogical features such as recommended readings, discussion questions, activities and relevant websites. Essential reading for postgraduate students in developmental psychology, education, social work and social policy, its lucid style makes complex theoretical concepts accessible to readers at all levels, including those with limited background in psychology.

Rosalyn H. Shute, PhD, is an Adjunct Professor of Psychology in the Flinders University Institute for Mental Health and Wellbeing, College of Education, Psychology and Social Work, Flinders University, Adelaide, Australia. Her research expertise lies broadly in clinical child psychology and paediatric psychology/child health and wellbeing, and she is an experienced teacher of developmental psychology and clinical child/paediatric psychology.

Phillip T. Slee, PhD, is Emeritus Professor in Human Development in the Flinders University Institute for Mental Health and Wellbeing, College of Education, Psychology and Social Work at Flinders University, Adelaide, Australia. He is a trained teacher and registered psychologist. His main areas of interest include childhood bullying/aggression, conduct disorders, stress and teacher education, and he has a particular interest in the practical and policy implications of his research.

International Texts in Developmental Psychology

Series editor: Peter K. Smith, Goldsmiths College, University of London, UK.

This volume is one of a rapidly developing series in *International Texts in Developmental Psychology*, published by Routledge. The books in this series are selected to be state-of-the-art, high level introductions to major topic areas in developmental psychology. The series conceives of developmental psychology in broad terms and covers such areas as social development, cognitive development, developmental neuropsychology and neuroscience, language development, learning difficulties, developmental psychopathology and applied issues. Each volume is written by a specialist (or specialists), combining empirical data and a synthesis of recent global research to deliver cutting-edge science in a format accessible to students and researchers alike. The books may be used as textbooks that match on to upper level developmental psychology modules, but many will also have cross-disciplinary appeal.

Each volume in the series is published in hardback, paperback and eBook formats. More information about the series is available on the official website at: https://www.routledge.com/International-Texts-in-Developmental-Psychology/book-series/DEVP, including details of all the titles published to date.

Published Titles

Children's Literacy Development: A Cross-Cultural Perspective on Learning to Read and Write, 3rd edition
By Catherine McBride

Global Impacts on Childhood Social Development: Building Resilience Amid Conflict, Environmental Degradation, and Climate Change
By Charles N. Oberg and Hopewell R. Hodges

Child Development: Theories and Critical Perspectives, 3rd edition
By Rosalyn H. Shute and Phillip T. Slee

Child Development

Theories and Critical Perspectives

Third Edition

Rosalyn H. Shute and Phillip T. Slee

Routledge
Taylor & Francis Group
LONDON AND NEW YORK

Designed cover image: Getty Images @Alistair Berg

Third edition published 2026
by Routledge
4 Park Square, Milton Park, Abingdon, Oxon, OX14 4RN

and by Routledge
605 Third Avenue, New York, NY 10158

Routledge is an imprint of the Taylor & Francis Group, an informa business

First edition published by Hodder Education 2003
Second edition published by Routledge 2015

British Library Cataloguing-in-Publication Data
A catalogue record for this book is available from the British Library

ISBN: 9781032938080 (hbk)
ISBN: 9781032938011 (pbk)
ISBN: 9781003567738 (ebk)

DOI: 10.4324/9781003567738

Typeset in Times New Roman
by Newgen Publishing UK

Access the Support Material: https://resourcecentre.routledge.com/books/9781032938080

Contents

Figures, Tables and Boxes

Figures

Tables

Boxes

Preface

The world has changed a great deal since this book was first published in 2003, but opportunities still abound for child development theorizing, both to enhance understanding of the human condition and to guide efforts to promote children's healthy development. However, we also recognize voices that are strongly critical of developmental psychology and its negative impact on many children around the world. Right from the first edition, we felt that such critiques were important to include, as they were generally found in journal articles and specialist books but not in child development textbooks, which adopted a standard scientific perspective; this situation has hardly changed. This decision meant we were then confronted with the tensions characterizing scientific and critical debate concerning the nature and role of developmental theory. This, in turn, raised for us the significant question of whether one is able to articulate a middle ground for developmental theory. Is there a position that takes the best that modernism has to offer while also accommodating critical views? We are hopeful that, as the narrative of the third edition unfolds, readers will be challenged and encouraged to consider such issues in addition to the more familiar ones about nature–nurture and continuity–discontinuity in development.

As colonial statues topple, developmental psychology (often now called developmental science) must take a hard look at its history and the negative, as well as positive, outcomes that have emerged. Today, there is exciting progress in biological aspects, such as the role of epigenetics, tempered by concern that greater attention needs to be paid to ethics, and that psychology in general has become too 'biologized'. A literature largely based on narrowly focused mini-theories lies alongside a discernible movement towards theoretical integration that treats children holistically. Older theories sometimes gain fresh influence. There is greater, though not universal, acceptance of qualitative research; this can be crucial for understanding the perspectives of those growing up in a world that is now more appreciated as complex and culturally and gender-diverse, while backlashes against such diversity also emerge, creating challenging conditions for many children and those who care for them. However, many psychology students miss out on education about qualitative methods, or are even taught that they have no place in the field.

Our aim is to cast some light on all such matters, which means that it remains essential to apply philosophical, historical and cultural perspectives to child development theorizing. Other texts provide a detailed exposition of many of the classical theories of child development; while we certainly outline these, we focus in the main upon more recent critiques and trends, including issues of epistemology—theory of knowledge. The material in every chapter has been extensively updated. We have added a new chapter on theorizing about children's digital worlds, hoping to provoke new lines of thought in this important area that is expected to encompass more of the world's children over time. Overall, we aim to create an understanding of where the field of developmental child psychology has come from, and how different theories rise, decline and rub off on one another, using Stephen Pepper's 'worldviews' as a guiding framework. We give a little historical or personal background on many theorists to give a flavour of the times in which their ideas were developed. Hopefully, this book will help make better sense of where we stand at this particular point in history, when the multiplicity of theories and research approaches can be quite confusing.

Over the years, we have sought guidance from students, colleagues and reviewers about what they would like to see in a book like this. There seems to be agreement that there is no similar one. Primarily, students want to understand better how the theories fit together. They also feel that the university culture of critique leaves them with only a sense of 'what is wrong' with theories, and they also want to know 'what is right'. They like the illustrative boxes, so we have retained this feature. Aspects appreciated by colleagues and reviewers include the book's thorough yet concise nature, readability, anecdotes, use of metaphors and good coverage of women theorists. It is also valued as a handbook for lecturers. We continue to avoid an 'undergraduate' feel by placing aids to learning at the back of the book, while each chapter has its own reference list for ease of access.

We anticipate that most of our readers will be higher-level undergraduates, honours and postgraduate students of psychology, though the book also has much to interest those studying in related fields. Those on the cusp of making decisions about their careers are likely to be especially interested in the implications of their studies for policy and practice. These issues are certainly not neglected and, indeed, both authors have a keen background in applied issues. Phillip is a registered psychologist, trained history teacher, educator of teachers, and developer of internationally used peaceful schools programs. Rosalyn is the former head of a university psychology department and for many years taught developmental psychology, coordinated and taught on professional postgraduate psychology courses and provided paediatric psychology services to children and families.

We thank our Routledge editor Molly Selby and colleagues for inviting us to write this new edition, as well as the proposal reviewers, whose feedback was enormously helpful. We have incorporated many of their ideas, but not all, given the space constraints, and of course we take responsibility for those editorial decisions. We thank Routledge for allowing us some extra space in this edition, but make no claim to be comprehensive. Much important material and many influential names have been omitted (if yours is one, please forgive us!), and we can provide only a limited number of examples of empirical studies relevant for the various theories. We have tried, however, to select these (including some from our own work) to illustrate some important themes and trends in the developmental path of theorizing in the field, as well as creating a sense of connection between different theories. We also hope that our location in the Antipodes has helped to give a broader perspective than found in many texts; we have included numerous examples and viewpoints from Australasia and around the world.

We are grateful to the late Professor Peter Smith for his invitation to write the original text and for his helpful comments on drafts of the first two editions. Peter was quietly inspirational and always supportive, editing with a light touch. We are very sorry that we just missed out on being able to receive his input to this edition, but are glad to have known and worked with him. He leaves a lasting legacy of work relevant for the wellbeing of children and adolescents. We are also thankful to Wilhelmina Drummond for supplying her illustration of the Māori model of human development, Elen Shute for assistance with the original version of Figure 2.1 (now updated) and Ffion Shute for checking our summary of childhood in classical times.

Since the second edition Phillip and Elizabeth have welcomed a breath of fresh air into their lives in terms of grandchild Bonnie; their three (now somewhat older) boys—Matthew, Nicholas and Christopher—continue to provide a helpful distraction for Phillip from writing, with their own adventures into this wide world. Rosalyn continues her well-balanced retirement life, appreciating the loving support of Jason, Steffan, Elen, Bich Anh, Ffion and Trystan, with lively conversations often providing food for academic thought!

Rosalyn Shute and Phillip Slee
Adelaide, 8 July 2025

1 The nature of developmental psychology

Introduction

Some of our readers may be habitual 'preface-skippers', and if you are one, we encourage you to turn back to the Preface so that the rationale for this book and our general approach to this third edition are clear. We further set the context in this and the following chapter.

Founded in the 19th century, psychology is a relatively young discipline compared with, for example, philosophy and physiology (Stevens, 2020). From the outset, it wholeheartedly aligned itself with the natural sciences and embraced a positivist philosophy whereby objective knowledge is seen to be derived from logic, reasoning and science. The post-positivism that characterizes mainstream psychology today takes a slightly different perspective that recognizes researcher biases and that knowledge is not absolute, but it still aims for objectivity and favours theory-testing through quantitative research examining the relationships between variables.

Within psychology, the area concerned with how the individual grows and changes from conception until death is known as developmental psychology or (increasingly) developmental science, with child development being one special avenue of interest, or subdiscipline. We use the word 'child' generically to include all stages of development from conception through infancy, early, middle and late childhood, and adolescence, while acknowledging that not all cultures think about children in this way. We can further note the stage of 'emerging adulthood', first proposed by Jeffrey Arnett in 2000 as a response to changing social conditions in some countries, covering the distinct developmental challenges and opportunities for those aged 18–25 (Tanner and Arnett, 2016).

We have laid out some historical 'milestones' in developmental psychology in the Student Resources section, but it is in the body of the text that the underlying theoretical cross-fertilizations and debates are expounded. One ongoing challenge is to consider whether theoretical diversity or integration is the way of the future. Another is how to embrace a more critical outlook regarding the theories and assumptions underpinning the field. While research is often aimed at improving the lives of children (e.g. Sommer *et al.*, 2024), strong critique has come from Britain's Erica Burman, who contends that much developmental psychology has damaged

DOI: 10.4324/9781003567738-1

children around the world, and that '[any] general model tends to obscure the complexity of practices and contexts of development, and the structurally diverse character of the economic, cultural and interpersonal relationships that produce these varied developments' (Burman, 2012: 127). Burman and others, such as Indian writer Sunil Bhatia (2020), are, further, proponents of 'decolonizing' the field. We will return to these issues in due course.

Several broad questions are addressed in this text:

1. How do children change as they develop?
2. What factors influence the developmental changes?
3. What individual differences exist in development?
4. What is the nature of the relationship between children and their social milieux?
5. In considering a theory, what are its social justice implications?

We encourage readers to return to these questions as a way of reviewing the nature of the theories presented, as well as using the provided discussion questions, activities and websites.

The nature of developmental change

We can consider this in the light of certain questions raised over the decades. They are identifiable in various theories and provide a useful heuristic for understanding development.

- Heredity versus environment.
- Continuity versus discontinuity of development.
- Similarity versus uniqueness.
- Stability versus instability of attributes.
- Activity versus passivity of behaviour.
- Thinking versus feeling.
- An individual versus social focus.

Heredity versus environment

Everyday observations reveal similarities and dissimilarities between people, such as in their personality, mental capacity or emotional make-up. Are such characteristics innate or shaped by environmental forces after birth (or even before it)? The controversy engendered by this question has often been referred to as the nature–nurture (or nature–culture) debate. At various times, one or another view predominated (see Sameroff, 2010, for a historical overview). It is now widely accepted that heredity and environment must interact in order to produce behaviour. The issue is becoming less about how far each contributes to development, and more about how they combine. Research in epigenetics is especially relevant here. However, what has been called 'the interactionist consensus' has also been critiqued as often reducing development to biology (Stetsenko, 2019).

Furthermore, some theorists, such as Soviet psychologist Lev Vygotsky and the United States' Esther Thelen, maintained that nature and culture do not 'interact' but are inseparable.

Continuity versus discontinuity

The second important issue is whether development is gradual (continuous) or occurs in sudden leaps (discontinuous). The continuous viewpoint emphasizes slow methodical changes over time, like a tree growing steadily from a small seedling, with no sudden transformations or changes into another form. Some psychological theories and theory-informed practice, such as behaviourist theories and behaviour therapy, draw heavily upon the notion of continuity. An alternative viewpoint emphasizes discontinuity, the analogy here being a caterpillar changing into a butterfly. Theories such as those of Jean Piaget and Sigmund Freud emphasize a stage-like or discontinuous view of human development.

The use of the concept of stages differs between theories. Thus, in Erik Erikson's psychosocial theory it is broad, descriptive and evocative and does not 'refer clearly to anything definite or measurable in behavior' (Meadows, 1986: 19), whereas the use of the term in other psychological theories is more specific. In Piaget's theory, during the child's sensori-motor stage, for example, it is generally possible to clearly identify observable aspects of a child's thinking. A well-known instance is that a favourite toy hidden from a 6-month-old infant under a cloth will not elicit a search reaction, the child acting as though 'out of sight is out of mind'.

In order to enhance the descriptive and explanatory power of stage theories the following have been proposed as desirable to achieve:

- Specification of the behaviours subject to age changes that make up the stages (Meadows, 1986).
- Clear establishment of the relationship between structure and behaviour at any one stage (Kagan, Kearsley and Zelazo, 1978).
- A clearly explained relationship between the structure of one stage and the succeeding stage (Kagan *et al.*, 1978).
- Explanation of the factors contributing to the child's movement from one stage to the next (Meadows, 1986), such as through biological maturation or environmental input.

Similarity versus uniqueness

One view is that people are essentially similar despite superficial differences. Much developmental psychology concerns a search for general principles (the *nomothetic* approach). Swiss psychiatrist and psychologist Carl Jung (1923), however, was particularly interested in 'individuation' or the development of differences in people's preferred ways of attending to the world and making decisions. His thinking about psychological 'types' led to later work identifying the 'Big Five' personality traits. For example, German sixth-graders who are more conscientious, agreeable, extraverted, open and emotionally stable are more likely to later take an academically inclined secondary school path (Tetzner, Becker and Bihler, 2023). This exemplifies the *idiographic* approach.

Stability versus instability

Freud's psychoanalytic theory suggests that an individual's personality is largely shaped during the early years of childhood (Saracho, 2023). An alternative outlook is that an individual's characteristics are constantly changing, as in Erikson's (1963) theory. He proposed that a person continues to develop throughout the lifespan, being faced with certain normative crises (e.g. adolescent identity formation) that must be addressed before they can proceed to the next stage. For example, following the dismantling of apartheid in South Africa, norms changed so that Black youth became more confident of their cultural identity than did White adolescents (Thom and Coetzee, 2004).

Activity versus passivity

One view presents the individual as an agent: someone who takes responsibility for their behaviour; is understood as capable of acting for certain purposes or goals; attaches some freedom of choice to their acts; and may cite reasons for behaviour that are often guided by values (Battye and Slee, 1985). As the 20th century progressed, this view of child development gained influence (e.g. Bruner, 1986), the theorizing of Albert Bandura (e.g. 2006) being particularly noteworthy.

Alternatively, development can be considered as shaped by powerful forces that are largely beyond the individual's control. The person is thus seen as essentially a passive/reactive organism, a perspective promulgated by learning theory (Gauld and Shotter, 1977).

Thinking versus feeling

Writers such as Piaget emphasized the study of children's thinking while theorists such as Freud and Erikson focused on emotional (affective) development. More recent research, including longitudinal work, has shown that cognition and emotion are interdependent from infancy, and that one function of affect is to regulate cognitive processing (Bell, 2024; Storbeck and Clore, 2007).

Individual versus social focus

Some theories, such as learning theory and Piagetian theory, focus on the individual. Indeed, this approach largely characterizes the history of developmental psychology. Others, such as Vygotsky's sociocultural theory, Esther Thelen's dynamic systems theory, Urie Bronfenbrenner's ecological theory and feminist theories, embrace the social milieu as crucial for understanding how children develop.

A commentary on these controversies about developmental change

The either-or nature of these controversies suggests that one or the other represents the 'right' nature of development, that is discoverable, an idea long rejected by US developmental psychologist Willis Overton (1998: 113). Instead, he suggested, the focus may be best shifted away from 'which one' questions, to the nature of functioning of the opposing concepts and their relationship, as we noted with regard to the emotion/cognition association. Another example is that continuity and discontinuity may not be mutually exclusive, but depend on how fine-grained the analysis is. Overton and colleagues have further developed their thinking in favour of holistic approaches to understanding and studying development (Witherington *et al.*, 2018).

Despite their 'either-or' nature, the classical developmental theories do convey a 'sense of the richness and complexity of human beings, in contrast to the oversimplifications that are often evident in more narrowly empirical research' (Rose and Fischer, 1998: 123). A contrasting, critical, perspective decries the value of theory, which is 'taken [by postmodernists] to be a conceit of modernist knowledge seekers who imagine (and can only imagine) an epistemology of truth—of foundational, transhistorical knowledge' (Morawski, 2001: 436). We believe that both traditional and critical approaches can make valuable contributions to developmental psychology and later in the chapter we discuss further the nature and advantages of theories.

What is development?

This reasonable question is not so easy to answer. Broadly, human development is about the totality of changes that a person undergoes over time. 'Ontogeny', a more biological term, similarly encapsulates the developmental history of an individual organism, human or otherwise. Overton (2006) identified two broad types of developmental change:

1. *Transformational change* involves the emergence of novelty. An example is the single-celled zygote differentiating into ever more complex forms.
2. *Variational change* describes the individual differences that occur in development—e.g. the age by which a child walks in relation to the norm.

Overton saw these as reciprocal and complementary, arguing that 'transformational systems produce variation and variation transforms the system' (Overton, 2006: 28).

The (post-)positivist view has historically tended to see development as a linear unfolding of potential. This has been strongly challenged by those seeing development as often very non-linear and in a continual state of flux. For example, Mark Howe and Marc Lewis (2005: 248) suggested that 'ontogeny cannot be considered hard-wired in any sense, but rather emergent, unpredictable, and always coupled with environmental events'. Also relevant is Paul Baltes' (1987) lifespan approach, which views development as a change in adaptive capacity, which might mean loss as well as gain. A push to include the environment has also come from non-western perspectives, such as Cameroonian Bame Nsamenang's definition of developmental psychology as 'the science of human development in context' (1999: 163); this emerged from his African experience that development is about growing in social competence and learning to share responsibilities in the family and community. This throws a further spanner into the definitional works as it moves away from the typical western focus on 'the individual' as the subject of change; in addition, certain scholars have criticized developmental science's future-focus, to the neglect of the here-and-now.

The question (of what development is) is inextricably linked with two further questions: what is it that develops, and how? The 'what' can be considered relatively narrowly, such as Piaget's schemas, or more broadly, in terms of different facets of development. For example, attachment theorists focus on emotional development and ethologists on evolved innate behaviours, while for others cognitive development is central.

As for the 'how' of change, this is extensively considered in the following chapters. For example, Piaget focused on how the developing child constructs their own knowledge as a largely solitary activity, while Vygotsky theorized that children's cognitive abilities develop through interaction with others, although these theories may be best seen as complementary (Lourenço, 2012). Different theories suggest that different mechanisms are 'responsible' for certain outcomes, such as a child's level of cognitive development, but what exactly is meant by a 'mechanism'? Lauren Ross' (2022) philosophical view is that mechanisms, in whatever field of scientific study, are causal structures with the following features:

1. They consist of interacting lower-level parts that make up a higher-level whole.
2. They focus on fine-grained causal relationships between the parts.
3. They often adopt mechanical terminology such as one factor exerting a 'force' on another.

Deon Benton (2022) has considered the nature of mechanisms, in developmental science specifically. According to him, a mechanism:

1. is an active, dynamic multistage process;
2. has a beginning stage, intermediate stages and an end stage, each being necessary, and jointly sufficient to lead to the end stage;
3. is time-dependent, or unfolding;
4. has stages that behave regularly, i.e. are always the same under the same conditions;
5. has productive continuity, i.e. no gaps in the stages;
6. has stages that consist of entities (nouns) and activities (verbs), with activities happening to entities, as when an infant *tracks* (verb) a *moving target* (noun);
7. causes changes in the developing organism from greater simplicity to greater complexity, that are long-lasting.

While mechanisms may be discussed within a variety of developmental theoretical frameworks, some theories are particularly identified as 'mechanistic', and we will say more about this in Chapter 4. Psychology's concern with mechanisms reflects the discipline's focus on causative explanations, although whether these 'exist in nature' or are ways of categorizing our perceptions is a matter of philosophical debate (Teo, 2018). In Thomas Teo's opinion, the focus on causality has reduced psychology simplistically to the study of variables and their interrelationships, excluding the historical, cultural, political and economic realities underpinning matters of social concern and social justice. David Witherington *et al.* (2018) see developmental psychology's focus on mechanisms as drawing on an outdated reductionist worldview, with recent thinking moving towards a concern with holism and multiple forms of explanation.

Lifespan development

Our subject matter of the early years is where the major focus of developmental psychology lay for many years. Freudian theory, for example, in emphasizing the significance of the first years as formative, implies that changes in adults are of little relevance to developmental psychology, being largely cultural and lacking the age-linked and universal qualities that often characterize developmental theories.

By contrast, others such as Erikson emphasized that human development continues across the life-cycle. Simplistically, lifespan development is 'the study of the development of living organisms from conception to the end of life' (Overton, 2010: 4) but, as Overton further noted, a more in-depth examination highlights the underpinning complexities. Typically, lifespan theories consider age-related areas of study (e.g. infancy) in the context of various dimensions (e.g. biological and cognitive) against the background of the various systems within which the individual develops, such as family and school.

Such systemic views characterize development in a number of important ways (Shanahan, Sulloway and Hofer, 2000). First, they emphasize lasting malleability, and there is now evidence that the underlying mechanisms vary between individuals and across the lifespan (Voss *et al.*, 2017). Second, in adopting a more contextual 'life-history' view of development, account can be taken of secular trends such as changes in the onset of puberty, the health status of children and extended periods of education. Third, the greater appreciation of individual differences afforded by complex systems approaches has restricted the degree to which developmental psychology is looking for generalizability.

Benton's (2022) point that developmental mechanisms move towards complexity differs from Baltes' (1987) view that development may sometimes entail loss. For Benton, for example, memory loss after a head injury is regression, not development. It seems reasonable, though, to suggest that rehabilitation constitutes development, as it is a move towards greater complexity. It is also adaptation, in Baltes' sense, when a person has to learn new ways of managing after a loss, such as learning sign language after loss of hearing.

A lifespan perspective, coupled with longitudinal research, paved the way for development to be increasingly understood in terms of cascades and trajectories (or pathways). Ross (2022) describes cascades as causal explanations that are distinguishable from her definition of mechanisms, by virtue of having a trigger and a high likelihood of progression from the trigger to a particular end point. The third feature is sequential amplification—you may remember the R_0 ('R nought') reproduction number that we became familiar with when epidemiologists first explained mathematically how contagious COVID-19 was. Commonly, in developmental science there is no identified trigger moment; rather, a cascade is broadly seen as a process of building on prior states, involving multiple interacting mechanisms, and with any identified milestone being just one specific point in the course of ongoing development. In discussing this, Laura Guo and colleagues (2023) give the example of a 'babbling cascade' in which a baby's hearing of its own babbles, in concert with imitation and feedback from adults, prompts language development. They also note the sequential amplification that Ross identifies as a core feature of cascades, such that small differences in language acquisition in infancy result in large differences in later academic achievement.

Individual variations in genetic and environmental factors contributing to cascades put children on different trajectories of development. For example, the use of violent behaviour over time follows several different patterns in terms of the age when it begins and whether it increases, is stable, or declines; repeated adverse childhood experiences (ACEs) act cumulatively to increase the risk of violent behaviour in youth (Salo, Appleton and Tracy, 2021). Cascades have strong implications for the value of early intervention (Masten and Cicchetti, 2010).

A lifespan approach is also highlighted in considering the stage of emerging adulthood, when certain 'marker' events (such as finding a life partner and first employment) are likely to occur, that are related to identity and are more firmly imprinted in memory than earlier and later events (Tanner and Arnett, 2016). A further recent extension of the lifespan perspective is the concept of two-generation approaches to childhood development (Sommer *et al.*, 2024). This recognizes that children's development is intimately linked with that of their parents, and aims to focus on synergies in service provision that promote healthy development in both caregivers and children.

Why study child development?

A dominant theme, as verified by an examination of the contents pages of relevant journals, is that of raising children. This ongoing concern arose from the writings of 17th- and 18th-century philosophers such as John Locke and Jean-Jacques Rousseau, and religious writers such as John Wesley.

Through the study of children we may also come to understand adult behaviour better. As John Milton commented in *Paradise Lost*: 'The childhood shows the man as morning shows the day.' Gabriel Compayré, a 19th-century French educationalist, similarly suggested that '[i]f childhood is the cradle of humanity, the study of childhood is the cradle and necessary introduction to all future psychology' (Compayré, 1896: 3).

From a somewhat different perspective, Charles Darwin believed that the child was the link between animal and human species. The birth of his son (nicknamed 'Doddy') prompted Darwin to begin a diary description of Doddy's development—a 'baby biography', on which he published a paper in the journal *Mind* 37 years later (see Chapter 3). By observing the development of the infant, Darwin believed some understanding could be reached of the species itself. For example, in *The Expression of the Emotions in Man and Animals*, Darwin argued that emotional expression was basically a physiological matter and that expressive gestures were largely universal and innate:

> Everyone who has had much to do with young children must have seen how naturally they take to biting when in a passion. It seems instinctive in them as in young crocodiles, who snap their little jaws as soon as they emerge from the egg.
>
> *(Darwin, 1872/1965: 241–2)*

Gene Medinnus (1976) identified four main reasons for studying children:

1. An intellectual curiosity concerning natural phenomena.
2. The need to gain information to guide children's behaviour.
3. To increase our ability to predict behaviour.
4. The need to understand our own (adult) behaviour.

The last three points have an underlying political motivation: to guide children towards becoming good adult citizens without costly behavioural problems, and with the happiness of the citizenry a relatively recent concern (Sameroff, 2010). Missing from the list is any suggestion that research might be aimed at promoting children's wellbeing. A more critical view of the research enterprise might also add that we need to bear in mind factors such as adult agendas, social structures, power differences, and children's right to have their voices heard and respected. In addition, we must question how representative of the world's children are the studies that we typically read in developmental journals (see Box 1.1). Julie Robinson (2024) has summarized the challenges facing scholars from low- and middle-income countries, such as western-thinking editors and reviewers, and limitations in training opportunities, funding and internet access.

BOX 1.1 ARE CHILD DEVELOPMENT JOURNALS BIASED AGAINST RESEARCH FROM THE MAJORITY WORLD?

Researchers working in 'Majority World' countries (also known as the 'Global South' or low- and middle-income countries) have written about their experiences of attempting to publish in high-impact child development journals. We quote part of their description below, beginning with their opening example of an editor's response:

> 'While your research is important and the South African context interesting, I do not see [journal name] as an ideal fit for this paper. I would suggest looking to a journal focused exclusively on international research.' … The repeated implication in the reasons we are given for rejection … is the results would not be generalizable. Yet this rationale does not seem to impede publication of studies with samples from Minority countries, despite their under-representation of the global child population. This was not an isolated incident; co-authors on this paper working in Colombia, Brazil, and Greece have received similar responses from journals and are often directed to local journals to publish. Indeed, in a moment of uncommon transparency in relation to this issue with non-generalizability of findings, one editor went so far as to tell one co-author from Colombia that 'It would be a mistake for other countries to use this study as a model.' It is hard to imagine researchers conducting work in the United States, United Kingdom, Canada, Australia, or Western Europe being told that their work is not a good fit for reasons of geography. Co-authors on this paper who publish using data from Majority and Minority countries note a distinct difference in the nature, number, and receptiveness of comments received from (or prior to) review.
>
> *(Draper et al., 2023: 2)*

What is a theory?

We finish this chapter by considering the nature of theories and how they might be evaluated. In current popular discourse, we often hear the word 'theory' used disparagingly, as in 'that's only a theory', thereby suggesting that it has no necessary relationship to facts. As defined by *The Cambridge Dictionary*, a fact is 'something that is known to have happened or to exist, especially something for which proof exists, or about which there is information'. Research into child development is uncovering facts at a rate that sometimes outstrips our ability to integrate them into a coherent framework. Facts are very important as building blocks of science. However, just as a pile of bricks does not make a house, a collection of facts does not make a science: 'A theory may be considered as a way of binding together a multitude of facts so that one may comprehend them all at once' (Kelly, 1963: 18). But to backtrack a little …

The word 'theory' has its origins in the Greek *theoria*—contemplation, spectacle, mental conception. US academic Jerry Harvey (in Williams, 1976) related theory to 'fantasy', suggesting that it is quite inferior to practice. As noted by Jill

Morawski (2001), though, any understanding of the concept should look to embed it in historical context. In relation to psychology, theory has held a rather uneasy place. From a logical-positivist perspective, 'a judiciously crafted theory, sparse and logically pristine, could be submitted to hypothetico-deductive method; that is, it could yield tidy hypotheses for laboratory testing', although theory unrestrained has frequently resulted in 'profligate claims about human nature' (Morawski, 2001: 434–5). Paul Meehl observed that psychological theories are less prone to becoming either well-accepted or else rejected, in comparison with the natural sciences:

> There is a period of enthusiasm about a new theory, a period of attempted application to several fact domains, a period of disillusionment as the negative data come in, a growing bafflement about inconsistent and unreplicable empirical results, multiple resort to ad hoc excuses, and then finally people just sort of lose interest in the thing and pursue other endeavors.
>
> *(Meehl, 1978, cited in Sanbonmatsu, Neufeld and Posavac, 2025: 2)*

Moreover, theory has existed uncomfortably alongside practice. Theory was distinguished from practice by the philosopher Francis Bacon (1626, cited in Marias, 1967), while 'praxis' is practice informed by theory (Williams, 1976: 268), as discussed in detail in our final chapter.

'Metatheory' is a concept that has increasingly been referenced in the child development literature to apply to broad groupings of theories with similar core assumptions (for example, theories that draw on systems thinking). Other terms used for much the same idea include theoretical 'approaches', 'traditions' or 'orientations'; they are often 'isms', as in organicism and behaviourism, and are sometimes underpinned by metaphors. Metatheories are similar to 'paradigms'. More specific theories, sometimes called mini-theories or micro-theories, can be located within broader metatheoretical frameworks, and it is from these that specific, testable propositions can be derived.

This approach is based upon the philosophy of science articulated by Hungarian Imre Lakatos (Ketelaar and Ellis, 2000), which provides a broad framework for making decisions about whether to accept or reject a theory. The post-positivist view that science proceeds by falsification of hypotheses (Popper, 1959) remains well-accepted in psychological research. However, Lakatos proposed that falsification should not be used to reject a theory, only to reject specific statements derived from the theory. For Lakatos, a metatheoretical core is surrounded by a 'protective belt' of middle-level theories and auxiliary hypotheses that give rise to specific, testable statements. In this way, competing statements derived from the same basic metatheory may be tested. Rather than experimental results leading to all-or-none acceptance or rejection of the basic metatheory, they contribute to evaluation of the performance of the protective belt—to a decision about whether the 'research program' in general is progressive or degenerative. The Lakatosian approach would perhaps stave off a tendency to become disillusioned with theories in the way that Meehl observed.

An area where the theory–metatheory distinction has been sharply drawn is in certain feminist critiques of evolutionary psychologists, with some of the latter accused of confusing 'research theories' with higher-level metatheories in a way that muddles conceptual discussions about the conclusions to be drawn from research evidence. Another area where the distinction arises is in considering diversity versus integration in developmental theorizing, a matter on which we expand in Chapter 15.

Various other writers have suggested criteria for evaluating developmental theories, but we can identify little consensus. We suggest that readers might apply a number of criteria concerning change, based on the key points raised earlier in this chapter.

- How well do the theories explain how children change as they develop? What empirical support is provided for their explanations?
- How do the theories account for the various factors, such as culture, that influence developmental change?
- How well do the theories account for individual differences in children's development?
- Is the explanation parsimonious?
- What are the social justice implications of the theory?

Michael Green and John Piel (2009) discussed the dilemma facing practitioners in deciding whether to be an eclectic or a purist in selecting theoretical frameworks for applied purposes. The advantages of eclecticism include the ability to match theory selection to human needs, permitting individualization, and avoiding distortion by forcing people to fit a certain theory. Purists, on the other hand, point out the logical inconsistencies between different theories, particularly with regard to the nature of the newborn, the role of the environment, the organism–environment relationship and the location of the change mechanism. These writers felt unable to determine the best approach but, overall, believed that the purists have the stronger arguments.

Conclusion

The relatively short history of developmental psychology has been characterized by several either-or controversies that we will meet in discussing the various theories that have been devised. Distinguishing between a theory and its underlying metatheoretical (philosophical) assumptions is crucial, an issue we will pursue further in due course. The traditional post-positivist approach that still largely characterizes the field has been subject to critical analysis, and theorizing itself has not escaped criticism. However, theories and metatheories help to bring coherence and meaning to otherwise disparate 'facts'. An optimistic view is that, if critiques of developmental science are acted upon, 'the future of our field can be a producer and a product of a more humane and just world' (Lerner, 2015: 172).

References

Baltes, P. B. 1987. Theoretical propositions of life-span developmental psychology: on the dynamics between growth and decline. *Developmental Psychology 23*(5): 611–26. https://psycnet.apa.org/record/1988-01055-001

Bandura, A. 2006. Toward a psychology of human agency. *Perspectives on Psychological Science 1*(2): 164–80. https://doi.org/10.1111/j.1745-6916.2006.00011.x

Battye, P. and Slee, P. T. 1985. The demise of the person in social work. *Australian Social Work 38*: 23–9. www.tandfonline.com/doi/abs/10.1080/03124078508549892

Bell, M. A. (ed.). 2024. *Child development at the intersection of emotion and cognition*. Washington, DC: American Psychological Association.

Benton, D. T. 2022. The elusive 'Developmental Mechanism': what they are and how to study and test them. Developmental Review 65: 101034. www.sciencedirect.com/science/article/abs/pii/S0273229722000247

Bhatia, S. 2020. Decolonization and coloniality in human development: neoliberalism, globalization and narratives of Indian youth. Human Development 64(4–6): 207–21. https://doi.org/10.1159/000513084

Bruner, J. 1986. *Actual minds, possible worlds*. Cambridge, MA: Harvard University Press.

Burman, E. 2012. Un/thinking children in development: a contribution from northern antidevelopmental psychology. *Psychology: The Journal of the Hellenic Psychological Society 19*(2): 125–43. https://doi.org/10.12681/psy_hps.23612

Compayré, G. (Trans.). 1896. *The intellectual and moral development of the child*. New York: Appleton.

Darwin, C. 1872/1965. *The expression of the emotions in man and animals*. Chicago: University of Chicago Press.

Draper, C. E., Barnett, L. M., Cook, C. J., Cuartas, J. A., Howard, S. J., McCoy, D. *et al.* 2023. Publishing child development research from around the world: an unfair playing field resulting in most of the world's child population under-represented in research. *Infant and Child Development 32*: e2375. https://doi.org/10.1002/icd.2375

Erikson, E. H. 1963. *Childhood and society*. Harmondsworth: Penguin.

Gauld, A. and Shotter, J. 1977. *Human action and its psychological investigation*. London: Routledge and Kegan Paul.

Green, M. G. and Piel, J. A. 2009. *Theories of human development: a comparative approach*. Abingdon: Routledge.

Guo, L. X., Pace, A., Masek, L. R., Golinkoff, R. M. and Hirsh-Pasek, K. 2023. Cascades in language acquisition: re-thinking the linear model of development. *Advances in Child Development and Behavior 64*: 70–95. https://doi.org/10.1016/bs.acdb.2022.11.004

Howe, M. L. and Lewis, M. D. 2005. The importance of dynamic systems approaches for understanding development. *Developmental Review 25*: 247–51. https://doi.org/10.1016/j.dr.2005.09.002

Jung, C. G. 1923. *Psychological types*. London: Routledge Kegan Paul.

Kagan, J., Kearsley, R. B. and Zelazo, P. R. 1978. *Infancy: its place in human development*. Cambridge, MA: Harvard University Press.

Kelly, G. A. 1963. *A theory of personality*. New York: Norton.

Ketelaar, T. and Ellis, B. J. 2000. Are evolutionary explanations unfalsifiable? Evolutionary psychology and the Lakatosian philosophy of science. *Psychological Inquiry 11*: 1–21. https://psycnet.apa.org/doi/10.1207/S15327965PLI1101_01

Lerner, R. M. 2015. Promoting positive human development and social justice: integrating theory, research and application in contemporary developmental science. *International Journal of Psychology 50*(3): 165–73. https://doi.org/10.1002/ijop.12162

Lourenço, O. 2012. Piaget and Vygotsky: many resemblances, and a crucial difference. *New Ideas in Psychology 30*: 281–95. https://psycnet.apa.org/doi/10.1016/j.newideapsych.2011.12.006

Marias, J. 1967. *History of philosophy*. New York: Dover Publications.

Masten, A. S. and Cicchetti, D. 2010. Developmental cascades. *Development and Psychopathology 22*: 491–5. https://doi.org/10.1017/S0954579410000222

Meadows, S. 1986. *Understanding child development*. London: Hutchinson.

Medinnus, G. R. 1976. *Child study and observation guide*. New York: Wiley.

Morawski, J. G. 2001. Gifts bestowed, gifts withheld: assessing psychological theory with a Kochian attitude. *American Psychologist 5*: 433–40. https://psycnet.apa.org/doi/10.1037/0003-066X.56.5.433

Nsamenang, B. 1999. Eurocentric image of childhood in the context of the world's cultures. *Human Development 42*(3): 159–68. https://doi.org/10.1159/000022622

Overton, W. F. 1998. Developmental psychology: philosophy, concepts, and methodology. In W. Damon and R. M. Lerner (eds), *Handbook of child psychology: theoretical models of human development*. Fifth edn. Vol. 1. New York: Wiley, 107–89.

Overton, W. F. 2006. Developmental psychology: philosophy, concepts and methodology. In R. M. Lerner (ed.), *Handbook of child psychology: theoretical models of human development*. Sixth edn. Vol. 1. New York: Wiley, 18–88.

Overton, W. F. 2010. Life-span development: concepts and issues. In W. F. Overton and R. M. Lerner (eds), *Handbook of life-span development: cognition, biology, and methods across the lifespan*. Vol. 1. Hoboken, NJ: Wiley, 1–29.

Popper, K. 1959. *The logic of scientific discovery*. Abingdon: Routledge.

Robinson, J. A. 2024. Editorial: research priorities concerning formal and informal learning in low- and middle-income countries. *Frontiers in Psychology 15*: 1391089. https://doi.org/10.3389/fpsyg.2024.1391089

Rose, S. P. and Fischer, K. W. 1998. Models and rulers in dynamical development. *British Journal of Developmental Psychology 16*: 123–31. https://doi.org/10.1111/j.2044-835X.1998.tb00752.x

Ross, L. N. 2022. Cascade versus mechanism: the diversity of causal structure in science. *British Journal for the Philosophy of Science*. www.journals.uchicago.edu/doi/10.1086/723623

Salo, M., Appleton, A. A. and Tracy, M. 2021. Childhood adversity trajectories and violent behaviors in adolescence and early adulthood. *Journal of Interpersonal Violence 37*(15–16): NP13978–NP14007. https://doi.org/10.1177/08862605211006366

Sameroff, A. 2010. A unified theory of development: a dialectic integration of nature and nurture. *Child Development 81*: 6–22. https://psycnet.apa.org/doi/10.1111/j.1467-8624.2009.01378.x

Sanbonmatsu, D. M., Neufeld, B. and Posavac, S. S. 2025. There is no theory crisis in psychological science. *Journal of Theoretical and Philosophical Psychology*. Advance online publication. https://dx.doi.org/10.1037/teo0000301

Saracho, O. N. 2023. Theories of child development and their impact on early childhood education and care. *Early Childhood and Education Journal S1*: 15–30. https://doi.org/10.1007/s10643-021-01271-5

Shanahan, M. J., Sulloway, F. and Hofer, S. M. 2000. Change and constancy in developmental contexts. *International Journal of Behavioral Development 24*: 421–7. https://psycnet.apa.org/doi/10.1080/016502500750037964

Sommer, T. E., Franchett, E., Yoshikawa, H. and Lombardi, J. 2024. A global call for two-generation approaches to child development and caregivers' livelihoods. *Child Development Perspectives 18*(4): 204–14. https://doi.org/10.1111/cdep.12516

Stetsenko, A. 2019. Cultural-historical activity theory meets developmental systems perspective: transformative activist stance and natureculture. In A. Edwards, M. Fleer and L. Bøttcher (eds), *Cultural-historical approaches to studying learning and development*. Singapore: Springer, 249–62. https://doi.org/10.1007/978-981-13-6826-4_16

Stevens, L. (ed.). 2020. *Introduction to psychology and neuroscience*. Halifax, NS: Dalhousie University. Creative Commons Attribution 4.0 International License. https://caul-cbua.pressbooks.pub/intropsychneuro/

Storbeck, J. and Clore, G. L. 2007. On the interdependence of cognition and emotion. *Cognition and Emotion 21*(6): 1212–37. https://doi.org/10.1080/02699930701438020

Tanner, J. L. and Arnett, J. J. 2016. The emergence of emerging adulthood. In A. Furlong (ed.), *Routledge handbook of youth and young adulthood*. Second edn. London: Taylor & Francis.

Teo, T. 2018. The consequences of 'positivism' in psychology. In T. Teo, *Outline of theoretical psychology*. London: Palgrave Macmillan, 103–32.

Tetzner, J., Becker, M. and Bihler, L.-M. 2023. Personality development in adolescence: examining big five trait trajectories in differential learning environments. *European Journal of Personality 37*(6): 744–64. https://doi.org/10.1177/08902070221121178

Thom, D. P. and Coetzee, C. H. 2004. Identity development of South African adolescents in a democratic society. *Society in Transition 35*: 183–93. https://doi.org/10.1080/21528586.2004.10419113

Voss, P., Thomas, M. E., Cisneros-Franco, J. M. and de Villers-Sidani, E. 2017. Dynamic brains and the changing rules of neuroplasticity: implications for learning and recovery. Frontiers in Psychology 8. https://doi.org/10.3389/fpsyg.2017.01657

Williams, R. 1976. *Keywords: a vocabulary of culture and society*. New York: Oxford University Press.

Witherington, D., Overton, W. F., Lickliter, R., Marshall, P. J. and Narvaez, D. 2018. Metatheory and the primacy of conceptual analysis in developmental science. *Human Development 61*: 181–98. https://doi.org/10.1159/000490160

2 Ways of knowing about children

Introduction

We devote this chapter to discussing some ways of knowing about children: knowing them from various philosophical and theoretical perspectives, knowing them in a cultural sense and knowing them as beings within historical contexts. We consider these three factors in turn, while also recognizing that they are intertwined. For example, the life stage of 'emerging adulthood' is explicitly related to recent cultural change in some societies, with extended periods of formal education, expanding career opportunities for women and greater acceptance of premarital sex (Tanner and Arnett, 2016). The chapter aligns with Patricia Miller's view that theorists 'are products of their culture, and thus hold implicit beliefs and assumptions that lead them towards particular questions, explanations, hypotheses, and interpretations of data' (Miller, 2022: 3). The role of theorists in the construction of knowledge is illustrated by cross-cultural researchers Pierre Dasen and Alastair Heron's comment that the stages of children's development in the Ivory Coast and France were identical, but varied in cultural content: 'Depending on our theoretical orientations, we may be struck by the similarities or the differences!' (cited in Harkness and Super, 2020: 104).

History

Sumerian civilization—dating from the 4th millennium BCE and regarded as foundational for western societies—valued education and established schools; boys and girls could aspire to be doctors, judges, businesspeople or priests. When Babylonian and Assyrian cultures became predominant, women progressively lost rights and girls were only prepared for domesticity or the priesthood; an Assyrian girl challenging male authority could be killed, and females became legally almost invisible (Isselhardt, 2001). Ancient Athens stressed educating boys into the laws and cultural mores of the time; girls' education was generally domestic, weaving being an important skill (Woida, 2024). Everything old is new again: in the 21st century, girls in various parts of the world are missing out on education because of violence, abductions or, in Afghanistan, outright bans beyond primary school (United Nations, 2023).

DOI: 10.4324/9781003567738-2

In Roman times, the father (*pater familias*) had autocratic rule over the extended family and was responsible for educating children; the law also required him to ensure that obviously 'deformed' infants were put to death (Jolowicz, 1952). For centuries children were regarded as property, particularly of their fathers, with paternalism and patriarchy significant elements in parent–child relationships. The Greek philosopher Aristotle considered human beings as 'ethically equal', but 'the justice of a master or a father is a different thing from that of a citizen, for a son or slave is property, and there can be no injustice to one's own property' (Russell, 1974: 186).

Further insight comes from later European philosophers such as Thomas Hobbes, John Locke, Jean-Jacques Rousseau and John Stuart Mill. Hobbes, writing in the 17th century, argued that children were cared for solely because they were capable of serving their father and should be assigned a position of complete dependence. 'Like the imbecile, the crazed and the beasts over … children … there is no law' (Hobbes, 1931: 257). The implication is that children have no natural rights and no rights by social contract, because they lack the ability to make formal contracts or to understand their consequences.

Locke considered children as under their parents' jurisdiction until they were capable of fending for themselves. Until then, children were thought to lack understanding and therefore were unable to assert their will (Russell, 1974). Unlike Hobbes, Locke believed that both adults and children possessed certain natural rights, which needed protection. Parental benevolence was believed sufficient to ensure that children's rights were protected. Locke's outlook replaced the proprietary aspect of parenthood with the concept of children as God's property: until they developed adult capacities for reasoning and understanding, parents were under a God-given obligation to care for them. By implication, where parents failed to fulfil this obligation, the state would be empowered to do so. Laws elaborated between 1300 CE and 1800 CE prescribed the relationship between parent and child in terms of trust (Fraser, 1976). The parent's rights came from the state, which reserved the right to intervene and protect children's rights and interests. However, while the court would protect children's interests, it could not present their grievances and had no guarantee of independent representation.

Education of children began to play a stronger role. In Europe, influenced by Swiss philosopher Rousseau (1712–1778), the second half of the 18th century saw the establishment of community schools. Frederick the Great introduced compulsory learning in Prussia as early as 1763 (Koops, 2015).

In 19th-century England, Mill wrote of liberty and the importance of educating the working class; eclipsing the earlier philosophical work of Mary Wollstonecraft, he was among the first to promote equal status for men and women. However, he did not extend liberty to 'barbarians' or children. Sharon Stanley (2017) believes his views on children have been little analysed, and suggests that his outlook was based on drawing an untenable line between childhood dependence and autonomy in adulthood.

The late 18th and 19th centuries in Europe were also witness to the dramatic social and economic changes wrought by the Industrial Revolution. Children, in large part, fared very poorly. Schorsch (1979) noted that children as young as 4 worked in the cotton mills of England, while:

> [a] child over seven worked from sunrise to sunset six days a week with two and a half days off a year; children between six and sixteen earned slightly more than half a woman's wages and only a fourth of a man's.
>
> *(Schorsch, 1979: 143)*

The 19th-century French writer Emile Zola, in his novel *Germinal* (1885/1979) depicts 12-year-old children working alongside their fathers and older siblings in the mineshafts of France. Eventually, child labour laws were enacted, first in Britain in 1833, to protect children from the excesses and exploitation of the Industrial Revolution. The nature of childhood as viewed by western society was beginning to change. Increasing emphasis was given to education and distinguishing young children's special needs. It was not until the final quarter of the 20th century that mandatory reporting of child abuse came into effect in various countries, along with changing societal attitudes (Bross and Mathews, 2013).

In 1960 (translated into English in 1962), French historian Philippe Ariès argued that childhood, as by then understood in western society, was a relatively recent phenomenon. Anita Schorsch too observed that 'thinkers of the 16th century, and of the preceding centuries as well, agreed that the child is nothing more than a lower animal—"the infant mewling and puking in the nurse's arms" as Shakespeare put it baldly but succinctly' (Schorsch, 1979: 11). On this view, in medieval Europe the prevailing image was of the child as chattel or piece of property of the parent and state, with early death so likely that parents emotionally distanced themselves. Seen thus, the child did not count for much in the eyes of society, as a 16th-century rhyme indicates:

> Of all the months the first behold,
> January two-faced and cold
> Because its eyes two ways are cast
> To face the future and the past.
> Thus the child six summers old
> Is not worth much when all is told.
>
> *(Schorsch, 1979: 23)*

Although, importantly, Ariès pioneered studies on the history of childhood and highlighted cultural changes in such understanding, his perspective on medieval childhood became regarded as too extreme, or plain wrong. Nicholas Orme concluded that medieval parents, just like those of ancient times and today, loved their children and grieved for their loss (Orme, 2001). Also contrasting with Ariès' view is the idea that, at various times throughout European history, the infant has been revered as an embodiment of New Testament depictions of 'sinlessness', as illustrated by the representations of infants and young children by Renaissance painters.

Taking a critical perspective, Erica Burman (2018) observes that the shift from 'the working child' to 'the schooled child' delegitimated the socio-political knowledge of young workers. She says this continues in the case of street-connected children, a term recognized by the United Nations for children who live (or survive) on the streets.

In western societies today, social systems such as education and justice are based on understanding of children's abilities at different ages, to which developmental psychology contributes. Laura Tisdall criticizes the field and other 'psy' disciplines for promoting such use of chronological age; she sees it as an unrecognized form of ageism, originating from 18th-century Anglo-American concepts of personhood that position children as dependent, irrational non-persons (Tisdall, 2022). She points out that in certain African societies relative seniority, not chronological age, was historically central to social relations, although colonized youth sometimes adopted western norms in order to challenge gerontocracies.

Jieyu Liu (2022) has examined how the experience of childhood changed across three generations in 20th-century China. While the value of children as 'family helpers' reduced strongly, western models of the 'modernization' of childhood in China, seen as moving towards 'individualization', did not hold up. Rather, the third (only-child) generation experienced greater parental regimentation under the influence of neoliberalism. Furthermore, the value of girls increased as a result of the one-child policy.

Japan is another culture where a historical perspective has been found valuable. For example, in the late 17th century Confucian moral teachings were used to advise parents, but this later expanded to include advice on childcare, health and education, at a time when the rulers were making an effort to produce 'an obedient and productive working class' (Kojima, 1996: 377).

Australian Indigenous history has largely been ignored (or denied) by official accounts (Collard, 2000; Marr, 2023). Participants in the *Footprints in Time* longitudinal study of the development of Australian Indigenous children say that an important reason for remaining involved is to be able to write their own history (Thurber *et al.*, 2018).

Overall, we can see that the status of children, attitudes towards children, and the value society attaches to children are best understood in historical context. Today, children are considered to have rights, with the International Convention on the Rights of the Child adopted by the United Nations in 1989 and ratified by all countries except the United States. Burman (1996) pointed out the tension between the cultural imperialism promoted by the globalization of rights, and localized cultural understandings. A philosophical view of children that she has discussed more recently is 'childism'; this invites adults to attend to children's subjectivities and reconsider child–adult relations and what adults can learn from children, as exemplified by young climate activists (Burman, 2023). She contrasts this with 'child as method', an anti-psychological version of child scholarship which is not about children's subjectivities, but re-situates the child in the geopolitical world and uses the notion of childhood to address other agendas.

Culture

William Kessen (1979) regarded children and child psychology as 'cultural inventions', highlighting that we cannot easily separate the influence of culture from any discussion of the nature of children and families. For example, Marilyn Fleer investigated Australian Aboriginal conceptions of 'family', noting that '[t]he child is not an individual unit, but rather a part of a tightly woven family system that is bound together by a real sense of obligation' whereby many different family and community members have responsibility for 'looking out for each other' (Fleer, 2004: 60–1).

In the mid-19th-century United States the cultural construction of the child was embodied in child actors and actresses and reflected in their role in national theatre, which 'became a marketplace for national esteem, and child actresses became marketable signifiers of what the country needed to escape or deny' (Mullineaux, 2012: 284). A Chinese example is the portrayal of the 20th-century child in literature as a sign of national hope and prosperity and (commodity-like) as a bearer of national and political messages (Jones, 2011). The popular press of the time proclaimed the talents of the child actors as markers of 'national integrity, sophistication and spirit' (Jones, 2011: 283).

In the mid-20th-century United States, anthropologist Margaret Mead promoted an appreciation of the role played by culture in development. In her book *Culture and Commitment* (1970) she called upon knowledge she had gleaned from studying children in Manus, Bali and New Guinea, following their lives into adulthood. The influence of culture on children's development became a thriving area of interdisciplinary research in the last decades of the 20th century, with collaborations between cross-cultural psychologists and anthropologists challenging 'context-free' studies of child development.

According to Sara Harkness and Charles Super (2020) interest waned in the wake of postmodern critique that researchers cannot escape their own cultural frame of reference. Analysis of articles in the *Journal of Cross-Cultural Psychology* in 2010 showed that, over 40 years, the subject matter had shifted away from child development towards social psychology and personality (Cretchley, Rooney and Gallois, 2010). However, various versions of 'cultural' theory, inspired by Lev Vygotsky, became more prominent, seeing culture not as 'influencing' development, but as an inseparable constituent of it.

The mix of the population should be considered when examining the effects of culture on child development. For example, Fleer's (2004) work addressed how, through colonization, western mainstream concepts of family were inappropriately brought to bear on early childhood education services for Aboriginal children. Another instance is that western theories of how migrants 'acculturate' to their new setting often assume that there is a dominant culture, but this is not always so: African countries, for example, are often made up of various tribes, overlaid by complex histories of colonization (Adams and van de Vijver, 2017).

The effects of globalization are also relevant. The developing identities of adolescent girls in Belize, Central America, are influenced not just by local culture, such as religion, but by exposure to international media; they accept some overseas ideas (e.g. that gendered violence constitutes abuse) but reject others (e.g. the western ideal that thinness is attractive) (Gibbons, Poelker and Hasbun, 2021). In terms of perceptions of childhood, Burman has opined that 'global capitalist agendas [play] out via the concern for children' (Burman, 2012: 127).

In summary, although cross-cultural developmental research has arguably become less popular, 'cultural' developmental psychology is thriving, accepting the central role of culture in shaping how children develop and, indeed, in shaping our very views of children, childhood and families. Today, the word 'culture' is sometimes applied to mean 'cultural diversity', encompassing identities related to gender, ethnicity, and so forth, that are often subject to discrimination; Harkness and Super suggest that, just as in much cross-cultural research, methods used often 'fail to capture local meanings' (2020: 110). The growing appreciation that there is no universal way in which children grow up has encouraged reference to 'childhoods' rather than 'childhood' (Blume Oeur and Varga, 2024). Nevertheless, the story told by Majority World researchers in Box 1.1 indicates an ongoing obsession with 'generalizability' in the western-dominated field, which also often fails to see the lack of generalizability of its own research products.

Philosophy of science

The word 'science' comes from the Latin *scientia*, meaning 'knowledge'. The philosophy of science has significant ramifications for the theoretical and conceptual foundations of developmental psychology. Worldviews concern ways of knowing (epistemology) and issues of reality (ontology) (Overton, 2007). 'In the broadest sense of the term a world view helps people interpret, understand and bring some order to their lives' (Slee, 1987: 8). Thus, worldviews help to shape how we use terms like 'knowledge', 'information' and 'science'. That is, they help to specify the types of theory used in research and to identify problems worthy of study and the required methodology (Lerner, 1986).

'Common sense' has often initially prompted and informed the interpretation of behaviour, such as Charles Darwin's observations regarding the emergence of emotions in children, or Jean Piaget's careful recording of the behaviour of his children in relation to their use of their senses and motor activity to acquire knowledge. These scientists attempted to systematically bring some order and coherence to their observations, such as by gathering further examples or experimenting in an attempt to reproduce the initial findings.

As child development became a matter of scientific study in western societies, this went hand in hand with the development of an empirical methodology that clearly separated the observer from the observed, in the best interests of the scientific endeavour. The child was objectified, in the spotlight of this critical gaze. The exercise involved a gendered division of labour: 'Women were excluded from the investigative enterprise because they were declared constitutionally incapable of regarding their children with the requisite objectivity' (Burman, 1994: 12). Such critical perspectives draw our attention to the various factors shaping the study of child development.

While developmental psychology never hesitated to draw upon disciplines such as biology, anthropology and sociology, advances in the philosophy of knowledge were largely ignored (Teo, 1997). This rather curious omission occurred despite influential writers and researchers in the field, such as Piaget, having epistemology as the basis for their work. Thomas Teo suggested that the primary reason for this neglect was the rise and dominance of empiricism, particularly as reflected in mainstream North American psychology.

Empiricism is a philosophy of science and a worldview that has shaped the conduct of the science of child study. The dominant western model of 'reality' draws heavily upon a belief in a particular view of the scientific method as the only valid approach to the acquisition and understanding of a systematic body of knowledge. In modelling itself upon the natural sciences, the empirical method of child study has placed great importance on searching for causes of behaviour, with an emphasis on reducing the complexity of behaviour to its basic components. In 1974 Urie Bronfenbrenner famously observed that some 76 per cent of child development research was of an experimental laboratory nature, contrasting with only 8 per cent that used naturalistic observation.

While the empirical method eschews interpretation, at the beginning of the 20th century psychology struggled with the method of *Verstehen*, or understanding, as a methodology. Ultimately, the method drowned in the sea of empiricism, which became the dominant scientific discourse in psychology in general and developmental psychology in particular. With the advent of feminism and postmodern thinking towards the end of the 20th century, the role of interpretation began to undergo a re-examination in relation to understanding human development, although post-positivism remains the predominant approach. However, Teo (2018) believes that psychology as a discipline today is better characterized in terms of 'naïve empiricism' rather than positivism, in its implicit assumptions—for example, that value-free research and neutral research methods are possible.

Images of children

As we have outlined, history, culture and the philosophy of science play significant roles in shaping how we view children and adolescents. We can draw out several 'images' of children influenced by one or more of these factors: the experiential child, the iniquitous child and the virtuous child (see Figure 2.1).

The experiential child is a mainstream view identifiable in the psychological literature. Inherent in this view is the notion that the newborn infant is a *tabula rasa* or blank slate, a concept arising from the worldview of empiricism, the primary influence being Enlightenment ('Age of Reason') English philosopher Locke (1632–1704). Empiricism did much to replace scholasticism—a worldview of a God-ruled static cosmos. Empiricism advocates that all knowledge is derived from experience.

> Let us suppose the mind to be, as we say white paper, void of all characters, without any ideas; how comes it to be furnished? Whence comes it by that vast

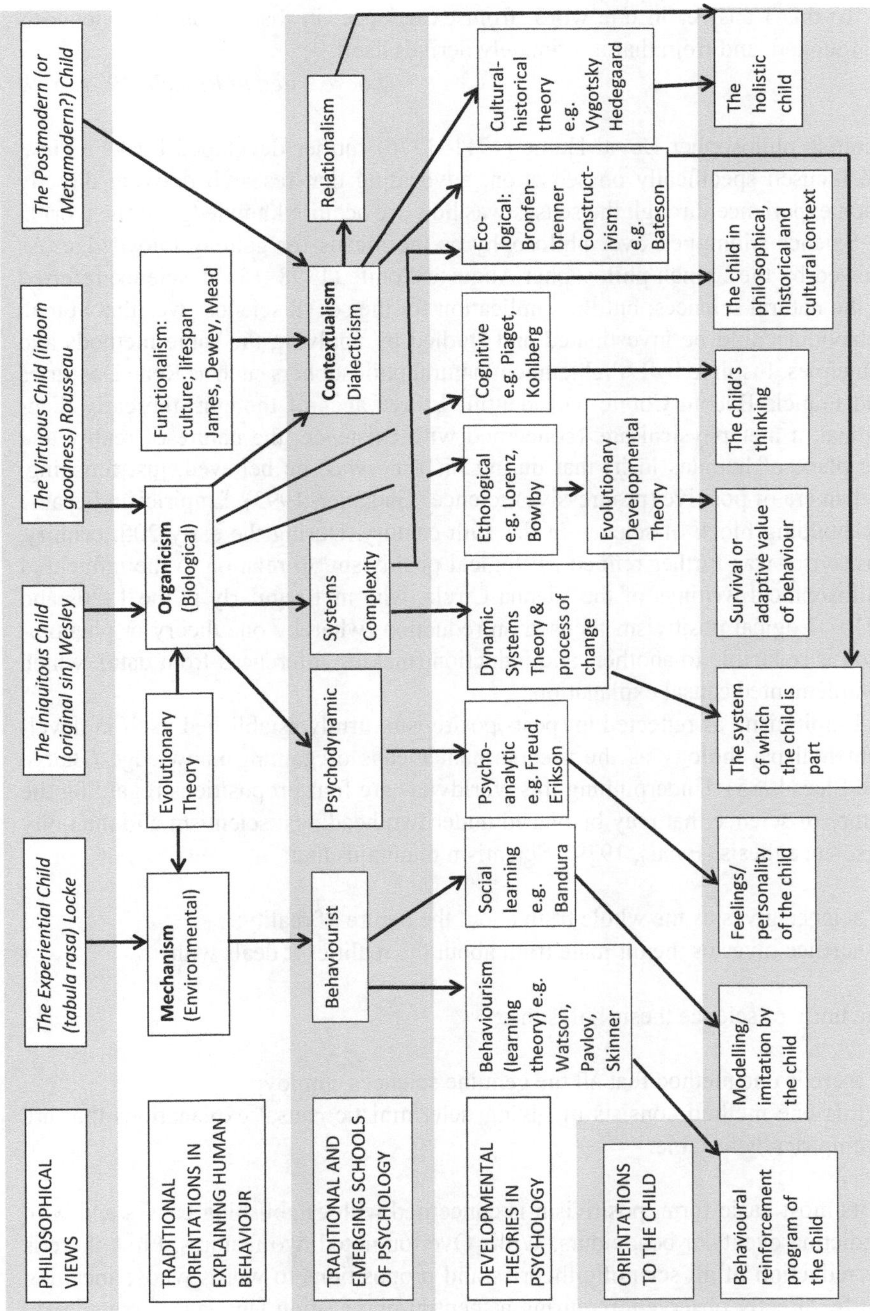

Figure 2.1 Images of children
Adapted from Slee (2002)

> store, which the busy and boundless fancy of man has painted on it with an almost endless variety? Whence has all the materials of reason and knowledge? To this I answer in one word; from experience: in that all our knowledge is founded, and from that it ultimately derives itself.
>
> *(Locke, cited in Russell, 1974: 589)*

Scottish philosopher David Hume (1711–1776) further developed Locke's view. He focused specifically on sensation, advocating that research drawing directly upon experience through the senses was how we acquire knowledge of the world.

Science triumphed over philosophy as the means for gaining knowledge. As viewed by the French philosopher Auguste Comte (1798–1857), science referred to the natural sciences, but the implication for the social sciences was that human behaviour could be investigated and studied by applying the same methods and principles. Inspired by Enlightenment natural philosophers such as René Descartes and Francis Bacon, Comte had identified three ages of thought: the early theological; a metaphysical age (concerned with existence, the nature of reality and the place of humans in it) that during his time was, he believed, just finishing; and an era of positive (progressive) science (Gadamer, 1993). Empiricism became the building block of science in the 19th century. During the early 20th century, positivism was further refined as 'logical positivism' in relation to the influential philosophical writings of the Vienna Circle, who met regularly in the 1920s and 1930s. Logical positivism focused on reduction (whereby one theory or phenomenon is reducible to another) and induction (making inferences from data), which complemented causal explanation.

Empiricism, as reflected in (post-)positivism, firmly established itself in developmental psychology as the predominant means of gaining knowledge (Battye and Slee, 1985). Underpinning this worldview are four propositions regarding the nature of science that may be placed under two headings: scientism and the unity of science thesis (Evans, 1979). Scientism maintains that:

- science gives us the whole truth about the nature of reality;
- science gives us the ultimate truth about the realities it deals with.

The unity of science thesis holds that:

- there is one method that all the genuine sciences employ;
- this one method consists of giving deterministic causal explanations that are empirically testable.

In its most basic form, positivism is concerned with establishing causes and with predicting events or behaviours. Willis Overton noted two features. First, there is the reduction of all scientific theories and propositions to words whose meaning can be directly observed, requiring a 'neutral observation language – completely objective, and free from subjective or mind-dependent interpretation'. Second, 'to be scientifically meaningful, any universal propositions (e.g. hypotheses, theories, laws) had to be demonstrably nothing more than summary statements of the pristine observations themselves' (Overton, 1998: 158).

This outlook presented humans as passive or inert organisms whose behaviour is shaped by external forces. That is, at birth the infant is a *tabula rasa* and the environment determines all that the child becomes. A modern exponent of this view was Burrhus F. Skinner. Nevertheless, as pointed out by philosophers Stephen Laurence and Eric Margolis (2024), a mind that was truly a blank slate would be incapable of learning anything, and empiricists do accept that there must be some innate general-purpose cognitive mechanisms that permit learning to occur.

A second view of children, as iniquitous, accepts the proposition regarding the inherent sinfulness of humankind (see Figure 2.1). Because the child is thought to be born into original sin, the task of the parents becomes that of breaking the child's will, so that they submit to the will of parents and God (see Box 2.1). In the Puritan tradition of 17th- and 18th-century England and the United States, the inherent sinfulness of the child was an accepted outlook of educators and the establishment generally. The English churchman John Wesley (1703) wrote forcefully:

> Break their wills betimes, begin this work before they can run alone, before they can speak plain, perhaps before they can speak at all … Let a child from a year old be taught to fear the rod and to cry softly; from that age make him do as he is bid, if you whip him ten times running to effect it. If you spare the rod you spoil the child; if you do not conquer you ruin him.
>
> *(Cited in Southey, 1925: 304)*

Wesley's views were incorporated into regulations for running a girls' boarding school. Faint-hearted parents intending to enrol their children were warned off. The girls' daily life included a 4 am rise, an hour of religious instruction followed by public worship, breakfast and then the school day, which ended at 5 pm, with no time for play (Cleverley and Phillips, 1976). A later exploration of the iniquitous view of the child is found in William Golding's novel *Lord of the Flies* (1954), in which a group of boys is stranded on a desert island; free of the restraint of traditional culture and adult supervision, the iniquitous nature of the children comes to the fore.

BOX 2.1 CHILDREN AND PUNISHMENT

There was an old woman who lived in a shoe;
She had so many children she didn't know what to do.
She gave them some broth without any bread;
Then whipped them all soundly and sent them to bed.

(English nursery rhyme dating from the 18th century or earlier)

UNICEF (2023) reports that corporal punishment is still legal in schools in 63 states, covering half the global school-aged population. It has no benefits and impedes learning. Experiencing it is associated with aggression, antisocial behaviour, adult criminality and an increased likelihood of using it as a parent, contributing to a cycle of violence. The murderous Pol Pot regime in mid-1970s Cambodia spawned such intergenerational violence, now being countered culturally through the teachings of specially trained Buddhist monks, both in pagodas and as online social influencers. The idea that some children, or some kinds of children, are 'born bad' can persist today and be manifest in forms such as genocide, forced migration and conversion therapies (Linick, 2022).

Contrast this with the idea of the virtuous child (Figure 2.1). An exponent of this ideal was Rousseau. He took issue with Locke's ideas about children, proposing instead the concept of an innocent child whose development was powerfully directed by nature. He thereby affirmed children's inherent goodness. Rousseau also rejected Locke's notion of the rational child, arguing that reasoning capacity does not develop until around age 12. In his novel *Emile* (1762), Rousseau applied his ideas to education: 'God made all things good; man meddles with them and they become evil' (Rousseau, 1762/1914, Book 1: 5). He believed that in educating the innocent and amoral child, it made no sense to punish them for wrongdoing: 'Before the age of reason we do good or ill without knowing it, and there is no morality in our action' (Rousseau, 1762/1914: 34).

As we noted previously, Rousseau's views influenced the establishment of community schools in Europe. They were reflected too in the later thinking of the educator A. S. Neill (1968), who also rejected the idea of original sin or evil and advocated non-interference in children's education. He believed in some innate driving force that would lead children to make the best decisions if left to their own devices. An example is a group of six boys shipwrecked on a desert island in 1963, far from their Tongan home. Unlike their fictional counterparts, they organized themselves with foraging, gardening, cooking, standing guard, and musical and sporting activities until they were rescued 15 months later (Bregman, 2021). Burman has discussed another view of children as 'innocent', in the form of a theory that children's 'innocence', and adult efforts to keep them so through deception, is a way that adults maintain fantasies about the nature of society (see video in Student Resources).

David Elkind (1987) presented a case for a fourth contemporary outlook: the 'competent infant'. This view presents 'infants and young children as having much more capacity to learn academic skills than children, regardless of background, actually have' (Elkind, 1987: 8). Elkind argued that this view had been adopted by such educators as Jerome Bruner, with his now famous statement in 1962 that it is possible to teach any child any subject matter at any age in an intellectually responsible manner. Elkind believed that Bruner may not have appreciated how sincerely parents and educators would take up this statement as a rallying call. A new optimism was generated regarding the capabilities and competencies of the infant that, in Elkind's view, overstepped the mark. However, in recent years a growing body of evidence from carefully designed experiments has supported the view that infants are much more capable than previously understood (Baillargeon, Scott and Bian, 2016).

Metaphors, theories and metatheories

In considering different theoretical orientations to child development, some writers have drawn upon the work of philosopher Stephen Pepper (1942) on metaphor. While metaphors can be non-linguistic (e.g. ritual or gestural), it is the linguistic metaphors which have gained most attention. The literature on metaphor has a long history in western civilization, e.g. Aristotle's *Rhetoric and Poetics*. Paul Rosenblatt (1994: 12) held that '[a] metaphor is a figure of speech in which a word or phrase that ordinarily applies to one kind of object or idea is applied to another, thus suggesting a likeness or analogy between them'. For example, if someone says, 'My lawyer is a well-paid shark' (Carston and Wearing, 2011: 300), this transfers the meaning attached to a shark (a predator) to the lawyer. George Lakoff and Michael Johnson (1980) suggested that metaphor is a common everyday facet of language which guides our thinking regarding a wide variety of topics.

Two traditional orientations to behaviour that flow from the experiential, iniquitous and virtuous views of children are the mechanistic and organismic (Figure 2.1). Pepper (1942) identified these as two of four worldviews that are underpinned by 'root metaphors'. Roger Dixon and Richard Lerner (1992) identified these as two metatheoretical traditions in developmental psychology.

For theories within the mechanistic tradition, such as behaviourism, the root metaphor is the machine, with some force (e.g. hydraulic) operating through a system to bring predictable outcomes; the environment is all-important in shaping what we become and how we develop. Notions of classical science or 'Newtonianism' in the 17th and 18th centuries highlighted an image of a 'world in which every event was determined by initial conditions that were, at least in principle, determinable with precision. It was a world in which chance played no part, in which all the pieces came together like cogs in a cosmic machine' (Toffler, 1984: xiii).

The organismic tradition encompasses a wide range of theories, such as Piaget's, drawing upon the notion of the iniquitous or virtuous child, or the competent child, or a mixture of these. The organismic view does not consider the newborn as a blank slate: for example, infants may differ in temperament. The root metaphor for organicism is the living, growing organism, unique in its own right, but whose development is significantly shaped by mutual influence and the patterning of its parts. Although humanistic theory can be considered as following this tradition, we do not cover it as it did not focus upon child development; however, we can note in passing that the meaning of 'humanism' has been subject to change, and that a recent 'posthumanist' philosophical movement has, in fact, been applied to childhood (Burman, 2018), but is beyond the scope of the present discussion. We do cover ethological, psychoanalytic, cognitive and constructivist theories. In addition, dialectical theories (such as Vygotsky's) could be regarded as organismic, but can also be seen as bridging mechanistic and organismic theories, with the organism and the environment in mutually influential interaction, or even as inseparable elements of development. Dixon and Lerner (1992) categorized dialectical theories separately from organicism.

Systems, or complexity, approaches to development could be considered in the organismic tradition, although, like dialecticism, they emphasize mutual interaction between the organism and the environment. In fact, the notion of a system should perhaps be considered as a separate orientation from those suggested by Pepper. Rollo Browne suggested several possible metaphors, including that of the organic or 'open system' that has a focus on 'self regulation to balance internal needs and external demands' (Browne, 1996: 11). Broadly, a system is a holistic entity with interacting parts that reorganize and transform over time and may give rise to new properties not possessed by the parts themselves. The writings of Gregory Bateson (1972), deriving principally from cybernetic theory, significantly shaped the development of systems theories. So too did the writing of Paul Watzlawick and colleagues in distinguishing between first- and second-order change: first-order change represents a western positivist ideal of change as orderly, predictable and progressive; second-order change can be sudden and spontaneous, resulting in the emergence of unpredictable new patterns and behaviours (Watzlawick, Weakland and Fisch, 1974).

Pepper's other root metaphors are contextualism and formism. The root metaphor for contextualism is the act in context, or the historical act. Contextualism is concerned with placing the developing child within a historical time and culture, and Dixon and Lerner (1992) identified it as a separate metatheoretical tradition. Contextualists such as John Dewey and George Herbert Mead laid some of the groundwork for more recent sociocultural and Indigenous approaches. For example, for Dewey the essential problem is 'to understand the relation between universal aspects of human nature and its different forms of expression in different social circumstances or arrangements' (Cahan, 1992: 207).

Formism concerns classification. It draws upon the metaphor of the similarity of objects and highlights their classification into discrete and hierarchical categories. The world is seen to consist of 'things' or 'entities' which can be classified using some scheme or system, as in psychiatric diagnostic systems. Formism does not appear to link with any particular theoretical tradition and thus does not appear in Figure 2.1. However, attempts to classify theoretical approaches are in themselves expressions of formism. While groupings of theories are convenient, they are not always clear-cut. We do not expect all readers to endorse the scheme in Figure 2.1 but we offer it as a useful heuristic for understanding the relationships between various developmental theories.

Dixon and Lerner (1992) identified evolutionary theory, especially Darwinian theory, as playing a seminal role in the five metatheoretical traditions they identified (organicism, mechanism, contextualism, psychodynamic and dialectical).

Missing from this list is 'relationalism'— we consider it alongside dialecticism, though it can be considered as a metatheory in itself.

Pepper's root metaphors have been subject to relatively little investigation, exceptions being Steven Hayes, Linda Hayes and Hayne Reese (1988), Super and Harkness (2003) and David Shwalb and colleagues (2010). More recently, Saeed Karimi-Aghdam (2016) has applied Pepper's work to a consideration of Vygotskian theory as an interplay between organicism and contextualism, while Zhuanglin Hu (2023) has revisited Pepper's metaphors in relation to cognition. It is perhaps sufficient here to use them to help us understand the various lines of thought and the distinctions between them that have informed our theoretical understanding of child development.

Modernism, postmodernism and metamodernism

Psychology in general, and child development in particular, remain strongly rooted in modernism, a cultural and philosophical movement influenced by the Enlightenment and particularly identified with the late 19th and early 20th centuries. Hence, as we have noted, scientific thinking has guided these fields for many years, with a focus on objectivity, causality and seeking for truth, with quantitative methods predominant.

Postmodernism, arising in the later 20th century, challenged modernism as naïve, and promoted a subjective, critical and pluralistic worldview that favoured qualitative research. Influential postmodern thinkers included those in the German critical-theoretical tradition (Jürgen Habermas and Klaus Holzkamp), the French postmodernists (Jean-François Lyotard, Jacques Derrida and Michel Foucault) and a broad range of feminist and ethnic theorists (Teo, 1997).

William Tierney (2001) identified five attributes underpinning postmodern thinking. The first relates to the conceptualization of knowledge, which is not understood as something that is 'discovered' as though it is there somehow waiting to be unearthed, but is understood as being constructed. Social constructionism (a sociological view) maintains that knowledge is produced by people working in groups and is thus a social product with a political basis (Tierney, 1996: 359). Tierney commented that it is therefore no accident that science has been a largely male enterprise, ignoring women's concerns or interpreting them in a patriarchal manner (Tierney, 2001).

The second attribute of postmodernism relates to its challenge to modernism's faith in science and the efforts that it expends in analysing underlying assumptions and frameworks. The epistemological position of modernism with its positivist assumptions has been contrasted with postmodernism's 'critical questioning, and often outright rejection, of the ethnocentric rationalism championed by modernism' (Cooper and Burrell, 1988: 92, cited in Tierney, 2001). Central here is the idea of 'power' and that knowledge is not something neutral but is part of the scientific endeavour.

The third attribute relates to the contrasting identities of the modernist and postmodernist scientist. Compare the popular image of the nameless and faceless scientist labouring away in a laboratory with the 'fractured nature of the post-modern identity' (Tierney, 2001: 362).

A fourth attribute of postmodernist knowledge relates to the chaos, uncertainty and disorganization which a great deal of postmodern thinking encourages. This is in direct contrast to the causal, linear modernist thinking searching for certainty and predictability. Tierney suggested that the political and cultural underpinnings of postmodern thinking significantly broadened our understandings about the nature of knowledge.

Finally, some schools of postmodern thought prioritized the study of meaning-making while others (e.g. feminism) critically analysed oppressive social forces (Kilicoglu and Kilicoglu, 2020; Pipere and Martinsone, 2022). In that vein, Burman (2017) has long been a conspicuous contributor to the 'deconstruction' of child psychology.

What would a 'postmodern child' look like? We suggest that this child is one understood in philosophical, historical and cultural context; one who is listened to and valued for themself rather than simply as a means of understanding the adult condition; one whom the researcher strives to understand without exploitation, and whom the practitioner seeks to help in a full understanding of the social and historical contexts within which the child, practitioner and other relevant parties operate. This book's title (and the very structure of this chapter) indicates our willingness to embrace both modern and postmodern perspectives, but this remains very unusual in child development texts. Critiques of traditional schools of thought appear in various chapters. But even as we were advocating in our 2015 edition for greater consideration of critical viewpoints, some writers (in other fields) were already declaring postmodernism dead! Indeed, the term itself is less commonly encountered today, although the principles remain influential.

We continued efforts to unite the two perspectives in our 2022 book on paradigms for understanding school bullying, drawing on a 'grey systems theory' argument that different social research paradigms may not be as much in opposition as previously supposed (Javanmardi, Liu and Xie, 2019), and that a complex systems approach may offer a way forward (Shute and Slee, 2022). We have since discovered that such moves are in accord with a broader philosophical movement called 'metamodernism', that arose in fields such as art and architecture around the turn of the millennium. Two recent prominent proponents in the social sciences are sociologist Daniel Görtz and psychologist Gregg Henriques. This recent philosophy does not seek to replace modernism or postmodernism, but to negotiate between the two, swinging like a pendulum to question both the 'universality, totality and the truthfulness of modernism' and the 'fragmentation and scepticism of postmodernism' (Kilicoglu and Kilicoglu, 2020: 496). It has been argued that, just as children's development moves through increasingly sophisticated stages, so cultural change is moving from modernism, through postmodernism to metamodernism, which has been described as 'a kind of integrated pluralism' (Henriques, 2020). Although it has yet to penetrate child development theorizing, one can see its promise through the analysis of Turkish authors Gokhan and Derya Kilicoglu (2020) of Nordic (progressive) schooling through a metamodern lens.

A more familiar movement within psychology that is in keeping with metamodernist principles is the increasing use of mixed-method (complementary quantitative and qualitative) research (Shute and Zschorn, 2018). A philosophical approach that falls between post-positivist and interpretivist approaches is 'critical realism', that accepts pluralism of methodology; we will say more about this in Chapter 15.

Conclusions

While acknowledging the positivist heritage of developmental psychology and its western roots, we have also deliberately embedded theoretical thinking in the context of the intertwined aspects of history, culture and philosophy. In contextualizing theory in this manner we believe that it provides a richer account and understanding of influential theories of the past and in the world of the 21st century. As beautifully expressed by James Garfield, the 20th president of the United States, 'History is but the unrolled scroll of prophecy'.

References

Adams, B. G. and van de Vijver, F. J. R. 2017. Identity and acculturation: the case for Africa. *Journal of Psychology in Africa 27*(2): 115–21. www.tandfonline.com/doi/full/10.1080/14330237.2017.1301699

Ariès, P. 1962. *Centuries of childhood*. New York: Vintage Books.

Baillargeon, R., Scott, R. M. and Bian, L. 2016. Psychological reasoning in infancy. *Annual Review of Psychology 67*: 159–86. https://doi.org/10.1146/annurev-psych-010213-115033

Bateson, G. 1972. *Steps to an ecology of mind*. London: Ronald Press Ballantine.

Battye, P. and Slee, P. T. 1985. The demise of the person in social work. *Australian Social Work 38*: 23–31. www.tandfonline.com/doi/abs/10.1080/03124078508549892

Blume Oeur, F. and Varga, D. 2024. Colonialism, racism, and childhoods: introduction. *American Behavioral Scientist*. https://doi.org/10.1177/00027642241268546

Bregman, R. 2021. *Humankind: a hopeful history*. New York: Bloomsbury.

Bronfenbrenner, U. 1974. Toward an experimental ecology of human development. *American Psychologist 32*: 513–31.

Bross, D. C. and Mathews, B. 2013. The Battered-Child Syndrome: changes in the law and child advocacy. In R. Krugman and J. Korbin (eds), *C. Henry Kempe: a 50 year legacy to the field of child abuse and neglect*. Dordrecht: Springer, 39–50. https://doi.org/10.1007/978-94-007-4084-6_6

Browne, R. 1996. Metaphors and system interventions: open and closed systems. Part 1. https://psychodramaaustralia.edu.au/sites/default/files/rollos_paper_with_modifications_-_metaphors-and-systems-interventions-open-closed-systems-part-12.pdf

Burman, E. 1994. *Deconstructing developmental psychology*. London: Routledge.

Burman, E. 1996. Local, global or globalized? Child development and international child rights legislation. *Childhood 3*: 45–66. https://doi.org/10.1177/0907568296003001004

Burman, E. 2012. Un/thinking children in development: a contribution from northern antidevelopmental psychology. *Psychology: The Journal of the Hellenic Psychological Society 19*(2): 125–43. https://doi.org/10.12681/psy_hps.23612

Burman, E. 2017. *Deconstructing developmental psychology*. Third edn. London: Routledge.
Burman, E. 2018. Towards a posthuman developmental psychology of child, families and communities. In M. Fleer and B. van Oers (eds), *International handbook of early childhood education*. Dordrecht: Springer, 1599–620. https://doi.org/10.1007/978-94-024-0927-7_83
Burman, E. 2023. Child as method and/as childism: conceptual-political intersections and tensions. *Children and Society 37*: 1021–36. https://doi.org/10.1111/chso.12615
Cahan, E. D. 1992. John Dewey and human development. *Developmental Psychology 28*: 205–14.
Carston, R. and Wearing, C. 2011. Metaphor, hyperbole and simile: a pragmatic approach. *Language and Cognition 3*(2): 283–312. https://doi.org/10.1515/LANGCOG.2011.010
Cleverley, J. and Phillips, D. C. 1976. *From Locke to Spock*. Melbourne: Melbourne University Press.
Collard, K. 2000. Aboriginal culture. In P. Dudgeon, D. Garvey and H. Pickett (eds), *Working with Indigenous Australians: a handbook for psychologists*. Centre for Aboriginal Studies Curtin University of Technology, Perth, Western Australia, 21–6.
Cretchley, J., Rooney, D. and Gallois, C. 2010. Mapping a 40-year history with Leximancer: themes and concepts in the *Journal of Cross-Cultural Psychology*. *Journal of Cross-Cultural Psychology 41*(3): 318–28. https://doi.org/10.1177/0022022110366105
Dixon, R. A. and Lerner, R. M. 1992. A history of systems in developmental psychology. In M. H. Bornstein and M. E. Lamb (eds), *Developmental psychology: an advanced textbook*. Third edn. Hillsdale, NJ: Erlbaum, 3–58.
Elkind, D. 1987. The child yesterday, today and tomorrow. *Young Children 42*(4): 6–11.
Evans, C. S. 1979. *Perceiving the person: a look at the human sciences*. Illinois: IVP.
Fleer, M. 2004. The cultural construction of family involvement in early childhood education: some Indigenous Australian perspectives. *The Australian Educational Researcher 31*(3): 51–68. https://link.springer.com/article/10.1007/BF03249528
Fraser, B. G. 1976. The child and his parents: a delicate balance of rights. In R. Helfer and C. H. Kempe (eds), *Child abuse and neglect: the family and the community*. Cambridge, MA: Ballinger, 315–33.
Gadamer, H. G. 1993. *Über die Verborgenheit der Gesundheit*. Frankfurt am Main: Suhrkamp.
Gibbons, J. L., Poelker, K. E. and Hasbun, K. 2021. My social, political, and hybrid self: identity in Central and South America. In B. G. Adams and F. J. R. van de Vijver (eds), *Non-western identity: identity in a changing world*. Cham: Springer, 49–72. https://doi.org/10.1007/978-3-030-77242-0_4
Golding, W. 1954. *Lord of the flies*. Boston: Faber & Faber.
Harkness, S. and Super, C. M. 2020. Culture and human development: where did it go? And where is it going? *New Directions for Child and Adolescent Development 173*: 101–19. https://doi.org/10.1002/cad.20378
Hayes, S. C., Hayes, L. J. and Reese, H. W. 1988. Finding the philosophical core: a review of Stephen Pepper's world hypotheses: a study in evidence. *Journal of the Experimental Analysis of Behavior 50*: 97–111.
Henriques, G. 2020. What is metamodernism? *Psychology Today*, 17 April. www.psychologytoday.com/au/blog/theory-knowledge/202004/what-is-metamodernism
Hobbes, T. 1931. *Leviathan*. Oxford: Basil Blackwell.
Hu, Z. 2023. Root metaphor. In *Metaphor and cognition. Peking University linguistics research*. Vol. 8. Singapore: Springer, 99–108. https://doi.org/10.1007/978-981-99-3852-0_10

Isselhardt, T. R. 2001. Ancient girlhoods: Babylon and Assyria. *Girl Museum Inc.* www.girlmuseum.org/ancient-girlhoods-babylon-and-assyria/

Javanmardi, E., Liu, S. and Xie, N. 2019. Exploring the philosophical paradigm of grey systems theory as a postmodern theory. *Foundations of Science 25*: 905–25. https://doi.org/10.1007/s10699-019-09640-5

Jolowicz, H. F. 1952. *Historical introduction to the study of Roman law*. Cambridge: Cambridge University Press.

Jones, A. F. 2011. *Developmental fairy tales: evolutionary thinking and modern Chinese culture*. Cambridge, MA: Harvard University Press.

Karimi-Aghdam, S. 2016. Rethinking Vygotskian cultural-historical theory in light of Pepperian root metaphor theory: dynamic interplay of organicism and contextualism. *Human Development 59*(5): 251–82. https://doi.org/10.1159/000452719

Kessen, W. 1979. The American child and other cultural inventions. *American Psychologist 34*: 815–82.

Kilicoglu, G. and Kilicoglu, D. 2020. The birth of a new paradigm: rethinking education and school leadership with a metamodern 'lens'. *Studies in Philosophy and Education 39*: 493–514. https://doi.org/10.1007/s11217-019-09690-z

Kojima, H. 1996. Japanese childrearing advice in its cultural, social, and economic contexts. *International Journal of Behavioral Development 19*: 373–91. https://doi.org/10.1177/016502549601900209

Koops, W. 2015. No developmental psychology without recapitulation theory. *European Journal of Developmental Psychology 12*(6): 630–9. https://doi.org/10.1080/17405629.2015.1078234

Lakoff, G. and Johnson, M. 1980. The metaphorical structure of the human conceptual system. *Cognitive Science 4*: 195–208.

Laurence, S. and Margolis, E. 2024. *The building blocks of thought: a rationalist account of the origins of concepts*. Oxford: Oxford University Press.

Lerner, R. M. 1986. *Concepts and theories of human development*. Second edn. New York: Random House.

Linick, J. 2022. Attachment: theory, application, & clinical tools. In A. N. Marsh and L. J. Cox (eds), *Not just bad kids*. np: Academic Press, 39–66. https://doi.org/10.1016/B978-0-12-818954-2.00001-8

Liu, J. 2022. Childhood in urban China: a three-generation portrait. *Current Sociology Monograph 70*(4): 598–617. https://journals.sagepub.com/doi/10.1177/0011392120985861

Marr, D. 2023. *Killing for country*. Melbourne: Black Inc.

Mead, M. 1970. *Culture and commitment*. New York: Doubleday, Garden City.

Miller, P. H. 2022. Developmental theories: past, present, and future. *Developmental Review 66*: 101049. https://doi.org/10.1016/j.dr.2022.101049

Mullineaux, N. 2012. Our genius, goodness, and gumption: child actresses and national identity in mid-nineteenth-century America. *Journal of the History of Childhood & Youth 5*(2): 283–308. https://dx.doi.org/10.1353/hcy.2012.0021

Neill, A. S. 1968. *Summerhill*. Harmondsworth: Penguin.

Orme, N. 2001. *Medieval children*. New Haven: Yale University Press.

Overton, W. F. 1998. Developmental psychology: philosophy, concepts, and methodology. In W. Damon and R. M. Lerner (eds), *Handbook of child psychology: theoretical models of human development*. Fifth edn. Vol. 1. New York: Wiley, 107–89.

Overton, W. F. 2007. A coherent metatheory for dynamic systems: relational organicism-contextualism. *Human Development 50*: 154–9. https://doi.org/10.1159/000100944

Pepper, S. 1942. *World hypotheses: a study of evidence*. Berkeley: University of California Press.

Pipere, A. and Martinsone, K. 2022. Metamodernism and social sciences: scoping the future. *Social Sciences 11*: 457. https://doi.org/10.3390/socsci11100457

Rosenblatt, P. C. 1994. *Metaphors of family systems theory*. New York: The Guilford Press.

Rousseau, J. J. 1762/1914. (Trans. B. Foxley). *Emile on education*. New York: Basic Books.

Russell, B. 1974. *History of Western philosophy*. London: George Allen & Unwin.

Schorsch, A. 1979. *Images of childhood*. New York: Mayflower.

Shute, R. H. and Slee, P. T. 2022. *School bullying and marginalisation: harmonising paradigms*. Singapore: Springer Nature.

Shute, R. H. and Zschorn, M. 2018. Exploring parents' attributions about their child's physical disability: the benefits and challenges of qualitative research in the context of psychology. *Sage Case Studies in Psychology*. http://dx.doi.org/10.4135/9781526444127

Shwalb, D. W., Shwalb, B. J., Hyun, J-H., Chen, S-J., Kusanagi, E., MacKay, R. and Wilkey, B. 2010. *Maternal beliefs, images, and metaphors of child development in the United States, Korea, Indonesia, and Japan*. Hokkaido: Research and Clinical Center for Child Development, Hokkaido University.

Slee, P. T. 1987. *Child observation skills*. Beckenham: Croom Helm.

Southey, R. 1925. *The life of Wesley*. Vol. 2. London: Humphrey Milford.

Stanley, S. 2017. John Stuart Mill, children's liberty, and the unraveling of autonomy. *The Review of Politics 79*: 49–72. https://doi.org/10.1017/S0034670516000723

Super, C. M. and Harkness, S. 2003. The metaphors of development. *Human Development 46*: 3–23. https://doi.org/10.1159/000067782

Tanner, J. L. and Arnett, J. J. 2016. The emergence of emerging adulthood. In A. Furlong (ed.), *Routledge handbook of youth and young adulthood*. Second edn. London: Taylor & Francis, 50–6.

Teo, T. 1997. Developmental psychology and the relevance of a critical metatheoretical reflection. *Human Development 40*: 195–210. https://psycnet.apa.org/doi/10.1159/000278723

Teo, T. 2018. The consequences of 'positivism' in psychology. In T. Teo, *Outline of theoretical psychology*. London: Palgrave Macmillan, 103–32.

Thurber, K. A., Olsen, A., Guthrie, J., McCormick, R., Hunter, A., Jones, R. *et al.* 2018. 'Telling our story … creating our own history': caregivers' reasons for participating in an Australian longitudinal study of Indigenous children. *International Journal for Equity in Health 17*: 143. https://doi.org/10.1186/s12939-018-0858-1

Tierney, W. G. 1996. The academic profession and the culture of the faculty: a perspective on Latin American universities. In K. Kempner and W. G. Tierney (eds), *The social role of higher education: comparative perspectives*. New York: Garland Publishing, 11–26.

Tierney, W. G. 2001. The autonomy of knowledge and the decline of the subject: postmodernism and the reformulation of the university. *Higher Education 41*: 353–72. https://doi.org/10.1023/A:1017588907541

Tisdall, L. 2022. State of the field: the modern history of childhood. *History 107*(378): 949–64. https://doi.org/10.1111/1468-229X.13318

Toffler, A. 1984. *Future shock*. London: Random House.

UNICEF. 2023. *Ending corporal punishment in schools to transform education for all children*. https://endcorporalpunishment.org/wp-content/uploads/2023/05/Ending-corporal-punishment-in-schools-to-transform-education-for-all-children.pdf

United Nations. 2023. *The world is failing 130 million girls denied education: UN experts*. www.ohchr.org/en/press-releases/2023/01/world-failing-130-million-girls-denied-education-un-experts

Watzlawick, P., Weakland, J. H. and Fisch, R. 1974. *Change: principles of problem formation and problem resolution*. New York: Norton.

Woida, K. L. 2024. Children in Ancient Greece: a comprehensive summary. *Crunch Learning*. https://crunchlearning.com/children-in-ancient-greece/

Zola, E. 1885/1979. (Trans. L. Tancock). *Germinal*. Harmondsworth: Penguin Books.

3 From Darwin to DNA

Biologically based theories of development

Introduction

Human behaviour today is frequently examined through a biological lens. Described as psychology's most recent paradigm shift, it succeeded cognitivism that in turn ousted behaviourism (Campbell, 2012). The core assumption is that explanations for human behaviour and development can be found through an understanding of genetics, brain function, hormones and the like, although biology by no means excludes environmental influences; for example, environmental changes are central to natural selection.

Was Darwin really the forefather of developmental psychology?

Darwin has been described as 'having attained sainthood (if not divinity) among evolutionary biologists' (Gould and Lewontin, 1979: 589). His evolutionary theory has been identified as the precursor of five major families of developmental theory: mechanism, organicism, contextualism, psychodynamic theories and dialecticism (Dixon and Lerner, 1992). The first three we can recognize in terms of Stephen Pepper's worldviews, as discussed in the previous chapter, while the other two are closely related to organicism. Developmental psychology texts often claim Darwin to be the forefather of scientific child study, although other 'fathers' have also been recognized (Koops, 2015). Furthermore, in focusing on Darwin, it should not be forgotten that the polymath Alfred Russel Wallace independently proposed a similar evolutionary theory, both being presented together to the Linnaean Society in 1858; the appearance of Wallace's work shocked Darwin into finally writing *On the Origin of Species* (1859), which became highly influential.

Darwin's strong impact on psychology encompassed continuity between human and animal minds, the importance of individual differences, adaptation to the environment and a broadening of investigative methodologies (Charlesworth, 1992). However, William Charlesworth contended that, in developmental psychology specifically, Darwin's influence was 'weak, indirect and somewhat distorted' (1992: 7). He highlighted the field's lack of attention to natural selection, its focus being on proximate factors and ontogeny (individual life histories), rather than ultimate factors and phylogeny (changes over evolutionary time). However, evolutionary

DOI: 10.4324/9781003567738-3

speculation soon became more attractive to developmental psychologists than Charlesworth perhaps imagined.

Focusing on Britain, Paula Hellal and Marjorie Lorch (2010) underscored the influence on child study of Darwin's *Mind* paper based on his biography of his baby son Doddy. He revisited his old notes after reading a paper by French philosopher Hippolyte Taine, concerning infant language acquisition. Darwin observed instinctive biting behaviours in his son, offering the crocodile analogy we mentioned previously, but also regarding the infant's ability to associate concepts as superior to that of the cleverest family dog. Gestures and some understanding of speech preceded word production, which he considered unsurprising since both occur in some animals. He linked the complexity of human communication with the coevolution of the brain. As an eminent scientist, Darwin brought the study of infants out of the domestic sphere, and before the 19th century closed, James Sully had called for *Mind*'s readers to undertake large scale infant development studies, and had helped found the British Child Study Association. Hellal and Lorch concluded that 'developmental psychology emerged out of evolutionary biology through the theory of Charles Darwin, in contrast to other fields of psychology which have their early scientific roots in experimental psychophysics or psychopathology' (Hellal and Lorch, 2010: 12).

William Koops (2015) credits Darwin's contemporaries Ernst Haeckel and Wilhelm Preyer as originating developmental psychology in Europe. Haeckel famously, and wrongly, proposed that 'ontogeny recapitulates phylogeny', which nevertheless stimulated further theorizing. Preyer, Koops maintains, authored the first truly developmental study in 1882. By the turn of the millennium evolutionary developmental (evo-devo) psychology was being hailed as an emerging area of interdisciplinary inquiry. Forerunners can be identified, however, in the fields of ethology and sociobiology.

Ethology

Ethology was 'the leading biological discipline within behavioral research in the 20th century' (Gräfe and Stuhrmann, 2022: 10). From the 1920s and 1930s, three European Nobel-prize-winning zoologists, Konrad Lorenz, Niko Tinbergen and Karl von Frisch, became highly influential in the understanding of animal behaviour (e.g. Lorenz, 1981; Tinbergen, 1973; von Frisch, 1973) and, later, human development. The ethologists studied innate behaviours (instincts) which fitted animals for survival, examining these both in the natural environment and the laboratory. A central concept was the 'critical period' (later modified to the more flexible 'sensitive period')—a time early in life when the presence of certain environmental conditions is crucial for an instinct to be properly realized (Sluckin, 1970). For example, newly hatched chicks normally become attached to, or imprinted upon, their mother over the first day, but may become imprinted on a suitable alternative (readers will doubtless be familiar with photographs of Lorenz being followed around by goslings).

Such ethological concepts influenced researchers into early parent–child relationships, such as Britain's John Bowlby and Robert Hinde. Ethology values observation and description of natural events, and Hinde (1992a) regretted developmental psychology's neglect of this approach in favour of theory-derived hypothesis-testing. In the late 1960s, biologist Barbara Hold innovatively applied ethological methods to studying children's social ranking behaviour in Munich kindergartens (Odenwald, 2022). Prominent ethologist Irenaeus Eibl-Eibesfeldt saw the study of young children as potentially a way of identifying innate, universal, evolved abilities that would act as a counterpoint to the *tabula rasa* then favoured by behaviourists (Odenwald, 2022). Nicholas Blurton Jones (1972) was also influential in promoting ethological methods to provide objective descriptions of children's behaviour.

Although ethologists were interested in innate behaviours, they (like developmental psychologists) were nevertheless more interested in proximate than ultimate factors (Charlesworth, 1992). The latter were not ignored, however, by ethologists or other scholars they influenced: Bowlby proposed that attachment had evolved because of pressure from predators, while later ethologists argued that attachment behaviours increased individuals' fitness in the context of complex parental investment in offspring (Hess and Petrovitch, 2000).

Although it is often said that ethology as a discipline is over, it can alternatively be seen to now encompass all biologically based studies of animal behaviour (Gräfe and Stuhrmann, 2022). The term would rarely be applied to child study today, although papers on both human and animal behaviour are welcomed by the recently established journal *Frontiers in Ethology*. See Box 3.1 for an example of children's behaviour that has parallels in other species.

BOX 3.1 CHILDREN, CHIMPS AND OCTOPUSES PUNISH FREELOADERS

Cooperation within and between species is widespread in the animal kingdom, puzzling Charles Darwin as seemingly at odds with natural selection. Children as young as 4 are willing to punish those who do not contribute fairly to a collaborative activity. The early emergence of such behaviour has been taken to indicate that such behaviour may be part of humans' natural endowment as a species (Yang *et al.*, 2018).

Chimpanzees will also work together for a food reward, cooperation being much more common than competitive behaviour (Suchak *et al.*, 2016). Aggression is often a dominant animal punishing a freeloader who tries to steal food that others have worked together to obtain.

Similar behaviour has even been observed in octopuses (*Octopus cyanea*) working with partner fish in hunting (Sampaio *et al.*, 2021). The fishes perform a 'cooperative dance', with some actively flushing out prey for the octopus. Some opportunistic fish stand to benefit without actively contributing to the hunt, and *Octopus cyanea* often actively 'punches' them with one arm. The octopus might be imposing a cost on the uncooperative fish, that might also teach them to better cooperate, resulting in benefits to both species.

Sociobiology

In the mid-1970s, a far more radical view about the role of biological heritage was proposed: that animals, including humans, and their behaviour, exist merely to provide the means for their genes to survive and reproduce. This new discipline—sociobiology—was initiated by US entomologist Edward O. Wilson (1975)—'Mr Ant'. He was criticized for not sufficiently considering mammalian females or cooperation, and for a weak attempt at applying his theory to humans. The notion that human behaviour is subservient to genes (which compete with other genes for survival) was encapsulated in the title of English ethologist Richard Dawkins' (1976) book *The Selfish Gene.* Sociobiologists argued that, in addition to 'survival' (natural selection), 'sexual selection' would also confer an evolutionary advantage (competition for mates with same-sex members and selective mating with opposite-sex members). More specifically, 'sexual strategies theory' concerned the human psychological processes involved in sexual selection. Sociobiologists argued that, since males can produce numerous gametes (sperm) the best strategy for their genes' survival would be to impregnate many females, with a low subsequent investment in personally parenting these many offspring. By contrast, females, with their smaller reproductive potential, would best ensure their genes' survival through choosiness about their children's father and investing heavily in raising their fewer offspring. Hence greater male promiscuity and the primary role of females in parenting were seen as biological imperatives. Furthermore, aggression between males was regarded as a natural consequence of competition for females. It was even proposed that if a man discovered that his spouse had had sexual relations with another man, then jealousy to the point of murder (of the woman or her lover) could be seen as biologically sensible (Freedman, 1979). Feminists were outraged at such biological apologies for sexist and violent behaviour, and theorists (feminist and otherwise) mounted various arguments against sociobiology. Notably, Richard Lerner and Alexander von Eye (1992) critiqued three of its major tenets.

First, they took issue with sociobiologists' use of homology. For example, arguments for greater human male promiscuity and even rape were based on fruit fly and monkey behaviours. Yet similarities in observed behaviours (as in Box 3.1) provide no proof of evolutionary connectedness and are more appropriately seen as analogies. Neither do such similarities provide evidence for how far the behaviours are genetically constrained or produced.

Second, Lerner and von Eye critiqued the use of heritability estimates. These, varying between 0 and 1, represent an estimate of the *variation in genetic inheritance between individuals*. However, sociobiologists sometimes implied that the higher the estimate, the more a behaviour is genetically determined. Lerner and von Eye clearly illustrated this misinterpretation: imagine a law permits men, but not women, to be elected to government office; eligibility could then be absolutely predicted by possession of an XX or XY pair of chromosomes, giving a perfect heritability estimate of 1. Clearly, this is not evidence that eligibility for office is genetic, yet this is exactly how heritability estimates of various behavioural traits have often been interpreted. Conversely, universal traits such as the capacity for language or having ten fingers have zero *heritability* but are clearly *inherited*. The neuroscientist Steven Rose maintained that 'heritability estimates are simply meaningless when applied to complex human behavioural traits' (2001: 144). Misunderstanding of heritability indices remains a problem for public policy (Muthukrishna, 2024).

A third contentious principle was the assumption that what exists is necessarily an adaptation, a point previously addressed by biologists Stephen Jay Gould and Richard Lewontin (1979), using a now-famous architectural analogy. Cathedrals have rounded arches in their ceilings creating triangular spaces containing designs which fit the space perfectly; while no one would argue that the arches were placed there *in order to* provide spaces for the designs, biologists frequently made similar arguments for the evolutionary origins of animal structures and behaviours. Likewise, post hoc explanations for the evolutionary pressures which may have determined various forms and functions may be no more scientifically valid than a Rudyard Kipling *Just So* story (see Box 3.2: a distinctly Lamarckian evolutionary theory is apparent, which today's epigenetics research suggests may not be quite so far-fetched after all!). Lerner and von Eye concluded that the problems with sociobiological theory were so great that it was irrelevant for understanding human development or sex differences.

BOX 3.2 THE ELEPHANT'S CHILD

Kipling's *Just So* bedtime stories, like this one, 'explained' how various animals developed certain features.

> Then the Elephant's Child put his head down close to the Crocodile's musky, tusky mouth, and the Crocodile caught him by his little nose, which up to that very week, day, hour, and minute, had been no bigger than a boot, though much more useful. … Then the Elephant's Child sat back on his little haunches, and pulled, and pulled, and pulled, and his nose began to stretch … and at last the Crocodile let go of the Elephant's Child's nose with a plop that you could hear all up and down the Limpopo … he … wrapped it all up in cool banana leaves, and hung it in the great grey-green, greasy Limpopo to cool. … The Elephant's Child sat there for three days waiting for his nose to shrink, but it never grew any shorter … the Crocodile had pulled it out into a really truly trunk same as all elephants have today.
>
> *(Kipling, 1902/1975: 45–6)*

Altruism posed a challenge for 'selfish genes', though that metaphor confuses biology with morality. Altruism occurs when an organism reduces its own survival chances by helping others, such as by sharing scarce food resources. E. O. Wilson's early explanation that such behaviour benefited the group (*group selection theory*) was undermined by the argument that non-altruistic individuals would have greater survival chances, wiping out altruism genes. *Kin selection theory* explained why individuals are most likely to show altruism to close relatives; however, it did not explain the common human practices of adopting non-related children and cooperating with non-relatives. Therefore, *reciprocal altruism theory* was proposed, whereby assisting others may yield benefits through returned favours (Okasha, 2013). This necessitates monitoring interactions in order to calculate the likelihood of later reciprocity (a cost-benefits analysis). Support for this theory includes an experiment which found that the degree to which a 5-year-old child is prosocial towards an unrelated classmate depends on how prosocial that child has previously been towards them (House *et al.*, 2013).

These various altruism theories assumed that evolution occurs through individual selection. References to group selection became so unfashionable that scholars avoided the term, even if their work demonstrated the phenomenon. E. O. Wilson's co-authored 2007 paper examining this history began with a quotation from Darwin:

> [A]lthough a high standard of morality gives but a slight or no advantage to each individual man and his children over the other men of the same tribe ... an increase in the number of well-endowed men and an advancement in the standard of morality will certainly give an immense advantage to one tribe over another.
>
> *(Darwin 1881, cited in Wilson and Wilson, 2007: 328)*

Darwin's original insight had been lost amidst sociobiological disputes that resulted in avoidance of the very word 'sociobiology' by some. Wilson and Wilson presented detailed arguments and evidence accrued over four decades supporting Darwin's position (also noting that Dawkins eventually admitted his error in rejecting group selection[1]). Their summary statement runs: 'Selfishness beats altruism in single groups. Altruistic groups beat selfish groups' (Wilson and Wilson, 2007: 335). In other words, multilevel selection occurs, and the combined effects of individual and group selection must be considered, on a case-by-case basis. Multilevel selection, they concluded, 'provides a comprehensive framework for understanding human sociality' (2007: 343).

Evolutionary developmental (evo-devo) psychology

Despite the backlash against evolutionary approaches sparked by sociobiological theory, evolutionary theory gained new influence in psychology. It has been described as a metatheory, or broad perspective (Tate, 2013) within which more specific theories can be developed and tested (Buss and Schmidtt, 2011). The goals of evolutionary *developmental* psychology are 'to identify the genetic and ecological mechanisms that shape the development of … phenotypes and ensure their adaptation to local conditions' (Geary and Bjorklund, 2000: 57). The interplay between genetic and ecological conditions to determine the phenotype (physical and behavioural characteristics) is known as epigenetics; imprinting is a good example. Like sociobiology, evo-devo psychology draws upon evidence from animal (especially primate) species, from fossil records of ancestors of *Homo sapiens* and from a consideration of modern hunter-gatherer societies. It is concerned with not just the 'what' but the 'why' of human behaviour (Machluf, Liddle and Bjorklund, 2014).

Evo-devo psychologists divide the lifespan into stages defined by differences in physical development, social dependence and social goals. Humans have the longest juvenile period of any mammal and have evolved a 'social brain' that supports the complexity of human social relationships (e.g. Dunbar, 1992). An important presumed function of the extended pre-adult period is the opportunity to practise survival and reproduction skills (for example, competition for mates, a *deferred adaptation*), through play, social interactions and exploration of the environment. Social and cognitive immaturity may themselves be adaptive for shorter-term survival. An example of such an *ontogenetic adaptation* is children's short auditory memory span, that might aid language comprehension by reducing the amount of information to be processed (Geary and Bjorklund, 2000). David Bjorklund (2018) also identified *conditional adaptations*, involving developmental pathways responsive to environmental conditions. Broadly, any cognitive or behavioural adaptations that increase the chances of surviving the hazardous early years would tend to be selected for, resulting in a species-typical pattern of development (Machluf *et al*., 2014).

In infancy and childhood, attachment to parents is seen as the central social relationship, functioning to keep the young organism alive by keeping it close to parents and increasing the level of parental investment in their offspring. Individual differences in quality of attachment (e.g. Ainsworth and Wittig, 1969) are taken as evidence that attachment is an epigenetic process. However, an exclusive focus on parents overlooks the potential evolutionary role of others, especially grandmothers, in helping to raise children, as highlighted by anthropologists (see Box 3.3). Furthermore, Judith Rich Harris (2013) argued that peers are a far more influential feature of children's environment than are parents.

BOX 3.3 THE GRANDMOTHER HYPOTHESIS

Kristen Hawkes explained the Grandmother Hypothesis as follows.

> It is often assumed that the steady increase in life expectancy over the past century and a half has resulted in a larger proportion of older people than ever before. … But … it is levels of fertility, not life expectancy (mortality) that shift the proportion of elders in a population. …

> [In contrast to other primates, in] both historical and hunter-gatherer populations a third or more of women are usually beyond the age of 45. … Developments in evolutionary life-history theory suggest that, instead of help *for* older members of the population, it is help *from* postmenopausal grandmothers that accounts for the age structure of human societies. … In an ancestral population that was shifting from chimpanzee-like feeding [at weaning] to hard-to-handle foods, the more vigorous elder females could help more, thereby increasing the representation of their vigour in descendant generations, shifting rates of ageing, and lengthening average adult lifespans.
>
> *(Hawkes, 2004: 128, original emphasis)*

As children grow older, the shift from parents towards peers, especially same-sex peers, is seen as preparatory for adult reproductive activities. For example, boys' social relationships are concerned with status and dominance, which may be preparatory for competition for mates, while girls' more intimate relationships perhaps foster a supportive network for later parenting activities (Geary and Bjorklund, 2000). This traditional sex-typed interpretation required modification considering research (e.g. Crick and Bigbee, 1998) which broadened the definition of aggression from physical and verbal types to social forms more typical of girls, such as spreading rumours. Thus David Geary and Bjorklund acknowledged that girls also compete, proposing that this perhaps lays the groundwork for later competition for mates. Competition between teenage girls over boyfriends is one trigger for social aggression (Owens, Shute and Slee, 2000). Evolutionary theory has also been applied to understanding of adolescent bullying as often adaptive rather than dysfunctional, serving both boys' and girls' physical, sexual and dominance goals (Volk *et al.*, 2012).

Evolution has also been applied to cognition. In 1983, US philosopher Jerry Fodor expounded a 'modularity of mind' theory—an exemplar of Pepper's (1942) formism metaphor, based upon dividing the mind into separately functioning cognitive categories. Evolutionary psychologists further proposed that hierarchically organized modules of the mind have evolved to process both social and ecological aspects of the world (Geary, 1998, cited in Geary and Bjorklund, 2000). This is a 'core-knowledge' developmental theory. Modules regarding the social world are divided into those concerning social groups and those which are individually based, such as theory of mind (the ability to ascribe mental states to self and others). Ecological modules are divided into the biological and the physical. While their underlying neural structures are seen as inherent, they develop as children initiate activities and gain competence in 'folk psychology, folk biology and intuitive physics' (Geary and Bjorklund, 2000: 62). In other words, epigenetic processes are responsible for phenotype. The notion of sensitive periods is incorporated, with the additional suggestion that these may be related to the position of modules/submodules in the hierarchy, being shorter and earlier for lower-level than higher-level modules.

A goal of evo-devo psychology is to understand how biases and constraints on behaviour determined by evolutionary pressures are relevant for the modern world (Geary and Bjorklund, 2000). For example, while all children are biologically predisposed to learn language, reading is a cultural expression of language (Snowling, 2000) and thus inherently more difficult to learn.

Some dangers of the evolutionary perspective we have alluded to already. Hinde (1992b) warned against drawing simplistic and anthropomorphic parallels between animal and human behaviour, e.g. human children are more disturbed by spending separation from their mother in a strange environment, while monkey infants are more disturbed by remaining in the familiar group. Thus, animal data should be used to suggest principles testable in humans. However, Lynne Segal (2001) viewed evolutionary-based tales of wicked step-parents (with their lack of genetic investment in their step-children), competitive men and nurturing women as clichés repackaged as new insights. Others maintained that, while human evolutionary history clearly empowers and limits behaviour, this is so general as to be unhelpful in considering most specific human behaviours (Rose and Rose, 2001).

Furthermore, Alice Eagly and Wendy Wood (2013) identified considerable evidence *against* predictions based on sexual selection theory, suggesting that evolutionary theorists had ignored this in favour of the few confirmatory studies. David Buller's (2005) critique was based upon illogical interpretations of empirical results. Johan Bolhuis *et al.* (2011) presented evidence against the central arguments of some influential evolutionary psychologists, that:

- our Pleistocene past has shaped today's human mind (the Pleistocene was very variable, with humans living various lifestyles);
- human evolution has been 'too gradual' to adapt to modern conditions (genetic studies have shown substantial recent changes);
- human psychological mechanisms are universal, e.g. infants' fear of strangers (the human mind is very malleable according to environmental conditions);
- the mind has numerous evolved cognitive modules (domain-general mechanisms are more plausible).

For interested readers, Timothy Ketelaar and Bruce Ellis' (2000) article discusses whether evolutionary explanations are unfalsifiable. Those with a philosophical bent we refer to a recent book presenting a rationalist case favouring a nativist explanation of cognitive concepts, which also argues against the 'core knowledge' theories of the mind often espoused by evo-devo psychologists (Laurence and Margolis, 2024).

Christine Legare and colleagues note that many developmental psychologists now draw upon evolutionary theory without using the term. They also contend that Bjorklund's work would be enhanced by a greater consideration of cultural transmission and variation (Legare, Clegg and Wen, 2018). Indeed, Michael Muthukrishna (2024) favours the 'cultural brain hypothesis' that gives a central role to cultural transmission of knowledge and skills (e.g. knowing how to cook food, which has changed the human digestive system), explaining the human dominance of the planet and holding the key to solving our existential problems. Paul Smaldino's (2019) theory offers another recent evolutionary take on the formation and operation of cooperative human groups (see Box 3.4).

BOX 3.4 THE HERMIONE DILEMMA

Paul Smaldino (2019) argues that finding the best people to cooperate with is an essential aspect of human survival and evolution, and that this involves signalling 'who we are' to others. He illustrates this by considering the characters in J. K. Rowling's popular Harry Potter fantasies.

> Clever and resourceful Hermione wants to fight the Dark Lord Voldemort, and luckily she has a bevy of helpful would-be heroes just waiting to assist her! On her left is the one and only Harry Potter: holder of the most telling of scars, Harry is brave, talented, and buoyed by throngs of admirers and supporters. On her right is bumbling Neville Longbottom: kind-hearted but clumsy, socially isolated, and possibly a bit dim. Which of these two should she choose to join her in her quest to rid the wizarding world of evil? The problem here is categorically not how to pick the cooperator instead of the free rider. Instead, the difficulty is to choose the best cooperator, given the task at hand and Hermione's extant personality and skill set. Hermione is doing more than choosing a cooperator. She is choosing a collaborator: someone with whom she will have at least partially aligned goals and with whom she will coordinate to generate synergistic benefits. To make her choice, Hermione is aided by the overt and tacit signals sent by Harry and Neville, advertising their vices and virtues.
>
> *(Smaldino, 2019: 110)*

Behaviour genetics: a focus of the nature–nurture debate

Behaviour genetics rose to prominence following the Human Genome Project, which mapped the genes on human chromosomes and discovered the complete sequence of nucleotides on each gene. Sequencing was declared complete in 2003 (Schmutz *et al.*, 2004) and in 2024 it was stored for posterity on a memory crystal and deposited in a salt cave in Austria (University of Southampton News, 2024).

The notion that genes set limits on development has existed for decades, with the 'reaction range' bounded by the upper and lower limits of possible developmental outcomes (Gottesman, 1974). For example, chicks only become imprinted on objects if they possess certain size and movement characteristics, normally fulfilled by the mother. US psychologist Sandra Scarr (1992) promoted the concept of the 'average expectable environment' whereby, assuming a 'normal' environment, genes will express their potential, and environmental changes such as extra stimulation will have no effect. Only if the environment is outside the range of normality—e.g. in abusive families—will such environmental change significantly change behavioural outcomes. Furthermore, organisms would shape their own environments by 'niche-picking', with genotypes driving experiences.

Similar was Robert Plomin's 'environmental genetics' (e.g. Hetherington, Reiss and Plomin, 1994). He discussed behavioural differences between siblings, which are often very apparent despite their sharing 50 per cent of genetic material and being raised in the same family. Plomin maintained that the other 50 per cent causes children to respond to similar events differently and also evokes differing parental responses. This 'nonshared environment' therefore creates different outcomes.

Such theories gave genetics a much more predominant place in explaining behavioural differences. For example, Scarr's theory implied that children could be reassigned to different families and would turn out much the same. Such interpretations lead to profound conclusions. For instance, differences in parenting style then matter little—if parents are 'good enough' the child will develop as genes dictate. Furthermore, provided the environment is not very deviant, early enrichment programs for families would be a waste of resources.

Such conclusions were challenged by Diana Baumrind (1993), who undertook seminal research in the United States on the effects of parenting styles on children's development. She strongly disputed Scarr's notions, maintaining that her heritability estimates suffered from implausible basic assumptions, underdeveloped constructs, inadequate measures of family environment and unrepresentative populations. For example, the heritability estimates came from extraordinary populations, mainly twins and adoptees, and a 'good enough' environment appeared to be any non-abusive one. Baumrind cited evidence to support her counter-proposition that '[a]ll nonabusive environments above the poverty line are not equally facilitative of healthy development' (1993: 1299). Scarr accepted that her theory excluded individuals with disadvantaged circumstances or restricted life choices. Baumrind suggested that such individuals are the norm worldwide, the absence of disadvantage not being equivalent to having a rich environment. She disputed Scarr's assumption that the same ontological principles apply within all cultures: 'What is "normal" or "expectable" in one culture frequently is anathema in another' (1993: 1301): parents from different cultural backgrounds rear their children very differently, necessarily limiting the generalizability of heritability indices. Baumrind maintained that negative social or genetic factors can be attenuated by parents, but they will not be open to interventions if they believe the situation is genetic and unmodifiable.

Gert-Jan Vreeke (2000) questioned the value of behaviour genetics studies in matters of development, echoing the critiques of heritability estimates, and criticizing the use of additive statistical methods, since genotypes are translated into phenotypes by 'complex, dynamic and nonlinear' processes (Vreeke, 2000: 40). He maintained that Scarr's and Baumrind's interpretations could be reconciled if we accept that genes and the environment are interactive.

The bioecological model (Bronfenbrenner and Morris, 1998) gave a more important place to environmental influences on development. Urie Bronfenbrenner's

(1979) earlier ecological model was highly influential in emphasizing the multiple and interacting social and environmental systems influencing children's development. His bioecological model proposed instead that it is appropriate and ongoing interactions with the environment which enable genes to exert their potential to a greater or lesser degree. These proximate processes drive development, and their quality will affect heritability estimates.

Research and theorizing later focused on this notion of gene–environment interactions with regard to sensitivity to context (e.g. Boyce and Ellis, 2005). Children's reactions to being raised in adversity differ, some suffering long-term ill-effects while others demonstrate greater resilience. The diathesis-stress or dual-risk theory (e.g. Sameroff, 1983) maintains that children with a genetic or constitutional vulnerability will have poorer outcomes in the face of adversity. Using a Swedish metaphor, Boyce and Ellis (2005) proposed that the situation is more complex, characterizing children as 'dandelions' or 'orchids'. Dandelions thrive quite well in good or poor conditions but are never stunning. Orchids, by contrast, suffer badly in the wrong conditions, but bloom magnificently in the best ones. Similarly, it seems that some children have especially *good* outcomes in very supportive conditions, but particularly *poor* outcomes if circumstances are adverse. They are said to be more 'biologically sensitive to context'. The level of sensitivity is long-term, and seen as an outcome of the interaction between genetic predisposition and rearing environment, which either 'tunes up' their sensitivity to context or 'tunes it down'. Furthermore, it is seen as evolutionarily adaptive to possess a stress system that can be matched to the environment. Accumulating evidence supports the theory, although studies pitting it against diathesis-stress theory in efforts to understand the development of children born preterm (e.g. Gould *et al.*, 2022) have yielded no consistent results. The theory has shifted the focus from psychopathology to thriving—something that may be motivating for parents receiving help in raising vulnerable children (Pluess and Belsky, 2012) and is commensurate with the 'positive psychology' movement (e.g. Seligman *et al.*, 2005).

Research on behavioural development has again been revolutionized by technological progress in genomics, enabling a move away from twin-type studies to the direct measurement of DNA. Research investigating the relationship between specific gene variants and developmental outcomes was finding very small effects. Rather, thousands of genes simultaneously influence phenotypical behavioural traits. Genotyping (measuring) millions of genetic variants is now done easily and cheaply (Armstrong-Carter, Wertz and Domingue, 2021), enabling the creation of databases drawn from millions of individuals. Specifically, *polygenic scores* can be calculated in 'genome wide association studies' that scan the entire genomes of many individuals to identify which collections of genes are associated with specific phenotypes, such as educational attainment or personality. Published data on very large samples enable researchers to apply an algorithm to their own smaller samples to estimate polygenic scores.

Polygenic scores research with families has shown that genetic effects may not be simply direct (such as through affecting brain development) but also operate indirectly via the environment. For example, reading to pre-schoolers promotes their early literacy skills (Galea *et al.*, 2024), and mothers with polygenic scores related to higher educational attainment provide more of such behaviour, accounting for a portion of the child's academic attainment at age 18, over and above their direct genetic inheritance (Wertz *et al.*, 2019). Emma Armstrong-Carter *et al.* (2021) suggest that such research now offers a way of examining Scarr's suggestion of decades previously that individuals with stable behavioural trajectories might have a particular genetic predisposition towards them. This field of research is offering new opportunities for studying both direct and indirect intergenerational transmission, as well as examining the crucial timings during development for interventions to support children at risk. However, genome wide association studies raise ethical considerations and to date are restricted in the populations studied (Ambrosino *et al.*, 2024). A World Health Organization report provides guidance on the ethical use of genomics, covering matters such as informed consent, social justice, data stewardship and accountability (World Health Organization, 2024).

Brain, behaviour and epigenetics in development

Brain–behaviour relations were relatively neglected by developmental psychologists during most of the 20th century, but a proliferation of new information occurred with the advent of non-invasive technologies for studying brain functioning (van der Molen and Ridderinkhof, 1998). In the limited space available, we will cover a few basic theoretical issues, including an increased role for epigenetics.

It is often assumed, and promulgated in populist literature, that genes determine brain structure, which in turn determines behaviour. Differences in brain structure may be interpreted as providing evidence of fundamental, inherited individual differences in neurology which underlie observed behavioural differences. Such findings may be favoured for publication over failures to replicate them or over cultural explanations for behavioural differences, so that the evidence for inherited differences may be much weaker and more contradictory than initially apparent (e.g. Gilbert and Gilbert, 1998; Rippon, 2019). In fact, there is good reason to believe that the structure of the human brain is determined epigenetically. The young child has many more synaptic connections in the cerebral cortex than in adulthood, and it seems that experience determines which are retained and which lost.

Animal and human studies have established that brain structure is changed by early experience, whether with especially stimulating environments (e.g. Rosenzweig, 1996) or deprivation, such as a lack of normal visual experience (e.g. Tees, 1986; Westall and Shute, 1992). While young brains are malleable, this plasticity is constrained by external factors, such as exposure to a normal environment, and internal factors, such as the progressive development of the brain from deeper to more superficial areas.

These issues are illustrated by child trauma specialist Bruce Perry's (1997) theory of the neurodevelopmental aspects of violence. He stressed humans' evolution as social animals, with individual survival dependent upon nurturing by the clan. Most of the brain has evolved to subserve necessary social relationships, and the early caretaking experience is instrumental in determining how the brain becomes organized, from the more primitive brainstem and midbrain, through the limbic system and up to the complex neocortex. The latter becomes increasingly able to modulate the functions of the more primitive parts. However, experiences such as early exposure to neglect or violence may disturb the development of the lower parts of the brain, which in turn influence the development of the higher parts, given the brain's hierarchical structure. The modulating effect of the higher influences is therefore reduced, leading to effects such as increased anxiety and a predisposition to violence.

Perry argued that biological markers (e.g. certain blood chemicals) associated with violent behaviours may not reflect genetic differences between individuals but are biochemical *outcomes* of brain structures and processes determined by early experience. However, genes are not irrelevant: whether a boy raised by abusive parents becomes a violent youth depends on whether he has a particular gene variant (Caspi *et al.*, 2002). This accords with the diathesis-stress theory. Perry's view incorporates the notion of sensitive periods as demonstrated by human and animal studies of brain development.

Perry and colleagues' more recent work has investigated the timing of early stress, such as exposure to domestic violence or caregiver neglect, on several developmental outcomes (Hambrick, Brawner and Perry, 2019). Severe lack of responsive parenting in the first two months was associated with disruption of autonomic nervous system functioning and self-regulation (e.g. mood and sleep); this early effect would be expected based on Perry's theory, given brainstem involvement in such basic life functions. Stress during later infancy and childhood was associated with lower cognitive functioning, while stress during childhood was associated with the quality of relational functioning such as attachment and empathy.

Recent theorizing about brain development has made explicit reference to epigenetics, definitions of which vary. Following the biologist Conrad Waddington (1942), developmental psychologists have long used the term to refer broadly to development as a function of gene–environment interactions, with a sense that although development is plastic, options become increasingly narrowed as development proceeds down particular channels (is 'canalized'). With increased understanding of genetics, and an 'explosion' of biological epigenetics research (Miller, 2010), narrower, but debated, definitions have been adopted. Animal studies have shown that genes in various cells of the body can be 'switched on', 'switched off', or expressed more or less strongly, as a result of early experiences. The switching may occur:

- in networks of interacting genes;
- only in certain types of cell or more widely through the body;
- briefly or be long-lasting;
- with brief or long-lasting effects.

The genetic changes may even be passed on to subsequent generations, with the DNA sequence unaltered (that the changes can be inherited underpins one strict definition of an epigenetic trait). In a seminal paper by Canadian researchers Michael

Meaney and Moshe Szyf's team it was shown that rat pups' stress response systems can be 'tuned up' or 'tuned down' in response to their early environment (Weaver *et al.*, 2004), like 'orchid' children in particular. More attentive rat mothers produce less reactive offspring. Furthermore, these effects seem to be mediated by changes to the neural system that forms part of the complex web of bodily systems involved in responses to stressors. In addition, an evolutionary perspective has been proposed. Long-term effects of being raised in adverse circumstances, such as anxiety, used to be viewed as pathological remnants of (presumed) prehistoric conditions of greater physical threat, when high reactivity would have been useful. A newer suggestion is that it is adaptive to possess a stress response system that becomes attuned early in life to the level of environmental stressors.

Szyf's team also showed that brains from suicided people with a history of early abuse differ epigenetically from those who suicided without such history, specifically in an area of the brain concerned with mood regulation (Labonte *et al.*, 2012). Although limited by its correlational nature, the study offered a starting point for increasing understanding of the epigenetic changes that might underlie Perry's theory about early abuse.

Neural epigenetics was also invoked regarding cognitive development, by Annette Karmiloff-Smith (2012). She contrasted *domain-general* with *domain-specific* theories of cognitive development. A prime example of a domain-general theory is Jean Piaget's, with assimilation, accommodation and equilibration underlying all aspects of cognition, begging the question of why children can have strengths and weaknesses in their cognitive profile. A domain-specific theory is Geary and Bjorklund's, which sees the evolved neural substrates for the various domains as being 'fleshed out' in interaction with experiences. Karmiloff-Smith proposed an alternative that is both subtle and profound: that the inherited brain mechanisms are not *specific* for the various domains but are *relevant for* them or *biased towards* them. This 'neuroconstructivist' approach holds that, depending on the environment, the neural systems develop (epigenetically), and localization of form and function gradually emerge as neuronal pruning occurs and the developing neural systems compete with one another through means such as the selection of cell types, and variety in their density and interconnectedness. The brain is thus seen as self-organizing, with domains as end points, not starting points, and it is therefore perfectly possible for a child to show strength in one area, such as numerical understanding, but weakness in another, such as language. That there exists a degree of brain plasticity necessary for such a model is strikingly demonstrated by the fact that early removal of the entire left hemisphere (because of a tumour) allows the right one to largely take over its usual language functions (Danelli *et al.*, 2013). It must nevertheless be appreciated that the long-term outcome of early brain damage is not always good and depends greatly on its nature and timing (Anderson, Spencer-Smith and Wood, 2011).

Marked progress occurred in understanding early brain development with the discovery of two genes instrumental in determining the migration of neurons from the middle of the brain to form the outer cortical layer, in the first 18 months of life (Cappello *et al.*, 2013). More broadly, epigenetic processes are increasingly seen to lie at the heart of neural development and functioning: 'The billions of neurons in a single brain have the same DNA sequence yet are differentiated for their diverse functions through epigenetic programming during pre- and postnatal development and possibly throughout life' (Murgatroyd and Spengler, 2011). Technology now enables study of the molecular cell processes that underlie the epigenetic development of different anatomical and functional regions of the human brain (Cadwell *et al.*, 2019).

A crucial aspect of neural developmental processes is related to imprinting. This ethological term was applied to epigenetic changes to genotype brought about by the action of the parental gametes (sperm and ova) (Tzschentke and Plagemann, 2006). Around birth, these changes affect physiological control systems in the young organism, by creating feedback loops that involve lifelong neurological changes (as in the stress system). This time of feedback loop formation is a critical or sensitive period, with the environment playing a role. These epigenetic changes may be either adaptive or pathological ('imprinting disorders'). Tatton-Brown-Rahman syndrome, for example, is caused by disruption of epigenetic regulation that results in intellectual impairment and, often, autism spectrum disorder, schizophrenia and associated behavioural problems (Ng, Kalinousky and Harris, 2023).

While epigenetics is increasingly influencing developmental theorizing, caution is warranted. Human brains are understandably hard to come by for studying the detailed mechanisms involved, and enthusiasm for applying epigenetics to a broad range of human traits may be outstripping knowledge (Miller, 2010) or being misapplied to ethics and social justice issues (Huang and King, 2018). However, recent advances in epigenetics research are also seen as creating potential for improved therapies for neurodevelopmental and neuropsychological disorders (Ng *et al.*, 2023), and for promoting family contexts and parenting practices that support children's healthy psychological development (Barreto-Zarza and Arranz-Freijo, 2022).

The medical model

Why are we considering a perspective on children's behaviour which is not a theory, not developmental and not psychological? We consider a critical approach essential, given the real impact a medical perspective has on the lives of many children whose behaviour is considered problematic, particularly in the west. Psychology students may be introduced to a medical diagnostic approach to children's behavioural and emotional problems but how this accords (or otherwise) with psychological theories of child development seems rarely addressed. Students and practitioners must try and make sense of the professional dilemmas that arise. For example, author RHS has worked as a hospital paediatric psychologist, conceptualizing cases within theoretical frameworks such as systems theory and learning theory. However, the official hospital summary records required cases to be described as medical (psychiatric) diagnoses which were irrelevant to how the case was conceptualized and managed. Recording of contextual causes was actively discouraged, in favour of individual diagnoses, thereby implying that the problem was inherent in the child.

One way in which a psychiatric diagnostic system could be characterized chimes with this experience: as 'a kind of "convenient fiction" to enable communication, collaboration, and care' (Pickersgill, 2013: 524). Even if convenient, the effects of such a 'fiction' would be profound.

The pervasiveness of the medical model in western societies may encourage certain behaviours to *become* seen by the public as problematic and needing medical attention. A prime example is ADHD, possibly 'the most common mental health condition on Earth' (Hooton, 2024). Several decades ago, parents having trouble managing their children's behaviour began to present their children (and sometimes themselves) as suffering from ADHD (Searight and McLaren, 1998). ADHD illustrates the application of medical diagnoses to children's (and adults') behaviour, as laid out in various editions of the *Diagnostic and Statistical Manual of Mental Disorders (DSM)* of the American Psychiatric Association (APA, 2013)—another example of Pepper's 'formism' metaphor.

The *DSM* was drawn up in 1952 as a descriptive taxonomic system explicitly claimed to be atheoretical, to enable its use by practitioners favouring different theoretical orientations. However, some suggest that it is impossible to devise an explanatory system devoid of underlying theoretical assumptions. Those underlying the *DSM* project include viewing mental disorder as a subset of medical disorder, with each illness defined by certain behavioural criteria endowed with biological significance, removing them from any broader contextual considerations. In fact, psychiatrist Sami Timimi (2018) argues that psychiatric diagnoses are rarely explanatory, but descriptive and circular (I have these symptoms, therefore I have condition X; the cause of my symptoms is condition X). Peter Butler claimed that 'despite the cool neutrality of its language, the diagnostic project was *intended* from its inception to lead to a progressive exclusion of non-biologically focused systems of explanation (psychological, psychosocial, psychoanalytic) from authoritative psychiatric discourse' (Butler, 1999: 21, original emphasis). Butler and others have argued that successive changes to *DSM* classifications, rather than being driven by scientific evidence, as claimed, have been heavily influenced by sociocultural factors. The eventual removal of homosexuality as a mental disorder in 1974, in the face of changing societal attitudes, was a prime example. In the 2022 *DSM-5-TR* version, terminology changed from 'cross-sex treatment' for gender dysphoria to the more positive 'gender-affirming treatment'. Another example is that the shift from *DSM*-IV to *DSM*-5 in 2013 brought different autism-related diagnoses under the single umbrella of 'autism spectrum'; responding to the concerns of advocates about 'losing' their diagnoses and associated services, the *DSM*-5 encouraged clinicians to include such individuals in the new diagnosis—hardly the action of a neutral and objective revision process (Cooper, 2014).

ADHD again provides a good illustration of the ongoing trend to view children's problematic behaviours as medical conditions. ADHD has often been 'uncritically accepted as a neurobiological condition' (Reid and Maag, 1997: 13), with children's problematic behaviours regarding attention, impulsivity and high activity levels attracting a medical label and a drug-based solution (usually the psychostimulant methylphenidate). ADHD has long been a contentious diagnosis.

Proponents found it necessary to draw up an international consensus statement confirming its acceptance as a neurobiological condition (Barkley *et al.*, 2002). This in turn was critiqued by Timimi and 33 co-endorsers (2004), who pointed out the lack of any biological marker for the condition, any effect of medication specific to those diagnosed with ADHD, or any effect of medication beyond four weeks. Yet, in the United States, between 2003 and 2011 there was a 28 per cent increase in medicated ADHD (Visser *et al.*, 2014). The wide acceptance of the medical perspective in Australia, too, has marginalized non-medical professionals, including child psychologists, whose very area of expertise is children's behaviour (Atkinson and Shute, 1999; Prosser *et al.*, 2002); medication levels more than doubled over the five years up to 2022, with 3.2 million prescriptions issued (Hooton, 2024) in a population of 27 million, and one in ten people estimated to 'have' ADHD. Several decades ago, it was observed that increased demands in some countries for children's educational achievement, together with declining education and mental health budgets, was increasing the pressure for children's behaviour problems to be treated medically (Searight and McLaren, 1998); in Australia today, professional and lay opinions are expressed that ADHD is a wealthy people's condition, with expensive specialist clinics proliferating and medication sought especially by the parents of private high school students approaching their final examinations, in which the diagnosis earns them extra time (Hooton, 2024). To counteract the expense and delays of appointments with psychiatrists or paediatricians, Australian general medical practitioners are increasingly able to access training in ADHD diagnosis and management.

Such trends are part of a general pattern in western societies of 'medicalization' of non-disease states, with relief sought for discomforts and distress which would formerly have been tolerated (Searight and McLaren, 1998). In the case of ADHD, its wide acceptance as a neurobiological condition treatable by medication has led to a neglect of possible environmental causes, a lack of concern about medication side-effects and the promotion of a culture in which a pill is the solution to life's problems (Timimi *et al.*, 2004). The media's role in such medicalization is demonstrated by an analysis of Australian newsprint articles about ADHD between 1999 and 2009 (Harwood *et al.*, 2017). Social media too are purported to be spreading self-diagnosis and encouraging demands for treatment, with psychiatrists critical of ADHD diagnoses reporting feeling like pariahs (Hooton, 2024). Brenton Prosser (2024) sees debates about whether ADHD is 'real' as unhelpful, and advocates for the use of guidelines aimed at achieving a more consistent approach to diagnosis and treatment.

If indeed the intention of the *DSM* project was to edge out alternative theoretical perspectives on mental and behavioural problems, it has succeeded; it can be difficult for the alternative perspectives on child development considered in this book to be brought to bear effectively to address children's behavioural and emotional problems. However, the production of the *DSM*-5 in 2013 coincided with a rash of critical books as new diagnostic criteria were set to cast an even wider net; for example, continuing to grieve for a loved one could be seen as pathological within weeks of the death, leading to accusations that *DSM*-5 medicalized normal sorrow.

The project's credibility was further undermined by the finding that most of the various panels involved in the *DSM*-5 revision had a majority of members with a financial interest in the pharmaceutical industry (Cosgrove and Krimsky, 2012); the further term 'pharmaceuticalization' was coined for reframing or creating pathologies for the benefit of that industry (Pickersgill, 2013). There were even rumblings from the US National Institutes of Mental Health that alternatives to the *DSM* might be considered as more suitable for underpinning future research efforts, but a joint statement with the American Psychological Association soon papered over any cracks. The British Psychological Society went much further, comprehensively repudiating the *DSM* and similar diagnostic systems as a basis for clinical practice, favouring broad-based case formulation instead (British Psychological Society, 2011). For an account of the *DSM*-5 disputes placed in a complex historical context, see David Pilgrim (2014) and Martyn Pickersgill (2013), who concluded that:

> Diagnostic entities are powerful things, shaping society and individual subjectivities; it is, then, precisely for this reason that we should concern ourselves with what they are and with what they do.
>
> *(Pickersgill, 2013: 524)*

An even stronger statement follows:

> The only way I can see to move forward from this disaster is for commissioning and payment of services to stop being based on diagnoses and for the accompanying narrow biomedical model of mental health to be scrapped.
>
> *(Timimi, interviewed by Maisel, 2016)*

In 2024, Australia's world-first National Disability Insurance Scheme did, in fact, move from a service model based on diagnosis of physical and psychological conditions, to one based on need for functional or early intervention support. Diagnoses (e.g. concerning autism or developmental delay) may form part of the evidence for long-term disability, but eligibility depends on functional assessment (National Disability Insurance Scheme, n.d.). Alternatives to psychiatric diagnosis exist, for addressing mental distress and behavioural difficulties (Johnstone and Boyle, 2018). For children specifically, the hypothesis-testing approach of Martin Herbert (2006) offers a strong framework for assessment and intervention.

Finally, we can mention the increasing profile of neurodiversity, which is often ranged against the medical model (a deficit approach). It concerns acceptance of people as having different ways of thinking and learning (McLennan *et al.*, 2025). Despite the biological implication of the term, these authors found that most research that explicitly uses it is qualitative, and addresses matters of identity and wellbeing, focusing on adults rather than children. People often self-identify and there is no consensus on terminology or scope. Future research may concentrate on better ways to support children who experience the world differently from the majority (see Chapter 13).

Conclusions

The writings of Darwin were influential in establishing the field of child development and, with the advent of new technologies for studying genetics and brain function, biological approaches to psychological development are gaining further credence. Epigenetics research is giving impetus to the reconciliation of genetic and experiential approaches to development, and the relevance of culture and cooperation for human evolution is being explored. Biologically plausible theorizing about development is to be welcomed. However, the ongoing tendency to conceptualize children's behavioural and emotional problems as medical conditions raises serious concerns.

A major attraction of evolutionary and other biological approaches to behavioural development may be that they provide psychology with a yearned-for basis in the physical sciences (Miller, 1999). Joan Miller noted that such approaches edge out culture, which does not just *contribute* to psychological processes, but is a qualitative *determinant of the patterning* of those processes. Criticisms of evolutionary approaches that see the mother–child attachment relationship as an 'inherent glue' have also been raised, as divorcing the reproductive experiences of women from oppressive historical and political realities (Franzblau, 1999), as well as neglecting cultural diversity. We will meet such critical approaches in later pages.

Note

1 Dawkins denied this and a series of complex exchanges followed. Tanghe (2023) concludes that Wilson and Wilson were essentially correct.

References

Ainsworth, M. D. S. and Wittig, B. A. 1969. Attachment and exploratory behaviour of one-year-olds in a strange situation. In B. M. Foss (ed.), *Determinants of infant behaviour*. Vol. 4. London: Methuen, 113–36.

Ambrosino, E., Abou Tayoun, A. N., Abramowicz, M., Zilfalil, B. A., Boughtwood, T., Hamdi, Y. *et al.* 2024. The WHO genomics program of work for equitable implementation of human genomics for global health. *Nature Medicine 30*: 2711–13. https://doi.org/10.1038/s41591-024-03225-x

American Psychiatric Association. 2013. *Diagnostic and statistical manual of mental disorders*. Fifth edn. (*DSM-5*). Arlington: American Psychiatric Association.

Anderson, V., Spencer-Smith, M. and Wood, A. 2011. Do children really recover better? Neurobehavioural plasticity after early brain insult. *Brain 134*: 2197–221. https://doi.org/10.1093/brain/awr103

Armstrong-Carter, E., Wertz, J. and Domingue, B. W. 2021. Genetics and child development: recent advances and their implications for developmental research. *Child Development Perspectives 19*: 57–64. https://doi.org/10.1111/cdep.12400

Atkinson, I. and Shute, R. 1999. Managing ADHD: issues in developing multidisciplinary guidelines. *Journal of Psychologists and Counsellors in Schools 9*(2): 119–28. https://doi.org/10.1017/S1037291100003976

Barkley, R. A., Cook, E. H., Diamond, A., Zametkin, A., Thapar, A., Teeter, A. *et al.* 2002. International consensus statement on ADHD. *Clinical Child and Family Psychology Review 5*(2): 89–111. https://doi.org/10.1023/a:1017494719205

Barreto-Zarza, F. and Arranz-Freijo, E. B. 2022. Family context, parenting and child development: an epigenetic approach. *Social Sciences 11*(3): 113. https://doi.org/10.3390/socsci11030113

Baumrind, D. 1993. The average expectable environment is not good enough: a response to Scarr. *Child Development 6*: 1299–317. https://doi.org/10.1111/j.1467-8624.1993.tb02954.x

Bjorklund, D. F. 2018. Developing adaptations. *Developmental Review 38*: 13–35. http://dx.doi.org/10.1016/j.dr.2015.07.002

Blurton Jones, N. 1972. *Ethological studies of child behaviour*. Cambridge: Cambridge University Press.

Bolhuis, J. J., Brown, G. R., Richardson, R. C. and Laland, K. N. 2011. Darwin in mind: new opportunities for evolutionary psychology. *PLoS Biology 9*(7): e1001109. https://doi.org/10.1371/journal.pbio.1001109

Boyce, W. T. and Ellis, B. J. 2005. Biological sensitivity to context: I. An evolutionary developmental theory of the origins and function of stress reactivity. *Development and Psychopathology 17*(3): 271–301. https://doi.org/10.1111/j.1467-8721.2008.00571.x

British Psychological Society. 2011. *Response to the American Psychiatric Association: DSM-5 development*. London: British Psychological Society. https://dxrevisionwatch.com/wp-content/uploads/2012/02/dsm-5-2011-bps-response.pdf

Bronfenbrenner, U. 1979. *The ecology of human development: experiments by nature and design*. Cambridge, MA: Harvard University Press.

Bronfenbrenner, U. and Morris, P. A. 1998. The ecology of developmental processes. In R. M. Lerner (ed.), *Handbook of child psychology: theoretical models of human development*. Fifth edn. Vol. 1. New York: Wiley, 993–1027.

Buller, D. J. 2005. Evolutionary psychology: the emperor's new paradigm. *Trends in Cognitive Sciences 9*(6): 277–83. https://doi.org/10.1016/j.tics.2005.04.003

Buss, D. M. and Schmidtt, D. P. 2011. Evolutionary psychology and feminism. *Sex Roles 64*: 768–87. https://doi.org/10.1007/s11199-011-9987-3

Butler, P. V. 1999. Diagnostic line-drawing, professional boundaries, and the rhetoric of scientific justification: a critical appraisal of the American Psychiatric Association's *DSM* project. *Australian Psychologist 34*: 20–9. https://doi.org/10.1080/00050069908257420

Cadwell, C. R., Bhaduri, A., Mostajo-Radji, M. A., Keefe, M. G. and Nowakowski, T. J. 2019. Development and arealization of the cerebral cortex. *Neuron 103*: 980–1004. https://doi.org/10.1016/j.neuron.2019.07.009

Campbell, A. 2012. The study of sex differences: feminism and biology. *Zeitschrift für Psychologie 220*(2): 137–43. https://doi.org/10.1027/2151-2604/a000105

Cappello, S., Gray, M. J., Baduel, C., Lange, S., Einsiedler, M., Srour, M. *et al.* 2013. Mutations in genes encoding the cadherin receptor-ligand pair DCHS1 and FAT4 disrupt cerebral cortical development. *Nature Genetics 45*(11): 1300–8. https://doi.org/10.1038/ng.2765

Caspi, A., McClay, J., Moffitt, T. E., Mill, J., Martin, J., Craig, I. W. *et al.* 2002. Role of genotype in the cycle of violence in maltreated children. *Science 297*(5582): 851–4. https://doi.org/10.1126/science.1072290

Charlesworth, W. R. 1992. Darwin and developmental psychology: past and present. *Developmental Psychology 28*: 5–16. https://psycnet.apa.org/doi/10.1037/0012-1649.28.1.5

Cooper, R. 2014. *Diagnosing the Diagnostic and Statistical Manual of Mental Disorders*. London: Karnac Books.

Cosgrove, L. and Krimsky, S. 2012. A comparison of *DSM*-IV and *DSM*-5 panel members' financial associations with industry: a pernicious problem persists. *PLOS Medicine*. https://doi.org/10.1371/journal.pmed.1001190

Crick, N. R. and Bigbee, M. A. 1998. Relational and overt forms of peer victimization: a multiinformant approach. *Journal of Consulting and Clinical Psychology 6*: 337–47. https://doi.org/10.1037//0022-006x.66.2.337.

Danelli, L., Cossu, G., Berlingeri, M., Bottini, G. Sberna, M. and Paulesu, E. 2013. Is a lone right hemisphere enough? Neurolinguistic architecture in a case with a very early left hemispherectomy. *Neurocase 19*(3): 209–31. https://doi.org/10.1080/13554794.2011.654226

Darwin, C. 1859. *On the origin of species*. London: John Murray.

Dawkins, R. 1976. *The selfish gene*. Oxford: Oxford University Press.

Dixon, R. A and Lerner, R. M. 1992. A history of systems in developmental psychology. In M. H. Bornstein and M. E. Lamb (eds), *Developmental psychology: an advanced textbook*. Third edn. Hillsdale: Erlbaum, 3–58.

Dunbar, R. I. M. 1992. Neocortex size as a constraint on group size in primates. *Journal of Human Evolution 20*: 469–93. https://doi.org/10.1016/0047-2484(92)90081-J

Eagly, A. and Wood, W. 2013. Feminism and evolutionary psychology: moving forward. *Sex Roles 69*: 549–56. https://doi.org/10.1007/s11199-013-0315-y

Fodor, J. A. 1983. *Modularity of mind: an essay on faculty psychology*. Cambridge, MA: MIT Press.

Franzblau, S. H. 1999. Historicizing attachment theory: binding the ties that bind. *Feminism and Psychology 9*: 22–31. https://doi.org/10.1177/0959353599009001003

Freedman, D. G. 1979. *Human sociobiology: a holistic approach*. New York: Free Press.

Galea, C., Robidoux, S., Salins, A., Noble, C. and McArthur, G. 2024. The impact of shared book reading on children and families: a study of Dolly Parton's Imagination Library in Tamworth, Australia. *Journal of Research in Childhood Education*: 1–30. https://doi.org/10.1080/02568543.2024.2322731

Geary, D. C and Bjorklund, D. F. 2000. Evolutionary developmental psychology. *Child Development 71*: 57–65.

Gilbert, R. and Gilbert, P. 1998. *Masculinity goes to school*. St. Leonards, New South Wales: Allen & Unwin.

Gottesman, I. I. 1974. Developmental genetics and ontogenetic psychology: overdue entente and propositions from a matchmaker. In A. Pick (ed.), *Minnesota symposium on child psychology*. Minneapolis: University of Minnesota Press, 55–80.

Gould, J., Di Fiore, C., Williamson, P., Roberts, R. M., Shute, R. H., Collins, C. T. and Makrides, M. 2022. Diathesis-stress or differential susceptibility? Comparing the theories when determining the outcomes for children born preterm. *Acta Psychologica 224*: 103533. https://doi.org/10.1016/j.actpsy.2022.103533

Gould, S. J. and Lewontin, R. C. 1979. The spandrels of San Marco and the Panglossian paradigm: a critique of the adaptationist programme. *Proceedings of the Biological Society of London 205*: 581–98. https://doi.org/10.1098/rspb.1979.0086

Gräfe, S. and Stuhrmann, C. 2022. Histories and ethology: methods, sites, and dynamics of an unbound discipline. *Berichte zur Wissenschaftsgeschchichte 45*(1–2): 10–29. https://doi.org/10.1002/bewi.202200026

Hambrick, E. P., Brawner, T. W. and Perry, B. D. 2019. Timing of early-life stress and the development of brain-related capacities. *Frontiers in Behavioral Neuroscience 6*(13): 183. https://doi.org/10.3389/fnbeh.2019.00183

Harris, J. R. 2013. Where is the child's environment? A group socialization theory of development. *Psychological Review 102*(3): 458–89. https://psycnet.apa.org/doi/10.1037/0033-295X.102.3.458

Harwood, V., Jones, S., Bonney, A. and McMahon, S. 2017. Heroic struggles, criminals and scientific breakthroughs: ADHD and the medicalization of child behaviour in Australian newsprint media 1999–2009. *International Journal of Qualitative Studies on Health and Well-being 12*: 1298262. https://doi.org/10.1080/17482631.2017.1298262

Hawkes, K. 2004. The grandmother effect. *Nature 428*: 128–9. www.nature.com/articles/428128a

Hellal, P. and Lorch, M. 2010. Darwin's contribution to the study of child development and language acquisition. *Language & History 53*: 1–14. https://doi.org/10.1179/175975310X12640878626147

Herbert, M. 2006. Clinical diagnosis and assessment: theoretical considerations. In M. Herbert (ed.), *Clinical child and adolescent psychology*. np: Wiley, 6–31.

Hess, E. H. and Petrovitch, S. B. 2000. Ethology and attachment: a historical perspective. *The Behavioral Development Bulletin 9*: 14–19. https://psycnet.apa.org/fulltext/2014-55592-005.html

Hetherington, E. M., Reiss, D. and Plomin, R. (eds). 1994. *Separate social worlds of siblings: the impact of nonshared environment on development*. Hillsdale, NJ: Erlbaum.

Hinde, R. A. 1992a. Developmental psychology in the context of other behavioral sciences. *Developmental Psychology 28*(6): 1018–29. https://psycnet.apa.org/doi/10.1037/0012-1649.28.6.1018

Hinde, R. A. 1992b. Commentary. *Human Development 35*: 34–9. https://doi.org/10.1159/000277111

Hooton, A. 2024. Why has everyone suddenly got ADHD? *The Age*, 9 March. Reproduced by the Australian Psychological Society at https://psychology.org.au/about-us/news-and-media/aps-in-the-media/2024/why-has-everyone-suddenly-got-adhd

House, B., Henrich, J., Sarnecka, B. and Silk, J. B. 2013. The development of contingent reciprocity in children. *Evolution and Human Behavior 34*: 86–93. https://doi.org/10.1016/j.evolhumbehav.2012.10.001

Huang, J. Y. and King, N. B. 2018. Epigenetics changes nothing: what a new scientific field does and does not mean for ethics and social justice. *Public Health Ethics 11*: 69–81. https://doi.org/10.1093/phe/phx013

Johnstone, L and Boyle, M. 2018. The Power-Threat-Meaning Framework: An alternative non-diagnostic conceptual system. *Journal of Humanistic Psychology 65*(4). https://doi.org/10.1177/0022167818793289

Karmiloff-Smith, A. 2012. Perspectives on the dynamic development of cognitive capacities: insights from Williams syndrome. *Current Opinion in Neurology 25*(2): 106–11. https://doi.org/10.1097/WCO.0b013e3283518130

Ketelaar, T. and Ellis, B. J. 2000. Are evolutionary explanations unfalsifiable? Evolutionary psychology and the Lakatosian philosophy of science. *Psychological Inquiry 11*: 1–21. https://psycnet.apa.org/doi/10.1207/S15327965PLI1101_01

Kipling, R. 1902/1975. *Just so stories*. London: Piccolo.

Koops, W. 2015. No developmental psychology without recapitulation theory. *European Journal of Developmental Psychology 12*(6): 630–9. https://doi.org/10.1080/17405629.2015.1078234

Labonte, B., Yerko, V., Gross, J., Mechawar, N., Meaney, M. J., Szyf, M. and Turecki, G. 2012. Differential glucocorticoid receptor exon 1B, 1C and 1H expression and methylation in suicide completers with a history of childhood abuse. *Biological Psychiatry 72*: 41–8. https://doi.org/10.1016/j.biopsych.2012.01.034

Laurence, S. and Margolis, E. 2024. *The building blocks of thought: a rationalist account of the origins of concepts*. Oxford: Oxford University Press.

Legare, C. H., Clegg, J. M. and Wen, N. J. 2018. Evolutionary developmental psychology: 2017 redux. *Child Development 89*(6): 2282–7. https://doi.org/10.1111/cdev.13018

Lerner, R. M. and von Eye, A. 1992. Sociobiology and human development: arguments and evidence. *Human Development 35*: 12–33. https://psycnet.apa.org/doi/10.1159/000277110

Lorenz, K. Z. 1981. *The foundations of ethology*. New York: Springer Verlag.

Machluf, K., Liddle, J. R. and Bjorklund, D. F. 2014. An introduction to evolutionary developmental psychology. *Evolutionary Psychology 12*(2): 264–72. https://journals.sagepub.com/doi/full/10.1177/147470491401200201

Maisel, E. R. 2016. Sami Timimi on ADHD, autism and children's mental health. *Psychology Today*, 1 April. www.psychologytoday.com/us/blog/rethinking-mental-health/201604/sami-timimi-adhd-autism-and-childrens-mental-health

McLennan, H., Aberdein, R., Saggers, B. and Gillett-Swan, J. 2025. Neurodiversity: a scoping review of empirical research. *Neurodiversity 3*. https://doi.org/10.1177/27546330251337874

Miller, J. G. 1999. Cultural psychology: implications for basic psychological theory. *Psychological Science 10*(2): 85–91. https://doi.org/10.1111/1467-9280.00113

Miller, G. 2010. The seductive allure of behavioral epigenetics. *Science 329*: 24–7. www.science.org/doi/10.1126/science.329.5987.24

Murgatroyd, C. and Spengler, D. 2011. Epigenetics of early child development. *Frontiers in Psychiatry 2*: Article 16. https://doi.org/10.3389/fpsyt.2011.00016

Muthukrishna, M. 2024. ABC radio interview with James Carleton. www.abc.net.au/listen/programs/godforbid/michael-muthukrishna-evolution-anthropology/104264964

National Disability Insurance Scheme (Australia) (n.d.). www.ndis.gov.au/applying-access-ndis/how-apply/information-support-your-request/types-disability-evidence

Ng, R., Kalinousky, A. and Harris, J. 2023. Epigenetics of cognition and behavior: insights from Mendelian disorders of epigenetic machinery. *Journal of Neurodevelopmental Disorders 15*: Article 16. https://doi.org/10.1186/s11689-023-09482-0

Odenwald, J. 2022. Ethologists in the Kindergarten: natural behavior, social rank, and the search for the 'innate' in early human ethology (1960s–1970s). *Berichte zur Wissenschaftsgeschchichte 45*(1–2): 87–111. https://doi.org/10.1002/bewi.202100022

Okasha, S. 2013. Biological altruism. In E. N. Zalta (ed.), *The Stanford Encyclopedia of Philosophy. Fall 2013 Edition.* http://plato.stanford.edu/archives/fall2013/entries/altruism-biological/

Owens, L., Shute, R. and Slee, P. 2000. 'Guess what I just heard…': indirect aggression among teenage girls in Australia. *Aggressive Behavior 26*: 67–83. https://psycnet.apa.org/doi/10.1002/(SICI)1098-2337(2000)26:1%3C67::AID-AB6%3E3.0.CO;2-C

Pepper, S. 1942. *World hypotheses: a study of evidence*. Berkeley: University of California Press.

Perry, B. D. 1997. Incubated in terror: neurodevelopmental factors in the 'Cycle of violence'. In J. D. Osofky (ed.), *Children in a violent society*. New York: Guilford, 124–49.

Pickersgill, M. D. 2013. Debating *DSM*-5: diagnosis and the sociology of critique. *Journal of Medical Ethics 40*: 521–5. https://doi.org/10.1136/medethics-2013-101762

Pilgrim, D. 2014. Historical resonances of the *DSM*-5 dispute: American exceptionalism or Eurocentrism? *History of the Human Sciences 27*(2): 97–117. https://doi.org/10.1177/0952695114527998

Pluess, M. and Belsky, J. 2012. Prenatal programming of postnatal plasticity? *Development and Psychopathology 23*: 29–38. https://doi.org/10.1017/S0954579410000623

Prosser, B. 2024. ADHD prescribing has changed over the years – a new guide aims to bring doctors up to speed. *The Conversation*, 4 October. https://theconversation.com/adhd-prescribing-has-changed-over-the-years-a-new-guide-aims-to-bring-doctors-up-to-speed-240313

Prosser, B., Reid, R., Shute, R. and Atkinson, I. 2002. Attention Deficit Hyperactivity Disorder (ADHD): special education policy and practice in Australia. *Australian Journal of Education 46*: 65–78. https://doi.org/10.1177/000494410204600106

Reid, R. and Maag. J. W. 1997. Attention deficit hyperactivity disorder: over here and over there. *Educational and Child Psychology 14*: 10–20. http://dx.doi.org/10.53841/bpsecp.1997.14.1.10

Rippon, G. 2019. *The gendered brain: the new neuroscience that shatters the myth of the female brain*. London: Bodley Head.

Rose, H. and Rose, S. 2001. Much ado about very little. *The Psychologist 14*(3): 428–9.

Rose, S. 2001. DNA is important – but only in its proper place. *The Psychologist 14*(3): 144–5. www.bps.org.uk/psychologist-issue/2001/march/psychologist-march-2001

Rosenzweig, M. R. 1996. Aspects of the search for neural mechanisms of memory. *Annual Review of Psychology 47*: 1–32. www.sciencegate.app/document/10.1146/annurev.psych.47.1.1

Sameroff, A. J. 1983. Developmental systems: contexts and evolution. In W. Kessen (ed.), *Handbook of child psychology*. Vol. 1. *History, theory and methods*. New York: Wiley, 237–94.

Sampaio, E., Seco, M. C., Rosa, R. and Gingins, S. 2021. Octopuses punch fishes during collaborative interspecific hunting events. *Ecology 102*(3): e03266. https://doi.org/10.1002/ecy.3266

Scarr, S. 1992. Developmental theories for the 1990s: development and individual differences. *Child Development 6*: 1–19. https://psycnet.apa.org/doi/10.2307/1130897

Schmutz, J., Wheeler, J., Grimwood, J., Dickson, M., Yang, J., Caoile, C. *et al.* 2004. Quality assessment of the human genome sequence. *Nature 429*(6990): 365–8. https://doi.org/10.1038%2Fnature02390

Searight, H. R. and McLaren, A. L. 1998. Attention-Deficit Hyperactivity Disorder: the medicalization of misbehavior. *Journal of Clinical Psychology in Medical Settings 5*(4): 467–95. https://psycnet.apa.org/doi/10.1023/A:1026263012665

Segal, L. 2001. Main agendas and hidden agendas. *The Psychologist 14*(8): 422–3.

Seligman, M. E., Steen, T. A., Park, N. and Peterson, C. 2005. Positive psychology progress: empirical validation of interventions. *American Psychologist 60*(5): 410–21. https://doi.org/10.1037/0003-066X.60.5.410

Sluckin, W. 1970. *Early learning in man and animal*. London: Allen & Unwin.

Smaldino, P. E. 2019. Social identity and cooperation in cultural evolution. *Behavioural Processes 161*: 108–16. https://doi.org/10.1016/j.beproc.2017.11.015

Snowling, M. 2000. *Dyslexia*. Second edn. Oxford: Blackwell.

Suchak, M., Eppley, T. M., Campbell, M. W., Feldman, R. A., Quaries, L. F. and de Waal, F. B. M. 2016. How chimpanzees cooperate in a competitive world. *PNAS 113*(36): 10215–20. https://doi.org/10.1073/pnas.1611826113

Tanghe, K. 2023. Did Dawkins recant his selfish gene argument against group selection? *Theoretical Biology Forum 116*(1–2): 75–86. http://hdl.handle.net/1854/LU-01HAKN6FBQPS2G693S41S64A38

Tate, C. C. 2013. Addressing conceptual confusions about evolutionary theorizing: how and why evolutionary psychology and feminism do not oppose each other. *Sex Roles. 69*: 491–502. https://doi.org/10.1007/s11199-012-0226-3

Tees, R. C. 1986. Experience and visual development: behavioral evidence. In W. T. Greenough and J. M. Juraska (eds), *Developmental neurobiology*. New York: Academic Press, 317–61.

Timimi, S. 2018. Attention-deficit hyperactivity disorder: a critique of the concept. *Irish Journal of Psychological Medicine 35*(3): 257–9. https://doi.org/10.1017/ipm.2018.9

Timimi, S. and 33 co-endorsers. 2004. A critique of the international consensus statement on ADHD. *Clinical Child and Family Psychology Review 7*: 59–63. www.brown.uk.com/diagnosis/timimi.pdf

Tinbergen, N. 1973. *The animal in its world: explorations of an ethologist, 1932–1972*. Vols 1 & 2. Cambridge, MA: Harvard University Press.

Tzschentke, B. and Plagemann, A. 2006. Imprinting and critical periods in early development. *World's Poultry Science Journal 62*(4): 626–37. www.tandfonline.com/doi/abs/10.1017/S0043933906001176

University of Southampton News. 2024. Human genome stored on 'everlasting' memory crystal. www.southampton.ac.uk/news/2024/09/human-genome-stored-on-everlasting-memory-crystal-.page

van der Molen, M. W. and Ridderinkhof, K. R. 1998. The growing and aging brain: life-span changes in brain and cognitive functioning. In A. Demetriou, W. Doise and C. van Lieshout (eds), *Lifespan developmental psychology*. Chichester: Wiley, 35–100.

Visser, S., Danielson, M. L., Bitsko, R. H., Ghandour, R. M., Perou, R. and Blumberg, S. 2014. Trends in the parent-report of health care provider-diagnosed and medicated Attention-Deficit/Hyperactivity Disorder: United States, 2003–2011. *Journal of the American Academy of Child & Adolescent Psychiatry 53*: 34–46. https://doi.org/10.1016/j.jaac.2013.09.001

Volk, A. A., Camilleri, J. A., Dane, A. V. and Marini, Z. A. 2012. Is adolescent bullying an evolutionary adaptation? *Aggressive Behavior 38*: 222–38. https://doi.org/10.1002/ab.21418

von Frisch, K. 1973. Decoding the language of the bee. *Nobel Lecture*, 12 December. www.nobelprize.org/uploads/2018/06/frisch-lecture.pdf

Vreeke, G.-J. 2000. Nature, nurture and the future of the analysis of variance. *Human Development 4*: 32–45. https://doi.org/10.1159/000022654

Waddington, C. H. 1942. Canalization of development and the inheritance of acquired characters. *Nature 150*: 563–5. https://doi.org/10.1038/150563a0

Weaver, I. C., Cervoni, N., Champagne, F. A., D'Alessio, A. C. Sharma, S., Secki, J. R. *et al.* 2004. Epigenetic programming by maternal behavior. *Nature Neuroscience 7*: 847–54. https://doi.org/10.1038/nn1276

Wertz, J., Belsky, J., Moffitt, T. E., Belsky, D. W., Harrington, H., Reut, A. *et al.* 2019. Genetics of nurture: a test of the hypothesis that parents' genetics predict their observed caregiving. *Developmental Psychology 55*: 1461–72. https://psycnet.apa.org/doi/10.1037/dev0000709

Westall, C. and Shute, R. 1992. OKN asymmetries in orthoptic patients: contributing factors and effects of treatment. *Behavioural Brain Research 49*: 77–84. www.sciencedirect.com/science/article/abs/pii/S0166432805801962

Wilson, D. S. and Wilson, E. O. 2007. Rethinking the theoretical foundation of sociobiology. *The Quarterly Review of Biology 82*(4): 327–48. www.journals.uchicago.edu/doi/full/10.1086/522809

Wilson, E. O. 1975. *Sociobiology: the new synthesis*. Cambridge MA: Harvard University Press.

World Health Organization. 2024. *Guidance for human genome data collection, access, use, and sharing*. https://iris.who.int/bitstream/handle/10665/379554/9789240102149-eng.pdf?sequence=1

Yang, F., Choi, Y.-J., Misch, A., Yang, X. and Dunham, Y. 2018. In defense of the commons: young children negatively evaluate and sanction free riders. *Psychological Science 29*(10): 1598–611. https://doi.org/10.1177/0956797618779061

4 Mechanism, behaviourism and beyond

The whole is equal to the sum of its parts

Introduction

Daniel Weiskopf observed that '[w]e are in the midst of a mania for mechanisms' (Weiskopf, 2011: 313). We will shortly explain what he meant, before describing the work of a number of influential theorists including Ivan Pavlov, John Watson, Mary Cover Jones, Burrhus F. Skinner and Albert Bandura. The worldview for their theories is 'mechanism' (Pepper, 1942), although Bandura came to see a need for a more cognitive and organismic approach to learning. The root metaphor is 'the universe as a machine, composed of discrete pieces operating in a spatio-temporal field' (Reese and Overton, 1970: 131). After outlining the philosophical background to these ideas, we consider the rise of behaviourism and then discuss how other theoretical views came to modify it, including Bandura's theorizing and information processing models.

Philosophical background

The philosophical issue of the relationship between mind and body is relevant for a consideration of mechanism. Plato (*c*.429–*c*.347 BCE) adopted a dualist position, arguing that the two were different entities. He considered the body as temporal but the mind as having greater permanence, as ideas live on through generations. In his book *Utopia*, the mind was to be cultivated by education to bring some reason and order into what are often seen as chaotic ideas. Plato's theory of 'Ideas' (or 'thoughts') was developed in *The Republic*. He was seeking to understand the essence of things—the distinction between reality and appearance. Plato's cave allegory represents, symbolically, the structure of reality. The cave represents the world as perceived by the senses, as indistinct shadows cast on its walls by a fire, which are all that people chained in the cave since childhood can see as others pass by, who name the objects casting the shadows. The outside world represents the true world perceived by reason, or the world of Ideas. The difference is one of appearance and reality. Plato's identification of the mind–body split is indirectly linked to the rise of experimental science in the modern era, since the mechanistic approach rejects introspection as a method appropriate for a behavioural scientist. Subjectivism and speculation regarding entities that cannot be directly observed

DOI: 10.4324/9781003567738-4

or measured are believed to have no place in an empirical behavioural science. As a rationalist, Plato sought to solve problems using deductive reasoning (drawing specific conclusions from general premises) as opposed to inductive reasoning (forming general theories from specific observations). Deriving knowledge from reason he saw as superior to that derived from sense perceptions alone. Plato set the scene for further debate, including Descartes' somewhat different approach to mind–body dualism in terms of the mental and physical as being different kinds of substance, that still has echoes in psychology and psychiatry today (Thibaut, 2018).

Behaviourism developed in the context of the rise to prominence in the 19th century of Newtonian science, which replaced the medieval view of a living, organic, spiritual universe with a mechanistic vision of reality. In the Newtonian view, the earlier interpretation of the world based upon introspection, revelation, reason and ordinary experience was abandoned in favour of rigid determinism and linear causality. Science delimited knowledge to a worldview constrained by statistical probability, value-free research and quantification.

Mechanism is commonly associated with causation, as we discussed in Chapter 1 with reference to the recent philosophical work of Lauren Ross and Deon Benton. Indeed, Weiskopf's comment referred to earlier, about a 'mania for mechanisms', relates to efforts to produce explanations for psychological (and other) phenomena; specifically, to explain an entity or system's ability, propensity or exercise of capacity, such as Weiskopf's ability to identify a lime, or the capacity of a neuron to produce an action potential. While eliciting causative mechanisms is a central concern of developmental psychology in general, the theories we discuss here have specifically been identified as 'mechanistic'.

Possibly no other perspective on child development has been subjected to such scrutiny as behaviourism, the approach to development forming the core of the present chapter. William James was severely critical of this approach ('structuralism'), because he considered it to provide a narrow and artificial view of human behaviour. As Frances Horowitz observed, 'It has been declared obsolete, overthrown, and outmoded. Yet, paradoxically, this object of derision, behaviorism, has given us our most unassailable behavioral laws' (Horowitz, 1987: 62). Not only has it largely stood the test of time, but its underlying principles have given rise to powerful behavioural technologies, such as those used to assist people with cognitive and physical impairments.

Also relevant are three metaphors identified by Richard Mayer (1996) in relation to theories of learning and instruction: learning as response-strengthening; learning as information processing; and learning as knowledge construction. We can also note here that social-cognitive and information processing approaches share with behaviourism an underpinning deterministic outlook towards developmental theory, that is, whatever facet of development we are considering, for every effect there is an identifiable antecedent cause that can be discovered in terms of its constituent elements.

Another philosophical view associated with the development of behaviourism was 'materialism' (or physicalism), holding that all facts are ultimately dependent on physical processes, hence scientific principles could be applied to the study of living organisms. To this end, physical and chemical laws were the basis of explanation—for example, physiology was reduced to chemistry. It was in this intellectual climate of scientism, materialism and reductionism that pioneer psychologists such as Sigmund Freud and Ivan Pavlov were educated.

The mechanistic worldview has had a revival in the 21st century in the form of 'neo-mechanism'. In-depth coverage can be found in a book by Diego Leite (2021), who has discussed a mechanistic theory of human cognition that requires an understanding of a foundational mechanistic theory of complex biological systems.

Ivan Pavlov (1849–1936) and the conditioned reflex

Pavlov was born in a small town in central Russia, the son of a clergyman. He turned from theological studies to obtain degrees in natural science and medicine, then travelled in Europe and studied with other scientists. He founded the Institute of Experimental Medicine in St Petersburg in 1890 and became its lifelong director. In 1904 he was the first Russian scientist to be awarded the Nobel Prize. Pavlov held a rather negative view of the new discipline of psychology, believing his own contribution fell within the field of physiology; he 'only became a psychologist when he was dragged across the gulf from physiology to psychology by a phenomenon revealed during studies of digestion' (Corr and Perkins, 2006: 368).

Pavlov's discovery of classical conditioning as a way of viewing the functioning of the nervous system remains his greatest contribution to psychology. In the course of his physiology experiments Pavlov observed certain irregularities in the normal functioning of the digestive glands of dogs. Sometimes a dog would start to secrete digestive juices as soon as it saw the person who customarily fed it. Pavlov's preliminary experiments were conducted by simply showing the dog bread before giving it bread to eat. Eventually the dog would begin to salivate on seeing the bread. Salivation with the bread in its mouth was a natural digestive reflex, while salivation at the sight of the bread was learned—that is, a conditioned reflex (CR).

Further experimentation clarified the conditioning process. For example, a bell (conditioned stimulus) was repeatedly sounded before food (unconditioned stimulus) was placed in a dog's mouth to produce salivation (unconditioned reflex) until eventually the sound of the bell alone caused salivation (CR). Pavlov grasped that the importance of his discovery of the CR lay in the potential it provided for reducing complex behaviour to basic elements. Thus, his work lay well within the prevailing empirical paradigm of the time. As he wrote:

> We are becoming better acquainted with the fundamental mode of conduct with which the animal is born – with congenital reflexes, heretofore usually called instincts. We observe and intentionally participate in building new reactions on the fundamental conduct in the form of so called habits and associations, which now increase, enlarge, become complicated and refined. According to our analysis these are also reflexes, but conditioned reflexes.
>
> *(Pavlov, 1928/1970: 18)*

This concept of associative learning or associationism has a long history dating back to Aristotle (Mackintosh, 2003). From a scientific, empirical point of view, the significance of the discovery of the CR lay in its potential to explain human behaviour, for '[t]he conditioned reflexes which accumulate progressively during the individual life of animals and man are formed within the cerebral hemispheres' (Pavlov, 1928/1970: 20). Later in his career Pavlov worked to link the CR to an understanding of human neuroses. New understandings regarding neurology overrode Pavlov's theory that excitation and inhibition occur on the surface of the cortex: it became understood that the transmission of neural impulses occurs along neurons and across synapses. Pavlov's theory has also been criticized for suggesting that all behaviour is the sum of accumulated CRs, but it does not appear that he made such a suggestion (Pavlov, 1932). Others, such as Watson, were certainly interested in such an idea.

As well as his Nobel Prize, Pavlov received the following praise from biologist and 'father of science fiction', H. G. Wells:

> If 'A' is drowning on one side of a pier and 'B' is equally drowning on the other, and you have one lifebelt, to which of the two would you like to throw it? Which would I save, Pavloff or [playwright] Shaw? What is the good of Shaw? And what is the good of Pavloff? Pavloff is a star which lights the world, shining above a vista hitherto unexplored. Why should I hesitate with my lifebelt for one moment?
>
> (*Wells, 1927: 1*)

John Broadus Watson (1878–1958) and behaviourism

Watson was born on a farm near Greenville, South Carolina, United States. His PhD in psychology was completed at the University of Chicago where he subsequently lectured. Later he became a professor at Johns Hopkins University. Watson has been described as 'combative and articulate, a real fighter who dismissed the psychology that existed at the time' (Moore, 2008: 1). A scandalous divorce led to his dismissal, and in 1920 he left for New York, moving out of the academic world to apply his knowledge very successfully to the world of advertising. However, he continued to write psychology articles for popular magazines such as *Harper's* and *Cosmopolitan*. Watson strongly rejected introspection in favour of the principles of objective observation of behaviour, and placed emphasis on the importance of the environment in shaping human development.

The first psychological laboratories set up in Germany and the United States defined psychology as the study of consciousness, with introspection as the principal method of study. However, critics quickly identified that subjects could not agree reliably on the description of sensation, images and feelings. At the same time, Freud was arguing that important aspects of the mind were not in consciousness. In North America a literal revolution was occurring in the study of human behaviour. Numerous researchers were making a significant contribution to the understanding of human development, utilizing basic tenets of the scientific method. Watson called behaviourism a 'purely American production' (1914: ix).

Briefly, Watson's method involved a great deal of emphasis on objective observation. Drawing upon his experience as a student of animal behaviour, Watson claimed that the subject matter of psychology was not consciousness but behaviour:

> Psychology as the behaviorist views it is a purely objective, experimental branch of natural science. Its theoretical goal is the prediction and control of behavior. Introspection forms no essential part of its methods, nor is the scientific value of its data dependent upon the readiness with which they lend themselves to interpretation in terms of consciousness. The behaviorist attempts to get a unitary scheme of animal response. He recognizes no dividing line between man and brute.
>
> *(Watson, 1913: 158)*

He emphasized environmental stimuli (such as a loud noise or praise from a teacher) and the response (such as a startled reaction or on-task pupil behaviour). Watson's view of behaviour is therefore often called stimulus-response (S-R) psychology. He argued that the only inherited features of behaviour were simple physiological reflexes such as the knee-jerk reflex, crediting all else to learning. Hence, his claim:

> Give me a dozen healthy infants, well formed and my own specified world to bring them up in and I'll guarantee to take any one at random and train him to become any kind of specialist I might select – doctor, lawyer, artist, merchant-chief, and yes even beggar-man and thief, regardless of his talents, penchants, abilities, vocation and race of his ancestors.
>
> *(Watson, 1930: 104)*

We can see a similar Confucian belief in the importance of the environment for shaping a child, in the story of Mencius' mother (see Box 4.1). Watson was heavily influenced by the work of Pavlov, and wanted to explain how all complex behaviours, of both animals and humans, were the result of conditioning by their environment.

BOX 4.1 THE MOTHER OF MENCIUS: A STORY IN THE CONFUCIAN TRADITION

This widely known story originated from Liu Xiang's *Biography of Exemplary Women*, 1922.

> It was said that Mencius was raised by his mother alone because his father died when he was little. Their first house was near a cemetery, so young Mencius imitated the performances of obsequies. His mother thought that this was not good for the child, so she moved to a place near a market. In

> this environment, Mencius thus imitated butchers' activities. His mother was again dissatisfied and moved to a place near a temple and school. Mencius thus learned to perform rituals and practise etiquette, for he often saw people doing so. By now the mother of Mencius was happy and decided to stay there permanently. This story illustrates a widely accepted belief in Chinese society that what children played typically reflected their surroundings and the things they encountered in their daily lives.
>
> *(Bai, 2005: 14)*

One of the most frequently cited learning theory experiments in psychological literature was conducted in 1920 by Watson and his research assistant Rosalie Rayner. They had already tested Little Albert, at 9 months, finding that he showed no fear reactions when confronted suddenly with a white rat, rabbit, dog, monkey masks, cotton wool and so on. That is, in learning theory terms, the stimuli were neutral. They discovered that, when a metal bar was struck with a hammer behind Albert, the loud sound (unconditioned stimulus) made him cry. When Albert was 11 months old, a white rat was presented to him and as he reached for it the bar was struck behind his head. Little Albert jumped and fell forward with his face in the mattress. When he reached for the rat again and his hand touched it, the bar was struck and again he fell forward and began to whimper. The experiment was stopped at this point. One week later, when the rat was presented he would not reach for it. When the rat was pushed nearer he reached for it very tentatively. Thus, Watson and Rayner demonstrated learning in infancy through a process of conditioning.

Rayner was implicated in the scandal that led to Watson's dismissal from Johns Hopkins University, after letters from the married Watson to Rayner found their way into the newspapers. They later married. Another interesting aside is that he reported suffering from an anxiety attack while at the University of Chicago. He observed that this experience 'in a way prepared me to accept a large part of Freud when I first began to get really acquainted with him around 1910' (Watson, 1936: 274). Watson first used William James' habit theory to explain psychoanalysis and later used Pavlov's notion of classical conditioning. He hoped ultimately to assimilate psychoanalysis into behaviourism (Rilling, 2000), as shown in Box 4.2.

BOX 4.2 WATSON TAKES AIM AT FREUD AND INTROSPECTIONISM

This is Carol Magai and Susan McFadden's take on Watson's views on introspectionism and psychoanalysis.

> Watson wanted no competitors and took aim at his rivals. Both Freudian psychoanalysis and introspectionism came under his fire. He

regarded psychoanalysis as a rather occult enterprise, and berated its reliance on untestable hypothetical constructs and mystical notions such as 'the unconscious'. Many of Freud's observations, he felt, could be rendered in more behavioral terms. For example, affection could be restated as an 'organic sensory response', and transference as 'stimulus generalization'. Introspectionism, which was more deeply entrenched in American psychology, had to be more forcibly rooted out. In a letter to Robert Yerkes, Watson wrote that he had been experimenting with conditioning in humans and was elated to find that 'it works so beautifully in place of introspection … that it deserves to be driven home; we can work on the human being as we can on animals and from the same point of view'.

(Magai and McFadden, 1995: 98)

Horowitz noted that evaluating Watson's contribution to developmental psychology is problematic given that many psychologists suggest that 'he was, at best, a psychologist concerned only with defining psychology as a natural science and, at worst, a dogmatist who went far beyond his data to popularize his beliefs about development' (Horowitz, 1992: 360). Watson certainly acknowledged the biological functions of the human organism (Horowitz, 1992), but his theory focused on learning as almost entirely responsible for behavioural development. In sum:

> Watson's developmental model was exceedingly simple, containing no discussion of stages and little of sequences; there was no consideration that learning principles were in any way influenced by the age of the child. Furthermore, the developmental progression, despite the nod to structural change as variable, was linear and cumulative.
>
> *(Horowitz, 1992: 361)*

Watson's theory provided a basis for shaping the nature of psychological thought in the early 1900s, particularly in North America. In fact, he was hailed as a 'second Moses' for achieving the 'promised land' of behaviourism (Magai and McFadden, 1995: 98). He also influenced parenting at the time, providing the following advice in a book on child care:

> There is a sensible way of treating children. Treat them as though they were young adults. Dress them, bathe them with care and circumspection. Let your behavior always be objective and kindly firm. Never hug and kiss them, never let them sit in your lap. If you must, kiss them once on the forehead when they say goodnight. Shake hands with them in the morning. Give them a pat on the head if they have made an extraordinarily good job of a difficult task. Try it out. In a week's time you will be utterly ashamed of the mawkish, sentimental way you have been handling it.
>
> *(Watson, 1928: 81–2)*

Rosalie seems to have been conflicted about these views (Smirle, 2013). In a joint publication they referred to 'too much motherly love' as detrimental to children's development but she also wished her sons to experience some coddling.

Watson's research with infants suggested that there are three innate emotional (visceral) reactions—fear, rage and love. His sons later claimed that their strict upbringing led to difficulty in managing emotions; one of them died from suicide and the other attempted it (Smirle, 2013). In a paper based on an interview with Watson's surviving son, James Watson recalled that his father showed more affection for animals than people, but hated cruelty to either (Hannush, 1987). Watson did compare children favourably with the subjects of his comparative psychology experiments, commenting that a baby could be 'more fun to the square inch than all the frogs and rats in creation' (Buckley, 1989, cited in Magai and McFadden, 1995).

John Malone and Andrés Garcia-Penagos suggested that Watson has become mythologized as someone who frightened a baby in the interests of science and was an arrogant self-promoter who focused too strongly on the role of conditioned reflexes. They argued that a careful consideration of his writings shows that the focus on S-R reflexes was not as narrow as often assumed: stimuli and responses could be 'temporally-dependent entities, depending on the phenomena involved' (Malone and Garcia-Penagos, 2014: 3). Stimuli could include the Russian Revolution and Easy Divorce, while responses might be Joining the Church, acquiring a skill or writing a book. Furthermore, they said, Watson never claimed that the mind cannot be measured, but that there *is no mind* as the mind/body distinction (as established by Plato and Descartes) is false; thinking is a kind of doing, in tune with the embodied cognition theories of today. We recommend this article as considering other misunderstood aspects of Watson's theorizing. The authors also suggested that although the charge of arrogant self-promotion against Watson is justified, it did ensure that behaviourist ideas were disseminated and he popularized psychology through his non-academic publications (James regarded his widowed father as quiet and inoffensive). John Malone (2014) also contended that although Watson championed behaviourism he was not its founder as there were numbers of predecessors; however, Hayne Reese (2014) disputed that the emergence of behaviourism was inevitable without Watson who, he said, should indeed be recognized as its founder.

Mary Cover Jones (1896–1987) and behaviour therapy

Jones has been described as 'one of the most remarkable people in the history of Psychology' (Krasner, 1988: 91). As a parent, educator, psychologist and researcher she emphasized that children were individuals who benefited by educational opportunities suited to their needs. Like Rayner, Jones worked for Watson as a research assistant. She was not comfortable with the ethical aspects of Watson's work with Little Albert (although Watson had some reservations about it himself, this did not prevent him from joking that if Albert had problems later in life, some psychoanalyst would probably attribute it to a sexual neurosis) (Magai and McFadden,

1995). Jones was more interested in the question of whether Watson's procedure could be reversed—whether a child with a phobia could be cured using conditioning principles. Working with children aged 3 years she published research in 1924 demonstrating that the fear of furry objects could be deconditioned, her study with 'Little Peter' becoming widely cited (Jones, 1924). Her work was seminal, representing the establishment of behaviour therapy. Her research also provided the basis for Skinnerian operant conditioning, Wolpean desensitization and Bandurian modelling. She was dubbed by Joseph Wolpe 'the mother of behaviour therapy' and yet she ultimately became less remembered than Watson (Magai and McFadden, 1995). Procedures she developed continue to be used. For example, R. D. Zettle (2003) reported the successful use of systematic desensitization in the treatment of maths anxiety disorders. Increasingly, the principles are applied through the use of virtual reality (Fayaz Hussain and Chenna Reddy, 2023).

Despite her enormous influence on behaviourism, it was in longitudinal work that Jones focused most of her career. She later said that she would no longer be satisfied with treating a child's phobia without considering their total complexity as a person, and without following up their longer-term progress, which is very much in accord with 21st-century approaches to children's development and wellbeing.

Burrhus Frederick Skinner (1904–1990) and operant conditioning

Skinner was born in Pennsylvania and attended Hamilton College in Clinton, New York, majoring in English. Apparently disillusioned with his writing skills, he went to New York City to live in Greenwich Village for six months, then studied psychology at Harvard. His interest in psychology was piqued by a diverse range of individuals including Pavlov, Watson and philosopher Bertrand Russell.

Behaviourism as developed by Skinner came to be known as operant conditioning. One of the most basic differences between operant and classical conditioning is that the latter applies to reflexes (respondent behaviour) and the former to voluntary behaviour. Thus, when a dog salivates in response to food the salivation is a reflex or a 'respondent'. Operants, in contrast, are said to be emitted rather than elicited. Thus, operants operate on, or have an effect on, the environment, and are not necessarily associated with any particular stimulus, as with the babbling of a young baby.

A central term relevant to operant conditioning is that of 'consequences'. Put simply, the consequences following a response may either increase or decrease the probability of a further response or responses. If the consequence produces a repetition of the response or an increase in the frequency of responding, it is described as reinforcing or rewarding. Should the consequence result in suppression or reduction of the behaviour, the consequence is described as punishing.

Reinforcement can be positive or negative. With positive reinforcement the frequency of response increases because it is followed by consequences that the subject finds rewarding. For example, if a dog receives a biscuit for running to its owner on hearing a whistle, this increases the likelihood of a repetition of this behaviour when the owner whistles. With negative reinforcement the frequency of a response increases because the response removes, or enables the organism to avoid, a negative or painful stimulus. For instance, a child completes a homework assignment to avoid being kept in after school.

The analysis of operantly conditioned behaviour has its foundations in laboratory studies of animals such as rats and pigeons, in the famous cage-like apparatus known as a Skinner box. While moving around, the animal inadvertently depresses a lever, which releases food into a tray and turns on a light. The food serves as a reinforcer to the hungry animal, which will depress the lever again to obtain more food (reinforcement). The lever-pressing is an operant, since it does not occur in response to any known stimulus. The experimenter may 'shape' the subject's behaviour by rewarding successive approximations to the desired behaviour.

Food is an example of a primary reinforcer. Secondary reinforcers are previously neutral stimuli (such as the light in the Skinner box) that acquire reinforcing properties when paired with primary reinforcers. Some reinforcers—general reinforcers—acquire the capacity to reinforce many behaviours; for humans, these include praise, social prestige, power and money. Various schedules of reinforcement (e.g. continuous, intermittent) are available for conditioning behaviour and each has a different impact on establishing and maintaining the behaviour in question. Generally speaking, the variable interval schedules tend to elicit a high response rate because of the unpredictability of knowing when one will be rewarded (watch individuals playing poker machines).

Skinner's interest in the environmental conditions surrounding an organism was reflected in how his daughter was raised in infancy (see Box 4.3).

BOX 4.3 PARENTING SKINNER STYLE

Skinner reported in some detail the raising of his daughter Deborah in a device he designed and called the baby tender.

> For our second child, Deborah, I built a crib-sized living space that we began to call the 'baby tender'. It had sound absorbing walls and a large picture window. Air entered through filters at the bottom and after being warmed and moistened, moved by convection upward through and around the edges of a tightly stretched canvas, which served as a mattress. [A small fan blew the air if the room was hot.] A strip of sheeting 10 yards long passed over the canvas, a clean section of which could be cranked into place in a few seconds.
>
> *(Skinner, 1979: 30)*

Deborah was introduced to the baby tender from the very first weeks of life and slept in it more or less regularly until she was two and a half years old. Skinner claimed that the tender's soundproofing enabled Deborah to sleep well and protected her from infection. Skinner's initial reporting of his invention in *The Ladies Home Journal* in October 1945 generated considerable controversy, including a comparison of the project with the Skinner box. Contrary to rumour, Deborah did not eventually suicide but grew up to become a successful artist.

There are three essential principles associated with traditional behaviourism. As noted in Chapter 2, it is argued that the organism at birth is a *tabula rasa*, and little attention is paid to internal cognitive structures. Second, it is believed that the principles of learning and conditioning apply across all species. Finally, the learner is essentially passive in the face of the conditioning process.

Watson, as we have seen, saw behaviourism as a natural science. However, this was attributed more strongly to Skinner by William Baum (2011), who said that this is what makes radical behaviourism 'radical' (Baum, 2011). Baum further noted that behavioural events are natural events with no agency—'they just happen'. Moreover they can be explained by other natural events and this does not require any reference to inner states or other variables intervening between stimulus and response.

Some researchers cast doubt on the extent to which the principles enunciated in behavioural theory could be applied. For example, Elsie Bregman (1934) found that it was possible to condition a child with fear if the conditioned stimulus was a live animal—like a rat—but not if it was an inanimate object. Martin Seligman (1972) linked conditioning to evolutionary theory, noting that birds are more easily conditioned to visual stimuli and human infants to verbal stimuli, suggesting that we come into the world 'prepared' in some way. Seligman further suggested that this preparedness may have survival value, as in the fear of snakes. It raises the interesting question of whether many of the behaviourist experiments, such as that with Little Albert, have fortuitously tapped into elements such as the 'preparedness' of the organism to be conditioned. Similarly, research by Robert Bolles (1970) found that pigeons do not 'simply peck' at a small lighted key, but are actually pecking in an attempt to eat it. Such considerations led to the development of 'ecological learning theory', which focused not just on 'how' learning happens, but 'what' is learned, in an adaptive and evolutionary sense (Davey, 1989), as discussed in Chapter 5 in relation to the work of the Gibsons.

Skinner's theory evolved towards a more functional than mechanistic view of behaviour, in the sense that it was intended to be very applied (Schlinger, 1992). Skinner's work utilizing the principles he had developed emerged in the 1950s when he began applying his science to education. The impetus was a visit to his younger daughter's fourth grade arithmetic class in 1953 (Smith and Morris, 2004). In his own words:

> Possibly through no fault of her own, the teacher was violating two fundamental principles: the students were not being told at once whether their work was

> right of wrong (a corrected paper seen twenty-four hours later could not act as a reinforcer), and they were all moving at the same pace regardless of preparation or ability.
>
> *(Skinner, 1983: 64)*

As a result, in short time he developed a teaching machine based on principles of behaviour derived from his research, for teaching spelling and arithmetic.

His principles continue to be used. The *Journal of Applied Behavior Analysis* is still published, and a paper by Maya Fallon *et al.* (2025) is an example of the use of behavioural methods with children with autism. Since, unfortunately, such children are highly subject to peer bullying, this study trained them in self-protection skills, using simulated situations. These included learning to report threats of physical or material harm, to respond to an unkind remark with a disapproving comment and, if a second unkind remark follows, to move away from the bullying person and engage in a different activity.

Although Richard DeGrandpre (2000: 722) saw operant principles as having become only 'a marginal force in contemporary psychological science', their usefulness in studying child development should not be underestimated. For example, an analysis of studies on conditioned kicking responses in infants aged 2-4 months was used to show that socio-economic status does not affect infant learning at that early age (Gerhardstein *et al.*, 2012). Jiaxi Hu (2024) has advocated for the continuing value of operant conditioning in helping children to develop positive behaviour patterns, while also considering ethical issues.

Albert Bandura (1925–2021) and social learning theory

Bandura was born in Alberta, Canada to parents of Polish and Ukrainian descent. He emigrated to the United States in 1949 and obtained his PhD in clinical psychology from the University of Iowa. He moved beyond classical and operant conditioning as explanations for learning to a third possibility, in terms of imitation: social learning theory (Bandura, 1971, 1986; Bandura and Walters, 1963). Bandura and Richard Walters' *Social Learning and Personality Development* (1963) broadened the scope of social learning theory with the now familiar principles of observational learning and vicarious reinforcement:

> Learning would be exceedingly laborious, not to mention hazardous, if people had to rely solely on the effects of their own actions to inform them of what to do. Fortunately, most human behavior is learned observationally through modeling: from observing others, one forms an idea of how new behaviors are performed, and on later occasions this coded information serves as a guide for action.
>
> *(Bandura and Walters, 1963: 22)*

Their research called attention to the importance of imitation and role models in learning. Their classic 1963 study featured a laboratory situation where nursery school children watched a woman (the 'model') play with toys and a life-size plastic 'Bobo' doll. In the experimental condition, she played quietly with the toys for a minute and then began to hit, kick and sit on the doll, with accompanying vocalizations such as 'Pow!' and 'Sock him in the nose!' In the control condition she simply played quietly with the toys. Neither the woman nor the watching children were directly reinforced. After the woman had left the room, each child in turn was left alone with the toys. Children who had observed the aggressive model were more likely than the control group to act aggressively. These results could not be predicted by operant conditioning theories since there was no apparent reinforcement for the children's behaviour. The reviews of research in this field suggest a causal link between exposure to violence and increases in aggressive behaviour (e.g. Anderson, 2004).

> There is consistent evidence that violent imagery in television, film and video, and computer games has substantial short-term effects on arousal, thoughts, and emotions, increasing the likelihood of aggressive or fearful behaviour in younger children, especially in boys. The evidence becomes inconsistent when considering older children and teenagers, and long-term outcomes for all ages.
>
> *(Browne and Hamilton-Giachritsis, 2005: 5)*

A later review concluded that there is strong evidence that children's risk of behaving aggressively is influenced by social learning, from both parents and peers, over and above other environmental factors and genetics (Goodnight, Wilhoit and Receveur, 2017).

Generally, Bandura believed that existing learning theory models were too mechanistic: 'Much of the early psychological theorizing was founded on behavioristic principles that embraced an input–output model linked by an internal conduit that makes behavior possible but exerts no influence of its own on behavior' (Bandura, 2001: 2). In this view, human behaviour is shaped and controlled automatically and mechanically by environmental stimuli. That is, behaviourism is seen primarily as a theory of performance control, rather than a theory of learning. While it can explain how learned imitative behaviour can be shaped by the prospect of a reward, it cannot explain how new response structures are developed as a result of observation. As such, the mechanistic approach undervalued the potential of individuals to affect their own behaviour. Following earlier theorizing by E. C. Tolman (see later), in Bandura's theory, psychological development is neither driven by inner forces nor shaped by external stimuli. Rather, symbolic, vicarious and self-regulatory processes play a significant role. For example, it was proposed that '[s]ocial learning theory posits that the experience of physical abuse will lead to later aggression to the extent that it makes aggressive responses salient in one's response repertoire as efficacious in leading to positive outcomes' (Dodge, Bates and Pettit, 1990: 259; also see Box 2.1).

By the 1970s Bandura was becoming aware that an important element was missing not only from the prevalent learning theories of the day but from his own social learning theory. In 1977 he published a paper 'Self-efficacy: Toward a Unifying Theory of Behavioral Change', in which he identified the important piece of that missing element: self-belief. With the publication of *Social Foundations of Thought and Action: A Social Cognitive Theory*, Bandura (1986) advanced a view of human functioning that accords a central role to cognitive, vicarious, self-regulatory and self-reflective processes in human adaptation and change. People were viewed as agents who were proactive, self-reflecting and self-regulating, and not simply reactive organisms shaped by environmental forces or driven by inner psychic impulses. Theoretically, human behaviour was viewed as the product of an interaction among personal, behavioural and environmental influences. For example, how people interpret the results of their own behaviour informs and alters their environments and the personal factors they possess which, in turn, inform and alter subsequent behaviour. This is the foundation of Bandura's conception of *reciprocal determinism*. This is the view that behaviour, personal factors (in the form of cognition, affect and biological events) and environmental influences create interactions that result in a *triadic reciprocality*. Bandura altered the label of his theory from social learning to social *cognitive* both to distance it from prevalent social learning theories of the day and to emphasize that cognition plays a critical role in people's ability to construct reality, self-regulate, encode information and perform behaviours.

Bandura continued to develop his work, and elaborated on the idea of human consciousness: 'Consciousness is the very substance of mental life that not only makes life personally manageable but worth living' (Bandura, 2001: 3). He posited that it is 'functional consciousness' that means the individual is very active in choosing, sorting, storing and accessing the information needed to make choices regulating everyday living.

He also focused on the concept of human agency:

> To be an agent is to intentionally make things happen by one's actions. Agency embodies the endowments, belief systems, self regulatory capabilities and distributed structures and functions through which personal influence is exercised, rather than residing as a discrete entity in a particular place.
>
> *(Bandura, 2001: 2)*

He referred to a substantial body of research supporting the view that perceived self-efficacy motivates and guides one's actions.

> Perceived self-efficacy is defined as people's beliefs about their capabilities to produce designated levels of performance that exercise influence over events that affect their lives. Self-efficacy beliefs determine how people feel, think, motivate themselves and behave. Such beliefs produce these diverse effects through four major processes. They include cognitive, motivational, affective and selection processes.
>
> *(Bandura, 2000: 75)*

Bandura (2001) was also particularly concerned about what he called the 'biologizing of psychology' and the overemphasis on evolutionism. He was further concerned that, 'the geneticization of human behavior is being promoted more fervently by psychological evolutionists than by biological evolutionists' (Bandura, 2001: 19). Kay Bussey and Bandura (2004) elaborated Bandura's theory in terms of the effects of culture in shaping gender role development.

Bandura was a prolific researcher and writer, publishing his last book entitled *Moral Disengagement: How People Do Harm and Live with Themselves* in 2016 (Zsolnai, 2016). It dealt with the psychological mechanisms employed by individuals, corporations and governments to persuade themselves and/or others that their actions are not harmful and are justified. A collection of papers detailing his profound effect on education was published two years after his death (Schunk and DiBenedetto, 2023).

Information processing

This approach to understanding human development and cognition draws on the metaphor of the human mind as a computer, which is why Tracey Gurbin (2015) sees it as presenting a 'machinist' perspective. As Bandura (2001: 2) noted, the line of theorizing associated with behaviourist principles 'was eventually put out of vogue by the advent of the computer, which likened the mind to a biological calculator'. The theory draws on the thinking of earlier writers such as Tolman (1932), a professor of psychology at the University of California, Berkeley. Although honoured in his day, he is now less well-known than Watson, Skinner or Bandura, but deserves due acknowledgement for his contribution to mainstream psychological thought and, on a personal level, for standing up courageously for academic freedom in the United States' McCarthy era in the 1950s.

Tolman's theory is variously referred to by terms such as 'molar behaviourism', 'purposive behaviours', 'sign learning' and 'cognitive behaviourism' (Malone, 1990). He and Bandura are sometimes considered as neo-behaviourists. Tolman stressed the purposive features of behaviour and the cognitive aspects. Influenced by Gestalt theorizing that directly challenged structuralist views, he stressed broad, molar descriptions of behaviour, analysing it in common-sense units such as 'cooking a meal' rather than breaking it up into a string of separate actions (Hill, 1963). Very importantly, he introduced the idea of the 'intervening variable' to psychology. Previously, behaviourists viewed anything intervening between stimulus and response as just another response, whereas Tolman introduced the notion of cognitions as intervening between the two. In doing so, he made the concept of cognition more 'respectable' within behaviourism (Hill, 1963). Through experiments with rats learning routes in mazes, he introduced the notion of 'cognitive maps', a term now widely used to apply to mental models in general. His notion of intervening variables is central to information-processing models, as will become apparent.

The information-processing approach in psychology has been used to address such issues as the organization of thinking, cognitive strategies in problem-solving and the role of memory in learning. The general view of information-processing theorists is that, over time, a person develops an increasingly complex and more sophisticated 'computer' (mind) for solving problems, a computer that stores more and more knowledge and develops ever better strategies for solving problems.

The early conceptions of information processing were introduced in the 1960s and 1970s, largely in response to the response-strengthening metaphor (Mayer, 1996, 2003), such as when reinforcement is viewed as strengthening a response; the response-strengthening notion has persisted but been subject to criticism (Simon, Bernardi and Cowie, 2020). With the development of theorizing around constructivism, the limitations of earlier information processing models became apparent because they suggested that human cognition and understanding was a passive-reactive process that did not easily accommodate how individuals actively construe their understandings and cognitions in a meaning-making manner.

Yuko Munakata (2006) identified four information processing approaches to development: production systems, i.e. computer-based tools using 'if-then' rules to study cognition and artificial intelligence; neural networks; dynamic systems; and ad hoc models. All focus on continuity rather than stages. We discuss dynamic systems theorizing in Chapter 10, but a wider consideration of information processing research is beyond the present scope. We give one example of a neural network study in Box. 4.4

BOX 4.4 BIOLOGICAL NEURAL NETWORKS AND TRAUMA IN CHILDREN

Neural networks can either refer to biological networks of neurons connected by synapses, or to artificial networks based on mathematical models, as used in artificial intelligence (AI). Donald Hebb proposed in 1949 that neural connections in the brain are remodelled by experience, and this 'Hebbian theory' of synaptic plasticity is supported by many studies (Zhao and Willing, 2018; also see Chapter 3). This concept underlies a study by Megan Klabunde and associates in 2024 that examined scans of the brains of children who have experienced trauma, to examine whether they had become 'wired up' in specific ways (Ireton, Hughes and Klabunde, 2024; also see Bruce Perry's work in Chapter 3). They used AI to identify patterns in fMRI scans from 14 studies, with half the children having trauma histories. The study revealed disruptions to brain networks concerned with self-perceptions and cognitive processing, in traumatized children, that were likely to affect emotions and impair learning and empathy.

Information processing examines how animals and humans use information from their environment to direct their behaviour. For example, imagine you are a child at school leaving the classroom at recess. You get up from your desk as the bell rings and jostle with several other children in the doorway to be first to the handball courts. As you run to the courts you decide to leave eating your snack until later. Approaching the courts, you see they are already in use by some children you do not know very well. You drop to a walk looking to see how far into the game they are. Noticing it is almost finished, you decide to ask if you can play next. Like the computer, the human mind takes in and encodes information, acts on the information, stores it and is capable of retrieving the information and generating responses. A simplified model of information processing is shown in Figure 4.1.

Considering our example, note that the young child is faced with a potentially infinite amount of information impacting on the sensory system as they leave the classroom. They must *select* the most significant information and then *interpret* it. The child must *infer* the motives and behaviour of the children already playing handball then *match* or accommodate their behaviour to suit that of the other children. They must *selectively attend* to certain behaviours of the children and ignore others.

A number of critical claims by Jean Piaget regarding problems of conservation and transivity (the ability to comprehend relationship properties between objects or concepts) have to do with the interaction of the *amount* of information a child receives with the *kind* of information (Bryant and Trabasso, 1971). For example, the likelihood of a child providing a correct response to a conservation problem is partly a function of how much information there is and how varied it is. Research

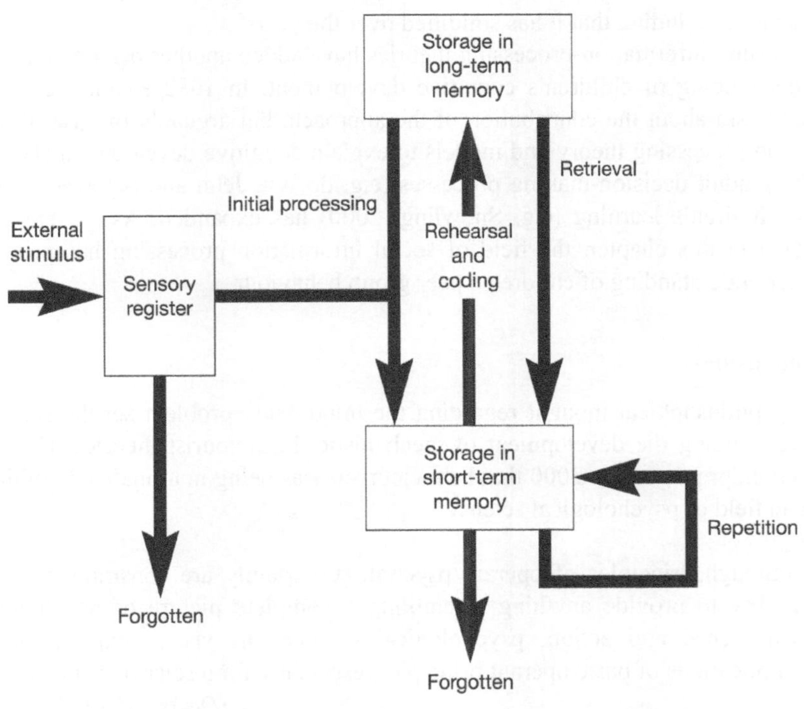

Figure 4.1 A simplified model of information processing

by Daniel Keating and Bruce Bobbitt in 1978 found 'evidence that late childhood and very early adolescence are a prime time for maturation of the information processing system' (Keating, 1980: 242).

Dodge *et al.* (1990) and Nicki Crick and Kenneth Dodge (1994) examined children's social adjustment using an information-processing approach. Thus the child is seen as confronting a particular problematic situation, such as solving an interpersonal conflict with another child via serial cognitive processes that allow them to generate effective responses. Dodge proposed five sequential steps:

- Encoding, which refers to the individual's ability to attend to and perceive social cues.
- Interpretation, or understanding the meaning of the cues.
- Response generation, in order to ascertain which response is most applicable, from a repertoire of responses.
- Response evaluation.
- Enactment of the chosen response.

Elizabeth Lemerise and William Arsenio (2000) reviewed the research relating to social information processing, concluding that the field had attempted to integrate the cognitive and social aspects of children's development in order to provide a better understanding of their behaviour. More recently, Yair Ziv and Einat Elizarov (2019) have reviewed the evidence for Crick and Dodge's model of social processing, concluding that it has solidified over the years.

In sum, information-processing theories have added another perspective to our understanding of children's cognitive development. In 1982 Keating expressed scepticism about the contribution of the approach, but arguably the use of information processing theory and models to explain cognitive development (Halford, 2005), adult decision-making processes (e.g. de Wit, Jehn and Scheppers, 2013) and children's learning (e.g. Snowling, 2000) has expanded. As we have also shown in this chapter, the field of social information processing has promoted better understanding of children's peer group behaviour.

Conclusions

Early philosophical thought regarding the mind–body problem set the scene for understanding the development of mechanistic, behaviourist theories. However, DeGrandpre argued in 2000 that behaviourism was being marginalized within the broad field of psychological science:

> although principles of operant psychology certainly are constrained in their ability to provide anything resembling a complete picture of psychological experience and action, psychological science has yet to exploit the full implications of basic operant principles, especially for a science of meaning.
>
> *(DeGrandpre, 2000: 721)*

There is little doubt that mechanism has elicited, and continues to elicit, strong and polarized opinion regarding its contribution to theoretical development and, more particularly, regarding its contribution to understanding and explaining human development. There is also certainly little doubt that the significant corpus of knowledge it has created continues to be applied in areas such as clinical psychology, health and education.

Tolman set a precedent for introducing cognition into behaviourism. While information-processing theories and Bandura's work both have their origins in the mechanistic school of thought, we have seen how these represented a move towards greater organicism. Furthermore, in emphasizing the notion of personal agency, Bandura attempted to provide a fuller and richer account of human development.

References

Anderson, C. A. 2004. An update on the effects of playing violent video games. *Journal of Adolescence 27*: 113–22. https://doi.org/10.1016/j.adolescence.2003.10.009

Bai, L. 2005. Children at play: a childhood beyond the Confucian shadow. *Childhood 12*: 9–32. https://doi.org/10.1177/0907568205049890

Bandura, A. 1971. *Psychological modeling: conflicting theories.* Chicago: Aldine- Atherton.

Bandura, A. 1977. Self-efficacy: toward a unifying theory of behavioral change. *Psychological Review 84*(2): 191–215. https://psycnet.apa.org/doi/10.1037/0033-295X.84.2.191

Bandura, A. 1986. *Social foundations of thought and action: a social-cognitive theory.* Engelwood Cliffs: Prentice-Hall.

Bandura, A. 2000. Exercise of human agency through collective efficacy. *Current Directions in Psychological Science 9*: 75–8. https://doi.org/10.1111/1467-8721.00064

Bandura, A. 2001. Social cognitive theory: an agentic perspective. *Annual Review of Psychology 52*: 1–26. http://dx.doi.org/10.1146/annurev.psych.52.1.1

Bandura, A. 2016. *Moral disengagement: how people do harm and live with themselves.* New York: Worth Publishers.

Bandura, A. and Walters, R. H. 1963. *Social learning and personality development.* New York: Holt Rinehart and Winston.

Baum, W. M. 2011. What is radical behaviorism? A review of J. Moore's *Conceptual foundations of radical behaviorism. Journal of the Experimental Analysis of Behavior 95*: 119–26. https://doi.org/10.1901/jeab.2011.95-119

Bolles, R. C. 1970. Species-specific defence reactions and avoidance learning. *Psychological Review 77*: 32–48. https://doi.org/10.1037/h0028589

Bregman, E. O. 1934. An attempt to modify the emotional attitudes of infants by the conditioning response technique. *Journal of Genetic Psychology 45*: 169–78. https://psycnet.apa.org/doi/10.1080/08856559.1934.10534254

Browne, K. and Hamilton-Giachritsis, C. 2005. The influence of violent media on children and adolescents: a public-health approach. *The Lancet 365*: 702–10. https://doi.org/10.1016/S0140-6736(05)17952-5

Bryant, P. E. and Trabasso, T. 1971. Transitive inferences and memory in young children. *Nature 232*: 456–8. https://doi.org/10.1038/232456a0

Bussey, K. and Bandura, A. 2004. Social cognitive theory of gender development and functioning. In A. H. Eagly, A. E. Beall and R. J. Sternberg (eds), *The psychology of gender*. Second edn. New York: Guilford Press, 92–119.

Corr, P. J. and Perkins, A. M. 2006. The role of theory in the psychophysiology of personality: from Ivan Pavlov to Jeffrey Gray. *International Journal of Psychophysiology 62*(3): 367–76. https://doi.org/10.1016/j.ijpsycho.2006.01.005

Crick, N. R. and Dodge, K. A. 1994. A review and reformulation of social information-processing mechanisms in children's social adjustment. *Psychological Bulletin 115*: 74–101. https://doi.org/10.1037/0033-2909.115.1.74

Davey, G. 1989. *Ecological learning theory*. London: Routledge

de Wit, F. R. C., Jehn, K. A. and Scheepers, D. 2013. Task conflict, information processing, and decision-making: the damaging effect of relationship conflict. *Organizational Behavior and Human Decision Processes 122*(2): 177–89. https://doi.org/10.1016/j.obhdp.2013.07.002

DeGrandpre, R. J. 2000. A science of meaning: can behaviorism bring meaning to psychological science? *American Psychologist 55*: 721–39. https://doi.org/10.1037/0003-066X.55.7.721

Dodge, K. A., Bates, J. E. and Pettit, G. 1990. Mechanisms in the cycle of violence. *Science 250*: 1678–83. http://dx.doi.org/10.1126/science.2270481

Fallon, M. J., Luczynski, K. C., Rodriguez, N. M., Felty, C. and Rahaman, J. A. 2025. A preliminary analysis of teaching children with autism spectrum disorder self-protection skills for bullying situations. *Journal of Applied Behavioral Analysis*. https://doi.org/10.1002/jaba.2938

Fayaz Hussain, G. and Chenna Reddy, P. 2023. Exposure therapy in the treatment of phobias using virtual reality. In A. Kumar, G. Ghinea and S. Merugu (eds), *Proceedings of the third international conference on cognitive and intelligent computing.* Vol. 2. ICCIC 2023. Singapore: Springer, 229–39. https://doi.org/10.1007/978-981-97-9266-5_23

Gerhardstein, P., Dickerson, K., Miller, S. and Hipp, D. 2012. Early operant learning is unaffected by socio-economic status and other demographic factors: a meta-analysis. *Infant Behavior and Development 35*(3): 472–8. https://doi.org/10.1016/j.infbeh.2012.02.005

Goodnight, J. A., Wilhoit, S. A. and Receveur, A. 2017. Social learning theory and the development of aggression. In P. Sturmey (ed.), *The Wiley handbook of violence and aggression*. New York: Wiley, 1–13.

Gurbin, T. 2015. Enlivening the machinist perspective: humanising the information processing theory with social and cultural influences. *Procedia-Social and Behavioral Sciences 197*: 2331–8. https://doi.org/10.1016/j.sbspro.2015.07.263

Halford, G. S. 2005. How many variables can humans process? *Psychological Science 16*: 70–6. https://doi.org/10.1111/j.0956-7976.2005.007

Hannush, M. J. 1987. John B. Watson remembered: an interview with James B. Watson. *Journal of the History of the Behavioral Sciences 30*: 137–52. https://doi.org/10.1002/1520-6696(198704)23:2%3C137::AID-JHBS2300230204%3E3.0.CO;2-Y

Hill, W. F. 1963. *Learning: a survey of psychological interpretations*. London: Methuen.

Horowitz, F. D. 1987. *Exploring developmental theories: toward a structural/behavioral model of development*. New York: Lawrence Erlbaum.

Horowitz, F. D. 1992. John B. Watson's legacy: learning and environment. *Developmental Psychology 28*: 360–7. https://doi.org/10.1037/10155-031

Hu, J. 2024. Operant conditioning in child psychology: understanding the influence of rewards and punishments on children's behavior. *Lecture Notes in Education Psychology and Public Media 44*: 259–65. http://dx.doi.org/10.54254/2753-7048/44/20230161

Ireton, R., Hughes, A. and Klabunde, M. 2024. A functional magnetic resonance imaging meta-analysis of childhood trauma. *Biological Psychiatry, Cognitive Neuroscience and Neuroimaging 9*: 651–70. https://doi.org/10.1016/j.bpsc.2024.01.009

Jones, M. C. 1924. A laboratory study of fear: the case of Peter. *Pedagogical Seminary 31*: 308–15.

Keating, D. P. 1980. Thinking processes in adolescence. In J. Adelson (ed.), *Handbook of adolescent psychology*. New York: Wiley, 211–46.

Keating, D. P. and Bobbitt, B. L. 1978. Individual and developmental differences in cognitive processing components of ability. *Child Development 49*: 155–67. https://psycnet.apa.org/doi/10.2307/1128604

Krasner, L. 1988. In memoriam. Mary Cover-Jones 1896–1982. *Behavior Analyst 11*: 91–2.

Leite, D. A. 2021. *The twenty-first century mechanistic theory of human cognition: a critical analysis*. New York: Springer Nature.

Lemerise, E. A. and Arsenio, W. F. 2000. An integrated model of emotion processes and cognition in information processing. *Child Development*: 71–107. https://doi.org/10.1111/1467-8624.00124

Mackintosh, N. J. 2003. Pavlov and associationism. *The Spanish Journal of Psychology 2*: 177–84. https://doi.org/10.1017/S1138741600005321

Magai, C. and McFadden, S. H. 1995. *The role of emotions in social and personality development: history, theory and research*. New York: Plenum.

Malone, J. C. 1990. *Theories of learning: a historical approach*. New York: Wadsworth Publishing Company.

Malone, J. C. 2014. Did John B. Watson really 'found' behaviorism? *The Behavior Analyst 37*: 1–12. https://doi.org/10.1007/s40614-014-0004-3

Malone, J. C. and García-Penagos, A. 2014. When a clear strong voice was needed: a retrospective review of Watson's (1924/1930) behaviorism. *Journal of the Experimental Analysis of Behavior 102*(2): 267–87. https://doi.org/10.1002/jeab.98

Mayer, R. E. 1996. Learning strategies for making sense out of expository text: the SOI model for guiding three cognitive processes in knowledge construction. *Educational Psychology Review 8*: 357–71. https://doi.org/10.1007/BF01463939

Mayer, R. E. 2003. Memory and information processes. In W. M. Reynolds and G. E. Miller (eds), *Handbook of psychology: educational psychology*. Vol. 7. New York: John Wiley & Sons, 47–57.

Moore, J. 2008. *Conceptual foundations of radical behaviorism*. Cornwall-on-Hudson: Sloan.

Munakata, Y. 2006. Information processing approaches to development. In D. Kuhn, R. S. Siegler, W. Damon and R. M. Lerner (eds), *Handbook of child psychology: cognition, perception, and language*. Sixth edn. np: John Wiley & Sons, Inc., 426–63.

Pavlov, I. P. 1928/1970. The discovery of the conditioned reflex. In W. H. Gantt, L. Pickenhain and C. H. Zwingman (eds), *Pavlovian approaches to psychopathology*. Oxford: Pergamon Press, np.

Pavlov, I. P. 1932. The reply of a physiologist to psychologists. *Psychological Review 39*: 91–127. https://doi.org/10.1037/h0069929

Pepper, S. 1942. *World hypotheses: a study of evidence*. Berkeley: University of California.

Reese, H. W. 2014. Commentary on Malone: who founded behaviorism? *Behavior Analysis 38*: 109–14. https://doi.org/10.1007/s40614-014-0020-3

Reese, H. W. and Overton, W. F. 1970. Models of development and theories of development. In L. R. Goulet and R. Baltes, *Life-span developmental psychology: research and theory*. New York: Academic Press, 116–50.

Rilling, M. 2000. John Watson's paradoxical struggle to explain Freud. *American Psychologist 55*: 301–12. https://doi.org/10.1037/0003-066X.55.3.301

Schlinger, H. D. 1992. Theory in behavior analysis: an application to child development. *American Psychologist 47*: 1396–410. https://doi.org/10.1037/0003-066X.47.11.1396

Schunk, D. H. and DiBenedetto, M. K. 2023. Albert Bandura's legacy in education. *Theory Into Practice 62*(3): 205–6. https://doi.org/10.1080/00405841.2023.2226560

Seligman, M. E. P. 1972. Phobias and preparedness. In M. E. P. Seligman and J. L. Hager (eds), *Biological boundaries of learning*. New York: Appleton-Century-Crofts, 577–84.

Simon, C., Bernardy, J. L. and Cowie, S. 2020. On the 'strength' of behavior. *Perspectives in Behavioral Science 43*(4): 677–96. https://pubmed.ncbi.nlm.nih.gov/33376947/

Skinner, B. F. 1979. My experience with the baby-tender. *Psychology Today 12*(10): 29–40. https://repository.library.georgetown.edu/handle/10822/783233

Skinner, B. F. 1983. *A matter of consequences*. New York: Knopf.

Smirle, C. 2013. Profile of Rosalie Rayner. In A. Rutherford (ed.), *Psychology's feminist voices multimedia internet archive*. https://feministvoices.com/profiles/rosalie-rayner

Smith, N. G. and Morris, E. K. 2004. A tribute to B. F. Skinner at 100: his awards and honors. *European Journal of Behavior Analysis 5*(2): 121–8. www.researchgate.net/publication/290114876_

Snowling, M. J. 2000. *Dyslexia*. Second edn. Oxford: Blackwell.

Thibaut, F. 2018. The mind-body Cartesian dualism in psychiatry. *Dialogues in Clinical Neuroscience 20*: 3. https://doi.org/10.31887/DCNS.2018.20.1/fthibaut

Tolman, P. H. 1932. *Purposive behaviors in animals and men*. New York: The Century Co.

Watson, J. B. 1913. Psychology as the behaviorist views it. *Psychological Review 20*: 158–77.

Watson, J. B. 1914. *Behavior: an introduction to comparative psychology*. New York: Norton.

Watson, J. B. 1928. *Psychological care of the infant and child*. New York: Norton.

Watson, J. B. 1930. *Behaviorism*. New York: Henry Holt.

Watson, J. B. 1936. Autobiography. In C. Murchison (ed.), *A history of psychology in autobiography*. Vol. 3. Worchester, MA: Clarke University Press, 271–8.

Weiskopf, D. A. 2011. Models and mechanisms in psychological explanation. *Synthese 183*: 313–38. https://link.springer.com/article/10.1007/s11229-011-9958-9

Wells, H. G. 1927. Mr. Wells appraises Mr. Shaw. *New York Times Sunday Magazine*, 1.

Zettle, R. D. 2003. Acceptance and commitment therapy (ACT) vs systematic desensitization in treatment of mathematics anxiety. *The Psychological Record 53*: 197–215. https://psycnet.apa.org/record/2003-05022-005

Zhao, L-R. and Willing, A. 2018. Enhancing endogenous capacity to repair a stroke-damaged brain: an evolving field for stroke research. *Progress in Neurobiology 163–4*: 5–26. https://doi.org/10.1016/j.pneurobio.2018.01.004

Ziv, Y. and Elizarov, E. 2019. Social information processing model. *The Encyclopedia of Child and Adolescent Development*, 1–13. https://doi.org/10.1002/9781119171492.wecad270

Zsolnai, L. 2016. *Moral disengagement: how people do harm and live with themselves*, by Albert Bandura. New York: Macmillan. *Business Ethics Quarterly 26*(3): 426–9. https://philpapers.org/rec/BANMDH

5 A rainbow is more than the sum of its colours

Beginnings of organicism

Introduction

Organicism is a philosophical position that has been applied to many areas including literature, architecture and politics. Concerning music, Holly Watkins (2017) observes that it gained a bad name because of its association with German nationalism. However, organicism arguably does not form a coherent intellectual tradition and has also been invoked as a rationale for progressive social policies, such as the introduction of child labour laws in the 19th century (Kucich, 2018).

Organicism draws upon the image of the growing organism whose development is significantly shaped by mutual influence and the patterning of its parts (Pepper, 1942). The basic metaphor is 'the organism, the living, organized system presented to experience in multiple forms' (Reese and Overton, 1972: 132). It is not the uniqueness of the individual child but the universal features of children that are important, though Robert Havighurst's theory does depart from this. Theories in this tradition emphasize internal regulation and organization, and the ability of the organism to organize and reorganize itself at different levels.

Organismic theorists have addressed numbers of different features underpinning development. First, children generally share some common features in relation to behaviours and capabilities; for example, children crawl before they walk. One of the principles of organicism is that the properties at one level of complexity (for instance, biological tissues) cannot be ascribed directly to their component parts but arise only because of the interactions among them, giving rise to *emergent properties*. Emergence can be considered as the spontaneous occurrence of something new as a result of the dynamics of the system. Second, there is commonality in the timing of the emergence of behaviours and abilities; for example, children generally start to crawl at around the same time. Third, while deviations from the general path of development may occur, they tend to be short-lived. Fourth, new abilities and capabilities of quite a different nature emerge from early behaviours, e.g. walking is a very different activity from crawling.

The organismic tradition has drawn heavily upon biological writings including evolutionary theory. Human development is conceptualized in terms of the interaction between genetic maturation and experience. Development unfolds according to a purpose or design—a teleological view—and is frequently conceptualized in

DOI: 10.4324/9781003567738-5

terms of discontinuous stages. Human beings are understood to be relatively active in seeking out and responding to a more or less passive environment. Generally, organismic theories espouse the idea that the organism is different from the sum of its parts, and the structural arrangement of the parts is quite significant. Richard Lerner (1983) summarized the organicist outlook as comprising viewpoints that are:

- epigenetic;
- antireductionist;
- qualitative;
- discontinuous;
- multiple and interactionist in nature.

The nature of organismic thinking can be understood in the light of some historically influential ideas. We will outline these before considering the views of some early organismic theorists.

Background ideas in Ancient Greek philosophy

Many central questions concerning child development theories are deeply rooted in philosophy. Of particular relevance for this chapter are vitalism and organicism, which we can contrast with atomism.

Vitalism proposed that the processes of life are not explicable by the laws of physics and chemistry alone and that life is in some part self-determining. Aristotle argued that if there is something distinctive about living entities it resides in their 'soul' which all living things (as opposed to non-living things) possess. What is particular about human beings is the rational part of the soul enabling us to think as we behave. To understand life, Aristotle held that we must understand purposefulness and we cannot understand the nature of parts without reference to the whole. He argued that wisdom is the understanding of the 'why of things', and to understand purposefulness he identified several kinds of cause, including final, or teleological, ones. These have two underpinning features: they explain things in terms of their ends and not their beginnings, and they incorporate the notion of 'goodness'. An activity is therefore understood by reference to its end point, which is considered beneficial (or not) for the agent whose activity is to be explained.

A reading of Greek philosophy also identifies organicism as a foundational theme: that the universe is an alive and orderly place. The *Timaeus* describes the world (*kosmos*) as a living being created by the 'Demiurge' (*ho demiourgos*) who follows an 'eternal pattern'. One important aspect of organicism is to see a fundamental unity in all things—to see beneath all diversity an unchanging unity. As John Davis observed, 'organicism is first and foremost a view about the essential connectedness of things in reality' (1998: 349). Another aspect is to see the whole as somehow different from its constituent elements. Following the Greek Stoic philosophers, as reported by Jeremy Collier (1904), the Roman Emperor Marcus Aurelius captured the essence of organicism in writing:

> What happens next is always intimately related to what went before. It is not a question of merely adding up disparate things connected by inevitable succession, but events are logically interdependent. Just as the realities are established in tune with one another, so in the world of sense, phenomena do not occur merely in succession, but they display an amazing affinity with one another.
>
> *(The Meditations, 167 CE)*

By contrast, we can consider atomism. Democritus, born around 460 BCE, argued that the universe is populated by two kinds of things: atoms and void with atoms being infinite in number, indivisible and solid and varying in shape. The objects of the world come into being through collision of the atoms in the void. Derived from this belief is the idea that the universe is divisible into simple and similar particles and that all wholes (forms) are fundamentally made up of these particles. The different concrete wholes, like rocks, trees, planets and air, are simply different configurations of these particles; and change in wholes, such as the growth of a rose from seed to flower, comprises only changes in the configurations of particles. This is by many accounts the antithesis of organicism; its modern-day manifestation is mechanism and—in psychology—behaviourism.

A brief note is warranted here of the concept of 'holism', generally attributed to South African General Jan Smuts (1926), though he did not clearly define it (Jörgenfelt and Partington, 2019). The *Oxford English Dictionary* definition is 'the tendency in nature to form wholes, that are greater than the sum of its parts, through creative evolution'. As we will discuss later, holism is perhaps more commonly framed in terms of whole–part relationships. It should be noted that, in relation to development, holism and organicism are most closely linked in relation to the living organism. With this background we now move to consider other proponents of organicism.

Background ideas from the 19th and 20th centuries

One influence on organismic theorizing was 'functionalism', a school of thought in psychology founded by leading US thinker William James (1890/1950). James was severely critical of structuralism (behaviourism) because he considered its outlook on human behaviour as narrow and artificial. He had been influenced by the thinking of Charles Darwin, who emphasized, through the mechanism of natural selection, the functional nature of the characteristics of animals. James argued that human consciousness similarly had a function, namely, to enable people to make rational choices. Through the 1940s, the views and research of several psychologists belonging to the functionalist school (e.g. Ames, 1951) gained attention. Adelbert Ames experimented with striking visual illusions such as the Ames room (Figure 5.1) which tricks the human visual system into misapplying shape and size constancy. Perception is therefore seen to occur as a result of the relationship between the observing person and the observed object. Context is the critical functional factor in helping us to interpret the world around us. Ames and

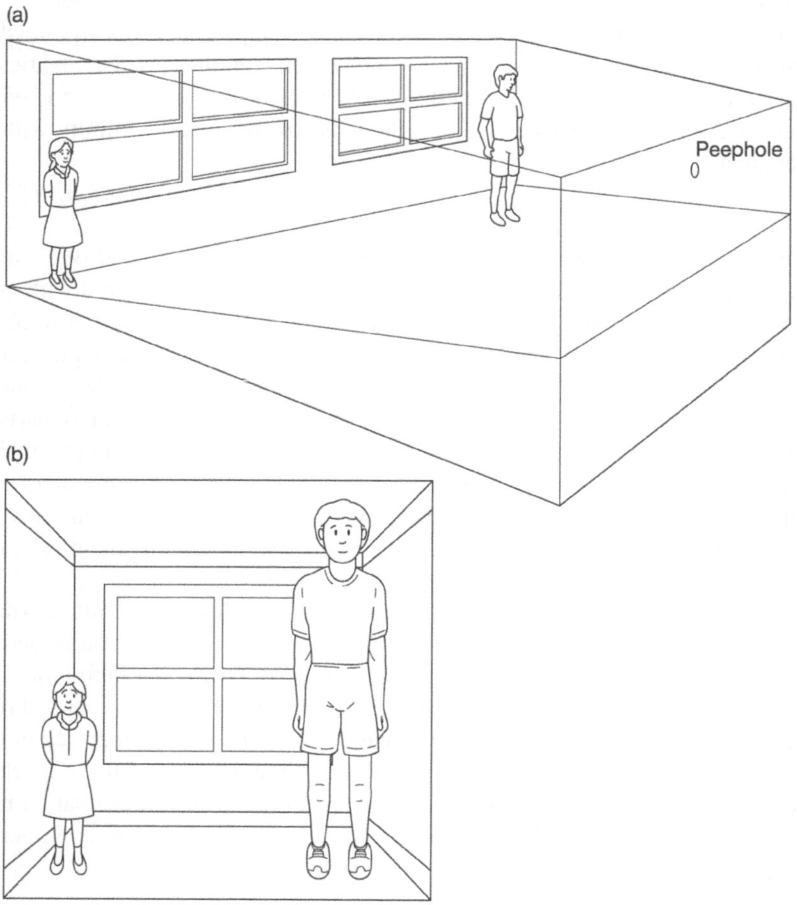

Figure 5.1 The visual illusion of the Ames room. Because the left-hand corner of the room shown in (a) is almost twice as far away from the viewer as the right-hand corner, the girl standing in the left-hand corner projects a smaller retinal image than the boy in the right even though they are both the same height in reality. When viewing the room through a peephole (b), we assume that we are looking at a normal room and that both children are the same distance: hence the illusion of the impossibly different relative sizes of the children

other functionalists argued against the idea that we can ever know anything as it 'really is': we can know things only in their relationship to us.

Also relevant is Gestalt psychology. This emerged in Austria and Germany in the early 20th century, beginning in 1912 with Max Wertheimer's publication of a study demonstrating the illusion of movement when two separate lights are alternately switched on; the display constitutes a perceptual whole. Gestalt psychology holds that the whole experience of a person is more than just the sum of its parts: it is a phenomenon in its own right. Kurt Koffka (1925) and Wolfgang Köhler (1927) were also influential, Koffka rejecting what he called 'crude materialism':

> This materialistic solution is astonishingly simple. It says: The whole problem is illusory. There are not three kinds of substance or modes of existence, matter, life, and mind; there is only one, and that is matter, composed of blindly whirling atoms which, because of their great numbers and the long time at their disposal, form all sorts of combinations, and among them those we call animals and human beings.
>
> *(Koffka, 1935: 6)*

The Gestaltists pointed out, for example, that red, green and blue light combine to produce white, but experiencing these colours is not the same as experiencing white. From his well-known experiments with apes, Köhler (1927) argued that animals and humans learn through insight (and not just through trial and error, as maintained by behaviourists). That is, in Köhler's terms there is a tendency to focus on the relationships between parts and not just the parts themselves. Gestaltists argued for the study of relationships, form and pattern, and were vehemently opposed to the reductionist claims of physiological psychology and the structuralist psychology of E. B. Titchener: this claimed that mental experiences could be analysed into elementary units such as sensations, feelings and thoughts, and if we could only objectively examine our experience we would discover that what come to the forefront are sensations (strong), images (fainter than sensations) and affect. Gestaltists, by contrast, argued that the basic units of consciousness are 'things', not sensations; thus, we see cars and people and buildings because of the innate perceptual equipment we have, and we do not construct them from sensations, images and affects and behaviourist 'laws of association' (see Chapter 4). Challengingly, Koffka, in wrestling with the Gestalt view, called psychology (particularly aspects of the US version) a 'very unsatisfying science'. In presenting the argument for a Gestalt he suggested that:

> If psychology can point the way where science and life will meet, if it can lay the foundations of a system of knowledge that will contain the behaviour of a single atom as well as that of an amoeba, a white rat, a chimpanzee, and a human being, with all the latter's curious activities which we call social conduct, music and art, literature and drama, then an acquaintance with such a psychology should be worth while and repay the time and effort spent in its acquisition.
>
> *(Koffka, 1935: 14)*

The work of US psychologist Eleanor J. Gibson (1910–2002) also provides some key concepts that will further broaden our understanding of organismic theories of cognitive development. Gibson is well known for her elegant experimental studies examining perception, such as the well-known 'visual cliff' studies (Gibson and Walk, 1960). Another classic experiment conducted by Gibson and her husband James (Gibson and Gibson, 1955) provided a foundation for the introduction of a different way to understand learning. Study participants had the opportunity to compare and contrast a series of graphic 'scribbles' against a standard 'scribble'. Viewers became aware of variations in the nature of the scribbles, their performance improving with the number of trials allowed. Unlike the learning described by behaviourists, which is seen to involve the forming of associations, the Gibsons' research suggested that the simple opportunity to improve perception permitted learning. Furthermore, there was no reinforcement, as behaviourism demands (Pick, 1992). An important concept for the Gibsons was 'differentiation': 'Our perception improves because we come to detect or differentiate more of the aspects, features, and nuances of the tremendously complex stimulation that impinges upon us' (Pick, 1992: 788).

Another central element was 'affordance'. James Gibson (1979) applied this term to the particular perceptual arrangements an organism possesses, such that the properties of any sensed object are perceived so as to optimize the species' survival. Thus, how objects are perceived depends on their meaning to the organism (Johansson, von Hofsten and Jansson, 1980). For example, 'holes afford hiding in, cups afford drinking out of, trees afford climbing' (Dennett, 2017, cited in Bruineberg and van den Herik, 2021). Box 5.1 addresses the child's search for meaning in stories.

BOX 5.1 THE CHILD'S SEARCH FOR MEANING IN STORIES

The idea that perception involves 'meaning-making' was an important element of Eleanor Gibson's thinking and research. Studies over several years have shown the benefits for language development of shared story-reading with young children, and that repeated exposure to the storyline and pictures appears to facilitate children's memory search for novel labels (Sénéchal, 1997); this echoes the Gibsons' work on multiple exposure to 'scribbles', whereby perception deepens over sessions. More recently, attention has turned to the meaning that children find in film. From a positive psychology perspective, de Leeuw *et al.* (2024) interviewed 66 children aged 4–15 years after they had watched the Disney/Pixar film *Inside Out*, a film about emotions that was informed by psychologists and that used the classical 'hero's journey' format. The film was found to be meaningful to the children as they were moved and inspired by the 'moral beauty' of the story; the film had encouraged them to follow the journey of Riley, the protagonist, and to gain the same insights that she had gained along the way. The authors suggest that film can offer children accelerated access to life experiences and the development of wisdom, which Aristotle had suggested as a benefit of story-telling more than two thousand years ago.

We now turn to a number of prominent early theories that highlighted the 'stage-like' aspect of development that characterizes organicism, beginning with the work of Stanley Hall.

Gerald Stanley Hall (1844–1924) and adolescence

Hall was born in a small town in Massachusetts in the United States. He became a seminarian, later studying theology and philosophy in Europe. In 1884 Hall was appointed as Professor in Psychology and Pedagogy at Johns Hopkins University. Influencing his psychology was a profound religious belief:

> The Bible is being slowly re-revealed as man's great text-book in psychology, – dealing with him as a whole, his body, mind, and will, in all the larger relations to nature, society,– which has been so misappreciated simply because it is so deeply divine.
>
> *(Hall, 1885: 239)*

After moving to Clark University, Massachusetts, Hall focused on the use of questionnaires to gather data in a broad range of areas, but he is probably best known for his writings regarding adolescent development. Under Darwinian influence, he developed a social-biological framework to explain human development. An important idea was 'recapitulation', drawing upon the work of Ernst Haeckel (1874), who argued that an embryo's ontogenetic progression mirrored phylogenetic history—the evolution of its species. Parenthetically, it is interesting that the British philosopher Herbert Spencer (1820–1903) also adopted the concept of evolution, advocating the idea that there takes place in the universe a continuous redistribution of matter and motion; evolution occurs when the integration of matter and motion are predominant, and devolution when the opposite occurs. Spencer had interpreted Darwin's theory to mean survival of the strongest individuals, although Darwin argued for *species*, not *individual*, survival. Spencer's 'social Darwinism' has been interpreted as justifying the use of force in the struggle for existence, but this was not the underlying feature of Darwin's theory. Hall's interpretation differed from Spencer's: he argued that until adolescence the child repeats through play and fear the evolution of human society, while environmental factors come to have a greater influence at adolescence (Hall, 1904).

In 1891 Hall initiated his child development research at Clark University (White, 1992) and produced *The Content of Children's Minds on Entering School*, establishing a tradition for measuring and observing children and summarizing findings in terms of age-based averages. Normative descriptive investigations were used to highlight similarities and differences in development. Sheldon White noted that Hall's two-volume *Adolescence: Its Psychology and its Relations to Physiology, Anthropology, Sociology, Sex, Crime, Religion and Education* (1904) went largely unread by the 1990s. The volumes were most often noted for popularizing views on three issues: recapitulation; adolescence as a time of 'storm and stress' (*Sturm und Drang*); and the claim for the 20th century's invention of 'adolescence'.

The term adolescence is derived from the Latin *adolescere*, which means 'to grow up' or 'to grow to maturity'. John Demos and Virginia Demos argued that 'the concept of adolescence, as generally understood and applied, did not exist before the last two decades of the nineteenth century', indicating that it was Hall's writing that promoted this view (Demos and Demos, 1969: 273). The change, storm and stress in adolescence, as seen by Hall, are characterized by:

> lack of emotional steadiness, violent impulses, unreasonable conduct, lack of enthusiasm and sympathy … previous selfhood is broken up … and a new individual is in the process of being born. All is solvent, plastic, peculiarly susceptible to external influences.
>
> *(Hall, 1904: 26)*

However, examination of some early writings indicates that, in fact, the idea commonly attributed to Hall that adolescence is a time of change is not at all new. Early writers noted particularly the impetuosity of youth. Eighth-century BCE Greek poet Hesiod's opinion would not be out of place today:

> I can see no hope for the future of our people if they are dependent on the frivolous youth of today for certainly all youth are reckless beyond words. … When I was a boy, we were taught to be discreet and respectful of elders, but the present youth are exceedingly wise and impatient of restraint.
>
> *(Hesiod, 8th century BCE)*

Aristotle's opinion was that:

> The young are in character prone to desire and ready to carry any desire they may have formed into action. Of bodily desires it is the sexual to which they are most disposed to give way, and in regard to sexual desire they exercise no self restraint. They are changeful too and fickle in their desires, which are transitory as they are vehement: for their wishes are keen without being permanent. … They are passionate, irascible, and apt to be carried away by their impulses.
>
> *(Aristotle, quoted in Demos and Demos, 1969: 633)*

Novelists have been particularly adept at picking up on the 'storm and stress' of adolescence, and such references certainly predate Hall. Claudio Violato and Arthur Wiley (1990) reviewed the images of adolescence in English literature from Geoffrey Chaucer (1342–1400) to Charles Dickens (1812–1870). They concluded that, in the main, literary works portray adolescence as 'a time of turbulence, excess and passion, which is consonant with Hall's (1904) depictions' (Violato and Wiley, 1990: 263). For example, in Shakespeare's *Romeo and Juliet*, the impetuous, passionate nature of youth is shown in the rapid betrothal of Romeo and Juliet and their respective suicides upon believing each other dead. The heightened sensitivity of adolescents was also vividly portrayed in the popular fiction writing of Sue Townsend in *The Secret Diary of Adrian Mole Aged 13 ¾*:

> The spot on my chin is getting bigger. It's my mother's fault for not having known about vitamins. I pointed out to my mother that I hadn't had my vitamin

C today. She said 'Go buy an orange'. So typical! Nigel came around today. He hasn't got a single spot yet. My grandma came by today. She squeezed my pimple. It has made it worse. I will go to the doctors on Saturday if the spot is still there. I can't live like this with everybody staring.

(Townsend, 1982: 21)

Nancy Galambos and Bonnie Leadbeater (2000), in a review of trends in adolescent research, observed an ongoing tendency to think of adolescence in terms of risks and opportunities. Challenges faced by young people concern their engagement in risky behaviours, and issues with poverty, homelessness and unemployment (Baumgartner, Valkenberg and Jochen, 2010). Young people take more risks than children or adults do, but understanding why is not straightforward (Slee, Campbell and Spears, 2012). While adolescent risk-taking was once ascribed to brain 'immaturity', a more recent view, based on studies that are larger-scale, longitudinal and more ecologically valid, is that adolescents are neurologically malleable, enabling adaptation to their changing inner and outer worlds; furthermore, contrary to common supposition, their risk-taking is more aligned with that of their parents than their peers (Abrams, 2022). Despite the popular conception of adolescence as a period of *Sturm und Drang*, the question is still raised regarding the validity of the idea (see Box 5.2).

In an extensive survey of young people aged 15–19, Mission Australia's Youth Survey report (2024) provides invaluable insights into young people's thoughts, experiences, concerns and solutions. The environment, equity and discrimination, the economy and financial matters, and mental health topped the issues they considered most important in Australia.

BOX 5.2 ADOLESCENT STORM AND STRESS—MYTH OR FACT?

As a trained secondary school history teacher, author PTS has a particular interest in the concept of 'storm and stress' as part of adolescence! The perception that adolescence is a particularly troubled time in the lifespan has a long history. Aristotle and Rousseau commented on the idea of the 'troubled adolescent' period and Hall promoted the idea particularly strongly. Arnett (1999) reviewed the evidence and concluded that there was evidence for a modified 'storm and stress' view in relation to the areas of conflict with parents, moodiness and increased risk-taking behaviour. Arnett concluded that it was less evident in more traditional cultures and hypothesized that in mainstream western cultures it was associated with globalization and increased emphasis on individualism. Hines and Paulson (2006) compared parental and teacher views of adolescent storm and stress. Their findings indicated that while both held views consistent with the idea of adolescence as a particularly troubled time, teachers held the views most strongly. They concluded that stereotypical beliefs regarding adolescence are maintained in western cultures which in turn may be associated with parenting and teacher practice. Buchanan *et al.* (2023), in their review of the concept, argued persuasively that the storm and stress view was outdated and should be replaced with a term or phrase that was more attuned to a 21st-century outlook, such as 'possibility and promise'.

Heinz Werner (1890–1964) and the orthogenetic principle

Werner arrived from Germany to teach at Clark University some 50 years after Hall had begun his work there. Werner published in a diverse range of areas and was 'a very modern thinker whose theoretical views were so at variance with normal professional practices that his message is yet to be heard' (Glick, 1992: 558). While the work of his contemporaries, such as Jean Piaget and Lev Vygotsky, continues to be evaluated and interpreted, the writings of Werner have been largely, but not entirely, overlooked.

Werner's views of development were influenced by Gestalt psychology and, more narrowly, by a particular school of Gestalt thinking emphasizing the 'developmental process of formation' (Glick, 1992: 559). Werner, with his strong background in biology and anthropology, argued that development was directional, supported by a basic survival drive and a desire to 'know'. While Werner shared an interest with Piaget in providing 'a developmental account of the a priori' (Glick, 1992: 559) he was more concerned with identifying growth principles or directions than with describing or discovering the nature of stages.

Werner elaborated his 'orthogenetic principle' (1948) as follows: 'Man, destined to conquer the world through knowing, starts out with confusion, disorientation, and chaos, which he struggles to overcome' (Werner and Kaplan, 1963: 5). While Werner's outlook in some ways reflects the recapitulation theory of G. S. Hall and the views of earlier philosophers such as Spencer, suggesting a move from a primitive to an advanced state, his theorizing was more sophisticated in many ways. He saw some 'directiveness' associated with development; the organism is motivated by a drive to survive and master its fate such that there is a movement towards ever greater differentiation. His research into human perception led him to conclude: 'We assume that organisms are naturally directed toward a series of transformations – reflecting a tendency to move from a state of relative globality and undifferentiatedness towards states of increasing differentiation and hierarchic integration' (Werner and Kaplan, 1963: 7). The orthogenetic principle refers to establishing the correct ('ortho') development ('genetic') in both physical and psychological development. The orthogenetic principle 'has radical implications that served to make Wernerian psychology fundamentally different from other developmental views' (Glick, 1992: 560). Significantly, it resulted in greater confusion regarding the topic of study because, as Glick observed, Werner did not begin with a topic of development such as language, but rather focused on the entity of development itself.

Hierarchical integration captures the increasing organization, or 'articulation' of responses and skills, for example, a baby's development of eating skills. First, the baby needs to be able to sit and focus on the food. As the child develops there is a move from the 'syncretic' (global) to the discrete as the child is increasingly able to separate out the various components. Thus, perception is combined with physical reaching skills to grasp a biscuit (cookie) and then bring it to the mouth. Two further orthogenetic principles were that of development moving from a state of rigidity to greater flexibility in order to influence the environment (as when the older child is able to reach inside a box of biscuits) and that of 'stability' such that the older child can concentrate for ever-longer periods.

There is some confusion regarding the status of Werner's theory, which may be better understood as a 'grand scale' theory (Glick, 1992). In this regard, it is not unlike dynamic systems theory, which also focuses on developmental processes in general rather than specific areas of development. There has been some revival of interest in Werner in the 21st century, with his life and work discussed by Jaan Valsiner (2012), and cited by Arnold Sameroff in developing his integrative developmental theory (see Chapter 15).

Gesell (1880–1961) and maturation

Arnold Lucius Gesell is a very significant figure in the history of developmental psychology. Trained under Hall at Clark University, Gesell (1946) went on to use innovative film techniques to chart the course of normal human development.

Gesell was relieved to find Darwinian views of development superseding theological ideas such as original sin, thus rescuing children from 'gloomier ideas of fixity and fate' (Thelen and Adolph, 1992: 369). Drawing on Darwin's emphasis upon the maturational component of development (Darwin, 1888/1959), Gesell did much to advance the charting of the growth of children.

Working during the early 20th century, Gesell embarked on the task of mapping the foetal, infant and early childhood behaviour of thousands of children. In the course of his work he established and standardized stages of development. His maturational view emphasized the natural unfolding of patterns of growth, which he believed was largely predetermined and self-regulated. His theory emphasized the 'lawfulness' of growth and consequently the ability to predict: 'Behavior is rooted in the brain and in the sensory and motor systems. The timing, smoothness and integration at one stage foretell behavior at a later age' (Gesell, cited in Knobloch and Pasamanick, 1974: 3). Gesell was well aware, however, of the multitude of factors impinging on a child that makes accurate prediction a risky venture.

Gesell identified the following four major fields of behaviour.

1. *Adaptive.* The most important field concerns the organizational component of behaviour, such as coordinating eye movements and reaching with the hand. Adaptive behaviour is the forerunner of later intelligence.

2. *Gross and fine motor*. This includes sitting, standing, walking, using fingers and manipulating objects.
3. *Language*. Gesell maintained that language also assumes distinct behaviour patterns and unfolds in a predetermined fashion, e.g. inarticulate vocalizations precede words.
4. *Personal and social*. This incorporates the reaction of children to their social world. However, according to Gesell, personal and social behaviour are determined by intrinsic growth patterns. Thus, while toileting is a cultural requirement shaped by social demands, the child's attainment of bladder and bowel control depends upon neuro-motor maturation.

According to Gesell, then, 'a child's development proceeds stage by stage in orderly sequence, each stage representing a degree or level of maturity' (cited in Knobloch and Pasamanick, 1974: 7). The view that body growth is strongly influenced by physical maturation is widely accepted (but see our discussion of dynamic systems theory in Chapter 10). However, the assertion that other important aspects of human development, such as personality, are similarly determined has attracted criticism. Esther Thelen and Karen Adolph (1992) conclude their overview of Gesell's work by acknowledging his lasting contribution to developmental theory, while noting the contradictions—for example, in his emphasizing the importance of genetics in determining development while at the same time recognizing the importance of the environment.

Gesell was an extraordinary 'stage' theorist: 'Who before or since has had the tenacity to describe 58 stages of pellet behavior, 53 stages of rattle behavior, and so on ...?' (Thelen and Adolph, 1992: 376). Gesell's maturational approach fell out of favour with the rise of Piaget, behaviourism and information-processing theories, but he probably laid the groundwork for the acceptance of Piaget's stage theory. The maturational approach is still apparent in clinical work with young children, where scales of developmental norms, based on work that Nancy Bayley began in the 1920s, continue to be used. For example, the Conners Developmental Milestones Scales (Conners, 2009) provide for an assessment of a young child's adaptive, communication and motor skills, play and pre-academic/cognitive skills.

Robert Havighurst (1900–1991) and developmental tasks

Another theorist who has made an important, if underrated, contribution to our contemporary understanding of child and adolescent development is Havighurst. He described development in terms of 'developmental tasks', or 'those things that constitute healthy and satisfactory growth in our society' (Havighurst, 1953: 2). In Havighurst's view, development is not one long slow uphill climb, but consists of steep gradients, where learning is difficult, and plateaux. One example is a child who must work hard to master the art of catching a ball, but who, having mastered the skill, can then 'coast' for years. Havighurst's theory addressed children's cognitive and other aspects of development. His views provide some contrast to cognitive-developmental and information-processing theories.

A question often asked of teachers or psychologists by parents, is 'How well is my child doing?' This is often answered in relation to developmental tasks. Evaluations generally reflect expectations based on pooled knowledge about child development that is transmitted from one generation to the next (Slee *et al.*, 2012). The expectations and concerns are often reflected in popular culture such as the milestones provided in child-rearing books. Havighurst explained developmental tasks thus:

> A developmental task is a task which arises at or about a certain period in the life of the individual, successful achievement of which leads to happiness and to success with later tasks, while failure leads to unhappiness in the individual, disapproval by society, and difficulty with later tasks.
>
> *(Havighurst, 1953: 2)*

Havighurst proposed that three forces set up certain developmental tasks for the individual.

- The biology of the individual, involving physical maturation, such as learning to walk or learning to relate to the opposite sex during adolescence.
- Cultural forces, such as learning to read and write.
- The personal values and aspirations of the individual, such as hoping to become a doctor or engineer.

He identified nine key tasks to be accomplished during early childhood, such as learning to walk, to eat solid food and to distinguish right from wrong. Nine tasks for middle childhood include learning the physical skills to play ordinary games and achieve personal independence. Havighurst identified ten developmental tasks during adolescence, including achieving mature relations with the opposite sex, achieving some economic independence, and selecting and preparing for an occupation.

In a later development of Havighurst's theory, Robert Selverstone (1989) proposed that the ten developmental tasks during adolescence may be clustered into four main categories.

- *Identity*. This involves the determination of the question 'Who am I?'
- *Connectedness*. This includes establishing relationships with peers.
- *Power*. This concerns the development of a sense of control and power.
- *Hope/joy*. This is achieved via the accomplishment of the previous three tasks.

According to Havighurst (1953), there is a right, or opportune, moment for teaching or developing a task. He also adopted a broad outlook about the nature of tasks, believing that they extend beyond the individual to the cultural-historical context in which the individual is developing. Hence, his was not a universalist theory. The Japanese researcher Hiroko Kanoh applied Havighurst's theory to teaching children about mobile (cell) phone use:

> [P]roviding direction to children in the use of mobile networks according to their developmental stage is as necessary as in scholastic learning. If this direction is given too early or too late, the effect will be reduced by half, but given at a specific developmental stage, it is likely to be effective.
>
> *(Kanoh, 2012: 232)*

Previously, after discussing Hall's work, we outlined the concerns of Australian youth as expressed in a 2024 survey. By comparison, we can examine here the concerns of Ukrainian youth, reflected in Havighurst's categories as listed by Selverstone and demonstrating the importance of the cultural-historical context. Young Ukrainians report serious war-related deterioration in their quality of life and mental health, disruption of social connections and education and (for some) accommodation and cost of living issues, along with cultural change (abandonment of Russian cultural exports and stronger national identity); they still hold hope for a rebuilt Ukraine (Zolkina and Fras, 2024).

At this point it is worthwhile revisiting the usefulness and validity of the concept of developmental stages such as 'adolescence' or 'youth'. As discussed earlier, organicism emphasizes the stages that help us identify and appreciate the nature of the challenges facing us as we grow and develop. However, alternatives to simple linear classification of the developmental process identified by normative transitions have been raised. For example, Johanna Wyn and Rob White emphasized that

> the focus on youth is not on the inherent characteristics of young people themselves, but on the construction of youth through social processes (such as schooling, families or the labor market). Young people engage with these institutions in specific ways, in relation to historical circumstances.
>
> *(Wyn and White, 1997: 9)*

Thus, for example, historians such as Robert Enright *et al.* (1987) have specifically argued that adolescence is a life stage created to meet the demands of industry for a skilled labour force. Furthermore, the notion of developmental tasks has been criticized as being merely descriptive. However, overall, it provides a means of understanding human development in a way that reflects a popular understanding: at particular times in our lives, we must address important developmental issues, and how effectively we fulfil these tasks has implications for current and future functioning.

Some 21st-century ideas drawing on the Gibsons' work

Although Patricia Miller (2022) has identified J. Gibson's work on affordances as having waned in influence in developmental psychology in recent years, it is very much alive in the fields of the philosophy of mind and embodied cognition that we will meet in Chapter 8 (Bruineberg and van den Herik, 2021). Although it has mainly been applied to adults, it certainly has developmental relevance, as we shall see.

Catherine Read and Agnes Szokolszky (2018) have drawn upon the (differing) theories of the two Gibsons, and recent research in biological organicism, to propose a novel developmental version of (adult) ecological psychology. They also draw on Werner's notion of 'differentiation' but observe that 'integration' is less well understood. Their principles include the following:

1. The organism and its environment are inseparable: the organism-environment system is what develops.
2. Information is a pattern in time and space that specifies a state of affairs of the organism-environment system; it does not involve a sender and receiver, as in engineering communication.
3. Perception and action are inseparable. 'Affordances depend on the action capabilities of the organism that change radically in the early stages of any altricial organism. For human infants affordances progress from those provided by caregivers [e.g. facial expressions, voice] gradually adding more of those affordances provided by the infant's own … actions' (Read and Szokolszky, 2018: 182).
4. 'Knowing' is direct, not computed unconsciously.
5. Experience brings about change in the ways of doing things, not in mental representations.

This list is not exhaustive, but the principles of organicism and affordance are clear. Furthermore, affordance has been examined in the context of robotics (Metta and Fitzpatrick, 2003): a humanoid system learned the different properties of objects (e.g. a toy car and a bottle) by prodding and poking, supporting J. Gibson's theory.

Systems thinking

Systems theory is a 20th-century scientific paradigm that has been used in conjunction with physical, biological and social systems (Minuchin, 1985). While systems thinking, with its notion of self-organization, has clear connections with the organismic metaphor described by Stephen Pepper (1942), its novel emphasis on holism and non-linear causality suggests that it should be considered a new developmental metaphor in itself. We have devoted Chapter 10 to it, but mention it briefly here given its organismic origins.

A prominent thinker here was the biologist Ludwig von Bertalanffy. Psychology in the first half of the 20th century was dominated by a positivistic-mechanistic-reductionistic approach, epitomized as the 'robot model of man' (Bertalanffy, 1968: 5–6). Bertalanffy was particularly interested in the application of systems theory to biological processes, making the following historical observation:

> As with every new idea in science and elsewhere, the systems concept has a long history. Although the term 'system' itself was not emphasized, the history of this concept includes many illustrious names. As 'natural philosophy,' we may trace it back to Leibniz; to Nicholas of Cusa with his coincidence of opposites; to the mystic medicine of Paracelsus; to Vico's and ibn-Kaldun's vision of history as a sequence of cultural entities or 'systems'; to the dialectic of Marx and Hegel, to mention but a few names from a rich panoply of thinkers.
>
> *(Bertalanffy, 1968: 408)*

He defined a system as a 'complex of interacting elements' (1968: 55). He was particularly interested in the relationship between the parts and the whole. An important contribution that he made was to identify 'open' and 'closed' systems. A closed system has no interaction with the surrounding environment (such as a chemical reaction in a closed container). An open system (such as a family) is one that interacts with the surrounding environment.

A number of developmentalists, including Arnold Sameroff (1983), recognized too the implications of the work of Ilya Prigogine and Gregoire Nicolis (1985) on self-organization in nonequilibrium systems. Thelen and Linda Smith noted that '[a]doption of such a systems model, with its assumptions of wholeness, self-stabilization, self-organization, and hierarchical organization, has implications for every aspect of developmental psychology' (Thelen and Smith, 1998: 575). There has indeed been strong interest in the application of systems theory to the study of children and the family. During the 1970s Gregory Bateson and colleagues developed and applied the ideas associated with general systems theory, in connection with research on families whose members had schizophrenia (Bateson, 1972). Later applications to families included work by Kenneth Kaye (1985) and Ylva Parfitt, Alison Pike and Susan Ayers (2013).

With the advent of systems thinking, a change in theoretical focus was observed in the fifth edition of the *Handbook of Child Psychology*, edited by William Damon and Richard Lerner (1998). There, Lerner observed 'a burgeoning interest not in structure, function, or content per se, but in change, in the process through which change occurs, and thus in the means through which structures transform and functions evolve over the course of human life' (Lerner, 1998: 1). This understanding captures features of dynamic systems theory, which has increasingly been applied to various areas of developmental psychology (Ashiabi and O'Neal, 2015; Mitra and Dangwal, 2021; Slee and Shute, 2025; Thelen and Smith, 1994).

Conclusions

In this chapter we have provided some important background to the worldview identified as 'organicism' (Pepper, 1942). It has a long history, as reflected in the earliest writings of Greek philosophers about concepts such as vitalism, though this idea of a 'vital force' is contentious: Jane Maienschein (1991) noted that, despite the admirable sentiment of organicism and its concern with the organism as a whole, it came to be associated with somewhat fuzzy thinking and serious questioning regarding what constitutes the 'life-force' or 'soul' of vitalism.

The emergence of new phenomena at each new level of organization that is not commensurate with a reduction to a lower level of organization is a feature of organicism. Lerner referred to the idea of 'epigenetic viewpoint', which

> denotes that at each higher level of complexity there emerges a new characteristic, one that simply was not present at the lower organizational level and thus whose presence is what establishes a new level as just that – a stage of organization qualitatively different from a preceding one.
>
> *(Lerner, 1983: 53)*

To that end, organismic theorists would generally endorse the Gestalt position that a rainbow is more than the sum of its colours. However, as we will outline in later chapters, particularly where we address dynamic systems, the whole is not only greater but 'different': 'Rather than focus on the functioning of individual parts that make up a larger whole, systems thinking looks at the way in which the parts interact with one another to create the larger whole' (Papero *et al.*, 2018: 2).

The organicist outlook also emphasizes that the individual's world moves through increasing levels of integration, that individuals are agents in constructing their reality and that there is some structural interdependence to the parts of development. The universal features of human development are emphasized, although Havighurst introduced a cultural-historical note. The notion of 'emergent properties' is not uncontested, either, as it creates difficulty for the more deterministic organicists. In the following chapter we continue to pursue the organicism metaphor in considering constructivist theories of development.

References

Abrams, Z. 2022. What neuroscience tells us about the teenage brain. *Monitor on Psychology*. American Psychological Association. www.apa.org/monitor/2022/07/feature-neuroscience-teen-brain

Ames, A. 1951. Visual perception and the rotating trapezoidal window. *Psychological Monographs 65*(7): 234. Available as book chapter at https://psycnet.apa.org/doi/10.1037/11303-012

Arnett, J. J. 1999. Adolescent storm and stress reconsidered. *American Psychologist 54*(5): 317–26. https://psycnet.apa.org/doi/10.1037/0003-066X.54.5.317

Ashiabi, G. S. and O'Neal, K. K. 2015. Child social development in context: an examination of some propositions in Bronfenbrenner's bioecological theory. *Sage Open 5*(2). https://doi.org/10.1177/2158244015590840

Bateson, G. 1972. *Steps to an ecology of mind.* London: Ronald Press.

Baumgartner, S., Valkenberg, P. M. and Jochen, P. 2010. Unwanted online sexual solicitation and risky sexual online behavior across the lifespan. *Journal of Applied Developmental Psychology 31*: 439–47. https://psycnet.apa.org/doi/10.1016/j.appdev.2010.07.005

Bertalanffy, L. von. 1968. *General system theory.* New York: George Brazillier.

Bruineberg, J. P. and van den Herik, J. C. 2021. Embodying mental affordances. *Inquiry*: 1–21. https://doi.org/10.1080/0020174X.2021.1987316

Buchanan, C. M., Romer, D., Wray-Lake, L. and Butler-Barnes, S. T. 2023. Adolescent storm and stress: a 21st century evaluation. *Frontiers in Psychology 14*: 1257641. https://doi.org/10.3389/fpsyg.2023.1257641

Collier, J. 1904. *The meditations of Marcus Aurelius*. London: The Walter Scott Publishing Company.

Conners, K. 2009. *Developmental milestones – parent scales*. Toronto: Multi-Health Systems. Also see www.wpspublish.com/conners-ec-conners-early-childhood

Damon, W. and Lerner, R. M. (eds). 1998. *Theoretical models of human development: handbook of child psychology*. Fifth edn. Vol. 1. New York: Wiley, 341–414.

Darwin, C. 1888/1959. *The life and letters of Charles Darwin* (Vol. 2, F. Darwin). New York: Basic Books.

Davis, J. B. 1998. Organicism. *Economics Faculty Research and Publications 454*. https://epublications.marquette.edu/econ_fac/454

De Leeuw, R. N. H., Weijers, A., Ahle, A-M. and Daalmans, S. 2024. How stories in the media can be meaningful in children's lives. *Media Psychology 27*(4): 479–502. https://doi.org/10.1080/15213269.2023.2247322

Demos, J. and Demos, V. 1969. Adolescence in historical perspective. *Journal of Marriage and Family 31*: 632–8. https://api.semanticscholar.org/CorpusID:144817217

Enright, R. D., Levy, V. M., Harris, D. and Lapsley, D. K. 1987. Do economic conditions influence how theorists view adolescents? *Journal of Youth and Adolescence 16*: 41–59. https://doi.org/10.1007/bf02138820

Galambos, N. L. and Leadbeater, B. J. 2000. Trends in adolescent research for the new millennium. *International Journal of Behavioral Development 24*: 289–94. https://doi.org/10.1080/01650250050118268

Gesell, A. 1946. The ontogenesis of infant behavior. In L. Carmichael (ed.), *Manual of child psychology*. New York: McGraw-Hill, 295–331. https://psycnet.apa.org/doi/10.1037/10756-006

Gibson, E. J. and Walk, R. D. 1960. The 'visual cliff'. *Scientific American 202*: 64–71. https://doi.org/10.1038/scientificamerican0460-64

Gibson, J. J. 1979. *The ecological approach to visual perception*. Boston: Houghton-Mifflin.

Gibson, J. J. and Gibson, E. J. 1955. Perceptual learning: differentiation or enrichment? *Psychological Review 62*: 32–41. https://psycnet.apa.org/doi/10.1037/h0048826

Glick, J. A. 1992. Werner's relevance for contemporary developmental psychology. *Developmental Psychology 28*: 558–65. https://psycnet.apa.org/doi/10.1037/0012-1649.28.4.558

Haeckel, E. 1874. *The evolution of man: a popular exposition of the principal points of human ontogeny and phylogeny* (2 vols.). International Science Library, NY: AI Fowler.

Hall, G. S. 1885. The new psychology. *Andover Review 3*: 239–48.

Hall, G. S. 1904. *Adolescence: its psychology and its relations to physiology, anthropology, sociology, sex, crime, religion and education*. Vols 1 and 2. New York: Appleton-Century-Crofts.

Havighurst, R. J. 1953. *Human development and education*. New York: Longman.

Hesiod. www.dsng.net/2005/06/youth-is-wasted-on-young.html

Hines, A. R. and Paulson, S. E. 2006. Parents' and teachers' perceptions of adolescent storm and stress relations. *Adolescence 41*(164): 597–614. https://psycnet.apa.org/record/2006-23510-001

James, W. 1890/1950. *The principles of psychology*. Vol. 1. New York: Dover.

Johansson, G., von Hofsten, C. and Jansson, G. 1980. Event perception. *Annual Review of Psychology 31*: 27–63. https://psycnet.apa.org/doi/10.1146/annurev.ps.31.020180.000331

Jörgenfelt, C. and Partington, H. 2019. A critical analysis of J. C. Smuts' theory of holism. *European Journal of Integrative Medicine 31:* 100980. https://doi.org/10.1016/j.eujim.2019.100980

Kanoh, H. 2012. The developmental stages of mobile network use: existence of the rule about mobile phone. In *E-Learn: world conference on e-learning in corporate, government, healthcare, and higher education.* Association for the Advancement of Computing in Education (AACE), 232–6. www.researchgate.net/publication/269872680_The_Developmental_stages_of_mobile_network_use_Existence_of_the_rule_about_mobile_phone

Kaye, K. 1985. Toward a developmental psychology of the family. In L. L'Abate (ed.), *Handbook of family psychology and therapy.* Homewood: Dow Jones-Irwin, 39–72.

Knobloch, H. and Pasamanick, B. 1974. *Gesell and Amatruda's developmental diagnosis: the evaluation and management of normal and abnormal neuropsychologic development in infancy and early childhood.* New York: Harper & Row.

Koffka, K. 1925. *The growth of mind.* New York: Harcourt Brace and World.

Koffka, K. 1935. *Principles of Gestalt psychology.* New York: Harcourt Brace.

Köhler, W. 1927. *The mentality of apes.* London: Routledge & Kegan Paul.

Kucich, J. 2018. Organicism. *Victorian Literature and Culture 46*(3–4): 791–5. https://doi.org/10.1017/S1060150318000852

Lerner, R. M. 1983. *Concepts and theories of human development.* New York: Random House.

Lerner, R. M. 1998. Theories of human development: contemporary perspectives. In W. Damon and R. M. Lerner (eds), *Handbook of child psychology.* Vol 1. *Theoretical models of human development.* Fifth edn. New York: Wiley, 1–24.

Maienschein, J. 1991. Morgan's regeneration, epigenesis, and (w)holism. In C. Dinsmore (ed.), *A history of regeneration research.* New York: Cambridge University Press, 133–49.

Metta, G. and Fitzpatrick, P. 2003. Better vision through manipulation. *Adaptive Behavior 11*(2): 109–28. https://doi.org/10.1177/10597123030112004

Miller, P. H. 2022. Developmental theories: past, present, and future. *Developmental Review 66*: 101049. https://doi.org/10.1016/j.dr.2022.101049

Minuchin, P. 1985. Families and individual development: provocations from the field of family therapy. *Child Development 56*: 289–302. https://psycnet.apa.org/doi/10.2307/1129720

Mission Australia 2024. Youth Survey. www.missionaustralia.com.au/publications/youth-survey

Mitra, S. and Dangwal, R. 2021. Evolution of the 'hole-in-the-wall': a status review. *Prospects 52*: 209–22. https://doi.org/10.1007/s11125-021-09552-y

Papero, D. V., Frost, R., Havstad, L. and Noone, R. 2018. Natural systems thinking and the human family. *Systems 6*: 19. https://doi.org/10.3390/systems6020019

Parfitt, Y., Pike, A. and Ayers, S. 2013. Infant developmental outcomes: a family systems perspective. *Infant and Child Development 23*(4): 353–73. https://doi.org/10.1002/icd.1830

Pepper, S. 1942. *World hypotheses: a study of evidence.* Berkeley: University of California Press.

Pick, H. L. 1992. Eleanor J. Gibson: learning to perceive and perceiving to learn. *Developmental Psychology 28*: 787–94. https://psycnet.apa.org/doi/10.1037/0012-1649.28.5.787

Prigogine, I. and Nicolis, G. 1985. Self-organisation in nonequilibrium systems: towards a dynamics of complexity. In M. Hazewinkel, R. Jurkovich and J. H. P. Paelinck (eds), *Bifurcation analysis.* Springer, Dordrecht. https://doi.org/10.1007/978-94-009-6239-2_1

Read, C. and Szokolszky, A. 2018. An emerging developmental ecological psychology: future directions and potentials. *Ecological Psychology 30*(2): 174–94. https://doi.org/10.1080/10407413.2018.1439141

Reese, H. W. and Overton, W. F. 1972. On paradigm shifts. *American Psychologist 27*(12): 1197–8. https://psycnet.apa.org/doi/10.1037/h0038064

Sameroff, A. J. 1983. Developmental systems: contexts and evolution. In W. Kessen (ed.), *Handbook of child psychology.* Vol. 1. *History, theory and methods*. New York: Wiley, 237–94.

Selverstone, R. 1989. Adolescent sexuality: developing self-esteem and mastering developmental tasks. *SIECUS Report 18*: 1–4. https://siecus.org/wp-content/uploads/2024/05/18-1.pdf

Sénéchal, M. 1997. The differential effect of storybook reading on pre-schoolers: acquisition of expressive and receptive vocabulary. *Journal of Child Language 24*: 123–38. https://psycnet.apa.org/doi/10.1017/S0305000996003005

Slee, P. T., Campbell, M. and Spears, B. 2012. *Child, adolescent and family development*. Third edn. Melbourne: Cambridge University Press.

Slee, P. T. and Shute, R. H. 2025. The school as a Complex Adaptive System (CAS). In P. K. Smith, S. P. Limber, V. Artinopolou and K. Breivik, *School bullying and the legacy of Dan Olweus*. Oxford: Wiley, 247–64.

Smuts, J. C. 1926. *Holism and evolution*. New York: Macmillan.

Thelen, E. and Adolph, K. E. 1992. Arnold L. Gesell: the paradox of nature and nurture. *Developmental Psychology 28*: 368–80. https://psycnet.apa.org/doi/10.1037/0012-1649.28.3.368

Thelen, E. and Smith, L. B. 1994. *A dynamic systems approach to the development of cognition and action*. Cambridge, MA: MIT Press.

Thelen, E. and Smith, L. B. (1998). Dynamic systems theories. In W. Damon and R. M. Lerner (eds), *Handbook of child psychology: theoretical models of human development*. Fifth edn. Chichester: John Wiley & Sons, 563–634.

Townsend, S. 1982. *The secret diary of Adrian Mole age 13¾*. London: Methuen.

Valsiner, J. 2012. Heinz Werner: a differentiation theory of development. In W. E. Pickren, D. A. Dewsbury and M. Wertheimer (eds), *Portraits of pioneers in developmental psychology*. np: Psychology Press, 37–49.

Violato, C. and Wiley, A. J. 1990. Images of adolescence in English literature: the Middle Ages to the modern period. *Adolescence 25*: 253–64. www.proquest.com/scholarly-journals/images-adolescence-english-literature-middle-ages/docview/195931874/se-2

Watkins, H. 2017. Toward a post-humanist organicism. *Nineteenth-Century Music Review 14*: 93–114. https://doi.org/10.1017/S1479409816000306

Werner, H. 1948. *Comparative psychology of mental development*. Chicago: Follett.

Werner, H. and Kaplan, B. 1963. *Symbol formation*. New York: Wiley.

White, S. 1992. G. Stanley Hall: from philosophy to developmental psychology. *Developmental Psychology 28*: 25–34. Republished at https://psycnet.apa.org/doi/10.1037/10421-014

Wyn, J. and White, R. 1997. *Rethinking youth*. London: SAGE.

Zolkina, M. and Fras, M. 2024. *Understanding Ukrainian young people's current concerns, needs and hopes: looking ahead to a future rebuilding of Ukraine*. British Council and London School of Economics. www.britishcouncil.org/sites/default/files/2024_ukraine_concerns_needs_hope_report_screen-compressed.pdf

6 The child as philosopher

Constructivism

Introduction

In continuing the presentation of theories associated with organicism, we introduce the field of thinking broadly referred to as constructivism. Some further background ideas include the philosophical notion of the world of ideas, George Kelly's personal construct theory and the psychological concept of cognition. We then address the important contributions made by Jean Piaget, Eleanor Maccoby and Jerome Bruner, and also consider the input that connectionism and theory of mind have made to theorizing about human development. We also touch again upon social cognitive theory although this was dealt with in more detail in Chapter 4.

Background ideas

We have already observed the contribution of Kurt Koffka to organismic thinking, and here it is appropriate to begin with a quote from his 1935 publication where he addressed the issue of the function of science, writing:

> To Summarise: the acquisition of true knowledge should help us to reintegrate our world which has fallen to pieces; it should teach us the cogency of objective relations, independent of our wishes and prejudices, and it should indicate to us our true position in our world and give us respect and reverence for the things animate and inanimate around us.
>
> *(Koffka, 1935: 5)*

This outlook leads us to consider the work of Karl Raimund Popper, born in 1902 in Vienna. He became one of the world's most influential philosophers, teaching at universities such as the London School of Economics and the Canterbury University College in Christchurch, Aotearoa/New Zealand. Popper proposed that the task of philosophy is to enrich our image of the world, arguing that the generally accepted picture involves a variation of mind–body dualism. He suggested that there are, in fact, three worlds:

DOI: 10.4324/9781003567738-6

> The first is the physical world or the world of physical states; the second is the mental world or the world of mental states; and the third is the world of intelligibles, or of *ideas in the objective sense*; it is the world of possible objects of thought: the world of theories in themselves, and their logical relations; of arguments in themselves; and of problem situations in themselves.
>
> *(Popper, 1972: 154)*

In 'World 1' we have physical reality, which we relate to with our five senses. 'World 2' is the inner world of thoughts, feelings and emotions, accessible through introspection. 'World 3' can be examined using the objective methods of logic and mathematics—similar to the Platonic realm of 'Ideas' (see Chapter 4). Writers such as Finn Tonnessen (1999) argued that cognitive psychology is located in World 3, and later we will see the emergence of connectionism as reflecting mental structures and models derived from logical and mathematical reasoning.

The 1960s and 1970s saw a significant shift towards cognitive psychology. Behaviourism had been the dominant influence in the 1940s and 1950s, particularly in North America. The early psychologists, including William James and Wilhelm Wundt, were certainly interested in aspects of cognition, including attention and memory, but the dominance of behaviourism discredited the study of the 'mind'. The behaviourist John Watson confidently wrote that after psychology accepted behaviourism, it could then be equated with the physical sciences: 'The findings of psychology … lend themselves to explanation in physico-chemical terms' (Watson, 1913: 177).

Despite Watson's prediction, the mid-20th century saw the emergence of a strong interest in cognitive processes, including children's cognitive development, social cognition and cognitive therapy. Influences bearing on this shift included George Kelly's personal construct theory. He posited two notions: '(1) that viewed in the perspective of the centuries, man might be seen as an incipient scientist, and (2) that each individual man formulates in his own way constructs through which he views the world of events' (Kelly, 1955: 12). This indicated that the personal constructs people hold lead them to understand and explain events in different ways, which in turn leads to different action. Personal construct psychology argued that individuals develop bi-polar dimensions of meaning, used to make sense of experience and anticipate the future. Each person psychologically constructs understandings of self, others and relationships, and continually evaluates whether these constructs effectively account for the world around them.

Beyond Kelly, methodological advances in the middle of the 20th century meant that it also became possible to study cognition without resort to introspection. For example, just as a rat bar-pressing in the context of a certain stimulus, such as a green light, would indicate that the subject was attending to the stimulus, a person pressing a button when a particular stimulus appears on a screen is taken as having consciously 'seen' it (though there are exceptions; for an interesting discussion of conscious and unconscious visual processing, see Jacobsen and Casco, 2022). All in all, there was an increasing research effort directed towards the understanding of cognitive development. Hans Kreitler and Shulamith Kreitler noted rather sceptically that 'the term "cognitive" has been used so widely that one might wonder whether there is anything in psychology that is not cognitive' (Kreitler and Kreitler, 1976: 4). Recognizing the plurality of cognitive science, George Miller presented a vision of a unified field concerned with 'the representational and computational capacities of the human mind and their structural and functional realization in the human brain' (Miller, 2003: 144).

In 1956, information-processing pioneers Allen Newell and Herbert Simon invented a 'thinking machine' that could create proofs for mathematical theorems. As they said, '[t]here is a growing body of evidence that the elementary information processes used by the human brain in thinking are highly similar to a subset of the elementary information processes that are incorporated in the instruction codes of … computers' (Newell and Simon, 1972: 282). In fact, cognitive psychologists have used the metaphor of the computer to compare with cognitive processes, which also serves to highlight the objectivity of their research (Tonnessen, 1999).

Jean Piaget (1897–1980) and cognitive developmental theory

Piaget is one of the most noteworthy figures in 20th-century developmental psychology. In fact, theories of cognitive development have been described as BP and AP—before and after Piaget (Flavell, Miller and Miller, 2002, cited in Barrouillet, 2015). He initially worked in the Jean-Jacques Rousseau Institute in Switzerland as a research coordinator and later became its Deputy Head. For decades, he was Director of the Bureau International de l'Éducation, the main aim of which was to promote peace and international understanding through education. His theory came to prominence as the influence of behaviourism was declining (Halford, 1989). For interested readers, Slee, Campbell and Spears (2012) have described the basic tenets of Piaget's theory in more detail. A number of early major reviews of Piaget's theory were provided by Harry Beilin (1992), Paul van Geert (1998) and John Flavell (1992), while Orlando Lourenço's (2012) reflections are also helpful.

Piaget's theory of children's cognitive development was at heart an epistemological one—that is, a theory of how we know what we know. However, as we shall explain later, Piagetian theory also embodies constructivism.[1] This maintains that meaning is constructed in our minds as we interact with the physical, social and emotional world of which we are part, with learning an active process unique to the individual. Piaget's notion of a 'schema', or mental knowledge structure through which the world is understood, became a central feature of cognitive psychology. This perspective contrasts sharply with objectivist views of the world which maintain that meaning exists in the world, to be discovered.

David Elkind (1974) identified three main phases in Piaget's theory.

1. From 1922 to 1928, Piaget was concerned with the ideas that children held about the physical world. In working with Alfred Binet on routine intelligence testing, Piaget's attention was caught by children's incorrect answers. Piaget developed and refined his clinical interview technique (*la méthode clinique*)

and discovered that children reasoned differently from adults and had literally different philosophies about the nature of the world (Elkind, 1971). Piaget was also concerned with the apparent egocentrism of young children and their often-observed inability to take in another's perspective.

2. The second period began in 1929 when he undertook the study of children's mental growth, prompted primarily by curiosity about his own children's development (Elkind, 1971). Issues such as object permanence were addressed.
3. From the 1940s, Piaget dealt with the child's understanding of concepts such as number, quantity and speed.

Piaget emphasized that the child is actively involved in their own development, hence the idea associated with Piagetian theory that the child is a 'little scientist'. Some have maintained that Piaget regarded the child as a rather solitary learner but, as we shall see, that understanding is not quite true. The child has a multitude of ideas about the world, which may be somewhat different from an adult's understanding. The child, in the course of education, is always learning and unlearning ideas such as the concepts of space, time, quantity and number. Finally, 'the child is by nature a knowing creature' and as such 'is trying to construct a world view of his own, and is limited only by his abilities and experience' (Elkind, 1971: 108). For an example from India, see Box 6.1.

BOX 6.1 HOLE-IN-THE-WALL COMPUTERS: CHILDREN TEACHING THEMSELVES

Children's natural curiosity and drive to experiment on the world has been drawn upon to bring computers and the internet to children without access to formal education. Physicist Dr Sugata Mitra began his 'minimally invasive education' experiment by placing a hole-in-the-wall computer in a New Delhi street adjoining a slum in 1999. With no direction or assistance from adults, children experimented together and learned to operate the computer. Within days they could create documents, browse the internet and paint pictures. The egg-timer icon they interpreted as 'Shiva's drum'. The project has been extended across India and to other nations such as Cambodia and Botswana. Further work (Inamdar, 2004) showed that rural children who used hole-in-the-wall computers scored only marginally lower on a Grade 8 computer science examination than children who had learned the material through the regular school curriculum.

This work established the notion of SOLES (self-organized learning environments) that draws upon systems theory (Mitra and Dangwal, 2021). While community-based set-ups become derelict for lack of funds, placing them in schools ensures sustainability, not because of teacher supervision (which is not provided), but because the computer is maintained.

There are two components to Piaget's theory, a stage-independent and a stage-dependent component (Honstead, 1968). In the former, Piaget addressed the issue of how cognitive development proceeds. He listed four factors to account for cognitive development, as follows:

1. *Maturation.* Piaget was a biologist by training and, from a biological perspective, viewed the developing child as maturing. At birth the immaturity of the infant's brain is a factor limiting cognition, but brain development (most rapid before birth) proceeds rapidly in the first two years after birth and continues to some extent for much longer.
2. *Experience.* Piaget argued that experience is of two kinds:
   (a) direct physical experience, such as playing with water and generally using the five senses to experience the world; and
   (b) mathematical experience, which occurs when the child reflects on the structure of experience and particularly on its logical and mathematical structure; according to Piaget and Bärbel Inhelder (1969), logico-mathematical experience comes from the child's acting on the world rather than from the experience itself.
3. *Social transmission.* This least developed part of Piaget's model led some to conclude, as noted earlier, that he viewed children as rather solitary learners. While he certainly emphasized the dialectic between the child and the physical world (which led some to regard him as a dialectical theorist), he 'included social interaction as a motivator of development, particularly through conflict of ideas between peers' (Meadows, 1986: 108).
4. *Equilibration.* This is probably the most basic of the four factors, being the process of achieving equilibrium between things that were previously understood and those not yet understood. Meeting something new, the child actively attempts to relate it to something known, that is, to assimilate it into an existing schema. When new information causes a schema to change, that is 'accommodation', and represents cognitive development.

Piaget's theory is also well known as a 'stage' theory of development. Four criteria for such theories were described by Inhelder (1975):

1. A period of formation and progressive organization of mental operations.
2. The progressive hierarchical development of one stage upon another.
3. Relative similarity on the attainment of each stage.
4. A directional and hierarchical nature.

As many of our readers will doubtless be aware, the stage-dependent component of Piaget's theory comprises four major stages, as described below. Each is identified in terms of the child's principal method of knowing.

1. *Sensori-motor period* (0–2 years). The child's primary method of knowing is through the actions they perform on the world in terms of the five senses.

2. *Pre-operational period* (3–7 years). The emergence of language, modelling and memory are key features, but cognitive limitations are evident and the child's thinking is dominated by perception rather than concepts (McGurk, 1975). For example, the child makes judgements in terms of how things appear to them, not how they actually are. If shown two balls of clay of equal size and weight, and one is then squeezed into a sausage shape, the child is likely to say that the sausage has more clay because it looks longer (i.e. because the child cannot yet 'conserve'). The child's acquisition of language signals the beginning of symbolic thought. Egocentrism is another element of the child's thinking; thus a girl may tell you she has a sister but deny that her sister has a sister.
3. *Concrete operations period* (7–11 years). Children's thinking attains greater flexibility, with grouping of ideas and logical deductive reasoning possible. However, operational groupings are limited to concrete objects such as blocks, clay and liquids and logical thought does not yet include verbal stimuli (Honstead, 1968: 139).
4. *Formal operations period* (11+ years). This is the final period of cognitive development. 'The hallmark of this stage is the child's ability to reason abstractly without relying upon concrete situations or events' (McGurk, 1975: 39).

For Piaget, the child is actively involved in seeking out information helping them understand the world. Piaget's theory has been labelled 'constructivist' (Gelcer and Schwartzbein, 1989) inasmuch as the child actively constructs the external world in acting upon it. Such a view contrasts with behavioural theories that emphasize the child's passivity. From a biological perspective, Piaget viewed development as progressive and directional. The invariant feature of his theory emphasized stage-like development, in which the manner of thinking at one level is qualitatively different from that at a later stage. Piaget exemplified the child's changing understanding with the response of Del, aged 7, when posed a question he himself had asked at 6: 'It's silly to ask that when it's so easy. It's silly. It doesn't go together. It's so [silly] that I don't understand a word of it' (Piaget, 1959: 223).

Critique of Piaget's theory

Graeme Halford observed that if the 1960s represented a period of optimism regarding the application of Piagetian psychology to understanding children's cognitive development, then the 1970s produced a reassessment resulting in some disillusionment. This can be attributed to research that challenged many of Piaget's assumptions regarding the nature of cognitive development, and to the failure of Piaget's research to reap the anticipated rewards in some applied areas (Halford, 1989). A critical overview of Piaget's theory can also be found in Zana Babakr, Pakstan Mohamedamin and Karwan Kakamad's 2019 paper. The following represents an overview of some of the major criticisms.

A feature of Piaget's experimental method, *la méthode clinique*, was his careful interviewing of the child. His child-centred approach in his earliest work consisted of an open-ended discussion with the child. It was a method allowing the deep meaning of children's responses to be accessed (Ducret, 1998). From an empirical perspective, Piaget's interview technique has been criticized as too subjective and value-laden. Criticism has also been directed at the reliance on verbal introspection of immature minds.

Another trenchant criticism has been directed at the sequence of stages and the nature of children's behaviour within them (Gardner, 1979). Major concerns have been expressed that a universal age/stage approach overlooks the part played by individual differences in mental and environmental factors in shaping a child's behaviour.

It has also been noted that Piaget tended to treat other people in the child's life as objects. Some authors suggest that this neglects the social competence of infants and the role of others as *social partners*. It is argued that such partnerships are important in promoting cognitive development (Eibl-Eibesfeldt, 1989; Xu and Kushnir, 2013), within specific cultural contexts (Babakr *et al.*, 2019); this was highlighted by theorists such as Lev Vygotsky (see Chapter 8), and Maccoby and Bruner (see below). Margaret Donaldson's (1978) work was also influential. Her most famous piece of research, the 'Naughty Teddy' study, showed how children's cognitive performance is influenced by their understanding of the social situation: children who seemed unable to conserve number using the standard procedure (when the experimenter moves the counters out of line) were often able to do so when, instead, a 'naughty teddy' swooped in and messed up the line.

Esther Thelen and Linda Smith observed that Piaget's theory was said to fit 'the orderliness of development on a large scale' (Thelen and Smith, 1994: 21). However, they argued that on a more detailed scale the theory fails to capture the 'complexity and messiness of cognitive development in detail' (1994: 21–2). In particular, they and others have challenged some central tenets of Piagetian theory, as follows:

1. *Children develop from an impoverished beginning state*. Research suggests that, in fact, the young infant is highly competent. This view of the infant encompasses the notion of the infant as 'active, competent and in some ways, in control, of his/her own learning' (Trevarthen, 2010: 119).
2. *There are global discontinuities in cognition across stages*. In fact, there is evidence of early precursors to abilities, including advanced abilities of the newborn relating to processing emotional information and speech sounds (Huotilainen, 2010).
3. *Cognitive growth is monolithic*. In fact, there is wide individual variation in development and competences. Outcomes depend on a dynamic interaction between the child and others, including the infant's and caregivers' motivations to engage with and respond to one another (Brinck and Liljenfors, 2013).

Thelen and Smith concluded that '[c]ognitive development does not look like a marching band; it looks more like a teeming mob' (Thelen and Smith, 1994: 22).

Piaget's standing in the 21st century

Despite such criticisms, Piaget's theory remains influential educationally and has become one of the best-known theories of child development. Howard Gardner acknowledged Piaget's tremendous contribution in the following terms:

> Whatever its ultimate scientific fate, Piaget's contribution has over the past few decades provided a major impetus for research in developmental psychology. Before Piaget began research into the child's special cognitive and conceptual powers most work consisted of either sheer descriptions of objective features of the child's existence (physical milestones, preferred activities, motoric activities), anecdotal accounts of individual children, including ones displaying unusual abilities or difficulties, or broadly speculative interpretations of the course of growth.
>
> *(Gardner, 1979: 73–4)*

Lourenço (2012) suggested that while Piaget could be considered a figure of the past, his theory and writings were continuing to inspire developmental thinking. A prominent example of a neo-Piagetian theorist was Robbie Case (1998), who combined a Piagetian approach with an information-processing one. According to his theory, as the brain develops and schemas become more automatic with practice, working memory capacity increases, allowing more advanced processing of information. Thus, children become able to undertake more complex cognitive tasks. The uneven nature of cognitive development noted by Thelen and Smith is accounted for in this formulation, as practice in one domain more than another would lead to uneven development across domains. See also our discussion in Chapter 3, regarding Annette Karmiloff-Smith's epigenetic approach.

Helena Marchand (2012) provided a comprehensive overview of Piagetian and neo-Piagetian theories in relation to education, and an overview of the neo-Piagetians has been provided by Gülşah Sevinç (2019), who points out that they enlarged upon, rather than contradicted, Piaget's theory. Jaime Dice and Meghan Dove (2011) used Piagetian theory to examine referential behaviour in infants—behaviours generally understood in the social cognitive literature to indicate that infants realize they are sharing attention to an object with another person. Also, Canadian-American Renée Baillargeon, in challenging Piaget's ideas about infant development (e.g. on object permanence), greatly expanded understanding of infant competence (e.g. Margoni, Baillargeon and Surian, 2018). A further legacy is Fei Xu and Tamar Kushnir's 'rational constructivism'. As they describe it, '[r]ational learners integrate prior beliefs, knowledge, and biases with new evidence provided by the environment' (Xu and Kushnir, 2013: 28). Learning is then seen as rational, inferential and statistical and they propose that this helps explain why infants learn so quickly.

Piaget's ongoing influence is indicated by the existence of an international Piagetian movement and a vast interdisciplinary secondary literature (Ratcliff, 2024). Nevertheless, Marc Ratcliff has observed a recent decline in empirical research based on Piaget's theory; he attributes this in part to a turning to newer theories and a change in academic culture whereby 'the reading unit of psychologists has become the article and the abstract and no longer the book' (Ratcliff, 2024: 29).

Connectionism

Connectionism first emerged as a force in the early 1980s and became influential in relation to research in language development, categorization and decision-making (Mahoney, 1993). Andy Clark (1993: ix) wrote optimistically that connectionism 'promises to be not just one new tool in the cognitive scientist's toolkit but, rather, the catalyst for a more fruitful conception of the whole project of cognitive science'. As Amanda Sharkey and Noel Sharkey (2019: 1) have observed, 'Connectionism has made an important contribution to the intriguing challenge of finding a physical basis for mind.' Connectionism is generally identified as a form of cognitive psychology, but there is no doubt that it also has much in common with behaviourism. Thus, neither distinguishes between the cognitive and the biological, both recognizing that learning entails changes to the nervous system (Tonnessen, 1999). Both can also explain gradual improvement through drill and repetition, trial and error, and gradual adjustment. Connectionism is linked to Popper's (1972) 'World 3', in that it is related to mathematical reasoning and the world of logic. The emergence of connectionism was associated with the development of supercomputers, and a number of models have been devised to account for developments in perception and cognition.

Connectionist models, often termed neural networks, have also been influenced by research on brain processing structures and attempt to explain how the brain works. At the most basic level, a connectionist network contains many simple, interconnected, processing units that transmit activation unidirectionally (Smith, 1996); the units are usually assumed to perform some simple computation. Athanassios Protopapas characterized a neural network as comprising interconnected units, or nodes, each of which can be assigned an 'activation value' (Protopapas, 1999: 414). It is therefore possible to identify the positive or negative sign of the input or output from a weighted algebraic sum of the units. The learning process is hypothesized to shape the weights on the interconnections among the units.

The description of neural networks in terms of 'units' and 'activation' 'leaves unanswered the question of what a unit represents semantically' (Smith, 1996: 898). A traditional conceptualization of memory invokes the metaphor of a filing cabinet wherein 'storage', 'search' and 'retrieval' represent accessible 'inscriptions'; by contrast, connectionist models do not have representations in discrete locations. Rather, 'the whole network of connection weights is a single representation that contains information derived from many past experiences' (Smith, 1996: 898).

In relation to cognitive development, William Ramsay, Stephen Stich and Joseph Garon (1991) commented that it was unquestionable that connectionism was already fostering major changes in how scientists conceived of cognition. Thelen and Smith (1994) saw it as intimately related to dynamic systems theory but observed that connectionist models fail as developmental theories in not seriously considering a number of issues, including how biology (including the brain) really works and how complex development actually is. Nevertheless, connectionism has been applied to efforts to understand cognitive development. For example, it has been applied to preschoolers' ability to understand 'false beliefs' —what another person believes about the location of an object moved in their absence (Berthiaume, Shultz and Onishi, 2013): a computer simulation based on a constructivist connectionist model successfully reproduced the transitions found in children's developing understanding. Connectionism shares with systemic theorizing the idea of emergence, is based on similar mathematical principles and they may be considered complementary (Smith and Samuelson, 2003). It has also been linked with artificial intelligence (Sun, 2014). According to Sharkey and Sharkey (2019) connectionism had its heyday in the 1990s but plateaued in the 2000s.

Theory of mind

The previous example (Berthiaume *et al.*, 2013) brings us to children's 'theory of mind' (ToM). David Premack and Guy Woodruff (1978) introduced this idea as part of their efforts to understand the cognitive and language abilities of chimpanzees: 'An individual has a theory of mind if he imputes mental states to himself and others' (1978: 515). It was a phrase adapted from writings relating to the philosophy of mind (e.g. Fodor, 1987). As we spend time with others we consider their feelings, thoughts and behaviour in order to try and understand why individuals behave as they do. Indications of the existence of theory of mind awareness are found in everyday language usage such as 'I think she was upset' or 'I'm sure you will like this'. To understand that children have a developing sense of another, researchers must first rule out the possibility that the child is (a) not behaving egocentrically (e.g. indicating that another child wants something based not on their knowledge of the other's desire but on their own desire) or (b) not simply using past experience to infer something about another child. Autism is a prominent area where ToM has been applied (Baron-Cohen, Leslie and Frith, 1985). See also Box 6.2, where ToM is applied to the issue of school bullying.

BOX 6.2 BULLYING AND THEORY OF MIND (TOM)

Claire Hughes and Sue Leekam (2004), reviewing ToM and its link with peer relations, including bullying, concluded that 'developments in theory of mind transform children's close relationships, but also highlight … the complexity of these socio-cognitive influences' (2004: 296). Certainly, a common portrayal of students who bully others, particularly in fiction, is of the bully as a rather 'powerful, but "oafish" person with little understanding of others' (Sutton, Smith and Swettenham, 1999: 117). Such a view is consistent with a social skills-processing view, suggesting that individuals might be deficient at any one of the five stages of information processing, including (a) social perception, (b) interpretation of cues, (c) goal selection, (d) response strategy generation, and (e) response decision. A bully might be thought of as lacking one or more of these 'social skills'. In contrast, Jon Sutton *et al.* (1999) suggested that some bullies might be very adept at using ToM to understand other individuals in order to manipulate and organize them. This theoretical viewpoint has attracted some debate about whether bullying arose because the bully *lacked* social skills or because they *were* socially skilled (e.g. Crick and Dodge, 1999). A longitudinal study has reported that, for boys only, greater and earlier ToM directly predicted greater bullying two years later (Fink *et al.*, 2020).

In an early major review of the field Flavell (1999) identified three main waves of research relating to children's knowledge about the mind. The first wave largely involved Piaget's theory and research. Piaget's argument concerning the essentially egocentric nature of children in the early stages of development indicated that children were restricted in their ability to appreciate the perspectives of others. Studies confirmed a gradual increase in children's perspective-taking abilities (Flavell, 1992).

A second wave of research related to children's metacognitive development, concerning knowledge about people as cognizers, the nature of different cognitive tasks, and possible strategies for solving problems (Flavell, 1999). How do children develop the capacity for 'thinking about their thinking'? Brinck and Liljenfors (2013) examined the development of metacognition in infants from a dynamic systems perspective, arguing that it arises in infancy out of mutual and reciprocal dyadic interaction of infant and caregiver.

The third, and now dominant, wave of research relates to ToM development. A virtual avalanche of research began in the 1980s, the more recent studies suggesting that well below the 3–5 age range (which has been the traditional focus of ToM research), even very young children possess such capacity, but fail to perform accordingly (Samson and Apperly, 2010). Nonverbal ToM tasks are easier for them than the verbal ones typically used in false-belief studies.

Several newer versions of ToM came into existence (Gallagher, 2004). The original version, largely based on false-belief tests, has been called 'theory-theory (TT)', whereby a folk theory of the minds of others is either seen as developing with experience or as 'coming on-line' at specific ages. By contrast, 'simulation theory (ST)' holds that there is no 'theory', as such, but that we mentally simulate another's mind based on our own; this draws upon the discovery of mirror neurons that activate when we see another person doing an action, as well as when we think about doing that action ourselves. There is also Shaun Gallagher's interaction theory (IT), which maintains that the use of TT and ST is rare, as we can mostly immediately perceive another's intentions by 'body reading', with both infants and animals able to do this without any sophisticated cognitive apparatus (Gallagher,

2004). The whole question of what ToM 'is' was raised by Ian Apperly (2012), with researchers variously implying that it is about concepts, or cognitive processes, or individual differences—all legitimate angles to take, but often requiring clearer articulation.

Henry Wellman (2018) has provided a comprehensive overview of the historical development of ToM and highlighted emerging areas of new research. For example, it now includes cultural and social aspects, and neural correlates, and investigates children above preschool age and adults, thus becoming more truly developmental (e.g. Liu *et al.*'s 2025 longitudinal study of brain–behaviour links in ToM from infancy into childhood).

We can finally note that mindfulness practice assumes a further hierarchical level above cognition and metacognition: 'meta-metacognition'. It involves deliberately damping down metacognition, and children are arguably developmentally unready for this (see Chapter 16).

Eleanor Maccoby (1917–2018): adding the 'social' to cognitive development

The extensive research interests of Eleanor Maccoby placed her at a particular advantage in psychology to integrate various theoretical influences. Maccoby (1980) acknowledged the influence of cognitive-developmental theory in shaping her views, hence her inclusion in the present chapter. However, she expressed a concern echoed by others, that 'the theory is too "cold" and does not give enough weight to the role of emotions in social development' (Maccoby, 1980: 31). She was also critical of stage theory, arguing instead that there are 'decision points' in children's lives and at such points various influences, such as the family, can lead any two children to follow different developmental patterns.

Born in Tacoma, Washington, of parents with 'alternative' beliefs (Stevens and Gardner, 1982), Maccoby's adolescent rebellion against her parents' values was possibly reflected in an early interest in psychology and in her belief that human behaviour could be studied empirically according to the objective methods developed by positivist sciences. In 1950 she began teaching at Harvard University. Although she later reported receiving little gender discrimination, Gwendolyn Stevens and Sheldon Gardner (1982) said she was unhappy in the rather patriarchal setting of that university (for instance, women were not permitted to enter the Faculty Club by the front door) (Chapter 12 discusses the androcentric nature of psychology at the time). She subsequently moved to Stanford University.

From an early stage in her career she was interested in studying children, including the effects of television. At various times her eclectic research interests also encompassed mother–child interaction, women's studies, gender, moral values, aggression, attachment and the relationship between intelligence and non-cognitive abilities.

In outlining her views of children's socialization, Maccoby acknowledged the influence of behaviourism and Freudian theory, particularly in relation to sex-role development. Perhaps most importantly, however, she identified a broad range of research influences shaping understanding of children's social development:

- Research involving trait theory, which has highlighted not just consistency, but the inconsistency of children's behaviour in various situations.
- Cognitive-developmental theory, which has alerted us to the manner in which children's thinking shapes their perception of events.
- Ethological theory and the associated concept of instincts, which raises the possibility of the predisposition of children to learn certain things, such as attachment.
- Temperament research, which created awareness of the dissimilarity of infants at birth.
- Cross-cultural research, which alerted developmental researchers to the influence of social structures such as the nature of the family unit, the economic basis of a society (e.g. agricultural or industrial), the role of men and women, and how a culture educates its members.

Broadly speaking, Maccoby's wide-ranging perspective reflected an awareness that the biology of the child should be taken into account, and that the child actively participates in the socialization process and also moves through various phases in developing a concept of the social self. One important feature of Maccoby's thinking (Maccoby, 1980) concerned the parents' role in aiding the child's social development. In this respect, her perspective is more consistent with that of Diana Baumrind than Sandra Scarr (see Chapter 3).

Jerome Bruner (1915–2016) and constructivism

Constructivism has deep philosophical roots. It can be dated back to the writings of Socrates, who claimed that by talking with each other and asking questions we can construct knowledge and understanding. It also has philosophical roots in the European tradition of thinking drawn from the philosophy of George Berkeley and Immanuel Kant, who emphasized the subjectivity of our perception, and it has been linked with the thinking of Piaget. Esther Gelcer and David Schwartzbein (1989) summarized two important assumptions of Piaget's theory: that there are different levels of knowing the same experience, and that the greater the level of abstraction, the more flexible is the individual's approach to problem-solving. Other key writers who have contributed to theory relating to constructivism include the Chilean biologist Humberto Maturana and his colleague Francisco Varela (1988), and the cybernetician Heinz von Foerster (2003). The systems thinking of Gregory Bateson also had an impact.

The central assertion of constructivism is that reality cannot be revealed to us in only one true way. It is through the process of construing that we come to know reality, as in Kelly's theory: 'each organism creatively constructs its world within the limits of whatever biological or environmental context it encounters' (Gelcer and Schwartzbein, 1989: 440). Constructivism emphasizes a proactive view of the individual who, as an observer, participates actively in the process of observation. It is through this process of active participation that the co-creation of meaning occurs. Such a proactive view of the person contrasts with much of mainstream psychology, which views the individual as reactive.

The North American psychologist Bruner (2017) criticized behaviourism's reliance on stimulus and response to explain development. His theory reflected a constructivist approach and was greatly influenced by the thinking of Piaget and Vygotsky (see Chapter 8). For example, for Vygotsky the process of knowing is shaped by those with whom we interact and mediated by community and culture. While Bruner's theory is similar to that of Piaget in many respects, it also differs in crucial aspects. For Bruner, language is intimately related to a child's cognitive growth. In his view, thinking would not be possible without language. Bruner (1987) also argued that the competencies of children are greater than Piaget's theory leads us to believe. He placed great emphasis on the child as a social being whose competencies 'are interwoven with the competences of others' (Bruner, 1987: 11). Bruner (1966) identified three major themes in understanding cognitive growth and the conditions that shape it. The first relates to how humans organize and represent their experience of the world. As detailed later, Bruner argued that children pass through three stages or modes of representing their world, each of which enables the child to represent the world in unique ways (Bruner, 1987).

A second theme relates to the impact of culture on development, as Vygotsky maintained. Bruner noted that cognitive growth is shaped as much 'from the outside in as the inside out' (Bruner, 1966: 13). A third major theme relates to the evolutionary history of humans: Bruner believed humans to be particularly suited to adapting to their environment by social, rather than morphological, means (Bruner, 1986).

In reading Bruner's work, several basic assumptions are evident. One of these is that reality is constructed. Bruner placed a great deal more emphasis than Piaget on the notion that humans actively construct meaning from the world. In *Actual Minds, Possible Worlds* Bruner cited Nelson Goodman's notion of a constructivist philosophy:

> Contrary to common sense, there is no unique 'real world' that pre-exists and is independent of human mental activity and human symbolic language; that which we call the world is a product of some mind whose symbolic procedures construct the world.
>
> *(Bruner, 1986: 95)*

This is consistent with postmodern philosophical ideas. Bruner argued that the idea that we construct the world should be quite congenial to developmental or clinical psychologists, who observe that humans can attach quite different meanings to the same event.

Another of Bruner's central assumptions is that development is culturally and historically embedded (Bruner, 1986; Bruner and Haste, 1987). In this way Bruner's outlook is closely aligned with that of Vygotsky. Culture is the means by which 'instructions' about how humans should grow are carried from one generation to the next (Bruner, 1987). That is, culture helps transmit knowledge and understanding.

Bruner and Helen Haste also observed that 'we are now able to focus on the child as a social being whose competencies are interwoven with the competencies of others' (Bruner and Haste, 1987: 11). They were critical of Piaget's legacy, which suggested that while the child is active in the construction of the world, the picture that emerges is one of a rather isolated child working alone at problem-solving tasks. They emphasized that the child is in fact a social operator who, through a social life, 'acquires a framework for interpreting experience, and learns how to negotiate meaning in a manner congruent with the requirements of a culture' (Bruner and Haste, 1987: 1).

The first of Bruner's (1966) proposed stages is *enactive representation*, equivalent to Piaget's sensori-motor period. Bruner argued, as did Piaget, that the infant gains knowledge about the world not from mental images but rather from action. Comparing the two theories, Bruner noted that Piaget regarded the 'first part in sensori-motor intelligence as one in which things are lived rather than thought' (Bruner, 1966: 17; Piaget, 1954). Bruner likened this type of intelligence to an irreversible and fixed succession of static images, each connected to an action. The child seems able to 'hold an object in mind by less and less direct manual prehension of it' (Bruner, 1966: 17). During the enactive stage infants can perform actions but do not know how they perform them. To this extent, Bruner agrees with Piaget. These ideas can be linked with Vygotsky and with current thinking about 'embodied cognition'.

Bruner's second stage of knowing, that of *iconic representation*, 'emerges when a child is finally able to represent the world to himself by an image or spatial schema that is relatively independent of action' (Bruner, 1966: 21) The word 'iconic' (today rather overworked) comes from the Ancient Greek word (*icon*) for likeness or image. A mental image is a genuine cognitive representation. It is representative of a body of information but takes a different form from that which it represents. In Bruner's (1966) view, iconic knowledge has a number of identifiable characteristics:

- It is inflexible.
- It focuses upon small details.
- It is self-centred in relation to having central reference to the child as an observer.
- It is subject to distortion because of the child's needs or feelings.
- Perception is closely tied to action or doing.
- Perception is unsteady in terms of the young child's unsteadiness of concentration.

Bruner and Piaget disagreed about the role of iconic representation in a child's thinking. In Bruner's theory the role of iconic knowledge is crucial to the explanation of conservation.

Bruner's third stage of knowing is *symbolic representation*: 'The idea that there is a name that goes with things and that the name is arbitrary is generally taken as the essence of symbolism' (Bruner, 1966: 31). Thus, while a picture of a beautiful landscape looks like a landscape, a written sentence describing it does not; the landscape is symbolized in the descriptive language. In Bruner's (1966) theory, symbolic representation is enhanced through language acquisition in particular. Without the ability to symbolize, the child will grow into adulthood dependent upon the enactive and iconic modes of representing and organizing knowledge of the world.

By emphasizing the constructive nature of cognitive development and the influence of cultural factors, Bruner added a richer dimension to our contemporary understanding of the nature of children's thinking and its development. For example, he proposed allowing students to 'discover' the connections between their learning and the relevance to themselves, thereby better remembering and making sense of information (Bruner, 1966). Used in Australian classrooms, 'guided discovery' scaffolded (appropriately supported) by the teacher provides students with greater autonomy in their learning (Reynolds, 2009). Bruner's work is further discussed in Chapter 8. He put forward the idea of the child's cognitive development in terms of agency, self-regulatory and self-reflective processes, which was in stark contrast to behavioural views.

Expressing similar sentiments to Bruner, Albert Bandura (2001) argued that nothing less than a paradigm shift had occurred in psychological theorizing, supplanting behaviourist theory with the view of the individual as an 'agent' with the capacity to intentionally make things happen by one's actions, as we noted previously: 'Consciousness is the very substance of mental life that not only makes life personally manageable but worth living. A functional consciousness involves purposive accessing and deliberative processing of information for selecting, constructing, regulating, and evaluating courses of action' (Bandura, 2001: 3).

Social-cognitive theory, which we discussed in Chapter 4, focuses upon transactions between cognition, behaviour and the environment (Bandura, 1997). A social-cognitive view of motivation proposes that during the process of instruction, such as during school lessons, students access knowledge about earlier motivational states, outcomes and emotions, which influences their readiness and willingness to learn (Winne, 1991). In Philip Winne's view, this motivational knowledge influences task selection and shapes the quality of students' involvement with a task, including their expenditure of effort and level of interest, and affects task persistence. Social-cognitive theory has been applied in a range of contexts, including the classroom, where it has been used to understand more about teachers' instructional strategies and students' knowledge about how to learn (Askell-Williams and Lawson, 2015).

Conclusions

The organismic worldview (Pepper, 1942) highlights the directional movement of the organism towards ever-increasing integration against the background of a dynamic, evolving context. As we have argued, all phenomena are interdependent. In this situation the child is an active constructor of reality and not merely responding passively. As an active individual, the child constructs interpretations of environmental events, and continually acts and interacts with the environment in order to construct and reconstruct experience. The child is viewed as a spontaneously active organism, and because some activities are not simply a response to external events it is not theoretically possible to predict all of an individual's behaviour. Acting like lay theorists, children are continually adapting their theories to fit ever-changing events in their world, altering the world in the process. However, the lay theories are by no means as neat and consistent as we might like to imagine (Basseches, 1989) and it is the very inconsistencies in children's theorizing that force them to act to resolve them.

While this approach takes into account the uniqueness of individuals and their active participation in their own development, two key limitations to organismic theories have been raised. One relates to the structural stage conceptions of development, which 'fail to reflect the complexity and diversity of individuals' meaning making' (Basseches, 1989: 189). The second limitation is a lack of explanation for how internal regulation, organization and self-organization relate to the developmental process, although this was a challenge to which systems theorists and the neo-Piagetians rose (Sevinç, 2019).

Note

1 Constructivism is concerned with an individual's psychology, whereas the sociological notion of 'constructionism' focuses on the societal level.

References

Apperly, I. 2012. What is 'theory of mind'? Concepts, cognitive processes and individual differences. *Quarterly Journal of Experimental Psychology 65*(5): 825–39. http://dx.doi.org/10.1080/17470218.2012.676055

Askell-Williams, H. and Lawson, M. 2015. Changes in students' cognitive and metacognitive strategy use over five years of secondary schooling. In *Educational futures: translating research into visions for transformative practice*. Hershey: IGI Global, 1–19.

Babakr, Z. H., Mohamedamin, P. and Kakamad, K. 2019. Piaget's cognitive developmental theory: critical review. *Education Quarterly Reviews 2*(3): 517–24. https://doi.org/10.31014/aior.1993.02.03.84

Bandura, A. 1997. *Self-efficacy: the exercise of control*. New York: Freeman.

Bandura, A. 2001. Social cognitive theory: an agentic perspective. *Annual Review of Psychology 52*: 1–26. https://doi.org/10.1146/annurev.psych.52.1.1

Baron-Cohen, S., Leslie, A. M. and Frith, U. 1985. Does the autistic child have a 'theory of mind'? *Cognition 21*: 37–46. https://psycnet.apa.org/doi/10.1016/0010-0277(85)90022-8

Barrouillet, P. 2015. Theories of cognitive development: from Piaget to today. *Developmental Review 38*: 1–12. http://dx.doi.org/10.1016/j.dr.2015.07.004

Basseches, M. 1989. Toward a constructive-developmental understanding of the dialectics of individuality and irrationality. In D. A. Kramer and M. Bopp (eds), *Transformation in clinical and developmental psychology*. New York: Springer-Verlag, 188–210.

Beilin, H. 1992. Piaget's enduring contribution to developmental psychology. *Developmental Psychology 28*: 191–204. https://psycnet.apa.org/doi/10.1037/0012-1649.28.2.191

Berthiaume, V. G., Shultz, T. S. and Onishi, K. H. 2013. A constructivist connectionist model of transitions on false-belief tasks. *Cognition 126*: 441–58. https://doi.org/10.1016/j.cognition.2012.11.005

Brinck, I. and Liljenfors, R. 2013. The developmental origin of metacognition. *Infant and Child Development 22*: 85–101. https://doi.org/10.1002/icd.1749

Bruner, J. 1966. *Studies in cognitive growth*. New York: Wiley.

Bruner, J. 1986. *Actual minds, possible worlds*. Cambridge, MA: Harvard University Press.

Bruner, J. 1987. *Child's talk*. New York: Norton.

Bruner, J. 2017. *A study of thinking*. Second edn. New York: Routledge.

Bruner, J. and Haste, H. 1987. *Making sense: the child's construction of the world*. London: Methuen.

Case, R. 1998. The development of central conceptual structures. In D. Kuhn and R. Siegler (eds), *Handbook of child psychology, cognition, perception and language*. Vol. 2. Fifth edn. New York: Wiley, 745–800.

Clark, A. 1993. *Associative engines: connectionism, concepts, and representational change*. Cambridge, MA: MIT Press.

Crick, N. R. and Dodge, K. 1999. Superiority is in the eye of the beholder: a comment on Sutton, Smith and Swettenham. *Social Development 8*: 128–34. https://psycnet.apa.org/doi/10.1111/1467-9507.00084

Dice, J. L. and Dove, M. K. 2011. A Piagetian approach to infant referential behaviors. *Infant Behavior & Development 34*(3): 481–6. https://doi.org/10.1016/j.infbeh.2011.04.003

Donaldson, M. 1978. *Children's minds*. Glasgow: Fontana.

Ducret, J. J. 1998. Jean Piaget 1970–80. Dix dernières années de recherches sur le constructivisme au Centre International d'Épistémologie Génétique. *Bulletin de Psychologie S1*(435): 343–75.

Eibl-Eibesfeldt, I. 1989. *Human ethology*. New York: Aldine de Gruyter.

Elkind, D. 1971. Cognitive growth cycles in mental development. *Nebraska Symposium on Motivation 19*: 1–31. https://psycnet.apa.org/record/1973-10840-001

Elkind, D. 1974. *Children and adolescents*. Second edn. London: Oxford University Press.

Fink, E., de Rosnay, M., Patalay, P. and Hunt, C. 2020. Early pathways to bullying: a prospective longitudinal study examining the influences of theory of mind and social preference on bullying behaviour during the first 3 years of school. *British Journal of Developmental Psychology 38*(3): 458–77. https://doi.org/10.1111/bjdp.12328

Flavell, J. H. 1992. Development of children's knowledge about the mental world. *International Journal of Behavioral Development 24*: 15–23. https://doi.org/10.1080/016502500383421

Flavell, J. H. 1999. Cognitive development: children's knowledge about the mind. *Annual Review of Psychology 50*: 21–45. https://doi.org/10.1146/annurev.psych.50.1.21

Fodor, J. A. 1987. *Psychosemantics: the problem of meaning in the philosophy of mind*. Cambridge, MA: Bradford Books/MIT Press.

Foerster, H. von. 2003. Cybernetics of cybernetics. In K. Krippendorff (ed.), *Communication and control*. New York: Gordon and Breach, 5–8. https://link.springer.com/content/pdf/10.1007/0-387-21722-3_13.pdf

Gallagher, S. 2004. Situational understanding: a Gurwitschian critique of theory of mind. In L. Embree (ed.), *Gurwitsch's relevancy for cognitive science*. Dordrecht: Springer, 25–44.

Gardner, H. 1979. Developmental psychology after Piaget: an approach in terms of symbolization. *Human Development 22*: 73–88. https://doi.org/10.1159/000272430

Geert, P. van. 1998. A dynamic systems model of basic developmental mechanisms: Piaget, Vygotsky, and beyond. *Psychological Review 105*: 634–77. https://philpapers.org/rec/VANADS-6

Gelcer, E. and Schwartzbein, D. 1989. A Piagetian view of family therapy: Selvini-Palazzoli and the invariant approach. *Family Process 28*: 439–56. https://doi.org/10.1111/j.1545-5300.1989.00439.x

Halford, G. S. 1989. Reflections on 25 years of Piagetian cognitive developmental psychology 1963–1988. *Human Development 32*: 325–57. https://psycnet.apa.org/doi/10.1159/000276484

Honstead, C. 1968. The developmental theory of Jean Piaget. In J. L. Frost (ed.), *Early childhood education rediscovered*. New York: Holt, Rinehart and Winston, np.

Hughes, C. and Leekam, S. 2004. What are the links between theory of mind and social relations? Review, reflections and new directions for studies of typical and atypical development. *Social Development 13*: 590–619. https://psycnet.apa.org/doi/10.1111/j.1467-9507.2004.00285.x

Huotilainen, M. 2010. Building blocks of fetal cognition: emotion and language. *Infant and Child Development 19*: 94–8. https://doi.org/10.1002/icd.658

Inamdar, P. 2004. Computer skills development by children using 'hole in the wall' facilities in rural India. *Australasian Journal of Educational Technology 20*(3): 337–50. https://doi.org/10.14742/ajet.1351

Inhelder, B. 1975. Some aspects of Piaget's genetic approach to cognition. In J. Gants and H. J. Butcher (eds), *Developmental psychology*. Harmondsworth: Penguin, 22–40.

Jacobsen, T. and Casco, C. 2022. A scientific approach to conscious experience, introspection, and unconscious processing: vision and blindsight. *Brain Science 12*(10): 1305. https://doi.org/10.3390/brainsci12101305

Kelly, G. A. 1955. *A theory of personality*. New York: Norton.

Koffka, K. 1935. *Principles of Gestalt psychology*. New York: Harcourt, Brace.

Kreitler, H. and Krietler, S. 1976. *Cognitive orientation and behaviour*. New York: Springer-Verlag.

Liu, Y., Moss, E., Ting, F. and Hyde, D. C. 2025. Neural sensitivity to others' belief states in infancy predicts later theory of mind reasoning in childhood. *Cortex 184*: 96–105. https://doi.org/10.1016/j.cortex.2024.11.023

Lourenço, O. 2012. Many resemblances, and a crucial difference. *New Ideas in Psychology 30*: 281–95. https://doi.org/10.1016/j.newideapsych.2011.12.006

Maccoby, E. 1980. *Social development: psychological growth and the parent-child relationship*. New York: Harcourt Brace Jovanovich.80

Mahoney, M. J. 1993. Introduction to special section: theoretical developments in the cognitive psychotherapies. *Journal of Consulting and Clinical Psychology 61*: 187–93. https://psycnet.apa.org/doi/10.1037/0022-006X.61.2.187

Marchand, H. 2012. Contributions of Piagetian and post-Piagetian theories to education. *Educational Research Review* 7(3): 165–76. https://doi.org/10.1016/j.edurev.2012.04.002

Margoni, F., Baillargeon, R. and Surian, L. 2018. Infants distinguish between leaders and bullies. *Proceedings of the National Academy of Sciences 115*(38): E8835–43. https://doi.org/10.1073/pnas.1801677115

Maturana, H. R. and Varela, F. J. 1988. *The tree of knowledge: the biological roots of human understanding*. Boston: New Science Library.

McGurk, H. 1975. *Growing and changing: a primer of developmental psychology*. London: Methuen.

Meadows, S. 1986. *Understanding child development*. London: Hutchinson.

Miller, G. A. 2003. The cognitive revolution: a historical perspective. *Trends in Cognitive Sciences 7*(3): 141–4. https://doi.org/10.1016/s1364-6613(03)00029-9

Mitra, S. and Dangwal, R. 2021. Evolution of the 'hole-in-the-wall': a status review. *Prospects 52*: 209–22. https://doi.org/10.1007/s11125-021-09552-y

Newell, A. and Simon, H. 1972. *Human problem solving*. Engelwood Cliffs: Prentice-Hall.

Piaget, J. 1954. *The construction of reality in the child*. London: Routledge and Kegan Paul.

Piaget, J. 1959. *Language and thought of the child*. London: Routledge.

Piaget, J. and Inhelder, B. 1969. *The psychology of the child*. New York: Basic Books.

Pepper, S. 1942. *World hypotheses: a study of evidence*. Berkeley: University of California Press.

Popper, K. 1972. *Objective knowledge: an evolutionary approach*. Oxford: Clarendon Press.

Premack, D. and Woodruff, G. 1978. Does the chimpanzee have a theory of mind? *Behavioural and Brain Sciences 1*: 515–26. https://psycnet.apa.org/doi/10.1017/S0140525X00076512

Protopapas, A. 1999. Connectionist modeling of speech perception. *Psychological Bulletin 125*: 410–36. https://psycnet.apa.org/doi/10.1037/0033-2909.125.4.410

Ramsay, W., Stich, S. P. and Garon, J. 1991. Connectionism, eliminativism, and the future of folk psychology. In W. Ramsey, S. P. Stich and D. E. Rumelhart (eds), *Philosophy and connectionist theory*. Hillsdale: Erlbaum, 199–228.

Ratcliff, M. J. 2024. Origins, trends and perspectives of historical-epistemological research on Piaget. *Integrative Psychological and Behavioral Science 58*: 23–34. https://doi.org/10.1007/s12124-023-09796-7

Reynolds, R. 2009. *Teaching studies of society and the environment in the primary school*. South Melbourne: Oxford University Press.

Samson, D. and Apperly, I. A. 2010. There is more to mind reading than having theory of mind concepts: new directions in theory of mind research. *Infant and Child Development 19*: 443–54. https://doi.org/10.1002/icd.678

Sevinç, G. 2019. A review on the neo-Piagetian theory of cognitive development. *Ankara University Journal of Faculty of Educational Sciences 52*(2): 611–31. https://doi.org/10.30964/auebfd.470159

Sharkey, A. J. C. and Sharkey, N. 2019. Connectionism. In *The Routledge companion to philosophy of psychology*. Second edn. np: Routledge, ch 12.

Slee, P. T., Campbell, M. and Spears, B. 2012. *Child, adolescent and family development*. Third edn. Melbourne: Cambridge University Press.

Smith, E. R. 1996. What do connectionism and social psychology offer each other? *Journal of Personality and Social Psychology 70*: 893–912. https://psycnet.apa.org/doi/10.1037/0022-3514.70.5.893

Smith, L. B. and Samuelson, L. K. 2003. Different is good: connectionism and dynamic systems theory are complementary emergentist approaches to development. *Developmental Science 6*(4): 434–9. https://doi.org/10.1111/1467-7687.00298

Stevens, G. and Gardner, S. 1982. *The women of psychology*. Vol. 2. *Expansion and refinement*. Cambridge, MA: Schenkman.

Sun, R. 2014. Connectionism and neural networks. In K. Frankish and W. M. Ramsey (eds), *The Cambridge handbook of artificial intelligence*. np: Cambridge University Press, 108–27.

Sutton, J., Smith, P. K. and Swettenham, J. 1999. Bullying and 'theory of mind': a critique of the 'social skills deficit' view of anti-social behaviour. *Social Development 8*: 117–27. https://psycnet.apa.org/doi/10.1111/1467-9507.00083

Thelen, E. and Smith, L. B. 1994. *A dynamic systems approach to the development of cognition and action*. Cambridge, MA: MIT Press.

Tonnessen, F. E. 1999. Options and limitations of the cognitive psychological approach to the treatment of dyslexia. *Journal of Learning Disabilities 5*: 386–95. https://doi.org/10.1177/002221949903200504

Trevarthen, C. 2010. What is it like to be a person who knows nothing? Defining the active intersubjective mind of a newborn human being. *Infant and Child Development 20*: 119–35. https://psycnet.apa.org/doi/10.1002/icd.689

Watson, J. B. 1913. Psychology as the behaviorist views it. *Psychological Review 20*: 158–77. https://psychclassics.yorku.ca/Watson/views.htm

Wellman, H. M. 2018. Theory of mind: the state of the art. *European Journal of Developmental Psychology 15*(6): 728–55. https://psycnet.apa.org/record/2018-54164-003

Winne, P. H. 1991. Motivation and teaching. In H. Waxman and H. Walberg (eds), *Effective teaching: current research.* Berkeley: McCutchan, 295–314. https://files.eric.ed.gov/fulltext/ED414355.pdf

Xu, F. and Kushnir, T. 2013. Infants are rational constructivist learners. *Current Directions in Psychological Science 22*: 28–32. https://doi.org/10.1177/0963721412469396

7 From Oedipus to attachment

The Freudian legacy

Introduction

Sigmund Freud (1856–1939) was born in Freiberg, Moravia (now in the Czech Republic), to Jewish parents and moved to Vienna with his family at the age of 4. He pursued a medical degree at the University of Vienna, focusing on neurology. Commencing psychology students often expect to hear a great deal about his theory, but find his work given only a minor place in psychology curricula which emphasize the scientific method and evidence-based psychology practice. Despite his interest in such methods (Gay, 1988), Freud's ideas were developed without scientific support, during the early 20th century. Despite—and possibly because of— this, Freud's concepts had great influence upon social science and the practice of psychiatry at the time: Freud may have tapped into ongoing desires to study subjective experience, which was then being rejected by psychologists as unscientific (Fisher and Greenberg, 1996).

By the end of that century, Freudian ideas had 'penetrated into the matrix of modern psychology and [were] continu[ing] to exert formidable influence' (Fisher and Greenberg, 1996: 6–7). Other appraisals variously declared him 'dead' (e.g. Kihlstrom, 2009) or, by contrast, 'the greatest psychologist since Aristotle' (Lothane, 2006: 285). However, English clinical psychologist and writer of Vienna-based mystery novels Frank Tallis (2023) has called for a more balanced approach to Freud's scientific standing.

With the benefits of hindsight, Freud's psychosexual theory of child development has to be seriously questioned. Nevertheless, empirical support has been found for some aspects, and his thinking was inspirational to others who have greatly influenced understanding of children's development, especially in infancy. Although in no way Freud's disciples, they reflected upon certain of his key insights and developed them in their own ways.

Freud's child development theory

Freud saw the child as entering the world already equipped with basic instincts to survive and reproduce, constituting the aspect of the psyche which he called the id. The ego was the part of the psyche in touch with reality, mediating between

DOI: 10.4324/9781003567738-7

the id and the superego, or conscience. In continuity with Darwinian theory, he applied notions of phylogenetic evolution to intrapsychic development (ontogeny) (Emde, 1992). He proposed that the functions of current actions could be understood through past history, placing great emphasis on early experience as laying the foundations for a series of developmental stages—something later taken much further by Jean Piaget.

The stages Freud delineated were psychosexual: the oral, anal, phallic, latency and genital. Each is defined by the zone of the body which is the focus of pleasure for the child (the exception being the latency stage, when sexual instincts lie dormant). His emphasis upon the sexual nature of children was considered outrageous at the time. Although one of Freud's most enduring legacies is his recognition of the significance of early experiences for later development, it is important to remember that Freud also emphasized the importance of hereditary and constitutional factors. However, the word 'genetic' as used by Freud means ontogenetic or epigenetic rather than gene-controlled (Hilgard, 1962).

Although various aspects of Freudian theory have implications for child development, the Oedipal theory is 'the skeleton of the psychoanalytic model' (Fisher and Greenberg, 1996: 118). In fact, these authors conceived of Oedipal theory as a collection of mini-theories about a range of developmental issues, such as family dynamics, identification with parents, moral development and sexual development. Freud doubtless saw his theory as a 'grand theory', and the tendency to consider it as a collection of mini-theories perhaps reflects later trends in theorizing.

From the vantage point of today's scientific psychology, it seems remarkable that a man who proposed a theory of child development built his theory on the basis of the recollections of his (mainly female) middle-class patients diagnosed with psychological disorders such as 'hysteria'. Their descriptions of childhood sexual experiences Freud originally took at face value, attributing their adult psychological symptoms to repressed sexual trauma. However, he renounced this 'seduction theory' in 1897, coming to see these women as expressing childhood sexual fantasies. Although working mainly with females, Freud took males as the developmental prototype (a reflection of his historical times), although we now know that, biologically speaking, the reverse is the case (Emde, 1992).

In describing the phallic stage, Freud drew upon the Greek myth of King Oedipus, who killed his father and married his mother. Freud theorized that the young boy, around the age of 4 or 5, harbours sexual impulses towards his mother, placing him in direct competition with his father for her affections; he fears that his father will castrate him as a punishment. To overcome this Oedipal conflict, the boy identifies with his father, in the course of which he internalizes his father's moral values and develops his own superego. Freud postulated that for girls, a parallel but necessarily somewhat different process occurs (Electra complex), with the girl believing she has already been castrated by her mother and moving towards her father as a love object; he has the potential to give her a baby in compensation for the presumed loss of her penis (the 'penis-baby equation'). Freud was less clear about how the female's conflict is resolved but maintained that it is more gradual and results in a weaker superego for girls. Freud saw normal adult psychological development as dependent upon the resolution of these early psychosexual conflicts, and theorized that adult neuroses and sexual dysfunctions result from a failure to do so.

Regarding the supposed fantasies of Freud's patients, John Bowlby later placed the emphasis back on reality, in early childhood experiences (Andrews and Brewin, 2000), and writers increasingly suggested that Freud's earlier interpretations of his patients' recollections as actual abuse were correct (e.g. Masson, 1984). Despite debate about the accuracy of childhood memories recovered in adult therapy, and the difficulty of establishing prevalence, international data suggest that around 18 per cent of girls and 8 per cent of boys experience sexual abuse (World Health Organization, 2023), reports emanating from around the globe. For example, the five-year Australian Royal Commission into Institutional Responses to Child Sexual Abuse Report (Commonwealth of Australia, 2017) found that religious institutions were subject to most allegations and responded inadequately, to say the least, leading to devastating lifelong impacts and suicides.

Seymour Fisher and Roger Greenberg (1996) undertook two very detailed reviews of the scientific literature to examine the empirical support for various aspects of Freudian theory. They found a considerable body of evidence supporting the 'Oedipal triangle' (child favouring opposite-sex over same-sex parent), but no evidence that a boy identifies with his father and adopts his values through fearing him. On the contrary, boys identify most strongly with warm and nurturing fathers. Evidence linking later sexual functioning with Oedipal notions is also lacking. Neither is there any evidence that boys develop stronger superegos than girls; Freud considered this to result from the depth of castration anxiety, with girls developing a weaker sense of justice and greater tendency to be swayed by their emotions (Fleming, 2006). In this respect, Freudian ideas of morality development, like those of Piaget and Lawrence Kohlberg, are androcentric. Moral development is influenced by a range of factors other than the father–child relationship (Fisher and Greenberg, 1996; Garrigan, Adlam and Langdon, 2018).

Overall, Fisher and Greenberg concluded that the empirical evidence for Freud's attempt to produce a grand theory of children's sexual and moral development was not strong. In a similar vein, Emde (1992) pointed out that both gender identity and moral development can be observed well before the time when Freud saw the Oedipus complex as becoming resolved; also, rather than having an attachment to one parent disrupted later by the other, children usually develop early ties of affection with both parents. Robert Emde also made the more general theoretical point that Freud, in keeping with understandings of physics at the time, saw mental processes in terms of entropy (tending towards lower levels of organization, as in drive reduction), which contrasts with contemporary notions that development tends towards *greater* complexity.

Despite its shortcomings, Freud's theory is echoed in later developmental (mini-) theories, particularly attachment theory (Emde, 1992) and reflected in the work of major developmental theorists such as René Spitz, John Bowlby and Mary Ainsworth, and in the development of the psychoanalytic approach to child therapy (e.g. Melanie Klein, Donald Winnicott and the object relations school). Also, Piaget learned from Freud's open-ended approach to inquiry and, in particular, his attention to what an individual's errors can reveal about their cognitions, as Freud discussed in *The Psychopathology of Everyday Life* (Freud, 1914/1940). We will now consider some important 20th-century child development theorists upon whom Freudian ideas had a particular influence.

Erik Erikson (1902–1994) and lifespan development

German-born US psychologist Erik Erikson developed Freud's theory into further stages in adulthood. This promoted the notion of lifespan development, which has been especially influential in US theorizing. Like Freud, Erikson saw development as resulting from conflicts; at each stage, their resolution could be more or less adaptive. Erikson's theory was psychosocial, viewing the ego not just as a mediator within the individual's psyche, but as an active promoter of development under cultural influence. Erikson's influential works included *Childhood and Society* (1950) and *Identity, Youth and Crisis* (1968); his work crops up in later chapters. Erikson's book on identity was celebrated 50 years after its publication; scholars drew inspiration with respect to a wide variety of topics such as epigenetics, identity processes in the digital age, and the implication of unconscious processes for identity development (Schachter and Galliher, 2018).

Object relations

Melanie Klein (1882–1960) was an influential figure from the 1920s to the mid-20th century in the object relations school of psychoanalysis. She trained therapists at the British Psychoanalytic Institute, emphasizing the potential of early loss for later psychopathology. A Kleinian 'object' is a loved thing or, especially, person. Unlike Freud, she saw fear of death as primary, not learned, and the underlying cause of anxiety. However, she provided few observations of how infants actually behave in separation situations (Bowlby, 1975). She saw anxiety as apparent right from the initial traumatic experience of birth, and internal conflict as the source of childhood emotional problems.

Others, such as Donald Winnicott, later developed Klein's approach, giving more emphasis to external factors. Winnicott (1953) discussed young children's attachment to inanimate objects. For instance, a young relative of author RHS carried around a toy rabbit for several years until all that was left was a small piece of blue cloth. Linus' blanket in the *Peanuts* cartoons is another example. Winnicott termed such objects 'transitional objects', maintaining that they demonstrated the beginnings of symbolic thought. In representing a love object, such as the mother or her breast, they characterize the infant's journey from subjectivity to objectivity.

Object relations theory forms a bridge between Freudian theory, with its intrapsychic emphasis, and family therapy, which emphasizes interrelationships between family members (Gladding, 1998). The influence of early object relations and the unconscious influence they may have on current relationships is recognized; these may lead to repeated dysfunctional patterns of interaction. Therapy aims to break these through assisting family members to gain insight. Training in object relations therapy remains available today (e.g. through the New York based Object Relations Institute, 2024). Scholarly interest continues, too, with the relationship between the theorizing of Klein and Winnicott addressed in a 2018 book (Abram and Hinshelwood, 2018).

Maternal deprivation

Important among the theorists whom Freud influenced was René Spitz (1887–1974), who emigrated from Europe to the United States in 1939, where he worked as a psychiatrist. Spitz is known through his work on 'maternal deprivation' of babies in orphanages in the 1950s. Spitz had met Freud in 1911 and regarded him as a mentor (Emde, 1992). However, unlike Freud, his theorizing arose from direct observations of infants, and his (for the time) innovative use of film strengthened the impact of his work (Spitz, 1952). Spitz also stressed a Darwinian influence, was a friend of ethologist Konrad Lorenz, and told Emde that he wanted his final words to be remembered as 'survival, adaptation, and evolution' (Emde, 1992: 354). Therefore we could perhaps equally well have placed Spitz's contribution in Chapter 3—a reminder of the multiple influences that impinge on any theorist's work—although it is certainly for his work on infant socialization that Spitz remains recognized.

In Spitz's day, unmarried motherhood was deeply shameful, and babies were often removed (sometimes forcibly) for adoption or institutional care. Spitz overturned notions that these institutionalized infants were sickly because their mothers were constitutionally morally inferior beings, and maintained instead that they failed to thrive because of a lack of mothering. His work on infant social smiling and on fear (more often now called wariness) of strangers around 8 months of age remains well-known. He also laid the foundations for a later thriving area of inquiry in proposing that reciprocity exists between infants and their caregivers—that a two-way flow of interaction occurs long before the child develops speech. Compared with Freud, Spitz's research methods were exemplary, but he was criticized even in his own time for poor reporting of experimental detail and lack of evidence for the reliability and validity of his measures. Nevertheless, his theory that maternal deprivation causes depression and apathy in infants was upheld by later work such as Bowlby's, although further refinements remained to be made, such as the recognition that infants are typically attached not only to their mother (Emde, 1992).

William Goldfarb, a New York psychologist, was another researcher influential in this area (cited in Bowlby, 1953). He compared the development of two groups of adolescents who had been surrendered by their mothers in infancy. Those who had spent their first three years in institutions were delayed in development in comparison with those who had been taken straight to foster homes. For example, their speech and social skills were poorly developed. These findings demonstrated that early deprivation could have long-lasting effects and suggested that there was a critical period for the development of such skills.

Decades later, this was subjected to more detailed examination in Bucharest through the only randomized controlled trial of ongoing institutional care versus high-quality foster care, for children under 3 years (Nelson, Fox and Zeanah, 2023). This study followed revelations that, in the 1980s, children in Romanian orphanages had suffered shockingly deprived conditions under the Ceauşescu regime's population policies (including bans on contraception and abortion). The children studied were followed up throughout their childhood and teenage years. Those randomly assigned to foster care were advantaged in terms of behaviour, IQ and brain development, and were less likely to be diagnosed with a psychiatric condition. Those fostered before the age of 2 had greater advantages, with timing (critical periods) varying for different aspects of development.

Although Spitz and Goldfarb are the names remembered for seminal work on maternal deprivation, the observations and practice of two South Australian women predated them by 70 years (see Box 7.1).

BOX 7.1 CATHERINE HELEN SPENCE (1825–1910) AND CAROLINE EMILY CLARK—ATTACHMENT PIONEERS

Spitz, Goldfarb and Bowlby are credited with establishing notions of infant institutionalization and maternal deprivation as developmentally damaging. Yet, in the 19th century, this issue was well-recognized in South Australia, as recorded by a Scottish-Australian pioneer of women's rights and children's welfare, Catherine Helen Spence. She wrote a book honouring Miss C. E. Clark, who had worked since the 1860s to establish a system of care for destitute children in family homes rather than institutions (Spence, 1907). At a time when unmarried mothers were vilified, legislation was enacted in 1881 to try and keep infants with their mothers: a woman entering the Destitute Asylum to have her baby would be contracted to stay with the baby for six months, 'giving it the natural nourishment', and Spence noted that 'affection grows strong during these six months' (Spence, 1907: 59). Where an infant could not be kept with its mother, it was boarded out to a foster mother: 'It is wonderful the love that grows up in the house where there is only one child placed' (1907: 62). Efforts were also made to maintain the child's relationship with its natural mother: 'the foster mother shows to the real mother all its pretty ways, encourages it to crow and laugh … and sometimes is the means of reconciling the mother to her relatives' (1907: 63). These images of happily attached 19th-century infants present a very different picture from those of the sickly infants observed in orphanages elsewhere in the world well into the 20th century.

Attachment theory

The beginnings

We have drawn upon Inge Bretherton's (1992) account in writing this section. John Bowlby (1907–1991), one of the originators of attachment theory, studied medicine and psychiatry, and also trained at the London Child Guidance Clinic and the British Psychoanalytic Institute. He disagreed with Klein's approach to child psychopathology, which emphasized internal conflict rather than external influences as the source of children's emotional problems. Later object relations theorists, such as Winnicott, were more in accord with Bowlby's views of the importance of early family relationships, although Bowlby preferred the term 'affectional bonds' to 'object relations' (Bowlby, 1975: 15).

Bowlby's interest in the importance of early attachment and loss developed originally from a couple of specific cases of children with emotional problems who had experienced early maternal loss (one used to follow him around the clinic, becoming known as his shadow). Later, he analysed over 40 case studies, concluding that the children's problems (including thieving) resulted from maternal deprivation. During the 1940s he began to put this research onto a more scientific footing when he developed some expertise in statistical analyses which enabled him to add some numerical support to his case study approach. After the Second World War he became director of London's Tavistock Clinic's Children's Department. Significantly, he renamed it the Department for Children and Parents and wrote one of the first papers on family therapy, about a method of his own devising (Bowlby, 1949).

Bowlby was commissioned by the World Health Organization to write a report on children displaced by the war, which appeared in 1951, and a later version appeared as the well-known book *Child Care and the Growth of Love* in 1953. It is interesting that in Bowlby's report for the World Health Organization, a Freudian influence is obvious in the language used, but certainly not in the concepts expounded (Bretherton, 1992). His basic tenet was that healthy mental development of the young child is dependent upon an ongoing warm, intimate relationship with the mother (or permanent mother substitute). The mother acts as the child's ego and superego, the child gradually taking over such functions as they become capable—a very different scenario from the internal and interpersonal conflicts which characterize the Oedipal processes described by Freud (see Box 7.2).

Bowlby's thinking was influenced by biological considerations and ethology, fruitful exchanges occurring between himself and ethologist Robert Hinde. He saw the organism's behaviour as controlled by a hierarchy of action plans which, in more complex organisms, are determined by a combination of innate factors and those which are flexible in the light of environmental circumstances. This reflected a movement towards cybernetic, rather than drive-reduction, models of behavioural control (Bretherton, 1992). He likened the psychological development of the infant to that of an embryo: just as early interference in embryonic development will have widespread ill effects, so the failure to establish an attachment relationship to a single individual in the first year of life will be very difficult to make good, as 'the character of the psychic tissue has become fixed' (Bowlby, 1953: 59). The notions of imprinting and critical periods in mother–infant relationships began to supplant the Freudian idea that the child is attached to the mother because she gratifies the child's oral needs. These ideas were later supported through animal research, such as Harry Harlow's well-known (but ethically notorious) research with infant rhesus monkeys, who preferred to cling to a terry-cloth 'mother' than to a wire one which provided milk (Harlow and Harlow, 1966); however, as pointed out by Julie Robinson (1999), it is possible that the terry-cloth mother assisted temperature regulation and was therefore still meeting the infant's physical, rather than attachment, needs. Bowlby and Harlow were introduced to each other by Hinde, and their work became mutually influential (Bowlby, 1969; van der Horst, Leroy and van der Veer, 2008).[1]

BOX 7.2 DID BOWLBY'S IDEAS ANTICIPATE VYGOTSKIAN THEORY?

The Soviet psychologist Lev Vygotsky and later workers such as Jerome Bruner maintained that children develop through interaction with more capable individuals, who gradually withdraw support for activities as the child becomes independently capable of them. Vygotsky's work had not been translated into English at the time Bowlby wrote the following passage. While the language is Freudian, the notion is distinctly Vygotskian (Bretherton, 1992).

> It is not surprising that during infancy and early childhood these functions are either not operating at all or are doing so most imperfectly. During this phase of life, the child is therefore dependent on his mother performing them for him. She orients him in space and time, provides his environment, permits the satisfaction of some impulses, restricts others. She is his ego and his super-ego. Gradually he learns these arts himself, and as he does, the skilled parent transfers the roles to him. This is a slow, subtle and continuous process, beginning when he first learns to walk and feed himself, and not ending completely until maturity is reached. … Ego and super-ego development are thus inextricably bound up with the child's primary human relationships.
>
> *(Bowlby, 1951, cited in Bretherton, 1992: 761)*

Like Winnicott, Bowlby discussed infants' attachment to inanimate objects, but took issue with Winnicott's explanation in terms of a symbolic shift from subjective to objective existence. His more parsimonious explanation was simply that certain components of attachment behaviour become directed towards such objects because the 'natural' object, such as the breast, is unavailable. He suggested the term ‘substitute object’ rather than ‘transitional object’. Bowlby’s interpretation was supported by later research showing that in Mayan society in Guatemala, where infants sleep with their mothers and feed at will during the night, such objects are almost unknown (Morelli *et al.*, 1992).

Bowlby later expanded upon the notions of separation from, and loss of, attachment figures (Bowlby, 1975), drawing on the work of Ainsworth, discussed below. An important theoretical advance in this connection was the introduction of the notion of ‘working models’ of the self and attachment figures. In other words, the child develops internal representations of the self and others, which guide their expectations about how others are likely to respond should they seek support from them. Bowlby suggested that this theory, taken together with Piagetian theory, provides a framework for understanding the psychoanalytic phenomenon of transference: the analyst is assimilated to the patient’s pre-existing model, which has not yet accommodated to incorporate how the therapist has in fact behaved towards the patient.

In contrast to Freud, Bowlby’s theorizing was supported by thorough empirical observations of mothers and children. However, his ideas were very critically received by influential members of the psychoanalytic movement at the time. Nevertheless, Bowlby’s work has supplanted that of psychoanalysis in its influence on modern child development theory, and his ideas about attachment have deeply influenced broader theorizing about grief and loss (Archer, 1999). Bowlby was concerned about the public policy implications of attachment and loss for children’s welfare and addressed issues such as adoption and the importance of mothers maintaining contact with their hospitalized children.

Another important figure in the development of attachment theory was James Robertson. He learned child observation skills working as a boilerman at a residential London nursery for children displaced by the Second World War, run by Freud’s daughter Anna. The skills Robertson developed were later used to good effect when he worked for Bowlby collecting data about the hospitalization of young children. Observing the plight of these children separated from their mothers, Robertson (1952, and later with his wife Joyce) made harrowing films which had the desired impact of bringing to public attention the hitherto unrecognized distress caused to young children through being separated from their parents, for example, through hospitalization or absence of their mother to give birth to another child.

Another person who joined Bowlby’s unit a little later was Mary Ainsworth (1913–1999), whose name has become almost synonymous with attachment theory. As Mary Salter, she had completed a dissertation on secure dependence of the young child on parents, and moved from Canada to London in 1950, where she became familiar with Bowlby’s work. She first studied mother–infant attachment in Uganda in the early 1950s, but did not publish the data for several more years, after moving to the United States and also renewing her intellectual collaboration with Bowlby.

Ainsworth made a very important contribution to attachment theory in two respects. She introduced the notion that the mother, or other attachment figure, provides a secure base from which the young child can explore the world. Second, she introduced the notion of parental sensitivity to child signals, paving the way for a later body of research on parent–infant communication. Ainsworth (e.g. Ainsworth and Wittig, 1969) is famed for developing an experimental protocol for examining infants' attachment to their mother, known as 'The Strange Situation'. The child is examined around the age of a year, first observed playing with their caregiver, usually the mother. The child's behaviour is then observed in several different situations: when a stranger enters the room; when the mother leaves; when the mother returns and the stranger leaves; when the mother leaves; when the stranger returns; and when the mother returns. On the basis of studies using this procedure, Ainsworth proposed that infants vary in the degree of security of their attachment relationship. 'Securely attached' infants explore the room freely in their mother's presence, protest at her absence and reunite joyfully with her; this is regarded as the optimal type of attachment relationship, resulting from sensitive parenting. 'Insecure-avoidant' infants are less distressed at separation and avoid the mother on her return, while 'insecure-resistant' babies are distressed throughout the procedure and respond to the mother's return with a mixture of relief and anger.

Ideas were shared between those interested in infant development and attachment. Bowlby was influential in convening regular meetings, which included those interested in comparative psychology, such as Harlow and Hinde. The proceedings appeared in *Determinants of Infant Behaviour*—a series of volumes edited throughout the 1960s by Brian Foss, whose own research interests lay in imitation and ethology.[2]

Work by psychiatrist Michael Rutter was later very influential in examining more closely the mechanisms involved in 'maternal deprivation'. In his 1972 book, he concluded that there were two separate aspects to the reported ill effects of separation: disruption of bonding with an attachment figure (not necessarily the mother) and privation of social, perceptual and linguistic stimulation. The former might occur in short-term situations, such as hospitalization, while the latter was a crucial factor in the case of the institutionalized infants studied by Spitz and Goldfarb. A particularly important aspect of Rutter's work was to point out that not all children are similarly affected by separations. Variables modifying the long-term response include the child's age, length of separation, whether there are other attachment figures available, whether the separation results from family discord, and the child's temperament. It was therefore becoming apparent that the developmental implications of attachment were much more complicated than previously supposed.

Later developments

Attachment theory became controversial as the 20th century progressed, with increasing numbers of western women maintaining both careers and motherhood (Domenico and Jones, 2006). The issue was raised as to whether separation from their mothers would damage young children's development. Bowlby had always maintained that the attachment figure could be a mother substitute, and his position was supported by later research indicating that infants could be satisfactorily attached to a wider circle of caregivers, including fathers, grandparents and others (e.g. Schaffer and Emerson, 1964).

Sandra Scarr and Judy Dunn (1987), like Rutter, concluded that the psychological disturbance of institutionalized children was due to a lack of human contact and stimulation, not the lack of a mother per se. Despite early reports by horrified outside observers of children raised communally in Israeli kibbutzim, systematic research indicated that they were no more disturbed than children raised by their parents in the United States. Nevertheless, Ora Aviezer *et al.* (1994) concluded, on the basis of assessments of attachment with the Strange Situation, that communal sleeping arrangements were problematic and 'unnatural'.

With regard to alternative (or, rather, supplementary) child care, Scarr and Dunn concluded that what matters is its quality. Good quality care means that the parents and other carers should collaborate to provide a 'consistent and agreeable world for the child' (1987: 187). Consistency involves having routines and not too many changes of carer. Children cared for consistently by others outside the family who are sensitive to their needs develop attachment relationships with them. Research indicating harmful effects of day care on infants mainly came from the United States, where the quality of such centres was not well-regulated and highly variable in comparison with some countries, such as Australia (Robinson, 1999), while attention was drawn to methodological criticisms of studies claiming negative effects and a tendency to make much of minimal negative findings (Ochiltree, 1994). We can add here that kibbutz-reared children experienced benefits, in terms of group skills and close peer relationships. As western working mothers became commonplace, the focus on quality care continued. For example, Jay Belsky and Michael Pluess (2011) found that adolescents with a history of experiencing low quality child care had more behaviour problems if they had also been difficult-temperament infants. Interestingly, they did not find evidence to support a 'sensitivity to context' explanation, as these difficult-temperament children did not have especially *good* adolescent outcomes if they had experienced the *highest* quality child care. In Australia in 2025 care quality became a matter of deep concern: providers (the majority being private businesses) often used a casualized workforce, and one case of sexual abuse led to hundreds of children needing STD checks, with parents becoming understandably anxious about male care workers (Mills-Bayne, 2025).

Robinson (1999) applied the notion of attachment to the 'stolen generations' of Australian Indigenous children removed from their families (see Chapter 11). She asked why many had such deep psychological disturbance if a child is capable of multiple attachments. For one thing, they experienced a range of stressors, such as racist attacks and various forms of abuse, as well as separation. Also, it is highly unusual for a child to simultaneously lose *all* attachment figures, as was usual in these cases. Even when siblings were removed together, it was often a deliberate policy to separate them. As Anna Freud found in studying war orphans, the peer group can provide attachment figures, and Indigenous people raised in institutions have commented that other children were their lifeline. However, Robinson observed that many children may have received minimal support from peers because they too were psychologically injured. These children also generally experienced multiple placements; if we assume, as Bowlby did, that attachment 'blueprints' can be updated through experience, then we might predict that multiple placements would lead children to develop internal working models of relationships as temporary. It would hardly be surprising, then, if such children grew up with difficulties in maintaining interpersonal relationships.

Despite various challenges, attachment theory has remained an important guiding concept in developmental psychology. The Strange Situation has continued to be used (with the addition of an extra type of attachment style—disorganized), although alternative, more naturalistic methods have also been developed. With the growing influence of lifespan approaches, attachment theory has also been adapted and applied to adults, under the assumption that early attachment schemas form a blueprint for other relationships. The Adult Attachment Interview was developed as a means of assessing attachment style in older children and adults (Main, Kaplan and Cassidy, 1985), opening up the issue of whether there is continuity in attachment. One longitudinal study, despite its rather misleading title, suggests not: while adopted children who experienced sensitive maternal support in both infancy and early adolescence were secure over the years, those who had experienced low maternal sensitivity in infancy but high sensitivity in adolescence shifted from low to high secure status (Beijersbergen *et al.*, 2012). This demonstration of plasticity presents an optimistic scenario in the face of less-than-ideal early parenting.

Freud theorized that attachment developed *as a result of* the satisfaction of instinctual drives such as hunger, a view later supported by some biologically orientated writers (the 'cupboard love' theory of attachment—Archer, 1999). Freud's granddaughter Sophie observed that, by contrast (and in line with the object relations school), some later psychoanalysts saw seeking attachment itself as the primary 'wired-in' motivational force of human beings (Freud, 1998). This is consistent with the ethological tradition, the 'social brain' theory, and the ideas of evolutionary psychologists that attachment theory can be seen as a major theoretical approach within the broader metatheoretical framework of evolutionary theory.

Bowlby saw grief as having evolved in relation to attachment. Attachment theorists later came to use the term attachment to apply not only to the child's attachment to the caregiving figure, but also the caregiver's connection to the child—so the term became used more broadly to apply to any affectional bonds (Archer, 1999). Viewed like this, attachment theory assists in understanding grief reactions to all kinds of losses. John Archer discussed the puzzling fact that, from an evolutionary perspective, grief appears maladaptive, resulting, for example, in immunosuppression and increased risk of ill health. However, temporary losses and separations from loved ones are much more common than permanent ones, and perhaps humans have evolved behaviours which serve the purpose of attempting to become reunited with the missing person—searching, calling, preoccupation, etc.—typical grief reactions. Thus grief becomes a by-product of the adaptive process of seeking to maintain important social relationships, and is the cost to be paid for the benefits of close relationships.

Criticisms from cultural and feminist perspectives

Attachment theory, like many other developmental theories, is open to the criticism that it has been developed within western societies and ignores alternative cultural perspectives (see Chapter 11), although Ainsworth's early work was in Uganda. Japanese infants are much more likely than US children to show resistance to the mother on her return; however, it has been questioned whether the Strange Situation is valid in Japan, as Japanese infants typically spend 24 hours a day with their mothers, so that the situation is especially strange for them (Miyake, Chen and Campos, 1985). Furthermore, attachment theory is based on western notions of individuation, with the child being gradually 'weaned' from dependence towards independence (Ritchie and Ritchie, 1979) (being expected to sleep alone at an early age is one manifestation of this). In most societies worldwide, the situation is different. In Polynesia, for example, a child is never required to identify with a single caretaking individual, but has multiple caregivers, including peers, and is expected to match their behaviour to various social environments, always having the choice to move from one to another. Indeed, in Indigenous families worldwide, the extended family plays an important role in child rearing and socialization (Muir and Bohr, 2019).

The Ritchies observed that '[m]illions of human beings have grown up without [attachment]' and query what western child development experts would make of 'a New Guinea tribe where any lactating female will happily feed a hungry child or even a pig' (1979: 155). Even in the west, children thrive under a variety of caretaking arrangements, as pointed out in a feminist critique of attachment theory (Birns, 1999). Indeed, being attached to several caregivers makes good evolutionary sense in case one attachment figure is unavailable for any reason (temporarily or permanently).

The idea that attachment theory is universally applicable has been criticized as wrong-headed and harmful to those from non-western cultures (Keller, 2018). Like developmental psychology in general, it originated from within WEIRD (western, educated, industrialized, rich and democratic) populations, which only represent about 5 per cent of the world's population (Henrich, Heine and Norenzayan, 2010). Heidi Keller points out, for example, that attachment is based on dyadic parent–child relationships where face-to-face communication is central, whereas in many cultures the infant's primary relationships are with other children, and relating to a wider social network is the norm; for instance, babies may be typically held facing the group, not the mother, but be in physically close contact with her and fully involved in her social activities. Furthermore, the emotional expressiveness central to attachment theory is not relevant to cultures where emotional displays (including emotional facial expressions) are not encouraged, and stranger wariness is not an observed behaviour nor reflected in cortisol (stress hormone) levels in, for example, sub-Saharan African groups. Keller presents a case study of the harm that can occur when western ideals of attachment are applied to those from other cultures (see Box 7.3).

BOX 7.3 THE MISAPPLICATION OF ATTACHMENT THEORY

The Bhattacharyas migrated from India to Norway and had two children. This is Heidi Keller's description of what followed.

> The nursery school became aware of tantrums by the 2-year-old son and eventually reported the family to the Norwegian Child Welfare Service (CWS), who visited the family's home for observations and video recordings. After several home visits over several months, the CWS decided to separate the two children from the parents because the parenting style of the mother did not conform with their ideas of appropriate parenting. Specifically, the mother raised a threatening palm to her son with a firm instruction to stop what he was doing, a common Indian parenting practice which was taken as a threat of physical abuse. Another point was that the 4-mo-old daughter did not look into her mother's eyes, which the investigator found peculiar. However, the CWS never talked to the mother about her parenting or voiced their impressions and concerns. With no prior announcement, the [children] were placed in state custody. ... After a long battle with the CWS over many years and the intervention of the Indian Government, Mrs. Bhattacharya, by then legally separated from her husband, received the custody of her children. ... The concept of sensitive, child-centered parenting that is regarded as a crucial condition for children's healthy development obviously was guiding the Norwegian Child Welfare Service.
>
> *(Keller, 2018: 11414)*

Rather than transporting western ideas to other cultures, it may be more meaningful to begin with understandings from other cultures themselves. In collectivist Japan, for example, the notion of *amae* (expectation of benevolence from others) might provide a more culturally appropriate framework than attachment for understanding social development (Rothbaum *et al.*, 2001). Nevertheless, findings from attachment research have been used to explain the abandonment of communal sleeping arrangements for children in Israeli kibbutzim (Sagi and Aviezer, 2001). Also see Box 7.4 for a positive transportation and adaptation of grief and loss theory by an Australian Aboriginal counsellor (Wanganeen, 2014).

BOX 7.4 ROSEMARY WANGANEEN'S 'GRIEFOLOGY'

This box was written jointly by author RHS and Rosemary Kudnarto Wanganeen, a proud South Australian Aboriginal woman. She has adapted western loss and grief theorizing for the purpose of explaining the individual, collective and intergenerational suppressed and unresolved grief that has compounded and complicated contemporary losses and unresolved grief. Rosemary has devised the term 'Griefology' for the grief and losses suffered by Aboriginal people as a result of Australia's invasion/colonization. Her intuitive research (1987–1992) has drawn upon her traumatic personal experiences suffered as a result of inhumane policies and practices, like the Stolen Generations of Aboriginal children. She combined this with experience gained from her work as an Aboriginal research officer with the Royal Commission into Aboriginal Deaths in Custody and her study with mainstream counselling services to develop her own holistic sociocultural theory: Seven Phases to Integrating Griefology©. The framework has been designed to capture culturally appropriate counselling, which can be modified for non-Aboriginal people as both groups seek reflective and creative ways to process their grief. Similarly, the framework is for educating non-Aboriginal service providers to deliver culturally appropriate services for Aboriginal people (https://lossandgrief.com.au/meet-rosemary/).

Critique of attachment theory has also emanated from feminism. Erica Burman (2008) criticized the whole 'project' of developmental psychology as focusing on mothers as providers of all that is best for their children, thereby acting to regulate women's lives. However, she valued psychoanalytic theory more broadly as a counterpoint to positivist developmental psychology. Also from a feminist perspective, Beverly Birns (1999: 19) critiqued attachment theory as follows: 'To believe that being a loving, sensitive mother to an infant can protect a child for life against the adversity of poverty, abuse, poor schools, uncaring neighborhoods and violent television, is both a theoretical and a practical mistake.' No one today who understands the notion of developmental cascades and cumulative adverse childhood events (see Chapter 1) would, in fact, make the claim that Birns suggested.

Finally, while attachment theory has been usefully applied to clinical practice, especially with young children, the evidence base is relatively small, especially concerning cross-cultural studies (Mesman, 2021, cited in Thompson, Simpson and Berlin, 2022), and there has been a warning that 'popularized misconceptions' have led to the theory being inappropriately used, at times, in therapy (Zilberstein, 2014: 97). Specifically, research does not support Bowlby's suggestion that conduct disorders such as aggression, lying and stealing result from attachment difficulties, and mislabelling a child's problems as an attachment disorder may have harmful results.

Nevertheless, Ross Thompson and colleagues (2022) conclude that attachment theorists and critics alike do agree on some basic points: the importance of early relationships for children's survival and development; that children form attachment relationships and other relationships important for development; and that all cultures must address the challenges of bringing children to adult functioning and reproductive maturity. This really takes us no further than our biological discussions in Chapter 3. Those authors conclude that much remains uncertain, despite the longevity of this theory's impact, and that the field of attachment may best be advanced by studying the commonalities and differences across cultures, by taking a lifespan perspective, and with a clearer focus on the concept of internal working models.

Conclusions

Writings about Freudian theory continue to appear. Often, they are from historical, philosophical, psychiatric or social perspectives, rather than directly related to current developmental psychology, although there is some interest in neurological correlates of Freudian theory. Some psychoanalytic practice continues, including with children, and has its own journals. Much has been written about what was wrong with Freudian theory. Philosopher B. A. Farrell (1951) described it as 'unbelievably bad' as a theory. John Kihlstrom (2009), despite acknowledging Freud's cultural influence on the 20th century as probably greater than that of Einstein, Lenin, Roosevelt, Picasso or the Beatles, saw Freudian theory as a 'dead weight' on that century's psychology.

By contrast, Tallis (2023) suggests that an era of 'Freud bashing' is ending, including fresh recognition of his Darwinian influence: Freud's 'life-preservation instincts' reflect natural selection, and his 'sexual instincts' match sexual selection, while 'repression' can be seen as adaptive in enabling cognitive and behavioural functioning to continue. Echoing British pioneer of sexuality studies, and Freud's contemporary, Havelock Ellis, Tallis suggests that even if Freudian theory is as imperfect as a broken necklace, we should continue to pick up some of the dropped pearls. Freud's work continues to influence developmental theorizing via some of the paths charted above. Some influential 'guiding ideas' include the notion of the continuity of development from infancy onwards (through stages), the idea that earlier influences on later behaviour occur at an unconscious level, and the suggestion that behaviour often results from attempts to resolve internal conflicts (Hilgard, 1962). Although the notion of 'the unconscious' is no longer considered tenable, there is a great deal of evidence for 'unconscious processes' (Scheepers and Derks, 2016; Westen, 1999). That these concepts remain broadly taken for granted in psychology is a measure of the depth of Freud's influence. His impact on the later development of attachment theory also remains as a major contribution to developmental psychology, and the notion of 'working models' of the self and others remains influential. Furthermore, attachment theory has been suggested as a potential integrating force underlying diverse schools of psychotherapy (Gold, 2011). Freudian theory also helped maintain some focus on emotional development in the face of radical behaviourism (Kihlstrom, 2009).

Finally, it is of interest that, like Burman (2008), Freud's granddaughter Sophie made a connection between Freudian theory and postmodernism (Freud, 1998). Similarly to Freud, the overriding concern of constructivist theorists and narrative therapists is with the idiosyncratic meaning that individuals make of their experiences. Steven Reisner (1999) too observed that Freud anticipated postmodernism, in his habit of proposing basic premises, elaborating on them, and then deconstructing them. So, while we noted earlier that Freud's theory was in many ways a reflection of its times, in this respect it can be said to have anticipated some later developments in psychological theorizing. Scholarly interest in Freud's work continues, with the launch of his revised complete psychological works, edited by Mark Solms, a neuropsychologist who studies links between brain science and psychoanalytic theory. The 24-volume work includes newly translated material and was celebrated with a conference in London in 2024.

Notes

1 Harlow, world-renowned for his monkey research, was a highly controversial figure, even being described as sadistic. In 1974, he said, 'I really don't like animals ... How could you like a monkey?' (Gluck, 1997). Present author RHS was told by someone familiar with his laboratory that his results were not as strong as he claimed, and he exaggerated them as he was confident that they were 'correct'. This anecdote is perhaps consistent with his further comment that, 'The only thing I care about is whether the monkeys will turn out a property that I can publish' (Gluck, 1997).

2 Present author RHS received undergraduate ethology lectures from Foss; on social occasions he would accompany himself on the piano and sing his own ditties on ethological themes, such as 'I'm a little fish' celebrating Tinbergen's famous stickleback research.

References

Abram, J. and Hinshelwood, R. D. 2018. *The clinical paradigms of Melanie Klein and Donald Winnicott: comparisons and dialogues*. London and New York: Routledge.

Ainsworth, M. D. S. and Wittig, B. A. 1969. Attachment and exploratory behaviour of one-year-olds in a strange situation. In B. M. Foss (ed.), *Determinants of infant behaviour*. Vol. 4. London: Methuen, 113–36.

Andrews, B. and Brewin, C. R. 2000. What did Freud get right? *The Psychologist 13*(12): 605–7. www.bps.org.uk/psychologist/what-did-freud-get-right

Archer, J. 1999. *The nature of grief: the evolution and psychology of reactions to loss*. London: Routledge.

Aviezer, O., van Ijzendoorn, M. H., Sagi, A. and Schuengel, C. 1994. 'Children of the Dream' revisited: 70 years of collective early child care in Israeli Kibbutzim. *Psychological Bulletin 116*: 99–116. www.marinusvanijzendoorn.nl/wp-content/uploads/2012/07/Aviezer-Van-IJzendoorn-Sagi-et-al-1994.-Psychological-Bulletin.-Collective-early-childcare-kibbutzim.pdf

Beijersbergen, M. D., Juffer, F., Bakermans-Kranenberg, M. J. and van IJzendoorn, M. H. 2012. Remaining or becoming secure: parental sensitive support predicts attachment continuity from infancy to adolescence in a longitudinal adoption study. *Developmental Psychology 48*(5): 1277–82. https://doi.org/10.1037/a0027442

Belsky, J. and Pluess, M. 2011. Differential susceptibility to long-term effects of quality of child care on externalizing behavior in adolescence. *International Journal of Behavioral Development 36*: 2–10. https://doi.org/10.1177/0165025411406855

Birns, B. 1999. Attachment theory revisited: challenging conceptual and methodological sacred cows. *Feminism and Psychology 9*: 10–21. https://doi.org/10.1177/095935359900 9001002

Bowlby, J. 1949. The study and reduction of group tensions within the family. *Human Relations 2*: 123. https://doi.org/10.1177/001872674900200203

Bowlby, J. 1953. *Child care and the growth of love*. Harmondsworth: Penguin.

Bowlby, J. 1969. *Attachment*. Harmondsworth: Penguin.

Bowlby, J. 1975. *Separation*. Harmondsworth: Penguin.

Bretherton, I. 1992. The origins of attachment theory: John Bowlby and Mary Ainsworth. *Developmental Psychology 28*(5): 759–75. https://psycnet.apa.org/doi/10.1037/0012-1649.28.5.759

Burman, E. 2008. *Deconstructing developmental psychology*. London: Routledge.

Commonwealth of Australia. 2017. Australian Royal Commission into Institutional Responses to Child Sexual Abuse Report. www.childabuseroyalcommission.gov.au/

Domenico, D. M. and Jones, K. H. 2006. Career aspirations of women in the 20th century. *Journal of Career and Technical Education 22*(2): 1–7. https://files.eric.ed.gov/fulltext/EJ901302.pdf

Emde, R. N. 1992. Individual meaning and increasing complexity: contributions of Sigmund Freud and Rene Spitz to developmental psychology. *Developmental Psychology 28*(3): 347–59. https://psycnet.apa.org/doi/10.1037/0012-1649.28.3.347

Erikson, E. H. 1950. *Childhood and society*. New York: Norton.

Erikson, E. H. 1968. *Identity, youth and crisis*. New York: Norton.

Farrell, B. A. 1951. The scientific testing of psychoanalytic findings and theory. *British Journal of Medical Psychology 24*: 35–41. https://doi.org/10.1111/j.2044-8341.1951.tb00393.x

Fisher, S. and Greenberg, R. P. 1996. *Freud scientifically reappraised: testing the theories and therapy*. New York: Wiley.

Fleming, J. S. 2006. *Piaget, Kohlberg, Gilligan, and others on moral development*. http://extendeddayresources.pbworks.com/w/file/fetch/107259768/Fleming%202005.pdf

Freud, S. 1914/1940. *The psychopathology of everyday life*. Harmondsworth: Penguin.

Freud, S(ophie). 1998. The baby and the bathwater: Freud as a postmodernist. *Families in Society: The Journal of Contemporary Human Services 79*(5): 455–64. https://doi.org/10.1606/1044-3894.726

Garrigan, B., Adlam, A. L. R. and Langdon, P. E. 2018. Moral decision-making and moral development: toward an integrative framework. *Developmental Review 49*: 80–100. https://doi.org/10.1016/j.dr.2018.06.001

Gay, P. 1988. *Freud: a life for our time*. New York: W. W. Norton & Company.

Gladding, S. T. 1998. *Family therapy: history, theory and practice*. Second edn. Upper Saddle River: Prentice-Hall.

Gluck, J. P. 1997. Harry F. Harlow and animal research: reflection on the ethical paradox. *Ethics & Behavior 7*(2): 149–61. https://doi.org/10.1207/s15327019eb0702_6

Gold, J. 2011. Attachment theory and psychotherapy integration: an introduction and review of the literature. *Journal of Psychotherapy Integration 21*(3): 221–31. https://psycnet.apa.org/doi/10.1037/a0025490

Harlow, H. F. and Harlow, M. K. 1966. Learning to love. *American Scientist 54*: 244–72.

Henrich, J., Heine, S. J. and Norenzayan A. 2010. The weirdest people in the world? *Behavioral & Brain Science 33*: 61–83. https://psycnet.apa.org/doi/10.1017/S0140525X0999152X

Hilgard, E. R. 1962. The scientific status of psychoanalysis. In E. Nagel, P. Suppes and A. Tarski (eds), *Logic, methodology and philosophy of science: proceedings of the 1960 International Congress.* Stanford University Press, 375–90. Reproduced in S. G. M. Lee and M. Herbert (1970), *Freud and psychology*. Harmondsworth: Penguin, 29–49.

Keller, H. 2018. Universality claim of attachment theory: children's socioemotional development across cultures. *Proceedings of the National Academy of Science USA. 6;115*(45): 11414–19. https://doi.org/10.1073/pnas.1720325115

Kihlstrom, J. F. 2009. Is Freud still alive? No, not really. https://www.ocf.berkeley.edu/~jfkihlstrom/freuddead.htm

Lothane, Z. 2006. Freud's legacy – is it still with us? *Psychoanalytic Psychology 23*(2): 285–301. https://doi.org/10.1037/0736-9735.23.2.285

Main, M., Kaplan, N. and Cassidy, J. 1985. Security in infancy, childhood, and adulthood: a move to the level of representation. *Monographs of the Society for Research in Child Development* 50(1–2): 66–104.

Masson, J. M. 1984. *The assault on truth: Freud's suppression of the seduction theory*. New York: Farrar, Straus & Giroux.

Mills-Bayne, M. 2025. Parents are feeling anxious about men in child care centres. Stronger rules would make everyone feel safer. *The Conversation*, 2 July. https://theconversation.com/parents-are-feeling-anxious-about-men-in-childcare-centres-stronger-rules-would-make-everyone-feel-safer-260282

Miyake, K., Chen, S. J. and Campos, J. J. 1985. Infant temperament, mother's mode of interaction, and attachment in Japan: An interim report. *Monographs of the Society for Research in Infant Development 50*(1–2): 276–97.

Morelli, G., Rogoff, B., Oppenheim, D. and Goldsmith, D. 1992. Cultural variation in infants' sleeping arrangements: questions of independence. *Developmental Psychology 28*: 604–13. https://psycnet.apa.org/doi/10.1037/0012-1649.28.4.604

Muir, N. and Bohr, Y. 2019. Contemporary practice of traditional Aboriginal child rearing: a review. *First Peoples Child & Family Review 14*: 153–65. https://fpcfr.com/index.php/FPCFR/article/view/378/310

Nelson, C. A., Fox, N. A. and Zeanah, C. H. 2023. Romania's abandoned children: the effects of early profound psychosocial deprivation on the course of human development. *Current Directions in Psychological Science 32*(6): 515–21. https://doi.org/10.1177/09637214231201079

Object Relations Institute. 2024. https://orinyc.org/

Ochiltree, G. 1994. *Effects of child care on young children: forty years of research.* Melbourne: Australian Institute of Family Studies.

Reisner, S. 1999. Freud and psychoanalysis: into the 21st century. *Journal of the American Psychoanalytic Association 47*(4): 1037–60. https://doi.org/10.1177/000306519904700403

Ritchie, J. and Ritchie, J. 1979. *Growing up in Polynesia.* Sydney: Allen & Unwin.

Robertson, J. 1952. A two-year-old goes to hospital [Film]. London: Tavistock Child Development Research Unit. www.robertsonfilms.info/

Robinson, J. A. 1999. Update on attachment theory and research. Paper presented to Child and Adolescent Mental Health Service, Norwich House: Adelaide, April 1999.

Rothbaum, F., Weisz, J., Pott, M., Miyake, K. and Morelli, G. 2001. Deeper into attachment and culture. *American Psychologist 56*(10): 827–8. https://psycnet.apa.org/doi/10.1037/0003-066X.56.10.827

Rutter, M. 1972. *Maternal deprivation reassessed.* Harmondsworth: Penguin.

Sagi, A. and Aviezer, O. 2001. The rise and fall of children's communal sleeping in Israeli Kibbutzim: an experiment in nature and implications for parenting. *Newsletter of the International Society for the Study of Behavioral Development 1*(38): 4–6.

Scarr, S. and Dunn, J. 1987. *Mother care/other care*. Harmondsworth: Penguin.

Schachter, E. P. and Galliher, R. V. 2018. Fifty years since 'Identity: youth and crisis': a renewed look at Erikson's writings on identity. *Identity 18*(4): 247–50. https://doi.org/10.1080/15283488.2018.1529267

Schaffer, H. R. and Emerson, P. E. 1964. The development of social attachments in infancy. *Monographs of the Society for Research in Infant Development* 29(3): 1–77.

Scheepers, D. and Derks, B. 2016. Revisiting social identity from a neuroscience perspective. *Current Opinion in Psychology 11*: 74–8. https://doi.org/10.1016/j.copsyc.2016.06.006

Solms, M. (ed.). 2024. *The revised standard edition of the complete psychological works of Sigmund Freud.* np: Rowman & Littlefield.

Spence, C. H. 1907. *State children in Australia: a history of boarding out and its developments*. Adelaide: Printed by Varolen and Sons Ltd.

Spitz, R. 1952. *Emotional deprivation in infancy study*. www.youtube.com/watch?v=z1eOpqV1fco

Tallis, F. 2023. We should still pick up the pearls: on the scientific status of Freud. *Brain 147*: 1115–17. https://doi.org/10.1093/brain/awad414

Thompson, R. A., Simpson, J. A. and Berlin, L. J. 2022. Taking perspective on attachment theory and research: nine fundamental questions. *Attachment & Human Development 24*(5): 543–60. https://doi.org/10.1080/14616734.2022.2030132

van der Horst, F. C. P., Leroy, H. A. and van der Veer, R. 2008. When strangers meet: John Bowlby and Harry Harlow on attachment behavior. *Integrative Psychology and Behavioral Science 42*: 370–88. https://doi.org/10.1007/s12124-008-9079-2

Wanganeen, R. 2014. Seven phases to integrating loss and grief. In P. Dudgeon, H. Milroy and R. Walker (eds), *Working together: Aboriginal and Torres Strait Islander mental health and wellbeing principles and practice.* Second edn. Canberra: Commonwealth of Australia, 475–92. https://indigenouspsyched.org.au/resource/seven-phases-to-integrating-loss-and-grief/

Westen, D. 1999. The scientific status of unconscious processes: is Freud really dead? *Journal of the American Psychoanalytic Association 47*: 1061–106. https://doi.org/10.1177/00030651999047000404

Winnicott, D. W. 1953. Transitional objects and transitional phenomena: a study of the first not-me possession. In L. Caldwell and H. Taylor Robinson (eds), *The Collected Works of D.W. Winnicott*. Vol. 4, 1952–1955. New York, 2016. Online edn, Oxford Academic, 1 December 2016. https://doi.org/10.1093/med:psych/9780190271367.003.0034

World Health Organization. 2023. *Lifetime prevalence of child sexual abuse*. www.who.int/data/gho/data/indicators/indicator-details/GHO/lifetime-prevalence-of-child-sexual-abuse-(-)

Zilberstein, K. 2014. The use and limitations of attachment theory in child psychotherapy. *Psychotherapy 51*: 93–103. https://doi.org/10.1037/a0030930

8 Dialecticism

The child developing in a social world

Introduction

We outline here the dialectical approach to development (especially Vygotsky's) and how it has influenced recent theorizing in development, education and disability. We also consider the political times that, together with his early death, made the story of Vygotsky's theorizing a very fraught and convoluted one that could easily have ended with his work lost forever. Vygotsky was a Soviet psychologist who developed his ideas over just ten years between the two World Wars before dying from tuberculosis, leaving many unpublished manuscripts. He therefore had little time to elaborate his theoretical framework, in contrast to the long-lived Piaget, who spent decades revising his theory. He ranks with Piaget as one of the two most influential developmental psychologists of the 20th century (Lourenço, 2012).

Dialectics has a very strong foundation in philosophical thinking across the Western and Eastern world (Mascolo *et al.*, 2024). In the 4th century BCE Plato used the term to describe the Socratic method of posing questions to an interlocutor in order to examine one's assumptions and basic concepts, thereby arriving at better versions. This generates knowledge by means of resolving contradictions, which involves ongoing activity and conflict, rather than passivity and stability (Riegel and Meacham, 1978). The German philosopher Georg Hegel (1770–1831) characterized the dialectic (shown in Figure 8.1) as a circular process, with the whole greater than the sum of the parts.

Michael Basseches (2005: 5) described dialectics as a 'family' of worldviews sharing three features: 'common emphases on change, on wholeness, and on internal relations'. Thomas Bidell (1988), in observing that complexity is an essential aspect of developmental processes, believed that many scientific challenges cannot be solved using a reductionist Cartesian paradigm, useful as that has been in science. In his view, dialectics is the opposite of reductionist philosophy and practice, and is needed to understand the rich complexity and fluidity of the interactions amongst the various elements as development proceeds.

DOI: 10.4324/9781003567738-8

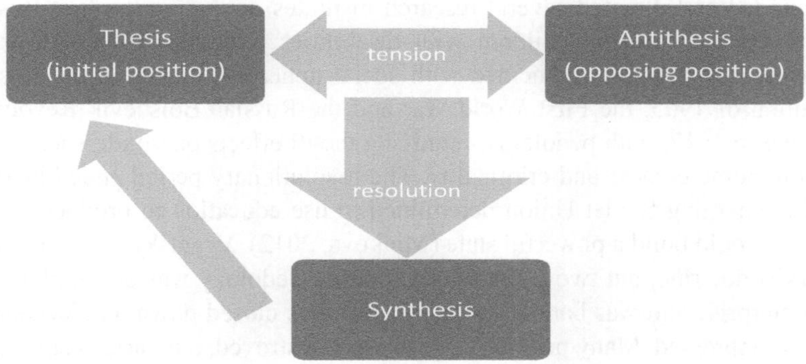

Figure 8.1 Hegel's dialectical process

Piaget (1896–1980) and dialectical theory

Although Piaget's theory falls into the organismic tradition, it has dialectical aspects. The child, through interaction with the world around and (to a lesser extent) the people in it, comes to experience and re-experience their understanding of how the world works. If new information fits an existing schema it is assimilated. For example, a child might observe that their Jack Russell terrier barks, and while a German Shepherd looks different it also barks and so fits the child's schema for 'dog'; a Basenji does not bark, but if the child comes to realize that it is also a dog, then the schema of 'dog' has enlarged (accommodated) to fit this new understanding. Assimilation and accommodation lead to cognitive growth and a state of equilibrium. A less well-developed aspect of Piaget's theory related to the role of peers; the child may be challenged by different perspectives and so must accommodate to manage different outlooks.

Juan Pascual-Leone and Janice Johnson (2017) proposed that in the late 1960s Piaget's thinking more strongly embraced dialectical thinking. That is, in better attempting to explain how a child moved from one stage to another Piaget proposed a constructivist outlook incorporating more strongly the interplay of the child with the world as they strive to resolve contradictions. Basseches (2005) suggested that dialectical thinking should not be considered as a process of achieving equilibrium, which represents a closed system of knowledge; dialectical thinking allows one to break through this isolation towards new knowledge.

Vygotsky (1896–1934) and dialectical theory

In the early 20th century, the science of 'pedology', or child development, thrived in Russia, and Alexander Nechaev opened the first laboratory of educational psychology in St. Petersburg in 1901 (Minkova, 2012). The intellectual context was therefore ripe to support the brilliance of Vygotsky, who has been called 'the

Mozart of psychology' (Roth and Jornet, 2017). He was not only a deep thinker but also founded and directed several research institutes, including the first Russian institute for the study of children with disabilities (Kozulin, 1988). However, the thriving of pedology coincided with social upheaval, including the Russian Revolution of 1905, the First World War and the Russian/Bolshevik Revolution beginning in 1917, with pedologists studying the ill effects on youth, such as disaffection, homelessness and criminality. The revolutionary period ended in 1923, with the emerging Soviet Union determined to use education to produce a 'new man' who could build a powerful state (Minkova, 2012). Vygotsky was committed to Marxist doctrine, but two years after his death, pedology was declared a bourgeois enterprise and was banned, with the institutes closed down and Vygotsky's writings suppressed. Many pedology works were destroyed, but various colleagues and students of Vygotsky protected his works, while some scholars toed the party line and became his critics. It was not until Nikita Krushchev, the First Secretary of the Communist Party, denounced Stalinism in 1956 that it became possible for his work to re-emerge. It had great influence on psychological theory and practice in his own country, especially in terms of the education of children with disabilities. The work of the 'Institute of Defectology' in using his principles to foster the development of deaf/blind children—even enabling some to enter university—was beautifully illustrated in the documentary film *The Butterflies of Zagorsk* (British Broadcasting Corporation, 1990).

In his lifetime he had intellectual exchanges with Piaget, but Vygotsky's main influence on western developmental psychology is much more recent, following from the translation of his last work into English. *Thought and Language* was published in English in 1962, with a foreword by Jerome Bruner. By the end of that decade, this text was set for present author RHS's undergraduate classes at London University but it took another decade for an edited and translated body of his work to appear as *Mind in Society*, in 1978, when the broader psychological community began to take notice. He now has a major place in undergraduate developmental textbooks, where his theory is typically compared and contrasted with that of Piaget. Possible reasons for his increased influence in the west included re-publications of his work in Russian and further translations into English, an increased exchange of ideas between US and former Soviet Union academics, and the relevance of his ideas for education (Wertsch and Tulviste, 1992). Also, his theoretical framework seemed to have come at the 'right time' in western scholars' thinking.

However, the work of James Wertsch and Michael Cole in the United States that did so much to bring international attention to Vygotsky's theorizing has been heavily criticized as mistranslating and altering his work. While being a laudable attempt to make his writings more understandable, it was impossible for readers of *Mind in Society* to know what was the original Vygotsky; it also distorted the crucial fact that his focus was on *teaching* (pedagogy) rather than *learning* (Barrs, 2022). Wolff-Michael Roth and Alfredo Jornet (2017) maintain that the rather neat presentations of Vygotskian theory in many textbooks ('the Vygotskian narrative') do not do justice to the complexity and development of Vygotsky's thinking in its epistemological and historical context. For example, Vygotsky critiqued his own early work and his later theorizing drew upon the philosophy of Baruch Spinoza (1632–1677), addressed the mind–body dichotomy and was moving towards a deeper consideration of the nature of consciousness (also see Yasnitsky, 2012, 2018).

Central to Vygotsky's theory is the notion that human cognition has its beginnings in social life. This idea seems to have come from previous thinkers such as Karl Marx and Pierre Janet, who was in turn influenced by the sociologist Émile Durkheim, and also George Herbert Mead (Wertsch and Tulviste, 1992). Vygotsky emphasized that the child develops cognitively through interactions with others, hence his theory is dialectical. He was critical of mainstream western views where the focus was on individual development, with collective functioning generally ignored.

Vygotsky's theory of child development has been summarized as involving four main principles:

- Children construct knowledge using cultural tools that become 'tools of the mind.'
- Development must always be studied in its sociocultural context.
- Learning can be organized in such a way that it promotes development.
- The development of language is central to the intellectual development of the child.

(Cole, in foreword to Bodrova and Leong, 2024: ix)

While this portrays Vygotsky's work as a theory of cognitive development (which it is, in part), Vygotsky was very much concerned with the whole child, eschewing dichotomies such as intellect *versus* affect, and doing *versus* thinking. In his preface to the English-language translation of *Thought and Language* in 1962, Bruner observed that Vygotsky's theory represented an enormous step up from understanding development in terms of classical Pavlovian conditioning. Vygotsky built upon Ivan Pavlov's notion of the 'second signal system' which 'provides the means whereby man creates a mediator between himself and the world of physical stimulation so that he can react in terms of his own symbolic conception of reality' (Bruner, in Vygotsky, 1934/1962: x). This has become of recent interest as Vygotsky's notion of *perezhivanie* (Cong-Lem, 2022): this is the idea that the environment does not have a deterministic influence on a child's development, but operates in a non-linear fashion through the prism of the child's own perspective, or 'how a child becomes aware of, interprets, [and] emotionally relates to a certain event' (Vygotsky, 1978, cited in Cong-Lem, 2022). The notion of *perezhivanie* is now being taken up by Russian scholars: Veraksa *et al.* (2022) found a relationship between young children's dialectical thinking and their understanding of emotions, while Gavrilova and Kornienko (2025) have applied it to a case study on the promotion of emotional development of two young siblings through the visual arts.

Vygotsky's theory was instrumental, cultural and genetic (Holaday, Lamontagne and Marciel, 1994). It was instrumental inasmuch as it claimed that '[p]eople actively modify the stimuli they encounter and use them as instruments to control conditions and regulate their own behavior' (Holaday *et al.*, 1994: 16). As such, a feature of Vygotsky's theory (like Piaget's) was that individuals are active agents in creating their own learning and development. The cultural aspect was expressed through the centrality he granted to language as a cultural tool in the development of thinking. The genetic aspect (in the developmental sense) was that, through interactions with others, higher order mental functions develop from lower order ones.

According to Vygotsky, child development is made up of periods of relatively stable growth, crises and transformation, which implies that development passes through qualitatively distinct stages. The development of an individual can come to a standstill or even regress. Based on Vygotsky's work, René van der Veer (1986: 528) described five stages in child development: infancy; early childhood; the preschool period; school age; and adolescence. Each is a so-called stable period preceded and concluded by a period of crisis. At around 12 months, the toddler faces a new period of crisis or transformation which is associated with the three new developments of walking, speech and emotional reactions. For Vygotsky, the child's language development is paramount, and he made a distinction between thought and speech development in the first two years of life. However, at about 2 years the two curves—of development of thought and speech—come together to initiate a new form of behaviour. In Vygotsky's view this is a momentous time in the toddler's cognitive development, when speech begins to serve intellect and thoughts begin to be spoken. The onset of this stage is indicated by two unmistakable objective symptoms: a sudden active curiosity about words and questions about every new thing; and the resulting rapid increase in the child's vocabulary.

Vygotsky also articulated a number of stages in children's conceptual development, derived from experimental work on the sorting of blocks varying in colour and shape (Vygotsky, 1934/1962). Pseudo-concepts predominate in the thinking of the preschool child. Superficially, the child appears to be using true concepts, but deeper probing reveals 'flawed' reasoning. The development of pseudo-concepts is very much directed by adult language, which enables an adult and a preschool child to communicate, but the underlying understandings may be quite different. True, abstract thought appears in adolescence, but earlier, more concrete, forms of thinking continue to operate. This latter point—that adolescents (and even adults) do not always, or even usually, operate at the highest level of abstraction, was also demonstrated through studies designed to test Piagetian ideas about intellectual development. Piaget's stage theory has very much overshadowed the stage aspects of Vygotskian theory, which is acknowledged most for its emphasis on the social, language-driven nature of cognitive development, and has been identified by some (e.g. Berk, 2013) as a continuity theory. Others have characterized it as incremental with intermittent crises, which is consistent with both Piagetian theory (assimilation and accommodation) and the notion of first- and second-order change in systems perspectives (see Chapter 10). Here, Aline Nardo's (2021) argument is helpful, in emphasizing that Vygotsky differentiated between 'learning' and 'development': the former is a process of cumulative change that occurs through everyday interaction with the world, while the latter is a qualitative 'leap', being a fundamental change in the individual-world unit, a transformation to a higher plane of thought that occurs through pedagogical interaction with another person, a teacher.

Egocentric speech

Particularly influential has been Vygotsky's discussion of 'egocentric speech'. Initially, the child's behaviour is controlled by verbal instructions from others, then later the child talks aloud, especially when difficulties arise—in effect, instructing the self. Finally, these instructions 'go underground' (to use Vygotsky's phrase) and become internalized as thought. Vygotsky gave an example to illustrate how the child's self-directed speech performs a controlling function. A child was drawing a streetcar when his pencil broke; he said, 'It's broken' and, using another pencil, proceeded to draw a *broken* streetcar after an accident (Vygotsky, 1934/1962). Thus, egocentric speech (which Piaget saw as a by-product of thought) becomes an integral part of the developmental process. His pupil Alexander Luria (who did much to preserve his legacy) and later researchers experimentally demonstrated the shift in children's development from speaking aloud while performing tasks, to muttering, to silence (e.g. Frauenglass and Diaz, 1985). The term private, or inner, speech later became preferred. A summary of Vygotsky's view of the relationship between thought, language and action is captured in Box 8.1.

BOX 8.1 VYGOTSKY AND THE RELATIONSHIP BETWEEN THOUGHT, WORD AND DEED

> The relation between thought and word is a living process; thought is born through words. A word devoid of thought is a dead thing, and a thought unembodied in words remains a shadow. The connection between them, however, is not a preformed and constant one. It emerges in the course of development, and itself evolves. To the Biblical 'In the beginning was the word,' Goethe makes Faust reply, 'In the beginning was the deed.' The intent here is to detract from the value of the word, but we can accept this version if we emphasize it differently: in the *beginning* was the deed. The word was not the beginning – action was there first; it is the end of development, crowning the deed.
>
> *(Vygotsky, 1934/1962: 153)*

Vygotsky was way ahead of his time here, as it is only recently that cognitive science has taken seriously the proposition that abstract concepts are built upon bodily interactions with the environment ('embodied cognition'). One study examined children's use of gestures to indicate spatial concepts (e.g. left, up) and the more complex metaphorical use of such spatial gestures to indicate time (e.g. now, tomorrow) (Iossifova and Marmolejo-Ramos, 2013). While sighted children made gestures such as pointing ahead that depended upon an appreciation of external landmarks, blind children were more likely to use their own body as a reference point (e.g. touching the head or chest), especially for temporal gestures, which were much more difficult for them to produce. The study showed that children's development of abstract concepts depends on the type of bodily interactions they have experienced with the world. With his deep interest in 'defectology', Vygotsky would not be surprised by these findings.

Although Vygotsky emphasized language, some activities (especially in certain cultures) are better learned by observation (Rogoff, 1990). Imagine, for example, trying to teach someone to knit through verbal instruction alone! But Vygotsky's theory did encompass all forms of cultural signs and symbols. Furthermore, he made special mention of the ability to imitate as being an important sign that the child is intellectually ready to understand the task at hand (Vygotsky, 1930/1978).

The zone of proximal development (ZPD)

The notion of 'developmental readiness' brings us to this other feature of Vygotsky's theory. He defined the zone of proximal development (ZPD) as 'the distance between actual developmental level as determined by independent problem solving and the level of potential development through problem solving under adult guidance or in collaboration with more capable peers' (Vygotsky, 1930/1978: 86). Thus, a standard mental test, such as an IQ test, measures independent problem solving (completed development), but does not capture the entirety of a child's ability, as two children with the same IQ might be able to reach different levels of performance under adult guidance. Furthermore, Vygotsky's perspective implies that a child's capacity to develop is not just a property of the child, but a shared property between the child and a particular guide (socially shared cognition). So, a child's ZPD might be more advanced with a guide who is more sensitive to the child's developmental needs.

Two important dimensions of the ZPD are 'joint collaboration' and 'transfer of responsibility'. 'Joint collaboration' is active, shared participation for the purpose of solving a problem. The adult, by virtue of greater understanding, actively facilitates or encourages the child in their own definition and redefinition of the problem to promote the achievement of a solution. 'Transfer of responsibility' refers to the adult's decreasing role in regulating and managing behaviour or task performance, with the child being given more opportunities to perform the task independently (Holaday *et al.*, 1994; Rogoff, 1986). While the notion of the ZPD has become influential in child development theory and education, it has also been criticized as circular: it cannot be defined a priori, but only in relation to the child's performance (it is not alone in this, with the behaviourist term 'stimulus' being criticized as only definable in relation to a response).

Despite its enormous influence, the ZPD was a relatively minor concept in Vygotsky's work. It has been elaborated, misunderstood and misrepresented. For example, the value of using peer collaboration as a learning method has been attributed to him, although he only mentioned it as a method (pairing with a higher-IQ child) to assess the ZPD (Gredler, 2012).

Vygotsky compared with Piaget

While there is a case for an element of dialecticism in Piaget's theory, it is fundamental to Vygotsky's. It is often said that the Vygotskian child is a 'little apprentice', in contrast to the solitary 'little scientist' of Piaget. From a Piagetian perspective, while procedures can be learned from others, this does not represent true understanding, which is demonstrated by unassisted performance (Wood, 1988/1998). However, as we observed previously, Piaget did maintain that social interactions between equals could be important for cognitive growth, especially regarding moral understanding. The European social psychologist Willem Doise (1990) took up the notion that social interaction can promote cognitive development under some circumstances, but based this on Piaget's theory, not Vygotsky's. He proposed (and demonstrated experimentally) that a child can develop cognitively if their schema comes into conflict with an alternative schema proposed by another person, provided circumstances permit the successful resolution of the cognitive conflict to produce a more advanced schema. For this to happen, the child must already have a certain level of competence; to translate this into Vygotskian terms, this would mean the task must be in the ZPD. Also, the nature of the social relationship must be one in which the cognitive conflict can be explored and resolved. Drawing upon Durkheim, Doise maintained that this can only happen in 'relations of cooperation' rather than 'relations of constraint'. In other words, if the other person uses their authority to impose their perspective on the child, cognitive growth will not occur. It is often peer relationships which permit the necessary cooperation, rather than the relationships with adults which Vygotsky saw as important for cognitive development. There is no real antagonism between the view of Piaget/Doise and the Vygotskian perspective if we take into account that an adult who uses authority to impose their view would also be an adult who, in Vygotsky's view, was not operating within the child's ZPD—and again, no cognitive progress would be expected.

A crucial difference between Piaget and Vygotsky remains, however. While Piaget acknowledged that the speech of another person could spark thoughts leading to cognitive growth, the real driver of that growth is the child's own activity. For Vygotsky, however, cognitive processes are directly derived from speech. The autonomy of the Piagetian child, versus the heteronomy of the Vygotskian one, has been characterized as the most important difference between the theories—something that should not be lost sight of amidst a growing tendency to emphasize their similarities (Lourenço, 2012). Orlando Lourenço has observed that the

Piagetian view reflects a social democratic ideal in contrast to Vygotsky's Marxist one, and he suggests that the two theories are complementary.

Scaffolding

The concept of sensitive guidance for development was taken up and elaborated by a number of workers, who applied the term 'scaffolding' to this (Bruner and Haste, 1987; Wood, 1988/1998; Wood, Bruner and Ross, 1976; Wood, Wood and Middleton, 1978). These researchers were inspired by Vygotsky's theory to examine the tutoring of young children by adults on tasks which the children were unable to perform alone. They discovered, for example, that mothers provided different levels of support for their children's performance on a block construction task, ranging from full demonstration of the task, through verbal instruction on how to do it, to simply encouraging the child to perform the task. Not all such tutoring was equally effective. For example, children often became frustrated with full demonstration (an example of adult imposition of a solution) or were given verbal instructions that were too difficult. It was found that children's learning was best promoted by providing assistance as soon as the child became stuck, and refraining from intrusive assistance when the child was making progress. David Wood called this 'contingent teaching': 'These mothers ensured that the child was not left alone when he was overwhelmed by the task, and also guaranteed him greater scope for initiative when he showed signs of success' (Wood, 1988/1998: 79). Scaffolding has been described as occurring when 'a more competent or able adult or peer adjusts the learning situation or task conditions … to produce appropriate understanding of a particular problem for a learner at a particular level of ability' (Rogoff and Gardner, 1984: 109).

Barbara Rogoff suggested that the term 'guided participation' is more inclusive than scaffolding. This term was used earlier by Albert Bandura and others to refer to assistance provided by a trusted and encouraging companion to help children and adolescents to overcome fears, such as fear of snakes (Bowlby, 1975: 226). As Rogoff used the term, it involves children with 'multiple companions and caregivers in organized, flexible webs of relationships that focus on shared cultural activities' (Rogoff, 1990: 98). This acknowledges that it is not just parents who participate in the process. In some societies, young children spend more time with older siblings and peers than with adults. Older siblings and peers can therefore play a particularly powerful role in younger children's development, an extreme view being that in all societies it is peers, rather than parents, who mainly influence children's development (Harris, 1995). This was not Vygotsky's own view, however.

In general terms, Rogoff suggested that the characteristics of guided participation are:

- The provision of a bridge between existing skills and knowledge and those needed to perform new ones.
- The provision of structure by the tutor.
- Active learning.
- Transfer of responsibility to the learner.

There need not be an intention by the tutor to teach. Learning can occur whenever children participate in helping more capable companions to perform everyday tasks (Rogoff, 1990).

These ideas have been applied educationally and, indeed, Bruner observed that Vygotsky's theory is as much a theory of education as of cognitive development. We noted above how Doise used Piagetian theory as a basis for understanding how peer collaboration on a task can lead to cognitive growth. By contrast, Vygotsky's theory provides a theoretical framework for understanding peer tutoring, in which a more expert child tutors another (Foot *et al.*, 1990). Children are certainly able to teach one another in this way, and there may be social, as well as cognitive, advantages to peer tutoring. However, children's ability to provide sensitive scaffolding, such as their ability to detect misunderstandings by their tutees, is limited by their own level of cognitive development (Foot, Shute and Morgan, 1997; Shute, Foot and Morgan, 1992).

Wood (1988/1998) cited evidence that experts, but not novices, when solving problems, report self-monitoring, self-correction and so forth—known as 'self-explanations'. When the self-explanation aspect is turned off in a computerized problem-solving simulation, the computer model loses flexibility and some powers of generalizability. Wood suggested that this supports the Vygotskian notion that self-talk (aloud or silent) plays a vital role in enabling individuals to solve taxing tasks. As Wood observed, '[l]anguage is not simply *what* we think about but part of the thinking process itself' (1988/1998: 108). The scaffolding concept was used to analyse some early preschool computer programs (Shute and Miksad, 1997), showing that verbal and cognitive skills, but not maths skills, improved over eight sessions as long as the programs had scaffolding deemed 'substantial' (as defined by Wood *et al.*, 1976).

Becoming conscious of one's thinking and becoming increasingly able to manage one's own thought ('thinking about thinking', or metacognition) has become an extensive area of inquiry in itself, with strong relevance for education (see, for example, Schneider and Artelt, 2010; also Shute, 2018, applying dialecticism and metacognition to school-based mindfulness programs). Emily Fox and Michelle Riconscente (2008), too, have discussed metacognition and self-regulation with respect to Vygotsky's theory.

The notion of scaffolding has been applied to the social as well as the cognitive sphere (e.g. Kaye, 1977). An interactive social relationship exists between parents and infants from a young age, but initially it tends to be the parent who 'does most of the work'. Later, responsibility is shared, while as infants grow older they increasingly initiate and manage social interactions. In the course of such interactions, 'shared meaning' develops between adults and infants (Schaffer, 1989).

Cognition and culture

An important feature of Vygotsky's theory, as the earlier quotation from Rogoff illustrates, is that it offers a link between individual cognitive development and the culture in which the child develops. Whereas the Soviet system was supposed to provide equal chances for everyone's development, Vygotsky and his student Luria found individual differences in cognitive performance between young adults and between those varying in ethnic group and geographical location, requiring explanation (Meacham, 1999). Although Vygotsky did not provide an extensive account of the notion of culture, in broad terms he saw it as being a product of human social activity over historical time.[1] Such activity produces cultural 'tools' consisting of sign systems such as language, writing, numerical systems and art. Through social interactions, these sign systems mediate between the culture and the developing individual, becoming incorporated into individual mental functioning. Vygotsky's theory, then, is not universalist. While this process is often understood in terms of the internalizing of social relations as psychological functions, Vygotsky (following Spinoza) in fact saw such functions as being *indivisible from* social relations, such that thought, or the mind, exists socially and this is the essence of humanity (Roth and Jornet, 2017). A connection can be seen here with recent '4 Es' philosophical views that the mind is:

- Embedded (culturally).
- Extended (e.g. connected with others' minds and technology).
- Embodied (developed through sensorimotor processes, not just brain-based).
- Enactive (created through action in the world) (Menary, 2010; see Box 8.1).

Vygotsky and Luria believed various cultures could be ranked in terms of how 'developed' they were, and western psychologists have often perceived their own culture as superior. This was illustrated by Joseph Glick's (1975) research with West Africa's farming Kpelle people, in which people were asked how to classify objects such as an orange, a potato, a hoe and a knife. They classified them functionally (potato and hoe, orange and knife—in the way Vygotsky described children as classifying objects early in development). The western, abstract response (classifying the tools together and the food items together)—which would gain more points on a typical IQ test—the Kpelle people said was how a fool would classify them. Later theorists developed ideas apparent in Vygotsky's own writings to argue that such differences in mental activity are better seen as characteristic of the specific setting in which they develop, and are qualitative differences rather than inherently 'better' or 'worse'. Along these lines, workers such as Wertsch and Tulviste (1992) proposed that individual mental functioning can best be seen as consisting of a 'cultural tool kit' of mental processes. The link which Vygotsky's theory creates between individual development and culture means that his theory became especially popular with cross-cultural psychologists (Rogoff and Morelli, 1989).

Although Vygotsky's theory is based on a *dialogue* between the individual and the social world, he placed most emphasis on how social processes shape individual development. More recent researchers have also emphasized the role of the developing individual in influencing the world. James Wertsch and Peeter Tulviste did not believe the notion of individual agency to conflict with Vygotsky's concepts, and united the two perspectives by proposing that the individual uses culturally derived tools to operate upon the world in new ways. Nevertheless, creativity is necessarily constrained by culture to be 'a new use for an old tool' (Wertsch and Tulviste, 1992: 555).

A more radical adaptation of Vygotsky's theory is the suggestion to change the ZPD to the ZCD (zone of collaborative development) in non-western education, where individuality is less relevant. This idea has been applied to moral education in Malaysia, where there is a challenge to implement this aspect of the national curriculum in multi-ethnic classrooms (Balakrishnan and Claiborne, 2012). Although children's personal reflections on moral dilemmas form part of the process, the emphasis is on reaching a shared moral language with those from other ethnic backgrounds, clans and religions.

Another challenged aspect of Vygotsky's work is his view that the cultural aspects of development initially operate separately from 'natural' development, with these two aspects only uniting around the age of 2. As Wertsch and Tulviste (1992) pointed out, much research has clearly demonstrated that, from the earliest days, infants develop under the influence of adult speech. Vygotsky, of course, did not have the benefit of such empirical findings in devising his theory.

How far Vygotsky saw development as being mechanistic rather than organismic is another aspect of his theory that has been given attention. Despite occasional phrases in Vygotsky's writings suggesting a mechanical influence of the social environment on the child's development, Wertsch and Tulviste are in no doubt that Vygotsky did not intend this. Rather, individual agency and social influence are intimately linked in the sense that individual actions are carried out by socially determined means.

Vygotky's 'defectology'

Vygotsky's revolutionary work on development in the context of disability has been relatively overlooked in recent years. He was 'stuck with' this unfortunate terminology that was well-established in Russia, and which suggested that a child with a disability is 'lacking' in relation to norms (in line with a typical biomedical perspective). He in fact had great insight in viewing such children as 'developing differently' (Bøttcher and Dammeyer, 2012). His view of development as progressing (or even regressing) in the course of an ongoing dialectical exchange between the child and the (socially mediated) environment captures how such differences can come about. Followers of his methods as depicted in *The Butterflies of Zagorsk* provided deaf/blind children with a social environment at a residential school. It provided them with alternative routes for cognitive development, such as through sign language, touch and use of any residual hearing or sight, always mindful of each child's ZPD. The individualized unfolding of development that he conceptualized is compatible with more recent understandings gained through a dynamic systems perspective (see Chapter 10) and epigenetics research. Box 8.1 is again useful in illustrating how children's physical abilities affect the way they come to perceive the world. Bøttcher and Dammeyer (2012) propose that

Vygotsky's theory offers a way to break down a dualistic understanding of a person with a disability and the rest of society.

Vygotsky, social constructivism and education

Constructivism has been a very influential perspective in western education since the 1980s, supplanting the more mechanistic behaviourist and information-processing approaches (Liu and Matthews, 2005). It is a postmodern perspective based on the idea that individuals do not perceive an objective world but create individual subjective constructions of it. While Piaget is seen as the originator of cognitive constructivism, Vygotsky is credited with being one of the founding influences on social constructivism (Pritchard and Woollard, 2010). It has been variously described as a theory, a 'church' of related theories, a paradigm, a metaphor for human learning, a powerful folk-tale and even as akin to a secular religion (Liu and Matthews, 2005). Educational practices based on social constructivism are seen as progressive and include child-focused learning and the use of one-on-one and small group learning. However, constructivism has been criticized as having poor empirical foundations, neglecting facts in favour of relativism and leading to a neglect of substantiated teaching methods such as those based on learning theory (Matthews, 2003).

Educational writings, though, often stray far from Vygotsky's original theory, and he is often misrepresented. There is a lack of appreciation of the philosophical underpinnings of his theory, leading to an individual-cultural dualism that is far removed from his view of these as functionally inseparable (Liu and Matthews, 2005). Furthermore, criticisms of social constructivism (e.g. Matthews, 2003) often reject it in terms of its most extreme relativist versions that do not reflect Vygotsky's writings.

Vygotsky a hundred years on

On the hundredth anniversary of the establishment of Vygotsky's psychology (2024), one is spoiled for choice in seeking to investigate the effect of Vygotsky's work on current scholarly thinking and praxis. Topics include: peer dialogue in the classroom; Marxism and Vygotskian theory; relevance for religious education; application to scholarly ethical/activist agendas; consciousness and education; metaphors in science education; materialism/idealism relationship in his theory; aesthetics and theatre studies; early childhood education; teacher professional development; and more. An approachable source for newcomers to Vygotsky's work in relation to early childhood education is the third edition of *Tools of the Mind* (Bodrova and Leong, 2024). A broader overview of his historical background and theorizing can be found in a paper written for non-specialists by Olga Vasileva and Natalia Balyasnikova (2019). Other recent contributors include Myra Barrs and John Richmond (2024) on Vygotsky the pedologist, and Peter Smagorinsky (2024) on 'defectology'. The truth of the statement that 'rumors of Vygotsky's scientific death are greatly exaggerated' (van der Veer, 2021: 795) seems indisputable.

S. L. Rubinstein (1889–1960) and constitutive relationalism

Sergei Rubinstein is a name still occasionally cited in philosophical works but is unlikely to be found in standard textbooks of developmental psychology. Yet he was another very prominent 20th-century Soviet philosopher and psychologist who played an important part in the development of dialectical theory. His cosmopolitan approach to life had him denounced as a non-patriot between 1948 and 1953. Particularly influential were books he wrote in 1940 and 1959 addressing some of the basic questions of psychology, especially the mind–body relationship (Meacham, 1999). He drew together Marxist-Leninist and Pavlovian ideas to create the notion that the mind develops through links between historical/cultural and biological aspects of development. As Jack Meacham (1999) explained, Rubinstein did not envisage this in terms of a mechanistic *interaction* between the separate entities of the brain and the sociohistorical world. Rather, the mind is a reflection of both nervous system activity and the material world and is always in a *transactional* state with them. Thus, the mind exists only in mutual relationship to these entities. This was his theory of 'constitutive relationalism'. In other words, it is the *relation* that is primary, and the entities in transaction cannot be understood—indeed, do not exist—in the absence of the relationship. Rubinstein focused particularly on morality and differentiated between 'acts' (towards objects) and 'deeds' (towards other humans). He argued that the self (or 'ethical subject') only exists in relation to one's deeds and presupposes the existence of another human being—one does not exist without the other, and each 'deed' recreates the self anew, so that the self is a task, or process, not a fixed entity (Lektorsky, 2013).

According to John Broughton and Klaus Riegel (1977), Rubinstein saw early development as driven by biological imperatives, with sociohistorical factors later becoming co-determinants. He noted that individuals transform their own environment, thereby creating new conditions for development (cf. 'niche-picking' in Chapter 3).

In recent years, relationalism has become regarded as a new metatheory, though prominent writings in the area do not acknowledge Rubinstein. Some echoes of Rubinstein's ideas (although not attributed to him or any other dialectical psychologist) are found in a discussion by Jane Herlihy and John Gandy (2002) about reductionism. They observed that the modern tendency is to consider neurobiological explanations of phenomena as the 'real' explanations, with an implicit belief that 'to rely on anything but the tangible, like brain matter, somehow implies unworldly and mystical thinking' (2002: 248). They suggested that explanations for any phenomenon can be given at different levels, such as biochemical, cognitive or behavioural. However, they proposed, it is wrong to imply that a neurological event *causes* a cognition or behaviour, and it is even misleading to speak of the relationship in terms of correlation. They posited that the biology and the psychology are only separable in the abstract and are actually two pieces of information about the same event. They conclude that psychologists should not, nor lead the public to, consider neurological explanations as superior to cognitive or behavioural ones; rather, we should think of human beings as 'moving from one psychophysical state to another, describable on different levels by different specialists. Causation flows between these states and not between the levels of description' (2002: 251). Their concerns reflect those of others, such as Bandura, about the 'biologizing' of behaviour.

Klaus Riegel (1925–1977): transactions in historical context

Riegel's contribution to dialectical developmental theorizing has been described by his associate Meacham (1999) and by Marinus van IJzendoorn, Luc Goossens and René van der Veer (1984). Riegel was born in Berlin but later worked as an academic psychologist in the United States. In the years leading up to his comparatively early death he developed an American form of 'double-dialecticism', disseminated through his university lectures, publications and conferences. Precursors of his theory included the work of Eduard Spranger (who proposed that individuals could only be understood in relation to their historical times), and it was Rubinstein, rather than Vygotsky, who influenced his thinking (*Thought and Language* but not *Mind in Society* appeared in English translation in Riegel's lifetime). Riegel's psychological theory lay in stark contrast to traditional psychology's concern with stability and the maintenance of equilibrium. Rather, his theory was specifically developmental. Drawing upon Rubinstein's theory, he proposed that aspects of the individual (biological, psychological, sociocultural and historical) are in transactional relationships—each being defined in relation to all the others (hence, doubly dialectical). A change in one aspect produces a crisis, the resolution of which results in development (which may be positive or negative). His theory was reflexive, in that he recognized that it should be applied to theorizing itself, which is therefore influenced by its historical times.

Developmental psychology he saw as not satisfactory in being ahistorical, with cross-sectional and longitudinal research designs not capturing such influences. He proposed mixed-longitudinal (time-lag) designs instead, that could capture the changing person in a changing environment. He also saw interdisciplinary work as necessary, especially making links with history specialists. Riegel's own times encompassed the Holocaust, the civil rights movement in the United States, and publication of Arthur Jensen's controversial work on genetics and intelligence; in fact, Riegel presented what was probably the first university course in Black psychology. Riegel's concern was therefore not with individuals' stability, but with their development in relation to sociocultural change. For Riegel, however, the environment for development was not just cultural, but determined by occurrences such as natural disasters, geography and the climate.

He decried the 'capitalist' developmental psychology that he saw as originating from Thomas Hobbes, John Locke, G. Stanley Hall and others, that he characterized as social-Darwinian (favoured by the English upper classes) that held up the young White adult male working in business or industry as the 'fittest', against which all others, including children, should be judged. By contrast, he identified a mercantile tradition in Europe, and philosophers such as Jean-Jacques Rousseau, as promoting the valuing of children for what they were.

Riegel (1973) commented on Piaget's theory, characterizing it as dialectical. However, he pointed out that Piaget applied the concepts of assimilation and accommodation most clearly to the development of early schemas, such as sucking and grasping. As the child develops, these processes fade out of Piaget's discussion, in favour of traditional logic in formal operations. Riegel argued that dialectical thinking is needed, for mature thought, which does not rely on formal logic, but concerns hypotheses about the real world. For example, the older child or adult understands that a particular event may be unfortunate from one person's perspective, but fortunate from that of another, so the event can be simultaneously both fortunate and unfortunate, just as an object may be both big and small, depending on the frames of reference applied. Judgements are therefore temporary, in flux, and subject to constant re-evaluation. Further, Riegel noted that although Piaget observed that some individuals 'fail' in formal operational thinking through a lack of relevant experience, he did not carry this through to an acknowledgement that thought develops in relation to the cultural-historical context.

We will expand on the sociocultural theme in Chapter 11. It is of interest that Riegel's work is now much less well known than Vygotsky's, perhaps because his emphasis on relativism is more explicit, and therefore presents a greater challenge to traditional (post-)positivist developmental psychology. Indeed, Broughton suggested that the critical perspective on developmental psychology offered by Riegel's dialecticism has been lost in its application to lifespan psychology. He maintained that this field has 'trivialized history … reducing it positivistically to a variable confounded with psychological change' (Broughton, 1987: 11).

Conclusions

We began this chapter with a consideration of the (debated) dialectical thinking of Piaget. In a much stronger sense, a dialectical approach to children's development was proposed by Vygotsky in the early 20th century but not taken up beyond the Soviet Union until decades later. The contributions of Rubinstein and Riegel also deserve mention, although it is Vygotsky's theory that has become the best known. However, the presentations and understandings of Vygotsky's theory have become distorted.

Three of Vygotsky's original contributions to our understanding of human development are his description of the crisis-like character of development, the importance he placed on the role of speech, and his emphasis on the social nature of the young child (van der Veer, 1986). He emphasized the heteronomous, rather than autonomous, nature of children's development. His work has inspired research on the crucial role of adults and (arguably) older peers in cognitive development, with a focus on process rather than structure. Vygotsky's dialectical theory, in providing a link between individual development and the social world, paved the way for a greater consideration of the role of culture and history in individual development. In this way, he provided inspiration for the development of the social constructivist movement. The breadth of his influence stretches even further when we realize that his protégé Luria established the field of neuropsychology (e.g. Luria, 1972).

It has also been suggested that the fields of cognitive science and artificial intelligence would benefit from a closer consideration of Vygotsky's theory (Lindblom and Ziemke, 2003).

Dialecticism represents a move in the direction of more holistic and systemic views of development. In this respect, Rubinstein's and Riegel's notion of constitutive relationalism is worthy of fresh consideration. We will meet these issues, and the work of some further neo-Vygotskians, in later chapters.

Note

1 Vygotsky's theory is sometimes wrongly conflated with cultural-historical activity theory (Cong-Lem, 2022).

References

Balakrishnan, V. and Claiborne, L. B. 2012. Vygotsky from ZPD to ZCD in moral education: reshaping Western theory and practices in local context. *Journal of Moral Education 41*(2): 225–43. https://doi.org/10.1080/03057240.2012.678056

Barrs, M. 2022. After Vygotsky. In M. Barrs, *Vygotsky the teacher*. London: Routledge, 203–26.

Barrs, M. and Richmond, J. 2024. Vygotsky the pedologist. In M. Barrs and J. Richmond, *The Vygotsky anthology*. London: Routledge, 89–107.

Basseches, M. 2005. The development of dialectical thinking as an approach to integration. *Integral Review 1*: 47–63. www.integral-review.org/documents/Development%20of%20Dialectical%20Thinking%201,%202005.pdf

Berk, L. 2013. *Child development*. Ninth edn. Boston: Pearson.

Bidell, T. 1988. Vygotsky, Piaget and the dialectic of development. *Human Development 31*(6): 329–45. https://psycnet.apa.org/doi/10.1159/000276332

Bodrova, E. and Leong, D. 2024. *Tools of the mind: the Vygotskian approach to early childhood education*. Third edn. London: Routledge.

Bøttcher, L. and Dammeyer, J. 2012. Disability as a dialectical concept: building on Vygotsky's defectology. *European Journal of Special Needs Education 27*(4): 433–6. https://doi.org/10.1080/08856257.2012.711958

Bowlby, J. 1975. *Separation*. Harmondsworth: Penguin.

British Broadcasting Corporation. 1990. *The butterflies of Zagorsk*. London: BBC Education and Training.

Broughton, J. M. 1987. An introduction to critical developmental psychology. In J. M. Broughton (ed.), *Critical theories of psychological development*. New York: Plenum, 1–30.

Broughton, J. M. and Riegel, K. F. 1977. Developmental psychology and the self. *Annals of the New York Academy of Sciences 291*: 149–67. https://doi.org/10.1111/j.1749-6632.1977.tb53067.x

Bruner, J. 1962. Introduction. In L. S. Vygotsky. 1934/1962. *Thought and language*. Cambridge, MA: MIT Press, v–x.

Bruner, J. and Haste, H. 1987. *Making sense: the child's construction of the world*. London: Methuen.

Cong-Lem, N. 2022. Vygotsky's, Leontiev's and Engeström's cultural-historical activity theories: overview, clarifications and implications. *Integrative Psychological and Behavioral Science 56*(4): 1091–112. https://doi.org/10.1007/s12124-022-09703-6

Doise, W. 1990. The development of individual competencies through social interaction. In H. C. Foot, M. J. Morgan and R. H. Shute (eds), *Children helping children*. Chichester: Wiley, 43–64.

Foot, H. C., Shute, R. H. and Morgan, M. J. 1997. Children's sensitivity to lack of understanding. *Educational Studies 23*(2): 185–94. https://psycnet.apa.org/doi/10.1080/0305569970230203

Foot, H. C., Shute, R. H., Morgan, M. J. and Barron, A-M. 1990. Theoretical issues in peer tutoring. In H. C. Foot, M. J. Morgan and R. H. Shute (eds), *Children helping children*. Chichester: Wiley, 65–92.

Fox, E. and Riconscente, M. 2008. Metacognition and self-regulation in James, Piaget, and Vygotsky. *Educational Psychology Review 20*: 373–89. https://psycnet.apa.org/doi/10.1007/s10648-008-9079-2

Frauenglass, M. H. and Diaz, R. M. 1985. Self-regulatory functions of children's private speech: a critical analysis of recent challenges to Vygotsky's theory. *Developmental Psychology 21*: 357–64. https://psycnet.apa.org/doi/10.1037/0012-1649.21.2.357

Gavrilova, M. and Kornienko, D. 2025. Perezhivanie as a source of children's development: case of emotional development intervention through visual arts. *Frontiers in Psychology 15*: 1476973. https://doi.org/10.3389/fpsyg.2024.1476973

Glick, J. 1975. Cognitive development in cross-cultural perspective. In F. Horowitz (ed.), *Review of child development research*. Vol. 4. Chicago: University of Chicago Press, 595–654.

Gredler, M. E. 2012. Understanding Vygotsky for the classroom: is it too late? *Educational Psychology Review 24*: 113–31. https://doi.org/10.1007/s10648-011-9183-6

Harris, J. R. 1995. Where is the child's environment? A group socialization theory of development. *Psychological Review 102*(3): 458–89. https://psycnet.apa.org/doi/10.1037/0033-295X.102.3.458

Herlihy, J. and Gandy, J. 2002. Causation and explanation. *The Psychologist 15(5)*: 248–51.

Holaday, B., Lamontagne, L. and Marciel, J. 1994. Vygotsky's zone of proximal development: implications for nurse assistance of children's learning. *Issues in Comprehensive Pediatric Nursing 17*: 15–27. https://doi.org/10.3109/01460869409078285

Iossifova, R. and Marmolejo-Ramos, F. 2013. When the body is time: spatial and temporal deixis in children with visual impairments and sighted children. *Research in Developmental Disabilities 34*: 2173–84. https://doi.org/10.1016/j.ridd.2013.03.030

Kaye, K. 1977. Toward the origin of dialogue. In H. R. Schaffer (ed.), *Studies in mother-infant interaction*. London: Academic Press, 89–117.

Kozulin, A. 1988. Reality monitoring, psychological tools, and cognitive flexibility in bilinguals: theoretical synthesis and pilot experimental investigation. *International Journal of Psychology 23*(1–6): 79–92. https://psycnet.apa.org/doi/10.1080/00207598808247754

Lektorsky, V. A. 2013. German philosophy and Russian humanitarian thought: Sergei Rubinstein and Gustav Schpet. *Russian Studies in Philosophy 52*: 82–99. https://doi.org/10.2753/RSP1061-1967520105

Lindblom, J. and Ziemke, T. 2003. Social situatedness of natural and artificial intelligence: Vygotsky and beyond. *Adaptive Behavior 11*(2): 79–96. https://doi.org/10.1177/10597123030112002

Liu, C. H. and Matthews, R. 2005. Vygotsky's philosophy: constructivism and its criticisms examined. *International Education Journal 6*(3): 386–99. https://files.eric.ed.gov/fulltext/EJ854992.pdf

Lourenço, O. 2012. Many resemblances, and a crucial difference. *New Ideas in Psychology 30*: 281–95. https://doi.org/10.1016/j.newideapsych.2011.12.006

Luria, A. R. 1972. *The man with a shattered world.* Harmondsworth: Penguin.

Mascolo, M. F., Shannon, N., Belolutskaya, A. and Shiyan, O. 2024. Dialectical thinking: concepts, research methodologies and its power and potential. In N. Shannon, M. F. Mascolo and A. Belolutskaya, *The Routledge international handbook of dialectical thinking*. New York: Routledge, 3–22.

Matthews, W. J. 2003. Constructivism in the classroom: epistemology, history, and empirical evidence. *Teacher Education Quarterly 30*(3): 51–63. www.jstor.org/stable/i23478285

Meacham, J. 1999. Riegel, dialectics, and multiculturalism. *Human Development 42*(3): 134–44. https://doi.org/10.1159/000022619

Menary, R. 2010. Introduction to the special issue on 4E cognition. *Phenomenology and the Cognitive Sciences 9*(4): 459–63. https://doi.org/10.1007/s11097-010-9187-6

Minkova, E. 2012. Pedology as a complex science devoted to the study of children in Russia: the history of its origin and elimination. *Psychological Thought 5*(2): 83–98. https://doi.org/10.23668/psycharchives.1903

Nardo, A. 2021. Exploring a Vygotskian theory of education and its evolutionary foundations. *Educational Theory 71*(3): 331–52. https://doi.org/10.1111/edth.12485

Pascual-Leone, J. and Johnson, J. 2017. Organismic-causal models 'from within' clarify developmental change and stages. In N. Budwig, E. Turiel and P. D. Zelazo (eds), *New perspectives on human development*. Cambridge: Cambridge University Press, 67–87. https://doi.org/10.1017/CBO9781316282755.006

Pritchard, A. and Woollard, J. 2010. *Psychology for the classroom: constructivism and social learning*. London: Routledge.

Riegel, K. F. 1973. *Dialectic operations: the final stage of cognitive development.* Princeton: Educational Testing Service.

Riegel, K. F. and Meacham, J. A. 1978. Dialectics, transaction, and Piaget's theory. In L. A. Pervi and M. Lewis (eds), *Perspectives in interactional psychology*. Boston: Springer, 23–47. https://doi.org/10.1007/978-1-4613-3997-7_2

Rogoff, B. 1986. Adult assistance of children's learning. In T. E. Raphael (ed.), *Contexts of school based literacy*. New York: Random House, 27–40.

Rogoff, B. 1990. *Apprenticeship in thinking: cognitive development in social context.* Oxford: Oxford University Press.

Rogoff, B. and Gardner, W. 1984. Adult guidance of cognitive development. In B. Rogoff and J. Lave (eds), *Everyday cognition: its development in social context.* Cambridge, MA: Harvard, 95–116.

Rogoff, B. and Morelli, G. 1989. Perspectives on children's development from cultural psychology. *American Psychologist 44*: 343–8. https://psycnet.apa.org/doi/10.1037/0003-066X.44.2.343

Roth, W-M. and Jornet, A. 2017. *Understanding educational psychology: a late Vygotskian, Spinozist approach*. Dordrecht: Springer Nature.

Schaffer, R. 1989. Early social development. In A. Slater and G. Bremner (eds), *Infant development.* Hove: Lawrence Erlbaum, 189–210.

Schneider, W. and Artelt, C. 2010. Metacognition and mathematics education. *ZDM Mathematics Education 42*: 149–61. https://doi.org/10.1007/s11858-010-0240-2

Shute, R. H. 2018. Schools, mindfulness, and metacognition: a view from developmental psychology. *International Journal of School & Educational Psychology 7 (sup1)*: 123–36. https://doi.org/10.1080/21683603.2018.1435322

Shute, R., Foot, H. and Morgan, M. 1992. The sensitivity of children and adults as tutors. *Educational Studies 1*: 21–36. https://doi.org/10.1080/0305569920180103

Shute, R. and Miksad, J. 1997. Scaffolding effects of computer-assisted instruction on the cognitive development of preschool children. *Child Study Journal 27*(2): 237–53.

Smagorinsky, P. 2024. Vygotsky, 'defectology', and inclusive education. In *L. S. Vygotsky and English in education and the language arts*. First edn. Vol. 1. London: Routledge, 238–56. https://doi.org/10.4324/9781003374848-17

van der Veer, R. 1986. Vygotsky's developmental psychology. *Psychological Reports 59*(2): 527–36. https://doi.org/10.2466/pr0.1986.59.2.527

van der Veer, R. 2021. Vygotsky's legacy: understanding and beyond. *Integrative Psychological and Behavioral Science 55*(4): 789–96. https://doi.org/10.1007/s12124-021-09652-6

van IJzendoorn, M. H., Goossens, F. A. and van der Veer, R. 1984. Klaus F. Riegel and dialectical psychology: in search for the changing individual in a changing society. *Storia e Critica della Psicologia 5*(1): 5–28. https://pubmed.ncbi.nlm.nih.gov/11611542/

Vasileva, O. and Balyasnikova, N. 2019. (Re)Introducing Vygotsky's thought: from historical overview to contemporary psychology. *Frontiers in Psychology 10*: 1515. https://doi.org/10.3389/fpsyg.2019.01515

Veraksa, N. E., Airapetyan, Z. V., Gavrilova, M. N. and Tarasova, K. S. 2022. The relationship between dialectical thinking and emotion understanding in senior preschool children. *Cultural-Historical Psychology 18*: 41–9. https://psyjournals.ru/en/journals/chp/archive/2022_n1/Veraksa_et_al

Vygotsky, L. S. 1930/1978. *Mind in society: the development of higher mental processes*. Cambridge, MA: Harvard University Press.

Vygotsky, L. S. 1934/1962. *Thought and language*. Cambridge, MA: MIT Press.

Wertsch, J. V. and Tulviste, P. 1992. L. S. Vygotsky and contemporary developmental psychology. *Developmental Psychology 28*(4): 548–57. https://psycnet.apa.org/doi/10.1037/0012-1649.28.4.548

Wood, D. 1988/1998. *How children think and learn*. Oxford: Blackwell.

Wood, D., Bruner, J. S. and Ross, G. 1976. The role of tutoring in problem-solving. *Journal of Child Psychology and Psychiatry 17*(2): 89–100. https://doi.org/10.1111/jcpp.1976.17.issue-2

Wood, D. J., Wood, H. A. and Middleton, D. J. 1978. An experimental evaluation of four face-to-face teaching strategies. *International Journal of Behavioral Development 1*(2): 131–47. https://doi.org/10.1177/016502547800100203

Yasnitsky, A. 2012. The complete works of L. S. Vygotsky: PsyAnima Complete Vygotsky project. *Dubna Psychological Journal 3*: 144–8. https://psyanima.su/journal/2012/3/2012n3a6/2012n3a6.2.pdf

Yasnitsky, A. 2018. *Vygotsky: an intellectual biography*. London: Routledge.

9 The historic event

Contextualism

Introduction

In this chapter we examine contextual theory and the theorists most strongly linked with it. Stephen Pepper used the term 'the real historic event' to encapsulate contextualism (Pepper, 1942: 232), which is generally associated with the writings of William James, John Dewey and Margaret Mead. We will consider all these as well as lifespan developmental psychology. We will also touch upon Urie Bronfenbrenner's theory, although his work is given fuller treatment in Chapter 10.

As shown in Figure 2.1 in Chapter 2, an important antecedent to contextualism was functionalism, 'a philosophical theory (or family of theories) concerning the nature of mental states' (Polger, 2012: 337). Janet Levin (2023) links functionalism to the writings of Aristotle, which presented the view that the human soul is a natural expression of the organized system comprising the human body; this is distinct from Plato's view that the soul can exist apart from the body. Thomas Polger contrasted functionalism with behaviourism:

> Functionalism allows that the inputs and outputs that characterize psychological states can be inputs from and outputs to and from other internal parts of the system—viz., subpersonal psychological states—in addition to stimulus inputs from the environment and overt behavioral outputs
>
> *(Polger, 2012: 338)*

It is generally recognized that psychology split from philosophy, establishing itself as a science, with the emergence of Wilhelm Wundt's laboratory and the championing of the controlled experiment as the modus operandi (e.g. Proctor and Warren, 2024). That said, as Howard Gardner observed, 'nearly every field begins as philosophy; and psychology continues to foreground its philosophical origins more faithfully than any other discipline' (Gardner, 1994: 182)—though Thomas Teo (1997) believed that psychology did not keep up with later philosophical developments. Dewey stated in his *Psychology as Philosophic Method*, 'what else can philosophy in its fullness be but psychology, and psychology but philosophy?' (Dewey, 1981: 116). In considering the philosophical underpinnings of contextualism, we accept Patricia Kahlbaugh's argument that 'contextualism is

DOI: 10.4324/9781003567738-9

based on assumptions fundamentally distinct from those of the dialectical (organismic) paradigm' (Kahlbaugh, 1989: 4). However, there is some commonality between Pepper's (1942) organismic and contextualism metaphors, in particular, the idea that 'reality is in constant flux' (Kramer and Bopp, 1989: 4). They also share an emphasis on placing activity in a given time and place. However, organicism places the focus on the developmental process of the organism, while contextualism includes the subjective context of both the observer and the observed in a certain social context.

A contextualist approach holds that developmental change involves reciprocal influence whereby an active organism is relating to a responsive context, thus individuals are both products and producers of their contexts (Lerner, 1976). Ralph Rosnow and Marianthi Georgoudi (1986) have identified four themes that are especially important in considering contextualism:

1. The historic event is the basic unit of analysis with a consequent focus on change and development. The root metaphor is the act in context, or the historical act, not meaning a thing that is finished, but 'doing as a thing that is being done, as in hunting, shopping or making love' (Hayes, Hayes and Reese, 1988: 100).
2. The context consists of all the conditions surrounding the event. The sociocultural context in which the event takes place provides meaning to the event.
3. Variability and chance are an integral part of contextualism because contexts themselves are ultimately developing and impermanent realities. This point alone differentiates contextualism from mechanism and organicism, which assume that the true order and unity of events can be determined probabilistically (Thayer, 1968).
4. Action and knowledge. The purposive and intentional nature of human action is emphasized in contextualism. Development, then, is an active participation in the construction of contexts that in turn impact upon any future action.

Box 9.1 illustrates that having a contextualist outlook influences how one perceives and acts in the world—in that case, in parenting children.

BOX 9.1 PARENTAL BELIEFS ABOUT CHILD DEVELOPMENT: THE ROOT METAPHOR OF CONTEXTUALISM

A steadily accumulating body of research demonstrates cultural differences in parental beliefs about child development, as we will see in Chapter 11. Ideas about appropriate parenting are determined not only by beliefs about childhood, but also by understanding of the psychology of how children grow (Sanson and Wise, 2001). Charles Super and Sara Harkness (2003) examined the role of Pepper's (1942) four root metaphors for explaining child-rearing behaviour, finding all four useful for explaining parental child-rearing beliefs.

The extent to which parents adopted one metaphor as a general model of child behaviour drew on their broad philosophical views and their exposure to, and experience with, a range of child-rearing behaviours as well as their education and training. Contextualism, with its focus on multiple determinants and perspectives, was favoured by parents with a higher level of education.

Functionalism: William James and Charles S. Peirce

Whether New York-born James (1842–1910) was a true contextualist is open to some debate, but his work certainly provides relevant background. As we observed in Chapter 5, James founded 'functionalism'. The brother of novelist Henry James, he was profoundly influenced by their theologian father, particularly in relation to his indifference to worldly success and his focus on addressing some of life's fundamental problems. James broke off from his Harvard University studies and spent time in Germany, experiencing bouts of ill-health, depression and suicidality. This period confirmed for him his deep and abiding interest in philosophy. He returned to Harvard, finished his medical degree and had an academic career there from 1872 to 1907. His 12-year task of writing *Principles of Psychology* was finally completed in 1890 and was a significant marker in the history of psychology.

An undergraduate friend was the philosopher Charles S. Peirce (1839–1914), whose writings focused strongly on the link between theory and practice and particularly the application of philosophy to everyday life. Cornelis de Waal (2003) provided some fascinating insight into the life and times of Peirce, a polymath whose scientific output ranged from calculating the shape of the earth and pioneering Shakespearean pronunciation, to inventing the electronic switch that would later be used in computers. Although brilliant, he died in poverty, at one stage living off leftover bread from a bakery. James helped pay off his debts.

Peirce's scientific work influenced his philosophy of the sciences and his view of the scientific method. He noted that '[a]lmost every proposition of ontological metaphysics is either meaningless gibberish – one word being defined by other words, and they still by others, without any real conception ever being reached – or else is downright absurd' (Peirce, 1958: 92). According to Peirce, truth was discovered using the scientific method and the next step was to apply it to solve everyday problems. Philosophical pragmatism embraced the idea that what is true will work, highlighting the practical usefulness of discovered truth. It informed the later writings of both James and Dewey. Peirce argued that pragmatism begins with beliefs which are conscious, deliberate habits of action: 'Our beliefs guide our desires and shape our actions. … The feeling of believing is a more or less sure indication of there being established in our nature some habit that will determine our actions.' Thus, our beliefs cause us to act in a certain way because of the perceived consequences (Peirce, 1958: 59).

James endeavoured to understand and apply Peirce's philosophy. For James, pragmatism was principally a way to evaluate truth claims, not by looking at the truth or falsity of a primary definition but by evaluating the claim in terms of its moral and aesthetic outcome. Second, for James it was a way of reconciling conflicting definitions of reality. People could still maintain their individual idiosyncratic beliefs if their outcomes led to common social behaviour agreed as acceptable (James, 1907). The pragmatic outlook appealed to those interested in using science to solve everyday problems, and to the frontier mentality of some developing western nations, such as the United States, in the early 20th century. Through Darwinian influence, James argued for adaptive function. According to James, the mind is revealed in habits, knowledge and perceptions:

> Sow an action and you reap a habit;
> Sow a habit and you reap a character;
> Sow a character and you reap a destiny.
> *(James, 1890)*

The mind is seen as constantly engaged in interaction with, and adaptation to, the environment. James emphasized the selective function of consciousness, holding that the 'stream of consciousness' includes ideas as well as relations among them. As a pragmatist, he argued that 'thoughts and feelings exist' (James, 1890, Vol. 1: vi).

Principles of Psychology aimed trenchant criticism at the structuralist psychology originating in Germany. James' main purpose was the development of a functional psychology whereby the intention was not to reduce psychology to its constituent elements, but rather to study consciousness as an ongoing process or stream. James critiqued the 'mind-stuff' theory that 'our mental states are composite in structure, made up of smaller states conjoined' (1890, Vol. 1: 145). Mind-stuff theory attempted to explain higher mental states by viewing them as the sum of lower ones:

> All the 'combinations' which we actually know are effects, wrought by the units said to be 'combined', upon some entity other than themselves … no possible number of entities (call them as you like, whether forces, material particles, or mental elements) can sum themselves together. Each remains in a sum, what it always was; and the sum itself exists only for a bystander who happens to overlook the units and to apprehend the sum as such.
> *(James, 1890, Vol. 1: 160–1)*

As similarly noted by Owen Flanagan, 'the mind cannot be identical to the sum of its parts because we need the mind to do the summing and to acknowledge the addition' (Flanagan, 1991: 42). Functionalism required the use of multiple methods to pursue answers to questions in both basic and applied psychological research (Crosby and Viney, 1990). In *The Meaning of Truth*, James wrote, 'To know an object is to lead to it through a context which the world provides' and 'Owing to the fact that all experience is a process, no point of view can ever be the last one' (James, 1907: 5). For example, he viewed scientific truth as changeable and the product of human perception (James, 1890), and that therefore no one could claim to discover 'Truth'. He believed that the important questions of human behaviour could best be understood holistically. In *Principles*, James (1909/1975, cited in Wozniak, 1995) saw human perception as central to understanding psychological questions. James argued that people uniquely construct the nature of the world in their minds on the basis of personal experiences and that history is shaped by individual constructions of experience.

Both mechanism and organicism assume some causal connection between events across some dimension, either temporal or spatial: 'Events are assumed to be systematically related such that each new state is both an improvement over and a transformation of the previous one' (Kahlbaugh, 1989: 77). James, however, did not advocate a theory of progress, but proposed that history was simply a collection of unrelated facts, without any assumption about what the end state would be, or that it would represent an improvement. In this respect, we can see a connection with dynamic systems theory.

In the 1940s, the views and research of a number of psychologists belonging to the functionalist school (such as Ames, 1951) garnered attention. Perception became seen as resulting from the relationship between the observer and the observed object, with context as the critical functional factor in helping us interpret the world around us. Functionalism continues to have a place in addressing children's behavioural difficulties, particularly in the case of children with disabilities and in educational settings (Box 9.2).

BOX 9.2 CAN TEACHERS FIGURE OUT THE FUNCTIONS OF PROBLEMATIC CLASSROOM BEHAVIOUR?

In 1997 it became mandatory in the United States for children's behavioural problems to be addressed using a support plan based on functional behavioural assessment (FBA). FBA assumes that behaviour serves some purpose for the child. It involves detailed observations of the child in the environment (typically, the classroom), normally requiring the time and expertise of a psychologist. Present author RHS, with an Australian and a US colleague, examined whether it was possible to train a teacher to undertake this process in an efficient, shortened way within the regular classroom context (Packenham, Shute and Reid, 2004).

We worked with a teacher who nominated two children with problematic behaviours, 8-year-old high-achiever Michelle who caused frequent disruption by calling out and excessive talking, and 9-year-old low-achiever Jack, who was often off-task. After brief training in analysing the behaviours, the situations leading up to them (antecedents), and the consequences, the teacher hypothesized that the function of Michelle's behaviour was seeking teacher attention, while Jack's behaviour was aimed at escaping from difficult work. New and appropriate ways of providing attention to Michelle were implemented, while Jack was given easier and more individually supported work tasks. Single case studies showed sustained improvements. Michelle's disruptive behaviour decreased from 34 per cent of observation periods to 10 per cent, while Jack's off-task behaviour dropped from 53 per cent to 24 per cent.

John Dewey (1859–1952): active minds in cultural settings

John Dewey was born in 1859 in Burlington, Vermont, growing up in a family that was active in the social community of that US state, with a democratic political vision. He strongly believed in groups of people problem-solving peacefully, through 'discussion, debate, and decision making' (Gutek, 2014: 78).

Reviewing Dewey's work, Emily Cahan (1992: 213) concluded that, 'Dewey is not well known to contemporary psychologists, nor did he exert a strong influence on the emergence of a disciplinary psychology'. Any perusal of educational or developmental psychology textbooks would suggest this claim still holds today. However, in reflecting on the role of history, culture and values in psychology, to redress some of its preoccupation with the collation of facts, there is a significant place for a greater understanding of Dewey's thinking.

Studying under G. Stanley Hall, and perhaps influenced by the writings of Jean-Jacques Rousseau, Dewey developed a rather idealist philosophy. This was somewhat tempered by Hall, who counselled against its excesses. Cahan noted Dewey's 'personal craving for a philosophical system in which parts related to a whole in a manner consistent with the new evolutionary biology with its emphasis on the organism in interaction with the environment' (Cahan, 1992: 206). To that end, Dewey shared much in common with James. Dewey's thinking capitalized on two prominent ideas of his time, namely biology's concept of the 'organism in the environment' and social psychology's emphasis on observing 'active minds in cultural settings'. Dewey's writings provided a counterbalance to much of the laboratory-based psychology of his day: 'folk-lore and primitive culture, ethnology and anthropology, all render their contributions of matter and press upon us the necessity of explanation' (Dewey, 1884: 57).

In 'The reflex arc concept in psychology' (1896), Dewey argued against the suggestion that human beings are mechanisms made up of separate parts. He also disagreed with a view of consciousness as the simple additive sum of discrete elements such as sensations. In a functional manner, Dewey did not believe that stimulus and response were separate, unrelated entities, instead arguing that they were 'functionally related to each other through purposeful activity' (Cahan, 1992: 208).

For example, consider a behavioural interpretation of a curious child learning not to put her hand in a flame; a simple association forms between the sight of the flame and the burn, resulting in future avoidance. Dewey would have a more functional explanation. The child would see the attractive dancing flame in a curiosity-arousing way and the flame would not be a passive thing at all. After touching it, the experience literally changes the flame holistically to a shining, hot painful object: it is our interaction with objects as a whole that gives them their meaning.

Development, then, is active participation in the construction of contexts that in turn impact on any future action. As Aaron Schutz observed, 'Dewey was convinced that understanding something involves seeing how it is connected with other things and events' (Schutz, 2001: 269). Authentic learning occurs in the midst of purposeful activity. In this regard he believed that the best learning occurred when instruction was geared to a student's interests and motivations. His approach to education involved student interest, student activity, group work and real-life experience. Thus, Dewey took a child-centred approach to education well before the introduction of open classrooms, discovery learning and the activity-based curriculum. His educational ideas are very relevant in the 21st century (Williams, 2017).

In 1896 Dewey established and created one of the most important educational experiments of the 19th and 20th centuries—the Laboratory School at the University of Chicago. Dewey believed strongly that it was from our experiences that we develop our theories about the world. He warned against the excesses and limitations of knowledge gleaned from laboratories (Cahan, 1992)—a view later expounded by Bronfenbrenner.

Daniel Fishman and Stanley Messer (2013) drew inspiration from the early pragmatism of James, Dewey and Peirce to suggest a 'bottom up', phenomenon-based, approach to applied psychology, rather than a 'top-down' approach that applies theories drawn from basic research. It involves an accumulation of single-case studies (quantitative or qualitative), from any theoretical background, to build databases addressing specific phenomena. A database could be interrogated or combined with information from larger-scale studies to form a unified knowledge base for understanding a phenomenon or addressing a problem.

Margaret Mead (1901–1978) and cross-cultural research

The US anthropologist Margaret Mead was born in Pennsylvania and is widely known for her cross-cultural research and writing, heralded by the publication of *Coming of Age in Samoa* in 1928. She was a prolific author and social commentator, and married Gregory Bateson, anthropologist and social historian, after they met on a field trip in New Guinea. They had one child, Catherine Bateson, herself a noted anthropologist.

Mead's ideas help us to appreciate the role played by culture in shaping our views of children and the family. In her book *Culture and Commitment* (1970) she called upon knowledge she had gleaned from studying children in Manus, Bali and New Guinea, following their lives into adulthood to identify three different kinds of culture: postfigurative, cofigurative and prefigurative.

1. *Postfigurative*. Children learn primarily from the collective experience and history of their forebears.
2. *Cofigurative*. Children learn from their peers.
3. *Prefigurative*. Adults are capable of learning from their children, as well as vice versa.

To make a connection here with Lev Vygotsky, we can see that his theory explicitly focused on the first type of learning and, to a minor degree, the second. However, his theory could be applied to the third type if we assume that, in some circumstances, children are more capable than adults. For example, author PTS valued computing advice from his young sons in preparing the previous edition of this book (and this time around, they still began with, 'Dad, have you tried turning it off and on?'!).

In her 1970 book, Mead mounted a powerful argument, based on years of anthropological research, to suggest that a number of conditions had combined to bring about the revolt of youth around the world at that time. First was the novel emergence of an identifiable world community characterized by sharing knowledge and an awareness of the dangers of nuclear annihilation. Second, advances in modern technology, while beneficial in some areas such as food production, were seriously challenging the planet's ecology. Third, advances in medical knowledge had reduced the pressure for population increase, which in turn freed women from devoting themselves entirely to reproduction, thereby changing their role in society and influencing the raising of children. Given these momentous changes, Mead believed people were living in a present unprepared for by their understanding of the past, when 'there were always some elders who knew more than any children in terms of their experience of having grown up within a cultural system. Today there are none' (Mead, 1970: 61). According to Mead, the young generation felt there must be better ways than those offered by the previous generation to deal with society's problems, and that they must find them; they recognized the crucial need for immediate action on world problems. She wrote:

> Now, as I see it, the development of a prefigurative culture will depend on the existence of a continuing dialogue in which the young, free to act on their own initiative, can lead their elders in the direction of the unknown. Then the older generation will have access to new experiential knowledge, without which no meaningful plans can be made. It is only with the direct participation of the young who have that knowledge, that we can build a viable future.
>
> *(Mead, 1970: 3)*

Of course, Mead wrote this in an era of student protests (e.g. against the Vietnam, or American, War), a reminder that her theory, like others, must be historically contextualized. Youth voices became quieter for some years—for example, cuts to public funding of universities obliged students in many countries to take employment as well as studying, leaving little time for civic participation. However, new impetus to youth protest was given by the global financial collapse of 2008, with neoliberal austerity measures galvanizing youth-led protests against global capitalism, with social media playing a central role in the formation and activities of movements such as 'Occupy' (Giroux, 2013). Within a few more years, 'School Strikes 4 Climate' saw rallies of school students massing around the world, though this movement became impeded by the COVID-19 pandemic (Slezak and Davis, 2023).

To summarize Mead's contribution, she added a strong voice and some semblance of balance to the nature–nurture debate, which until that time had favoured nature, although there has been considerable debate about the validity of her Samoan research, with suggestions that her adolescent participants 'pulled the wool over her eyes' in describing their sexual adventures (Freeman, 1996). We have presented her strong contribution in this chapter because of her sharp focus on culture in explaining differences in development.

Urie Bronfenbrenner (1917–2005) and the ecology of development

During much of the 20th century, there was an emphasis on child development as an individual process, to the neglect of social and cultural contexts (Oakley, 1972). During the 1970s, Bronfenbrenner (born in Moscow, Russia) began to address this, famously criticizing developmental psychology as 'the study of the strange behavior of children in strange situations with strange adults for the briefest possible period of time' (Bronfenbrenner, 1977: 513). He modestly claimed that the increasing attention paid to ecological context was not especially due to his work, but rather that his work represented an idea whose time had come (Bronfenbrenner, 1986). Nevertheless, his name remains the one that developmental psychologists most closely associate with the shift at the end of the 20th century towards recognizing the influence of environmental contexts on children's development, a shift that can be traced to the publication of *The Ecology of Human Development* in 1979. He argued that:

> The ecology of human development involves the scientific study of the progressive mutual accommodation between an active, growing human being and the changing properties of the immediate settings in which the developing person lives, as this process is affected by relations between these settings, and by the larger contexts in which the settings are embedded.
>
> *(Bronfenbrenner, 1979: 21)*

He envisaged the child as developing within a nested series of contexts, like a set of Russian dolls, although students of psychology often recall him as 'the man with the circles'—a reference to the two-dimensional visual representations of the interacting layers of the environment surrounding the child as a series of mutually influential concentric circles. With his recognition of the importance of broader contexts for development, he also advocated a closer connection between child development research and public policy. We say more about Bronfenbrenner in Chapter 11.

Lifespan development

Lifespan developmental psychology is a contextually oriented psychology with the core assumption that development is not completed upon reaching adulthood. Rather, ontogenesis continues across the entire life course, and the notion of development is adapted and used to encompass the idea of lifelong adaptive learning (Baltes, Lindenberger and Staudinger, 1998; Wohlwill, 1973). According to Paul Baltes (1987) lifespan developmental psychology is considered to involve the following:

- Flux and change by virtue of the consideration it gives to the growth and decline of the individual.
- A focus on the historical embeddedness of development.
- Development's location in cultural context.
- The plasticity of human development.

Daniel Levinson (1978) believed that Freud's Swiss protégé Carl Jung (1875–1961) should be considered the founder of the modern study of adult development, though Baltes *et al.* (1998) observed that the German approach to developmental psychology was always more lifespan orientated than that of the United States, Britain and some other European countries. Jung disagreed with Freud's emphasis on the early childhood years and intrapsychic conflicts, and placed more weight on development in the second half of life, and on the roles of religion, mythology and culture in shaping our lives. Baltes avoided the dichotomy:

> There can be no strong field of lifespan developmental psychology without a solid foundation in and connection to childhood. By the same token, the study of child development does not exist in a vacuum, but is vitally enriched by considering the aftermath of childhood.
>
> *(Baltes, 1979: 1)*

The lifespan approach, in contrast to the passivity of mechanism, views the individual as actively involved in their development, an idea relatively neglected by developmental psychology until about 1970 (Brandtstadter, 1998), with Michael Lewis and Leonard A. Rosenblum's (1974) proposition that infants affect their own development, and Richard Bell's (1978) milestone paper on infant socialization as a bi-directional process. However, the notion of the 'seasons' of life and the concept of transformation and perfectibility have a long history dating back to Aristotle's idea of action (i.e. when we choose to undertake an action we do so for some purpose), to the 'Renaissance Man' ideal and, latterly, to the German 'understanding psychology' of Wilhelm Dilthey (Brandtstadter, 1998).

Lives of all great men remind us
We can make our lives sublime,
And, departing, leave behind us
Footprints on the sands of time.
(Henry Wadsworth Longfellow,
A Psalm of Life, *1891)*

Baltes *et al.* (1998) also suggested that lifespan developmental psychology can be viewed in either a person-centred (holistic) or function-centred fashion. The former focuses on the person as a system and attempts to describe the stages or ages of development of the individual, while the latter focuses on attributes such as memory and tracks the development of those functions across the lifespan.

Authors including Erik Erikson (1968), Levinson and colleagues (1976) and Bernice Neugarten (1976) wrote about the concept of the 'life-cycle'. This term seems to be adopted from biology, where the development of the individual passes through a sequence of stages such as from egg to embryo, birth, sexual development, reproduction and death. It is cyclical in that it is repeated across generations. Levinson (1986), a colleague of Erikson, in attempting to describe the concept, compared it with 'life course' (the temporal unfolding of life over the years). 'Life-cycle' went beyond this, suggesting the unfolding of an underlying sequence or order of various phases or seasons of life, stressing that the individual grows and changes across the lifespan and is not doomed to live out the effects of early childhood experiences. Other theorists have identified turning points, tasks (Robert Havighurst) or, as Neugarten (1976: 1) described it, 'punctuation marks along the life-cycle' that impact on the individual's self-concept, or sense of identity, and usually require adaptation on behalf of the individual and those around them. Erikson's life-cycle stages are summarized in Table 9.1 (for further information, see Slee, Campbell and Spears, 2012).

Levinson (1978) proposed that the life-cycle evolves through a series of 'eras', each lasting approximately 25 years. During each era certain tasks present themselves and the extent to which they are accomplished determines how much satisfaction or turmoil the individual experiences. An era is a time of life in the broadest

Table 9.1 Erikson's psychosocial stages

Ages	*Stages*
Infancy	Basic trust versus mistrust
1.5–3.5 years (approx.)	Autonomy versus shame and doubt
3.5–5.5 years (approx.)	Initiative versus guilt
5.5–12 years (approx.)	Industry versus inferiority
Adolescence	Identity versus role confusion
Young adulthood	Intimacy versus isolation
Adulthood	Generativity versus stagnation
Maturity	Ego integrity versus despair

possible sense, each era using a distinctive character shaped by biological, psychological and social aspects. In moving from one era to the next, basic changes occur in the 'fabric of life' and the transition can take as long as six years. The major eras consist of preadulthood, early adulthood, midlife transition, middle adulthood and late adulthood. There is a limited amount of research to support the validity of Levinson's scheme of developmental periods, which were largely based on his impressionistic interpretations of his large amount of clinical interview material with men, although he later followed this up by considering with his wife the 'seasons of life' of women (Levinson and Levinson, 1996, published after his death) (see also Sheehy, 1976).

During childhood, major developmental achievements (such as walking and talking), which exert a major influence on the child's relationships with others, occur within a specific age range. In contrast, the developmental landmarks in adulthood (establishing a relationship, having children or becoming a grandparent) are neither age-linked nor universally experienced. While attaching specific time periods to adult life-events is less important at one level, at another level, the 'timing' of such events is often quite critical. Neugarten (1968) used the term 'social clock' to describe each culture's sense of timing for events such as marriage and childbearing. Neugarten believed that individuals are sensitive to being 'off-time', for example, bearing children later in life than expected in a particular culture.

Demographic changes in many industrialized and postindustrial western countries prompted Jeffrey Arnett (2000) to propose a new phase of life, between adolescence and adulthood (see Box 9.3). This is a clear reminder of the importance of the historical and sociocultural context in understanding lifespan development.

BOX 9.3 EMERGING ADULTHOOD

'In effect, a new period of life has opened up between adolescence and adulthood as a normative experience for young people in industrialised societies' (Arnett, 2000: 3). Jeffrey Arnett (e.g. 2007) cited the changing demographics in many western industrialized and postindustrialized countries, including a rise in the median age of marriage, an increase in women's age at first childbirth, and the proportion of young people completing tertiary education. Accordingly, emerging adulthood exists in cultures that postpone entry into adult roles and responsibilities until well past the late teens. Such countries require a high level of education for entry into the information-based professions and individuals postpone marriage and parenthood until well after schooling is completed.

Arnett proposed that the period between the end of adolescence and the early twenties had become long enough not to be a 'transition period' but a *life stage* in itself: 'emerging adulthood'. This is 'a period of life characterised for many young people by a high degree of change, experimentation, and instability as they explore a variety of possibilities in love, work, and worldviews' (Arnett, 2000: 3). Arnett suggested five characteristics that make emerging adulthood a distinct entity, being the age of:

- Identity explorations.
- Instability.
- Self-focus.
- Feeling in-between.
- A sense of possibilities.

Arnett's views have invoked considerable discussion in the lifespan development literature.

That lifespan approaches need to be culturally contextualized is also highlighted by the writing of Bame Nsamenang (2005), who proposed that in the African context human ontogenesis comprises three stages of selfhood. The first stage, spiritual selfhood, begins at conception or before that, if the culture believes in reincarnation of an ancestral spirit; it ends when the child is named and thus introduced into the community. This is followed by social selfhood, lasting until biological death; it has seven phases, concerned with developmental tasks that are intimately linked with culture, social integration and interdependence. An intelligent child, in African terms, is one who shows good social responsibility, with the peer group playing a central role in promoting this. The third stage of the life-cycle is that of an ancestor, who continues to influence the affairs of the living.

Conclusions

In this chapter we have focused on contextualism as a means for understanding human development, taking Pepper's (1942) idea that the root metaphor for contextualism can be expressed as 'the real historic event' in all its dynamic activity. To this end, we have examined the contributions of the functionalists, those who highlighted the significance of culture in understanding and interpreting development, and lifespan theorizing. There is no doubt that contextualism has had, and continues to exert, a strong impact on the study of child development. The twin notions of 'constant change' and 'embeddedness' emphasize change as promoting change. Richard Lerner and Imma de Stefanis (2000: 476) argued that 'the regulation by individuals of their relations with their complex and changing context is the process involved in successful development across life'. Contextualism was the theme of an international conference in 2025. It paves the way for a deeper consideration of cultural issues in children's development, which is the subject of Chapter 11.

References

Ames, A. 1951. Visual perception and the rotating trapezoidal window. *Psychological Monographs 65*(7): 1–32. https://psycnet.apa.org/doi/10.1037/h0093600

Arnett, J. J. 2000. Emerging adulthood: a theory of development from the late teens through twenties. *American Psychologist 55*(5): 469–80. https://psycnet.apa.org/doi/10.1037/0003-066X.55.5.469

Arnett, J. J. 2007. Emerging adulthood: what is it, and what is it good for? *Child Development Perspectives 1*(2): 68–73. https://psycnet.apa.org/doi/10.1111/j.1750-8606.2007.00016.x

Baltes, P. B. 1979. On the potential and limits of child development: life-span developmental perspectives. *Newsletter of the Society for Research in Child Development*, Summer, 1–4.

Baltes, P. B. 1987. Theoretical propositions of life-span developmental psychology: on the dynamics between growth and decline. *Developmental Psychology 23*(5): 611–26. https://doi.org/10.1037/0012-1649.23.5.611

Baltes, P. B., Lindenberger, U. and Staudinger, U. M. 1998. *Life-span theory in developmental psychology*. New York: Academic Press.

Bell, R. A. 1978. A reinterpretation of the direction of effects in studies of socialization. *Psychological Review 75*: 81–95. https://doi.org/10.1037/h0025583

Brandstadter, J. 1998. Action perspectives on human development. In W. Damon and R. M. Lerner (eds), *Handbook of child psychology: theoretical models of human development*. Vol 1. Fifth edn. New York: Wiley, 807–63.

Bronfenbrenner, U. 1977. Toward an experimental ecology of human development. *American Psychologist* July: 513–31. https://doi.org/10.1037/0003-066X.32.7.513

Bronfenbrenner, U. 1979. *The ecology of human development: experiments by nature and design*. Cambridge, MA: Harvard University Press.

Bronfenbrenner, U. 1986. Recent advances in research on the ecology of human development. In R. K. Silbereisen, K. Eyferth and G. Rudinger (eds), *Development as action in context: problem behavior and normal youth development*. New York: Springer-Verlag, 286–309.

Cahan, E. D. 1992. John Dewey and human development. *Developmental Psychology 28*: 205–14. https://doi.org/10.1037/0012-1649.28.2.205

Crosby, D. A. and Viney, D. W. 1990. *Toward a psychology that is radically empirical*. Paper presented at the 98th Annual Convention of the American Psychological Association, Boston, August 1990.

De Waal, C. 2003. Charles Sanders Peirce: the architect of pragmatism. *Philosophy Now 3*: 8–11.

Dewey, J. 1884. Kant and the philosophic method. *The Journal of Speculative Philosophy*, 16–174.

Dewey, J. 1896. The reflex arc concept in psychology. *Psychological Review 3*(4): 357–70. https://doi.org/10.1037/h0070405

Dewey, J. 1981. The structure of experience. In J. J. McDermott (ed.), *The philosophy of John Dewey*. Second edn. Vol. 1. Chicago: The University of Chicago Press, 1–325.

Erikson, E. 1968. *Identity, youth and crisis*. New York: Norton.

Fishman, D. B. and Messer, S. B. 2013. Pragmatic case studies as a source of unity in applied psychology. *Review of General Psychology 17(*2): 156–61. https://doi.org/10.1037/a0032927

Flanagan, O. 1991. *The science of the mind*. Second edn. Cambridge MA: MIT Press.

Freeman, D. 1996. *Franz Boas and the flower of heaven: Coming of age in Samoa and the fateful hoaxing of Margaret Mead*. Harmondsworth: Penguin.

Gardner, H. 1994. The stories of the right hemisphere. In W. D. Spaulding (ed.), *Integrative views of motivation, cognition and emotion.* Vol. 41. *The Nebraska symposium on motivation.* Lincoln: University of Nebraska Press, 57–69.

Giroux, H. A. 2013. The Quebec student protest movement in the age of neoliberal terror. *Journal for the Study of Race, Nation and Culture 19*(5): 515–35. https://doi.org/10.1080/13504630.2013.835510

Gutek, G. 2014. *Philosophical, ideological, and theoretical perspectives on education.* Second edn. New York: Pearson.

Hayes, S. C., Hayes, L. J. and Reese, H. W. 1988. Finding the philosophical core: a review of Stephen Pepper's world hypotheses: a study in evidence. *Journal of the Experimental Analysis of Behavior* 50: 97–111.

James, W. 1890. *The principles of psychology.* New York: H. Holt and Company.

James, W. 1907. *Pragmatism, a new name for some old ways of thinking: popular lectures on philosophy.* New York: Longmans Green and Co.

Kahlbaugh, P. E. 1989. William James' pragmatism: a clarification of the contextual world view. In D. A. Kramer and M. J. Bopp (eds), *Transformation in clinical and developmental psychology.* New York: Springer-Verlag, 73–88.

Kramer, D. A. and Bopp, M. J. 1989. *Transformation in clinical and developmental psychology.* New York: Springer-Verlag.

Lerner, R. M. 1976. *Concepts and theories of human development.* Reading, MA: Addison-Wesley.

Lerner, R. M. and De Stefanis, I. 2000. The import of infancy for individual, family and societal development. Commentary on the special section: does infancy matter? *Infant Behaviour and Development 22*: 475–82. https://doi.org/10.1016/S0163-6383(00)00020-5

Levin, J. 2023. Functionalism. In E. N. Zalta and U. Nodelman (eds), *The Stanford encyclopedia of philosophy* (Summer 2023 edn), https://plato.stanford.edu/archives/sum2023/entries/functionalism/

Levinson, D. 1978. *Seasons of a man's life.* New York: Random House.

Levinson, D. 1986. A conception of adult development. *American Psychologist 41*: 3–12.

Levinson, D. J., Darrow, C. M., Klein, E. B., Levinson, M. H. and McKee, B. 1976. Periods in the adult development of men: ages 18 to 45. *The Counseling Psychologist 6*: 21–4.

Levinson, D. J. with Levinson, J. D. 1996. *Seasons of a woman's life.* New York: Alfred A. Knopf.

Lewis, M. and Rosenblum, M. A. 1974. *The effect of the infant on its care-giver.* New York: John Wiley & Sons.

Longfellow, H. W. 1891. *A psalm of life.* np: Dutton.

Mead, M. 1928. *Coming of age in Samoa.* New York: William Morrow & Co.

Mead, M. 1970. *Culture and commitment.* New York: Doubleday, Garden City.

Neugarten, B. L. 1968. *Middle age and aging.* Chicago: University of Chicago Press.

Neugarten, B. 1976. Adaptation and the life cycle. *The Counseling Psychologist 6*: 16–20. https://doi.org/10.1177/001100007600600104

Nsamenang, B. 2005. Human ontogenesis: an indigenous African view on development and intelligence. *International Journal of Psychology*: 1–5. https://doi.org/10.1080/00207590544000077

Oakley, A. 1972. *Sex, gender and society.* Melbourne: Sun Books.

Packenham, M., Shute, R. and Reid, R. 2004. A truncated functional behavioral assessment procedure for children with disruptive classroom behaviours. *Education and Treatment of Children 27*: 9–25. www.jstor.org/stable/42899832

Peirce, C. S. 1958. The fixation of belief. In P. P. Wiener (ed), *Charles S. Peirce: selected writings*. New York: Dover Publications, 91–112.

Pepper, S. 1942. *World hypotheses: a study of evidence*. Berkeley: University of California.

Polger, T. W. 2012. Functionalism as a philosophical theory of the cognitive sciences. *Wiley Interdisciplinary Reviews: Cognitive Science 3*(3): 337–48.

Proctor, R. W. and Warren, A. D. 2024. Mechanism and contextualism in psychology. *Theory & Psychology 34*(3): 328–46. https://doi.org/10.1177/09593543241234654

Rosnow, R. L. and Georgoudi, M. (eds). 1986. *Contextualism and understanding in behavioral science: implications for research and theory*. New York: Praeger.

Sanson, A. and Wise, S. 2001. Children and parenting: the past hundred years. *Family Matters 60*: 36–45.

Schutz, A. 2001. John Dewey's conundrum. Can democratic schools empower? *Teachers College Record 103*: 267–302. https://doi.org/10.1111/0161-4681.00116

Sheehy, G. 1976. *Passages*. New York: Dutton & Co.

Slee, P. T, Campbell, M. and Spears, B. 2012. *Child, adolescent and family development*. Third edn. Melbourne: Cambridge University Press.

Slezak, M. and Davis, J. 2023. Ditching school to save the planet. *ABC News*, 18 November. www.abc.net.au/news/2023-11-18/climate-change-school-strike-protests-kids-demand-action/103112486

Super, C. M. and Harkness, S. 2003. The metaphors of development. *Human Development 46*: 3–23. https://doi.org/10.1159/000067782

Teo, T. 1997. Developmental psychology and the relevance of a critical metatheoretical reflection. *Human Development 40*: 195–210. https://doi.org/10.1159/000278723

Thayer, H. S. 1968. *Meaning and action: a critical history of pragmatism*. New York: Bobs-Merrill.

Williams, M. K. 2017. John Dewey in the 21st century. *Journal of Inquiry and Action in Education 9*: 91–102. https://files.eric.ed.gov/fulltext/EJ1158258.pdf

Wohlwill, J. F. 1973. *The study of behavioural development*. New York: Academic Press.

Wozniak, R. H. 1995. *Mind and body: Rene Déscartes to William James*. https://archive.org/details/9301710.nlm.nih.gov

10 Systems theories

Introduction

A 'system' can be broadly understood as an integrated whole whose essential properties arise from the relationships amongst the components. The word system is derived from the Greek *sunistánai*, meaning 'to cause to stand together'. Furthermore, systems thinking emphasizes that the properties of the system are properties of the whole which none of the parts possesses. This point takes us back to the early dichotomy between matter and form and Aristotle's belief that all around us is a combination of substance (e.g. matter) and form (e.g. pattern): form is immanent in matter (entirely within it).

There is no specific 'systems theory', but a family of theories that constitutes a very broad field of inquiry (Bausch, 2003; Peters, 2014), with the influence of organicism, Gestaltism and functionalism apparent (see Chapter 5). Ludwig von Bertalanffy's general systems theory (GST) can perhaps be considered to have the status of a fundamental metatheory that encompasses numbers of more specific theories, including various family therapy theories, ecological systems theory, dynamic systems theory, critical state theory and complex adaptive systems theory, all of which can help us to understand vexing problems in the world of today (see Box 10.1).

An important feature of systems theories is their transdisciplinary nature. This is at odds with the tendency towards neatly compartmentalizing the understanding of a phenomenon, instead proposing the necessity of embracing complexity. We begin with a broad description of the nature of systems thinking, placing it in historical context and linking it to other theoretical approaches. This accords with Bertalanffy's comment that, 'In order to evaluate the modern systems approach, it is advisable to look at the systems idea not as an ephemeral fashion or recent technique, but in the context of the history of ideas' (Bertalanffy, 1972: 407). In sum, as noted by David Peters:

> The theories and methods in systems thinking are each designed to address complex problems. They are complex because they involve multiple interacting agents, the context in which they operate keeps changing, because the manner

DOI: 10.4324/9781003567738-10

in which things change do not conform to linear or simple patterns, or because elements within the system are able to learn new things, sometimes creating new patterns as they interact over time.

(Peters, 2014: 2)

BOX 10.1 SYSTEMS THINKING AND 'WICKED' (HARD-TO-TAME) PROBLEMS

Sylvia Grewatsch, Steve Kennedy and Pratima (Tima) Bansal (2023) suggest that we are currently facing global environmental, economic and political challenges which can be described as 'wicked problems' because there is no simple cause or explanation for them. The problems are 'wicked' because of their complexity and interconnectedness, which renders them as not amenable to simple linear solutions. We have suggested the alternative term 'hard-to-tame' problems as some professionals strongly dislike using the word 'wicked', especially in the context of children's problems or disabilities (Shute and Slee, 2016).

Attempts at solutions call upon a more holistic approach frequently involving multiple stakeholders and an interdisciplinary outlook whilst appreciating that a systems outlook may be the way forward. As Grewatsch and colleagues note, 'The frequency and intensity of wicked problems are rising, as digital technologies and the mobility of people and things make the world increasingly interconnected and complex' (Grewatsch *et al.*, 2023: 722). Richard Beinecke (2016) has described the development of the phrase 'wicked problems', alerting us to the issue as it applies to school mental health programs. David Armstrong has applied the concept to the field of special education, arguing that this 'focus can stimulate innovations necessary for educational change and begin the process through which key problems in the field are addressed' (Armstrong, 2017: 229).

Early systems thinking

Systems thinking has been informed by a long and distinguished group of philosophers, writers and scientists. The early Greek philosopher Hesiod, writing in the *Theogony*, spoke strongly to the idea of order, and the world for Hesiod was an interconnected place:

> From Chaos came forth Erebus and black Night; but of Night were born Aether and Day, whom she conceived and bare from union in love with Erebus. And Earth first bare starry Heaven, equal to herself, to cover her on every side, and to be an ever-sure abiding-place for the blessed gods. And she brought forth long Hills, graceful haunts of the goddess-Nymphs who dwell amongst the glens of

> the hills. She bare also the fruitless deep with his raging swell, Pontus, without sweet union of love. But afterwards she lay with Heaven and bare deep-swirling Oceanus.
>
> *(Trans. Evelyn-White, 1914)*

Somewhat later in the era of classical Greece, Aristotle alerted us to the purpose of all things. The son of a physician to the Macedonian court, Aristotle too had a long association there and tutored Alexander the Great. Aristotle's interest in biology led him to advance the notion that all living things exist for a reason and have a purpose (*telos*) or direction to their life. His dictum that the 'whole is more than the sum of its parts' (*Metaphysica 10f-1045a*) is well-known and serves to highlight, by contrast, the reductionism inherent in behavioural approaches to psychology.

Stoicism added yet another dimension. The name is taken from the porch (*stoa poikilê*) in the Agora at Athens where the first generation of Stoic philosophers met and lectured. Roman stoicism (developed from earlier Greek thinking), informed by the views of Seneca, Epictetus and Marcus Aurelius, highlighted the need to live according to our ideals rather than reflect upon them. Stoic epistemology rejected reductionist thinking that focused on a single part of nature and instead emphasized the interconnected nature of things and the need for overarching 'cataleptic impression' (knowledge about the world arising from the gathering together of perceptions, memories and experiences).

Systems thinking also resonates with Indigenous worldviews that all things are interconnected, and the individual is not at the centre of matters. For example, in accord with the Māori worldview Ihirangi Heke and colleagues (2018) used systemic causal loop diagrams to develop a tool for Māori communities to apply to preventative health initiatives, as did Jennifer Browne and colleagues with Australian Aboriginal people: 'While systems science is relatively new in the Western world, elements of systems thinking have been strongly present in Aboriginal communities for thousands of years' (Browne *et al.*, 2021: 2).

General systems theory

It was Austrian-born Bertalanffy (1901–1972) who proposed the seminal idea of *Allgemeine Systemlehre* (general theory of systems, i.e. general systems theory—GST). In his early publication he argued that systems thinking was an alternative model to that of the prevailing positivist mechanistic view. Although a biologist, he was no stranger to psychology, counting among his close friends the developmental psychologist Charlotte Bühler (Weckowicz, 2000). In the 1930s he wrote that:

> Since the fundamental character of the living thing is its organization, the customary investigation of the single parts and processes cannot provide a complete explanation of the vital phenomena. This investigation gives us no information about the coordination of parts and processes. Thus the chief task of biology must be to discover the laws of biological systems (at all levels of organization).
>
> *(Bertalanffy and Woodger, 1933: 64)*

His writings as part of the famous Vienna Circle of philosophers proposed that understanding the biological nature of things necessitated new ways of thinking that went beyond the traditional methods of science that were dominated by a mechanistic view. The notion of entropy (running to disorder) was sharply at odds with the evolutionary view that the living universe was in fact evolving from disorder to increasing levels of complexity. To resolve this impasse Bertalanffy proposed the idea of 'open systems' in which entropy may not apply. He noted that:

> The 19th and first half of the 20th century conceived of the *world as chaos*. Chaos was the oft-quoted blind play of atoms, which, in mechanistic and positivistic philosophy, appeared to represent ultimate reality, with life as an accidental product of physical processes, and mind as an epi-phenomenon. It was chaos when, in the current theory of evolution, the living world appeared as a product of chance, the outcome of random mutations and survival in the mill of natural selection. In the same sense, human personality, in the theories of behaviorism as well as of psychoanalysis, was considered a chance product of nature and nurture, of a mixture of genes and an accidental sequence of events from early childhood to maturity.
>
> *(Bertalanffy, as quoted in Lilienfeld, 1978: 7–8)*

A number of characteristics of GST provide an understanding of the underlying principles:

- *Natural systems*. A natural system is one that has emerged over time, has not degraded and has been able to reorganize itself and manage challenges to its integrity.
- *Reduction to dynamics vs reduction to components*. Scientists typically attempt to understand complex systems by reducing them to their components and understanding their interrelationships. This contrasts with the reduction to dynamics where the attempt is to understand how a system reacts when it is exposed to a complex set of influences.
- *Emergent properties*. An emergent property becomes apparent only when its components are assembled. Emergence ceases when the component is removed from the system—e.g. an eye ceases to 'see' when removed from the body.

In further writings Bertalanffy suggested that some of the problems in implementing GST would be answered more fully in the future in four ways:

- With the application of dynamic systems theory and control theory to GST (1968).
- Through development of a mathematics of systems theory which could further expand explanations and understanding of processes of change within systems (1972).

- With increased understanding of the development and function of the brain and nervous system which Bertalanffy held would be the key to understanding individual humans as systems (1968).
- With recognition that GST would provide a basis for unity in science.

Ilya Prigogine (1917–2003)

This Moscow-born Belgian chemist was an important contributor to the development of systems thinking. Winning the 1997 Nobel Prize, his research into dissipative structures arising out of the nonlinear processes in nonequilibrium systems provided a comprehensive theory of change. The theory (Prigogine and Stengers, 1984) is underpinned by several key concepts:

1. *Systems and sub-systems*. All systems are composed of sub-systems which are in a continual state of fluctuation or change, which may not be reversible. At any one time the fluctuation may be so strong as to shatter the pre-existing order.
2. *Chaos and order*. At any 'singular moment' or 'bifurcation' the system may descend into 'chaos' or transcend to a higher level of organization or 'order', known as a 'dissipative structure' because it requires more energy to sustain it than the previous structure.
3. *Equilibrium*. In Newtonian thermodynamics all systems run down to disorder with energy dissipating over time. In the natural world, many systems are 'open', exchanging energy, matter or information with the environment. Prigogine discovered that entropy in a chemical system could be prevented by introducing energy into the system. Prigogine argued that a deterministic approach to unstable systems is not possible, and that prediction can only be made in terms of probabilities, not absolutes.

Gregory Bateson (1904–1980) and family systems

The ideas of English anthropologist Bateson were influential in emerging thinking about constructivism (see Chapter 6), and extended systems thinking to social phenomena in researching 'schizophrenic families'. This he did in association with the informal Californian 'Palo Alto group' of researchers and clinicians, for almost a decade from 1951. Adopting many of the ideas associated with GST, they identified several characteristics of families:

- Families are systems, having properties that are more than the sum of the properties of their parts.
- Families are open systems, which nonetheless are governed by rules.
- A family is a cybernetic system incorporating the important notion of feedback to family members.

Bateson and colleagues identified a feature of 'schizophrenic families' they called 'the double bind'. They argued that schizophrenia was not a disturbance within the individual, but a result of interactions and feedback loops. He provided the following example, of a son receiving contradictory messages from his mother:

> A young man who had fairly well recovered from an acute schizophrenic episode was visited in the hospital by his mother. He was glad to see her and impulsively put his arm around her shoulders, whereupon she stiffened. He withdrew his arm and she asked 'Don't you love me any more?' He then blushed, and she said, 'Dear, you must not be so easily embarrassed and afraid of your feelings'. The patient was able to stay with her only a few minutes more and following her departure he assaulted an aide and was put in the tubs.[1]
>
> *(Bateson, 1972: 217)*

Double-bind theory has not been extensively researched, and today schizophrenia is considered to have more complex causation (and in any case, Bateson may often have been dealing with patients who would later be more appropriately considered to have war-induced post-traumatic stress disorder). Nevertheless, his ideas were taken up strongly in the field of family counselling. 'The family could now be described as a system that had characteristics and organizing principles that were independent of the psychic structures of the individuals comprising the family' (Goolishian and Anderson, 1987: 529). The same principles can be applied to schools; Box 10.2 explains how a systemic approach can be applied to school bullying.

BOX 10.2 THE APPLICATION OF SYSTEMS THINKING TO SCHOOL BULLYING

Viewing bullying as 'collective in its nature, based on social relationships in the group' (Sutton, Smith and Swettenham, 1999: 97), one can apply many of the principles of systemic thinking. Thus, it can be argued that bullying is not a problem located solely within a particular individual (Pepler, 2006; Schott and Søndergaard, 2014; Slee and Shute, 2025). Conventional western mechanistic and causal ways of thinking direct us to search for the faulty or broken part—or problematic individual—in order to fix the 'problem'. Schools are, however, also based around systems, and systems within systems (e.g. community, home, school, year level, classroom and peer groups). The various systems interact, and within the systems individuals are viewed as active agents in construing their own world. From a systemic perspective, people are viewed in terms of their relationships with one another, rather than simply being understood principally on the basis of their individual development. A child's misconduct in school (e.g. bullying others) is understood to serve some purpose within the system or to reflect something about the system itself. The behaviour is not just the result of some inner psychic disturbance or carried out for some reward. The student's behaviour is, in a sense, a window through which we can look to understand their place in the system, and provides an important insight into the various roles and relationships within the system.

Bateson further contributed a number of concepts to contemporary systems thinking. One was that communication can occur across different levels, and that unhealthy communication often involves this, as in the double-bind example. Also, with a consuming interest in biology as well as human behaviour, Bateson wrote about connecting patterns. 'What pattern connects the crab to the lobster and the orchid to the primrose and all four of them to me? And me to you? And all six of us to the amoeba ...?' (Bateson, 1979: 16). He went on to describe the patterns which connect in terms of meta-patterns—patterns of patterns.

One line of family counselling based on Batesonian ideas was developed by the 'Milan Group' of psychologists, in their work with the families of people with anorexia nervosa (Selvini-Palazzoli *et al.*, 1978). In Adelaide, South Australia, the family counsellor Michael White, in the 1980s, developed an influential narrative approach to family therapy based on a unique blend of ideas drawn from Batesonian theory. Essentially the emphasis in narrative therapy is on the individual's (or family's) 'lived experience' and the meaning that is attached to it. The important point here is that the 'meaning' becomes 'the problem', rather than the person (or family), a procedure known as 'externalizing'. Author PTS worked for a year in the Calgary Family Therapy Centre (University of Calgary) which employed family systems thinking strongly influenced by Michael White's therapeutic approach. Box 10.3 gives a case example. David Denborough (2009) has outlined the legacy of Michael White to the field of family therapy.

BOX 10.3 A NARRATIVE THERAPY CASE

Author PTS reports this case study. A primary school age child was referred by his general practitioner for treatment for his anger and aggression as he had been suspended from school. His clinical notes indicated a history of physical assaults on his classmates and occasionally his teachers. The therapeutic team saw him and his family and worked to externalize his anger and aggression, giving a form and substance to 'Mr Angry'. Working across the school, classroom and family systems over a number of months he learned to not invite Mr Angry into his life and a graduated program was developed to overturn his school suspension. His parents and siblings became better at recognizing when he did not let Mr Angry into his life when faced with some frustration and were better able to point this positive development out to him. In follow-up visits his successes were celebrated and his set-backs were reflected upon as he learned how 'sneaky' and 'cunning' Mr Angry could be.

Patricia Minuchin (1985: 289) noted commonalities between family counselling and developmental psychology: 'Both disciplines regard the family as a primary focus for understanding human behavior and must find some way of conceptualizing the relationship between the family and the individual.' She went on to observe:

> Family therapy is based on systems theory. Although the field is characterized by theoretical argument and a diversity of alternative techniques for creating change the systems view of human functioning is well established. It shapes the nature of clinical work and generates data about children and families from a different perspective than that of developmental psychologists.
>
> *(Minuchin, 1985: 289)*

She summarized the principles of systems theory that are also relevant to developmental psychology:

- A system (e.g. a family) is an organized whole with each part of the system interdependent with the other parts.
- Patterns are circular, not linear. That is, the basic unit is the cycle of interaction, not a search for causation.
- A system has some stability of patterns.
- Evolution and change are a part of open systems whereby information is exchanged.
- Complex systems are made up of sub-systems, e.g. mother–father, child–child.
- There are boundaries between sub-systems.

From a systems perspective the individual is an interdependent, contributing part of the system that controls their behaviour. The emphasis is on studying the functioning of the individual as part of the system rather than on internal or intrapsychic processes. Such an approach emphasizes understanding the individual's functioning within context (Minuchin, 1985).

More recently Carolina Tinajero and Fernanda Páramo, in referring to systems thinking, have argued, perhaps somewhat optimistically, that '[d]evelopmental psychology seems to have come to an [sic] unifying theoretical framework which may make feasible to overcome the fragmentation so frequently referred to within the discipline' (Tinajero and Páramo, 2012: 457). They note that in the systemic outlook the emphasis is upon context, a matter highlighted by Urie Bronfenbrenner.

Urie Bronfenbrenner (1917–2005) and ecological systems theory

In the early 1970s Ann Oakley noted that 'the emphasis on childhood as an individual process unfolded from within has tended to neglect the impact on children and childhood of social and cultural contexts' (Oakley, 1972: 22). Socioecological models were introduced to urban studies by sociologists associated with the 'Chicago School' after the First World War, as a reaction to the narrow scope of most research conducted by developmental psychologists. Members of this School included the philosopher George Herbert Mead, with later writing and thinking associated with symbolic interactionists such as Herbert Blumer. Social ecology pays explicit attention to the social, institutional and cultural contexts of people–environment relationships, and these considerations lie at the heart of Bronfenbrenner's theorizing.

Bronfenbrenner's childhood move from the newly formed Soviet Union to the United States gave him his appreciation of how different environmental contexts affect children's development, and in 1970 he published *Two Worlds of Childhood: U.S. and U.S.S.R.* Later, in *The Ecology of Human Development* (1979) he proposed that:

> The ecology of human development involves the scientific study of the progressive mutual accommodation between an active, growing human being and the changing properties of the immediate settings in which the developing person lives, as this process is affected by relations between these settings, and by the larger contexts in which the settings are embedded.
>
> *(Bronfenbrenner, 1979: 21)*

These settings and contexts are as follows.

- *Microsystem*. This is made up of the individual characteristics of the child and the various settings within which the child is embedded, such as family, school and neighbourhood.
- *Mesosystem*. Here the focus is on the interrelationships between elements of the microsystem and contexts, for example, how a family responds to the school system and their experiences with it.
- *Exosystem*. Elements of the exosystem do not impinge on the child directly but influence the child through one of the microsystems.
- *Macrosystem*. This is composed of settings that refer to the much larger cultural or sub-cultural environment in which the child lives, and refers to the values and mores which are part of the broader environment.
- *Chronosystem*. Across the lifespan, how do events such as parental divorce or separation impact on the way a child develops?

Two important features of Bronfenbrenner's theory need to be taken into account in any evaluation or application. First, the foregoing description and images of the theory in the form of concentric circles is commonly taken to represent the child as a rather passive organism shaped and moulded by the environment, underplaying the dynamic, systemic interrelationships between the child and their contexts (for example, the child's seeking of ecological niches) that reflected Bronfenbrenner's view. Second, and very importantly, Bronfenbrenner later broadened his theory to be inclusive of biological aspects of development and to give more emphasis to the chronosystem (Bronfenbrenner and Morris, 1998). This version is more explicitly dynamic and even more holistic than the original theory, and so we will discuss it further in considering theoretical integration in Chapter 15, as well as exemplifying its application to sex/gender development in Chapter 12.

Bronfenbrenner regarded his theory as suitable for research in 'discovery mode' rather than 'verification mode', with propositions for testing being drawn (at least initially) more from theory than from research findings. This implies that one should be less concerned about falsely claiming to have found an effect (Type I error) than overlooking a 'real' effect (Type II error), since even a marginal finding may in fact be a useful pointer towards new discoveries. This is especially important given that, in development, small initial influences may become magnified over time (sequential amplification) and, ultimately, powerful predictors of outcome, as we saw in considering developmental cascades. Thus, as with systems approaches in general, Bronfenbrenner's theory challenges traditional hypothesis-testing and the use of linear statistics in developmental psychology, and critiques of his theory often refer to the difficulty of empirically testing his ideas. Systems-friendly methods do exist and we have discussed them elsewhere (Shute and Slee, 2022).

A shortcoming of his theory is that 'the precise relationships of systems to one another remain elusive' (Neal and Neal, 2013: 723). Jennifer Watling Neal and Zachary Neal maintain that the typical depiction of his theory disguises the fact that the various contexts actually overlap and network with each other. They draw attention to the work of Georg Simmel (1858–1918) on social networks, which held that the circles should be juxtaposed, not concentric. The Neals' re-theorizing of ecological systems theory turns the settings on their head, defining them in terms of interacting relationships rather than spatial features. This formulation, they argue, has the potential to better guide research based on ecological systems theory, by enabling improved operationalization and measurement, through the use of social networking methodology.

This relationships-based approach has something in common with 'social systems theory' as advanced by Niklas Luhmann (1997). This emphasizes that the basic element of all social systems is *communication*, or the synthesis of utterance (including physical movements as well as speech or writing), information and understanding. Communication is a social (and, as proposed by Luhmann, the only genuinely social) operation, which cannot be causally reduced to individual action. Social systems for Luhmann are not, therefore, systems of action, structured in terms of the thoughts and behaviours of individual actors, but systems of communications in which the communications themselves determine what further communications occur.

Bronfenbrenner's 1979 book is highly cited and his work continues to have great influence. For example, his theory has been applied to assist social workers in the United States to provide for the healthy development of children from immigrant families (Paat, 2013). One of his lasting contributions was as a founder of the US-wide *Head Start* program, aimed at supporting the development of preschool children from low-income families. The program has prepared millions of children for kindergarten and supported the development of those from the poorest families, especially in rural areas, yet in 2025 the incoming federal administration immediately froze its funding, sacked staff and closed several regional offices (Peeks and

Schneider, 2025). As we write, the *Head Start* system is reportedly in chaos (ironic in the present context!) and there are fears that defunding will become permanent.

Esther Thelen (1941–2004) and dynamic systems theory

In the fifth edition of the *Handbook of Child Psychology* edited by William Damon and Richard Lerner, Lerner commented that the focus in theoretical development had become 'a burgeoning interest not in structure, function, or content per se, but in change, in the process through which change occurs, and thus in the means through which structures transform and functions evolve over the course of human life' (Lerner, 1998: 1). This understanding captures the major features of dynamic systems theory (DST).

The founder of DST was Esther Thelen, a US zoologist and professor of psychology. She was described by her colleague Linda Smith as a 'maverick' because she rejected the traditional idea of intelligence in terms of symbolic reasoning, without considering the dynamic role of the physical world. She established a research program on motor development that gave rise to a new theory of child development and promoted the notion of 'embodied cognition' (refer back to Box 8.1) (Smith, 2006). Her theory drew upon the insights provided by systems thinking in a range of scientific disciplines, including Prigogine's and Bertalanffy's work: 'What we invoke here are the principles for the global properties of complex systems' (Thelen and Smith, 1994: 49).

Thelen and Smith aimed to meet six requirements for a developmental theory:

- Biological plausibility.
- To account for the origins of novelty.
- To reconcile global regularities with local variability, complexity and context-specificity.
- To integrate developmental data at many levels of explanation.
- To explain how local processes lead to global outcomes.
- To establish a theoretical basis for generating and interpreting empirical research.

Further:

> [T]he new science that can extract common principles in the behavior of chemical reactions, clouds, forests, and embryos is variously called the study of dynamic, synergetic, dissipative, nonlinear, self-organizing, or chaotic theories. (We adopt here dynamic systems as the descriptor to emphasize that these are systems that change continuously over time).
>
> *(Thelen and Smith, 1994: 50)*

As such, a dynamic system is any system whose behaviour at one point in time depends in some way on its state at an earlier point in time (Elman, 1998) and which therefore emerges from the interplay of many factors over time and is self-organizing (Clarke, 1997). Ideas of nonlinearity may be used to explain how apparently small transformations result in significant changes in the organism. DST shares a common origin with, and is an extension of, GST. Piaget's organismic theory also fits well with this perspective, but Thelen and Smith noted that much research inspired by his theory has been more concerned with structure than process. Other important theories which influenced their work include Edelman's (1992) theory of neuronal group selection and Eleanor Gibson's work in ecological psychology and the notion of affordance (see Chapter 5).

Thelen and Smith (1998) observed that a number of developmentalists including Arnold Sameroff (1983) had recognized the implications of Prigogine's theorizing: 'Adoption of such a systems model, with its assumptions of wholeness, self-stabilization, self-organization, and hierarchical organization, has implications for every aspect of developmental psychology' (Thelen and Smith, 1998: 575). To illustrate this point they cited the need for development to be contextualized, because the concept of open systems necessitates an interchange between the organism and the environment.

Drawing on the writings of numbers of researchers and clinicians such as Paul van Geert (1998), it is possible to identify a number of general assumptions that underpin DST. The first is that development is a transaction between the person and their environment, where the emphasis is on the dynamic interplay between them, producing change in both the individual and the environment.

The second assumption challenges the deterministic assumptions underpinning development, particularly the idea that a single or a few factors shape development. This is replaced with 'the new synthetic concept that unites determinism and indeterminism … the concept of complex order, emerging out of self-organization' (van Geert, 1998: 272).

The third assumption goes to the heart of challenging genetic determination (Pearson, 2006). Research in molecular biology questions the very nature of what we might understand to be a 'gene'. Evelyn Fox-Keller and David Harel (2007: 1) believed that 'the concept of the gene has begun to outlive its usefulness. Among the reasons generally given is the great difficulty that we encounter today in trying to reach any sort of consensus about what a gene actually is'. The suggestion is that in looking at a DNA sequence there is no locatable gene but rather a series of protein chains which, while separated spatially, operate in concert with the rest of the cell chemistry to influence development (Clarke, 1997). Nevertheless, the concept of 'the gene' does live on, but changes as knowledge increases (Portin and Wilkins, 2017).

The fourth assumption is that dynamic systems are seen as having properties of self-organization, resulting from the transactions within the system. As such, there is no one driving external factor or combination of factors that shapes development. To illustrate, early understandings of how infants learn to walk generally concluded that it was the result of the maturation of the nervous system. DST shed new light onto the process, emphasizing that, rather than the nervous system instructing the muscles in learning to walk, it is the dynamics of the movement of walking which instruct the nervous system.

A fifth assumption is that development, while subject to external and internal constraints, will settle into a preferred state called an 'attractor state', described as a set of physical properties towards which a system is attracted. As described by van Geert (2008), in a self-organizing open system, while a significant range of patterns is possible, the system settles into or prefers only a limited range of behaviours. (This can be linked to Annette Karmiloff-Smith's conceptualization of how brain modules develop—see Chapter 3.)

Thelen and Smith (1994) maintained that the appearance of development as being orderly, progressive, incremental and directional, giving the impression of a predetermined plan, is illusory. For example, the development of infants' ability to walk was long regarded as a series of invariant stages determined by maturation, as described by Arnold Gesell (see Chapter 5); Thelen and Smith presented evidence that, on closer inspection, development is much 'messier' than this, with component processes moving along in fits and starts, and sometimes regressing rather than progressing. On closer investigation, then, the grand plan disappears, as it does also if one examines cognitive development (Spencer, Perone and Buss, 2011). Effectively, group averages mask individual differences which are important for understanding the true nature of development, a point also made by Hinde (1992). Thelen and Smith observed that descriptions of typical developmental stages had become mistaken for explanations.

DST has been widely applied in the field of developmental psychology (Pepler and Craig, 2000; Slee, 2001; Slee and Shute, 2025; Thelen and Smith, 1994, 1998). At its heart DST is a mathematical theory; conventional linear equation modelling does not adequately address the complex and changing patterning of relationships. A number of other 'developmental systems theories' have also been developed, all of which reject the separation of nature from nurture and conceptualize development in terms of a dynamic interaction between multiple factors (Guanghui, 2025). Overall, DST has drawn on a rich and broad history of thought with regard to systems. As Bertalanffy predicted for GST, it has been informed by advances in neuroscience (Slee, Campbell and Spears, 2012); as new breakthroughs occur, the interaction between the brain, developing behaviour and the environment presents new challenges in terms of model building and empirical research. It is here that pivotal concepts of dynamic systems thinking such as self-organization provoke new ways of reasoning about how the growing child develops and changes. We consider further the integrative nature of DST in Chapter 15.

Critical state theory

As we have seen, in adopting systems thinking, developmental psychology has drawn upon insights from other disciplines, such as chemistry and biology. We speculate here that some recent advances in theoretical physics may in the future impinge upon our understanding of human development and behaviour as we increasingly take a systemic approach.

Science is traditionally concerned with predictability of events, yet, as we have seen, Prigogine warned that unstable systems create a difficulty here. Theoretical physicists carried out a wide range of studies during the 1980s and 1990s which showed that many natural events within complex systems are unpredictable (Buchanan, 2000). Catastrophic events such as earthquakes, major forest fires and species extinctions are not events which can be predicted and controlled, although the likelihood of occurrence of a particular-sized event can be calculated mathematically. The larger an event, the less likely it is to happen, but at any time the interacting factors underlying the event may reach a critical state of hidden instability such that an additional, minor change to the system can trigger a catastrophic event (in accord with the notion of emergence). For example, an extensive and intricate pattern of fault lines in the earth's crust may be balanced on the edge of instability, but this only becomes apparent when one small movement of the earth triggers a shift in the entire system; like a house of cards tumbling down as one card is placed slightly carelessly, the result is a massive earthquake.

Evidence is accumulating that these laws of non-equilibrium physics apply not just to events in the physical world, but to human activities such as stock market crashes and world wars. There seems no reason to suppose that these laws might not also apply to aspects of the developing individual, their family or community. Indeed, if we take a broad systemic view of development which includes cultural, historical and even evolutionary change, we can say that there is already strong evidence that development is subject to these influences.

Since we put these ideas forward in the first edition of this book, it has been proposed that critical state theory might be applicable to brain functioning. Gerhard Werner (2009) suggested that, just as cooling water 'suddenly' becomes ice, so abrupt transitions in brain states may occur. Taking the example of consciousness, he observed that a subjective state of awareness may happen suddenly, but the groundwork for it has been laid below the level of consciousness, with processing occurring at different levels of hierarchical organization. He likened activity in widely dispersed areas of the brain to a 'bucket brigade' whereby, if a state transition occurs at one level, the contents of the bucket (neural messages) are passed up to the next level, until a critical state is reached and consciousness emerges. The existence of such processes is consistent with patterns of brain activity found in EEG studies. The well-known 'cocktail party effect' perhaps affords an example here, whereby an overheard mention of one's name pops into consciousness out of an undifferentiated background hum of voices. Werner cited vision research that similarly suggests that activity in widely dispersed parts of the brain comes together to produce a response that takes account of the needs, goals and history of the whole system. Such an approach, combined with the principles of DST and an increasing understanding of epigenetics, holds considerable promise for our understanding of neural development and functioning. One suggestion is that the brain may operate at a level of near-criticality which, if it tips into disorder, represents mental illness (O'Byrne and Jerbi, 2022); in regarding this as a computational matter relevant for biological and artificial neural networks, these authors adopt a mechanistic perspective.

Complex adaptive systems

'Complex adaptive systems' (CAS) is a term that is increasingly used today as an umbrella term for a range of theories. CAS adopts the fundamental principles of systems theorizing that we have outlined, but the terminology draws attention to the adaptive potential of a system. A typical example is how certain ant colonies function to achieve an end that individual ants cannot, such as forming a bridge to cross a patch of water, the bridge being an emergent property at the macroscopic, or system, level. There can also be adaptation at the agent level. Agents in a system need to be relatively similar in order for a system to self-organize, as when a flow of traffic slows and speeds up in a wave-like manner; if a driver behaves too differently, such as failing to slow down in a way that correlates with other drivers, the result will be disruption to the emergent flow pattern, such as a crash. However, agents also need to have a degree of capacity to change if they are to individually adapt to ongoing changes in the system (Carmichael and Hadžikadić, 2019). These authors regard the terms learning, adaptation and evolution as essentially similar processes, though with learning as faster and easier and evolution as on a longer timescale and more permanent.

We have discussed CAS in relation to schools and bullying (Shute and Slee, 2022; Slee and Shute, 2025). Computer simulations with a few basic rules for agents have demonstrated emergent properties such as group 'bullying' (Mudrak and Kumar Semwal, 2015). Schools, education and educational psychology have also been described in CAS terms (Hilpert and Marchand, 2018; Jacobson, Levin and Kapur, 2019), and CAS theory applied to understand the sequence of events that determined whether a school-based health program was implemented as intended or went off the rails (Evans, Murphy and Scourfield, 2015). CAS has also been used to aid understanding of efforts to apply knowledge of early childhood development to the scaling-up of early childhood programs to a national level in several countries (Pérez-Escamilla *et al.*, 2018). Since outcomes of CAS cannot be known with certainty, this field has been called 'the Science of Surprise' (Carmichael and Hadžikadić, 2019). It is, at heart, an endeavour that cuts across disciplines and encourages new types of interdisciplinary collaboration (see Box 10.4)

BOX 10.4 21ST-CENTURY CHALLENGES FOR DEVELOPMENTAL PSYCHOLOGY

The following extract comes from a section of a textbook headed 'The emerging challenge to causal thinking'.

> All the sciences of Western industrialized society are based on a traditional mode of thought that can be traced back to Aristotle, at least, but was codified and established within the scientific enterprises of the seventeenth, eighteenth and nineteenth centuries. … This mode of thinking, amounting to a world-view, an article of faith in the way the world works, assumes direct linearity in causation. … Whether from the perspective of 'normal' science or the new sciences of complexity, the advantages of multidisciplinary studies of complex systems are impressive. The compartmentalized disciplines of modern science have each special strengths for investigating a circumscribed range of phenomena. None can exhaust the complexities of any aspect of the world, but each can specify the likely states of some variables, and the relationships between variables within parts of a given system.
>
> *(Dincauze, 2000: 35)*

After reading the present chapter, these ideas should sound familiar. However, this passage comes not from a developmental psychology text, but from a book on environmental archaeology. Issues concerning systems, complexity and the value of multidisciplinary collaboration have come to the forefront in many sciences concerned with change, such as meteorology, geology and epidemiology. In these respects, developmental psychology may find that it has more in common with these sciences than with other fields of psychology.

Conclusions

We have suggested that general systems theory constitutes a metatheory, the principles of which are drawn upon by a range of other theories, including family therapies, ecological systems theory, dynamic systems theory, critical state theory and complex adaptive systems. Model building and empirical research in this field is a dynamic and ongoing process and we have attempted to capture some of the vibrancy of current developments. Systems thinking provides a challenge to the positivism of traditional developmental psychology, but there is now an established strong focus on the application of systems theories to the study of children, the family and schools.

Systems thinking is best viewed in the context of the history of ideas. It became influential in various fields in the middle of the 20th century. While systems thinking shares with organicism a view of the individual as an active participant in their own development, it overcomes some limitations of organismic theories by detailing the processes of change and the complexity and diversity of the development of individuals and their communities. This focus on complexity, change and plasticity has moved developmental science beyond dualistic debates such as 'nature versus nurture' (Lerner, 2012). Systems thinking has also given a new prominence to the role of culture in human development, as no longer a mere backdrop, but as *part of the very fabric of human development*, operating in a co-constructive fashion. Systems thinking has also played a part in promoting the idea of embodied cognition—that cognition is not a brain-only phenomenon, but extends into the body and beyond into the technological and cultural worlds of the individual (Overton, 2013).

Note

1 Placing agitated psychiatric patients in a bath to calm them was once common practice.

References

Armstrong, D. 2017. Wicked problems in special and inclusive education. *Journal of Research in Special Educational Needs 17*(4): 229–36. https://doi.org/10.1111/1471-3802.12402

Bateson, G. 1972. *Steps to an ecology of mind*. London: Ronald Press Ballantine.

Bateson, G. 1979. *Mind and nature*. np: Flamingo.

Bausch, K. C. 2003. *The emerging consensus in social systems theory*. New York: Kluwer Academic Publishers.

Beinecke, R. H. 2016. Leadership for 'wicked' school mental health problems. In R. H. Shute and P. T. Slee (eds), *Mental health and wellbeing through schools*. London: Routledge, 15–26.

Bertalanffy, L. von. 1968. *General systems theory*. New York: Braziller.

Bertalanffy, L. von. 1972. The history and status of general systems theory. *The Academy of Management Journal 15*(4): 407–26.

Bertalanffy, L. von and Woodger, J. H. 1933. *Modern theories of development: an introduction to modern biology*. London: Oxford University Press.

Bronfenbrenner, U. 1970. *Two worlds of childhood: U.S. and U.S.S.R.* New York: Russell Sage Foundation.

Bronfenbrenner, U. 1979. *The ecology of human development: experiments by nature and design*. Cambridge, MA: Harvard University Press.

Bronfenbrenner, U. and Morris, P. A. 1998. The ecology of developmental processes. In R. M. Lerner (ed.), *Handbook of child psychology: theoretical models of human development*. Fifth edn. Vol. 1. New York: Wiley, 993–1028.

Browne, J., Walker, T., Brown, A., Sherriff, S., Christidis, R., Egan, M. *et al*. 2021. Systems thinking for Aboriginal health: understanding the value and acceptability of group model building approaches. *Population Health 15*: 100874. https://doi.org/10.1016/j.ssmph.2021.100874

Buchanan, M. 2000. *Ubiquity: the science of history or why the world is simpler than we think*. London: Weidenfeld & Nicolson.

Carmichael, T. and Hadžikadić, M. 2019. The fundamentals of Complex Adaptive Systems. In T. Carmichael, A. J. Collins and M. HadHadžikadižikadić (eds), *Complex Adaptive Systems: views from the physical, natural, and social sciences*. np: Springer, 1–16.

Clarke, J. E. 1997. A dynamical systems perspective on the development of complex adaptive skill. In C. Dent-Read and P. Zukow-Goldring (eds), *Evolving explanations of development: ecological approaches to organism-environment systems*. Washington, DC: American Psychological Association, 383–406.

Denborough, D. 2009. Some reflections on the legacies of Michael White: an Australian perspective. *Australian and New Zealand Journal of Family Therapy 30*: 92–108. https://doi.org/10.1375/anft.30.2.92

Dincauze, D. 2000. *Environmental archaeology*. Cambridge: Cambridge University Press.

Edelman, G. M. 1992. *Bright air, brilliant fire: on the matter of the mind*. New York: Basic Books.

Elman, J. L. 1998. Generalization, simple recurrent networks, and the emergence of structure. In *Proceedings of the 20th annual conference of the cognitive science society*. Mahwah: Erlbaum, 6.

Evans, R., Murphy, S. and Scourfield, J. 2015. Implementation of a school-based social and emotional learning intervention: understanding diffusion processes within complex systems. *Prevention Science 16*: 754–64. https://doi.org/10.1007/s11121-015-0552-0

Evelyn-White, H. G. E. 1914. *The theogony of Hesiod*. www.sacred-texts.com/cla/hesiod/theogony.htm

Fox-Keller, E. and Harel, D. 2007. Beyond the gene. *PLoS ONE 2*(11): e1231. https://doi.org/10.1371/journal.pone.0001231

Goolishian, H. and Anderson, H. 1987. Language systems and therapy. *Psychotherapy 4*(35): 529–38.

Grewatsch, S., Kennedy, S. and Bansal, P. 2023. Tackling wicked problems in strategic management with systems thinking. *Strategic Organization 21*(3): 721–32. https://doi.org/10.1177/147612702110386

Guanghui, C. 2025. Developmental systems theory. In Z. Kan (ed.), *The ECPH encyclopedia of psychology*. Singapore: Springer. https://doi.org/10.1007/978-981-97-7874-4_437

Heke, I., Rees, D., Swinburn, B., Waititi, R. T. and Stewart, A. 2018. Systems thinking and indigenous systems: native contributions to obesity prevention. *AlterNative: An International Journal of Indigenous Peoples 15*: 22–30. https://doi.org/10.1177/1177180118806383

Hilpert, J. C. and Marchand, G. C. 2018. Complex systems research in educational psychology: aligning theory and method. *Educational Psychologist 53*(3): 185–202. https://doi.org/10.1080/00461520.2018.1469411

Hinde, R. A. 1992. Developmental psychology in the context of other behavioral sciences. *Developmental Psychology 28*(6): 1018–29. https://psycnet.apa.org/doi/10.1037/0012-1649.28.6.1018

Jacobson, M. J., Levin, J. A. and Kapur, M. 2019. Education as a complex system: conceptual and methodological implications. *Educational Researcher 48*(2): 112–19. https://doi.org/10.3102/0013189X19826958

Lerner, R. M. 1998. Theories of human development: contemporary perspectives. In W. Damon and R. M. Lerner (eds), *Handbook of child psychology*. Vol. 1. Fifth edn. *Theoretical models of human development*. New York: Wiley, 1–24.

Lerner, R. M. 2012. Developmental science: past, present, and future. *International Journal of Developmental Science 6*: 29–36. https://doi.org/10.3233/DEV-2012-1210

Lilienfeld, R. 1978. *The rise of systems theory: an ideological analysis*. New York: Wiley.

Luhmann, N. 1997. *Die Gesellschaft der Cesellschaft*. Frankfurt: Suhrkamp.

Minuchin, P. 1985. Families and individual development: provocations from the field of family therapy. *Child Development 56*: 289–302. www.jstor.org/stable/1129720

Mudrak, G. and Kumar Semwal, S. 2015. Modeling aggression and bullying: a complex systems approach. *Studies in Health Technology and Informatics 219*: 187–91. https://doi.org/https://doi.org/10.3233/978-1-61499-595-1-187

Neal, J. W. and Neal, Z. P. 2013. Nested or networked? Future directions for ecological systems theory. *Social Development 22*(4): 722–737. https://doi.org/10.1111/sode.12018

Oakley, A. 1972. *Sex, gender and society*. Melbourne: Sun Books.

O'Byrne, J. and Jerbi, K. 2022. How critical is brain criticality? *Trends in Neurosciences 45*(11): 820–37. https://doi.org/10.1016/j.tins.2022.08.007

Overton, W. F. 2013. A new paradigm for developmental science: relationism and relational-developmental systems. *Applied Developmental Science 17*(2): 94–107. https://doi.org/10.1080/10888691.2013.778717

Paat, Y.-F. 2013. Working with immigrant children and their families: an application of Bronfenbrenner's ecological systems theory. *Journal of Human Behavior in the Social Environment 23*(8): 954–66. https://doi.org/10.1080/10911359.2013.80 20060007

Pearson, H. 2006. Genetics: what is a gene? *Nature 441*: 398–401. https://doi.org/10.1038/441398a

Peeks, C. and Schneider, A. 2025. 5 things to know about Head Start. *Centre for American Progress Report.* www.americanprogress.org/article/5-things-to-know-about-head-start/

Pepler, D. 2006. Bullying interventions: a binocular perspective. *Journal of the Canadian Academy of Child & Adolescent Psychiatry 15*: 16–20.

Pepler, D. J. and Craig, W. M. 2000. Making a difference in bullying. *LaMarsh Research Report # 60*. Toronto: York University.

Pérez-Escamilla, R., Cavallera, V., Tomlinson, M. and Dua, T. 2018. Scaling up integrated early childhood development programs: lessons from four countries. *Child Care Health and Development 44*: 50–61. https://doi.org/10.1111/cch.12480

Peters, D. H. 2014. The application of systems thinking in health: why use systems thinking? *Health Research Policy and Systems 12*: 1–6.

Portin, P. and Wilkins. A. 2017. The evolving definition of the term 'gene'. *Genetics 205*(4): 1353–64. https://doi.org/10.1534/genetics.116.196956

Prigonine, I. and Stengers, I. 1984. *Order out of chaos*. London: Flamingo.

Sameroff, A. J. 1983. Developmental systems: contexts and evolution. In W. Kessen (ed.), *Handbook of child psychology*. Vol. 1. *History, theory and methods*. New York: Wiley, 237–94.

Schott, R. M. and Søndergaard, D. M. 2014. Introduction: new approaches to school bullying. In R. M. Schott and D. M. Søndergaard (eds), *School bullying: new theories in context*. Cambridge: Cambridge University Press, 1–17.

Selvini-Palazolli, M., Cechin, G., Prata, G. and Boscolo, L. 1978. *Paradox and counter-paradox*. New York: Jason Aronson.

Shute, R. H. and Slee, P. T. 2016. Mental health and wellbeing through schools: thinking big, acting wisely. In R. H. Shute and P. T. Slee (eds), *Mental health and wellbeing through schools: the way forward*. Oxford: Routledge, 185–97.

Shute, R. H. and Slee, P. T. 2022. *School bullying and marginalisation: harmonising paradigms*. Singapore: Springer Nature.

Slee, P. T. 2001. *The P.E.A.C.E. Pack: a program for reducing bullying in our schools*. Adelaide: Flinders University.

Slee, P. T., Campbell, M. and Spears, B. 2012. *Child, adolescent and family development*. Third edn. Melbourne: Cambridge University Press.

Slee, P. T. and Shute, R. H. 2025. The school as a Complex Adaptive System (CAS). In V. Artinopoulou, P. K. Smith, S. P. Limber and K. Breivik (eds), *School bullying and the legacy of Dan Olweus*. np: Wiley, np. https://doi.org/10.1002/9781394173556.ch14

Smith, L. B. 2006. Movement matters: the contributions of Esther Thelen. *Biological Theory* 1: 87–9. https://link.springer.com/content/pdf/10.1162/biot.2006.1.1.87.pdf

Spencer, J. P., Perone, S. and Buss, A. T. 2011. Twenty years and going strong: a dynamic systems revolution in motor and cognitive development. *Child Development Perspectives* *5*(4): 260–6. https://doi.org/10.1111/j.1750-8606.2011.00194.x

Sutton, J., Smith, P. K. and Swettenham, J. 1999. Bullying and 'theory of mind': a critique of the 'social skills deficit' view of anti-social behaviour. *Social Development 8*: 117–27. https://doi.org/10.1111/1467-9507.00083

Thelen, E. and Smith, L. B. 1994. *A dynamic systems approach to the development of cognition and action*. Cambridge, MA: MIT Press.

Thelen, E. and Smith, L. B. 1998. Dynamic systems theories. In W. Damon and R. M. Lerner (eds), *Handbook of child psychology*. Fifth edn. New York: John Wiley and Sons Inc., 563–630.

Tinajero, C., and Páramo, M. F. 2012. The systems approach in developmental psychology: fundamental concepts and principles. *Psicologia: Teoria e Pesquisa 28*: 457–65. https://psycnet.apa.org/doi/10.1590/S0102-37722012000400011

van Geert, P. 1998. A dynamic systems model of basic developmental mechanisms: Piaget, Vygotsky, and beyond. *Psychological Review 105*: 634–77. https://doi.org/10.1037/0033-295X.105.4.634-677

van Geert, P. 2008. The dynamic systems approach in the study of L1 & L2 acquisition: an introduction. *The Modern Language Journal 92*: 179–99. https://doi.org/10.1111/j.1540-4781.2008.00713.x

Weckowicz, T. E. 2000. *Ludwig von Bertalanffy (1901–1972): a pioneer of general systems theory*. University of Alberta Center for Systems Research Working Paper 89-2. www.richardjung.cz/bert1.pdf

Werner, G. 2009. Viewing brain processes as critical state transitions across levels of organization: neural events in cognition and consciousness, and general principles. *Biosystems 96*: 114–19. https://doi.org/10.1016/j.biosystems.2008.11.011

11 Culture in development

Introduction

Anthropologist Margaret Mead's broad definition of culture was 'the whole complex of traditional behavior which has been developed by the human race and is successively learned by each generation' (Mead, 1937/2002: 17). A more recent, fuller version is:

> A group of people who share a set of values, beliefs, and practices; who have access to the same institutions, resources, and technologies; who have a sense of identity of themselves as constituting a group; and who attempt to communicate those values, beliefs, and practices to the following generation.
>
> *(Tudge, 2008: 3–4)*

A culture in developmental psychology is generally defined by national, regional or linguistic boundaries, but may be based on other criteria, such as religion, tribe or sexuality (e.g. queer cultures). Moreover, cultures change, necessitating a historical perspective. We may be unable to 'see' our own culture at all without exposure to others (Rogoff, 2001). Or, we may become more aware of it as contexts change, as illustrated by the words on a coffee mug belonging to a scientist's mother: 'I never think about being Jewish until I leave New York' (Smaldino, 2019: 108).

It has become a truism that most developmental psychology research has been with WEIRD (western, educated, industrialized, rich and democratic) samples, neglecting the majority of the world's children, as exemplified in Chapter 1 (Box 1.1). Although lamented from the early 1990s (Tudge and Freitas, 2012), little changed until recently. While the Anglosphere remains predominant, some highly influential theorists, such as Sigmund Freud, Jean Piaget and Lev Vygotsky, came from the non-English-speaking world, though it is through translations into English that their ideas became incorporated into mainstream developmental theorizing.

Pioneering African psychologist Bame Nsamenang pointed out that western writings have often applied a particular value system that prizes above all individualism and cognitive competence, implying that alternative notions of childhood are faulty (Nsamenang, 1995, 2005). This places traditional models and methods of developmental psychology at odds with the interdependence that is central to most

DOI: 10.4324/9781003567738-11

cultures, and neglects socioemotional development in favour of rational thought. One example of the inappropriate application of western-biased theories to a different culture is Lindy Wilbraham's trenchant critique of a South African textbook that followed the North American model: it treated AIDS-orphans through attachment theory, neglecting the adaptations made by child-led households. The orphans were seen as 'dangerously adrift after cataclysmic loss of a Western nuclear family ideal of unconditional nurturance of their innocence and potential; and furthermore, that the Government should "do something"' (Wilbraham, 2005: 74).

A distinction is often made between *etic* and *emic* cultural research (Helfrich, 1999). Etic research is cross-cultural and aims to elucidate general principles of behaviour or development, taking an outsider's perspective, and is generally quantitative. Emic research seeks an insider's perspective within a single culture or subculture, looking in depth at social meanings using qualitative methods. A useful mnemonic is that eTic is like a Telescope, looking from a distance, while eMic is like a Microscope, looking in close detail.

There has been a recent shift from 'cross-cultural' (etic) towards 'cultural' (emic) developmental psychology, largely under Vygotsky's influence, with a growing emphasis on Indigenous psychologies (plural), with some calling, further, for the 'decolonization' of developmental psychology. It seems, therefore, that when one tries seriously to address questions about culture and development, matters of philosophy, epistemology, ethics and politics inevitably arise (and sometimes clash!).

Early work on culture and development

First and foremost, Vygotsky is due credit for his seminal theorizing about cognitive development. For him, this was inseparable from the influence of more experienced members of the culture. The Vygotskian recognition of the importance of learning from others, and the co-construction of learning/development within the zone of proximal development (ZPD), is illustrated in Box 11.1.

BOX 11.1 LEARNING FROM ELDERS

Within New Zealand's Māori context, the teacher-pupil relationship is an intimate one based on high expectation with both the more learned and the learner working together on a set task. For example, a grandmother teaching her grand-daughter(s) about the mythology and art of finger weaving. … The pupil(s) and the teacher are in a position jointly to evaluate the ongoing process and development of their efforts. When the pupil proves that she has learned the necessary skills, knowledge and understanding to perform the task on her own, both teacher and pupil are then ready to move on to another task.

(Pere, 1982: 67)

Vygotsky theorized that the interpersonal becomes the intrapersonal, so that the way a person thinks is inculcated through (largely) linguistic interaction with others and is culturally determined. That cultural differences can operate even at the perceptual level was brought home to him when he discovered that, in Uzbekistan, visual illusions which fooled city folk did not work. One of the present authors once heard a non-Indigenous Australian woman interviewed about her time with a particular Australian Aboriginal group; she had abandoned her struggles to learn their language, because everything had to be contextualized in terms of 'where-I-am-in-the-journey-of-the-day', a way of thinking she found simply too alien.

Despite the overwhelming bias towards US samples and values, it is nevertheless the case that some very influential work recognizing the role of culture emerged from there, notably from individuals with strong overseas links. One was Margaret Mead, and another was Erik Erikson, who was born in 1902 in Germany of Dutch parents, and moved to the United States as an adult. He was influenced by Mead and by Freud (undergoing psychoanalysis with Freud's daughter, Anna). In his book *Childhood and Society* (1950), he described his work with the Sioux and Yurok, Indigenous peoples of North America. In contrast to then typical western approaches to Indigenous peoples as primitive or infantile, he recognized that they had their own ways of dealing with the world and raising children. He saw stages of development as marked by the resolution of normative crises resulting from the interaction between the biological plan for the species and the cultural environment.

Urie Bronfenbrenner, too, included culture as an overarching influence on development. His 1970 account of the importance of peers in the United States and Russia was greeted with great interest, although the same point had been made by cross-cultural psychologists, but gone unrecognized, for the previous 30 years (Ritchie and Ritchie, 1979). Later (in 1990) when Richard Shweder claimed to have started a new field called 'cultural psychology', M. H. Segall said this was like an explorer to Africa 'discovering' a lake and calling it Lake Rudolf, with no recognition that it had already been known to the local people (the Turkana) for centuries (Dasen, 2022).[1]

In contrast to Vygotsky's theory that culture is integral to development, researchers often saw sociocultural variables as something to be *controlled* to enable 'pure process' to be observed. A conceptual shift became apparent, however, towards seeing social environmental variables as something to be *studied* to understand development, as acknowledged by the later versions of Bronfenbrenner's theory:

> [I]t made no sense at all to control for ethnicity, social class, or household composition in an attempt to produce 'pure' process. No process occurs outside of a context. And if we want to understand context, we need to take it into account, not pretend to control it away.
>
> *(Steinberg et al., 1995, cited in Bronfenbrenner and Morris, 1998: 1016)*

Like Bronfenbrenner, dialectical psychologist Klaus Riegel developed his theory in the United States in the 1970s. Influenced by the Soviet-based work of Sergei Rubinstein, he maintained that it was inappropriate to focus on the isolated individual, who can only be understood in relation to historical and societal changes regarding issues such as demography, political structures and majority–minority group relations. Thus, the individual does not just exist within the boundaries of the body, but within a 'psychological space' that encompasses interactions with family, friends and the broader culture (Meacham, 1999).

In a similar vein, Joan Miller (1999) distinguished between ecological (etic) perspectives and the emic approach of cultural psychology, which is concerned with shared meaning systems, so that psychological notions such as 'mind', 'self' and 'emotion' are themselves culturally created and understood. Cultural practices are not all adaptive, but may be nonrational, such as when people refuse to eat certain edible animals for cultural reasons.

As noted in Chapter 3, culture itself can be seen as subject to evolutionary selection processes, rather than viewing humans as 'biologically complete hominids' who 'suddenly invented culture' (Miller, 1999: 87). So, apart from some innate propensities in infancy and some involuntary responses, development must, then, occur within a cultural setting for most psychological processes to develop. This more radical approach owes much to the views of the dialectical psychologists and presents a major challenge to Piagetian theory. Miller also pointed out the need to recognize that all research findings are dependent upon the underlying constructs, which may be culture specific. She suggested that cultural psychology may be best seen not as a separate area of inquiry, but as a perspective that can inform whatever psychological issue is under consideration. Even more strongly, Pierre Dasen, in discussing cognitive development, suggests that 'a profound ethnographic understanding is even the required basis for a good study' (Dasen, 2022: 790).

Wilhelmina Drummond (unpublished, 1990s) described three cultural models of human development. Interestingly, she took Bronfenbrenner's ecological theory as an example of a western model, though it was clearly atypical in explicitly setting out to be cross-culturally applicable. The systemic nature of Bronfenbrenner's model, with its dynamically interacting levels of analysis, has parallels with another model described by Drummond, specific to the Māori people of Aotearoa/New Zealand and developed by Pere (Figure 11.1) (also see Ministry of Health New Zealand, 2024). This is based on *Te Wheke*, or The Octopus, with tentacles representing various aspects of Māori life such as spirituality and *Mauri* (life principle), which includes respect for the environment. The intertwining tentacles represent connections between the various aspects, and the mutual reliance of the parts on one another is reminiscent of complex systems theory.

A major difference exists, however, between the Bronfenbrenner and Māori models: Bronfenbrenner places the individual centrally, whereas the Octopus's head represents the family unit. Factors unique to the individual are within a single tentacle; while inseparable from, and sharing sustenance with, the whole, the

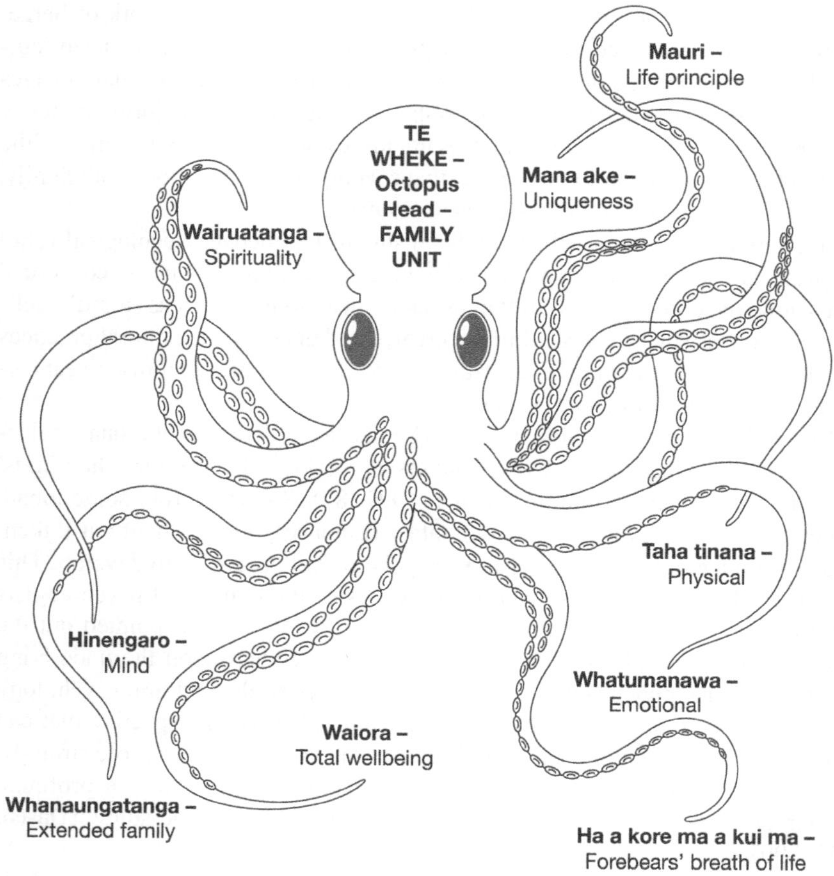

Figure 11.1 Te Wheke – the Octopus

individual is not central. By comparison, Bronfenbrenner's model still bears the hallmarks of western thinking.

Drummond also described a Philippine developmental model centring around Church, family and broader community, and reflecting aspects of both Asian identity and western colonial influence and, to western eyes, containing many paradoxes, such as the co-existence of strong women and machismo, and Christianity and belief in spirits. Jane and James Ritchie (1979) also observed apparent contradictions in Polynesian society, citing Robert Redfield's proposal that the very 'work' of culture might be to reconcile such inconsistencies. Drummond observed that Māori writing on human development has incorporated ideas such as Vygotsky's ZPD, and Bruner's scaffolding. These concepts are clearly consonant with their own cultural experiences, as illustrated by the finger-weaving example, and with these ideas still incorporated into the early childhood education curriculum.

Transmitting culture through child-rearing

Parental ethnotheories

Parental ethnotheories, or belief systems, have been proposed as a way of capturing the link between cultural forces and parenting practices (Harkness *et al.*, 2001). Researchers draw upon both anthropology and developmental psychology and note the need for tolerance of research methods from different traditions. This cross-cultural approach aimed to elicit the often-implicit theories that parents have about the correct way to raise children: 'Adults everywhere want their children to grow up not simply to be good human beings in universal terms but to be good people in their own cultural terms' (Ritchie and Ritchie, 1979: 147).

A cross-cultural study of infant temperament (de Vries, 1984) was (by chance) particularly telling about differing perceptions about children held by parents in some cultures, compared with western researchers' beliefs. Studying differences in infant temperament, researchers in the United States had established that infants vary in how easy or difficult they are to manage. The US temperament criteria were applied to infants of Masai parents (people of Kenya and Tanzania). Then, tragically, many infants died in drought, but the survivors were the 'difficult' babies, who had, presumably, demanded more frequent feeding. Furthermore, Masai parents valued assertiveness, perhaps the very characteristic that US parents regarded as difficult, but which promoted survival for the Masai. This illustrates the notion of 'goodness-of-fit' between a child's propensities and the environment in determining development (Thomas and Chess, 1977). Charles Super *et al.* (2008) later found both similarities and difficulties across several countries in parents' perceptions of children as 'difficult'.

David Shwalb *et al.* (2010) examined how mothers in the United States, Japan, South Korea and Indonesia view children's development, in accord with a range of metaphors and images of children (see Chapter 2). All saw children's development as under environmental rather than genetic influences (though not as 'blank slates'), and in unique, rather than universal, terms. Interestingly, they most strongly endorsed Stephen Pepper's formism metaphor—the least considered in this book as it is not clearly aligned with any theoretical tradition: mothers saw children as falling into different 'types', a view best corresponding with theories of temperament and personality, such as that of Carl Jung. Contextualism was the next most endorsed metaphor. Except for the Indonesian mothers, they saw children as 'pure' rather than 'mischievous', and all endorsed a 'gardening' metaphor for bringing up children. All except the Japanese mothers saw religious influence as important. Japanese mothers also perceived children as lonely. Overall, the results suggested that mothers' views of children's development are multifaceted and show both individual and cultural influences.

Ip *et al.* (2024) compared maternal perceptions of children's misbehaviour in the United States and mainland China. Both regarded social insensitivity as the least desirable behaviour. US mothers also focused on aggression and disruptive behaviours, while Chinese mothers were more concerned about cognitive and motivational issues. US mothers attributed misbehaviour to passing internal states and immaturity, while Chinese mothers blamed children's temperament and the social environment (as in the Confucian story of Mencius' mother in Box 4.1).

Cultural change over time

Attitudes towards children not only differ between cultures, but have altered historically, as illustrated by the changing views about children in China across three generations in the 20th century (see Chapter 2). There is similar evidence from Brazil. In the 1930s and 1940s, politeness, morality and good behaviour were encouraged; in the 1950s and 1960s, play, stimulation and tenderness were important; in the 1970s and 1980s, mothers spoke of dialogue, mutual understanding and children's wellbeing (Biasoli-Alves, 1997, cited in Tudge *et al.*, 2018).

Some recent work on culture and parenting has drawn upon the theoretical work of Çiğdem Kağıtçıbaşı, who hailed from Türkiye but also studied in the United States. She proposed that there may be universal features of optimal development that are important to understand, given that culture is fluid and the world is seeing many changes in contexts for development, such as rapid global urbanization. Devising universal standards is something she believed many developmental psychologists shrink from, for fear of being considered ethnocentric. She proposed that an integration of both the contextual and the global is needed (Kağıtçıbaşı, 2012).

Rather than seeing autonomy and relatedness as values at opposite ends of a continuum, she proposed two dimensions: agency (ranging from autonomy to heteronomy) and interpersonal distance/connectedness (ranging from separateness to relatedness). She suggested that a healthy model for children's development might be to aim for a good balance between these dimensions: promoting greater relatedness in societies that value autonomy, and greater autonomy in societies that value relatedness. This more balanced self she saw as better adapted to sociocultural change, such as increasing urbanization/modernization. Similarly, she suggested that a better balance between cognitive competence (valued by the west) and social competence (valued by the Majority World) is adaptive in a changing world.

Her theory therefore moved beyond considering cultures as lying on an 'individual–collectivism' continuum, which characterized theorizing about values in the 1980s. Kağıtçıbaşı's family change model, with its two orthogonal dimensions, creates four quadrants into which different types of families can fit (see Table 11.1). This was expanded to suggest two types of autonomy (Keller, 2012): encouraging children's thinking and planning (typical in North America and Europe) or being autonomous in practical tasks such as running errands, caring for stock and looking after younger siblings, which is more typical of rural cultures with less (formal) education.

Jonathan Tudge *et al.* (2018) found some evidence supporting Kağıtçıbaşı's theory, in Brazil: mothers from small towns more strongly valued relatedness, while those from capital cities fitted the autonomous-related pattern. Overall, Kağıtçıbaşı's theory has been described as 'part of a wider shift from studying

Table 11.1 Kağitçibaşi's model of family types

	heteronomous	*autonomous*
related	encourage obeying of elders/ following traditions and also close social connection	encourage some individual agency, especially in education and occupation, while also encouraging links with community and traditions
separate	a rarer family type that encourages the following of parental rules but not community connections	encourage individual agency but not links with broader community and traditions

cross-cultural differences in terms of external context (i.e. affluence, climate, modes of subsistence) to the analysis of such differences in terms of internal psycho-cultural parameters, especially values' (Poortinga, 2017: 5).

The role of fathers

Developmental psychology now considers more closely the role of fathers, rather than focusing mainly on the mother/child dyad. While studying fathers has a decades-long history (Paquette, Coyl-Shepherd and Newland, 2013), a boost has come from ecological and dynamic systems theories, whereby fathers are seen as part of the complexity impinging on children's development, within their cultural context. For example, religious beliefs in many Middle Eastern countries portray the father as the head of the household while in North America parents play an almost equal role in raising children (Afrooz, Asgharpour and Lotfi Kashani, 2022). Lee Gettler suggested that 'cultural dimensions and norms that shape men's developmental experiences as well as their social and economic roles in adulthood are potentially paramount in the expression of diverse biological responses to fatherhood' (Gettler, 2016: S38). The multidisciplinary work of Shwalb and colleagues in considering the changing roles of fathers (Shwalb, Shwalb and Lamb, 2013) and grandparents (Shwalb and Hossein, 2017) has taken account of research in languages other than English, showing increased father involvement in parenting in many communities (e.g. the Arab world) as gender roles are being reshaped by globalization. A recent review similarly points to the variable and changing role of the father across cultures and in relation to the social structure of the family; for example, in Asian countries such as Japan, Korea and China, economic problems have affected men's definition of fatherhood (Afrooz *et al.*, 2022)

Cultural and cultural-historical developmental psychology

Patricia Miller (2022) discerns a recent shift from cross-cultural developmental psychology (that compares cultures) to *cultural* developmental psychology, focused on how culture permeates all aspects of development. However, she comments, it is very difficult for westerners to make this shift from conceptualizing culture as something that *influences* the development of individuals, to viewing it as *constitutive*: 'the child-in-context is not fully assimilated into current theorizing and research' (Miller, 2022: 8).

US neo-Vygotskian Barbara Rogoff has been very influential in this change. Helen Hedges (2021) has drawn upon her work in considering early childhood education. She observes that classical theories such as those of Erikson and Piaget tend to treat learning as following development, whereas the dialectical view is the reverse (that learning leads development).[2] Based on intensive anthropological and developmental research within the same communities over decades, Rogoff's theorizing prioritizes the notion of 'learning by observing and pitching in': in other words, children learn by informal involvement in the everyday activities of their families and communities. Far from being inferior to formal education, it has several characteristics that promote development, being:

- Interactive, meaningful, and affective.
- Offering guidance, with assessment aimed at supporting an activity.
- Conversational (not didactic).
- Tailored to individual initiatives and interests.
- Driven by participants' active pursuit of knowledge, skills and innovation.

(Rogoff et al., 2016)

Hedges' view is that children's learning is non-linear, with complex trajectories, and needs peers and adults to support inquiry-driven learning. She uses the term 'working theories', representing the idea that children's current knowledge is temporary and adjusted by further experience. It empowers learners and is not based on the stages and norms that characterize much developmental psychology.

This paints a very different picture of education from that in many countries, especially as children grow older, with standardized curricula, extra tuition for many, and intensive examination of individual 'progress'. A review of quantitative studies has found that academic pressure is associated with mental health problems in adolescents, and although causality could not be established statistically (Steare *et al.*, 2023), adolescents themselves report that academic pressure has a major impact on their mental health (*The Lancet*, 2023). For example, in India, intensive hours of study leave little time for anything else and impact physical and psychological health; many students need psychiatric help for academic distress, which has been identified as the cause of increasing youth suicide there (Deb and Deb, 2023).

Another researcher who has, in recent decades, been influencing thinking in a Vygotsky-inspired direction in education is Denmark's Mariane Hedegaard. Her work is often described as 'cultural-historical theory' and takes account of the whole person (Chaiklin, 2019). Hedegaard maintains that development constitutes a change in a person's relation to the world, along Vygotskian lines (Libâneo and da Madeira Freitas, 2019). The extra step she takes (beyond both Vygotsky and Rogoff) is to consider the role of cultural values and practices within institutions such as schools and how these interact dynamically with children's sociocultural experiences in other institutions such as the family and community. For example, she has studied cultural practices within families by providing Danish children with instant cameras to photograph things of importance to them, and analysing the photographic and complementary observational data in terms of changes over time in the culturally important dinner setting (Hedegaard, 2018).

The importance of institutions for teaching/learning was highlighted for Hedegaard within Danish public schools, characterized by the presence of migrant and refugee children; she considered anthropologists as making an essential contribution to understanding. Teaching, for her, needs to be culturally sensitive and interactive, drawing upon students' lived experiences in various institutions and tailoring subject matter to be relevant for their everyday lives. She characterized this as a 'double movement' within the ZPD between the teacher's conception of the subject matter and students' everyday cultural knowledge.

José Libâneo and Raquel da Madeira Freitas (2019) suggest that Hedegaard's theory and her extensive research developing theory-based teaching practice would be valuable in enlightening a current debate in Brazil about the purpose of schooling. One view, they believe, over-values diversity and sees social care of the vulnerable as the main role of school, to the detriment of formal knowledge acquisition and equity. By contrast, they see Hedegaard's work as offering a means of promoting children's development through focusing on school-based knowledge that takes full account of its relationship with sociocultural practices.

Further theorizing that draws upon Vygotsky and that has been linked with Hedegaard and with Esther Thelen's dynamic systems theory is known as 'cultural-historical activity theory' or CHAT. While there are various versions (Cong-Lem, 2022), Anna Stetsenko explains hers in terms of development as not only nonlinear, transactional and probabilistic, 'but also, and importantly, a self-organizing process contingent on experiential history and activities of individuals themselves' (Stetsenko, 2019: 252). She sees the human world as a 'collective becoming', dynamic and tying together all generations. It is the foundation for each new person to exercise agency and develop in their own unique way, while also being deeply social. Nature and nurture (or culture) form an inseparable whole. The notion of internal and external 'factors' influencing development disappears, though such theorizing remains on the margins of the field, as Miller (2022) observed.

Critical approaches

During the 1960s and 1970s, critical psychology was developed in Germany by Klaus Holzkamp (1927–1995) and colleagues, emphasizing agency and emancipation (psychology that is not just 'about' people, but 'for' people). Thomas Teo (2013) argued that this movement could be understood, in part, as a backlash against US psychology and the Americanization of German psychology after the Second World War. The post-structuralists (e.g. Jacques Derrida and Michel Foucault) also took a questioning approach to the prevailing scientific means of understanding human affairs (Taylor, 2018). In 1987, Ronald Taft advised that developmental psychology would benefit greatly from taking into account alternative sources of information, including historical, demographic and anthropological, an opinion repeatedly expressed by (cross-)cultural theorists.

These approaches challenged the (post-)positivist epistemology that still underlies the education of most psychology students. The term 'critical psychology' covers various areas of endeavour, such as feminist psychology, which have been around for some years, but remain at the margins of the discipline (Shute, 2018). From a critical perspective, subjectivity, ethical and power issues are central, and qualitative methods predominate.

Decades ago, British developmental psychologist Erica Burman (1994/2008) first reviewed her field from a critical perspective. She observed that, in the mid-19th century, non-western peoples, along with infants and animals, were studied as examples of the 'primitive' mind, thus serving the perspective of European (especially British) imperialists that their own race was superior. This perspective continued well into the 20th century. Even Vygotsky, who did so much to foster understanding of the role of culture in individual thought, regarded some cultures as inferior (Wertsch and Tulviste, 1992).

Patricia Dudgeon and Harry Pickett (2000) observed that while psychology purports to be objective and apolitical, it is really a value-laden discipline that promotes individualism to the neglect of the community and family welfare which are central to many Indigenous cultures. Alternative psychological perspectives such as community, narrative and discursive psychology recognize issues such as multiple truths and social justice, and are explicitly concerned with social change and valuing the marginalized. Rather than speaking of a universal 'psychology', the possibility of specific psychologies is raised. For example, Carolin Demuth (2013) observed that negative emotional expressions in 20-month-olds gave German mothers and Cameroonian Nso mothers opportunities to interpret and frame the emotion in relation to their own cultural and historical norms.

A critical approach means considering history and cultural change relevant for the subdiscipline of developmental psychology itself. Carol Magai and Susan McFadden (1995) observed how the long-held view in western culture that the emotions are inferior to the intellect, and need to be tamed, is reflected in this history. For example, John Watson, of 'Little Albert' fame, advised parents to avoid 'mawkish sentimentality' in child-rearing. Watson's stance seemed to be influenced not only by prevailing western approaches to emotion, but by his own upbringing, which combined religious fundamentalism with a father dependent on alcohol and prone to violent outbursts. The topic of emotional development became increasingly neglected in the 20th century, being gradually squeezed out of child development textbooks. Researcher Carroll Izard reported difficulty in gaining funding and publications in the area: he received dismissive reviews of submitted papers and had to maintain his academic reputation by undertaking research on cognition. Similarly, present author PTS found it impossible to publish papers in psychology journals from his 1983 PhD thesis on mother–infant emotional relationships, and the first major paper was published in a journal of psychiatry.

Magai and McFadden also provided an enlightening analysis of how historical factors influenced 20th-century theorizing about the development of infant emotions. Watson's proposal that infants express three basic emotions (fear, rage and love) was disputed in the 1930s by Kathryn Bridges, who maintained that the emotions of young infants only become differentiated gradually through a process of conditioning. Her work was later criticized for its lack of descriptive detail of infant behaviour and use of institutionalized infants, who are unusually lacking in emotional expression, as René Spitz observed. Nevertheless, her theory was accepted for many years and completely overshadowed research by Charlotte Bühler, who demonstrated the existence of discrete emotions in infants. Her painstaking, detailed observational research and experiments included what was, in effect, the first demonstration of object permanence in infants. Yet this is firmly ascribed to Jean Piaget, whose work, in terms of experimental rigour, was arguably outstripped by Bühler's.

The influence of these three individuals on child development theory reflects historical factors, with Bühler working in the German language and remaining untranslated into English, while Piaget's work was translated from French into English from the 1930s onwards. With English-language publications the most influential in developmental psychology, Piaget became known as a 'giant' of developmental psychology, Bridges' notion of undifferentiated emotions held sway for many years, and Bühler's work has remained little acknowledged, even in German-language accounts of the history of emotional development, which have drawn upon English-language accounts.[3]

Magai and McFadden's historical exercise has great value. It shows that certain theories and theorists gain credence and others disappear because of cultural factors such as prevailing views about which topics are worthy of publication, what languages are influential and, as we shall see in Chapter 12, the sex/gender of the researcher. To use Bronfenbrenner's language, there may be much to be gained by paying closer attention to the chronosystem as it applies to the development of our subdiscipline.

Taking a critical perspective means moving beyond 'tolerance' of alternative approaches to appreciating their unique contributions. Given the different philosophical positions of various disciplines and subdisciplines, this is not easy to achieve. The present authors are only too aware of the disputes and rivalries that keep experts apart, and we have explored philosophical and practical ways of addressing this in the area of school bullying (Shute and Slee, 2022). Further promise lies in the recently introduced philosophy of metamodernism (see Chapter 2), that values the contributions of both etic and emic approaches. The use of mixed quantitative and qualitative methods is becoming more accepted within psychology, although some scholars may still avoid that terminology to describe their work, for fear that their papers will have a negative reception by journal editors and referees (Creamer and Reeping, 2020). These authors have identified a few writers as advocating for 'cycling' between quantitative and qualitative methods, which sounds very much like the 'pendulum' approach of metamodernism.

Indigenous psychologies

The United Nations does not define Indigeneity and has declared that Indigenous people have a right to self-identify (United Nations, 2013). In North America, some non-Indigenous people have been accused of fraudulently asserting Indigeneity; for example, in order to claim tax breaks or university scholarships, leading to debates about who has the right to determine that someone has Indigenous status (Simon, 2021). Australians who discover as adults that they have Indigenous ancestry generally find acceptance from the Indigenous and non-Indigenous communities, though sometimes there are clashes, such as when 'New Identifiers' are considered to be taking on roles to which they are not entitled (Watt and Kowal, 2019). The issue of Indigeneity is far from straightforward, then.

While there is no generally agreed definition, suggested criteria include historical continuity with pre-invasion/pre-colonial times, a strong link to territory/country, being a minority group, having a distinct language, culture and beliefs, and a commitment to passing on culture to subsequent generations. Teo (2013) maintains that the term 'Indigenous psychology' should not be reserved for minority or less powerful cultures, but refers to the specificities of *all* psychologies, including that which predominates in the United States.

Interest in Indigenous psychology—especially in the experience of Indigenous people themselves—is quite recent. Care must be taken that the concept is not used to marginalize non-western perspectives (Nsamenang, 2005). In the Australian case, western views about Aboriginal children's cognitive and motivational 'shortcomings' regarding education and the 'incompetence' of Aboriginal parents gave succour to arguments for the forced removal of Aboriginal children from their communities in the 20th century, in accordance with an assimilationist policy (as illustrated by the award-winning film *Rabbit-Proof Fence*). Evidence from Aboriginal people and others that many children (predominantly those of mixed ancestry) were indeed removed from their communities and placed in White families as recently as the 1970s, leading to intergenerational social and psychological problems, was presented in a Royal Commission report *Bringing Them Home* (Human Rights and Equal Opportunity Commission, 1997). Only after that report did psychology as a discipline begin to engage supportively and respectfully with Indigenous Australians (Bretherton and Mellor, 2006). Furthermore, some (White) influential Australian voices continued to question the existence of 'stolen generations' of Indigenous children, with the privileging by the dominant culture of written evidence over oral history further marginalizing the histories of Indigenous peoples. Although the Federal Government formally apologized in 2008 for past actions, Australia's 'culture wars' about what versions of Australian history should be privileged continued (Manne, 2009).

Indigenous psychologies can only thrive when members of a dominant culture are prepared to recognize the impact of colonialism, something that Indigenous groups advocate for in the form of 'truth-telling'. This is consistent with Riegel's perspective that individual development can only be understood in relation to cultural and historical change and the relations between majority and minority groups. As recently as 1988 the International Congress of Psychology was devoid of Indigenous content, a fact raised by a New Zealand community psychologist at the closing ceremony (Gridley *et al.*, 2000). This galvanized some Australian psychologists into action, so that by the turn of the millennium articles on Indigenous issues were published in journals of the Australian Psychological Society. Furthermore, non-traditional types of journal article and review processes were accepted, guidelines for psychologists working with Indigenous people had appeared and Aboriginal issues and presenters became regularly included in conferences. It also became usual for conferences to include a welcome from local Indigenous Elders, although we knew of one dispossessed Elder who would only 'greet', not 'welcome', visitors onto her traditional land on which our university was built. It is widely accepted across Australia that public gatherings express acknowledgement of the local Indigenous people. An effort by author PTS to similarly express respect to local traditional people at an overseas conference was met with puzzled looks from North American attendees! The editorial of a special issue on Indigenous issues of the journal *Australian Psychologist* (Sanson and Dudgeon, 2000) noted that in some of the articles the authors had chosen to be explicit about their own background. This recognition (and encouragement) of subjectivity represented a radical, and as yet, rare, shift from the 'objective' traditions of science.

Peoples with a history of colonization experience poorer wellbeing than their non-Indigenous counterparts because of the collective impact of policies such as child removals, and ongoing racism. For example, Indigenous Australians have lower life expectancies, more mental health problems, and greater rates of incarceration and suicide, including amongst youth (Newton *et al*., 2015). As identified in Canada, structural changes alone are insufficient to address the disadvantage of Indigenous children and families (Mussell, Cardiff and White, 2004): an Indigenous worldview is necessary that recognizes the role of culture in wellbeing and fully involves, and promotes, Indigenous leadership.

Some Australian health facilities are led by Indigenous people, one example being Rosemary Wanganeen's counselling service as described in Box 7.4. Efforts have also been made within mainstream services to 'Indigenize' practices to make them more culturally appropriate. However, Danielle Newton and colleagues identified a lack of culturally appropriate assessment instruments, and a greater focus on deficits than strengths. Some non-Indigenous psychologists therefore avoid using standard assessment methods with Indigenous clients. The Australian justice system, too, falls very far short of providing culturally appropriate services for young offenders; the punitive treatment of young Aboriginal offenders (many with neurological damage, often caused by foetal alcohol exposure) in some Australian detention facilities, and child deaths in custody, continue to make shocking headlines (Bourke, 2024).

Taking a positive approach, Heid *et al.* (2022) reviewed the literature on Indigenous youth and resilience in Canada and the United States, with the review of each paper including an Indigenous person. They found no equivalent to 'resilience', but there were related concepts such as 'walking a good path' and the teaching of values by grandfathers. Qualitative approaches that used youth-led definitions of stressors (e.g. substance use, loss of cultural identity) and resilience yielded important insights. For example, youth reported the importance of cultural pride and learning from nature and Elders. However, according to Cindy Blackstock *et al.* (2023), Canada's First Nations children are treated duplicitously by government that offers apology for past wrongs while deliberately continuing to act in a discriminatory and inequitable manner.

One remote Australian Aboriginal community wanted non-Indigenous health care providers to better understand their parenting practices, which proved similar to those of other Indigenous communities in Australia and elsewhere (Byers *et al.*, 2012). The qualitative methodology fitted culturally with the Aboriginal practice of 'yarning' (discussing, having a say, or storytelling). They explained that a central aspect is raising children to understand how they 'fit in' to their broad kinship network that is responsible for raising the child, as opposed to a nuclear family. In accord with critiques of attachment theory, they said babies never cry as they have many constant carers. They expect children to develop independence and learn through experimentation. They are praised for new skills such as starting to sit, but children are allowed to develop at their own pace and are given responsibility appropriate to their own level of maturity. Stepping out of line socially or getting in harm's way are addressed by teasing distraction or, occasionally, shaming, not by controlling commands. It was therefore alien to their culture to force children to take prescribed medication, casting light on a problematic health issue in the community. In many traditional cultures children are free to organize their own time and activities and develop self-reliance; the language of the Wintu people of California does not allow for coercion, so that, for example, one does not 'take a baby' somewhere but 'goes with the baby' (Lee, 1959).

The only longitudinal study of Australia's Indigenous children, *Footprints in Time*, running since 2008, uses mixed quantitative and qualitative methods (Rogers *et al.*, 2022). Teachers often report that they 'treat everyone the same', indicating a lack of awareness of cultural differences and student identity, though cultural activities are more common in areas with more Indigenous children. One parent in five reports experiencing racism at their children's school, and a quarter of Indigenous children are subjected to race-based bullying, especially in urban areas where the proportion of Indigenous children is lower. Parents overall feel that the primary school experiences of their children are better than their own had been.

An interesting example of (potential) Indigenization of children's services from Africa is Martin Musengi's (2023) discussion of *Ubuntu*, a pan-African view of thought that preceded, but resonates with, Vygotsky's work. It is based on wholeness, interdependence and harmony, and the idea that 'I am because you are'. It values overlap between communities. This extended historically to ethnic mobility and multilingualism rather than the European idea that one has a 'first' language, the notion of a 'foreigner' being unknown to many African communities. According to Musengi, '[t]he self-identity that individuals develop cannot be made sense of except by reference to the languages they use and the cultures that define them' (2023: 44). Musengi discusses this in relation to the education of deaf children, with *Ubuntu*, like Vygotsky, seeing such children as 'developing differently'. Colonialism disrupted traditional ways and imported western thinking into the education of the deaf. For example, it introduced the idea that one has a single main language, and that deaf people suffer loss, rather than taking a positive view of difference as illustrated by the African proverb: 'A disabled person is clever, he supports himself against a wall when dancing' (Musengi, 2023: 50). Musengi sees a parallel here with Vygotsky's concept of 'compensatory mechanisms' in the development of deaf children. He suggests that the dormant communitarian values of *Ubuntu* could revolutionize the education of deaf children in a culturally relevant manner. Further discussion about developmental psychology in Africa, and its relevance for translational science, can be found in Chapter 16.

Decolonizing developmental psychology

Musengi placed his discussion in the context of colonial legacies. A term used by him and others is 'coloniality', or the hidden power structures that continue to maintain oppressive and exploitative relations long after a nation's independence. For him, 'decolonization' of deaf education would involve the introduction of principles of *Ubuntu*.

Ignacio Martín-Baró (cited by Teo, 2013) argued for a Latin-American 'liberation' psychology that should be concerned with serving its populace, not with gaining acceptance by the rich countries of the world. Also, he said that 'pure' Indigenous psychologies are not possible because of the multiple interwoven factors that have changed them over time. Further, in this vein, is historian Josephine Quinn's (2024) argument that western culture itself has its roots not just in Greece and Rome, but in ancient civilizations around the world, with evidence for contact and cultural exchange stretching back over 4,000 years.

While this potentially expands our understanding of the global cultural origins of 'the West', it does not change the fact that more recent histories have been marked by colonization that continues to affect children today. A strongly argued paper about the need for decolonization of developmental psychology comes from a consideration of India, based on ethnographic research there, in the context of rapid contemporary globalization (Bhatia, 2020). Such globalization creates an impression of a 'shrinking' world and produces hybrid global/local identities. Young people are at the forefront, for example, working in call centres where they minimize their accents and take on western names. Sunil Bhatia says there are 356 million Indian youth, who are completely invisible in the field of developmental psychology, which is taught through a Eurocentric lens. 'Orientalism' was about European culture's concept of native peoples that underpinned their colonization and regulation. Charles Darwin, Francis Galton, G. Stanley Hall and Herbert Spencer are identified as culpable figures. Bhatia maintains that 'coloniality is alive in neoliberal globalization' (2020: 213) and reflected in conceptions of the self as a set of assets to be cultivated through, for example, networking, goal setting and seeking of expert advice (e.g. financial planners, life coaches). Some Indians are developing hybrid identities that blend this individualism with collectivism and a family orientation, which echoes Drummond's characterization of blended cultures in the Philippines, Kağıtçıbaşı's approach to families, and the construction of hybrid local/globalized identities by adolescents in Belize (see Chapter 2).

Decolonization, for Bhatia, is about addressing absences and coming to terms with colonial and racist history, including violence, land theft, slavery and Whiteness. Decolonization of developmental research involves interdisciplinary collaboration and an activist social justice perspective. Bhatia says:

> A decolonizing framework questions the dominance of science as the sole guarantor of truth and knowledge. Instead, it seeks to disrupt the coloniality of scientific knowledge as signifying valid method and highlights knowing that arises from indigenous communities, bearing witness to history of suffering, dismantling white supremacy, undoing coloniality, and focusing on modes of knowing that are rooted in lived experiences of communities.
>
> *(Bhatia, 2022: 218)*

An example of such an approach is the research of Ingrid Palmery and Stanford Mahati (2015) with unaccompanied child migrants entering South Africa from neighbouring countries. Using Burman's (1994/2008) work to reflect critically on the lives of these children, they shift the focus from the individual child to the historical and contextual conditions surrounding this migration. Their analysis moves beyond the question of 'cultural relevance' to acknowledge that 'developmental psychology arose at a moment of colonization in which notions of development were framed as a linear accomplishment with the child representing the underdeveloped savage' (Palmery and Mahati, 2015: 4). They argue that the migrant child imagined in South African law, that reflects its colonial origins and focuses on children's rights and the importance of care by the family, is at odds with the experiences of these unaccompanied children, whose lives are governed not by families but by the state and economic necessity. Returning them to the care of relatives is a state priority, driven by colonial ideals of childhood, assuming that they are refugees, orphans or have been trafficked. However, the children they interviewed had chosen unaccompanied border crossing for economic reasons, often encouraged by their families. Some live a cross-border existence, entering South Africa for cheaper education, groceries and even phone calls (supported by border guards, who know they will go back). Some participate in the economy by working as vendors at the borders. Policing and documentation checks are lax so, despite the laws, the children's independent activities appear to be broadly culturally sanctioned, even if state authorities seek to return them to relatives.

In the Canadian context Debra Pepler has been developing a community based approach in working with Canadian Indigenous peoples for over 35 years. She and colleagues emphasize the importance of researchers being trained to understand 'the intricacies and nuances of bringing the ethical guidelines to life through co-created research with Indigenous communities' (Riddell *et al*., 2017: n.p.).

In Australia the matter of decolonizing psychology has received some attention over the last decade. Cammi Murrup-Stewart and colleagues (2019) examined

Aboriginal perceptions of wellbeing programs. For Aboriginal people, a basic requirement is a collaborative and collectivist approach along with due recognition of intergenerational trauma in an historical context.

Ali *et al.* (2022) have offered an approach for non-Indigenous researchers based on two western theories that resonate with Indigenous worldviews—Bronfenbrenner's ecological systems theory and symbolic interactionism, which is concerned with the dynamic construction of meaning:

> The combination of both theories creates a paradigm that can provide a useful philosophical lens when researching with Indigenous peoples as they guide researchers to consider Indigenous affairs as a whole complex and dynamic system including socio-historical and political contexts from the perspectives of Indigenous peoples. This paradigm can enable non-Indigenous researchers to engage with Indigenous community members in ways that afford opportunities for their developing understanding of unique Indigenous ancient worldviews, knowledges and practices, how they influence the way Indigenous peoples act and interact and develop research in ways that are culturally valid and informative.
>
> *(Ali et al., 2022: 209)*

All this leaves open the question of how such issues can be taken into account in the teaching of developmental psychology. Decolonizing the psychology curriculum is a contentious issue, highlighted publicly and internationally by the movement to bring down statues of historical colonial figures (Phiri, Sajid and Delanerolle, 2023). These scholars maintain that some western academics distance themselves from the issue, ignore history, or actively reject the idea that psychology is western-centric. This echoes with the experience of author RHS in past decades, when our university introduced a course in 'globalization', but turned down an academic's proposal for a topic on the effects of globalization on Indigenous people.[4] Phiri *et al.* (2023) believe it is necessary for teachers and students to openly discuss brutal histories and their legacies, and that changes such as including readings or the occasional lecture from ethnic minority experts are trivial; rather, that a re-evaluation of westernized history is required—a complex and long-term task. Both the American Psychological Association and the British Psychological Society have held webinars on the subject, and the latter has produced a book of advice and resources for lecturers wanting to address colonialism in their teaching (British Psychological Society, 2020).

Conclusion

Understanding of the place of culture in development has undergone considerable transformation over the past hundred years. Cross-cultural work, including the study of parental ethnotheories, has been somewhat overtaken by a 'cultural' approach that owes its origins to Vygotsky, whose ideas have been developed by others such as Rogoff and Hedegaard. A critical approach to developmental psychology has raised the importance of considering historical factors in relation to cultures and Indigenous experiences, as well as the path of developmental psychology itself. The importance of interdisciplinary work and an appreciation of multiple methodologies has been emphasized by many cultural researchers. A shift from cross-cultural towards cultural research has occurred, that sees culture not as 'influencing' development, but being constitutive of it, though this change in thinking is far from complete. There is an increasing focus on Indigenous psychologies, and although finding 'pure' Indigenous post-colonial psychologies is considered impossible, efforts are being made towards the decolonization of developmental psychology, which necessitates acknowledgement by western scholars of the history and ongoing legacy of colonialism.

Notes

1 As reported by Dasen, it was originally called Lake Turkana, but this was a later appellation. Its original Indigenous name was *Anam a Cheper* and later *Anam Ka'alakol*, meaning 'the sea of many fish'.

2 See Nardo's argument in Chapter 8. Vygotsky also wrote of a child's 'readiness' as indicated by imitation in the ZPD, but in his terms this was readiness not to *learn* but to *develop* to a qualitatively different plane.

3 Today, there are still competing accounts of emotional development: basic emotions theories and the theory of constructed emotions (van Heijst *et al.*, 2023) that can be broadly likened to the theories of Bühler and Bridges respectively. Socioemotional development is now a major field of study, but the focus on 'emotional regulation' is perhaps an ongoing reflection of the western idea that the emotions are something to be tamed.

4 Having migrated from Wales to Australia, RHS had been invited to contribute a lecture on the colonization of Wales by the English; her Welsh mother-in-law would have been punished for speaking her native language at school. The after-effects still resonate, with the (English) UK Prime Minister in May 2025 saying that English is the only official language of the UK; in fact, Welsh also has official status in Wales.

References

Afrooz, G. A., Asgharpour, H. and Lotfi Kashani, F. 2022. The father's role in parenting: a comparison of different cultures and psychological perspectives. *Archives of Men's Health 6*(1): e1. https://doi.org/10.22037/mhj.v6i1.36795

Ali, T., Buergelt, P., Maypilama, E. L., Paton, D., Smith, J. A. and Jehan, N. 2022. Synergy of systems theory and symbolic interactionism: a passageway for non-Indigenous researchers that facilitates better understanding Indigenous worldviews and knowledges. *International Journal of Social Research Methodology 25*(2): 197–212. https://doi.org/10.1080/13645579.2021.1876300

Bhatia, S. 2020. Decolonization and coloniality in human development: neoliberalism, globalization and narratives of Indian youth. *Human Development 64*(4–6): 207–21. https://doi.org/10.1159/000513084

Blackstock, C., Libesman, T., King, J., Mathews, B. and Hermeston, W. 2023. Decolonizing first peoples child welfare. In C. Cunneen, A. Deckert, A. Porter, J. Tauri and R. Webb (eds), *The Routledge international handbook on decolonizing justice*. London: Routledge, 313–23.

Bourke, K. 2024. Why don't you care? *ABC News*, 19 October. www.abc.net.au/news/2024-10-19/fiona-stanley-hannah-mcglade-gerry-georgatos-cleveland-dodd-/104481052

Bretherton, D. and Mellor, D. 2006. Reconciliation between Aboriginal and other Australians: the Stolen Generations. *Journal of Social Issues 62*: 81–98. https://psycnet.apa.org/doi/10.1111/j.1540-4560.2006.00440.x

British Psychological Society. 2020. *Decolonising the curriculum – introducing multiple voices to inform and enrich learning*. Leicester: The British Psychological Society.

Bronfenbrenner, U. and Morris, P. A. 1998. The ecology of developmental processes. In R. M. Lerner (ed.), *Handbook of child psychology: theoretical models of human development*. Fifth edn. Vol. 1. New York: Wiley, 993–1028.

Burman, E. 1994/2008. *Deconstructing developmental psychology*. London: Routledge.

Byers, L., Kulitja, S., Lowell, A. and Kruske, S. 2012. 'Hear our stories': child-rearing practices of a remote Australian Aboriginal community. *Australian Journal of Rural Health 20*: 293–7. https://doi.org/10.1111/j.1440-1584.2012.01317.x

Chaiklin, S. 2019. Units and wholes in the cultural-historical theory of child development. In A. Edwards, M. Fleer and L. Bøttcher (eds), *Cultural-historical approaches to studying learning and development*. Singapore: Springer, 263–77.

Cong-Lem, N. 2022. Vygotsky's, Leontiev's and Engeström's cultural-historical (activity) theories: overview, clarifications and implications. *Integrative Psychological and Behavioral Science 56*: 1091–112. https://doi.org/10.1007/s12124-022-09703-6

Creamer, E. G. and Reeping, D. 2020. Advancing mixed methods in psychological research. *Methods in Psychology 3*: 100035. https://doi.org/10.1016/j.metip.2020.100035

Dasen, P. R. 2022. Culture and cognitive development. *Journal of Cross-Cultural Psychology 53*(7–8): 789–816. https://doi.org/10.1177/00220221221092409

Deb, S. and Deb, S. 2023. Positive youth development through holistic approach. In S. Deb and S. Deb (eds), *Handbook of youth development: policies and perspectives from India and beyond*. Singapore: Springer Nature, 3–34.

Demuth, C. 2013. Socializing infants toward a cultural understanding of expressing negative affect: a Bakhtinian informed discursive psychology approach. *Mind, Culture, and Activity 20*: 39–61. https://doi.org/10.1080/10749039.2012.719992

de Vries, M. W. 1984. Temperament and infant mortality among the Masai of East Africa. *American Journal of Psychiatry 141*: 1189–194.

Dudgeon, P. and Pickett, H. 2000. Psychology and reconciliation: Australian perspectives. *Australian Psychologist 35*(2): 82–7. https://doi.org/10.1080/00050060008260328

Erikson, E. 1950. *Childhood and society*. New York: Norton.

Gettler, L. T. 2016. Becoming DADS: considering the role of cultural context and developmental plasticity for paternal socioendocrinology. *Current Anthropology 57*(Supp. 13): S38–S51. https://psycnet.apa.org/doi/10.1086/686149

Gridley, H., Davidson, G., Dudgeon, P., Pickett, H. and Sanson, A. 2000. The Australian Psychological Society and Australia's Indigenous people: a decade of action. *Australian Psychologist 35*(2): 88–91. https://doi.org/10.1080/00050060008260329

Harkness, S., Super, C. M., Axia, V., Eliasz, A., Palacios, J. and Welles-Nyström, B. 2001. Cultural pathways to successful parenting. *International Society for the Study of Behavioural Development Newsletter 1*(38): 9–13. https://issbd.org/wp-content/uploads/2022/12/ISSBD_newsletter_01-1.pdf

Hedegaard, M. 2018. Children's cultural learning in everyday life exemplified at the dinner setting. In M. Fleer and B. van Oers (eds), *International handbook of early childhood education*. Dordrecht: Springer, 1525–40. https://doi.org/10.1007/978-94-024-0927-7_79

Hedges, H. 2021. Contemporary principles to lead understandings of children's learning: synthesizing Vygotsky, Rogoff, Wells and Lindfors. *Early Child Development and Care 191*(7–8): 1056–65. https://doi.org/10.1080/03004430.2020.1849169

Heid, O., Khalid, M., Smith, H., Kim, K., Smith, S., Wekerle, C. *et al.* 2022. Indigenous youth and resilience in Canada and the USA: a scoping review. *Adversity and Resilience Science 3*: 113–47. https://doi.org/10.1007/s42844-022-00060-2

Helfrich, H. 1999. Beyond the dilemma of cross-cultural psychology: resolving the tension between etic and emic approaches. *Culture and Psychology 5*(2): 131–53. https://doi.org/10.1177/1354067X9952002

Human Rights and Equal Opportunity Commission. 1997. *Bringing them home: the report of the National Inquiry into the Separation of Aboriginal and Torres Strait Islander Children from their Families*. Sydney: Commonwealth of Australia.

Ip, K. I., Heng, J. A., Lin, J., Shi, J. Li, W. and Olson, S. 2024. Parents' ethnotheories of the nature and causes of children's misbehaviors: a comparison of mothers across two cultures. *International Journal of Behavioral Development 48*(5): 385–97. https://doi.org/10.1177/01650254241239974

Kağıtçıbaşı, C. 2012. Sociocultural change and integrative syntheses in human development: autonomous-related self and social-cognitive competence. *Child Development Perspectives 6*: 5–11. https://doi.org/10.1111/j.1750-8606.2011.00173.x

Keller, H. 2012. Autonomy and relatedness revisited: cultural manifestations of universal human needs. *Child Development Perspectives 6*: 12–18. https://doi.org/10.1111/j.1750-8606.2011.00208.x

The Lancet. 2023. Editorial: time to take academic pressure seriously. *The Lancet* 7. www.thelancet.com/action/showPdf?pii=S2352-4642%2823%2900231-6

Lee, D. 1959. *Freedom and culture*. Englewood Cliffs: Prentice-Hall.

Libâneo, J. C. and da Madeira Freitas, R. A. M. 2019. Mariane Hedegaard's contribution to developmental didactics and to pedagogical research in the Brazilian context. In A. Edwards, M. Fleer and L. Bøttcher (eds), *Cultural-historical approaches to studying learning and development*. Singapore: Springer, 323–37. https://doi.org/10.1007/978-981-13-6826-4_21

Magai, C. and McFadden, S. H. 1995. *The role of emotions in social and personality development: history, theory and research*. New York: Plenum.

Manne, R. 2009. The history wars. *The Monthly*, November. www.themonthly.com.au/issue/2009/november/1270703045/robert-manne/comment

Meacham, J. 1999. Riegel, dialectics, and multiculturalism. *Human Development 42*(3): 134–44. https://doi.org/10.1159/000022619

Mead, M. (ed.). 1937/2002. *Cooperation and competition among primitive peoples*. Boston: Beacon Press.

Miller, J. G. 1999. Cultural psychology: implications for basic psychological theory. *Psychological Science 10*(2): 85–91. https://doi.org/10.1111/1467-9280.00113

Miller, P. H. 2022. Developmental theories: past, present, and future. *Developmental Review 66*: 101049. https://doi.org/10.1016/j.dr.2022.101049

Ministry of Health New Zealand/Manatu Hauora Aotearoa. 2024. *Te Wheke model of Mauri health*. www.health.govt.nz/maori-health/maori-health-models/te-wheke

Murrup-Stewart, C., Searle, A. K., Jobson, L. and Adams, K. 2019. Aboriginal perceptions of social and emotional wellbeing programs: a systematic review of literature assessing social and emotional wellbeing programs for Aboriginal and Torres Strait Islander Australians' perspectives. *Australian Psychologist 54*: 171–86. https://doi.org/10.1111/ap.12367

Musengi, M. 2023. Vygotskian resonances with the African worldview of Ubuntu for decolonial deaf education. *American Annals of the Deaf 168*: 37–55. https://doi.org/10.1353/aad.2023.a904166

Mussell, B., Cardiff, K. and White, J. 2004. *The mental health and well-being of Aboriginal children and youth*. Chilliwack, BC: British Columbia Ministry of Children and Family Development. www.academia.edu/69980742/The_Mental_Health_and_Well_Being_of_Aboriginal_Children_and_Youth_Annotated_Bibliography

Newton, D., Day, A., Gillies, C. and Fernandez, E. 2015. A review of evidence-based valuation of measures for assessing social and emotional well-being in Indigenous Australians. *Australian Psychologist 50*: 40–50. https://doi.org/10.1111/ap.12064

Nsamenang, A. B. 1995. Theories of developmental psychology for a cultural perspective: a view from Africa. *Psychology and Developing Societies* 7(1): 1–19. https://doi.org/10.1177/097133369500700101

Nsamenang, B. 1999. Eurocentric image of childhood in the context of the world's cultures. *Human Development 42*: 159–68. www.unige.ch/fapse/SSE/teachers/dasen/Nsamenang1999.pdf

Nsamenang, B. 2005. Human ontogenesis: an indigenous African view on development and intelligence. *International Journal of Psychology*: 1–5. https://doi.org/10.1080/00207590544000077

Palmery, I. and Mahati, S. 2015. Using deconstructing developmental psychology to read child migrants to South Africa. *Feminism and Psychology 25*(3): 347–62. https://doi.org/10.1177/0959353514562806

Paquette, D., Coyl-Shepherd, D. D. and Newland. L. A. 2013. Fathers and development: new areas for exploration. *Early Child Development and Care 183*(6): 735–45. https://doi.org/10.1080/03004430.2012.723438

Pere, R. M. 1982. Concepts and learning in the Maori tradition. *Working Paper No. 17*. Dept. of Sociology, University of Waikato, Hamilton, New Zealand.

Phiri, P., Sajid, S. and Delanerolle, G. 2023. Decolonising the psychology curriculum: a perspective. *Frontiers in Psychology*, 14 June. https://doi.org/10.3389/fpsyg.2023.1193241

Poortinga, Y. H. 2017. A majority world perspective on human development: commemorating the achievements of Çiğdem Kağıtçıbaşı. *European Journal of Developmental Psychology 15*(2): 131–8. https://doi.org/10.1080/17405629.2017.1406851

Quinn, J. 2024. *How the world made the West: a 4,000 year history*. London: Random House.

Riddell, J., Salamanca, A., Pepler, D., Cardinal, S. and McIvor, O. 2017. Laying the groundwork: a practical guide for ethical research with Indigenous communities. *International Indigenous Policy Journal 8*(2): 1–20. https://doi.org/10.18584/iipj.2017.8.2.6

Ritchie, J. and Ritchie, J. 1979. *Growing up in Polynesia*. Sydney: Allen & Unwin.

Rogers, J., Williams, K., Laurens, K. R. Berthelsen, D., Carpendale, E., Bentley, L. and Briant, E. 2022. *Footprints in Time longitudinal study of Indigenous children: primary school report*. Brisbane: Queensland University of Technology. https://eprints.qut.edu.au/235509/

Rogoff, B. 2001. The nature of culture. *Journal of Museum Education 26*(2): 6. https://doi.org/10.1080/10598650.2001.11510440

Rogoff, B., Callanan, M., Gutiérrez, K. D. and Erickson, F. 2016. The organization of informal learning. *Review of Research in Education 40*: 356–401. https://doi.org/10.3102/0091732X16680994

Sanson, A. and Dudgeon, P. 2000. Guest editorial: psychology, indigenous issues, and reconciliation. *Australian Psychologist 35*(2): 79–81. https://doi.org/10.1080/00050060008260327

Shute, R. H. 2018. *Clinical psychology and adolescent girls in a postfeminist era*. London: Routledge.

Shute, R. H. and Slee, P. 2022. *School bullying and marginalisation: harmonising paradigms*. Singapore: Springer.

Shwalb, D. W. and Hossain, Z. 2017. *Grandparents in cultural context*. New York: Routledge.

Shwalb, D. W., Shwalb, B. J., Hyun, J-H., Chen, S-J., Kusanagi, E., Satiadarma, M. *et al.* 2010. *Maternal beliefs, images, and metaphors of child development in the United States, Korea, Indonesia, and Japan*. Hokkaido: Research and Clinical Center for Child Development, Hokkaido University. www.researchgate.net/publication/43121344_Maternal_Beliefs_Images_and_Metaphors_of_Child_Development_in_the_United_States_Korea_Indonesia_and_Japan

Shwalb, D. W., Shwalb, B. J. and Lamb, M. E. (eds). 2013. *Fathers in cultural context*. New York: Routledge.

Simon, C. 2021. Fraudulent claims of indigeneity: Indigenous nations are the identity experts. *The Conversation*, 23 November. https://theconversation.com/fraudulent-claims-of-indigeneity-indigenous-nations-are-the-identity-experts-171470

Smaldino, P. E. 2019. Social identity and cooperation in cultural evolution. *Behavioural Processes 161*: 108–16. https://doi.org/10.1016/j.beproc.2017.11.015

Steare, T., Gutiérrez Muñoz, C., Sullivan, A. and Lewis, G. 2023. The association between academic pressure and adolescent mental health problems: a systematic review. *Journal of Affective Disorders 339*: 302–17. https://doi.org/10.1016/j.jad.2023.07.028

Stetsenko, A. 2019. Cultural-historical activity theory meets developmental systems perspective: transformative activist stance and natureculture. In A. Edwards, M. Fleer and L. Bøttcher (eds), *Cultural-historical approaches to studying learning and development*. Singapore: Springer, 249–62. https://doi.org/10.1007/978-981-13-6826-4_16

Super, C. M., Axia, G., Harkness, S., Welles-Nyström, B., Zylicz, P. O., Parmar, P. *et al.* 2008. Culture, temperament, and the 'difficult child': a study in seven western cultures. *International Journal of Developmental Science 2*(1–2): 136–57. https://doi.org/10.3233/DEV-2008-21209

Taft, R. 1987. Presidential address: cross-cultural psychology as psychological science. In C. Kağıtçıbaşı (ed.), *Growth and progress in cross-cultural psychology*. Berwyn, PA: Swets North America, 3–9.

Taylor, A. 2018. Engaging with the conceptual tools and challenges of poststructural theories. In M. Fleer and B. van Oers (eds), *International handbook of early childhood education*. Dordrecht: Springer, 91–114.

Teo, T. 2013. Backlash against American psychology: an Indigenous reconstruction of the history of German critical psychology. *History of Psychology 16*: 1–18. https://doi.org/10.1037/a0030286

Thomas, A. and Chess, S. 1977. *Temperament and development*. New York: Bruner/Mazel.

Tudge, J. R. H. 2008. *The everyday lives of young children: culture, class, and child rearing in diverse societies*. New York: Cambridge University Press.

Tudge, J. R. H. and Freitas, L. B. L. 2012. Internationalization, globalization and culture. *Psicologia e Sociedade 24*(3): 547–56.

Tudge, J. R. H., Martins, G. D. F., Merçon-Vargas, E. A., Dellazanna-Zanon, L. L., Piccinini, C. A. and Freitas, L. B. L. 2018. Children, families, and communities in Brazil: a cultural-ecological approach to child-rearing values and practices. In M. Fleer and B. van Oers (eds), *International handbook of early childhood education*. Dordrecht: Springer, 1503–23.

United Nations. 2013. *Indigenous peoples and the United Nations human rights system*. New York and Geneva: UN Human Rights Office of the High Commissioner. www.ohchr.org/sites/default/files/Documents/Publications/fs9Rev.2.pdf

Watt, E. and Kowal, E. 2019. To be or not to be Indigenous? Understanding the rise of Australia's Indigenous population since 1971. *Ethnic and Racial Studies 42*(16): 63–82. https://doi.org/10.1080/01419870.2018.1546021

Wertsch, J. V. and Tulviste, P. 1992. L. S. Vygotsky and contemporary developmental psychology. *Developmental Psychology 28*(4): 548–57. https://psycnet.apa.org/doi/10.1037/0012-1649.28.4.548

Wilbraham, L. 2005. Formula two – developmental theories and contexts in text boxes. *PINS 32*: 65–80. www.academia.edu/100308679/Formula_Two_Developmental_Theories_and_Contexts_in_Text_Boxes

van Heijst, K., Kret, M. E. and Ploeger, A. 2023. Basic emotions or constructed emotions: insights from taking an evolutionary perspective. *Perspectives on Psychological Science*. https://doi.org/10.1177/17456916231205186

12 Listening to different voices 1

Feminism, developmental psychology and backlashes

Introduction

Readers whose experience of developmental psychology is in the post-positivist 'mainstream' may find this chapter surprising, and later we will explore possible reasons. I (author RHS, the female half of our writing team) drafted this chapter and will occasionally use the first person where my own experiences exemplify broader cultural issues in relation to feminism and psychology. I have decided against adopting the once-common practice of differentiating between sex and gender, given the inseparability of nature and nurture (see Chapter 3) and the inconsistent use of these terms in psychology; I will instead generally adopt the term *sex/gender* (Radtke and Stam, 2016). I will not be using the controversial spelling 'womxn' that some feminists prefer.

Although not a feminist scholar, I was motivated to write a book addressing feminism in relation to clinical psychology practice with adolescent girls (Shute, 2018). This was because the field in which I spent much of my working life had remained stubbornly focused on 'fixing' the decontextualized individual, ignoring the social factors undermining girls' wellbeing. The (very masculine) metaphor of one British clinical psychologist, that I endorse, was that his profession kept patching people up with sticking plasters (band-aids) and sending them back into the trenches without dealing with the war (Harper, 2016). My book was positioned in the postfeminist era, while noting that we seemed on the cusp of a fourth wave of feminism. That proved to be so. US media mogul Harvey Weinstein's long-standing abusive behaviour towards women in the workplace finally became public, and his conviction as a sex offender followed in 2023. The online *#MeToo* movement became much more prominent as women and girls publicized the culture of harassment, assault and rape to which they were exposed. While it is too soon to know how far this latest seismic social change will influence developmental psychology, the time seems ripe for a fresh examination of feminism's contribution to the field.

The waves of feminism

Psychological theorizing, we have argued, is profoundly affected by its cultural-historical milieu. Here, we explore the changing cultural place of women and girls,

DOI: 10.4324/9781003567738-12

as highlighted by the various waves of feminism (or feminisms), that blend into one another. Historian Martha Rampton (2015) identified precursors in the ancient world, but 'first wave' feminism arose in the late 19th century, as western middle-class White women fought for suffrage and other legal rights. A global feminist wave with similar origins has played out in different ways under different regimes (Weldon *et al.*, 2023); see Box 12.1 for a South American example.

BOX 12.1 FEMINISM IN ARGENTINA

Marina Durano gives the following account of recent Argentinian feminism.

> In 2015, under the banner call of #NiUnaMenos (Not One Less), thousands of Argentinians, mostly women, marched towards the Plaza de Mayo in Buenos Aires to seek justice for all the women who died under brutal circumstances. Argentinians, like many in Latin America, call the phenomenon *femicidio*, highlighting the female victim whose murder is often, though not exclusively, perpetrated by an intimate partner.
>
> As #NiUnaMenos grew into a movement, Argentinian feminists expanded their initial calls to end abuse and violence to include other women's rights issues, like the legalization of abortion. The country's growing economic crisis is also disproportionately harming women. In Argentina, women are overrepresented among the poorest 20 percent of the population. Due in part to higher unemployment rates, large gender pay gaps, and other economic disadvantages, women are facing higher barriers to resiliency and survival. (Indeed, the movement has also linked increased anxiety and stress to a higher probability of being abused—as well as a lower probability of feeling able to leave an abusive environment.)
>
> *(Durano, 2020: n.p.)*

The second (western) wave in the 1960s focused on reproductive rights, women's restriction to domestic roles and objectification such as beauty pageants (Rampton, 2015). 'Sisterhood' was emphasized in fighting women's subjugation, and women's studies was established as a scholarly field, critiquing patriarchy, capitalism and normative heterosexuality. None of this touched my undergraduate psychology curriculum at the end of that decade; I commented rather uncertainly in an assignment that a study only had male participants, which might have affected the results, but I had never known this issue raised anywhere.

I became much more aware of the patriarchal tenor of the times in my first academic position in the UK in 1972. Having attended an all-girls school and a university college that had previously been women-only (and therefore still had plenty of female lecturers), I was taken aback in my first staff (faculty) meeting to find I was the only woman present. Also, I assumed as a woman that the (male) head of psychology of my old university college would be pleased to support a former student giving her first ever conference paper, but this belief was soon shattered: the previous evening the professor said he hadn't prepared his keynote speech and asked me about my talk; as I awaited my turn in the auditorium next morning, his opening speech opposed the case I was about to present. Afterwards, one woman was heard to comment that she didn't like me as I was 'too confident' (behaving against stereotype, though I was quaking inside). I was even more shocked to later learn that, in the same era, the entertainment at a major Australian psychology conference dinner had been a stripper!

Psychology was not untouched by second-wave feminism, however, with the American Psychological Association (APA) convening a taskforce in the 1970s to address sexism in psychotherapy. In the late 1980s I was serving on the Council of the British Psychological Society when a proposal was received to form a Psychology of Women section; it met strong resistance from those who saw no need for any separate consideration of women's psychology, but eventually succeeded. In the 1990s, a feminist-inspired psychotherapy conference was held in the United States and a book published (Worell and Johnson, 1997). According to Kera Lovell (2016), second-wave feminism neglected the role of adolescent girls, but primary sources in the United States showed that they were very active in challenging school control of their dress and advocating for access to male-dominated subjects. Although these early examples of 'girl power' were seen as inconsequential in the aftermath of the Second World War, they achieved real educational change.

Second-wave issues remained a focus in academia, but beyond it a complex third wave emerged in the 1990s, with 'sisterhood' replaced by the individualism of the neoliberal era. The achievements of earlier feminists became taken for granted, and many women rejected the feminist label (Genz and Brabon, 2009). Conservative media portrayed feminism as man-hating. Popular culture became a space for young women's self-expression, often through 'raunch' culture, with girls demonstrating their (albeit lower status) femininity through hyper-sexualized and consumerism-inspired dress and behaviour—'the postfeminist masquerade', hiding the patriarchal forces that promoted it (McRobbie, 2008). Sharon Lamb (2010) maintained that feeling sexually emboldened is not the same as being empowered, while Rosalind Gill warned that 'empowerment' is hard to identify in cultures that use the concept 'to sell everything from liquid detergents to breast augmentation surgery' (Gill, 2012: 736).

The term 'postfeminism' has multiple and contradictory meanings, covering both the backlash against the second-wavers and various new versions of feminism (Genz and Brabon, 2009). While the word 'feminism' became dirty to many (and known as 'the f word' in educational circles; Keddie, 2010), there was also a push for diversity and understanding of intersectionality, with concerns about the oppression of women of colour in the United States, and queer theory emerging. The 'boy turn' arose in the face of girls' increasing academic success, whereby boys became seen as the new educational victims—'recuperative masculinity politics' fuelled by a resurgence of the political right (Martino and Berrill, 2003). The disengagement of some boys was in fact due to the holding of male stereotypes, low self-discipline and reading much less than girls (Farkas and Leaper, 2016).

The fourth wave began around 2010 as a reaction against postfeminism. Some second-wave concerns re-emerged, highlighting violence against women. It became characterized by online activism, and the *#MeToo* movement (and similar versions around the world) focused on workplace harassment. Domestic and family violence became a greater topic of political discussion under pressure from activist women, such as through the Australian project *Counting Dead Women* that keeps a running tally of women killed by violence each year. Also see Box 12.2.

BOX 12.2 THE PÉLICOT CASE

In 2024, a brave French woman, Gisèle Pélicot, took her husband and 50 other men to court, choosing publicly open proceedings, which presented video evidence that her husband had repeatedly drugged her to unconsciousness over a decade, to allow these men to rape her (Nichols, Rimmer and Martin, 2024). The response of the town's mayor further illustrated local male attitudes: he said it could have been much worse, as she was unconscious, no children were involved and no one was killed (Harding, 2024). This horrific highlighting of a broader 'rape culture' (Burnett, 2016) demonstrated how much feminism still needs to achieve, especially in the face of the latest backlash, discussed later in this chapter.

Common themes of feminist theories

Feminist scholars come from various disciplines, and there is no single theory (DeKeseredy, 2011). Feminism can be seen as a metatheory within which more specific theories can be developed and tested (Tate, 2013). Judith Worell and Claire Etaugh (1994) discerned six common themes relevant for developmental psychology.

1. Most feminist theories challenge the tenets of traditional scientific inquiry. For example, science is regarded as not objective nor value-free. Various methods are judged useful, with qualitative inquiry especially valued.
2. There is a focus on women's lives and experiences. Women are seen as worthy of study apart from the standard of male norms, and sex/gender differences are examined from the perspective of socialized power differentials.
3. Power relations are regarded as the basis of patriarchal political social arrangements. For example, women's social status is seen as resulting from unequal power distribution and not their deficiencies.

4. Sex/gender is to be analysed, not taken to explain difference. We can add that it is now often seen as *constructed* through discourse, and that sex/gender diversity has become increasingly accepted, though with backlashes also occurring.
5. Language is considered important, including explicit naming of hidden phenomena such as 'sexual harassment' (a term coined in 1975), restructuring language to be inclusive, and reducing the (western) public–private polarity in women's lives.
6. Finally, there is a common concern with social activism, such as reconceptualizing theories, methods and goals, in the interests of promoting sex/gender justice.

In rejecting the epistemological underpinnings of traditional scientific inquiry, the dichotomy between the objective observer and the research participant breaks down (Wilkinson, 1998). Feminist-standpoint research aims to reduce the power differential favouring the researcher. In foregrounding participants' voices, qualitative methods such as interviews, focus groups and discourse analysis are preferred, although quantitative methods too can test feminist theory.

Feminism has focused on women rather than children and, clearly, such methods have limitations when working with children. Try holding a focus group with one-year-olds! Obviously, other methods, such as observation, are also needed. The concern with intersubjectivity remains, however; researchers must be conscious of their impact upon the child, as demonstrated by Margaret Donaldson and colleagues' classic 'Naughty Teddy' study.

A further extension of (adult-focused) feminist theorizing to girls is the application of the concept of intersectionality. The well-established practice in psychological science of investigating interactions between predictor variables perhaps primes it to accept intersectionality although, from a feminist viewpoint, participant subjectivity should be prioritized over researcher-chosen variables (Grabe, 2020). The concept of intersectionality seems to have been more readily taken up by developmental psychology than sociological child studies (Alanen, 2016). For example, Kelly Mulvey *et al.* (2018) found that young people experience bullying as especially harmful when based on both sex/gender and ethnicity. Study of the combined impact of these and other social identities (e.g. sexual orientation, immigrant status) is relevant for prevention and intervention in disadvantaged and diverse populations (Ghavami, Katsiaficas and Rogers, 2016).

Developmental psychology's gendered inheritance

Charles Darwin argued that 'only men are intelligent, creative and capable of learning' (Cohen, 2010: 162). His baby biography earned him the moniker 'the father of developmental psychology', but diary studies before his, many by women, were overlooked (Bradley, 1989, cited in Burman, 2008). A gendered approach soon saw only fathers possessing the necessary emotional detachment to study their children (Burman, 2008). Seymour Fisher and Roger Greenberg suggested that Sigmund Freud's penis-baby equation was about the female being obliged to 'construct an illusory maleness' (1996: 165) to orientate herself in an androcentric, phallically defined world.

Ellin Scholnick and Patricia Miller (2000) discussed the use of metaphor in developmental theorizing, as metaphors reflect choices about what to highlight. They described several metaphors reflecting masculine values (e.g. rationality, conflict and hierarchy). Later, they made a case for similarly analysing the concept of 'executive functioning' (Miller and Scholnick, 2015). Not only are socio-historical contexts ignored in this flourishing research area, but the ideal problem-solving child is autonomous and works speedily and efficiently, applying rationality to control their body and emotions. They suggest that the very term 'executive' 'places the competitive corporate model within the brain' (p. 271), disallowing that effective problem-solving may sometimes be best achieved through collaboration rather than a focused solo effort. Their analyses illustrate that the field of child development 'is associated with the rise of science and modernity, subscribing to a specific, gendered model of scientific practice' (Burman, 1994: 10). This history is illustrated by the testimony of Carol Gilligan.

Carol Gilligan (b. 1936)

Gilligan's revolutionary research on morality is well-known to psychology students. We can gain greater insight into her significance through an interview she gave to Ruthellen Josselson (2023).

Early in her career, Gilligan was a teaching assistant at Harvard University and research assistant to Lawrence Kohlberg, known for his theory of the stages of children's moral development, culminating in a justice orientation (Kohlberg, 1971). At the time of the *Roe v. Wade* decision of the US Supreme Court in 1973, legalizing abortion, Gilligan interviewed women about their moral decision-making concerning terminations, finding their moral reasoning very different from Kohlberg's model. It was not about justice but caring for others and considering who would be affected by the decision. Gilligan's best-selling 1982 book *In a Different Voice* (from which this chapter's title is taken) followed from an earlier paper of the same name. Coming in the second wave, it became a springboard for subsequent work on sex/gender, but Gilligan herself did not focus on such issues and never saw herself, at the time, as a feminist trailblazer. As Josselson writes:

> In listening closely to her participants in the abortion study, she was able to formulate that what was 'wrong' in psychology lay in the dominance of a particular frame of reference, a male one, in privileging independence over interdependence, reason over emotion, the self over relationships.
>
> *(Josselson, 2023: 128)*

Gilligan admired her colleagues Kohlberg and Erik Erikson but could hardly believe that they had omitted half the population from their theories; she realised then that culture can prevent you from seeing what is right before your eyes. Kohlberg said that her work was 'a B route through my stages' (indicating its perceived inferiority and emphasizing his ownership of the existing theory! [RHS]); she replied that her work *reframed* his stages. Erikson, too, did not believe he needed to rethink the stages of his life-cycle theory; she pointed out that he did, as he found the theory did not 'quite apply to women who join identity with intimacy' (Josselson, 2023: 129). Gilligan was told that her (qualitative) work was 'not psychology' and 'not science', and her colleagues did not include her findings in their lectures.[1]

Gilligan then undertook research with girls, coming to realize that the 'different voice' she had identified was the voice of resistance against patriarchy. Girls, women and some men, she argued, experience a conflict between what they have learned experientially, and the way they are culturally restricted in expressing that knowledge. An important example, from longitudinal interview research, was that girls would increasingly say, 'I don't know' as they approached adolescence (a frequently-uttered phrase often considered meaningless and omitted from interview transcripts). Close inquiry showed that this was a cover for *knowing* something but feeling obliged not to express it (Brown and Gilligan, 1992). Gilligan recognized this from her own initial reluctance to push her research findings forward in a non-receptive disciplinary culture. Gilligan has been credited with 'mapping the dynamics of resistance and accommodation in the face of sociocultural oppression', which extends her influence well beyond the study of women (Rogers and Way, 2021, cited in Josselson, 2023: 131).

Josselson observes that while second-wavers will immediately understand the profundity of the changes that Gilligan fostered, she could not, in the confines of her paper, reconstruct 'the pervasiveness of how women were viewed, stereotyped, and disparaged in this era' (Josselson, 2023: 132). She recommends that younger readers watch the US TV series *Mad Men.*

Psychology's response to feminism

Today, there are various groups concerned with the psychology of women, and thriving specialist international journals such as *Feminism and Psychology* and *The Psychology of Women Quarterly*, but it is uncommon to see an explicitly feminist perspective in articles in 'mainstream' journals. In the postfeminist era it was difficult to persuade young APA members of a need for feminism (Law, 2006), and the 2007 APA guidelines for psychological work with women and girls acknowledged their feminist history but did not explicitly espouse feminism. Research addressing girls' issues (e.g. body image, eating disorders) has flourished, frequently driven by concern about their demonstrably compromised wellbeing (in western countries) as they enter their teens (Marquez *et al.*, 2024), but rarely does it have an expressed feminist or social justice perspective. The influence that feminism has undoubtedly had in driving such research agendas is therefore often hidden.

The difficulty of shifting the culture of developmental psychology is exemplified by the efforts of Aurélie Athan and Heather Reel (2015) to offer students a more critical approach. Twenty years after Erica Burman's *Deconstructing Developmental Psychology* was first published, these US academics reflected on the role of mothers within developmental psychology. A long tradition had viewed 'the mother' simply as a vehicle for understanding the child; as they put it, succinctly, 'the child's success depends on the success of the mother' (Athan and Reel, 2015: 2). Her own subjectivity is often treated as secondary or irrelevant. They cite Burman's view that the mother, in developmental research, is paradoxically both powerful and invisible, exemplified by a Victorian photographic tradition in which the completely veiled mother becomes an anonymous background highlighting the solo infant on her lap.

Athan and Reel established a university graduate class and laboratory focusing on mothers' experiences. Many students soon dropped out, and others challenged the maternal focus, even when presented with relevant feminist scholarship. In five years, Athan and Reel never had a student cite Burman or question the developmental status quo. They wondered whether their work was subversive, flying in the face of 'the cult of childhood' (Burman, 1994), or whether students' resistance simply arose from their education that had 'placed knowledge generated by Bowlby, Ainsworth, and Harlow, among others, as more worthwhile' (Athan and Reel, 2015: 2). Furthermore, they noted, the more recent interest in mothers' experiences had focused on psychopathology, such as perinatal depression (and its effects on children), to the neglect of those who flourish, or have complex reactions, in transitioning to motherhood. They suggest that study in this field offers an alternative to the established feminist view of motherhood as 'oppressive' and could place mothers not just as creators of their children's development, but as *receivers* of it, in transactional and transformative ways. There is much to be gained, they propose, by transdisciplinary scholarship interweaving developmental paradigms with expertise in feminist, clinical, psychoanalytic (and other disciplinary) realms, and in which diverse methodologies contribute.

Reasons for developmental psychology's resistance to feminism

These include the gendered inheritance of developmental psychology, the more recent era of postfeminism, and feminism's focus on women rather than girls. Other factors are psychology's positivist inheritance, its individualist focus and the medicalization of distress (Shute, 2018), as elaborated below.

Psychology has long associated itself with the natural sciences, with ongoing ambitions for acceptance as a prestigious 'hard' science (Wilson, 2012). The current biological/neurological zeitgeist reflects this. This places psychology at odds with the philosophy of feminism and other critical approaches that embrace subjectivity and qualitative methods. The hegemonic focus on objectivity and quantification is maintained by course accreditation (Breen and Darlaston-Jones, 2010) and, we would suggest, enculturation into the scientific method that influences psychologists' identity as scientists.

Lorraine Radtke and Henderikus Stam wrote:

> [T]he marginalization of feminist scholarship within psychology is clearly relevant to the stagnation on the question of sex/gender differences as this body of

> work remains outside the conventional canon that students and researchers in the field are expected to know.
>
> *(Radtke and Stam, 2016: 178)*

Furthermore, feminism is an activist, social justice movement. Some maintain that psychology and politics should not mix, firmly distinguishing between 'what is' and 'what ought to be'. A critical perspective is that it is naïve to believe that such decontextualized, value-free research is possible.

Another reason for psychology's muted reception of feminism is the discipline's long history of focusing on the individual. Jill Morawski wrote: 'Masculinity and femininity research illustrates psychology's sustained reliance on the idea of bounded individuals whose life is independent of historical circumstance and is available to measurement' (cited in Radtke and Stam, 2016: 176). Despite notable exceptions (e.g. Lev Vygotsky's and Urie Bronfenbrenner's theories), a strong thread of individualism is exemplified by the theories of Burrhus F. Skinner and Jean Piaget.

Furthermore, clinical practice with girls, and related research, reflects a societal tendency to take a medical approach to distress (see Chapter 3). It is related to the desire to be 'scientific', although the *DSM*'s original scientific ambitions have arguably failed in reality (Demazeux, 2015). An individualized approach ignores the social environment impeding girls' wellbeing: gender-based violence; socio-economic disadvantage; subordinate social status; and caring responsibilities (World Health Organization, 2016). 'A culture that creates the circumstances for girls' distress and then "solves" it through medication does not make for a comfortable situation' (Shute, 2018: 56).

Theories of sex/gender development

Most early research and university teaching on sex/gender in the 1970s and 1980s focused on women, redressing the previous 'womanless' era; if students asked why there was no class on men's studies, they were informed (accurately) that all their other classes were basically about the psychology of men (Etaugh, 2016). Sex/gender more broadly became a subject of psychology studies (Maccoby and Jacklin, 1974) but was initially atheoretical. Studies of sex/gender differences between boys and girls emerged, but introductory psychology texts often proposed no explanations (Eagly *et al.*, 2012), despite the fact that (or perhaps because) the nature of such explanations was becoming hotly contested. The feminist thrust eventually led to studies of men, boys, masculinity and gender diversity. However, Radtke and Stam (2016) have described psychology's relationship with sex and gender as 'begrudging'.

Theorizing about sex/gender development brings two metatheoretical camps into sharp relief. On the one hand is evolutionary developmental psychology, which holds that evolutionary pressures for division of labour earlier in our evolutionary history predispose males and females to behave differently because of biological differences, the term 'sex differences' reflecting this. On the other hand are those emphasizing similarity between the sexes; even a 'strong' statistically significant difference in sex/gender attributes reflects a 67 per cent degree of overlap (Leaper, 2022). Feminist scholars maintain that gender is both socially constructed and 'performed', under the influence of sex-based differences in status and power.

Anne Campbell (2012) objected to feminist political critique of evolutionary psychology, drawing the distinction between what 'is' and moral judgements about what 'ought to be'. She took feminists to task for ignoring evidence for differences between male and female minds suggesting an evolutionary origin. For example, a hormonal basis for sex-typed behaviour is indicated by the reduction in women's empathy, trust and fear after testosterone administration. From the feminist side, Eagly and Wood (2013) demonstrated that many studies failed to support the predictions of sexual strategies theory about male–female mating preferences and accused some evolutionary psychologists of confirmatory bias in their interpretation of the evidence (also see Box 12.3).

BOX 12.3 BIAS IN THE STUDY OF GENITALIA

Biological studies of the evolution of genitalia are strongly biased towards studying males. This is not accounted for by easier access to male organs for study, but by 'enduring assumptions about the dominance of males in sex', who are therefore seen to 'lead' the evolutionary process (Ah-King, Barron and Herberstein, 2014). The bias actually strengthened after being pointed out in 2000, despite evidence of co-evolution of male and female genitalia. This research base provides a biased grounding for evolutionary psychologists seeking guidance from animal studies.

Eagly and Wood (2013) identified a need to bridge the evolutionary/nature and feminism/nurture divide and move towards a 'biosocial interactionist' theory of sex/gender. The Grandmother Hypothesis interested feminist scholars (see Box 3.3 in Chapter 3), but female researchers tended to study the menopause and male researchers to focus on sexual selection theory that views males as the main drivers of evolution (Saini, 2014). By and large, however, the feminism-evolutionary psychology debate has not focused on children's development.

By contrast, neuropsychology has thrown up plenty of disagreement about sex/gender differences in development. The gender-stereotypical assumptions and biases underlying much research led Cordelia Fine (e.g. 2013) to coin the term 'neurosexism'. Biologist Anne Fausto-Sterling (2012) found little evidence for an assumed sex-differentiated developmental path from genes to prenatal hormones to brain to behaviour. Annette Karmiloff-Smith's 'neuroconstructivist' approach offered an alternative (see Chapter 3).

There is, in fact, 'compelling evidence in favor of structural plasticity throughout life' (Leuner and Gould, 2010: 112). For example, a supposedly innate female inferiority on visuo-spatial skills was investigated with adolescent girls: three months of practice through the Tetris computer game produced measurable changes in neocortex thickness and neural activity (Haier *et al.*, 2009). Even short-term exposure to stereotypical misinformation about female visuo-spatial inferiority leads girls to perform worse, with a different pattern of neural activity, compared with girls given positive or neutral information (Wraga *et al.*, 2006). Such 'stereotype threats' demonstrate that any sex/gender differences found in patterns of neural activity can be contextual and quite fleeting.

That sex/gender differences in brain structure or activity may be functionally equivalent is rarely considered, and the basic assumption that there is a neat male/female binary divide is questionable (Hoffman and Bluhm, 2016). Brains are highly variable in organization, and do not develop into distinct 'male' and 'female' versions. Rather, while some characteristics of cell types or regions are more typical of males or females, these form very individualized mosaics (Joel *et al.*, 2015). These findings have contributed to a new suggestion about inheritance over generations (Fine, Dupré and Joel, 2017): that we do not only inherit genes, but environments, including social environments that are in some ways sex-differentiated and tend to be stable over generations. This removes selective pressure for brains to evolve in a sex-differentiated way as the environment itself supports the individual in developing adaptive behaviours.

Neuropsychologist Gina Rippon (2019) observes that brain plasticity findings are having little impact on discussion of sex differences, which tends to remain 'rooted in the deterministic past' (Rippon, 2016: 919). For example, Robyn Bluhm (2013) compared three studies on emotional control, imaging the prefrontal cortex: one found greater male neural activity, another greater female activity, and the third no difference, yet all concluded (stereotypically) that their results indicated greater cognitive emotional control in males.

How boys' and girls' brains and abilities turn out depends largely on how they '*spend their time*' (Eliot, 2009: 16, original emphasis). Past sex/gender differences in cognitive abilities have been diminishing or disappearing, while life lessons about emotional expression remain heavily gendered from birth (Eliot, 2009). Overall, there seem to be few innate sex-differentiated behavioural biases (Eliot, 2009), but these are greatly magnified—fortified, to use Fausto-Sterling's (2012) term—by socialization into gender roles (cf. developmental cascades in Chapter 1). This may explain differential neural changes over time between male and female adolescents experiencing chronic bullying (Connaughton *et al.*, 2024); females have greater increases in thickness in brain areas associated with emotional processing, while males have more changes in motor and sensory areas, which may reflect adaptation to different types of bullying experienced (more relational in girls and more physical in boys).

Greater male aggressiveness is often considered biologically pre-programmed, suggesting a bleak outlook for women and girls (as well as males) who are the victims of male violence. Male sex/gender has a very small, but significant, correlation with the tendency for six-month-old infants to bite, hit and resist being placed in a car seat—behaviours that correlate with later intentional aggression

(Hay *et al.*, 2014). However, very few infants show such behaviours (which puts Doddy Darwin in a minority!) and, by toddlerhood, being male no longer predicts aggression, whereas mothers' tendency towards antisocial behaviour does (we can also recall here the role of mothers in the cultural socialization of infant emotions, mentioned in the previous chapter). Most studies find that physically aggressive behaviour problems in very young children occur equally in girls and boys (Crick and Zahn-Waxler, 2003). Furthermore, a review of hormone studies found no evidence for teenage boys' 'testosterone-fuelled' aggression (Duke, Balzer and Steinbeck, 2014). Cordelia Fine's 2017 book *Testosterone Rex* addresses this issue. Aggressiveness as a quintessential male trait was also brought into question by the research into social forms of aggression more typical of females (e.g. Björkqvist and Niemelä, 1992).

Greater male competitiveness is also often assumed to be innate, and some scholars have argued that this is why there are more men in science (Gneezy, Leonard and List, 2009). While Uri Gneezy *et al.* confirmed greater male competitiveness in a non-western patriarchal culture (the Maasai of Tanzania), they found greater *female* competitiveness in a matrilineal one (the Khasi of India), suggesting the importance of societal structure in fostering sex/gender differences. Social roles theory holds that differences in male and female body strength and child-bearing ability have historically given males greater power and status and placed females into caring roles, and that this in turn influences aggressive attitudes and behaviours (Eagly and Steffen, 1986).

It has also been proposed that sex/gender differences in empathy arise from evolutionary parenting pressures underpinned by neurological differences (e.g. Christov-Moore *et al.*, 2014), implying that women's greater caring burdens are inevitable. However, as with other evolutionary-based explanations for sex/gender differences, much of the evidence is far weaker than generally supposed (e.g. Fine, 2013). Nor is female empathy 'fixed'; for example, empathic concern is lower in early adolescent girls a year after a period of parent–child conflict, while perspective-taking is protected from a similar drop if the girl is strongly connected to school (Batanova and Loukas, 2014).

To summarize, the evidence for essential, brain-based behavioural differences between men and women, and boys and girls, is weak, and understanding is growing that brain and behaviour are in a constant state of flux, with the brain developing through ongoing dynamic interactions with the environment. Rippon's (2019) award-winning book offers a very readable account of the 'myth of the female brain'.

Holistic frameworks for sex/gender development

Leaper (2000, 2022) has proposed a holistic approach to sex/gender development that is inclusive of feminism and numbers of developmental theories, and that can be regarded as a metatheoretical framework. Humans have evolved *adaptability* to different environments. At a broad level, these constitute Bronfenbrenner's macrosystem and include cultural values and practices such as patriarchy or egalitarianism, which provide constraints and opportunities for development. The macrosystem links to the home microsystem. Illustrating that western norms for parental division of labour are not biologically determined, Leaper cites Barry Hewlett's work within the egalitarian Aka culture of central Africa: mothers and fathers share child care and subsistence tasks, and infant care is not seen as 'feminine' but an 'adult' task. The microsystem provides the context in which children construct their understanding of gender, in accord with Vygotsky's sociocultural theory. While children tend to demonstrate similar behaviours in similar situations, in reality the early microsystems of boys and girls differ, with access to different play and toy activities (Lytton and Romney, 1991), through which children construct gender schemas and internalize gender norms (Bem, 1993). Insofar as these create asymmetrical representations of masculinity and femininity, they limit people's life opportunities. Leaper therefore regards the promotion of early sex/gender stereotyping as a form of discrimination.

An example is the heavily gendered television advertising of toys, with girls depicted indoors playing with toys concerned with 'family, friendship, and romance', but boys shown in diverse locations that suggest 'more opportunities, action, and life chances' (Kahlenberg and Hein, 2010: 844). Sex/gender stereotyping of children's toys and clothing has increased in recent years (Marcus, 2023), including gendered colour-coding ('pinkification') and make-up and sexy garments marketed for little girls. There have even been online plastic surgery games, raising feminist objections. This trend is troubling, not least because self-objectification leads to greater adolescent body shame, appearance anxiety and disordered eating, with girls more affected than boys (Slater and Tiggemann, 2010). Although western young men are more concerned with body image than their predecessors, images of muscular male bodies may create motivation to change, rather than dissatisfaction (McNeill and Firman, 2014).

Leaper also discusses children's tendency to self-segregate into same-sex/gender peer groups, given the opportunity, from early childhood until adolescence, when more mixing occurs unless there are cultural/religious constraints. He draws in part upon self-socialization theory, or shaping one's own life through personal and socially available opportunities (Shneewind, 2015). He further suggests that those children displaying behavioural tendencies that are most congruent with existing sex/gender stereotypes may become 'prototypes' within same-sex/gender peer groups that the majority of others emulate. Others, though, with dispositions not congruent with their assigned sex/gender may struggle to fit into groups and develop adjustment difficulties or experience bullying if they lack social support. Social identity theory (Tajfel and Turner, 1979) offers a way of understanding such ingroup and outgroup processes (Shute and Slee, 2022).

A somewhat similar metatheoretical framework, devised specifically for understanding gendered violence, was proposed by Jacquelyn White and Robin Kowalski (1998), with five nested interacting layers:

- Sociocultural (e.g. historical values and patriarchal social systems).
- Social networks (e.g. family, school).

- The dyadic perpetrator–victim relationship.
- Situational factors that promote or mitigate violence
- The intrapersonal (e.g. motives, personal characteristics).

Both frameworks are explicitly developmental and acknowledge patriarchy as an overarching influence. An attempt to diagrammatically capture such comprehensive frameworks is shown in Figure 12.1.

One approach to reducing sex/gender discrimination in the early years draws upon feminist-informed queer theory (Blaise and Taylor, 2012), based on the premise that there is no one way to 'perform' gender. Children's sex/gender stereotypes are seen to come from a society that views heterosexuality, dominant masculinity and subservient femininity as the norm, as reflected in the games (including romantic games) of even small children. Power differences are seen as created through sex/gender discourses. It is suggested that early childhood educators can change stereotypes by encouraging competing discourses in children's play and stories. This would be very different from the day in the 1980s when author RHS's daughter's class in the UK was provided with paper, one wet lunchtime, and told that the girls should draw houses and the boys should draw rockets!

There is now greater acceptance of sex/gender diversity in many countries, but in 2025 a presidential decree in the United States, based on poor understanding of biology, declared that there are only two sexes, male and female. Soon afterwards, a Scottish feminist group lobbying against trans women being regarded as women in the law celebrated the Supreme Court of the United Kingdom's ruling that being 'a woman' meant being biologically female. As such changes feed from the macrosystem (law) through the exosystem (e.g. trans health services) and on to the microsystems in which children develop (Figure 12.1), serious damage to many young (and older) people's mental health is a predictable consequence. Societal movements against sex/gender diversity (which may include some feminists), and against feminism itself, exemplify the backlash phenomenon.

Masculinist backlashes

We have mentioned several backlashes, including that of third wavers against second wavers, the boy turn in education, anti-trans activity, and postfeminism more generally. While this chapter was in preparation, Giséle Pèlicot's case was making international headlines (see Box 12.2), with crowds of French women outside the courthouse waving placards and thanking her for standing up for other assaulted women (all 51 accused men were found guilty and given jail sentences). For Australians, more local news was that some conservative parliamentarians were complaining that the Parliament House café was now selling gingerbread people instead of gingerbread men! While one might wonder about the priorities of public figures fussing over a sex/gender inclusive biscuit, these matters are not unrelated: while the French mayor minimized Giséle's trauma, the politicians railed against a biscuit that symbolized 'wokeness' and a small win for feminism/diversity. The emotional, aggrieved, nature of backlashes noted by Lucy Nicholas

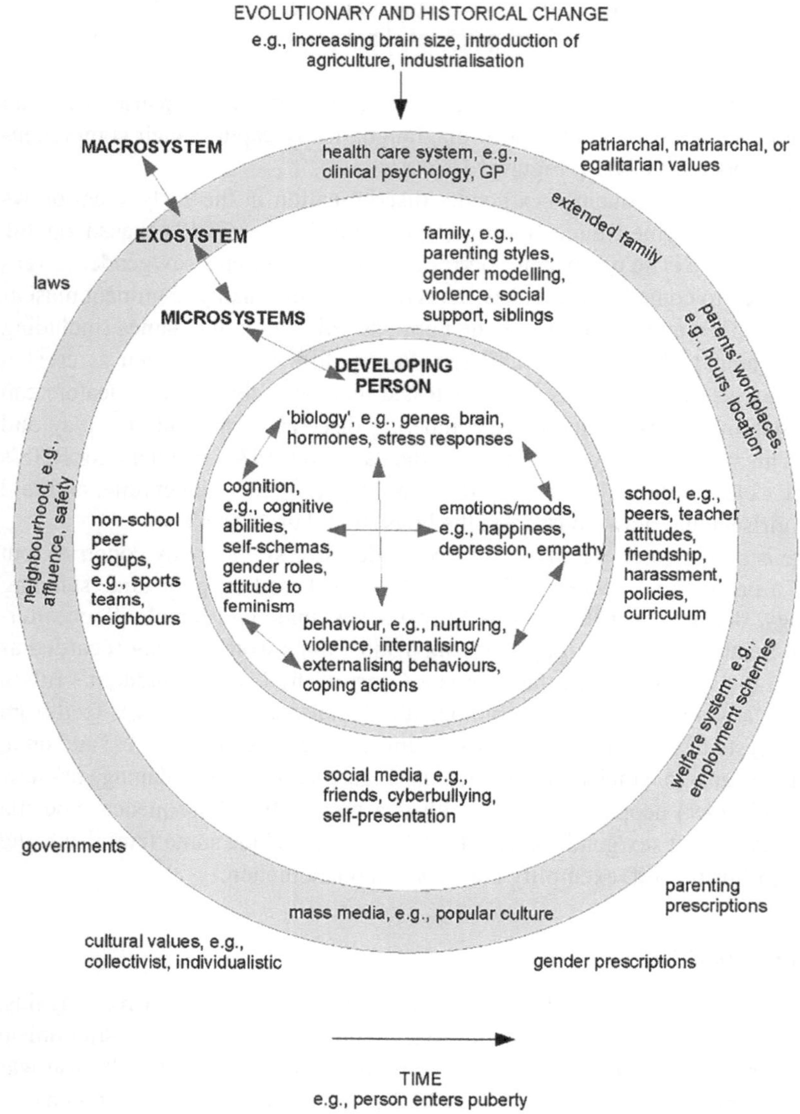

Figure 12.1 A holistic representation of sex/gender development. Reproduced from Shute (2018). This framework is broadly based upon Bronfenbrenner's ecological systems theory of development, but highlights examples of factors within the various hierarchical levels (macrosystem, exosystem, microsystems, and the developing person) that are especially relevant for sex/gender development. Subsystems within and between the various levels are mutually influential, though this is only shown for the inner level, the developing person. (Linkages between microsystems occur in what Bronfenbrenner called the 'mesosystem'.) In accord with western perspectives, where most research has taken place, the developing person is shown centrally, but this may be different in other cultures (see Fig. 11.1, the Maori octopus)

(2024) is illustrated by one of the politicians, who said he was fed up with having this kind of thing forced upon him.

Backlashes against feminism are acute phases that occur against a chronic background of anti-feminist attitudes and behaviours, when women and girls are perceived as making social progress (Haas and Binard, 2022; Nicholas, 2024). The overturning of *Roe v. Wade* in the United States in 2022 was a stark example of how hard-earned women's rights can never be taken for granted. To understand backlash, we need to examine masculinity (or masculinities) and masculinism.

In response to women's studies becoming established, men and masculinity studies also developed, involving both sociology and psychology, and the journal *Psychology of Men and Masculinity* launched in 2000. Two strands of psychological research emerged. One focused on traits (how far individuals exemplify idealized masculinity) and the other on social norms or ideology, as a cultural force underpinning gender relations, attitudes and beliefs that varies by time and place, with one version hegemonic at any particular point (Thompson and Bennett, 2015). Individuals internalize such cultural belief systems and these are measurable, including in adolescents, but are not regarded as (fixed) traits. Boys themselves are harmed by these norms, whether they try to live up to them or reject them (Shute, 2018).

Research in several countries has shown that their societies value particular male attributes (Hill *et al.*, 2020):

- Self-sufficiency.
- Acting tough.
- Being physically attractive, hypersexual and heterosexual.
- Enforcing rigid gender roles in the home.
- Controlling women.
- Using aggression when necessary.

Masculinism is an ideology that regards these as superior characteristics. However, in some countries, men perceive that society in general, and women, no longer value such attributes, and they are therefore more likely to express them in the company of their ingroup of other males (Iacoviello *et al.*, 2021). This is reflected in adolescent boys' groups, where they 'give each other shit' and 'frame emotional support as rational and problem-solving' (Nicholas, 2024: 3). Although more caring versions of masculinity exist, expressing these within male groups creates a sense of vulnerability. This can be successfully overcome through carefully managed group interventions, though outside the group context, boys may find implementing behaviour change difficult (Exner-Cortens *et al.*, 2021; McCormack and Anderson, 2010).

Also interesting is a recent study in two London schools with 10–11-year-old boys that found no homophobia or misogynist name-calling, very little bullying and no hegemonic form of masculinity (Swain, 2024). Rather, these boys displayed 'hybrid' identities that blended traditional masculine attributes such as confidence, athleticism and assertiveness with feminine-associated ones such as caring and being emotionally literate. We must therefore be alert to localized and changing versions of masculinity.

At the extreme end are those who overtly express male supremacy, including in online anti-feminist groups in the 'manosphere', keyboard warriors who troll outspoken women. Many adolescent boys today access the manosphere where they are exposed to charismatic leaders (influencers) who promote violence to women; many boys consider them 'cool', attracted to their neoliberal focus on 'money, achievement, material gain, the body, individualism and self-discipline' (Thomas-Parr and Gilroy-Ware, 2024: 239), and reflecting 'an aspirational, gendered self-hood' (p. 241) connected to themes of brotherhood/belonging. The misogynist element is playing out in Australian classrooms: girls and female and LGBTI+ teachers report increasingly misogynistic and defiant behaviours from boys, such as sexist comments and groups of boys making intimidating animal noises or even displaying Nazi symbols (Westcott, Roberts and Zhao, 2023). Girls feel unsafe and fear speaking up in class, and some female teachers are leaving the profession.

These attitudes are underpinned by an ongoing undercurrent of traditional, and entitled, masculinist views. In a large-scale Australian survey, almost half of young men believed that women often use accusations of sexual assault to get back at men. There have also been highly publicized cases in Australia and the UK of a culture in some elite boys' schools that normalizes the sexual assault of girls, which resulted in a feminist backlash from girls about consent education. This led to age-appropriate consent education being mandated in schools across Australia in 2023 (Woodley *et al.*, 2022).

Cross-fertilization between the manosphere and right-wing extremist groups is leading security agencies across the Global North to treat these forces as relevant for combating the radicalization of aggrieved young men, with sex/gender-based violence and acts of mass terrorism interrelated (Nicholas, 2024). As Nicholas (2017) has said, 'When you're accustomed to privilege, equality feels like oppression.'

Within masculinity studies, themes of identity and belonging are recognized as key to understanding backlash (Nicholas, 2024), as also identified for understanding gendered school bullying (Duncan, 1999; Shute and Slee, 2022). This represents a shift from the traditional individualist view of bullying, towards a more group-based understanding grounded in social norms. Social identity theory, successfully applied to school bullying (Ojala and Nesdale, 2004), offers one potential inroad into combating the radicalization of adolescent boys. For example, having social relationships outside the manosphere promotes disengagement (Munden, 2023), and this can be seen in terms of creating belongingness through alternative ingroups that do not endorse violence. The notion of generating emotional turning points for promoting deradicalization (Nicholas, 2024) is also interesting and could be examined from a psychological perspective.

Nicholas has written:

> The complex messages of contemporary masculinity damage men and boys, but they also damage women and girls, and queer and gender non-conforming people. The key difference is that gender causes women and gender-diverse

folks to harm themselves, but causes men to harm themselves, other men, women, and queer and gender-diverse people.

(Nicholas, 2024: 6)

Nicholas notes the challenging nature of addressing these issues, as masculinism is very adept at recuperation. Psychological theorizing about child and adolescent development has the potential to contribute to addressing these important social issues. Georgia Thomas-Parr and Marcus Gilroy-Ware suggest that feminism needs to be 'less market-driven and more inclusive and collective' (2024: 246) and to collaborate with boys in their need for agency and belonging.

The feminist decolonization of developmental psychology

In Chapter 11, we addressed the decolonizing of developmental psychology. Further complication is added when considering sex/gender in addition to culture. Indeed, decolonial work has marginalized sex/gender (Macleod, Bhatia and Liu, 2020) and, we might add, sidelined children in favour of women. An exception is Ayurdhi Dhar's (2020) discussion of girls' mental health in India and the slippery, shifting subjectivities of the girl child, that has many contradictory cultural influences and cannot be simply matched up with western psychological or psychiatric perspectives. Indeed, Dhar refers to the 'murder' of cultural knowledge that occurs when western concepts are uncritically applied to other cultures. Catriona Macleod *et al.* (2020) suggest that there is space for both local analyses (e.g. of intersectionality) and conversations that take place transnationally. Research such as that with unaccompanied child migrants to South Africa (see Chapter 11) paves the way for listening to children in colonized parts of the world. Heeding the different experiences of girls, boys and non-binary young people as a further aspect of decolonization is a challenging enterprise yet to be addressed.

Conclusion

Developmental psychology's androcentric perspective has gradually been eroded since Gilligan first challenged it in the 1970s, during the second wave of feminism, although she was not an activist but 'followed the data'. Burman's critical approach, from the 1990s, was also influential in feminist thought concerning child development. Sex/gender differences in children's development and topics of especial relevance for girls are now commonly addressed in the mainstream literature, but feminism is rarely cited as an influence, as developmental psychology remains heavily influenced by post-positivism. Feminist theorizing and research are thriving in psychology, but remain marginalized, and focus more on women than children. Holistic approaches to child development can incorporate feminism. Masculinity studies, established in response to women's studies, assist understanding of boys' development and the backlashes against feminism that continue to occur, to the detriment of girls, women and gender-diverse people (chillingly, in May 2025 the Pentagon ordered military leaders to remove all library books about gender, diversity and racism). Interventions have been devised to address harmful stereotypes and radicalization. The feminism-informed decolonization of developmental psychology is a complex matter ripe for future attention.

Note

1 Decades later, I (RHS) heard similar comments by some psychology academics and their students towards others who chose qualitative methods; indeed, one had to think very carefully about potential thesis examiners. Against the grain of my disciplinary context, I supported my own students in using mixed methods from the 1990s (that went well beyond the common practice of doing a bit of qualitative pilot work); with one of them, I wrote an invited piece giving advice to psychology students hoping to undertake qualitative research in a discipline that is still often hostile to it (Shute and Zschorn, 2018).

References

Ah-King, M., Barron, A. B. and Herberstein, M. E. 2014. Genital evolution: why are females still understudied? *PLOS Biology 12*(5): e1001851. https://doi.org/10.1371/journal.pbio.1001851

Alanen, L. 2016. 'Intersectionality' and other challenges to theorizing childhood. *Childhood 23*(2): 157–61. https://doi.org/10.1177/0907568216631055

American Psychological Association. 2007. Guidelines for psychological practice with girls and women. *American Psychologist 62*(9): 949–79. https://doi.org/10.1037/0003-066X.62.9.949

Athan, A. and Reel, H. I. 2015. Maternal psychology: reflections on the 20th anniversary of Deconstructing Developmental Psychology. *Feminism and Psychology 25*(3): 311–25. https://doi.org/10.1177/0959353514562804

Batanova, M. and Loukas, A. 2014. Unique and interactive effects of empathy, family, and school factors on early adolescents' aggression. *Journal of Youth and Adolescence 43*(11): 1890–902. https://doi.org/10.1007/s10964-013-0051-1

Bem, S. 1993. *The lenses of gender: transforming the debate on sexual inequality*. New Haven: Yale University Press.

Björkqvist, K. and Niemelä, P. (eds). 1992. *Of mice and women: aspects of female aggression*. San Diego: Academic Press.

Blaise, M. and Taylor, A. 2012. Using queer theory to rethink gender equity in early childhood education. *Young Children* January: 88–99. www.researchgate.net/publication/290316392_Using_queer_theory_to_rethink_gender_equity_in_early_childhood_education

Bluhm, R. 2013. Self-fulfilling prophecies: the influence of gender stereotypes on functional neuroimaging research on emotion. *Hypatia 28*(4): 870–86. https://doi.org/10.1111/j.1527-2001.2012.01311.x

Breen, L. J. and Darlaston-Jones, D. 2010. Moving beyond the enduring dominance of positivism in psychological research: implications for psychology in Australia. *Australian Psychologist 45*: 67–76. https://doi.org/10.1080/00050060903127481

Brown, L. M. and Gilligan, C. 1992. *Meeting at the crossroads: women's psychology and girls' development*. Cambridge, MA: Harvard University Press. https://doi.org/10.4159/harvard.9780674731837

Burman, E. 1994/2008/2016. *Deconstructing developmental psychology*. London: Routledge.

Burnett, A. 2016. Rape culture. In N. A. Naples (ed.), *The Wiley Blackwell encyclopedia of gender and sexuality studies*. Hoboken: Wiley, np. https://doi.org/10.1002/9781118663219.wbegss541

Campbell, A. 2012. The study of sex differences: feminism and biology. *Zeitschrift für Psychologie 220*(2): 137–43. https://doi.org/10.1027/2151-2604/a000105

Christov-Moore, L., Simpson, E. A., Coudé, G., Grigaityte, K., Iacoboni, M. and Ferrari, P. F. 2014. Empathy: gender effects in brain and behavior. *Neuroscience and Biobehavioral Reviews 46*(4): 604–27. https://doi.org/10.1016/j.neubiorev.2014.09.001

Cohen, C. 2010. Darwin on woman. *Comptes Rendus Biologies 333*: 2. www.sciencedirect.com/science/article/pii/S1631069109003072

Connaughton, M., Mitchell, O., Cullen, E., O'Connor, M., Banaschewski, T., Barker, G. J. *et al.* 2024. Bullying and early brain development: a longitudinal structural magnetic resonance imaging study from adolescence to early adulthood. www.biorxiv.org/content/10.1101/2024.09.11.611600v1

Crick, N. R. and Zahn-Waxler, C. 2003. The development of psychopathology in females and males: current progress and future challenges. *Development and Psychopathology 15*(3): 719–42. https://doi.org/10.1017/S095457940300035X

DeKeseredy, W. S. 2011. Feminist contributions to understanding woman abuse: myths, controversies and realities. *Aggression and Violent Behavior 16*: 297–302. http://dx.doi.org/10.1016/j.avb.2011.04.002

Demazeux, S. 2015. The ideal of scientific progress and the DSM. In S. Demazeux and P. Singy (eds), *The DSM-5 in perspective: philosophical reflections on the psychiatric Babel*. London: Springer, 3–24.

Dhar, A. 2020. The slippery and the sane: decolonizing psychology through a study of the Indian girl-child. *Feminism & Psychology 30*(3): 391–413. https://doi.org/10.1177/0959353520922419

Duke, S. A., Balzer, B. W. and Steinbeck, K. S. 2014. Testosterone and its effects on human male adolescent mood and behavior: a systematic review. *Journal of Adolescent Health. 55*(3): 315–22. https://doi.org/10.1016/j.jadohealth.2014.05.007

Duncan, N. 1999. *Sexual bullying*. London: Routledge.

Durano, M. 2020. The women's movement is leading reform in Argentina. *Open Society Foundations*, 6 March. www.opensocietyfoundations.org/voices/the-womens-movement-is-leading-reform-in-argentina

Eagly, A. H., Eaton, A., Rose, S. M., Riger, S. and McHugh, M. C. 2012. Feminism and psychology: analysis of a half-century of research on women and gender. *American Psychologist 67*(3): 211–30. https://doi.org/10.1037/a0027260

Eagly, A. H. and Steffen, V. J. 1986. Gender and aggressive behavior: a meta-analytic review of the social psychological literature. *Psychological Bulletin 100*(3): 309–30. http://search.proquest.com/docview/617238460?accountid=15115

Eagly, A. H. and Wood, W. 2013. Feminism and evolutionary psychology: moving forward. *Sex Roles 69*: 549–56. https://doi.org/10.1007/s11199-013-0315-y

Eliot, L. 2009. *Pink brain, blue brain: how small differences grow into troublesome gaps – and what we can do about it*. Boston: Houghton Mifflin Harcourt.

Etaugh, C. 2016. Psychology of gender: history and development of the field. *The Wiley Blackwell encyclopedia of gender and sexuality studies*. Hoboken: John Wiley, 3–24. https://doi.org/10.1002/9781118663219.wbegss442

Exner-Cortens, D., Wright, A., Van Bavel, M., Sitter, K. C., Hurlock, D., Carter, R. and Krause, P. 2021. 'To be a guy is to be human': Outcomes of the WiseGuyz program through photo-based evaluation. *Health Promotion Practice 22*(5): 659–69. https://doi.org/10.1177/1524839920976382

Farkas, T. and Leaper, C. 2016. Chivalry's double-edged sword: how girls' and boys' paternalistic attitudes relate to their possible family and work selves. *Sex Roles 74*: 220–30. https://doi.org/10.1007/s11199-015-0556-z

Fausto-Sterling, A. 2012. The dynamic development of gender variability. *Journal of Homosexuality 59*(3): 398–421. https://doi.org/10.1080/00918369.2012.653310

Fine, C. 2013. Neurosexism in functional neuroimaging: from scanner to pseudo-science to psyche. In M. Ryan and N. Branscombe (eds), *The SAGE handbook of gender and psychology*. Thousand Oaks: SAGE, 45–60.

Fine, C. 2017. *Testosterone Rex: unmaking the myths of our gendered minds*. London: Icon Books.

Fine, C., Dupré, J. and Joel, D. 2017. Sex-linked behavior: evolution, stability, and variability. *Trends in Cognitive Sciences 21*(9): 666–73. https://doi.org/10.1016/j.tics.2017.06.012

Fisher, S. and Greenberg, R. P. 1996. *Freud scientifically reappraised: testing the theories and therapy*. New York: Wiley.

Genz, S. and Brabon, B. 2009. *Postfeminism: cultural texts and theories*. Edinburgh: Edinburgh University Press.

Ghavami, N., Katsiaficas, D. and Rogers, L. O. 2016. Toward an intersectional approach in developmental science: the role of race, gender, sexual orientation, and immigrant status. In S. S. Horn, M. D. Ruck and L. S. Liben (eds), *Advances in child development and behavior*. Vol. 50. np: Elsevier Academic Press, 31–73. https://doi.org/10.1016/bs.acdb.2015.12.001

Gill, R. 2012. Media, empowerment and the 'sexualization of culture' debates. *Sex Roles 66*: 736–45. https://doi.org/10.1007/s11199-011-0107-1

Gilligan, C. 1982. *In a different voice: psychological theory and women's development.* Cambridge, MA: Harvard University Press.

Gneezy, U., Leonard, K. L. and List, J. A. 2009. Gender differences in competition: evidence from a matrilineal and a patriarchal society. *Econometrica, Econometric Society 77*(5): 1637–64. http://ideas.repec.org/a/ecm/emetrp/v77y2009i5p1637-1664.html

Grabe, S. 2020. Research methods in the study of intersectionality in psychology: examples informed by a decade of collaborative work with majority world women's grassroots activism. *Frontiers in Psychology: Hypothesis and Theory.* https://doi.org/10.3389/fpsyg.2020.494309

Haas, R. and Binard, F. 2022. Introduction: patriarchal backlashes to feminism in times of crisis: plus ça change, moins ça change. *European Journal of English Studies 26*(2): 163–75. https://doi.org/10.1080/13825577.2022.2091274

Haier, R. J., Karama, S., Leyba, L. and Jung, R. E. 2009. MRI assessment of cortical thickness and functional activity changes in adolescent girls following three months of practice on a visual-spatial task. *BMC Research Notes 1(*2): 174. https://doi.org/10.1186/1756-0500-2-174

Harding, A. 2024. Gisèle Pélicot: how an ordinary woman shook attitudes to rape in France. *BBC News*, 18 December. www.bbc.com/news/articles/cd75v8eqz44o

Harper, S. 2016. Beyond individual therapy. *The Psychologist 29*(6): 440–4. www.bps.org.uk/psychologist/beyond-individual-therapy

Hay, D. F., Waters, C. S., Perra, O., Swift, N., Kairis, V., Phillips, R. *et al.* 2014. Precursors to aggression are evident by 6 months of age. *Developmental Science 17*(3): 471–80. https://doi.org/10.1111/desc.12133

Hill, A. L., Miller, E., Switzer, G. E., Yu, L., Heilman, B., Levtov, R. G. *et al.* 2020. Harmful masculinities among younger men in three countries: psychometric study of the Man Box Scale. *Preventive Medicine 139*: 106185. https://doi.org/10.1016/j.ypmed.2020.106185

Hoffman, G. A. and Bluhm, R. 2016. Neurosexism and neurofeminism. *Philosophy Compass 11*(11): 716–29. https://doi.org/10.1111/phc3.12357

Iacoviello, V., Valsecchi, G., Berent, J., Borinca, I. and Falomir-Pichastor, J. M. 2021. Is traditional masculinity still valued? Men's perceptions of how different reference groups value traditional masculinity norms. *Journal of Men's Studies 30*: 20–7. https://journals.sagepub.com/doi/10.1177/10608265211018803

Joel, D., Berman, Z., Tavor, I., Wexler, N., Gaber, O., Stein, Y., *et al.* 2015. Sex beyond the genitalia: the human brain mosaic. *PNAS Proceedings of the National Academy of Sciences of the United States of America 112*(50): 15468–73. https://doi.org/10.1073/pnas.1509654112

Josselson, R. 2023. Developing a different voice: the life and work of Carol Gilligan. *Journal of Personality 91*: 120–33. https://doi.org/10.1111/jopy.12763

Kahlenberg, S. G. and Hein, M. M. 2010. Progression on Nickelodeon? Gender role stereotypes in toy commercials. *Sex Roles 62*: 830–47. https://doi.org/10.1007/s11199-009-9653-1

Keddie, A. 2010. Feminist struggles to mobilise progressive spaces within the 'boy-turn' in gender equity and schooling reform. *Gender and Education 22*(4): 353–68. https://doi.org/10.1080/09540250903289907

Kohlberg, L. 1971. From is to ought: how to commit the naturalistic fallacy and get away with it in the study of moral development. In T. Mischell (ed.), *Cognitive development and epistemology*. New York: Academic Press, 151–235.

Lamb, S. 2010. Feminist ideals for a healthy female adolescent sexuality: a critique. *Sex Roles 62*: 294–306. https://doi.org/10.1007/s11199-009-9698-1

Law, B. M. 2006. What feminism means today. *American Psychological Association*. www.apa.org/gradpsych/2006/09/feminism.aspx

Leaper, C. 2000. The social construction and socialization of gender during development. In P. H. Miller and E. K. Scholnick (eds), *Toward a feminist developmental psychology*. New York: Routledge, 127–52.

Leaper, C. 2022. Origins and consequences of childhood gender segregation: toward an integrative developmental systems model. In D. P. VanderLaan and W. I. Wong (eds), *Gender and sexuality development: Focus on sexuality research*. Cham: Springer, 159–205. https://doi.org/10.1007/978-3-030-84273-4_6

Leuner, B. and Gould, E. 2010. Structural plasticity and hippocampal function. *Annual Review of Psychology 61*: 111–40. https://doi.org/10.1146/annurev.psych.093008.100359

Lovell, K. 2016. Girls are equal too: education, body politics, and the making of teenage feminism. *Gender Issues 33*: 71–95. https://doi.org/10.1007/s12147-016-9155-8

Lytton, H. and Romney, D. M. 1991. Parents' differential socialization of boys and girls: a meta-analysis. *Psychological Bulletin 109*(2): 267–96. https://doi.org/10.1037/0033-2909.109.2.267

Maccoby, E. E. and Jacklin, C. N. 1974. *The psychology of sex differences*. London: Stanford University Press.

Macleod, C. I., Bhatia, S. and Liu, W. 2020. Feminisms and decolonising psychology: possibilities and challenges. *Feminism & Psychology 30*(3): 287–305. https://doi.org/10.1177/0959353520932810

Marcus, B. 2023. New report reveals how the marketing of toys reinforces gender stereotypes. *Forbes*, 1 December. www.forbes.com/sites/bonniemarcus/2023/12/01/new-report-reveals-how-the-marketing-of-toys-reinforces-gender-stereotypes/

Marquez, J., Taylor, L., Boyle, L., Zhou, W. and de Neve, J.-E. 2024. Child and adolescent wellbeing: global trends, challenges and opportunities. Chapter 3 in *World happiness report*. https://worldhappiness.report/ed/2024/child-and-adolescent-well-being-global-trends-challenges-and-opportunities/

Martino, W. and Berrill, D. 2003. Boys, schooling, and masculinities: interrogating the 'right' way to educate boys. *Educational Review 55*(2): 99–117. https://doi.org/10.1080/0013191032000072164

McCormack, M. and Anderson, E. 2010. 'It's just not acceptable any more': the erosion of homophobia and the softening of masculinity at an English sixth form. *Sociology 44*(5): 843–59. https://doi.org/10.1177/0038038510375734

McNeill, L. S. and Firman, J. L. 2014. Ideal body image: a male perspective on self. *Australasian Marketing Journal (AMJ) 22*(2): 136–43. https://doi.org/10.1016/j.ausmj.2014.04.001

McRobbie, A. 2008. *The aftermath of feminism: gender, culture and social change*. London: SAGE.

Miller, P. H. and Scholnick, E. K. 2015. Feminist theory and contemporary developmental psychology: the case of children's executive function. *Feminism & Psychology 25*(3): 266–83. https://doi.org/10.1177/0959353514552023

Mulvey, K. L., Hoffman, A. J., Gönültas, S., Hope, E. C. and Cooper, S. M. 2018. Understanding experiences with bullying and bias-based bullying: what matters and for whom? *Psychology of Violence 8*(6): 702–11. http://dx.doi.org/10.1037/vio0000206

Munden, H. P. 2023. Extremist group exits: what autobiographies by male right-wing formers reveal about identity transformation. *Behavioral Sciences of Terrorism and Political Aggression*. https://doi.org/10.1080/19434472.2023.2192771

Nicholas, L. 2017. Beyond quiet tolerance to diversity perspectives: when you're accustomed to privilege, equality feels like oppression. *Ethos 25*(4): 9–11. https://www.researchgate.net/publication/324166586

Nicholas, L. 2024. Young masculinities, masculinism, backlash, and the complexities of fostering change. *Journal of Applied Youth Studies 7*: 1–8. https://doi.org/10.1007/s43151-023-00109-8

Nichols, C., Rimmer, M. and Martin, P. 2024. Dominique Pelicot is a convicted rapist. He's also being investigated over an unsolved murder and attempted rape. *ABC News*, 21 December. www.abc.net.au/news/2024-12-21/dominique-pelicot-murder-investigation-gisele-pelicot-rape-trial/104753226

Ojala, K. and Nesdale, D. 2004. Bullying and social identity: the effects of group norms and distinctiveness threat on attitudes towards bullying. *British Journal of Developmental Psychology 22*: 19–35. https://doi.org/10.1348/026151004772901096

Radtke, H. L. and Stam, H. J. 2016. A history of psychology's complicated relationship to feminism: theorizing difference. In S. H. Klempe and R. Smith (eds), *Centrality of history for theory construction in psychology*. Cham: Springer International Publishing/Springer Nature, 167–85. https://doi.org/10.1007/978-3-319-42760-7_9

Rampton, M. 2015. *Four waves of feminism*. Pacific University, Oregon. http://www.pacificu.edu/about-us/news-events/four-waves-feminism

Rippon, G. 2016. The trouble with girls? Gina Rippon asks why plastic brains aren't breaking through glass ceilings. *The Psychologist 29*(12): 918–22. www.bps.org.uk/psychologist/trouble-girls

Rippon, G. 2019. *The gendered brain: the new neuroscience that shatters the myth of the female brain*. London: Bodley Head.

Saini, A. 2014. Menopause: nature's way of saying older women aren't sexually attractive? *The Observer*, 30 March. www.theguardian.com/society/2014/mar/30/menopause-natures-way-older-women-sexually-attractive

Schneewind, K. A. 2015. Socialization and education: theoretical perspectives. In J. D. Wright (ed.), *International encyclopedia of the social and behavioral sciences*. Second edn. np: Elsevier, 861–5. https://doi.org/10.1016/B978-0-08-097086-8.92071-3

Scholnick, E. K. and Miller, P. H. 2000. Engendering development: metaphors of change. In P. H. Miller and E. K. Scholnick (eds), *Toward a feminist developmental psychology*. New York: Routledge, 241–54.

Shute, R. H. 2018. *Clinical psychology and adolescent girls in a postfeminist era*. Abingdon: Routledge.

Shute, R. H. and Slee, P. T. 2022. *School bullying and marginalisation: harmonising paradigms*. Singapore: Springer Nature.

Shute, R. H. and Zschorn, M. 2018. Exploring parents' attributions about their child's physical disability: the benefits and challenges of qualitative research in the context of psychology. *Sage Research Methods Cases Part 2*. https://doi.org/10.4135/9781526444127

Slater, A. and Tiggemann, M. 2010. Body image and disordered eating in adolescent girls and boys: a test of objectification theory. *Sex Roles 63*: 42–9. https://doi.org/10.1007/s11199-010-9794-2

Swain, J. 2024. Popular boys, the ideal schoolboy, and blended patterns of masculinity for 10- to 11-year-olds in two London schools. *British Educational Research Journal 50*: 614–31. https://doi.org/10.1002/berj.3936

Tajfel, H. and Turner, J. C. 1979. An integrative theory of intergroup conflict: In W. G. Austin and S. Worchel (eds), *The social psychology of intergroup relations*. Monterey: Brooks/Cole, 33–7.

Tate, C. C. 2013. Addressing conceptual confusions about evolutionary theorizing: how and why evolutionary psychology and feminism do not oppose each other. *Sex Roles 69*: 491–502. https://doi.org/10.1007/s11199-012-0226-3

Thomas-Parr, G. and Gilroy-Ware, M. 2024. Im/perceptible boyhood in a post-Andrew Tate world. *Australian Feminist Studies 39*: 119–20, 229–50. https://doi.org/10.1080/08164649.2025.2460822

Thompson, E. H., Jr. and Bennett, K. M. 2015. Measurement of masculinity ideologies: a (critical) review. *Psychology of Men & Masculinity 16*(2): 115–33. http://dx.doi.org/10.1037/a0038609

Weldon, S. L., Lusvardi, A., Kelly-Thompson, K. and Forester, S. 2023. Feminist waves, global activism, and gender violence regimes: genealogy and impact of a global wave. *Women's Studies International Forum 99*: 1–10. https://doi.org/10.1016/j.wsif.2023.102781

Westcott, S., Roberts, S. and Zhao, X. 2023. The problem of anti-feminist 'manfluencer' Andrew Tate in Australian schools: women teachers' experiences of resurgent male supremacy. *Gender and Education 36*(2): 167–82. https://doi.org/10.1080/09540253.2023.2292622

White, J. W. and Kowalski, R. M. 1998. Male violence toward women: an integrated perspective. In R. G. Geen and E. Donnerstein (eds), *Human aggression: theories, research, and implications for social policy*. San Diego: Academic Press, 203–28. https://doi.org/10.1016/B978-012278805-5/50009-2

Wilkinson, S. 1998. Focus groups in feminist research: power, interaction, and the co-construction of meaning. *Women's Studies International Forum 21*: 111–25. www.sciencedirect.com/science/article/abs/pii/S0277539597000800

Wilson, T. D. 2012. Stop bullying the 'soft' sciences. *Los Angeles Times*, 12 July. www.latimes.com/opinion/la-xpm-2012-jul-12-la-oe-wilson-social-sciences-20120712-story.html

Woodley, G., Jacques, C., Jaunzems, K. and Green, L. 2022. Mandatory consent education is a huge win for Australia – but consent is just one small part of navigating relationships. *The Conversation*, 21 February. https://theconversation.com/mandatory-consent-education-is-a-huge-win-for-australia-but-consent-is-just-one-small-part-of-navigating-relationships-177456

Worell, J. and Etaugh, C. 1994. Transforming theory and research with women: themes and variations. *Psychology of Women Quarterly 18*(4): 443–50. https://doi.org/10.1111/j.1471-6402.1994.tb01041.x

Worell, J. and Johnson, N. G. (eds). 1997. *Shaping the future of feminist psychology: education, research, and practice*. Washington, DC: American Psychological Association.

World Health Organization. 2016. *Growing up unequal: gender and socioeconomic differences in young people's health and well-being*. www.who.int/europe/publications/i/item/9789289051361

Wraga, M., Duncan, L., Jacobs, E. C., Helt, M. and Church, J. 2006. Stereotype susceptibility narrows the gender gap in imagined self-rotation performance. *Psychonomic Bulletin & Review 13*: 813–19. https://doi.org/10.3758/BF03194002

13 Listening to different voices 2

The voices of children

Introduction

In developmental psychology research, the voices of children have been even more silent than those of women. Vicki Coppock (2011) suggested that feminism has influenced critical thinking about childhood: just as femininity has historically been understood as the opposite of, and inferior to, masculinity, so is childhood viewed in relation to adulthood. Erica Burman (2023) refers to this as 'childism' which parallels 'feminism' in advocating for child empowerment, and 'racism' in identifying prejudice against children. In this chapter we discuss recent moves in the direction of child empowerment, in the form of listening to children's voices (bearing in mind that this term includes adolescents). Linda Mahony *et al.*'s (2024) book exemplifies that 'listening to children' has become a rapidly developing multidisciplinary field.

The 'new sociology of childhood' and social constructivism

While childhood has been considered a topic worthy of scholarly attention within psychology since the 19th century, it only became prominent within sociology in the 1990s (Matthews, 2007). That discipline has, however, been much more progressive in taking seriously the notion that children have voices that should be heard. This perspective gained increasing traction, under the rubric of 'the new sociology of childhood' (NSC) (Matthews, 2007). Some have argued that in both sociology and psychology children have been seen as passive and vulnerable beings, acted upon by others rather than being social actors, and viewed as 'in the process of becoming' rather than 'being' (Heary and Guerin, 2006; Wyness, 2006); this view has been especially apparent in the tendency of US researchers to take a lifespan perspective on human development (Matthews, 2007). Sarah Matthews noted a greater research emphasis there than in other western countries on peer relationships, rather than on how the adult–child power differential affects children's development. The greater European focus on recognizing the effect of 'relations of constraint'—even in the cognitive work of Jean Piaget—can perhaps be traced back to the influence of the great French sociologist Émile Durkheim at the start of the 20th century (Doise, 1990). This reminds us of Thomas Teo's caveat

DOI: 10.4324/9781003567738-13

that the overwhelmingly large body of US-based research on child development must be interpreted in its cultural context.

An over-focus on the future may lead to neglect of the here and now and children's current wellbeing, as in the case of children's mental health potentially being compromised by high pressure to perform academically (*The Lancet*, 2023). A future focus is also relevant for children with disabilities, who may never reach milestones that children, or their parents, typically hope for. The most contented parents of children with severe disabilities are those who focus on enjoying their child in the here and now (Zschorn and Shute, 2016). And what about children who die? A major concern of bereaved parents is to make meaning of their child's life and death, which entails keeping alive the memory of an important family member who never had the chance to reach adult status (Darbyshire *et al.*, 2013).

The very use of the term 'the child' in scholarly literature has been criticized as objectifying children and implying that development takes a universal course (Greene, 2006), as does the term 'the voice of the child' rather than 'the voices of children'. Anthropology took a similar critical track; although US anthropology in particular has a long-standing research interest in childhood in different cultures, a commitment to listening to children's voices is more recent (James, 2007). Jane Murray has highlighted emerging issues including how to define 'children's voices', suggesting: 'views of children that are actively received and acknowledged as valuable contributions to decision-making affecting the children's lives' (Murray, 2019).

Such critiques adopt a social constructivist perspective (Sudarsan *et al.*, 2022). Although forerunners of social constructivism can be identified among some early thinkers, including Buddha (Pritchard and Woollard, 2010), it was a number of 20th-century writers who were especially influential. Foremost was Lev Vygotsky, with his dialectical theory emphasizing how an individual's constructions of reality develop within cultural contexts. George Kelly's (1955) personal construct theory, although not a child development theory, was also influential. Others credited with promoting social constructivism are the philosophers G. H. Mead in the 1930s and John Macmurray in the 1950s and 1960s (Lock *et al.*, 1989). Adopting a social constructivist position means accepting that children in different cultures experience childhood differently. A universal view of childhood is not possible, and children's experiences will differ in terms of how they view their relationships, rights and responsibilities. The changing views of childhood over time (Ariés, 1962; Musgrove, Leahy and Moruzi, 2019) reinforce the difficulty of producing universal truths. If we subject the very notion of children's voices to such analysis, the complexity becomes apparent:

> Voice is a social construct operating in a cultural context where shared meaning is negotiated. This immediately raises problems for children's voice because in order to have influence, their voice has to transcend the cultural boundaries of childhood and negotiate a shared understanding in the adult world, yet much of children's voice is not expressed in words – least of all

> adult words – and the rich tapestry of their non-verbal communication frequently goes unheard.
>
> *(Kellett, 2010: 196)*

Later, we will explore recent work attempting to overcome these difficulties, including the link with children's agency.

The argument just outlined that children have been wrongly viewed as passive beings can be challenged. Biologically speaking, humans are certainly altricial mammals, entering the world dependent upon the care, nurturing and protection of older members of society. While the sociological concern with 'socialization' of youngsters into the ways of their culture did have an 'acted-upon' emphasis, it has long been recognized in child psychology that children, despite their dependence, have agency from infancy. Sheila Greene (2006) suggested that some critics of developmental psychology had not appreciated this history. Jean Piaget's view of the child as a little scientist experimenting upon the world is a prime example of seeing children as actors, although his interest was in epistemology, not children themselves (Greene, 2006). Infant cognition is an important area in which the competence, rather than inferiority, of children has been highlighted. The phrase 'the competent infant' gained currency in the 1970s as new research methods enabled infant capabilities to be examined (refer back to Figure 2.1). This field has continued to produce revelations about the abilities of babies. For example, from 10 months of age, babies show surprise when a big animated block (with an eye and mouth) bows and gives way to a smaller one, showing that by this age babies understand how social dominance normally plays out when two actors have conflicting goals (Thomsen *et al.*, 2011). Such research findings emanating from child psychology gave strong impetus to the development of the NSC.

The NSC highlighted the fact that children do not simply passively accept and ape the attitudes and behaviours of their elders (as the 'socialization' approach suggested) but transform them. William Corsaro (2005) proposed the term 'reproductive interpretation' for this process. One example is the contribution of children to the development of creole languages. These arise where speakers of different languages are brought together as a new community and form a new language adapted from elements of their mother tongues; although children's role in the creation of creoles may have been overplayed, it does appear that they are the ones primarily responsible for regularizing the grammar as the creole develops (Hudson Kam and Newport, 2009). Erica Burman (2018), too, has emphasized that children have agency, although this may not be recognized by adults, as in the case of children we have mentioned previously: street-connected children, and the African children who voluntarily cross national borders for economic benefits, yet may be returned to their families by the authorities.

That children have agency is not questioned in some cultures. For example, when an outsider asked a Wintu mother why the hair of her 18-month-old had not been cut, she replied that he had not asked for that to be done, although the child did not yet have the language to make such a request (Lee, 1959). Anthropologist Dorothy Lee also described a Chinese way of 'toilet-training' a baby, which involved the mother tuning in to signals that the baby was about to empty its bladder and responding accordingly, so that the baby 'trained itself' at an early age: 'his autonomy has remained inviolate, because his mother has had the sensitivity and the patience to "listen" to him' (Lee, 1959: 8).

The United Nations Convention on the Rights of the Child (UNCRC, 1989)

This widely ratified Convention (UNICEF Australia, n.d.) was another spur to the development of the NSC. The idea that children should be 'seen and not heard' still has echoes today, but is very much at odds with international perspectives as laid out in the Convention (Mahony *et al.*, 2024), which places a binding obligation on states to attend to children's views in all matters that affect them, 'being given due weight in accordance with the age and maturity of the child' (Article 12) and to grant children freedom of expression through any media of the child's choice (Article 13). An example of how this is translated into local requirements is that, in special education in England, the relevant code of practice as drawn up in 2015 included an obligation on local authorities to include children and, further, that parental views could not be used as a proxy for those of their children (Bloom *et al.*, 2020).

As simplistically appealing as Article 12 is, hearing children's voices is difficult in practice (Hayes, 2024). Professionals often lack an understanding of children's rights and the necessary skills and tools to effectively 'listen to children' (Bloom *et al.*, 2020). In the past few years, there has been an explosion of scholarly discussion about the nature of 'children's voice' (or 'voices') and the challenges that listening presents for research and practice, especially with young children and those with disabilities, as reflected in Mary Kellet's quote above.

While Article 12 is clear that a child's age and maturity may place limits on the weight to be placed on their views, a 2009 recommendation was added that there should be a presumption that a child is capable of forming their own views and that these should be recognized by states parties; however, this is not legally binding (Murray, 2019). Nevertheless, much effort is being expended on exploring ways to listen to even the youngest and communicatively challenged children.

The Convention itself has been criticized for taking a universal, westernized, approach to children's needs, but the universalism/relativism debate, as applied to children's rights, has been seen by Afua Twum-Danso (2008) as creating an impasse that is not helpful for improving children's lives on the ground. She proposed that what is needed is a localized understanding of global discourse about children's rights, derived from research with children as well as adults, as illustrated by research in Ghana: younger relatives are always perceived as children, even if they are grown up, married and living separately with their own children, while Ghanaian children themselves view childhood in terms of respect and obedience to elders—indeed, they see the ability to respect and obey as children's rights.

Various countries have in place mechanisms to protect the rights of young people, such as a Children's Ombudsman/Commissioner, legal guardians or non-government organizations. In the authors' home state of South Australia there is an Office of the Guardian of Children and Young People.

Empowerment of children

In the 21st century, the concept of empowerment began to gain increasing importance in the social work field, being described as a new paradigm taking over from a problem-solving approach that viewed clients as having deficits needing to be 'fixed' (Guo and Tsui, 2010). The empowerment perspective is in tune with the positive psychology movement, which seeks to emphasize and work from people's strengths rather than pathologizing them (e.g. Seligman, 2002). Empowerment has been conceptualized in various ways, such as differentiating between a subjective sense of power and an actual ability to influence, which is similar to the point made in the previous chapter with regard to adolescent girls' participation in raunch culture. In considering the various ways in which adults might empower children through collaboration, Harry Shier (2001) drew upon Vygotskian theory, with listening to children as the lowest level, and sharing decision-making power and responsibility with them as the highest. He later revised his model, as we discuss later.

It was usual in the past for psychological research to use mothers' perspectives about their children rather than seeking children's own views, but 'child-centred research' has become more common. In recent decades, standardized questionnaires have been developed on many topics to access young people's own views, being child-appropriate in their language and content (Heary and Guerin, 2006). However, giving children 'a voice' is generally understood to be best achieved through more open-ended, qualitative research methods such as interviews, focus groups, children's drawings and the use of photographs ('photovoice', as used by author PTS to study bullying and school violence in India) (Epstein *et al.*, 2006; Hedegaard, 2018; Skrzypiec, Slee and Sandhu, 2015). Another example was a study that asked 8–12-year-old Irish children to take photographs representing their wellbeing, while another group was responsible for categorizing them and identifying missing elements (Gabhainn and Sixsmith, 2006); the themes were loved people, activities, food and drink, and animals/pets, all of which they saw in an integrated fashion as 'the way I live'. Qualitative research methods are diverse but have in common a concern with 'meaning' (Braun and Clarke, 2024). They continue to be subject to controversy concerning how study quality should be judged; for example, some journals reject articles that use a 'checklist' approach to rigour, while others require one (Braun and Clarke, 2024).

Of course, determining how to involve children in research and important life decisions, and how to act upon their input, is not straightforward. Allison James (2007) raised the risk that children would be 'listened to' in a way that simply confirmed old prejudices. Children's 'voices' quoted in research, for example, have still been edited and contextualized by the adult researchers, and she suggested that this was not sufficiently acknowledged (in her field of anthropology, at least). A recent issue that has arisen internationally concerns the banning of mobile phones in schools. Jack Reed and Catherine Dunn (2024) have considered this in relation to the guidance issued to English schools. Echoing Durkheim, they discuss the epistemological need to distinguish the dominant group (e.g. policy makers, politicians, educators) from subordinated social actors (young people). They conclude with a set of recommendations underpinned by 'identifying the inescapable nature of technological entanglements, the role and importance of promoting digital literacy in the classroom, and how fostering collaborative partnerships between various stakeholders' can best contribute to the development of a nuanced and strategic approach to the matter, to which we return in the next chapter.

One way of empowering young people has been a governance approach, whereby their input is sought by the reference groups of various organizations. The Charter of Rights for Children and Young People in South Australia was formally launched in 2006, tabled in Parliament in 2010 and is protected by law. It comprises a list of 20 aspirational conditions (e.g. wellbeing, education, safety) that all children and young people should have to be safe, happy and well. Children and young people helped shape the Charter and it reflects what is important to them and a commitment to work from a foundation of state, national and international children's rights, including the UNCRC. The Charter guides the South Australian Government, local government, and other organizations to make decisions that affect children and young people. That said, care must be taken that the voices of those from certain social groups are not privileged over others (Cooper, 2023).

The notion of 'empowerment' has been critiqued with regard to a situation with profound consequences for children: the making of custody and parenting plans in the case of family breakdown. For signatories to the UNCRC, the child must have separate legal representation and the child's opinions must be heard. Although the United States is not a signatory, how to involve children in the process is nevertheless of concern, and Richard Warshak (2003) criticized the most radical type of 'empowerment' of children in making this important decision, which lies at a much higher order of responsibility than simply being 'heard' (Shier, 2001). Seeking and honouring children's preferences in this context Warshak saw as flawed, as they may not have the maturity to make a considered decision. For example, children's expressed preferences (to live primarily with one parent or the other) may be based upon pressure from a parent, or upon transient issues such as a recent argument with a parent with whom a child has a long-term warm relationship, or a preference for a permissive parent who allows behaviours such as late bedtimes or alcohol consumption, that are not *in the best interest of the child*. This very phrase has been criticized by some as being often abused in order to maintain adult oppression of children (Coppock, 2011). Warshak's caution, though, suggests that a critical approach to children's welfare needs to be tempered by taking account of insights gained from research that focuses on longer-term outcomes. Warshak suggests that listening to the *collective* voices of children, as expressed through research, is one appropriate path, though it is unlikely that many critical theorists would accept that. A more personalized method he approved was to appoint a guardian who listens to a child's perspectives and speaks in the child's best interest, especially in contexts where parenting plans may be trialled and the child provides feedback on the experience.

We now turn to more radical ways of eliciting children's voices in both professional and research contexts, that have recently been given scholarly attention. These methods are inclusive of the youngest children and those with challenges in communication.

The voices of children in early childhood education

The growth of early childhood education services has prompted increasing research interest in examining children's experiences in such settings (Hayes, 2024). Qilong Zhang (2015) reviewed ten years of Australian and Aotearoa/New Zealand peer-reviewed articles on early childhood education. About half the articles did not require child-related data (e.g. they were about professional development), while over a third discussed the voice of the child. Some studies, however, could be classified as accessing 'pseudo-voice', whereby the data collected were 'about', not 'with' the child, such as psychometric and academic assessment, even though age-appropriate methods were used. In other cases, voice was unobtrusively inferred by observations; for example, children's previous drawings might be examined, rather than being generated with the child as part of the research process. Zhang used the term 'surveyed voice' for another type of study, whereby informal age-appropriate interviews or focus groups were held. Finally, there was co-constructed voice, where the researcher's presence was participatory and obtrusive, aimed at gaining understanding of the child's lived experience, such as through child-led tours, map-making, collaborative drawing and use of photographs taken with disposable cameras. Zhang concluded that the rhetoric of voice is not necessarily matched by practice, and that it would be better to explicitly disclaim trying to access children's voices rather than making a tokenistic effort.

The Reggio Emilia philosophical approach to early childhood education has spread from its Italian origins to other parts of the world. It accepts that the views of even the youngest children can be signalled in many ways, such as by words, silences, body language and drawings, that skilled educators can pick up on, and encourage young children to activate their voice (Hayes, 2024). Drawing upon Urie Bronfenbrenner and Pamela Morris' bioecological model, Nóirín Hayes suggests that shared acts of meaning, such as turn-taking in activities with babies, provide opportunities for learning about their culture, and that children need space and encouragement to express their views, be listened to, and have their views acted upon. The creation of a supportive pedagogical environment that is developmentally and individually appropriate is seen as central to enabling children's voices to be heard. However, practicalities such as staff time-pressure and a focus on 'investment return' (Murray, 2019) may interfere with ideal practice, a pressing issue in the largely private child-care 'industry' in Australia. Also, creating a democratic environment, and the necessary disruption to the usual adult-child power imbalance, can be 'disconcerting for some, and alarming for others' (Hayes, 2024: 833).

Franco Carnevale's hermeneutic approach

Franco Carnevale (2020) runs a research program in Canada called VOICE (Views on Interdisciplinary Childhood Ethics). He focuses attention on these issues by presenting several case studies that raise questions about what 'listening to children' means in practice, and how it relates to children's agency. For example, 10-year-old William understands that his cancer is very serious, but tells his nurse that he dislikes hospital and chemotherapy, which he is only doing for the sake of his parents, but doesn't want them to know to avoid upsetting them. Maria is aged 15 and anorexia nervosa is compromising her vital functions; she wants to lose more weight but has been restrained for the insertion of a nasogastric feeding tube.

Carnevale sees legalistic approaches based on developmental stages and cognitive maturity as outdated, unhelpful and oppressive, instead favouring transactional models. He does not (indeed, cannot) offer simple solutions to these difficult situations, but argues for a hermeneutic (interpretative) approach that seeks to understand what is meaningful to the child in the situation. This means considering children's perspectives and capacity to participate in discussions and decision-making. He contrasts this against a common view (that he calls 'psychosocial') that 'listening to children' means no more than expressing compassion and offering comfort. Rather, children's voices should carry ethical weight in decision-making about them. This approach, which takes account of political aspects (e.g. adults' greater power), he conceptualizes as 'thick', by contrast with a 'thin' perspective that takes what children say, and adults' understanding of it, at face value, rather than seeking deeper (moral) meaning.

Carnevale's hermeneutic approach involves considering ontogeny (what voice 'is', as 'thick'), epistemology (how children's voices can be known, through interpretation) and methodology. The latter is guided by questions about sources of information, such as identifying relevant documents or who should be consulted, and analytical questions, such as interview probes for a particular purpose.

Children who communicate differently: *Your Voice Your Choice*

Ashley Bloom and colleagues (2020) have devised a specific toolkit, based on emotional reactions, for eliciting the voices of children with speech and communication challenges, in order to gain information about how they feel about aspects of their schooling and support systems. Their philosophical framework is critical realism, which takes a path between positivism and interpretivism, in accepting that there is a 'reality' but that it cannot always be observed and may be seen differently by different individuals. This means accepting dominant narratives but analysing and exploring them for the operation of power and challenging them 'according to the practices and outcomes that they permit and inhibit' (Bloom *et al.*, 2020: 175). The kit consists of a purple felt mat incorporating a ladder (scale) and various emotional symbols that can be attached with Velcro, such as a thumbs-up sign, smiley face and other emotional expressions. Photographs or illustrations are used to represent aspects of the child's life at school. The child can stick the various symbols and images onto the mat or respond verbally if they wish. The kit is used contextually, which means initially spending time in the school and gaining the perspectives of teachers and, if possible, parents, through interviews, informal discussions and official documents. This enables the practitioner to develop propositions (similar to hypotheses) to focus the work, and to use specific items and interview questions with the toolkit that are relevant for the individual child, and that enable rival explanations to be examined.

The adult provides scaffolding, in accord with Vygotsky's zone of proximal development, often enabling a child to reach a higher level of emotional and cognitive expression than they could access without support. This is how their voice is enabled to be heard. One case the authors describe is a good illustration of how the process works and provides information that enables changed practice with the child (see Box 13.1).

BOX 13.1 A CASE STUDY OF *YOUR VOICE YOUR CHOICE*

Ashley Bloom and colleagues have described the following case study.

> Nathan was an example of a child who was reluctant or unable to provide verbal information. The interviewer was advised by the class teacher that Nathan would refuse to talk because he had 'refused to work or talk … for months' and was said to often refuse to talk to people he did not know particularly well. However, Nathan was able to engage with the activity while offering limited vocal communication throughout his interview. For instance, he showed that social situations made him feel angry, he disliked working in groups and he became worried when working with his teaching assistant. In contrast, listening to music calmed him down, he felt very happy around animals, and art and music were his preferred subjects. Triangulation through the supporting features of the YVYC toolkit, such as the interviewer observations and proxy perceptions, agreed with his feelings across many of the areas discussed, supporting the validity of his sentiments without requiring further detail. As a result, the case study was able to explore how the school might use the information to differentiate his work more successfully (for example, by focusing on his relational needs and motivational interests). However, without more information, the limits of the YVYC tool became apparent. For instance, it was unclear why he felt so angry, disliked social situations, and felt unable to talk to others. The answers to these questions were hypothesised and discussed within the case study using information from the additional perspectives drawn out by YVYC toolkit.
>
> *(Bloom et al., 2020: 189)*

The voices of children in research

Prompted by the UN Convention, there has been a growing trend to include children in research that is relevant for them, in the interest of democracy and respecting the voices of children as members of society. Indu Sudarsan *et al.* (2022) have provided a theoretical framework for considering children's research participation by applying a social constructionist approach. In keeping with Vygotskian theory and the NSC, this sees children as active, competent beings who come to understand the world through their interactions with others, within their social, cultural and historical context. These authors propose that constructivist grounded theory (Charmaz, 2016) offers a framework for the inclusion of children in research. This involves constant monitoring and comparison of findings and ongoing adjustment of the data collection process accordingly, to explore emerging issues. The researchers' population of concern was young Indians with asthma who were immigrants to Aotearoa/New Zealand, where implementation of the UN Convention has been slow, but where the Ministry of Vulnerable Children has been seeking child input. The chief researcher was an Indian nurse, who thus occupied an insider, emic position in some respects, but an etic position in other ways (e.g. not having children with asthma herself). Reflexive memo-keeping concerning the changing positioning of the researcher and the co-construction of experiences with children was a core aspect of the work. With younger children, methods included drawings, photographs, storytelling and puzzles, according to the child's interests; these methods were also available to older children if they preferred them to conversation. Parents were invited to be present, but a challenge was the authoritarian style of Indian parenting and the cultural expectation that children will obey adults (refer also to Box 6.3), and parents sometimes disagreed with children's statements, making it difficult to hear their voices (though it would have provided information about the family context). The project yielded details about children's experiences in managing their asthma, such as children's and parents' knowledge and attitudes about the use of inhalers.

The term 'participation' is sometimes used rather than 'voice' or 'listening'. Eija Sevón and colleagues (2023) undertook a systematic literature review of participatory research with young children, focusing on data collection methods. The context was often early childhood education, but health care, climate change and sustainability were also addressed. The aforementioned theoretical framework of Shier was often cited, as was that of his predecessor Roger Hart (1992), who devised a *Ladder of Children's Participation*, the top rung being child-initiated decisions shared with adults, and consultation at the lowest level. Hart also noted types of non-participation, including tokenism, manipulation and children as 'decoration'. Sevón *et al.* identified 75 peer-reviewed papers. The commonest approach was to use multiple methods, such as the Mosaic approach (Clark, 2005), followed by visual methods, such as those noted previously, based on the Reggio Emilia approach. Language-based and playful methods were also used. Eleven studies could be classified as involving the child as co-researcher, with active collaboration and learning together, and children variously identifying research themes, developing research questions and collecting data. Although ethical issues were carefully attended to, few studies gave children feedback on the study findings.

Bonnie Nastasi (2020) has considered research with children about their psychological wellbeing, that respects their rights and voices and sensitively takes account of cultural issues. Noting that most such research comes from America (meaning the United States), she critiques the tendency of researchers to assume that their research findings are universally applicable. Her conceptual foundations, like those of others considering cultural developmental matters, include Bronfenbrenner's and Vygotsky's theories and also come from anthropology and public health. We offered definitions of culture at the beginning of Chapter 11, but Nastasi's is as follows: 'Culture [is] a dynamic system of meanings, knowledge, and actions that provides actors collectively, interpersonally, and individually with community-legitimized strategies to construct, reflect upon, and reconstruct their world and experience, and guide behavior' (Nastasi, 2020: 579). Shared meanings and individual variations are both subjects to consider. She and colleagues have designed a Participatory Culture-Specific Intervention Model. Their wellbeing model includes interaction between individual-personal factors (culturally valued competencies, personal resources and personal vulnerabilities) with cultural-ecological factors (cultural norms, social-cultural stressors and resources, and socialization agents and practices). Initially, researchers frame their etic perspective based on a range of types of information, but this is then adjusted using ethnographic methods with key stakeholders. Partnerships with these cultural experts work to devise mixed-method research to develop culturally specific theory that guides interventions (adapted to the culture) and evaluation. They have also devised methods to enable cross-cultural work across multiple countries, avoiding the imposition of western definitions of mental health, indeed, avoiding that very term. Both qualitative data and quantitative data about social networks (ecomaps) are collected. They have found both common and unique factors when comparing cultures. For example, close relations with peers, family and teachers are widely identified as supportive resources, while certain others in the community are identified as a threat to wellbeing. Specific stressors include, for those living in the Amazon rainforest of Brazil, the impact of rainy weather such as being stuck indoors and electricity cuts, while children from southern Sri Lanka mentioned tsunamis, drought and monsoons as stressful events. Nastasi has drawn up a list of competencies needed for cross-cultural researchers, that includes an understanding of children's rights and knowledge of culturally sensitive research methods.

Harry Shier's revised *Pathways to Participation*

We end this chapter with Shier's revised model of children's participation, that followed his cross-cultural experience with child coffee-plantation workers in Nicaragua, where he lived for seven years, until 2008 (Shier, 2010). Out of touch with his old field of youth studies, he did not know initially that his model had become widely cited, but his experience in Nicaragua brought the realization that his previous work in the UK was very narrowly based and, like other studies in the Global North, tended to be about children's participation in public services such as education. By contrast, those in the Global South often live in extreme poverty, have little or no access to such services, and are widely regarded as 'public actors'. While child rights may be recognized by laws, the reality can be very different, and Shier's description of the conditions for some child coffee workers, including danger and, often, no pay, seems to amount to exploitation, though he does not use that word. However, their rights are defended by a non-government organization which has a vision of children as taking control of their own development and as capable of organizing themselves. It supports them in doing so, offering training and workshops and specifically supporting girls' rights.

Shier took away ten key learnings from this experience:

1. Children become empowered as a result of a long-term process of personal development.
2. Children's competence should be assumed.
3. Children and youth have a central community role as peer educators.
4. Children can have leadership roles.
5. Children can advocate for, and defend, their rights.
6. Children can be proactive and autonomous, even in adult-dominated spaces.
7. Children's participation in such spaces must be valued and not tokenistic.
8. Children should not be manipulated into direct action according to adult agendas, but supported to use various media (e.g. theatre, radio) to campaign for their own causes (literally, to have their voices heard).
9. Adult facilitators need to be trained to offer support that is appropriate (one can again invoke 'scaffolding' here).
10. As a result of child action, adults' attitudes can change, and adults realize they can learn from children (cf. Margaret Mead's prefigurative culture, in Chapter 9).

A group of Nicaraguan youth workers drew up a representation of children's participation in the form of a tree (Figure 13.1). This really amounts to a locally devised, rights-based model of children's development. The family is seen as the seed from which the tree grows, and the seedling is strengthened by participation in the community outside the home. The tree grows in the fertile soil of the UN Convention and other legal frameworks, and the strong trunk consists of children's developing understanding of their rights and competencies. The branches are the various activity groups and spaces in which children participate over the years, and the leaves are empowered children and young people. The fruits are respect, equality, respect for human rights, development and peace. (A second edition of the handbook in which this article appeared became available in 2023 but does not include the model.)

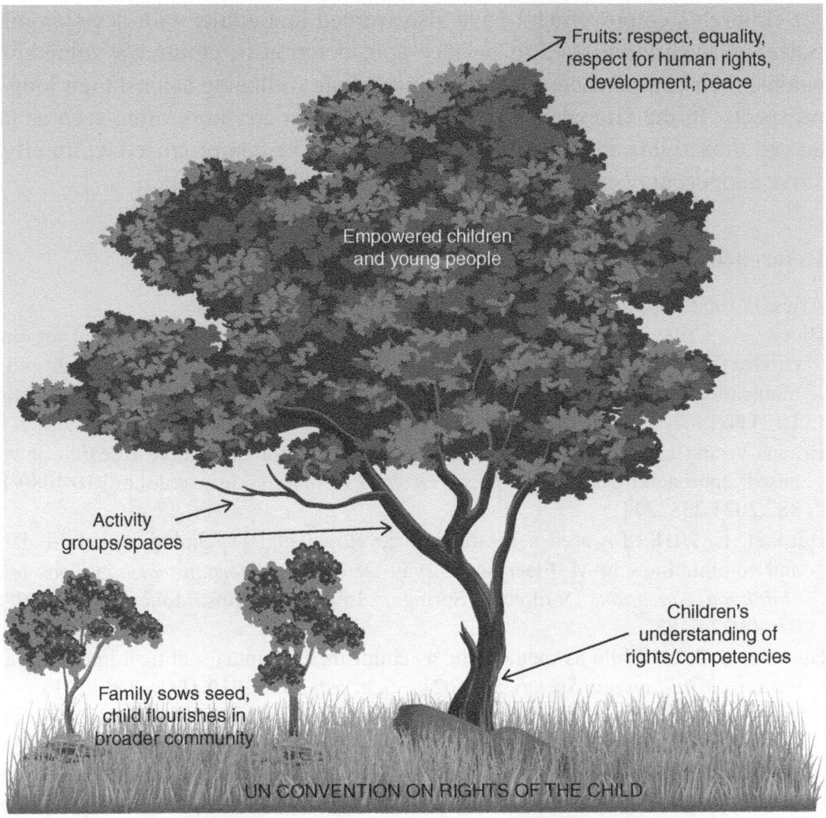

Figure 13.1 Nicaraguan perspective on children's rights-based development

Conclusion

Psychological theories promoted social constructivism, and developmental research findings further contributed to changing sociological views of children in the direction of understanding them as competent agentic beings. Together with impetus from the UN Convention on the Rights of the Child, these changing perspectives led to an increasing emphasis on listening to children's voices, in research and practice, but especially in early childhood education. While older children's perspectives on various matters can be accessed to some degree by standard quantitative psychological research methods such as questionnaires, children's voices, as generally understood, are considered to be best addressed by qualitative methods, especially those based on co-construction of meaning between adults and children. Methods are becoming available that can access the 'voices' of children in various ways that do not depend on the spoken word.

Much research is contextualized in the Global North, and some who advocate for children's empowerment have also warned that adults with decision-making power over children need to balance consideration of children's vulnerabilities against their competencies, and their immediate wellbeing against their long-term prospects. In the Global South, although children are more often seen as public actors, their rights and agency may nevertheless be compromised; culturally sensitive support may enable their voices to be heard.

References

Ariés, P. 1962. *Centuries of childhood.* New York: Vintage Books.

Bloom, A., Critten, S., Johnson, H. and Wood, C. 2020. Evaluating a method for eliciting children's voice about educational support with children with speech, language and communication needs. *British Journal of Special Education 47*(2): 170–207. https://doi.org/10.1111/1467-8578.12308

Braun, V. and Clarke, V. 2024. Reporting guidelines for qualitative research: a values-based approach. *Qualitative Research in Psychology*. https://doi.org/10.1080/14780887.2024.2382244

Burman, E. 2018. Towards a posthuman developmental psychology of child, families and communities. In M. Fleer and B. van Oers (eds), *International handbook of early childhood education.* Dordrecht: Springer, 1599–620. https://doi.org/10.1007/978-94-024-0927-7_83

Burman, E. 2023. Child as method and/as childism: conceptual-political intersections and tensions. *Children and Society 37*: 1021–36. https://doi.org/10.1111/chso.12615

Carnevale, F. A. 2020. A 'thick' conception of children's voices: a hermeneutical framework for childhood research. *International Journal of Qualitative Methods 19*: 1–9. https://doi.org/10.1177/1609406920933767

Charmaz, K. 2006. *Constructing Grounded Theory: a practical guide through qualitative analysis*. London: SAGE.

Charmaz, K. 2016. The power of constructivist grounded theory for critical inquiry. *Qualitative Inquiry 23*(1): 34–45. https://doi.org/10.1177/1077800416657105

Clark, A. 2005. Ways of seeing: using the Mosaic approach to listen to young children's perspectives. In A. Clark, A. T. Kjørholt and P. Moss (eds), *Beyond listening: children's perspectives on early childhood services*. Bristol: Policy Press, 29–49. https://us.sagepub.com/sites/default/files/upm-binaries/43997_9781446207529.pdf

Cooper, V. 2023. Child focused research: disconnected and disembodied voices. *Childhood 30*: 71–85. https://doi.org/10.1177/09075682221132084

Coppock, V. 2011. Children as peer researchers: reflections on a journey of mutual discovery. *Children & Society 25*: 435–46. https://doi.org/10.1111/j.1099-0860.2010.00296.x

Corsaro, W. 2005. *The sociology of childhood.* Second edn. Thousand Oaks: Pine Forge Press.

Darbyshire, P., Cleghorn, A., Downes, M., Elford, J., Gannoni, A., McCullagh, C. and Shute, R. 2013. Supporting bereaved parents: a phenomenological study of a telephone intervention programme in a paediatric oncology unit. *Journal of Clinical Nursing 22*(3–4): 540–9. https://doi.org/10.1111/j.1365-2702.2012.04266.x

Doise, W. 1990. The development of individual competencies through social interaction. In H. C. Foot, M. Morgan and R. H. Shute (eds), *Children helping children.* Chichester: Wiley, 43–64.

Epstein, I., Stevens, B., McKeever, P. and Baruchel, S. 2006. Photo elicitation interview (PEI): using photos to elicit children's perspectives. *International Journal of Qualitative Methods 5*(3): 1–11. https://doi.org/10.1177/160940690600500301

Gabhainn, S. N. and Sixsmith, J. 2006. Children photographing well-being: facilitation of participation in research. *Children in Society 20*(4): 249–59. https://doi.org/10.1111/j.1099-0860.2005.00002.x

Greene, S. 2006. Child psychology: taking account of children at last? *The Irish Journal of Psychology 27*(1/2): 8–15. https://doi.org/10.1080/03033910.2006.10446223

Guo, W. and Tsui, M. 2010. From resilience to resistance: a reconstruction of the strengths perspective in social work practice. *International Social Work 53*(2): 233–45. https://doi.org/10.1177/0020872809355391

Hart, R. A. 1992. *Children's participation: from tokenism to citizenship*. Florence: Unicef International Child Development Centre. https://digitallibrary.un.org/record/227219

Hayes, N. 2024. 'It's not fair': hearing the voices of young children. *International Journal of Primary, Elementary and Early Years Education 3–13 52*(6): 830–42. https://doi.org/10.1080/03004279.2024.2332862

Heary, C. and Guerin, S. 2006. Research with children in psychology: the value of a child-centred approach. *The Irish Journal of Psychology 27*(1/2): 6–7. https://doi.org/10.1080/03033910.2006.10446222

Hedegaard, M. 2018. Children's cultural learning in everyday life exemplified at the dinner setting. In M. Fleer and B. van Oers (eds), *International handbook of early childhood education*. Dordrecht: Springer, 1525–40. https://doi.org/10.1007/978-94-024-0927-7_79

Hudson Kam, C. L. and Newport, E. L. 2009. Getting it right by getting it wrong: when learners change languages. *Cognitive Psychology 59*: 30–66. https://doi.org/10.1016/j.cogpsych.2009.01.001

James, A. 2007. Giving voice to children's voices: practices and problems, pitfalls and potentials. *American Anthropologist 109*(2): 261–72. https://psycnet.apa.org/doi/10.1525/aa.2007.109.2.261

Kellett, M. 2010. Small shoes, big steps! Empowering children as active researchers. *American Journal of Community Psychology 46*: 195–203. https://doi.org/10.1007/s10464-010-9324-y

Kelly, G. 1955. *The psychology of personal constructs*. New York: Norton.

The Lancet. 2023. Editorial: time to take academic pressure seriously. *The Lancet* 7. www.thelancet.com/action/showPdf?pii=S2352-4642%2823%2900231-6

Lee, D. D. 1959. *Freedom and culture: essays*. Hoboken: Prentice-Hall.

Lock, A., Service, V., Brito, A. and Chandler, P. 1989. The social structuring of infant cognition. In A. Slater and G. Bremner (eds), *Infant development*. Hove: Lawrence Erlbaum, 243–71.

Mahony, L., McLeod, S., Salamon, A. and Dwyer, J. 2024. Why the voices of young children matter. In L. Mahony, S. McLeod, A. Salamon and J. Dwyer (eds), *Early childhood voices: children, families, professionals*. Cham: Springer, 3–16. https://doi.org/10.1007/978-3-031-56484-0_1

Matthews, S. H. 2007. A window on the 'new' sociology of childhood. *Sociology Compass 1*: 322–34. https://doi.org/10.1111/j.1751-9020.2007.00001.x

Murray, J. 2019. Hearing young children's voices. *International Journal of Early Years Education 27*: 1–5. https://doi.org/10.1080/09669760.2018.1563352

Musgrove, N., Leahy, C. P. and Moruzi, K. 2019. Hearing children's voices: conceptual and methodological challenges. In N. Musgrove, C. P. Leahy and K. Moruzi (eds),

Children's voices from the past. Cham: Macmillan, 1–25. https://doi.org/10.1007/978-3-030-11896-9_1

Nastasi, B. K. 2020. Applying child-rights-respecting research to the study of psychological wellbeing: global and local examples. In B. K. Nastasi, S. N. Hart and S. C. Naser (eds), *International handbook on child rights and school psychology*. Cham: Springer Nature, 577–90. https://doi.org/10.1007/978-3-030-37119-7_36

Pritchard, A. and Woollard, J. 2010. *Psychology for the classroom: constructivism and social learning*. London: Routledge.

Reed, J. and Dunn, C. 2024. Postdigital young people's rights: a critical perspective on the UK government's guidance to ban phones in England's schools. *Postdigital Science and Education*: 1–10. https://link.springer.com/article/10.1007/s42438-024-00464-6

Seligman, M. 2002. *Authentic happiness*. New York: Free Press.

Sevón, E., Mustola, M., Siippainen, A. and Vlasov, J. 2023. Participatory research methods with young children: a systematic literature review. *Educational Review*. https://doi.org/10.1080/00131911.2023.2215465

Shier, H. 2001. Pathways to participation: openings, opportunities and obligations. *Children in Society 15*(2): 107–17. https://doi.org/10.1002/chi.617

Shier, H. 2010. Pathways to participation revisited. In B. Percy-Smith and N. Thomas (eds), *A handbook of children's and young people's participation: perspectives from theory and practice*. London: Routledge, 215–29. https://www.harryshier.net/docs/Shier-Pathways_to_Participation_Revisited_Handbook.pdf

Skrzypiec, G., Slee, P. and Sandhu, D. 2015. Using the PhotoStory Method to understand the cultural context of youth victimisation in the Punjab. *The International Journal of Emotional Education 7*: 52–68. https://eric.ed.gov/?id=EJ1085609

Sudarsan, I., Hoare, K., Sheridan, N. and Roberts, J. 2022. Giving voice to children in research: the power of child-centered constructivist grounded theory methodology. *Research in Nursing and Health 45*: 488–97. https://doi.org/10.1002/nur.22231

Thomsen, L., Frankenhuis, W. E., Ingold-Smith, M. and Carey, S. 2011. Big and mighty: preverbal infants mentally represent social dominance. *Science 331*: 477–80. https://doi.org/10.1126/science.1199198

Twum-Danso, A. O. 2008. *Searching for the middle ground in children's rights: implementing the Convention on the Rights of the Child in Ghana*. PhD thesis, Centre of West African Studies, University of Birmingham. https://etheses.bham.ac.uk/id/eprint/453/1/TwumDanso08PhD.pdf

UNICEF Australia. *The United Nations Convention on the Rights of the Child*. www.unicef.org.au/united-nations-convention-on-the-rights-of-the-child

Warshak, R. A. 2003. Payoffs and pitfalls of listening to children. *Family Relations 52*(4): 373–84. https://psycnet.apa.org/doi/10.1111/j.1741-3729.2003.00373.x

Wyness, M. 2006. *Childhood and society: an introduction to the sociology of childhood*. New York: Palgrave Macmillan.

Zhang, Q. 2015. The voice of the child in early childhood education research in Australia and New Zealand: a systematic review. *Australasian Journal of Early Childhood 40*(3): 97–104. https://doi.org/10.1177/183693911504000313

Zschorn, M. and Shute, R. H. 2016. 'We are dealing with it the best we can': exploring parents' attributions regarding their child's disability using the 'Four Ws' framework. *Clinical Child Psychology and Psychiatry 21*(3): 416–31. https://psycnet.apa.org/doi/10.1177/1359104515614071

14 Theorizing about children's digital worlds

Introduction

> Digital detox urged for children who are aggressive, hospitalised when parents pull plug on devices.
>
> *(Australian Broadcasting Corporation headline, posted 11 July 2024)*

This headline typifies concerns often expressed about the effects of digital technology on children's development and wellbeing. Globally, one child in three (under 18 years) uses the internet (UNICEF, 2017, 2019), therefore the majority of the world's children, including most in sub-Saharan Africa, do not live in a digital world, with fewer than one in 20 school-age children from the world's poorest families having a home internet connection (UNICEF, 2024). This creates a concerning digital divide between various communities and individuals (Kitsara, 2022; UNICEF 2020). This chapter relates to the one third of young people who *do* have access to digital devices, such as 96 per cent of young Europeans. In his book *Faster: The Acceleration of Just About Everything* James Gleick (2000) highlighted the speed of myriad exchanges made possible by technology even as the millennium turned. For digitally connected children—a term generally encompassing adolescents in this book—a quarter of a century later, the word 'ubiquity' captures their experiences, especially of social media. After a brief overview of the development of the digital world, we revisit our argument that three major factors help shape views of children's development: history, culture and the philosophy of science. We then consider some theories offering different ways of understanding children's development in the digital age.

A brief history of the digital age

The term 'digital' has been described as 'complex, multilayered, hyped and overused', meaning different things to different people, but can be seen as a mindset concerned with the use of technology and data (Tardieu *et al.*, 2020). Computing technologies date back to the 1940s, while the internet arose out of

DOI: 10.4324/9781003567738-14

the Advanced Research Projects Agency (ARPA) funded and supported by United States President Dwight Eisenhower, and embedded in the Cold War of the 1950s–1960s. The United States was intent on maintaining dominance in the face of Russian pioneering breakthroughs in various fields including space (e.g. the launch of Sputnik 1, the first artificial Earth satellite, in 1957).

The development of email technology (in the late 1960s and early 1970s) is considered to have arisen from the ARPA's facilitating the development of networks between ARPANET computers, enabling messages between users. US computer programmer Ray Tomlinson originated email technology—soon realized to be a convenient way for gossiping in real time and to meet, make and maintain 'friendships' online and beyond. As the poet William Butler Yeats wrote: 'There are no strangers here; Only friends you haven't yet met.'

The growth of the internet was exponential. People were now using it to message each other, read news and swap files. In 1989, British computer scientist Tim Berners-Lee proposed a new way of structuring and linking all the information on the computer of CERN, the international particle-research laboratory in Geneva, Switzerland: the World Wide Web. This allowed the entry of non-academics and provided for the development of web pages. By 1995 the internet and the World Wide Web were established phenomena—connectivity was everything.

The rise of social media

The further development of the internet is illustrated in Figure 14.1, resulting in the creation of Social Networking Sites (SNSs). Sixdegrees.com, in 1997, provided the opportunity to link with friends, make new friends and create personal profiles. While this SNS closed in 2000, it was quickly replaced by sites such as Myspace and Facebook, the latter developing its own sustainable business model. The various sites enabled users to access an online space where uploaded content could be shared and commented upon. Additionally, SNSs are used to market and advertise. Specific sites are designed to appeal to certain demographics (e.g. LinkedIn is aimed at professional and semi-professional communities).

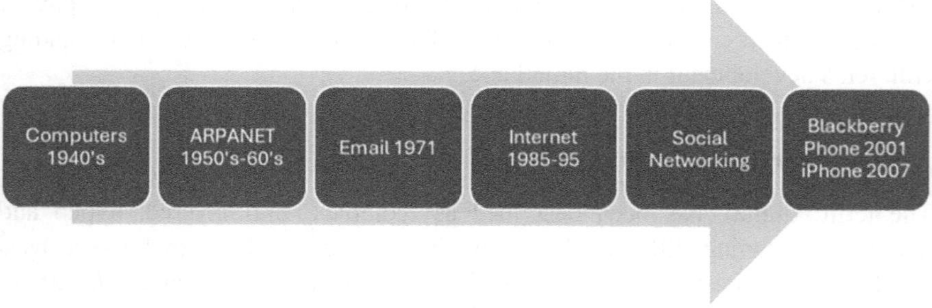

Figure 14.1 Timeline of digital social networking

Older people today remember life before the internet, laptop computers and smartphones, when one had to physically access information from library books and use a house phone or public phone box to communicate with distant others in real time. Different generations entered the digital world at different points in time. Almost everyone born after 1980 and living in communities where digital technology has long been an integral part of economic and social activities is regarded as a digital native. They may be introduced to such technology while very young (see Box 14.1) and cannot imagine life without it (Khalaf *et al.*, 2023). However, supposed 'digital natives' often struggle with information overload and digital literacy (Campbell *et al.*, 2024).

BOX 14.1 A BABY IN THE DIGITAL WORLD

In 2024 author PTS was visiting Japan. At dinner one evening, at a nearby table a young mother with her 8-month-old baby was enjoying time with two girlfriends. PTS noticed that the baby (seated on the mother's lap) was intensely focused on what he believed was her iPhone, propped up on the table about 30 cm away. At one point the phone fell over and the baby immediately became quite agitated and began to cry, whereupon the mother propped up the phone again and the baby calmed and began watching it intently. PTS then noticed that it was indeed an iPhone and on the screen were 6–7 'human eyes' moving randomly around the screen. Many questions arise from this observation. Is this type of interaction of a baby with technology beneficial or not (and to whom)? Does this interaction have implications for attachment? What is the baby learning from this interaction? Do parents understand the benefits or otherwise of providing this type of stimulation?

The internet provides young people with a means for exchanging information, being entertained, socializing, completing schoolwork and conducting research. Use of mobile devices may occupy seven hours a day or more (Gilmore *et al.*, 2017) though a more modest figure from Australia indicated that teenagers were spending an average of 14.4 hours per week online for activities including doing research, accessing videos, movies and music, chatting with friends and engaging in online gaming (Australian eSafety Commissioner, 2021). Furthermore, 55 per cent of children had communicated with strangers online while 12 per cent had met someone face-to-face after meeting online. YouTube and Flickr facilitate media sharing, enabling the uploading of pictures and video. Blogs provide the opportunity for online forums, and microblogging via Twitter (now X) provides short updates sent to anyone subscribed to receive them on a particular topic.

Internet slang originated in the early days of the internet and often is adapted from other cultures. It is used in SNSs, chat rooms, and generally by the online community. Examples include:

LOL: laugh out loud. In France, 'mdr' stands for 'mort de rire', meaning dying of laughter. In Thailand the number 5 signifies the letter 'h' so 555 is 'ha ha ha'.
BTW: by the way.
GTG and G2G: got to go.
Rizz: short for 'charisma', an ability to charm someone.

Another aspect of digital communication is the use of emoji, following the emergence of the yellow Smiley in the 1960s, which became an aspect of popular culture. Emoji help to compensate for a lack of nonverbal visual cues in text communications, and this has become a topic of research in itself (Bai *et al.*, 2019).

The advent of artificial intelligence (AI) has added another level to online communication, and another digital divide, with the United States and China leading the field (Kitsara, 2022). AI includes technologies enabling computers to perform various advanced functions, including the ability to see, understand and translate spoken and written language, analyse data and make recommendations. It aims to replicate human thought processes and decision-making through computer algorithms. Examples of AI include online assistants (e.g. Chatbox, Siri, Alexa, Cortana), used by smartphones and social media platforms. Concerns arise that algorithms further entrench privilege, such as being biased against Black people (Green, 2022). When it works well AI is very useful (see Box 14.2, for example), but the information that generative AI harvests from the internet is only as good as what is available, some of which is nonsense; even solid information may be turned into garbage, as when author RHS came across nonsensical AI-generated summaries of her book chapters. More dangerously, a browser search seeking advice on Australian native edible plants yielded a web page that was obviously AI-generated and listed not only non-Australian plants, but poisonous ones. It also referred to Australians 'gathering in the shade beneath the soursobs'; you would have to be pixie-sized to meet your friends under that invasive garden weed! These examples raise questions about how far internet users, including children, can differentiate between accurate and misleading information, especially with the rise of convincing deepfakes. Finland leads media literacy for children, with a policy since 2013 for integrating it into the curriculum throughout their schooling (Steiner, 2025). In 2025 the United Arab Emirates introduced AI into the curriculum from kindergarten onwards, including technical and ethical aspects, advantages, risks and limitations (Gulf Insider Education, 2025). A serious concern for scientific research is the possibility of some journal reviewers using undeclared AI, undermining the peer review process (Barker, 2025). AI also raises much more profound questions about where the world is heading in the 21st century in relation to the 'reckless' fusion of humans and machines (Harvey, 2024). AI has been found capable of learning about vulnerabilities in human decision-making and influencing people's decision-making (Dezfouli, Nock and Dayan, 2020).

BOX 14.2 ARTIFICIAL INTELLIGENCE AND CHILD DEVELOPMENT

The media is awash with headlines—often alarming—regarding the emergence of AI as a driving force in our daily lives. Consider these, from *Science Daily*:

'Truly autonomous AI is on the horizon'
'Physician's medical decisions benefit from chatbot'
' "Embodied energy" powers modular worm, jellyfish robots'
'AI can detect serious neurologic changes in babies in the NICU using video data alone'.

Australian researcher Toby Walsh in his book *Faking It: Artificial Intelligence in a Human World* has observed that AI researchers have different views of the definition, although 'most of us will agree that it is about trying to get computers to do tasks that, when humans do them, we say require intelligence. These include perceiving the world, reasoning about the world and learning about the world' (Walsh, 2023: 3). In a scoping review of AI in early childhood teaching Jiahong Su and Weipeng Yang (2022) concluded that AI had significantly improved young children's concepts regarding AI and computer skills, and enhanced their other skills such as creativity and emotion control. AI has also been advocated for use in developmental monitoring, particularly where in-depth assessments relating to a young child's physical, cognitive and social development are needed, but are time-consuming and labour-intensive.

There is also a multidisciplinary field called 'developmental robotics' (Lungarella *et al.*, 2003), which has pulled away from the mind-as-computer metaphor of cognitive science to embrace ontogenetic development as an experience-based process, as exemplified by the theorizing of Jean Piaget and Eleanor Gibson. It draws upon the principles of complexity, epigenetics and embodied cognition, both to create robotic systems that develop like babies, being more autonomous, adaptable and sociable, and to use robots to investigate embodied models of development. Attention to ethical matters is essential in order to avoid a dystopian future (Torresen, 2018).

Overall, the rise of digital technology has deeply changed the way many young people manage and think about their lives, compared with past generations. We can recall Kurt Riegel's dialectical view that development must always be understood in historical context, and that he invented time-lag analyses accordingly (see Chapter 8). The use of this and other longitudinal methods has been called for, given that young people's social media use is developing so rapidly (Smith, Leonis and Anandavalli, 2021). As Hubert Tardieu and colleagues have written:

> We act as we do, we engage as we do, and the world runs as it does thanks to the pervasiveness of digital technologies. This trend is expected to continue such that, in a few years, the world (including human beings) will be an inseparable continuum of the physical and the virtual. Digital will cease to be a discernible thing because it will just be an integrated part of a new norm.
>
> *(Tardieu et al., 2020: 7)*

Culture and social media

Caleb Carr and Rebecca Hayes commented that '[w]hile scholars assume an inherent understanding of social media based on extant technology, there is no commonly-accepted definition of what social media are, both functionally and theoretically, within communication studies' (Carr and Hayes, 2015: 2). Author PTS asked his three young adult sons what 'social media' meant; their replies included Facebook, TikTok, YouTube, email, blogging and Twitter. Middle son Nick defined social media as 'a collective group of members of the public who use the internet to talk and interact with people'. Overall, their descriptions accord with a common understanding that the term refers to channel characteristics (e.g. Bluesky or Facebook). Other definitions refer to digital/online communication, collaboration and networking. Carr and Hayes (2015: 8) offer: 'Social media are Internet-based channels that allow users to opportunistically interact and selectively self-present, either in real-time or asynchronously, with both broad and narrow audiences who derive value from user-generated content and the perception of interaction with others.' One strength of this more comprehensive definition is that it captures four key elements that have drawn much research attention:

- Interaction, e.g. cyberbullying.
- Self-presentation, e.g. body image issues.
- Audience, e.g. feedback regarding one's postings.
- Real time, in terms of the immediacy of the medium.

Social media differ from television and newspapers in significant ways, enabling interaction and the creation and uploading of one's own messages and images. In turn, recipients can respond in almost real time, providing commentary and forwarding the messages to their own circle.

In Chapters 2 and 11 we emphasized that culture is an essential factor in shaping how societies view and raise children, and here we consider the limited research relating to cultural influences on social media. We have cited different definitions of culture in previous chapters, and one used in the context of social media is 'a system of socially constructed symbols and meanings, premises, and rules, pertaining to communicative conduct' (Philipsen, 1997: 126). Drawing on that definition, Todd Sandel and Bei ('Jenny') Ju (2019) suggested that social media use does vary culturally, such as Chinese users being impacted by internet censorship and therefore struggling to shape the reporting of important events. Sandel and Ju argue that culture is 'created' and provides guidance on how to act/interact/look in social settings. For example, social media are replete with 'idealized' images, such as thinness being emphasized in western societies for women's bodily appearance. This opens up the possibility that young people at crucial stages in their emotional, social and physical development, in appraising their own appearance against those on social media, may be more prone to poor mental health and eating disorders.

Hye-Ryeon Lee *et al.* (2014) explored the role of social media in relation to body image, through a cultural lens. They posited that in collectivist cultures such as Korea people will more strongly adhere to social norms than in more individualistic cultures such as the United States; while they found some similarities between the two cultures, using social media for appearance-related status-seeking was only apparent in Koreans.

In an Australian report, 400 Aboriginal and Torres Strait Islanders were surveyed about their media habits (McNair, 2014). The findings indicated that young Indigenous people have a higher media use than non-Indigenous Australians, as confirmed by a later study (Hefler *et al.*, 2019). Possible explanations include the level of social disadvantage, including educationally, along with exposure to violence, high levels of incarceration and remote living conditions. Despite potential negative aspects of their social media use, a literature review concluded that:

> Indigenous young people use social media to help form, affirm and strengthen identity, to feel a sense of power and control over their own lives and to make and continue community and family connections. This shows the potential for social media to be used in beneficial ways.
>
> *(Rice et al., 2016: 13)*

In a study of New Zealand Māori youth, it has been observed that '[i]n a growing corner of the internet, rangatahi (young) Māori are finding and creating a place to gather, to discuss, and to explore their indigeneity' (Green, 2020: ii). That is, the internet is providing opportunity for them to develop as they navigate between Māori and Pākehā (White) worlds. An interesting cross-national study reported that young Māori people living in Australia benefit from the opportunity to develop and maintain their identity online: 'Ma-ori language use in social media among them incorporated a mix of English, Ma-ori te reo/Ma-ori language, text-speak and slang, contributing to their sense of cultural identity while living in another country' (Harwood, 2015).

Philosophy of science and the digital age

As one particular worldview, the dominant role of empiricism in mainstream psychology influences theory, shapes methodology and identifies the types of problems worthy of study in any field, including child development.

One way of viewing digital technology is encapsulated in Martin Heidegger's thinking (1954/1977). He argued that technology in itself is not 'bad' but that we should not confuse its appearance with its 'essence' (what it is). Technology provides us with a particular way of revealing or understanding the world that is based on a deterministic or scientific outlook. Heidegger identified two essential types of thinking here: calculative thinking, which is about the production of something and the getting of results; and meditative thinking, which encapsulates pausing to reflect in order to deepen one's awareness and understanding of the nature of one's thoughts. We could liken calculative thinking to a modern deterministic outlook that has come to represent the conduct of science today.

In gathering data about children from social media, some salient characteristics of the information have been identified: 'The nature of social media determines that its data significantly differs from the data in traditional data mining. … Social media data is big, noisy, incomplete, highly unstructured and linked with social relations' (Tang, Chang and Liu, 2014: 1). 'Big' refers to the idea that while social media may not have much data on any one individual, the quantity of data overall is huge. For example, in 2024 there were 500 million tweets per day. Social media data are 'linked' via social relations and hence not independent. They are also 'noisy'; for example, it is difficult to distinguish between users who are 'friends' versus 'acquaintances'. Jiliang Tang and colleagues also highlight the unstructured nature of social media data such that individuals may upload large bodies of text or short tweets and the language may incorporate abbreviations. Finally, data are incomplete; for example, uploads by any individual on Facebook rarely contain identifiable demographic information. Overall, this description of social media data can be referred back to Heidegger's central notion that, in relation to technology, the 'appearance' does not equate to its 'essence'. This distinction is important for understanding what rapidly emerging social media technology tells us in terms of the data being generated by and about children and their development. The limitations of internet-based research are discussed in Georgia Thomas-Parr and Marcus Gilroy-Ware's manosphere study cited in Chapter 12. Since such data can only be very partial, this highlights the need to access complementary data directly from young people, whether using typical psychological quantitative methods (e.g. to assess attitudes) or qualitative methods aimed at accessing the meaning of social media in the lives of young people.

Bertrand Russell (a philosopher, though not a self-identifying one), from the 1920s onwards, addressed the implications of technological change, observing its great promise for improving wellbeing, but only if a range of conditions were met, including shared prosperity and the abolition of war (Leach, 2020; Russell, 1976). Russell's perspective, decried as utopian, still seems so today. It often feels that the development of the digital world is running ahead unchecked, but it is crucial to maintain a critical perspective on science and technology. In 1976 computer scientist Joseph Weizenbaum warned against 'simplistic worldviews inherent in granting imperial rights to science', fearing that this could replace human social values and lead to irreversible undesirable consequences (cited in Pedersen and Brincker, 2021). These authors suggest that the choice today is not between getting with the program of 'big tech' and nostalgia for a past analogue age, but active engagement with questioning how information technology can support human ethics, and not allowing technology to dismantle the civic values guiding everyday human lives. In this multidisciplinary endeavour, in which philosophy and psychology have a part to play, working to understand the impact of technology on the very development of young humans is an essential component.

Theoretical perspectives on children's digital worlds

An evolutionary perspective

One way of understanding the impact of digital technologies, especially social media, on children's development takes us back to a theme in Chapter 3: the social nature of human beings. 'Humans are an exquisitely social species' (Blakemore, 2010: 744) that cannot thrive without relationships with others, with a brain that is theorized to have evolved to support this social life. 'Hanging out', being present with others at small- and large-scale events and communicating, chatting, joking, singing and playing games are all part of people's social selves. Social media use illustrates a veritable explosion of humankind's capacity to 'hang out'.

In understanding the nature of social networks consideration is needed of structure. Alistair Sutcliffe *et al.* (2012) have classified networks into different levels based on the degree of intimacy and support, extending from an intimate level to a broader active network moving to the level of clan or kin. The anthropologist Robin Dunbar proposed that there exists a cognitive limit on human groups, of about 150 individuals, based on the relationship between group size and relative neocortex size in other primates, compared to humans (Dunbar, 1992). In Figure 14.2 the top layers identify our closest ties (intimate family members and best friends), while

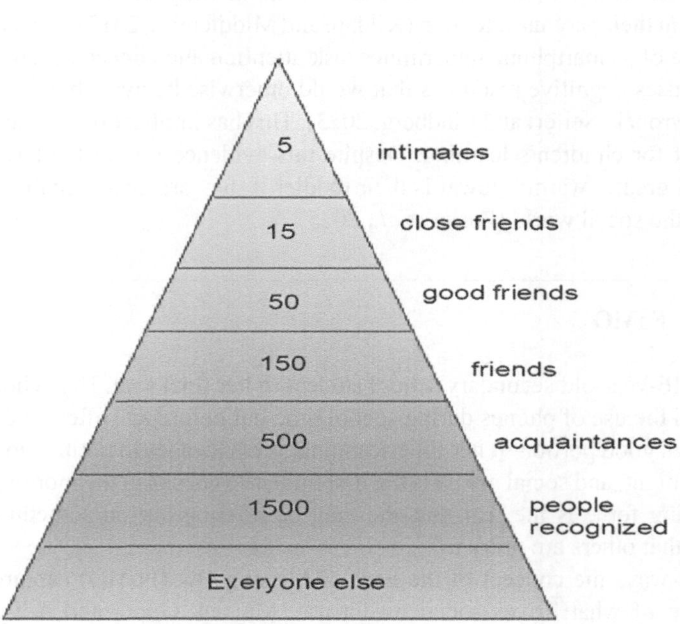

Figure 14.2 Structured layers of human social networks (based on Dunbar, 2012)

the lower layers represent individuals who are still important to us, but with whom we are less connected. Establishing and maintaining relationships requires time and effort, helping to explain why we have less time to spend with lesser connected individuals (Dunbar, 2012). Dunbar's number has been heavily critiqued but a study examining the Twitter exchanges of over 1.7 million users confirmed that Twitter users 'can entertain a maximum of 100 – 200 stable relationships' in support for Dunbar's prediction. 'The "economy of attention" is limited in the online world by cognitive and biological constraints as predicted by Dunbar's theory' (Gonçalves, Perra and Vespignani, 2011:1). Acquaintances, or 'weak ties', are nevertheless important to maintain as they create a sense of community and are a broader source of information than the 'bubble' of our nearest and dearest (Klein, 2025).

One feature of young people's access to digital communication includes the minute-by-minute monitoring of friends' (and strangers') movements as well as sharing one's own space and location with others via social networks (see Box 14.3, about fear of missing out). The attributes of the new media platforms now 'constitute the life-worlds of billions of people across the planet' (Hassan and Sutherland, 2017: 1). In part, this explains the behaviour of people in relation to social media. For example, author PTS lives near a national park and on any day witnesses adults walking with their attention focused on their mobile phones, striding past the koala in the tree, the musk lorikeets feeding on the blossom or the kangaroo grazing! Author RHS is always disappointed to see parents on public transport similarly ignoring their young children, losing the opportunity to share conversation about the passing scenes. A literature review showed that such distracted parents are less sensitive to their children, and that children engage in risky behaviours in their efforts to regain their parents' attention (Kildare and Middlemiss, 2017). Indeed, the mere presence of a smartphone undermines task attention and concentration, indicating that it uses cognitive resources that would otherwise be available for other matters (Skowronek, Seifert and Lindberg, 2023). This has implications not just for parenting, but for children's learning. Despite this evidence for 'technoference', parents report greater warmth towards their toddler if they are also digitally well-connected to the social world (Fusha *et al.*, 2025).

BOX 14.3 FoMO

Katie is a 16-year-old secondary school student in her final year. Her school has banned the use of phones during school time but before and after school she spends a good portion of her time scanning, often awakes to notifications during the night, and social media is the first thing she checks in the morning. A motivating force is the fear that she may be missing out on something important that others are privy to.

In some ways the concept of the Fear of Missing Out (FoMO) captures the essence of what drives social media use. Mayank Gupta and Aditya Sharma's review noted, '(FoMO) is a unique term introduced in 2004 to describe a phenomenon observed on social networking sites. FoMO includes two processes; firstly, perception of missing out, followed up with a compulsive behavior to maintain these social connections' (Gupta and Sharma, 2021: 4881). Today, more than ever, people are exposed to much detail about what others are doing, and are faced with continuous uncertainty about whether they are doing enough or if they are where they should be in their life. As social beings this helps create concerns that missing out possibly places you at a disadvantage. This may be why people often prioritize an incoming phone call over a face-to-face conversation they are having. The nature and strengths of people's social networks have been linked with emotional wellbeing across the lifespan. For example, while younger individuals may have a wider and more diversified social network than older individuals, research is clear that older individuals' social networks are equally important. For example, feelings of loneliness are directly related to satisfaction with one's social network (Kemperman *et al.*, 2019). Przybylski *et al.*'s 2013 paper used Social Determination Theory (SDT) as a framework for understanding FoMO; this theory by Edward Deci and Richard Ryan (1985; Ryan and Deci, 2000) regards autonomy, competence and relatedness as basic human needs affecting motivation and wellbeing.

An identity perspective

Paul Smaldino's evolutionary theory (see Box 3.4) emphasized that human social worlds are very much tied up with the formation of groups that provide a sense of identity, as we saw previously in discussing culture. Social identity theory and self-categorization theory aid understanding of how people identify with ingroups and differentiate themselves from outgroups, and engage with others accordingly, in a dynamic fashion. Children engage in these processes from a young age, increasingly digitally, and potential outcomes include bullying and harmful social comparisons, but also social support, friendship and a sense of belonging and identity (Shute and Slee, 2022). Granic, Morita and Scholten (2020) cite evidence that young people create and curate a network of social relationships online that is far more extensive than could otherwise be achieved. SNSs provide many opportunities for self-definition. 'Nowadays, social networks provide new platforms for the self-presentation, the self-realising as a person, as a representative of a certain gender, for identifying femininity or masculinity in the context of adolescent socialisation' (Durmishi and Durmishi, 2022: 28).

Drawing on Erik Erikson's theory that identity formation is the core task of adolescence, Granic *et al.* (2020) have explored the role of social media use in achieving connectedness/a sense of belonging and personal agency, and attaining a coherent balance between these to produce a life narrative about who one is. A recent large-scale Australian survey found that adolescents with moderate levels of social media use have mental health and wellbeing on a par with, or better than, that of low-level users (Orygen, 2025). Digital platforms offer positive opportunities for connection and agency, but this needs balancing against negative effects, such as anxiety about social comparisons, and a lack of agency when manipulated online by marketers or sexual predators. In 2025 Australia introduced a world-first law banning children from holding social media accounts before the age of 16.

Neurological perspectives

We established in Chapter 3 that how children's brains develop depends very much on how they spend their time. It is therefore reasonable to ask how neurological development is affected by spending a great deal of time using digital devices.

There has been considerable concern expressed by adults (often not digital natives) about 'screen time' and suggestions, including from governments, that this should be limited, especially in young children (Arabiat *et al.*, 2023). A study in Delhi of 370 15–18-month-olds found that only one had not been exposed to screens, and some had begun as young as 2 months (Meena, Gupta and Shah, 2020). Excessive screen time is associated with cognitive difficulties in preschoolers, together with microstructural abnormalities in white matter, in neural tracts that support language and executive functioning; however, generally 'poor parenting' has been proposed as an alternative explanation (Srivastava and Patkar, 2023). Reviewing the literature, these authors also noted a finding from France that language development was most advanced in 2-year-olds who had an intermediate amount of screen time (i.e. there was a U-shaped function). They also observed that, although there is no suggestion that excessive screen time causes autism spectrum disorder, these children are very drawn to screens and this seems to impede development of their communicative and self-control abilities.

Overall, there is little research as yet on screen time in relation to brain development, but there is a consensus that greater use at a young age seems to impede language development (Hutton *et al.*, 2024). In general, scholarly opinion has moved away from the broad notion of 'screen time' towards a functional theoretical framework that encompasses why and how young people engage with digital media, and how this interacts with lives offline (Granic *et al.*, 2020).

Another neurological aspect is the brain's reward system. Neuroimaging studies show that the adolescent brain in humans (and some other animals) is particularly sensitive to reward. This may have advantages, such as boys' social inclusion through online gaming, or symbolic rewards for progress in online foreign language learning programs. However, it also creates an 'addiction' risk, with SNSs deliberately designed to be addictive, such as through 'likes', that expose users to advertising that generates income for the platform. For a review of research on digital media and the developing brain, see Hutton *et al.* (2024).

The medical model

Online communication has rapidly emerged as a primary means of youths' (15–24 years) social interactions throughout the richer parts of the world, with upwards of 95 per cent daily using SNSs such as Snapchat, Instagram and YouTube (Tankovska, 2021). We have also seen how hard it is for people to tear themselves away from mobile phones to deal with other matters. In Chapter 3 we noted that the dominance of the medical model in western societies may encourage certain behaviours to *become seen* as problematic and needing medical attention. The Royal Australian and New Zealand College of Psychiatrists has now identified a new mental health condition called Problem Internet Use (PIU), suggesting that it could be considered an addictive condition (internet addiction), and that individuals experiencing problematic use at this level may require input from mental health or addiction services (RANZCP, 2018).

However, the term 'addiction' remains highly contentious. The American Psychiatric Association replaced it with the preferred term 'dependence' in the *DSM*-IV. The fifth edition (*DSM*-5) does include internet gaming disorder (IGD) as a diagnosable condition. Underpinning the medical model is a broad and increasing range of research exploring the association between Internet Addiction Disorder (IAD) and physical and psychological functioning. For example, Hong-Xia Zhang *et al.* (2013) reported significant associations between adolescent diagnosis with IAD and levels of norepinephrine, which is released by the adrenal gland in response to stress or low blood pressure, and elevated scores on self-reported anxiety.

Learning and cognitive theories

Burrhus F. Skinner identified a number of reinforcement schedules that increase or decrease the probability of a behaviour being repeated, whether by a pigeon, a rat or a human. Indeed, the online world has been called a 'Skinner Box for the modern human' (Lindström *et al.*, 2021). Intermittent reinforcement is particularly effective at maintaining a behaviour, as used by designers of gambling sites. It is often suggested that the same principle applies to keeping people active, sometimes obsessively, on social media, checking and re-checking on whether their post has yielded responses such as 'likes', which act as social rewards. Björn Lindström *et al.* (2021) tested this hypothesis by applying a computational method to analyse over a million social media posts, and to run an online experiment. Their results supported the proposition that behaviour on social media is in accord with the principles of reward learning, with individual differences in strategies for balancing effort against reward.

A cognitive approach can be applied to multitasking, which involves neuropsychological processes in the prefrontal cortex and corpus striatum. In offline life, this might metaphorically amount to 'walking and chewing gum at the same time'. In the digital world, it is often a question of attention-switching, whether a real-life conversation disrupted to answer a ringing phone, or competing tasks on a digital device, such as a child doing a homework assignment on a laptop while receiving intermittent alerts from their social media account. College students who multitask in class spend more time studying outside class and achieve lower academic results; in other words, multitasking is not efficient (Bellur, Nowak and Hull, 2015). A review of multitasking in adolescents and adults concluded that it does not always affect the quality of work but should be avoided for the undertaking of complex tasks or if it causes stress, especially to young children (Fröhlich and Lehmkul, 2018).

From a Piagetian perspective, children would be expected to be able to experiment online and develop cognitively. Indeed, the 'hole- in-the-wall' computer experiment exemplified this (see Box 5.1). However, leaving children, especially young children, online alone potentially exposes them to coming across distressing or damaging content such as violence (e.g. videos of beheadings, or pornography that portrays male violence to women). Device settings can be used to minimize such risks, though many children are adept at bypassing them.

From a Vygotskian perspective, emphasis shifts to the cultural, social and joint construction of knowledge and meaning involving the child and others. Children's cognitive development depends on shared learning experiences with adults, in the zone of proximal development. This suggests the importance of adults sharing online experiences with children, both to enhance their development and to ensure their safety, rather than (literally) leaving them to their own devices. UNICEF (2019) and collaborators have produced a research-based toolkit, *Global Kids Online*, that views parents as mediators and supporters. In early childhood education, studies of teachers and children experiencing digital technologies together have yielded a number of perspectives (Undheim, 2021). For example, that digital play is real play, even if the keyboards and phones are dummies used imaginatively.

Philosophical argument has been made (building upon Vygotsky's thinking) that cognition is not bounded by brain or body but should include artifacts such as mobile phones, iPads and laptops, thereby facilitating the development of complex mental processing. Not only do we interact with this technology and modify it to better suit our purposes, but the technology in turn interacts with us, modifying our behaviour and cognition in a reciprocal fashion. That is, there is a dynamic interaction involving the brain, body and the world. A rather confusing array of terms has been applied to this general idea, including 'extended cognition' (Clark and Chalmers, 1998), 'distributed intelligence' (Pea, 1993), 'distributed cognition' (Hutchins, 1995) and 'embodied cognition' (Wilson, 2002). We highlighted in Box 8.1 that Vygotsky was well ahead of his time in proposing that abstract concepts are built upon bodily interactions with the environment; this has an affinity with dynamic systems theory, in modelling the brain, body and environment as a single system whose elements cannot be prised apart when solving a cognitive task (Thelen and Smith, 1994).

We end this section with an outline of Stephen Downes' (2022) consideration of the role of theorizing in distance and open education, which we suggest may also be applicable to children's learning in the digital world. He points out dissatisfaction with old mechanistic 'learning theories' that focused on the development of cognitive schemas through transmission of content. By contrast, the digital environment is about context and community, is affected by cultural and social norms, and helps to create identities. That is, learning is more than 'cognitive'. He draws upon constructivism, connectionism and dynamic systems theory. He also cites embodied cognition as a newer way of thinking about learning, which covers not just the technology, but the community that it opens up: '"I store my knowledge in my friends" is an axiom for collecting knowledge through collecting people' (Stephenson, cited in Downes, 2022: 10). He concludes: 'While it would perhaps be nice to expect simply causal explanations rooted in deep cosmic laws or principles, it may be that these are simply not forthcoming. The universe might not, after all, be like a machine' (Downes, 2022: 15).

Social cognitive theory (SCT)

Albert Bandura's theory replaced the mechanistic association theories of Ivan Pavlov and Skinner, and drive reduction theories, proposing instead a model of human behaviour incorporating cognitive, vicarious, self-regulatory and self-reflective processes, as captured in his book *Social Foundation of Thought: A Social Cognitive Theory* (1986). As SCT claims to be a general theory of human behaviour, it may be applicable to a complex array of social media behaviour.

One of the key principles of SCT is observational learning. The presence of 'attractive' online models, including social influencers, on various platforms provides participants with extensive opportunity to imitate their behaviour, whether in terms of appearance, clothing or political views. For example, there are literally scores of studies demonstrating that exposure to thin-ideal media images increases western girls' dissatisfaction with their bodies, as well as negative affect (for example, see Tiggemann and Slater, 2013). Another example is the radicalization of adolescent boys by influencers in the manosphere (see Chapter 12).

Another key principle of SCT is self-efficacy. An individual's beliefs about the impact they can have upon the world is paramount for realizing that impact. Social media's facilitation of the production of one's own messages and images while providing the opportunity for immediate extensive dissemination allows for the feeling that, volitionally, one is interpersonally communicating with a large number of people; this, in turn, may enhance the immediacy of messages and an individual's potential for social influence. Shaoxiong Fu and Hongxiu Li (2022) have used SCT to explain why Facebook users disengage from this platform. They identified three relevant factors: (1) technology overload; (2) information overload; and (3) social overload. They recommend that platforms looking to overcome such problems give users more control, such as options to turn off comments, block group information and hide others' posts.

Social development theory

Based on Urie Bronfenbrenner's theory, this takes account of the social ecology of health and wellbeing (Catalano and Hawkins, 1996). Marilyn Campbell *et al.* (2024) used it as a theoretical basis for reviewing the evidence concerning the pros and cons of banning/permitting mobile phone use in schools, with regard to children's learning and wellbeing. For example, does cyberbullying increase or decrease when phones are banned? Are phones a distraction from learning? Findings were disparate and inconclusive, with no randomized controlled trials found and a variety of ban types examined (e.g. total or partial). Much remains to be learned in this area, in order to guide policy decisions, though the finding that the mere presence of a mobile phone detracts from cognitive performance even in adults sends a warning message concerning children's education.

Systems approaches

Jessica Navarro and Jonathan Tudge (2023) propose that Bronfenbrenner's bioecological theory needs to be adapted into 'neo-ecological theory', that takes account of technology and the digital era by dividing microsystems into the physical and virtual. Without doing so, they say, children will again be studied 'doing strange things in strange situations', as the virtual world of proximate processes will not be taken account of by scholars. They particularly note demand characteristics, i.e. the more observable characteristics of the person, such as appearance, that invite or discourage reactions. They suggest that these are especially important in virtual contexts where self-presentation is curated, but also limited in the mesosystem of family, friends and others that constitute the audience.

Complex adaptive systems (CAS) theorizing has been applied to the introduction of new technologies in workplaces. It represents a move from top-down introduction of changes that workers must assimilate, to a view of these individuals as actively initiating and responding to changes in a constant process of adaptation (Hasgall and Ahituv, 2018). The school can similarly be regarded as a CAS (Slee and Shute, 2025). Changes such as banning mobile phones without consulting students is top-down. Nevertheless, children will actively adapt, and it is important to monitor both positive and negative changes and to be prepared for unanticipated outcomes to emerge, in accordance with CAS.

The voices of children

The final sections above touch tangentially on children's voices. It seems that changes to children's lives regarding technology use are often made top-down, with adults making decisions on limited evidence, sometimes driven by political considerations based on public perceptions (see Box 14.4). We can refer again here to the matter of children's rights to be listened to about matters that affect them (see Chapter 13). UNICEF (2019), in considering the digital worlds of children, emphasizes children's rights and the importance of listening to their views about the advantages and harms of digital connectedness. Decision-making can take their views into account in association with available research evidence and, we suggest, adults' wisdom drawn from their own longer-term life experiences (Newman, 2025).

BOX 14.4 BANNING SOCIAL MEDIA FROM SCHOOLS

Media reports highlight the ongoing public debate regarding young people and social media. One outcome concerns the development of and/or advocacy for strategies to protect young people from the negative influence of social media, such as restricting the age of children's access and banning of phones during school hours. In the authors' home state of South Australia the state Education Department introduced an 'off and away' policy in public secondary schools in 2024. The policy was introduced in a staged way, with some schools choosing to bring it in earlier. It applies to mobile phones and personal devices including smart watches, iPads, tablets and personal laptops. Schools implemented the policy in various ways. In August 2024 the Department released a media report claiming that the school phone ban was a success, citing a 63 per cent decline in reported critical incidents concerning social media, in comparison with the previous year, and a 10 per cent reduction in incidents of violence such as kicking and punching, 54 per cent fewer behavioural issues and a 44 per cent reduction in policy compliance problems. There was also reportedly an immediate demand for extracurricular activities and clubs to be available in break times, while more physical activity and face-to-face conversations were observed. Author PTS attended a forum where many young people tried to speak against the ban, but were given little time. Anecdotally, students have adapted, after initial resistance: 'over the weeks I slowly grew into it' (Brodie, 15); 'the socialisation levels have definitely improved' (Hannah, 16); 'students are more engaged with the teacher' (Tenzin, 16); 'my tendency to pick up my phone and just scroll through social media has … changed a bit' (Leelu, 17) (Osborne and Wakim, 2024).

In Australia mobile phones are now effectively banned in public schools across all states and territories, raising the important question of the state of evidence for such policy. Marilyn Campbell *et al.*, in a scoping review of global evidence for such action, concluded that there was 'little to no conclusive evidence that "one-size-fits-all" mobile phone bans in schools resulted in improved academic outcomes, mental health and wellbeing and reduced cyberbullying. Findings were nuanced and complex' (Campbell *et al.*, 2024: 258). Furthermore, serious consideration needs to be given to the inclusion of children themselves in research that is relevant for them, in the interest of democracy and respecting the voices of children as members of society.

Conclusion

We are at a point in history where populations in wealthier societies are still adapting to rapidly changing information technologies, while others have yet to access these. Many young people now live in worlds that are online/offline hybrids. The risks and opportunities offered are quite different from the worlds of their forebears which gave rise to many developmental theories. Scholars are only in the starting blocks when trying to understand how this new reality affects children's development. For example, surprisingly, studies of children's digital competence have paid little attention to developmental aspects (Kreuder *et al.*, 2024). Although we have barely scratched the surface in this chapter and are unable here to explore solutions to problematic aspects of the digital age, we hope our preliminary suggestions will promote further thought about how developmental theorizing might form a basis for future research on children's digital worlds.

References

Arabiat, D., Al Jabery, M., Robinson, S., Whitehead, L. and Mõrelius, E. 2023. Interactive technology use and child development: a systematic review. *Child: Care, Health and Development 49*: 679–715. https://doi.org/10.1111/cch.13082

Australian eSafety Commissioner. 2021. *Children's online lives*. www.esafety.gov.au/research/mind-gap/childrens-online-lives

Bai, Q., Dan, Q., Mu, Z. and Yang, M. A. 2019. Systematic review of emoji: current research and future perspectives. *Frontiers in Psychology 10*: 2221. https://doi.org/10.3389/fpsyg.2019.02221

Bandura, A. 1986. *Social foundations of thought and action*. Englewood Cliffs: Prentice-Hall.

Barker, T. H. 2025. 'Vague, confusing, and did nothing to improve my work': how AI can undermine peer review. *The Conversation*, 10 March. https://theconversation.com/vague-confusing-and-did-nothing-to-improve-my-work-how-ai-can-undermine-peer-review-251040

Bellur, S., Nowak, K. L. and Hull, K. S. 2015. Make it our time: in class multitaskers have lower academic performance. *Computers in Human Behavior 53*: 63–70. https://doi.org/10.1016/j.chb.2015.06.027

Blakemore, S. J. 2010. The developing social brain: implications for education. *Neuron 65*(6): 744–7. https://doi.org/10.1016/j.neuron.2010.03.004

Campbell, M., Edwards, E. J., Pennell, D., Poed, S., Lister, V., Gillett-Swan, J. *et al.* 2024. Evidence for and against banning mobile phones in schools: a scoping review. *Journal of Psychologists and Counsellors in Schools 34*(3): 242–65. https://doi.org/10.1177/20556365241270394

Carr, C. T. and Hayes, R. A. 2015. Social media: defining, developing, and divining. *Atlantic Journal of Communication 23*: 46–65. https://doi.org/10.1080/15456870.2015.972282

Catalano, R. F. and Hawkins, J. D. 1996. The social development model: a theory of antisocial behavior. In J. D. Hawkins (ed.), *Delinquency and crime: current theories*. New York: Cambridge University Press, 149–97.

Clark, A. and Chalmers, D. 1998. The extended mind. *Analysis 58*: 7–19. https://doi.org/10.1111/1467-8284.00096

Deci, E. L. and Ryan, R. M. 1985. *Intrinsic motivation and self-determination in human behavior*. New York: Plenum.

Dezfouli, A, Nock, R. and Dayan, P. 2020. Adversarial vulnerabilities of human decision-making. *Psychological & Cognitive Science 117*(46): 29221–8. https://doi.org/10.1073/pnas.2016921117

Downes, S. 2022. Newer theories for digital learning spaces. In O. Zawachi-Richter and I. Jung (eds), *Handbook of open, distance and digital education*. Singapore: Springer, 1–18. https://doi.org/10.1007/978-981-19-0351-9_8-1

Dunbar, R. I. M. 1992. Neocortex size as a constraint on group size in primates. *Journal of Human Evolution 22*: 469–93. https://doi.org/10.1016/0047-2484(92)90081-J

Dunbar, R. I. M. 2012. Social networks: human social networks. *New Scientist*, 3 April, iv–v. www.newscientist.com/article/mg21428590-400-social-networks-human-social-networks/

Durmishi, L. and Durmishi, A. 2022. A philosophical assessment of social networks' impact on adolescents' development in conditions of unlimited access to information. *Futurity Philosophy 1*(2): 27–41. https://doi.org/10.57125/FP.2022.06.30.03

Frölich, J. and Lehmkuhl, G. 2018. Multitasking: Gewinn oder 'Zeitfalle'? – Eine Übersicht zum medialen Multitasking bei Kindern und Jugendlichen [Multitasking: an asset or a 'time trap'? Overview of media multitasking in children and adolescents]. *Z Kinder Jugendpsychiatr Psychother 46*(5): 431–43. [In German]. https://doi.org/10.1024/1422-4917/a000575

Fu, S. and Li, H. 2022. Understanding social media discontinuance from social cognitive perspective: evidence from Facebook users. *Journal of Information Science 48*: 544–60. https://doi.org/10.1177/0165551520968688

Fusha, D., Corkin, M. T., Peterson, E. R. and Henderson, A. M. E. 2025. Calls over cuddles: is technoference associated with lower parental warmth? *Journal of Applied Developmental Psychology 97*: Article 101740. https://doi.org/10.1016/j.appdev.2024.101740

Gilmore, A. K., Wilson, S. M., Skopp, N. A., Osenbach, J. E. and Reger, G. 2017. A systematic review of technology-based interventions for co-occurring substance use and trauma symptoms. *Journal of Telemedicine and Telecare 23*(8): 701–9. https://psycnet.apa.org/doi/10.1177/1357633X16664205

Gleick, J. 2000. *Faster: the acceleration of just about everything*. New York: Vintage Books.

Gonçalves, B., Perra, N. and Vespignani A. 2011. Modeling users' activity on twitter networks: validation of Dunbar's number. *PLoS One 6*(8): e22656. https://doi.org/10.1371/journal.pone.0022656

Granic, I., Morita, H. and Scholten, H. 2020. Beyond screen time: identity development in the digital age. *Psychological Inquiry 31*(3): 195–223. https://doi.org/10.1080/1047840X.2020.1820214

Green, B. 2022. Escaping the impossibility of fairness: from formal to substantive algorithmic fairness. *Philosophy and Technology 35*: Article 90. https://doi.org/10.1007/s13347-022-00584-6

Green, J. 2020. *Maori Instagram: the social media lifeworlds and decolonising practices of rangatahi Maori*. Master of Arts thesis. University of Otago, Dunedin, New Zealand.

Gulf Insider Education. 2025. www.gulfeducationinsider.com/uae-to-introduce-mandatory-ai-subject-in-schools-from-2025-what-does-this-mean-for-teachers/

Gupta, M. and Sharma, A. 2021. Fear of missing out: a brief overview of origin, theoretical underpinnings and relationship with mental health. *World Journal of Clinical Cases 9*(19): 4881–9. https://doi.org/10.12998/wjcc.v9.i19.4881

Harvey, M. D. B. 2024. *The age of humachines: big tech and the battle for humanity's future*. Arlington: Steady State Press.

Harwood, A. 2015. Horis, neffs and aunties: social media, language and identity for young Ma-ori in Australia. *Journal of Migration & Culture 6*: 7–21. https://doi.org/10.1386/cjmc.6.1.7_1

Hasgall, A. and Ahituv, N. 2018. Implementing continuous adaptation to technology innovation in complex adaptive organizations. *Journal of High Technology Management Research 29*: 35–45. https://doi.org/10.1016/j.hitech.2018.04.004

Hassan, R. and Sutherland, T. 2017. *Philosophy of media*. London: Routledge.

Hefler, M., Kerrigan, V., Henryks, J., Freeman, B. and Thomas, D. P. 2019. Social media and health information sharing among Australian Indigenous people. *Health Promotion International 34*(4): 706–15. https://doi.org/10.1093/heapro/day018

Heidegger, M. 1954/1977. *The question concerning technology*. New York and London: Garland.

Hutchins, E. 1995. *Cognition in the wild*. Cambridge, MA: MIT Press.

Hutton, J. S., Piotrowski, J. T., Bagot, K., Blumberg, F., Canli, T., Chein, J. *et al.* 2024. Digital media and developing brains: concerns and opportunities. *Current Addiction Reports 11*: 287–98. https://doi.org/10.1007/s40429-024-00545-3

Kemperman, A., van den Berg, P., Weijs-Perrée, M. and Uijtdewillegen, K. 2019. Loneliness of older adults: social networks and the living environment. *International Journal of Environmental Research and Public Health 16*(3): 406. https://doi.org/10.3390/ijerph16030406

Khalaf, A. M, Alubied, A. A., Khalaf, A. M. and Rifaey, A. A. 2023. The impact of social media on the mental health of adolescents and young adults: a systematic review. *Cureus 15*(8): e42990. https://doi.org/10.7759/cureus.42990

Kildare, C. A. and Middlemiss, W. 2017. Impact of parents' mobile device use on parent-child interaction: a literature review. *Computers in Human Behavior 75*: 579–93. https://doi.org/10.1016/j.chb.2017.06.003

Kitsara, I. 2022. Artificial intelligence and the digital divide: from an innovation perspective. In A. Bounfour (ed.), *Platforms and artificial intelligence*. Cham: Springer, 245–65. https://doi.org/10.1007/978-3-030-90192-9_12

Klein, N. 2025. The small-world illusion: overestimating the frequency of in-person interactions with acquaintances. *Organizational Behavior and Human Decision Processes 186*: 104387. www.sciencedirect.com/science/article/pii/S0749597824000797

Kreuder, A., Frick, U., Rakoczy, K. and Schlittmeier, S. J. 2024. Digital competence in adolescents and young adults: a critical analysis of concomitant variables, methodologies and intervention strategies. *Humanities and Social Sciences Communications 11*: Article 48. https://doi.org/10.1057/s41599-023-02501-4

Leach, S. 2020. Russell on technology and common sense. *Human Affairs 30*: 518–25. https://doi.org/10.1515/humaff-2020-0044

Lee, H.-R., Lee, H. E., Choi, J., Kim, J. H. and Han, H. L. 2014. Social media use, body image, and psychological well-being: a cross-cultural comparison of Korea and the United States. *Journal of Health Communication 19*(12): 1343–58. https://doi.org/10.1080/10810730.2014.904022

Lindström, B., Bellander, M., Schultner, D. T., Chang, A., Tobler, P. N. and Amodio, D. M. 2021. A computational reward learning account of social media engagement. *Nature Communications 12*: Article 1311. https://doi.org/10.1038/s41467-020-19607-x

Lungarella, M., Metta, G., Pfeifer, R. and Sandini, G. 2003. Developmental robotics: a survey. *Connection Science 15*(4): 151–90. https://doi.org/10.1080/09540090310001655110

McNair. 2014. Media use amongst Aboriginal and Torres Strait Islander people. https://mcnair.com.au/wp-content/uploads/Media-Usage-amongst-Aboriginal-and-Torres-Strait-Islander-People-McNai....pdf

Meena, P., Gupta, P. and Shah, D. 2020. Screen time in Indian children by 15–18 months of age. *Indian Pediatrics 57*: 1033–6. www.indianpediatrics.net/nov2020/nov-1033-1036.htm

Navarro, J. L. and Tudge, J. R. H. 2023. Technologizing Bronfenbrenner: neo-ecological theory. *Current Psychology 42*: 19338–54. https://doi.org/10.1007/s12144-022-02738-3

Newman, S. 2025. Valuable 'old lady' lessons children need to know. *Psychology Today*, January. www.psychologytoday.com/us/blog/singletons/202501/valuable-old-lady-lessons-children-need-to-know

Orygen. 2025. *New data indicates moderation is key for social media use by teens*. www.orygen.org.au/About/News-And-Events/2025/New-data-indicates-moderation-is-key-to-social-med

Osborne, T. and Wakim, M. 2024. Jury still out on whether school phone bans help kids learn, reduce bullying. *ABC News*, 15 August. www.abc.net.au/news/2024-08-15/is-mobile-phone-ban-in-schools-helping-students-learn/104218850

Pea, R. D. 1993. Practices of distributed intelligence and designs for education. In G. Salomon (ed.), *Distributed cognitions: psychological and educational considerations*. Cambridge: Cambridge University Press, 47–87.

Pedersen, E. O. and Brincker, M. 2021. Philosophy and digitization: dangers and possibilities in the new digital worlds. *SATS 22*: 1–9. https://doi.org/10.1515/sats-2021-0006

Philipsen, G. 1997. A theory of speech codes. In T. L. Albrecht (ed.), *Developing communication theories*. New York: SUNY Press, 119–56.

Przybylski, A. K., Murayama, K., DeHaan, C. R. and Gladwell, V. 2013. Motivational, emotional, and behavioral correlates of fear of missing out. *Computing and Human Behavior 29*: 1841–8. https://doi.org/10.1016/j.chb.2013.02.014

RANZCP. 2018. *The impact of media and digital technology on children and adolescents*. www.ranzcp.org/clinical-guidelines-publications/clinical-guidelines-publications-library/the-impact-of-media-and-digital-technology-on-children-and-adolescents

Rice, E. S., Haynes, E., Royce, P. and Thompson, S. C. 2016. Social media and digital technology use among Indigenous young people in Australia: a literature review. *International Journal for Equity in Health 15*(81). https://doi.org/10.1186/s12939-016-0366-0

Russell, B. 1976. *The impact of science on society*. London: Dover.

Ryan, R. M. and Deci, E. L. 2000. Self-determination theory and the facilitation of intrinsic motivation, social development, and well-being. *American Psychologist 55*: 68–78. https://doi.org/10.1037//0003-066x.55.1.68

Sandel, T. L. and Ju, B. 2019. Social media, culture, and communication. In J. Nussbaum (ed.), *Oxford research encyclopedia of communication*. New York and Oxford: Oxford University Press.

Shute, R. H. and Slee, P. T. 2022. Towards Complex Adaptive Systems (CAS). In *School bullying and marginalisation: harmonising paradigms*. Singapore: Springer Nature, 229–49.

Skowronek, J., Seifert, A. and Lindberg, S. 2023. The mere presence of a smartphone reduces basal attentional performance. *Scientific Reports 13*: 9363. https://doi.org/10.1038/s41598-023-36256-4

Slee, P. T. and Shute, R. H. 2025. The school as a Complex Adaptive System (CAS). In P. K. Smith, S. P. Limber, V. Artinopolou and K. Breivik (eds), *School bullying and the legacy of Dan Olweus*. Oxford: Wiley, 247–64.

Smith, D., Leonis, Y. and Anandavalli, S. 2021. Belonging and loneliness in cyberspace: impacts of social media on adolescents' well-being. *Australian Journal of Psychology 73*: 12–23. https://doi.org/10.1080/00049530.2021.1898914

Srivastava, C. and Patkar, P. 2023. Digital technology and brain development. *Journal of Indian Association for Child and Adolescent Mental Health 19*: 21–6. https://doi.org/10.1177/09731342231178632

Steiner, H. 2025. Finland teaches 6-year-olds how to spot disinformation – and they might be better at it than you. *Fortune*, 29 January. https://fortune.com/2025/01/29/finland-teaches-6-year-olds-to-spot-disinformationand-internet-hoaxes-media-literacy/

Su, J. and Yang, W. 2022. Artificial intelligence in early childhood education: a scoping review. *Computers and Education: Artificial Intelligence 3*: 100049.https://doi.org/10.1016/j.caeai.2022.100049

Sutcliffe, A., Dunbar, R., Binder, J. and Arrow, H. 2012. Relationships and the social brain: integrating psychological and evolutionary perspectives. *British Journal of Psychology 103*: 149–68. https://doi.org/10.1111/j.2044-8295.2011.02061.x

Tang, J., Chang, Y. and Liu, H. 2014. Mining social media with social theories: a survey. *SIGKDD Explorations Newsletter 15*: 20–9. https://doi.org/10.1145/2641190.2641195

Tankovska, H. 2021. Percentage of US population who currently use any social media from 2008 to 2019. *Statista*. www.statista.com/statistics/273476/percentage-of-US-population-with-a-social-network-profile

Tardieu, H., Daly, D., Esteban-Lauzán, J., Hall, J. and Miller, G. 2020. The birth of digital—a brief history of digital technologies. In H. Tardieu, D. Daly, J. Esteban-Lauzán, J. Hall and G. Miller (eds), *Deliberately digital: future of business and finance*. Cham: Springer, 3–7. https://doi.org/10.1007/978-3-030-37955-1_1

Thelen, E. and Smith, L. B. 1994. *A dynamical systems approach to the development of cognition and action*. Cambridge, MA: MIT Press.

Tiggemann, M. and Slater, A. 2013. NetGirls: the internet, Facebook, and body image concern in adolescent girls. *International Journal of Eating Disorders 46*: 630–3. https://doi.org/doi:10.1002/eat.22141

Torresen, J. 2018. A review of future and ethical perspectives of robotics and AI. *Frontiers in Robotics and AI 4*: 75. https://doi.org/10.3389/frobt.2017.00075

Undheim, M. 2021. Children and teachers engaging together with digital technology in early childhood education and care institutions: a literature review. *European Early Childhood Education Research Journal 30*(3): 472–89. https://doi.org/10.1080/1350293X.2021.1971730

UNICEF. 2017. *Children in a digital world*. www.unicef.org/media/48601/file

UNICEF. 2019. *Growing up in a connected world*. www.unicef.org/innocenti/reports/global-kids-online-growing-connected-world

UNICEF. 2020. Two thirds of the world's school-age children have no internet access at home, new UNICEF-ITU report says. (Press release). www.unicef.org/press-releases/two-thirds-worlds-school-age-children-have-no-internet-access-home-new-unicef-itu

UNICEF. 2024. Protecting and prioritizing children's rights and safety in digital environments: a call to action. www.unicef.org/innovation/stories/protecting-childrens-rights-in-digital-environments

Walsh, T. 2023. *Faking it: artificial intelligence in a human world*. Collingwood, Vic: La Trobe University Press/Black Inc.

Wilson, M. 2002. Six views of embodied cognition. *Psychonomic Bulletin Review 9*(4): 625–36. https://doi.org/10.3758/bf03196322

Zhang, H. X., Jiang, W. Q., Lin, Z.G., Du, Y. S. and Vance A. 2013. Comparison of psychological symptoms and serum levels of neurotransmitters in Shanghai adolescents with and without internet addiction disorder: a case-control study. *PLoS One*, 3 May, e63089. https://doi.org/10.1371/journal.pone.0063089

15 Putting it all together

Towards theoretical integration

Introduction

Our developmental psychology students are not alone in wanting a better sense of the 'whole picture' when it comes to theorizing. For about a century, there have been calls for an overarching theoretical framework encompassing psychology (Sanbonmatsu, Neufeld and Posavac, 2025). These authors have, further, considered criticisms that psychological theorizing is in a state of crisis because theories are of 'poor quality'. First, they say there is no 'crisis', as the matters of concern have been discussed for decades. They then argue that psychological theories (and those in related disciplines such as anthropology and sociology) can never match up to the benchmark of the physical sciences because human phenomena are demonstrably much more complex, with generalizability always limited. Although theories are often sketchy, they facilitate the production of testable models. Furthermore, these authors maintain, and as shown in the foregoing pages, theories have built up cumulatively and generated an enormous body of knowledge that can be applied to solving important social and behavioural problems.

We have tried to indicate how various schools of developmental thought are related, as suggested in Figure 2.1 and expanded upon in the text. This chapter addresses efforts aimed at theoretical integration, in an era of many mini-theories.

Philosophical considerations

First comes a bigger-scale question: is it viable to bring together traditional scientific theories and critical perspectives, as we have advocated? After all, the philosophical bases of the two are generally regarded as incompatible, and scholars usually fall into one camp or the other. While scientists seek objective truth, a postmodern perspective as articulated by Gergen (2001) holds that all knowledge is relative, and that there is no such thing as reality, but only individuals' constructions of reality. Thus, any perspective on child development, including ones derived from scientific inquiry, would be no better than any other. The result would appear to be an unhelpful anarchy and nihilism. Indeed, as Jack Martin and Jeff Sugarman (2000: 400) observed, taking such views literally, psychology and education are not only problematized, they are liquidated! Yet it is hard to disregard the fact that,

DOI: 10.4324/9781003567738-15

without bringing critical perspectives to bear, developmental psychology would be even more ethnocentric, androcentric, ignorant of its history and disempowering to its research community than it already is. We have previously described ourselves as sitting rather uncomfortably on the fence; however, our metaphorical straddling was cushioned by realizing that we were not alone. Martin and Sugarman observed that some psychologists

> resonate to postmodern themes of difference, plurality, peculiarity and irregularity as refreshing changes from past adherence to sameness, regularity and strict rationalism … in effect, having labored within the straightjacket of modernity, they enjoy the full ludic romp of postmodernism's radical problematizing without really believing its full social constructionist and deconstructive implications for themselves and their everyday and professional practices.
>
> *(Martin and Sugarman, 2000: 398)*

They considered it rather sensible to resist a forced choice between 'the unsustainable myths of modernity on the one hand and some of the more excessively radical medicine of postmodernism on the other' (Martin and Sugarman, 2000: 400). They proposed a middle-ground philosophical perspective, drawing upon the work of Lev Vygotsky and Margaret Mead amongst others.

On this view, the non-human world of physical and biological objects ('natural kinds') really exists, independently of the humans who study it. 'Human kinds' also exist, but are themselves heavily implicated in this reality: as humans are aware and reflective, their actions and ways of being are affected by the classification of societies and cultures and by their own reactions to these classifications. Thus, their actions are influenced not only by their culture, but by their own unique experiences within it. Their reflections and actions may in turn change the available societal classifications (e.g. changes to *DSM* prompted by advocacy groups). The implications for a rapprochement between reality-based science and postmodern constructivism is captured in the following extract:

> In the dynamic, developmental scenario we have painted, the possibility of reflexive subjectivity is developmentally emergent within human embeddedness in real and preexisting physical, biological and sociocultural contexts. Although precise forms of emergent subjectivity are necessarily historically and contextually contingent and thus variable, some such emergence (given the physical, biological, and sociocultural conditions of human existence) is existentially inevitable.
>
> *(Martin and Sugarman, 2000: 403)*

This exemplifies a metatheoretical approach to the social sciences called 'critical realism' (Archer *et al.*, 2016). Broadly, it is a post-positivist philosophy in that it accepts ontological realism (that there is an objective world) but blends this with epistemological relativism (that our knowledge about the world is inevitably fallible and contextualized). Nevertheless, social science can still 'make claims about reality which are relatively justified, while still being historical, contingent, and changing' (Archer *et al.*, 2016: 7). This aligns well with our approach.

We can further consider the perspective of a mid-20th-century US philosopher of science whose work is having a revival today: Wilfrid Sellars. The view of his work presented here is that of Michael Hicks (2020), commenting on Sellars' 1962 essay, 'Philosophy and the scientific image of man'. Hicks maintains that Sellars has sometimes been seriously misunderstood, but that what he actually did was to critique previous philosophical ideas that 'the unity of intellectual endeavour' is a *given*. Rather, Sellars saw working out 'how things hang together' as the broad ongoing *task* for philosophy, which entails considering the clash between the 'scientific image' and the 'manifest image' (as things appear to us). The latter encompasses folk wisdom, common sense and philosophy. These images are two different ways that humankind has developed for understanding itself in the world. The scientific image eschews the manifest, although historically it emerged from it. Sellars used the metaphor of stereopsis, with the overall vision fusing the scientific and the manifest. Hicks regards Sellars as having a realist view of a pluralist, patchwork scientific image, given the variety of sciences and their procedures. A scientist may understand their own scientific neighbourhood very well, but not necessarily its place in the bigger scientific endeavour; that is a 'higher-level integrative project' (Hicks, 2020: 9386). Although many scientists happily remain in their local area and what it offers, for Sellars, we should not be satisfied until we reach unity, therefore the task of philosophers (and reflective disciplinary specialists) is to aim for greater coherence through productive and creative work.

What can developmental psychologists take from this? Some will prefer to stay in their local theoretical area, but others may choose to participate in the broader integrative project. This might mean bringing together different scientific theories to make better sense of a situation, one example being Campbell Leaper's (2022) multi-theory framework for conceptualizing gender development (see Chapter 12). Or, it might mean working at the philosophical level to reduce the 'clash' between the scientific and manifest images, such as Martin and Sugarman proposed. It seems clear that what is 'manifest' must be highly variable, depending, for example, on historical point in time, developmental stage, gender or culture. Tahir Ali *et al.*'s union of two western theories to improve cross-cultural research by creating greater compatibility with the cultures and beliefs of Indigenous peoples is an example of a 'stereoscopic' view that works to unite the scientific with the manifest (see Chapter 11).

Unlike scientism, which sees science as the basis for all knowledge, including ethics and politics (Gobbo and Marcheselli, 2023), Hicks suggests that ethico-political matters lie in Sellars' manifest image, and this would include the social justice matters that concern those bringing a critical eye to developmental science. The patchwork pieces of the scientific image, though diverse, generally engage quantification, while the manifest image includes multifarious subjective meanings and the epistemologies and associated (usually qualitative) procedures that investigators bring to bear on understanding them (Willig, 2012). Hence, a stereoscopic fusion of science with the insights of critical investigators can help to create a more just developmental science.

A different metaphor, that of a pendulum swinging between modernism and postmodernism, comes from 'metamodernism' (see Chapter 2). Other very helpful philosophical viewpoints are those of Willis Overton and Anna Stetsenko, discussed later.

The Tower of Babel

Marc Lewis (2000: 36) noted developmental psychologists' difficulty in making sense of the proliferation of theoretical approaches: a 'Tower of Babel' (Lewis, 2000: 36). Little wonder, then, that students are equally perplexed! The traditional (meta)theoretical orientations have each contributed unique insights to the corpus of understanding regarding human nature and human behaviour, but have produced very diverse accounts of development (Lewis, 2000).

Within the various schools, there is further diversity. Ethologist Robert Hinde (1992) commented that although psychology gained scientific respectability by 'aping physics', the strengths of the standard scientific approach can also be weaknesses. Science proceeds by analysis, neglecting synthesis. Over the years, there was a gradual breaking up of psychology into subdisciplines, which tended to divorce developmental psychology from other relevant areas such as social and clinical psychology and also isolated it from related disciplines. This tendency towards 'regressive fragmentation' (Bevan, 1994) has been seen by some as inevitable and healthy (Sternberg and Grigorenko, 2001).

R. Keith Sawyer (2000) too lamented the isolation of psychology from other fields, reflecting the reductionist paradigm of methodological individualism—the study of mental activity in isolation from social or cultural context. Sawyer suggested that this would ultimately render psychology redundant, reducing explanations of human behaviour to a biomedical level. Indeed, attempts to reduce explanations of human development and behaviour to genetics had already occurred, in sociobiology—paradoxically, claimed as a unifying force, since all aspects of human activity and development were seen as ultimately aimed towards the single end of gene reproduction (Lerner and von Eye, 1992). This is an explanation in terms of ultimate function, whereas most of the theories in this book offer explanations in terms of *mechanisms*, which rarely span different levels of analysis.

Concerns continued about developmental psychology's fragmentation and isolation (Leaper, 2011), although connections with biology have bucked that trend. Furthermore, developmental psychology itself moved away from 'grand theories' towards many mini-theories. For example, Marion Underwood worried that the field of aggression was in danger of following memory research—into a stage of personalized theorizing 'in which theories become much like toothbrushes in that everyone must have one of her own' (Underwood *et al.*, 2001: 275). Franz and Sabine Weinert appeared resigned to this: 'The time of the "large theories" and broad theoretical controversies is past. Micromodels and microtheories have dominated the field for some time' (Weinert and Weinert, 1998: 25). Similarly, in her book on child development theories, Patricia Miller concluded that '[a]lthough it is tempting to tidy up the assortment of theories presented here by offering an orderly set of conclusions, that aim is unrealistic' (Miller, 1993: 426).

Leaper (2011) took a critical, reflexive approach to the psychological issues impeding theoretical integration. For example, under social identity theory (Tajfel and Turner, 1979), a developmental psychologist may hold a social identity, and derive self-esteem, as an advocate of a particular theory; this would create a bias against 'outgroups' such as advocates of alternative theories, leading to a highlighting of differences, rather than similarities. This would clearly favour fragmentation. Other factors Leaper identified include a tendency to focus on a few explanatory variables, the burgeoning literature causing information overload and an inability to keep up, organizational pressures to specialize, the use of different terms for similar phenomena, and a lack of incentives (for example, thesis examiners and journal reviewers are likely to favour their own perspectives over novel attempts to broaden theories).

Despite the apparent surrender of some to the dominance of mini/micro-theories—a trend that Miller (2022) sees as having continued—there has also been a discernible thrust towards integration in the 21st century. Robert Sternberg and Elena Grigorenko (2001) called for a 'unified psychology', citing the well-known Indian parable of the blind men touching various parts of an elephant and each conceiving of it as a very different creature. They cited work from the 1950s by philosopher Isaiah Berlin which drew upon another animal analogy, in the words of the Greek poet Archilocus: 'The fox knows many things, but the hedgehog knows one big thing.' They called for a more hedgehog-like approach to psychology, consonant with Hinde's view that this need not be through the old 'grand theory' approach, but through interlevel and interfield theories. Interlevel theories seek to bridge more fundamental levels of analysis (e.g. basic learning principles) with more molar levels (e.g. language learning). Interfield theories combine approaches, such as biological and psychological, to problems. Sternberg and Grigorenko advocated a 'converging operations approach' in which psychology operates on the basis of phenomena under investigation, rather than separate fields of inquiry, with varieties of perspectives and methodologies applied. An example is the present authors' book that explicitly aims to harmonize different bullying paradigms (Shute and Slee, 2022). The difficulty of such enterprises, given the valuing of narrow specialization, has long been acknowledged (Shute and Paton, 1992; Sternberg and Grigorenko, 2001). This situation can frustrate practitioners, who do not work with 'children doing strange things in strange situations' (to paraphrase Bronfenbrenner), but with real, whole children, with their physical endowment, cognitions, emotions and behaviours, within their families, peer groups, schools and broader cultures. We now turn to various trends in developmental psychology that have moved theorizing towards the more integrative view that many seek.

Integrative trends in developmental theorizing

Theory bridging

This has been proposed by Leaper (2000, 2022) and is illustrated by his theory of gender development, which pulls together several theories to offer a fuller explanatory framework than any of them could do alone. Leaper (2011) advocates for the integration of theories of social and cognitive development, while also acknowledging the many obstacles. He believes attempts at 'knitting together' theories with common or complementary elements should be encouraged, to offer more complete explanations of development. He gives the example of social cognitive theory (e.g. Bandura and Bussey, 2004) and gender schema theory (a form of cognitive-developmental theory; Martin and Halverson, 1981). Advocates of these two theories have fiercely defended their own position, yet both highlight observational learning and hold that people's interpretations of events are influenced by their beliefs. They are also complementary, with social cognitive theory adding to gender schema theory by explaining how social sanctions against cross-gender behaviour differentially impact boys and girls. Leaper suggests that similar efforts could incorporate different levels of analysis (biological and cultural approaches).

Transactionalism/reciprocal influence

Alexander Thomas and Stella Chess (1977) suggested that how an infant's temperament influences later development depends on the 'goodness of fit' between the child's temperament and the physical and social environment. This connects with Vygotskian and neo-Vygotskian concepts: the zone of proximal development will be greater if the child is interacting with a person sensitive to their level of development, who provides appropriate scaffolding. This exemplifies a growing appreciation within developmental psychology that children's social relationships are *transactional* (Sameroff, 2009). This notion was invoked by Aurélie Athan and Heather Reel in their efforts to encourage moving away from seeing mothers as affecting children's development, to considering how the two-way mother/child relationship might also influence maternal subjectivity (see Chapter 12). This concept of mutual influence has provided a bridge between mechanistic and organismic theories of development, as also reflected in Albert Bandura's theorizing (see Chapter 4).

Reciprocal influence can also be considered between levels. Hinde (1992), in expressing concern about fragmentation, commented that the child's physiology and psychology are embedded in a network of immediate social relationships, broader society, the physical environment, sociocultural values and so forth. These levels have their separate properties but dynamically interact. Contemporaneously, present author RHS proposed a multilevel model of childhood chronic illness, citing systems theorizing and evidence of reciprocal interlevel influences, such as biological factors affecting the child psychologically (e.g. physical illness might have emotional effects) and psychological factors influencing biology (as when a chronic illness is affected by stress) (Shute and Paton, 1990, 1992). Hinde did not cite general systems theory or Urie Bronfenbrenner's ecological theory, but elements of both are apparent in his description. As an example of the limitations of existing theories, Hinde mentioned the inadequacy of modelling and reinforcement to explain the finding that early experiences of parenting are translated into later long-term behaviour changes such as how a child interacts with peers; cognitive intermediaries such as 'internal working models' of the self, others and the world can help to bridge the gap (for a recent discussion, see Linick, 2022). This approach, couched in terms of mutually influential systems, integrates research from cognitive psychology, developmental psychology and psychopathology.

In considering evidence for reciprocity within and between different levels of analysis, we can also revisit the theme of gene–environment interactions discussed in Chapter 3. Not only has it been shown that genes can influence the environment in which the child develops (e.g. through niche-picking), but the environment can change gene expression, through epigenetic processes. Both Gert-Jan Vreeke (2000) and Bronfenbrenner and Pamela Morris (1998) took issue with suggestions that genes are the major determinants of developmental outcome, maintaining instead that an interactive, or dynamic, developmental view best accords with the evidence. Vreeke proposed that the distance between a genotype and the ultimate phenotype grows larger, because the phenotype is reached via a network of epigenetic, nonlinear processes.

These examples illustrate the rising acceptance of notions of interaction and transaction in developmental theorizing. Similar trends have occurred in other fields such as social psychology (Doise, 1986; Hogg, 1992). Ideas about interaction and transaction certainly seemed to represent considerable progress, and these terms were described by Thelen and Smith as 'everyone's comfortable buzzwords, and the proffered "solution" to the nature-nurture dichotomy' (Thelen and Smith, 1994: xv). However, as we shall explain further later, these writers, and others, maintain that these ideas in fact provide no such solution.

Family therapy and beyond

Family therapy must be credited with taking up, at an even earlier stage (from the 1940s), notions of mutual influence, within the specific area of the family (see Chapter 10). Schools of family therapy were developed by psychologists, psychiatrists and social workers (Gladding, 1998). They varied in many ways, such as whether emphasizing historical family factors or present symptoms, the length of therapy, the nature and strength of their theoretical basis and the specific therapeutic emphases and techniques; however, all, to a greater or lesser degree, were based on addressing psychological problems by considering reciprocal influences between family members, rather than focusing on individual factors. The idea that repetitive patterns of interaction develop over time is crucial to family therapy, which is aimed at identifying and changing such patterns when they are dysfunctional. The term 'circularity' is often used to refer to these patterns, but 'recursion' may better capture the notion that repeated patterns within systems are never actually identical (Breunlin, Schwartz and Kune-Karrer, 1992).

While those who devised family therapy took pride in their breadth of vision, later clinical developments saw even family therapy as too narrowly focused. Douglas Breunlin *et al.* (1992) developed a 'metaframework' approach. They pointed out that most family therapy models ignored the intrapsychic aspects of family members, yet at times these may need addressing. Furthermore, systems beyond the family (such as the peer group) are sometimes important for understanding their role in the presenting problem. They observed that it is especially ironic that, although claiming to be anti-reductionist, family therapy gave a reductionist account of the environmental context, as consisting of just the family. Similarly, influenced by Bronfenbrenner's theory, 'multisystemic therapy' was devised, based on considering the broader ecological systems in which children and adolescents develop (Henggeler *et al.*, 1998). It is effective in especially difficult clinical situations, such as working with youth in the juvenile justice system (Zajac, Randall and Swenson, 2015).

Some family therapists have created an even more encompassing view, which is also developmental, taking into account recent knowledge in epigenetics and neuroscience, such as the effect of early stressors on the developing brain. This 'ecobiodevelopmental' view of mental health emphasizes the importance of early detection and prevention of mental health problems, especially through addressing the quality of parent–child relationships (Patterson and Vakili, 2013). Notably, the highly fragmented field of psychotherapy has generated considerable interest in theoretical integration, with an international Society for the Exploration of Integrative Psychotherapies being formed (Zarbo *et al.*, 2016).

Lifespan psychology

From the 1970s lifespan psychology extended the study of development from childhood into the adult years. Overton defined lifespan development as 'the scientific study of systematic intraindividual changes—from conception to the end of life—of an organism's behavior, and of the systems and processes underlying those changes and that behavior' (2010: 4). Forerunners included Erik Erikson, Charlotte Bühler and Carl Jung. The influence of lifespan approaches is reflected in a trend towards research that is longitudinal and that examines developmental trajectories (e.g. Tremblay *et al.*, 2004).

The lifespan approach also represented a move towards a unifying metatheoretical developmental framework, with Paul and Margret Baltes among its foremost exponents. Paul Baltes believed a single developmental theory was impossible but identified the lifespan approach as a family of theories with common elements (Baltes, 1987; see Chapter 9). Broadly, development is seen as a change in adaptive capacity, whether positive or negative. Baltes described the approach as complex and pluralist. It is holistic in its multidisciplinarity, its contextualism and its view of the individual's life course as an unfolding and connected narrative.

Biopsychosocial models

While lifespan psychology encouraged a longer-term perspective, Bronfenbrenner's ecological systems theory promoted greater breadth. Ironically, though, he accepted that his original theory was too narrow: while it emphasized the nested environmental contexts in which children develop, it neglected the characteristics of the developing person, including biological and psychological aspects (Bronfenbrenner and Ceci, 1994; Bronfenbrenner and Morris, 1998). George Engel (1977) had proposed a comprehensive 'biopsychosocial' approach to medicine, recognizing reciprocal interactions between the person's biology, psychology and social contexts; this was increasingly supported by health psychologists during the 1980s. Consistent with this move were the trends we noted above towards comprehensive and systemic approaches coming from those with applied interests in child development, especially child health, where a major concern was to promote good adjustment in the face of particular developmental challenges.

Bronfenbrenner's theory evolved from the ecological model into his 'bioecological model' (Bronfenbrenner and Morris, 1998). The original theory had prompted many studies of 'context without development' (Bronfenbrenner and Morris, 1998: 994) and needed much more emphasis on developmental *processes*, giving pride of place to proximate processes—interactions between the organism and social environment which are the primary mechanisms for development. However, the revision also allowed for development through interaction with the non-social world (à la Piaget) and saw proximate processes varying as a function of aspects of the developing *person*, their *environmental contexts* and *time*. Bronfenbrenner and Morris further categorized person characteristics into *dispositions*, *resources* and *demand characteristics*, concepts which they also applied to the nested environmental systems such as the microsystem.

The concept was also introduced that features of the environment may not just foster, but interfere with, proximate processes, incorporating the idea that developmental outcomes represent competency or dysfunction; this reflected a growing interest in factors that contribute to risk for, or resilience against, poor developmental outcomes (an issue we take up in the final chapter). An increased concern with time (the chronosystem) was apparent, as reflected in Bronfenbrenner and Morris' definition of development as 'stability and change in the biopsychological characteristics of human beings over the life course and across generations' (Bronfenbrenner and Morris, 1998: 995). A link with evolutionary theory was made, in the assumption that biological and evolutionary factors both set limits to, and provide imperatives for, development. For a recent Bronfenbrenner-inspired holistic model see Figure 12.1. Jessica Navarro and Jonathan Tudge have further expanded bioecological theory into neo-ecological theory, that includes the digital world (see Chapter 14).

Dynamic systems theory (DST)

Melanie Mitchell's definition of a complex system serves to remind us of systems principles. It has 'large networks of components with no central control and simple rules of operation give rise to complex collective behavior, sophisticated information processing, and adaptation by evolution or learning' (Mitchell, 2009: 25). The term 'dynamic systems theory' was introduced to describe a new and well-articulated theory of development (Thelen and Smith, 1994; see Chapter 10), though we can detect the idea of systemic interdependence in Aesop's times (see Box 15.1) and in Indigenous worldviews. DST is strongly based upon the principles of general systems theory which means that, despite its name, it is not unique in its dynamic emphasis. As with Bronfenbrenner's bioecological theory, central notions are holism, mutual influence within and between traditionally separate levels of analysis, and a focus on process rather than structure. However, the two theories differ markedly in the emphasis placed upon biology. Although Bronfenbrenner came to acknowledge the biological (specifically, the genetic) contribution to development, he did not detail biological processes at all. On the contrary, Esther Thelen and Linda Smith set out deliberately to create a biologically valid theory; they explicitly rejected models of development which used machine or computer analogies and instead used biologically appropriate terminology. They questioned the common usage of the term 'biological' to refer exclusively to genes, neurology, hormones, etc.—the things that psychologists call 'biological bases' of behaviour. They argued that aspects of the environment, such as social environments that enable language to develop, are no less biological.

BOX 15.1 AESOP'S FABLE OF MUTUAL INTERDEPENDENCE

> The members of the Body once rebelled against the Belly. 'You,' they said to the Belly, 'live in luxury and sloth, and never do a stroke of work; while we not only have to do all the hard work there is to be done, but are actually your slaves and have to minister to all your wants. Now, we will do so no longer, and you will have to shift for yourself for the future.' They were as good as their word, and left the Belly to starve. The result was just what might have been expected: the whole Body soon began to fail, and the Members and all shared in the general collapse. And then they saw too late how foolish they had been.
>
> *(From Aesop's Fables, 1979)*

Thelen and Smith also argued that the notion of a 'plan for the adult' encapsulated in the genes is illogical, as is any 'plan' encoded in the environment. Both these extreme views, they maintained, lead to an impossible infinite regress of coded instructions for development, which is not solved by interactionism: a theory of development must explain how novelty and complexity in structure and function arise, and the answer 'through gene–environment interactions' does not explain *how* new forms and behaviours come about. Their answer is that one must not explain development from a top-down plan, but from the bottom up, an approach adopted by developmental robotics (see Chapter 14). Various factors interact to create novelty as described for general systems theory—so that new properties emerge, rather than being predetermined. An important feature of this is that some abilities may be present but hidden, only coming into play when other aspects of development catch up and enable them to operate. For example, infants can step with alternate legs on a treadmill from early infancy, if their weight is supported; normally, this ability is not apparent until they can also support their own weight and balance in order to walk (Thelen, Fisher and Ridley-Johnson, 1984). This conception helps to address one of developmental psychology's perennial questions—does development happen in discrete stages or is it continuous? The answer may be that it is both, with continuity in sub-abilities or attributes leading to relatively sudden change as the sub-abilities operate together to form an emergent property.

From the perspective of DST, Thelen and Smith said that one of the questions which had long vexed psychologists—what is innate and what is learned?—is uninteresting. This echoes earlier comments by the aptly-named Jeffrey Gray (1985) that the fondness psychologists have of (false) dichotomies often stands in the way of understanding the phenomena at hand. Psychologists are as fond of linear causality and traditional research and analytic methods as they are of dichotomies; such approaches do not lend themselves well to investigations in the mould of dynamic systems, and this presents some real challenges for developmental psychology. For a discussion about systems-friendly research methods, see Shute and Slee (2022).

The integrative power of dynamic systems theory was summed up in a tribute to Thelen by Smith: 'Traditionally, psychologists have considered action, learning, and development as distinct processes. Thelen … argued and showed us in her work how this conceptualization is wrong. For action, for mind, there is but one dimension of time' (Smith, 2006: 89).

Evolutionary developmental psychology

Evo-devo psychology is another approach with the potential to act as an integrating force. David Geary and David Bjorklund (2000) described it as an emerging interdisciplinary field, a sister discipline to evolutionary developmental biology, with the goals of identifying 'the social, psychological, cognitive, and neural phenotypes that are common to human beings, and to other species, and to identify the genetic and ecological mechanisms that shape the development of these phenotypes and ensure their adaptation to local conditions' (Geary and Bjorklund, 2000: 57).

This definition makes it clear that this field is inclusive of all aspects of development traditionally studied separately. Geary and Bjorklund (2000) proposed a hierarchically organized system of modules and submodules of the mind which enable the individual to manage the social environment (e.g. theory of mind) and the natural environment (e.g. spatial representation). These modules are said to have evolved to subserve survival and reproduction. This level of explanation is, of course, like genetic determinism, concerned with ultimate functions of behaviour and development, rather than with mechanisms, understanding of which must draw upon other theoretical frameworks. In making this point, Robin Dunbar (2001) applauded the potential of evolutionary psychology to 'weld together the innumerable cracks that threaten to tear psychology apart' (2001: 421).

Following Imre Lakatos, Timothy Ketelaar and Bruce Ellis (2000) argued that evolutionary theory has the status of a progressive metatheory, in being able both to accommodate major anomalous findings and to generate novel predictions and explanations.

There have been some attempts from feminist scholars to unite feminism with evolutionary psychology. Alice Eagly and Wendy Wood (2013) put forward a 'biosocial constructionist' theory of gender. On this theory, ancient ecological and social selection processes have acted on the female–male division of labour, which is constrained, but not determined, by major bodily sex differences such as females' bearing of children and males' greater body size and strength. The division of labour forms the basis for the social construction of gender roles that in turn reinforces division of labour. Complex neural and hormonal systems underlying male–female behavioural differences are assumed to have evolved to fit societal demands. These systems have built on more ancient mammalian systems but have become adapted to life in complex social groups where understanding of the self and others is crucial. These evolved abilities allow an understanding of gender expectations and permit the cumulative development of culture. The theory allows for human appreciation of the possibility of social change towards greater gender equality.

Charlotte Tate (2013) also attempted to integrate evolutionary psychology and feminism. She drew attention to confusion between metatheories and research theories by some prominent evolutionary psychologists, who had argued that studies that do not support sexual strategies theory do not invalidate the broad thrust of supportive research. Tate says this treats sexual strategies theory as a metatheory rather than the research theory that it is. Metatheories are not falsifiable, but more or less useful, and provide a 'trellis' for research theories and operational definitions. Tate sees the evolutionary psychology and feminist metatheories as not incompatible, when genes are seen as providing the first step and experiential variables the second step in a developmental process, with the separate contributions of the steps to gender similarities and differences possible to be analysed. This provides a framework for the development and empirical testing of specific research theories that straddle the steps. A book that sets out to initiate exchanges of ideas on these issues is *Evolution's Empress*, edited by Maryanne Fisher, Justin Garcia and Rosemarie Chang (2013).

In discussing cross-cultural developmental research and efforts to counteract the historical focus on WEIRD (western, educated, industrialized, rich and democratic) samples, Dorsa Amir and Katherine McAuliffe (2020) have suggested an approach that draws its questions from theoretical frameworks that are evolutionarily plausible and that consider both ultimate and proximate levels of analysis. Seeking 'universals' (or, as they prefer, following Barbara Rogoff, 'regularities') should be blended with in-depth ethnographic work, requiring interdisciplinary collaboration.

Evo-devo psychology has been subject to criticisms that we discussed in Chapter 3. Furthermore, critical approaches to scientific inquiry encourage a healthy scepticism about taken-for-granted archaeological assumptions used to support such theorizing; for example, a feminist approach encourages close inquiry into the truth of tales of brave, strong (male) hunters. Archaeological sites with large animal bones are more highly valued than those without them; there has thus been a privileging, in research, of carnivory and hunting over other nutritional strategies such as gathering plant materials or trapping small animals (Dincauze, 2001). Bones from Czech Upper Palaeolithic sites indicate that mammoth meat was largely scavenged or came from weak individuals, while hares and foxes were commonly eaten, together with plants, fruits, seeds and starchy tubers; evidence of cord and other woven materials indicates that the technology for making net traps was available (Stringer, 2012). One might therefore question how much evolutionary pressure really came from hunting. It has also been proposed that where hunting of large animals did occur, its purpose was achieving and validating male status, that is, it was cultural.

If the overall position that evo-devo psychology acts as a metatheory is accepted, this adds philosophical weight to the argument that it has the potential to act as a unifying force across many diverse areas of psychology. Given the suggestion that Darwinian theory was the starting point for the various schools of developmental theory, it is fascinating that the wheel has turned full circle and the evolutionary approach is now proposed as a means of reunification.

Dialectical psychology

Vygotsky is remembered for uniting cognition with culture, and was very much concerned with the child in a holistic fashion, rejecting dichotomies such as doing *versus* thinking (see Chapter 8). For him, the mind was indivisible from social relations. This presaged later '4 Es' philosophical perspectives on the mind, as did the constitutive relationalism of Sergei Rubinstein. On this view, the mind reflects nervous system activity and the material world, which are always in transaction and inseparable; the relationship is primary. Klaus Riegel expanded Rubinstein's theory in bringing together the biological, psychological, sociocultural and historical aspects of the person to understand their development; change in any one affects all the others, which suggests that developmental theorizing must be cohort-specific. Relationalism grew from dialectical psychology and is now seen as an anti-reductionist metatheory. It is reflected in the move from 'cross-cultural' to 'cultural' psychology, such as in the work of Mariane Hedegaard on education and social cultural activity theories such as that of Stetsenko (see Chapter 11 and later in the present chapter). Such broadening of perspectives encourages multidisciplinary cooperation that goes beyond 'developmental science' (that largely reflects psychology/cognitive neuropsychology links) to also embrace the humanities.

Arnold Sameroff (2010) produced a very interesting, unified theory of development based on dialecticism (citing Riegel), making theoretical links with the development of developmental science itself. It is impossible to do justice to it in a summary, but basically it conceptualizes development metaphorically as a double helix of nature and nurture intertwined, that progresses over time through cycles that are repetitive, but each a bit different because it builds on the changes of the previous cycle (hence, it is represented as a helix rather than a circle). Following Heinz Werner, development proceeds from a global to a more differentiated state within a cycle, interspersed with integration then further differentiation at a higher level (similar to Piaget's assimilation and accommodation). The theory unifies personal change, context, regulation and representational models of development.

The relational metatheory of Willis Overton

While Leaper's suggestions for theory bridging are at the level of specific theories, Willis Overton has taken a metatheoretical approach (Overton, 2010, 2014; Overton and Ennis, 2006; Witherington *et al.*, 2018). Although it is philosophical, we have saved it up for the end of the chapter as it helps to make sense of the preceding disparate material. Despite the ongoing trend towards the dominance of micro-theories, Overton observed, in 2014, that there seemed to have been a paradigmatic shift in developmental science towards a relational developmental systems (RDS) perspective, whereby the unit of analysis is the person and environment in a mutual, fused relationship. A reader who has worked their way through the present book may have derived a sense of this shift, reflected in Sameroff's unified theory and culminating in the publication of the first edition of a *Handbook of Integrative Developmental Science* (Mascolo and Bidell, 2020).

Overton says that, despite the focus on context in the RDS approach, the *conceptual* context for theorizing has been overlooked and, indeed, marginalized as an 'unwanted intruder' into the scientific endeavour (cf. Sellars' clash of images). It is reflected in the failure to teach students about the history of developmental science and its philosophical underpinnings. Therefore, he believes, developmental science has progressed little, in this regard, since early 20th-century neo-positivism and the mid-20th-century Popperian view that science is only about hypothesis-formation and refutation. One gets a sense that, in his later years, Overton has been on a mission to correct this!

He mentions Thomas Kuhn, Lakatos and others who identified a hierarchical/nested 'contextual network of concepts that form an intertwined or fused indissociable feature of any broad scientific research program, paradigm, or tradition' (Overton, 2014: 324). An abbreviated description of his scheme follows and is illustrated in Figure 15.1. To start at the bottom of the hierarchy, there lies the domain of inquiry, or phenomenon of interest, as understood by people's most immediate, common-sense observations, but that can be studied by experimental or observational methods. Above this are the specific theories and models that refer to the empirical world. Above that are more general, mid-range metatheoretical concepts, including 'rules' that determine what is acceptable by way of theory and therefore constrain theoretical and observational discourse; an example is 'the living organism is a dynamic

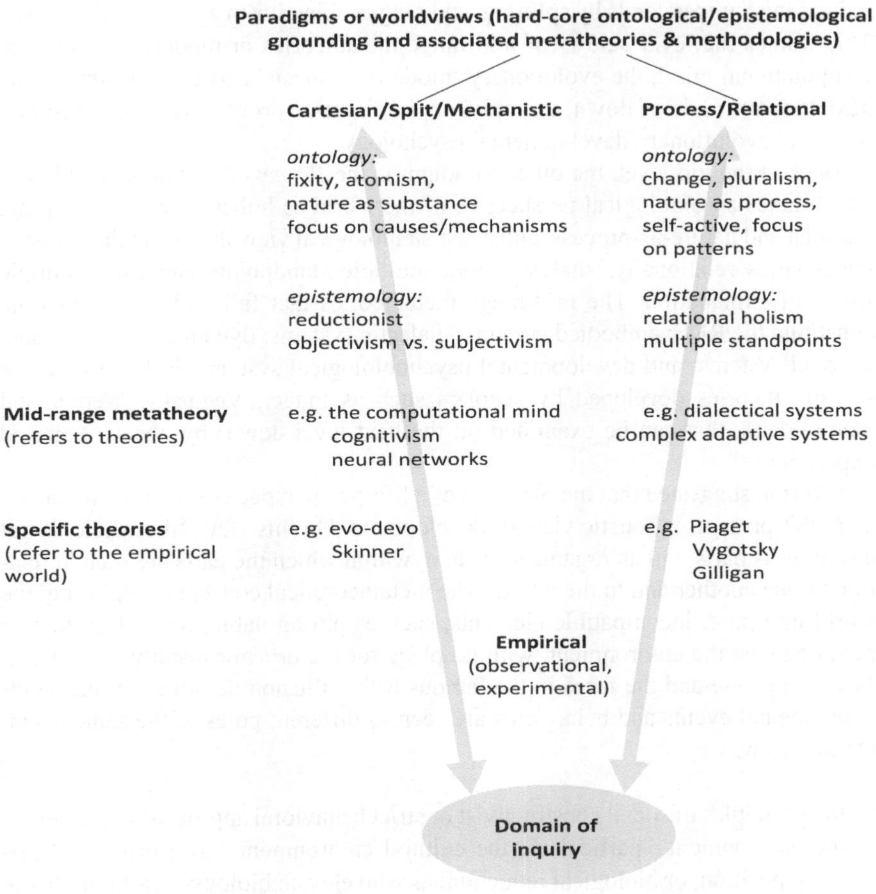

Figure 15.1 Overton's levels of empirical, theoretical and metatheoretical discourse in developmental psychology (based on text and diagrams in the various papers by Overton and colleagues)

system', which would rule out theoretical concepts such as 'stimulus' and 'response' but allow those such as 'self-organization' and 'environmental resources'. The most general level of background concepts lies at the top metatheoretical level: the 'hard core' ontological/epistemological grounding and associated metatheories and methodologies that constitute paradigms or worldviews. Overton's central point is that developmentalists confuse metatheory with theory, and what presents as theoretical debate is often, in fact, *metatheoretical* debate that cannot be addressed by empirical investigation, but only by philosophy. Tate's critique of some evolutionary theorists' position, outlined earlier, is an example.

Overton identifies a metatheoretical divide at this overarching level, that now characterizes developmental science. On one hand is what he calls the *Cartesian/Split/Mechanistic* paradigm. This takes an ontological view of the world as atomistic, static and nature-as-substance, and an epistemological view that is reductionist, understands by splitting, and ranges objectivism against subjectivism. This frames the level below (of mid-range metatheories or models), such as the computational mind, the evolutionary 'modern synthesis' and cognitivism. At the next, theoretical, level down, examples are information processing, cognitivist theories and evolutionary developmental psychology.

Back at the top level, the other paradigm is the *Process/Relational* worldview, which takes an ontological perspective of the world as holistic, active, changing, pluralist and nature-as-process, and an epistemological view that is (again) holistic, understands relationally, analyses from multiple standpoints and uses multiple forms of explanation. The mid-range metatheories that fall under this umbrella constitute the RDS: embodied systems; dialectic systems; dynamic systems; transactional systems; and developmental psychobiological systems. Below that come specific theories developed by scholars such as Piaget, Vygotsky, Werner and many others, that can be examined (at the next level down) by observation and experiment.

Overton suggested that the blending of a lifespan perspective with relationalism and DST presents a holistic view of development. On this view, 'the whole' is not a sum of its parts, but an organized system, within which the parts are seen in relation to one another and to the whole. The metatheoretical concept of 'splitting' the world into pure, incompatible elements, such as pitting nature against nurture or genes against the environment, with no place for reciprocal causality, is rejected. Just as the vase and the faces in the famous Rubin illusion do not exist independently, mental events and behaviours are seen as different poles of the same event. On this view,

> the principles of social constructivist or strict behavioral approaches that elevate the environment—particularly the cultural environment—to a privileged primary position, or biological reductionists who elevate biology—particularly the brain—to a privileged primary position lead to seriously incomplete approaches to inquiry.
>
> *(Overton and Ennis, 2006: 148)*

Interaction must be seen not as cooperation between separate parts, but as 'interpenetration' (as represented by the contrasting dots in the yin and yang symbol; Figure 15.2). We met these ideas in the 'constitutive relationalism' of Rubinstein, although he is not cited by Overton and colleagues. Linear views of development must then give way to complex, dynamic ones, in accord with DST. Seeking understanding by analysis into parts is not precluded, but sight must not be lost of the interrelationships between them. It is a question of what 'standpoint' is adopted.

The idea of 'standpoints' can be traced back to Renaissance philosopher Nicholas of Cusa, who drew upon Plato's philosophy to suggest that we can see the world from various standpoints which are not in opposition to one another, but complementary. This he referred to as *coincidentia oppositorum*, an idea that so appealed to Ludwig von Bertalanffy that he wrote a book about Cusa (Weckowicz, 2000).

Figure 15.2 Yin and yang symbol, illustrating interpenetration *(https://www.publicdomainpictures.net/en/view-image.php?image=196877&picture=yin-yang-symbol)*

When biology, the person and culture are seen as 'interpenetrating' parts, then a biopsychosocial lifespan approach can be said to exist. These three aspects co-evolve, or co-construct one another, with the psychological emerging from relatively undifferentiated biological and cultural beginnings, to then also play its part in the development of the organism into increasingly complex systems over the lifespan. Taking this perspective, the reductionism of the post-positivist era is replaced with multidisciplinary and multimethod approaches to understanding that offer complementary, not privileged, perspectives.

Overton and Ennis (2006) proposed relational metatheory as a way of uniting cognitive-developmental and behaviour-analytic approaches to development. They did this by addressing the incompatibility of the underlying metatheoretical assumptions, of organicism on the one hand and mechanism on the other. They began by re-casting modern behaviour-analytic theory as contextual, rather than mechanistic, in nature. Then they applied the notion of standpoints that are different, but not mutually exclusive. Hence, cognitive-developmental theory focuses on action-in-the-world through the person who acts, while behaviour-analytic theory focuses on the environmental contingencies affecting those acts, offering complementary views of the same event.

Another example concerns epigenesis as probabilistic and not deterministic, which is

> consistent with a Process-Relational research paradigm, with its emphasis on process, activity, change, emergence, and self-organization. Probabilistic

> epigenesis emphasizes that the roles played by any part process of a Relational-Developmental system – gene, cell, organ, organism, physical, social or cultural environment – is a function of all coacting parts and processes of the system. … As such, probabilistic epigenesis provides a powerful antidote to enduring attempts to partition developmental cause or explanation into individual elements, such as nature or nurture, genes or environment, inherited or acquired.
>
> *(Witherington et al., 2018: 189)*

This example, they suggest, demonstrates that the 'interaction debates' are metatheoretical, and can only be resolved through conceptual, not empirical, analysis.

Another matter discussed by these authors strikes us as very profound, yet generally unrecognized in developmental psychology: the matter of baselines. This refers back to our earlier discussions about the role of philosophy, history and culture in theorizing. 'What researchers choose to empirically sample necessarily depends on a set of pre-empirical assumptions that guide their notions of "normality"' (Witherington *et al.*, 2018: 194). They argue that psychology takes as its basis 'the Western ideal of the dispassionate, scientific or reflective attitude, considered the pinnacle of "civilized functioning"' that can be traced directly back to Descartes and that takes WEIRD samples as the baseline for psychological functioning. What is needed, they say, is a perspective on humans over time, and as social mammals, and the taking on board of Indigenous perspectives that are relational. Western thinking is seen as 'piecemeal' by many cultures. The Ngarrindjeri people of South Australia see children as developing in communities where 'Our Lands, Our Waters, Our people, All Living Things are connected', and where there is an 'essential link between the wellbeing of Ngarrindjeri individuals, families, communities, and the place-based consciousness/pedagogy through connection to lands and waters' (Hemming and Rigney, 2011: 352).

We can note here international concerns that many children today are growing up divorced from such connection with nature. Terhi Arola *et al.* (2023) observe that this is a developing field of research, in relation to children's wellbeing; it uses a plethora of different methods and attention is still needed to developing a coherent conceptualization and operationalization of nature connectedness and its relationship with children's wellbeing, and they advocate for more participatory approaches. Relatedly, Witherington and colleagues add to their philosophical paper: 'In a time of planetary ruin by the dominant culture, it may be especially appropriate for psychologists to re-examine their metatheoretical framework for conceptualizing baselines' (Witherington *et al.*, 2018: 196).

Anna Stetsenko: beyond relationalism

While valuing the insights of relationalism, Stetsenko believes that it could be elevated to another level by taking a Vygotskian, (updated) Marxist approach to metatheory and worldviews. This would involve rejecting the current zeitgeist that dismisses 'grand narratives' but, ironically, amounts to a flawed 'new grand synthesis' based on 'resurrected tenets of sociobiology, innatist linguistics, narrowly conceived neuroscience, orthodox cognitivism, and the test-and-control, knowledge transmission-based educational models' (Stetsenko, 2016: 284). She proposes a unified approach to human development that considers matters of knowledge production and human agency and that recognizes the commitment to egalitarianism that strongly underpinned Vygotsky's theorizing. As such, she sees the future of human development theorizing as embracing a political commitment to social change.

Conclusion

We have observed two different trends in developmental theorizing: fragmentation on one hand, and strong moves towards more holistic, integrative and relational approaches on the other. We often find psychologist colleagues much more comfortable with small models which are directly testable by standard research methods—in line with the world of mini-theories that encapsulates much psychological research. While we believe that working strictly in one's local scientific neighbourhood certainly yields useful information, our practitioner backgrounds mean we are much more excited by the current thrust towards theoretical integration and are appreciative of the enormous intellectual effort that goes into this. This integrative work, and the bigger-picture matter of the melding of scientific and critical perspectives, presents significant challenges. We have discussed elsewhere (Shute and Slee, 2022) systems-based procedures for promoting collaboration between people with different worldviews to achieve common purpose and action, a matter discussed further in the final chapter. These integrative endeavours demand that developmental psychology give much greater consideration to philosophical matters than has hitherto been the case.

We finish this chapter by pondering how we would respond to a student query: 'Having completed a third edition of your book on theories, what do you believe about how children develop?' Given the current state of the field, we cautiously propose this answer:

Children's development can be understood:

- by grounding psychology in philosophy and drawing on related fields such as anthropology;
- in terms of humans' evolution as highly social primates;
- positioned in relation to culture and history;
- in a limited way, by linear and causal thinking;
- better, by appreciating that human development comprises a responsive, dynamic complex system whose 'agents' (child and others) co-evolve in an environmental context;
- as emergent, self-organizing, adaptive, difficult to predict and irreducible to its component parts.

References

Aesop. 1979. (Trans. V. S. Vernon Jones). *Aesop's fables*. London: Heinemann.

Amir, D. and McAuliffe, K. 2020. Cross-cultural, developmental psychology: integrating approaches and key insights. *Evolution and Human Behavior 41*: 430–44. https://doi.org/10.1016/j.evolhumbehav.2020.06.006

Archer, M., Gorski, P., Porpora, D. and Smith, C. 2016. What is critical realism? *Perspectives 38*(2): 4–9. www.asanet.org/wp-content/uploads/2023/11/Perspectives-2016-vol38-issue2.pdf

Arola, T., Aulake, M., Ott, A., Lindholm, M., Kouvonen, P., Virtanen, P. and Paloniemi, R. 2023. The impacts of nature connectedness on children's well-being: systematic literature review. *Journal of Environmental Psychology 85*: 101913. https://doi.org/10.1016/j.jenvp.2022.101913

Baltes, P. B. 1987. Theoretical propositions of life-span developmental psychology: on the dynamics between growth and decline. *Developmental Psychology 23*(5): 611–26. https://psycnet.apa.org/doi/10.1037/0012-1649.23.5.611

Bandura, A. and Bussey, K. 2004. On broadening the cognitive, motivational, and sociocultural scope of theorising about gender development and functioning: comment on Martin, Ruble, and Szkrybalo (2002). *Psychological Bulletin 130*: 691–701. https://psycnet.apa.org/doi/10.1037/0033-2909.130.5.691

Bevan, W. 1994. Plain truths and home cooking: thoughts on the making and remaking of psychology. *American Psychologist 49*: 505–9. https://psycnet.apa.org/doi/10.1037/0003-066X.49.6.505

Breunlin, D. C., Schwartz, R. C. and Kune-Karrer, B. M. 1992. *Metaframeworks: transcending the models of family therapy*. San Francisco: Jossey-Bass.

Bronfenbrenner, U. and Ceci, S. J. 1994. Nature-nurture reconceptualized in developmental perspective: a bioecological model. *Psychological Review 101*: 568–86. https://psycnet.apa.org/doi/10.1037/0033-295X.101.4.568

Bronfenbrenner, U. and Morris, P. A. 1998. The ecology of developmental processes. In R. M. Lerner (ed.), *Handbook of child psychology: theoretical models of human development*. Vol 1. Fifth edn. San Francisco: Jossey-Bass, 535–84.

Dincauze, D. 2001. *Environmental archaeology*. Cambridge: Cambridge University Press.

Doise, W. 1986. *Levels of explanation in social psychology*. Cambridge: Cambridge University Press.

Dunbar, R. 2001. Darwinising ourselves. *The Psychologist 14*(8): 420–1.

Eagly, A. H. and Wood, W. 2013. Feminism and evolutionary psychology: moving forward. *Sex Roles 69*: 549–56. https://doi.org/10.1007/s11199-013-0315-y

Engel, G. L. 1977. The need for a new medical model. *Science 196*(4286): 129–36. https://doi.org/10.1126/science.847460

Fisher, M. L., Garcia, G. R. and Chang, R. S. 2013. *Evolution's empress: Darwinian perspectives on the nature of women*. New York: Oxford University Press.

Geary, D. C and Bjorklund, D. F. 2000. Evolutionary developmental psychology. *Child Development 71*: 57–65. https://psycnet.apa.org/doi/10.1111/1467-8624.00118

Gergen, K. 2001. Psychological science in a postmodern perspective. *American Psychologist 56*(10): 803–13. https://psycnet.apa.org/doi/10.1037/0003-066X.56.10.803

Gladding, S. T. 1998. *Family therapy: history, theory and practice*. Second edn. Upper Saddle River: Prentice-Hall.

Gobbo, G. and Marcheselli, V. 2023. *Science, technology and society: an introduction*. Cham: Palgrave Macmillan.

Gray, J. A. 1985. A whole and its parts: behaviour, the brain, cognition and emotion. *Bulletin of the British Psychological Society 38*: 99–112.
Hemming, S. and Rigney, D. 2011. Ngarrindjeri *Ruwe/Ruwar:* wellbeing through caring for country. In R. H. Shute, P. T. Slee, R. Murray-Harvey and K. L. Dix (eds), *Mental health and wellbeing: educational perspectives*. Adelaide: Shannon Research Press, 351–4.
Henggeler, S. W., Schoenwald, S. K., Borduin, C. N., Rowland, M. and Cunningham, P. B. 1998. *Multisystemic treatment of antisocial behavior in children and adolescents*. New York: Guilford.
Hicks, M. R. 2020. Wilfrid Sellars and the task for philosophy. *Synthese 198*: 9373–400. https://doi.org/10.1007/s11229-020-02646-8
Hinde, R. A. 1992. Developmental psychology in the context of other behavioral sciences. *Developmental Psychology 28*(6): 1018–29. https://psycnet.apa.org/doi/10.1037/0012-1649.28.6.1018
Hogg, M. 1992. *The social psychology of group cohesiveness: from attraction to social identity*. New York: New York University Press.
Ketelaar, T. and Ellis, B. J. 2000. Are evolutionary explanations unfalsifiable? Evolutionary psychology and the Lakatosian philosophy of science. *Psychological Inquiry 11*: 1–21. https://psycnet.apa.org/doi/10.1207/S15327965PLI1101_01
Leaper, C. 2000. The social construction and socialization of gender during development. In P. H. Miller and E. K. Scholnick (eds), *Toward a feminist developmental psychology*. New York: Routledge, 127–52.
Leaper, C. 2011. More similarities than differences in contemporary theories of social development? A plea for theory bridging. *Advances in Child Development and Behavior 40*: 337–78. https://psycnet.apa.org/doi/10.1016/B978-0-12-386491-8.00009-8
Leaper, C. 2022. Origins and consequences of childhood gender segregation: toward an integrative developmental systems model. In D. P. VanderLaan and W. I. Wong, (eds), *Gender and sexuality development: focus on sexuality research*. Cham: Springer, 159–205. https://doi.org/10.1007/978-3-030-84273-4_6
Lerner, R. M. and von Eye, A. 1992. Sociobiology and human development: arguments and evidence. *Human Development 35*: 12–33. https://psycnet.apa.org/doi/10.1159/000277110
Lewis, M. D. 2000. The promise of dynamic systems approaches for an integrated account of human development. *Child Development 71*: 36–43. https://psycnet.apa.org/doi/10.1111/1467-8624.00116
Linick, J. 2022. Attachment: theory, application, & clinical tools. In A. N. Marsh and L. J. Cox (eds), *Not just bad kids*. np: Academic Press, 39–66. https://doi.org/10.1016/B978-0-12-818954-2.00001-8
Martin, C. L. and Halverson, C. F. 1981. A schematic-processing model of sex typing and stereotyping in children. *Child Development 52*: 1119–34. https://psycnet.apa.org/doi/10.2307/1129498
Martin, J. and Sugarman, J. 2000. Between the modern and the postmodern: the possibility of self and progressive understanding in psychology. *American Psychologist 55*(4): 397–406. https://psycnet.apa.org/doi/10.1037/0003-066X.55.4.397
Mascolo, M. F. and Bidell, T. R. (eds). 2020. *Handbook of integrative developmental science*. Abingdon: Routledge.
Miller, P. H. 1993. *Theories of developmental psychology*. New York: Freeman.
Miller, P. H. 2022. Developmental theories: past, present, and future. *Developmental Review 66*: 101049. https://doi.org/10.1016/j.dr.2022.101049
Mitchell, M. 2009. *Complexity: a guided tour*. Oxford: Oxford University Press.

Overton, W. F. 2010. Life-span development: concepts and issues. In W. F. Overton (ed.), *The handbook of life-span development*. Part 1. *Cognition, biology and methods*. Wiley Online Library. https://doi.org/10.1002/9780470880166.hlsd001001

Overton, W. F. 2014. The Process-Relational paradigm and Relational-Developmental-Systems metamodel as context. *Research in Human Development 11*: 4323–31. https://doi.org/10.1080/15427609.2014.971549

Overton, W. F. and Ennis, M. D. 2006. Developmental and behavior-analytic theories: evolving into complementarity. *Human Development 49*: 143–72. https://doi.org/10.1159/000091893

Patterson, J. E. and Vakili, S. 2013. Relationships, environment, and the brain: how emerging research is changing what we know about the impact of families on human development. *Family Process 53*: 22–32. https://doi.org/10.1111/famp.12057

Sameroff, A. (ed.). 2009. *The transactional model of development: how children and contexts shape each other*. Washington, DC: American Psychological Association. https://doi.org/10.1037/11877-000

Sameroff, A. 2010. A unified theory of development: a dialectic integration of nature and nurture. *Child Development 81*: 6–22. https://psycnet.apa.org/doi/10.1111/j.1467-8624.2009.01378.x

Sanbonmatsu, D. M., Neufeld, B. and Posavac, S. S. 2025. There is no theory crisis in psychological science. *Journal of Theoretical and Philosophical Psychology*. Advance online publication. https://dx.doi.org/10.1037/teo0000301

Sawyer, R. K. 2000. Connecting culture, psychology and biology: essay review on Inghilleri's *From subjective experience to cultural change*. *Human Development 43*: 56–9. https://doi.org/10.1159/000022658

Shute, R. and Paton, D. 1990. Chronic childhood illness: the child as helper. In H. C. Foot, M. J. Morgan and R. H. Shute (eds), *Children helping children*. Chichester: Wiley, 327–52.

Shute, R. and Paton, D. 1992. Understanding chronic childhood illness: towards an integrative approach. *The Psychologist: Bulletin of the British Psychological Society 5*: 390–4.

Shute, R. H. and Slee, P. T. 2022. *School bullying and marginalisation: harmonising paradigms*. Singapore: Springer.

Smith, L. B. 2006. Movement matters: the contributions of Esther Thelen. *Biological Theory 1*: 87–9. https://doi.org/10.1162/biot.2006.1.1.87

Sternberg, R. J. and Grigorenko, E. L. 2001. Unified psychology. *American Psychologist 56*(12): 1069–79. https://psycnet.apa.org/doi/10.1037/0003-066X.56.12.1069

Stetsenko, A. 2016. Moving beyond the relational worldview: exploring the next steps premised on agency and a commitment to social change. Commentary on Karimi-Aghdam. *Human Development 59*(5): 283–9. https://doi.org/10.1159/000452720

Stringer, C. 2012. *The origin of our species*. London: Penguin.

Tajfel, H. and Turner, J. 1979. An integrative theory of intergroup conflict. In W. G. Austin and S. Worchel (eds), *The social psychology of intergroup relations*. Monterey, CA: Brooks-Cole, 94–109.

Tate, C. C. 2013. Addressing conceptual confusions about evolutionary theorizing: how and why evolutionary psychology and feminism do not oppose each other. *Sex Roles 69*: 491–502. https://doi.org/10.1007/s11199-012-0226-3

Thelen, E., Fisher, D. M. and Ridley-Johnson, R. 1984. The relationship between physical growth and a newborn reflex. *Infant Behavior and Development 7*: 479–93. https://psycnet.apa.org/doi/10.1016/S0163-6383(84)80007-7

Thelen, E. and Smith, L. B. 1994. *A dynamic systems approach to the development of cognition and action*. Cambridge, MA: MIT Press.

Thomas, A. and Chess, S. 1977. *Temperament and development*. New York: Bruner/Mazel.

Tremblay, R. E., Nagin, D. S., Séguin, J. R., Zoccollito, M., Zelazo, P. D., Boivin, M. *et al.* 2004. Physical aggression during early childhood: trajectories and predictors. *Pediatrics 114*: e43–e50. https://doi.org/10.1542/peds.114.1.e43

Underwood, M. K., Galen, B. R. and Paquette, J. A. 2001. Hopes rather than fears, admirations rather than hostilities: a reply to Archer and Bjorkqvist. *Social Development 10*(2): 275–80. https://doi.org/10.1111/1467-9507.00165

Vreeke, G. J. 2000. Nature, nurture and the future of the analysis of variance. *Human Development 4*: 32–45. https://doi.org/10.1159/000022654

Weckowicz, T. E. 2000. Ludwig von Bertalanffy (1901–1972): a pioneer of general systems theory. *University of Alberta Center for Systems Research Working Paper*. www.richardjung.cz/bert1.pdf

Weinert, F. E. and Weinert, S. 1998. History and systems of developmental psychology. In A. Demetriou, W. Doise and C. van Lieshout, *Life-span developmental psychology*. Chichester: Wiley, 1–33. https://api.semanticscholar.org/CorpusID:141796181

Willig, C. 2012. Perspectives on the epistemological bases for qualitative research. In H. Cooper, P. M. Carnic, D. L. Long, A. T. Panter, D. Rindskopf and K. J. Sher (eds), *APA handbook of research methods in psychology*. Vol 1. *Foundations, planning, measures and psychometrics*. Washington, DC: APA, 5–21.

Witherington, D., Overton, W. F., Lickliter, R., Marshall, P. and Narvaez, D. 2018. Metatheory and the primacy of conceptual analysis in developmental science. *Human Development 61*: 181–98. https://doi.org/10.1159/000490160

Zajac, K., Randall, J. and Swenson, C. C. 2015. Multisystemic therapy for externalizing youth. *Child and Adolescent Psychiatric Clinics of North America 24*(3): 601–16. https://doi.org/10.1016/j.chc.2015.02.007

Zarbo, C., Tasca, G. A., Cattafi, F. and Compare, A. 2016. Integrative psychotherapy works. *Frontiers in Psychology 6*: 2021. www.frontiersin.org/journals/psychology/articles/10.3389/fpsyg.2015.02021

16 Nothing is as practical as a good theory

Introduction

As the 21st century advances, there is serious concern about conditions for many children across the globe, with wellbeing, mental and physical health, and education impacted by multiple factors (Phillips and Ritchie, 2025). Despite Kurt Lewin's maxim as reflected in this chapter's title, we may well question the usefulness of child development theory for addressing problems that can seem monumental.

As evidenced throughout the preceding chapters, developmental psychology is almost embarrassed by an excess of riches in relation to theoretical development, and we have seen many real-life applications. Another example, in Box 16.1, uses the theoretical concept of affordance in a program for addressing delay in infants' motor development.

BOX 16.1 THE CONCEPT OF 'AFFORDANCE' IN AN INTERVENTION FOR MOTOR DELAY

Affordance is 'the possibility for action arising from relations between an individual and the environment' (Babik et *al*., 2023: 101563). For example, a dining chair offers opportunities for sitting, climbing to gain a higher perspective, crawling underneath and pushing around. Objects in a home with a diverse range of affordances support many aspects of children's development. In Babik *et al.*'s study, the affordances that homes offered to infants aged 7–16 months with delays in motor skills development were assessed through carer questionnaires: for example, is there a variety of manipulable toys such as balls; physical space allowing free movement; stairs or slopes; the opportunity to play with other people? The children were randomly assigned to an intervention or a control group, all continuing with their regular therapy. The intervention involved twice-weekly 40–60-minute home sessions from a physical therapist, for three months, using games with three aims: to help children develop understanding of their own body and object affordances; to develop object permanence and understanding of means-ends

DOI: 10.4324/9781003567738-16

causality; and to improve joint attention skills. Children from higher socio-economic status (SES) homes and homes with enriched affordances were more advanced in motor skills, cognition and language. Higher SES and a home richer in affordances moderated (enhanced) the effect of the program and reduced motor delay severity. It was concluded that environmental interventions aimed at raising SES and increasing affordances may enhance children's global development by reducing the developmental risk caused by motor delay.

Such theory-informed practice is sometimes referred to as 'praxis'. Equally, we have seen that policy decisions can fly in the face of what theory and research suggest will promote children's positive development, as when migrant children are separated from their families at the Mexico/US border (Blume Oeur and Varga, 2024). Alternatively, practice promoting positive development can sometimes occur without a theoretical basis, as in the case of the South Australian infants who were fostered rather than institutionalized in the 19th century.

Sometimes, developmental theory is neglected in well-meaning efforts to promote children's wellbeing. A prime example has been the enthusiastic adoption of universal mindfulness programs by schools although developmental theory and research indicate that children (and perhaps adolescents) do not yet have the necessary cognitive equipment (meta-metacognition) and may even experience harm (Shute, 2018, 2019/2024). A recent meta-analysis focusing on emotional outcomes found these programs to be significantly less effective than those based on cognitive behavioural principles (Hayes *et al*., 2025). There has been a strong call to abandon such mindfulness programs, and other universal mental health programs with low effectiveness, and to direct resources towards tailored psychological help for those who need it (Andrews and Foulkes, 2025). However, Daniel Hayes and colleagues concluded that, although effect sizes for programs reducing anxiety and depression are small, they are still worthwhile at a population level.

The gap between theory, research and practice has been a long-standing concern (Dodge, 2011; Joyce and Cartwright, 2020). As Jack Shonkoff put it, '[t]he transmission of knowledge from the academy (science) to the domains of social policy and practice is a formidable task' (Shonkoff, 2000: 101). Furthermore, the value of such one-way transmission is questionable in an era that recognizes reciprocity between multiple stakeholders. In this final chapter we turn to a more in-depth discussion of the links between theoretically driven child development research and practice, against a backdrop of the contribution of the philosophy of science.

Applied psychology and the nature of knowledge

Evidence-based practice (EBP) and evidence-informed practice (EIP) are commonplace terms in western public policy discourse and raise the issue of what counts as 'good' evidence on which practice should be based. EBP relates to the medical model, advocating rigorously evaluated, tightly controlled and experimentally evaluated evidence while, in contrast, EIP accesses various sources, including research, professional expertise and participant preferences (Kumah *et al.*, 2022). Reflecting Plato's distinction between beliefs and knowledge, a researcher may see a teacher's opinions about best practice as inferior to the knowledge gained from supposedly dispassionate scientific study. The empiricists such as John Locke posited that reliable knowledge exists outside the individual and that humans acquire knowledge through the senses, while the rationalists, such as René Descartes and Immanuel Kant, argued that reason is more important than experience and that the senses cannot be trusted to provide reliable knowledge. Such ideas continue to shape western philosophy, and form the basis for the scientific approach that there is discoverable knowledge 'out there'.

The rise of constructivism and postmodern theorizing about knowledge introduced a very different outlook, entertaining multiple forms of knowledge that are not discoverable, but built by people. The implications of this worldview for practice are exemplified by narrative therapy, which views clients (including children) as agentic and experts in their own lives; it accepts that people have many abilities that will assist them to address their problems (Jørring and Jensen, 2018). Some contemporary critical influences on child development theory include Indigenous and feminist theories, decolonization and children's rights, that need to be borne in mind in applications.

Wilfrid Sellars' philosophical vision of bringing together the scientific and manifest images, and integrative theories (see Chapter 15), point us towards adopting mixed methods for evaluation of interventions, and not 'chopping up the child' in service delivery. The UK Government's approach to wellbeing recognizes that most mental health problems begin in childhood and are related to physical health; it places a responsibility on every health and care professional to look after the whole person (UK Office for Health Improvement & Disparities, 2022).

The role of universities in creating knowledge is also crucial. Western universities have generally engaged in the conduct of science to develop and test theories and hypotheses. Tierney (2001) summarized the modernist paradigm as encapsulating linear, causal reasoning with an overarching search for theories and universal truths. Consistent with positivism, the university was once generally represented as a community of scholars dispassionately engaged in the pursuit of knowledge unfettered by political or social constraints. Just how far political influence can, in fact, go was plainly seen in the actions of the incoming US administration in 2025, which, for example, placed pressures on Harvard (a private university) not to enrol overseas students and even demanded that Australian collaborators with US researchers should declare their agreement with new US policies, such as accepting that 'there are only two sexes'.

That the university is the sole repository of knowledge had already been challenged in a postmodern context in which the term 'knowledge society' implied that knowledge is produced by and across society (Stehr, 1994). Moreover, 'contemplative knowledge' that seeks to 'describe the world, to represent the world'

Table 16.1 Attributes of Mode 1 and Mode 2 knowledge production

Mode 1	*Mode 2*
Academic context	Context of application
Disciplinary	Transdisciplinary
Homogeneity	Heterogeneity
Researcher autonomy	Reflexivity/social accountability

(Barnett, 2000: 410), so prized by universities, became increasingly understood as only one of *many* types of knowledge (Gokulsing and DaCosta, 1997; Wing On, 2014). This shift was highlighted by Laurens Hessels and Harro van Lente (2008) (see Table 16.1). Mode 1 knowledge production conforms to more traditional university modes while Mode 2 supplements it, using transdisciplinary collaborations and reflexivity. We will say more shortly about the challenges facing universities.

Shonkoff (2000) identified three related but separate cultures working to address issues facing children and adolescents. Scientists are engaged in theory building, hypothesis testing and research, whereas the culture of policy is driven by political, economic and social imperatives, where science is just one viewpoint, and often not the most influential. Finally, the culture of practice refers to domains where clinical judgement or professional experience is valued, which may or may not be based on scientific evidence or bear any relationship to policy imperatives. The tensions among these three cultures are neatly summarized as follows:

> Science is focused on what we do not know. Social policy and the delivery of health and human services are focused on what we should do. Scientists are interested in questions. Scholars embrace complexity. Policy makers demand simplicity. Scientists suggest that we stop and reflect. Service providers are expected to act.
>
> (*Shonkoff, 2000: 528*)

Current challenges facing universities

Richard Fabes *et al.* (2000) described a model of developmental research in terms of Bronfenbrenner's ecological theory. The researcher is at the centre of the organizational system, driven to research by interests and motivation. The microsystem considers those who impact directly on the researcher, including family, colleagues and professionals. The exosystem encompasses community interests and funding agencies, while the macrosystem taps into cultural practices and beliefs, including the politics of the particular time and place. The research endeavour is seen, then, to reflect the many forces to which it is subject.

In many countries, including in Europe, North America, Australasia and the UK, under neoliberal policies, public universities have become increasingly corporatized since the 1980s, competing for students and funding, and with satisfaction of learners and external stakeholders at the forefront of 'window-dressing' marketing; outside pressures (whether coercive, normative or mimetic) lead the managerial class in universities to change academics' teaching and knowledge production practices (Parker, 2011; also see Richard Hil's 2012 book *Whackademia*). The utility value of research has risen, with an increasing focus on preparing students for practice, with more internships and international exchange opportunities, aimed at developing workforce-ready 'soft skills' through experience, rather than just the acquisition of 'hard knowledge' based on fact and evidence (Franco-Ángel, Carbali and Velasco, 2022).[1] Knowledge production is increasingly aimed at commercialization and university self-funding as public funding is reduced (Parker, 2011, 2022). The emerging entrepreneurial role of universities encompasses knowledge production concerning the 'bio-economy', aiming at addressing climate change and other contemporary societal challenges (Tiron-Tudor, Nistor and Ştefănescu, 2018).

On the basis of both the scientist- and scholar-practitioner models discussed below, and a critical perspective, it can be argued that there should be a broader exchange of knowledge, with the opportunity for fieldwork practice to inform research and theory. Indeed, this has already happened in the case of Indigenous psychologies, following from disillusionment with the ability of traditional services to deliver benefits to Indigenous peoples (see Chapters 7 and 11). There is no doubt that the discipline of developmental psychology faces major challenges if it is to achieve this end more broadly:

> Put simply, a scholar's knowledge must be integrated with the knowledge that exists in communities in order to understand fully the nature of human development and, based on this constructed knowledge, to develop and sustain ethical actions that advance civil society.
>
> *(Lerner, Fisher and Weinberg, 2000: 27)*

Universities and researchers are increasingly being challenged to bridge the research–practice gap. This imperative is reflected in practical ways through collaborative research and funding involving industry and universities (as per the bio-economy), a move further stimulated by the reductions in public funding. Numbers of writers advised caution, maintaining that the academic community was being 'largely silenced as a source of dissent and independent critical thought' (Miller and Philo, 2002: 44). These authors warned that as the linkage between universities and government and corporate bodies strengthened, such external forces would exert increased control over research findings and the research agenda itself. In relation to this danger, author PTS has been directly involved in numbers of university–industry collaborative grants. In the finalization of contracts keen attention is given to intellectual property, particularly the ability of the university researchers to publish their findings (in some cases adverse ones). Happily enough, this has been resolved in every instance, but the article by Shonkoff (2000) resonates with this personal experience.

We are similarly aware that researchers with young people in the United States have been constrained by some funding bodies not to focus upon findings that would offend the gun lobby. Furthermore, different lobby groups generate contrasting explanations for events such as school shootings (Smith-Walter *et al.*, 2016). In response to the Sandy Hook shootings, the National Rifle Association concluded that more guns were needed, while the Brady Campaign to Prevent Gun Violence insisted that restricting access to firearms was essential.

David Miller and Greg Philo (2002: 45) commented that '[i]f academics are to give any lead or guidance on such pressing social issues, the universities and research councils must assert their independence from the state'. Corporate sponsorship must not allow the corporations to suppress publications or findings, especially where the findings are not supportive of their product or service. George Albee's editorial stand declared: 'The integrity of psychological science is based on the academic freedom to explore fundamental questions about the nature of human behaviour, thoughts, feelings, and social process' (Albee, 2002: 161).

Yet, the incoming 2025 administration in the United States launched an extraordinary assault on science, scientists and diversity programs, including services for transgender people; adding to the previous restrictions on women's reproductive services came the slashing of foreign aid that supports the wellbeing of the most marginalized, and effects immediately began to reverberate around the world (*Science*Insider, 2025). However, following political pressure on science under the 2016 administration, concerned US scientists had continued to advocate for evidence-based practice (Carter *et al*., 2019). By contrast, Lan Murdock and colleagues (2024) identified opportunities for translational research in the UK with the election of a government that valued evidence-based practice. Nevertheless, there is disquiet that the US example, tied to culture wars, is being exported: in 2025 the Vice-Chancellor of Cardiff University in Wales announced the closure of several humanities departments[2] (Shipton, 2025). She also said, 'I am convinced we need to think very hard about the future of the social sciences … Big Data is only one way in which the social sciences might be diminished in the future'. She added, with ill-informed reference to epigenetics, 'If things like poverty have a genetic explanation, the taken-for-granted approaches and conceptual frameworks we use as social scientists to explain poverty will need to be reworked.'

Despite the enormous challenges facing scientists and universities, what can be done, in practical terms, to address the matter of how theory relates to the effective application of developmental science for promoting a civil society (Shonkoff and Bales, 2011)? A number of frameworks have been developed.

Models of theory–practice links in psychology

The scientist-practitioner model

In 1950 the formulation of this model (Raimy, 1950) was facilitated by US government funding for rehabilitation of those returning from service in the Second

World War. The 1949 Boulder Conference had essentially produced a model of education and training rather than professional practice. As a result, there was a call for clinical psychologists to be trained as both scientists and practitioners (Shapiro, 2002). The body of psychological knowledge then resided principally with university academics. The scientist-practitioner model certainly found critics: 'one of the bottom-line issues is whether it is viable to train students to be scientists generally and researchers specifically when, at the core, these students enter training to be practitioners' (Gelso, 2006: 3).

Ian John's critical voice argued that the prevailing positivist influence on Boulder 'enabled academic psychologists, the exponents and self-declared custodians of these procedures, to position themselves as the arbiters of psychological knowledge claims of any kind' (John, 1998: 25). The implications for scientific practice were reflected in 'a form of instrumental or technical rationality that proceeds by rigorous deduction of prescriptions for practice from these generalizations' (John, 1998: 26). Furthermore, the diversity of incompatible theories provides a daunting challenge not only to developmentalists, but to educators and other practitioners working with children (Green and Piel, 2009; Lewis, 2000).

Those such as John (1994, 1998) drew attention to the range of knowledges jostling for a voice in the postmodern dawn. Debate turned to a consideration of how sociocultural forces influence psychological research and practice (e.g. Slee and Murray-Harvey, 2007). Given that the fostering of free inquiry is (or was!) the very business of universities, John (1998) regarded it as ironic that it was through a dominant positivist outlook that universities were training psychologists. The alternative term 'scholar-practitioner' focused on the skills of relating to clients, without implying that practitioners must necessarily engage in research; in recent times, Marius Drugaș (2023) has suggested that science and practice-based knowledge should go hand in hand.

Despite the critiques, the scientist-practitioner model remains a strong force. For example, the accreditation of Australian university graduate courses in clinical psychology and other specialities, while no longer foregrounding the term 'scientist-practitioner', very much embrace its principles; significantly, there is also now an emphasis on client safety and a biopsychosocial approach that respects cultural issues (Australian Psychology Accreditation Council, 2019).

Clinical child psychology practice did not arise from developmental psychology theory, but from applied work in child mental health (psychiatry) and education (child guidance). The scientist-practitioner model forged stronger links between developmental theory/knowledge and clinical applications. For example, learning theory, social learning theory and research on parenting styles have all been very influential in the development of parenting programs. Nancy Murdock (2006) called for greater appreciation of the critical role of theory—whether at a 'grand' level or at a middle-theory level—in the integration of science and practice; at its most basic, when a practitioner faces a specific problem, they must be able to conceptualize it more abstractly in order to connect the issue with a broader body of knowledge, although the use of diagnostic systems can detract from the application of theory (see Chapter 3).

Developmentally appropriate practice (DAP)

DAP was introduced in 1987 by the National Association for the Education of Young Children (NAEYC) in the United States and, with revisions, remains the guiding framework for the education of young children there (e.g. Copple and Bredekamp, 2009; NAEYC, n.d.) and in other western(ized) countries (Sanders and Farago, 2018). It is

> grounded in the research on child development and learning and in the knowledge base regarding educational effectiveness. From this knowledge base, we know a great deal about how children develop and learn at various ages and what approaches and conditions tend to work best for them.
>
> *(Copple and Bredekamp, 2009: 33)*

DAP was mainly introduced to counter an increased academic focus in early childhood centres, where the term generally refers to children's meaningful engagement in learning activities using hands-on support material; children are seen as actively constructing their own knowledge, in Piagetian fashion. The underlying assumption that knowledge and theory generated through research directly inform best practice in working with children has been questioned. In defending their position, advocates noted that, to develop a DAP curriculum, three areas must be addressed: age appropriateness; individual appropriateness; and social and cultural appropriateness (Aldwinckle, 2001). These are all highlighted by the NAEYC today. That is, DAP practice has expanded from an individual focus to being informed by a broad range of theoretical and research insights (Sanders and Farago, 2018). However, DAP recommendations have been criticized as contradictory, in acknowledging the importance of culture while also providing specific context-free recommendations for practice (Sanders and Farago, 2018). Teachers' use of theory has been little studied, but the most highly educated Australian early childhood teachers favour cultural-historical theory, while those with a technical qualification draw more upon social learning theory (Suryani and Fleer, 2024). Box 16.2 addresses culturally appropriate practice in African early childhood education.

BOX 16.2 WHAT IS DEVELOPMENTALLY APPROPRIATE PRACTICE IN AFRICA?

Winnie Mucherah and Teresia Mbogori (2019) have drawn on Lev Vygotsky's sociocultural theory and Erik Erikson's identity theory to suggest ways for making early educational practice more 'appropriate' for the African context. They observe that even for countries that gained independence from colonial masters decades ago, their influence is still very present in that textbooks describe 'optimal' development in western terms. Through internalization of colonial standards, English is often more highly valued than local languages, and children may still be beaten for using these. Alphabet books may begin with 'A is for apple', although most rural African children have never seen one! The message is clearly sent through the education system that children's own languages are inferior, damaging their African identity. Children are also being denied the cognitive advantages of being efficiently multilingual at an early age.

In Africa, they suggest that there needs to be an intentional examination of the education curriculum to promote more culturally appropriate teaching. It should reflect Africa's collectivist values and promote ethnic pride and identity, that is linked to higher self-esteem, greater connectedness to school and positive social functioning. Children can be praised for using their local language(s), and for wearing cultural outfits and natural/braided hair. There is a need for more books with African authors and main characters who are African so that children can see themselves represented. Africa's wealth of music and dance should be woven into the everyday life of schools, they suggest, and not reserved for special occasions.

Applied developmental science (ADS)

The establishment of ADS began with a meeting of delegates at Fordham University in New York in 1991 (Fisher and Lerner, 1994). Its purpose is to utilize descriptive and explanatory knowledge about human development in the interests of pursuing preventative or enhancing interventions. The field has expanded considerably, and a recent discussion emphasizes its interdisciplinary nature and potential to address the issues facing vulnerable children, as a result of poverty, premature birth, abuse, crime, ethnic conflicts and so forth (Guanghui, 2024).

Richard Lerner, Celia Fisher and Richard Weinberg (2000) identified three characteristics of ADS: it has direct implications for the actions of individuals, families and policy-makers; it has a focus on change across the lifespan; and it stresses the utilization of a diversity of research methods. Lerner and Fisher (2014) expressed optimism that ADS could be used to enhance the development and well-being of all individuals across the lifespan. In large part they attributed their optimism to advances in biological understanding, including evolution and epigenetics, which they believed to have substantial implications for human health and welfare. By contrast is a critical perspective that, in practice, developmental psychology has been damaging for children around the world. Erica Burman has written:

> [The] injustices, exclusions and pathologisation of the discourse of development are writ small in the story of what happens to children and their families while, reciprocally, the story of individual development is writ large in the story of national and international development.
>
> *(Burman, 2012: 127)*

For example, it is one thing to show through research that the mental health of Palestinian children is seriously damaged by ongoing conflict, and impacted by their mothers' mental health (Massad, Khammash and Shute, 2017), but quite another to resolve the underlying political tensions. As we write, families and children in Gaza are simply struggling to survive and access the basics of life (UNICEF, 2025). Clearly, developmental science alone cannot address such massive problems, which are entangled with many forces including history and politics, as emphasized by the dialectical theorist Klaus Riegel.

ADS and the scientist-practitioner model both aim to address important social issues for young people such as the impact of violence, crime and poor mental health, while also raising challenges for the traditional keepers of knowledge—the universities—regarding better understanding of the nature and type of knowledge they are pursuing. Universities are also being asked to address the ability of such knowledge to successfully address the various and immediate problems facing the world; for example, in 2025 the authors' university established an evidence-based 'wicked problems' initiative (also refer back to Box 10.1). As Fisher *et al.* observed, 'One of the defining characteristics of applied developmental science (ADS) is that theory, research, and its application in the real world are interwoven, each informing and enriching the other' (2013: 54).

This perspective created a growing interest in fostering 'outreach scholarship' (Gonzales-Kruger *et al.*, 2000). An important focus is that of contextualized knowledge (Lerner *et al.*, 2000), which promoted a change in the typical ontology within scholarship (i.e. a greater focus on 'relationism' or 'relationalism'), recognizing existence as contingent on the specifics of the physical and social conditions that exist at a particular moment of history (Overton, 1998; Pepper, 1942). In the 1980s, Alvin Toffler critiqued the long-standing mechanistic worldview dominating scientific inquiry, instead conceiving of science as 'an open system embedded in society and linked to it by very dense feedback loops. It is powerfully influenced by its external environment and, in a general way, its development is shaped by cultural receptivity to its dominant ideas' (Toffler, 1984: xii–xiii). Knowledge separated from its context is not, then, basic knowledge. For example, China's boom in developmental psychology research is mostly basic research that does not consider issues for young people in a changing social environment in which the labour force has been diverted from rural China to the cities (Guanghi, 2024). The contextual perspective has led Kathryn Joyce and Nancy Cartwright (2020) to change the question about evaluating practice from 'does it work?' to 'does it work *here*?'

Developmental resilience science

Ann Masten and Andrew Barnes (2018) have highlighted the role of 'developmental resilience science' as a framework for applied work with individual children, families, communities and care systems. Challenge can be positive for development, but more severe or frequent adverse childhood experiences (ACEs) are not. A study guided by the idea of cumulative risk and several developmental theories is shown in Box 16.3.

BOX 16.3 A CUMULATIVE RISK APPROACH TO A PARENTING PROGRAM FOR PARENTS OF AT-RISK CHILDREN

A Danish study used the concept of cumulative risks to examine the effect of the Incredible Years Parent Training program on disruptive child behaviour (Greve, Fentz and Trillingsgaard, 2024). Many studies had shown that cumulative risk is a better predictor of children's adjustment (e.g. criminal activity, mental health) than individual risk factors. Several developmental theories were apparent in the study, relating to non-optimal parenting practices: the use of punishment rather than praise (operant conditioning) and less sensitive responding to children (attachment theory). Also, the program took a cognitive-behavioural approach consisting of weekly sessions for one or both parents or a parent and grandparent, and included video examples, facilitated group discussions and sharing of experiences (social learning theory). Parental markers of low SES were: single parenthood; unemployment; low income; low education; and teen pregnancy. Very few had all five risks and so were excluded from the analysis. It was found that, unexpectedly, the effect of cumulative risk on program outcome was negligible: families with 0–4 risks benefited equally, in terms of reduction of disruptive child behaviour. The study added to evidence that this particular parenting program embraces families across the SES spectrum, in the Danish context.

Guided by the latest wave of resilience research that is integrative, drawing upon dynamic systems theory and complex adaptive systems, they define resilience as 'the capacity of a system to adapt successfully to challenges that threaten the function, survival or future development of the system' (Masten and Barnes, 2018: 1). Resilience does not reside within the child, but depends on their connections with other people and systems that provide 'back-up' in the face of ACEs. Education for workers needs to focus on understanding of 'dose' (severity of adversity) and the cumulative effects of ACEs, and the various protective and 'promotive' (positive) factors (and their timing) that have been selected for through biological and sociocultural evolution and identified through research. Examples are effective parenting, nurturing carers, optimism, meaning-making, agency, well-functioning communities and schools, and cultural traditions. The framework for interventions that Masten and Barnes identify includes:

- Mission with positive goals
- Models and measures that include promotive and protective factors as well as positive criteria for evaluating success
- Methods to mitigate risk, boost assets, and mobilize adaptive systems
- Multi-sector and multi-level alignment to create synergy for change
- Maximizing leverage for change by strategic timing and targeting.

(Masten and Barnes, 2018: 8)

A remarkable story of a resilient child is outlined in Box 16.4.

BOX 16.4 ANTONIO SALAZAR-HOBSON: A RESILIENT CHILD

Antonio was a Mexican child living with his Spanish-speaking fruit-picker parents and 13 siblings in Arizona. Mute until 3, he was kidnapped at 4 by a paedophile couple who whisked him off to California and abused and sex-trafficked him for five years. He attempted to hang himself at 9. The authorities failed to look for him, which could easily have been done, but, he says, missing brown children were not news. He later became a happily married man with two children, and a prominent labour lawyer fighting for the underprivileged. How was that possible?

He attributes it strongly to the deep love of his mother, who provided a happy home for the children, with warm family rituals such as their breakfast routine. He also believes that, as a mute child, he was a deep thinker. After the kidnap, he selected some bricks representing his family members and spoke to them in Spanish every day, sure he would find them again and determined to retain the language of his culture. Fearing the authorities, his captors sent him to school, where he worked hard and did well, books providing an escape. His despairing suicide attempt, while trafficked to a ranch harbouring well-to-do paedophiles, was noticed by one man who comforted him and threatened the owners with the police, so he was sent away. He met Cesar Chavez, a labour activist, who recognized his ability and gave him a fresh purpose: to become a labour lawyer. The resilience factors identified by research are clearly seen in his story, told in his memoir, *Antonio, We Know You.*

Other frameworks for promoting evidence-based practice

Implementation science

> If we keep on doing what we have been doing, we will keep on getting what we have been getting.
>
> *(Wandersman et al., 2008: 171)*

Joseph Durlak and Emily DuPre (2008), in reviewing the literature on preventative mental health studies, found that only a minority reported on their implementation process and that 'the magnitude of mean effect sizes [is] at least two to three times higher when programs are carefully implemented and free from serious implementation problems than when these circumstances are not present' (Durlak and DuPre, 2008: 340). Research later confirmed that the quality of the implementation of mental health programs in primary schools influences their effectiveness

(Dix *et al.*, 2012; Slee *et al.*, 2009, 2012). Traditionally, research had paid more attention to other methodological issues (such as experimental design, reliability of measurements and statistical power), with the assumption that the participants received the intervention(s) as intended. Durlak and DuPre's review identified eight aspects of implementation:

1. *Fidelity*: how far the innovation corresponds with the originally intended program (adherence, compliance, integrity, faithful replication).
2. *Dosage*: how much of the original program has been delivered (quantity, intervention strength).
3. *Quality*: how well different program components have been conducted.
4. *Participant responsiveness*: how much the program stimulates the interest or holds the attention of participants.
5. *Program differentiation*: how far the program's theory and practices can be distinguished from other programs (uniqueness).
6. *Control monitoring*: comparing differences to non-participating schools and their outcomes.
7. *Program reach*: (participation rates, program scope) refers to the rate of involvement and representativeness of program participants.
8. *Adaptation*: changes made to the original program during implementation.

Interventions are influenced by ecological factors such as the socio-economic and cultural environment (Slee and Murray-Harvey, 2007), affecting people's responses to an intervention and ultimately its success. Celene Domitrovich *et al.* (2008) described contextual factors influencing the implementation of new programs at three levels—policy, school and individual. One way to accommodate contextual factors is through qualitative information. For example, Domitrovich and Mark Greenberg urged that when 'schools consider program adoption, they should talk with other schools already using the program to gain local insights into the practical issues associated with its implementation' (Domitrovich and Greenberg, 2000: 208). Neil Humphrey *et al.* (2016) pointed out that developer evaluations find stronger results, which may be because there is better implementation, but also possibly because of bias, so independent evaluation is also called for.

Before Australia's *KidsMatter* primary schools mental health program was rolled out nationally, a framework for implementation was developed based on Domitrovich *et al.*'s (2008) recommendations. This included those implementing the intervention and those providing the support in gauging aspects of fidelity, dosage and quality of delivery. A series of indicators was collated from the various data sources in the evaluation to create an innovative 'Implementation Index' (Slee *et al.*, 2009). This enabled classification of schools according to the quality of their implementation and identification of the particular features of schools categorized as 'performing well', in order to detect indicators of exemplary practice. Evaluations of the implementation index clearly demonstrated its utility, highlighting links between the quality of the implementation and outcomes associated with the level of change in mental health functioning of the students (Askell-Williams, Slee and van Deur, 2013; Dix *et al.*, 2012).

Ultimately, following the election of a new Australian government in 2014, both the preschool and primary versions of *KidsMatter* were packaged together with several other government-funded programs under the umbrella title of Be You, with the intent of producing 'one single, national end-to-end education based program' (Beyond Blue, 2024). This organization provides online materials for short self-study modules on implementation. A more extensive training program is offered by the University of Melbourne, in the form of a six-month part-time graduate certificate in implementation science. Such arrangements do not incorporate a developer–implementer link, such as the project officers that used to be in schools to help teachers using *KidsMatter*.

In the light of their experience in Canada, Bonnie Leadbeater and Emilie Gladstone (2016) added further advice on taking a long-term, sustainable perspective on the implementation of school-based mental health programs. They emphasized the importance of program developers providing not just initial training, but ongoing support for users, and working to integrate the program into their routine activity and websites. For example, the *Big Talks for Little People* child mental health program (Slee, 2023) provides (a) on-line delivery of the lessons downloadable to teachers' smart-boards; (b) professional development prior to commencing the program (for which teachers can receive 2–3 hours towards their required yearly professional development; and (c) an on-line suite of teacher information sheets on topics such as trauma-informed teaching and ongoing professional support. This recently evaluated Australian program is being implemented nationally and internationally and calls upon implementation quality as a foundation stone for fostering positive outcomes (Slee, 2023; Slee, Pill and Agnew, 2025).

Other research too has underlined the importance of detailed attention to the school context in implementation. One informative study used a complex adaptive systems perspective to examine four schools in Wales that had sent teachers to a training course for a new mental health initiative; although all schools considered that they were fully implementing the program, only one adopted it sustainably, with careful study of the chain of events in each school highlighting several 'reinvention points' when implementation was compromised (Evans, Murphy and Scourfield, 2015). Joyce and Cartwright (2020) maintain that ensuring that a program fits into a specific context needs more than 'tinkering around the edges' and adopting good implementation practice; it requires the hard work of developing a context-local program plan. Also relevant is the delicate balancing act between implementing a program with fidelity, and adapting it to the local context (Lendrum, Humphrey and Greenberg, 2016). These authors suggest that, because fidelity has become the most studied aspect of implementation it has, in a circular way, become seen as the most important. They reframe the issue in terms of 'quality', operationalized as 'teacher preparedness, enthusiasm, and engagement with and responsiveness to students' (Lendrum *et al.*, 2016: 57). They showed this to be more predictive of outcomes than fidelity when both were measured together (Humphrey, Lendrum and Wigelsworth, 2014). Teacher attitudes towards evidence-based practice for student mental health are more positive if they have more knowledge about research methods, which has implications for pre-service and in-service teacher training (Kallitsoglou and Mahmud, 2023).

Quality assurance

Quality assurance is a widely used term across the physical and behavioural sciences. One definition is 'the determination of standards, appropriate methods and quality requirements by an expert body, accompanied by a process of inspection or evaluation that examines the extent to which practice meets the standards' (Murgatroyd and Morgan, 1993: 45). For example, the Australian Government has a National Quality Framework for regulating early childhood education and care, and funds an independent authority that supports states' and territories' regulatory authorities and pushes for continuous improvement (Australian Government Department of Education, n.d.).

Quality assurance is deeply grounded in the notion that theory gives rise to essential research which then informs the development of programs and practice, all designed to enhance the optimal development of children and young people. This process is anything but linear, as shown in Figure 16.1. The focus on quality is also evident in attempts to define, describe and improve meta-evaluations, that synthesize research of multiple studies, with free software available to assist with this (Cooke, 2024).

Prior to the national rollout of Australia's *KidsMatter* primary schools mental health promotion program, Slee *et al.* (2011) developed a quality assurance framework. It is summarized diagrammatically in Figure 16.2.

Figure 16.1 A quality assurance process

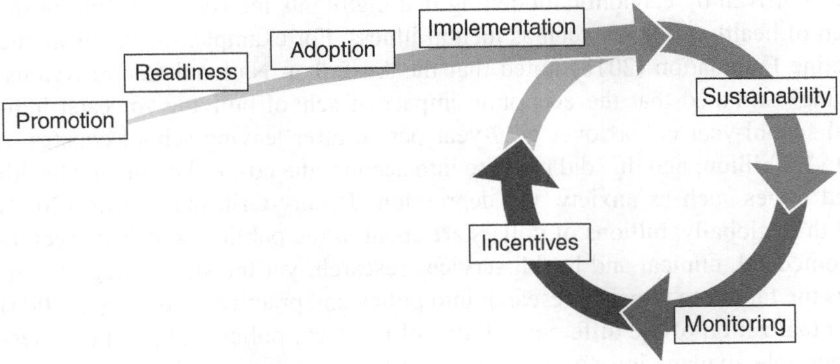

Figure 16.2 The seven-step model of *KidsMatter* quality assurance (adapted from Slee *et al.*, 2011)

Research–practice partnerships/co-design

Partnerships between researchers and those at the coal-face are becoming more common, such as in education (Joyce and Cartwright, 2020). They enable practitioners to identify matters of concern to them, so that researchers are then able to devise ways of studying the issue. The researchers focus on providing evidence-based knowledge, while the practitioners focus on implementation, but the process is one of co-design. This necessitates 'meaningful involvement of stakeholders in creating new knowledge and harnessing, mobilising, and transferring existing knowledge to support comprehensive and long-term solutions' (Iniesto, Charitonos and Littlejohn, 2022: 273).

Improvement science

This term is used in education for the study of variation in educational outcomes, to help discover and harness the factors that influence this variation (Joyce and Cartwright, 2020). Such information is shared through 'networked improvement communities' that provide practice-based evidence.

Translational science

Sussman *et al.* (2006: 18) saw this as 'an extended process of how research knowledge that is directly or indirectly relevant to health behavior eventually serves the public'. This reflects the fact that the commonest application of the term is to the medical sciences, in what used to be called 'bench to bedside' practice, but increasingly it is being applied to the behavioural sciences too. An alternative definition is that translational research 'seeks to integrate theories, methodologies, and frameworks from various disciplines across a team of researchers, [and] places emphasis on translation of findings in order to offer practical solutions to real-world problems' (Begerowski *et al.*, 2021: 1).

In no small part, the impetus for the increasing focus on translational science has been driven by economic modelling that highlights the cost to society of the burden of health problems such as mental illness. For example, the Alannah and Madeline Foundation (2018) noted that the Australian National Centre Against Bullying estimated that the economic impact of school bullying for each individual school-year cohort over a 20-year period after leaving school equates to AUD $1.8 billion; and this did not take into account the cost of key mental health related issues such as anxiety and depression. Jeremy Grimshaw *et al.* (2012) noted that, globally, billions of dollars are spent in the public and private sectors on biomedical, clinical and health services research, yet the single biggest concern is the failure to translate research into policy and practice. Shonkoff's (2000) conceptualization of the different cultures of research, policy and practice offers one possible explanation for translation failures. Unfortunately, the resultant evidence–practice gap provides less than optimal delivery of care, services and programs.

Grimshaw *et al.* (2012) identified five central questions relating to translational research, including:

1. What should be transferred (e.g. research papers or systematic reviews)?
2. To whom should research knowledge be transferred (e.g. consumers, professionals, policy-makers)?
3. By whom should research knowledge be transferred? (e.g. by an individual, group or organization)?
4. How should research knowledge be transferred (e.g. taking into account the barriers and facilitators)?
5. With what effect should research knowledge be transferred (e.g. to inform or educate)?

Some have focused on the barriers to effecting translational research. There are many reasons why scholars may be reluctant to participate, including 'differences in opinion about when the science is ready for translation, challenges associated with conveying discrepant findings, concern over maintaining appropriate boundaries between scholarship and advocacy, and a desire to avoid charges from peers of publicity seeking' (Shonkoff and Bales, 2011: 17).

Drawing on the research literature about groups and teams, Sydney Begerowski *et al.* (2021) have discussed the importance of well-functioning translational science teams, concluding that one size does not fit all. They emphasize the importance of 'establishing a shared vision, developing and maintaining clear expectations, cultivating team trust, and promoting effective communication' (Begerowski *et al.*, 2021: 3). They have devised some guiding questions for team development at four different research phases:

1. Development (e.g. has account been taken of the perspectives of all members from different disciplines?).
2. Conceptualization (e.g. are team members engaging in respectful disagreement?)

3. Implementation (e.g. do members understand their roles and those of others?).
4. Translation (e.g. have team goals for translation been agreed?).

A more complex soft-systems-based method for developing transdisciplinary teams, that takes account of different worldviews, was devised by Peter Checkland and Jim Scholes (1990) and is summarized in Figure 16.3.

One important difference in worldviews is the epistemological difference between quantitative and qualitative researchers. In an editorial in the *Journal of Child Psychology and Psychiatry*, Edmund Sonuga-Barke (2024) has noted the absence of qualitative studies in that journal, which he said was not surprising as the journal is an 'unashamedly … translational *science* journal' (Sonuga-Barke, 2024: 1255, original emphasis). Nevertheless, he argues that qualitative work has a complementary place in the translational science discovery–development–implementation cycle. Qualitative research is important in characterizing clinical phenomena from the perspective of clients, parents and professionals. Insights can be gained into what such stakeholders see as the most tractable aspects of mental health to help focus the intervention, and provide feedback on acceptability of, barriers to, and unintended consequences of, interventions. Qualitative material, he observes, also brings research findings to life, in a way that dry quantitative science often cannot, and enlightens scientists about their own taken-for-granted cultural assumptions.

Can program evaluation inform theory?

> [E]valuations of parenting programmes, if well conducted, can serve a dual aim: (1) to enhance children's and family functioning; and (2) to elucidate important developmental processes and mechanisms. The first aim is immediately obvious, but the second aim tends to get somewhat 'forgotten'.
>
> *(Deković et al., 2011: 64)*

The basic question one asks when evaluating any program is, 'Does it work?' (Deković *et al.*, 2011) or, according to Joyce and Cartwright (2020), 'Does it work *here*?' However, as Maja Deković *et al.* suggest, so much more can be achieved, if we also ask, 'Why does it work?' Taking parenting programs as an example, they suggest the usefulness of evaluations for testing theory. Often it is not clear what the crucial aspects of a complex program are, though numbers might be suggested by previous theory. Initially, the program must be both theory-based and well-implemented, or its value for theory-testing is useless. With a view to elucidating mechanisms of change, theory-testing can be done by measuring process variables and assessing their mediating role in determining outcomes. Preferably, one mediator would be evaluated against another. For example, if children's emotional or behavioural problems improve after a parenting program, is it because parents have become less harsh, more supportive, more confident or less stressed? We can add that testing moderating variables (such as affordance-richness, as described in Box 16.1) also helps guide understanding of mechanisms of change that can inform

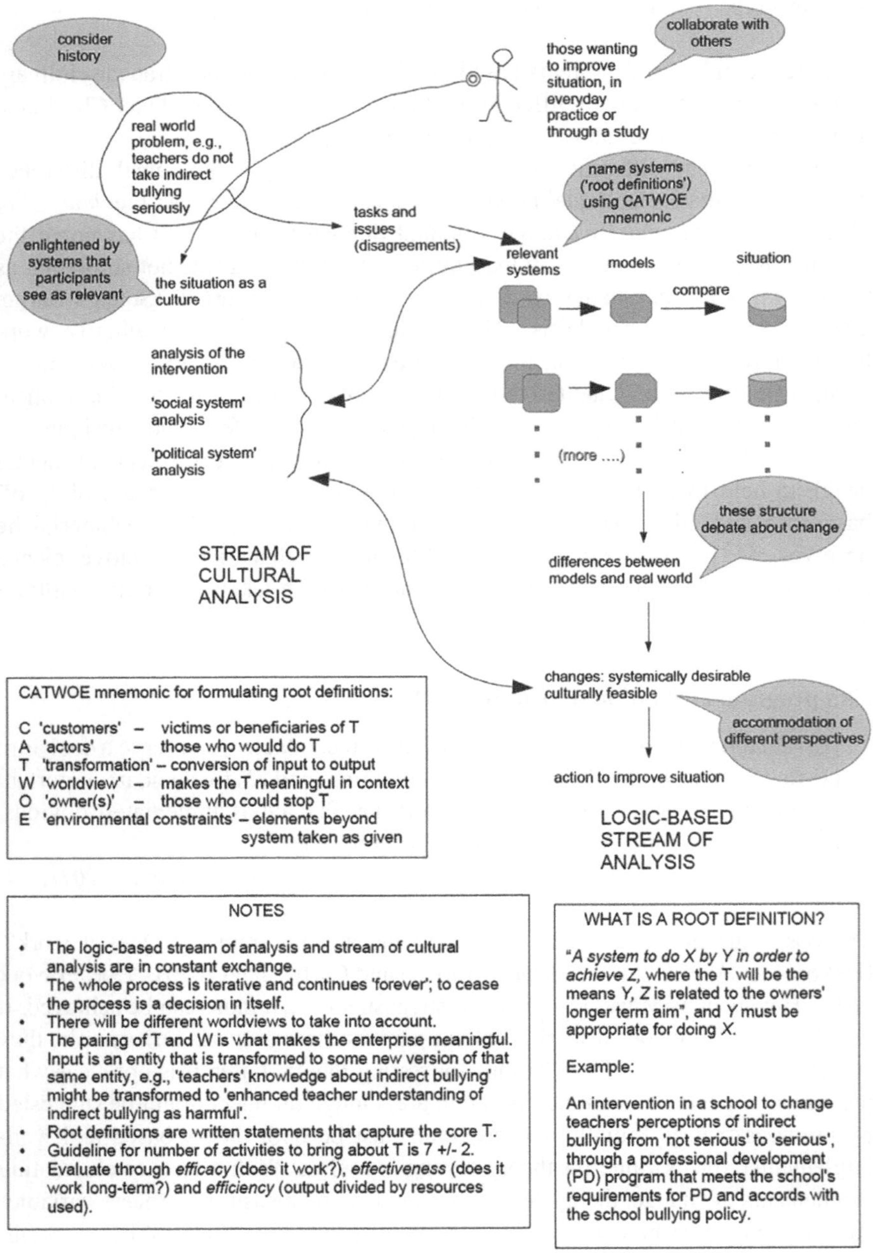

Figure 16.3 A soft-systems-based approach to multidisciplinary team development (Shute and Slee, 2022, adapted from Checkland and Scholes, 1990)

future practice. Furthermore, as we have seen, qualitative research can be highly informative about the reasons for the success or otherwise of interventions.

However, these standard methods, aimed at elucidating the mechanisms of change underlying interventions, are limited as they rely on linear assumptions, and we have seen how thinking has increasingly moved towards complexity. Matti Heino and colleagues (2021) have discussed the use of quantitative methods for evaluating behavioural interventions that take account of this. They introduce 'recurrence analysis', a kind of non-linear time-series analysis that can complement traditional investigations.

By designing programs in ways that make use of traditional or complexity-based methods, theory is refined and future programs can be better tailored. Hence, theory, research and practice are intimately entwined and mutually informative.

A final note: Stetsenko's approach to praxis

Anna Stetsenko (2016) perceives an intensifying 'end of theory' climate, driven by the imperative for evidence-based practice that we have discussed in this chapter. On the one hand, she observes a push to 'know the facts' that ignores their embeddedness in broader theoretical and sociocultural contexts and, on the other, a focus on locally contextualized practice that can neglect matters of theorizing about knowledge production. The result, she maintains, is 'a lack of exploration into the deeply-seated worldviews, philosophies, and grounding assumptions that in fact guide and underpin concrete investigations into human development' (Stetsenko, 2016: 284). In accord with the outline of her thinking as presented at the end of the previous chapter, she sees the future of praxis as being based on a true, not distorted, Vygotskian approach. This demands 'an activist commitment to *a sought-after future*' that bridges 'the gap between the narrowly understood natural science and the ideological-critical orientation aimed at social transformation in the process of theory-building (in overcoming the old-fashioned dualism of theory vs. practice)' (Stetsenko, 2016: 287, original emphasis). Her work offers a philosophically based starting point for a future that conjoins theory and practice in the interest of greater social justice for all the world's children.

Conclusion

In this final chapter we have returned to issues of knowledge: how it is created and used by various parties with an interest in promoting children's optimal development and wellbeing, and how the changing situation for universities plays a major role. In view of the billions of research dollars spent worldwide there is a growing demand to see how the knowledge created is translated into practice. The scientist-practitioner model, developmentally appropriate practice, applied developmental science and developmental resilience science variously act as guides for putting theoretical psychological knowledge about development into practice. Numbers of other relevant frameworks include implementation science, quality assurance and translational science. We have also seen that practice can feed back into theory, and that various writers highlight the value of using mixed methods or even methods that draw upon complexity. From a more critical perspective, we can appreciate that differences in professional cultures can create a barrier to effective translation of theory and research into policy and practice with children, within the complexities of the real world. Fortunately, ideas are available for working to overcome such barriers in the interest of creating well-functioning transdisciplinary teams. However, much remains to be done to develop praxis that brings together the traditional and critical perspectives that we have included in this book, with Stetsenko offering valuable insights.

We began this chapter querying the usefulness of child development theory for addressing problems that can seem monumental. In answer, we close with this eloquent reflection on the links between theory and practice by systems researchers Checkland and Scholes:

> Theory which is not tested out in practice is sterile. Equally, practice which is not reflective about the ideas upon which it is based will abandon the chance to learn its way steadily to better ways of taking action. Thus, theory must be tested out in practice; and practice is the best source of theory. In the best possible situation the two create each other in a cyclic process in which neither is dominant but each is the source of the other.
>
> *(Checkland and Scholes, 1990: xiv)*

Notes

1 But note that the development of 'soft skills' is able to be addressed scientifically (Shute, 2016).

2 This included music—hugely culturally important for Wales—which was later partially reinstated.

References

Alannah and Madeline Foundation. 2018. www.alannahandmadeline.org.au

Albee, G. W. 2002. Exploring a controversy. *American Psychologist 57*: 161–4. https://psycnet.apa.org/doi/10.1037/0003-066X.57.3.161

Aldwinckle, M. 2001. The DAP debate: are we throwing the baby out with the bath water? *Australian Journal of Early Childhood 26*: 36–9. https://doi.org/10.1177/183693910102600208

Andrews, J. L. and Foulkes, L. 2025. Debate: where to next for universal school-based mental health interventions? Time to move towards more effective alternatives. *Child and Adolescent Mental Health 1*(102–4). https://doi.org/10.1111/camh.12753

Askell-Williams, H., Slee, P. and van Deur, P. 2013. Social and emotional wellbeing programs: the nexus between sustainability and quality assurance. *The Psychology of Education Review 37*(2): 48–56. http://dspace.flinders.edu.au/dspace/

Australian Government Department of Education, n.d. *National quality framework*. www.education.gov.au/early-childhood/about/national-quality-framework

Australian Psychology Accreditation Council. 2019. *Accreditation standards for psychology programs*. https://apac.au/wp-content/uploads/2021/09/APAC-Accreditation-Standards_v1.2_rebranded.pdf

Babik, I., Cunha, A. B., Choi, D., Koziol, N. A., Hsu, L.-Y., Harbourne, R. T. *et al.* 2023. Socioeconomic status and home affordances moderate effects of motor delay and intervention. *Journal of Applied Developmental Psychology 87*: 101563. https://doi.org/10.1016/j.appdev.2023.101563

Barnett, R. 2000. University knowledge in an age of supercomplexity. *Higher Education 40*(4): 409–22. https://doi.org/10.1023/A:1004159513741

Begerowski, S. R., Traylor, A. M., Shuffler, M. L. and Salas, E. 2021. An integrative review and practical guide to team development interventions for translational science teams: one size does not fit all. *Journal of Clinical and Translational Science 5*. e198: 1–10. http://dx.doi.org/10.1017/cts.2021.832

Beyond Blue. 2024. *Planning for implementation*. https://beyou.edu.au/courses/planning-for-implementation

Blume Oeur, F. and Varga, D. 2024. Colonialism, racism, and childhoods: introduction. *American Behavioral Scientist*. https://doi.org/10.1177/00027642241268546

Burman, E. 2012. Un/thinking children in development: a contribution from northern antidevelopmental psychology. *Psychology: The Journal of the Hellenic Psychological Society 19*(2): 125–43. https://doi.org/10.12681/psy_hps.23612

Carter, J., Berman, E., Desikan, A., Johnson, C. and Goldma, G. 2019. The state of science in the Trump era: damage done, lessons learned, and a path to progress. *Centre for Science and Democracy*. www.ucsusa.org/sites/default/files/attach/2019/01/ucs-trump-2yrs-report.pdf

Checkland, P. and Scholes, J. 1990. *Soft systems methodology in action*. Chichester: Wiley.

Cooke, R. 2024. *Meta-analysis for psychologists*. Switzerland: Springer Nature.

Copple, C. and Bredekamp, S. (eds). 2009. *Developmentally appropriate practice in early childhood programs*. Washington, DC: National Association for the Education of Young Children.

Deković, M., Stolz, S., Schuiringa, H., Manders, W. and Asscher, J. J. 2011. Testing theories through evaluation research: conceptual and methodological issues embedded in evaluations of parenting programmes. *European Journal of Developmental Psychology 9*: 61–74. https://doi.org/10.1080/17405629.2011.611423

Dix, K. L., Slee, P. T., Lawson, M. J. and Keeves, J. P. 2012. Implementation quality of whole-school mental health promotion and students' academic performance. *Child and Adolescent Mental Health*, 3–26. https://psycnet.apa.org/doi/10.1111/j.1475-3588.2011.00608.x

Dodge, K. 2011. Context matters in child and family policy. *Child Development 82*: 433–42. https://psycnet.apa.org/doi/10.1111/j.1467-8624.2010.01565.x

Domitrovich, C. E. and Greenberg, M. T. 2000. The study of implementation: current findings from effective programs that prevent mental disorders in school-aged children. *Journal of Educational and Psychological Consultation 11*(2): 193–221. https://doi.org/10.1207/S1532768XJEPC1102_04

Domitrovich, C. E., Bradshaw, C. P., Poduska, J. M., Hoagwood, K., Buckley, J. A., Olon, S. *et al.* 2008. Maximising the implementation quality of evidence-based preventive interventions in schools: a conceptual framework. *Advances in School Mental Health Promotion 1*(3): 6–28. https://doi.org/10.1080/1754730X.2008.9715730

Drugaş, M. 2023. The scientist-practitioner and the scholar-practitioner model in psychology. *Psychological Thought: South-West University 'Neofit Rilski' 16*(2): 203–12. https://doi.org/10.37708/psyct.v16i2.904

Durlak, J. A. and DuPre, E. P. 2008. Implementation matters: a review of research on the influence of implementation on program outcomes and factors affecting implementation. *American Journal of Community Psychology 41*: 327–50. https://doi.org/10.1007/s10464-008-9165-0

Evans, R., Murphy, S. and Scourfield, J. 2015. Implementation of a school-based social and emotional learning intervention: understanding diffusion processes within complex systems. *Prevention Science 16*: 754–64. http://dx.doi.org/10.1007/s11121-015-0552-0

Fabes, R. A., Martin, C. L., Hanish, L. D. and Updegraff, K. A. 2000. Criteria for evaluating the significance of developmental research in the twenty-first century: force and counterforce. *Child Development 71*: 212–21. https://doi.org/10.1111/1467-8624.00136

Fisher C. B., Busch-Rossnagel, N. A., Jopp, D. S. and Brown, J. L. 2013. Applied developmental science, social justice, and socio-political well-being. *Applied Developmental Science 16*: 54–64. https://doi.org/10.1080/10888691.2012.642786

Fisher, C. B. and Lerner, R. M. 1994. Foundations of applied developmental psychology. In C. B. Fisher and R. M. Lerner (eds), *Applied developmental psychology*. New York: McGraw-Hill, 2–20.

Franco-Ángel, M., Carabali, J. and Velasco, M. I. 2022. The internship performance of undergraduate students: are hard or soft skills more important? *Industry and Higher Education 37*(3): 384–96. https://doi.org/10.1177/09504222221127213

Gelso, C. J. 2006. On the making of a scientist-practitioner model: a theory of research training in professional psychology. *Training & Education in Professional Psychology 1*: 3–16. https://psycnet.apa.org/doi/10.1037/1931-3918.S.1.3

Gokulsing, K. and DaCosta, C. 1997. *University knowledges as the goal of university education*. Lampeter: Edwin Mullen.

Gonzales-Kruger, G., Zamboanga, B. L., Carlo, G., Raffeli, M., Carranza, M., Hansen, D. J. *et al.* 2000. The Latino Research Initiative: a multidisciplinary and collaborative community-university outreach and scholarship model. *Great Plains Research 10*: 359–85. www.scopus.com/record/display.uri?eid=2-s2.0-0034426680&origin=inward&txGid=9fad4551bffd281e9abae06d623e79e5

Green, M. G. and Piel, J. A. 2009. Are theories compatible? In M. G. Green and J. A. Piel (eds), *Theories of human development: a comparative approach*. Abingdon: Routledge, 391–402.

Greve, L. T., Fentz, H. N. and Trillingsgaard, T. 2024. Cumulative risk predicting differential effectiveness of the incredible years parent-training. *Journal of Applied Developmental Psychology 95*: 101710. https://doi.org/10.1016/j.appdev.2024.101710.

Grimshaw, J. M., Martin, P., Eccles, M. P., Lavis, J. N., Hill, S. J. and Squires, J. E. 2012. Translation of research findings. *Implementation Science 7*: 2–17. http://dx.doi.org/10.1186/1748-5908-7-50

Guanghui, C. 2024. Applied developmental science. In K. Zhang (ed.), *The ECPH encyclopedia of psychology*. Singapore: Springer. https://doi.org/10.1007/978-981-99-6000-2_701-1

Hayes, D., Deniz, E., Nisbet, K., Thompson, A., March, A., Mason, C. *et al.* 2025. Universal, school-based interventions to improve emotional outcomes in children and young people: a systematic review and meta-analysis. *Frontiers in Child and Adolescent Psychiatry*. https://doi.org/10.3389/frcha.2025.1526840

Heino, M. T. J., Knittle, K., Noone, C., Hasselman, F. and Hankonen, N. 2021. Studying behaviour change mechanisms under complexity. *Behavioral Science 11*(5): 77. https://doi.org/10.3390/bs11050077

Hessels, L. K. and van Lente, H. 2008. Re-thinking new knowledge production: a literature review and a research agenda. *Research Policy 37*: 740–60. https://doi.org/10.1016/j.respol.2008.01.008

Hil, R. 2012. *Whackademia: an insider's account of the troubled university*. Sydney: NewSouth.

Humphrey, N., Barlow, A., Wigelsworth, M., Lendrum, A., Pert, K., Joyce, C. *et al.* 2016. A cluster randomized controlled trial of the Promoting Alternative Thinking Strategies (PATHS) curriculum. *Journal of School Psychology 58*: 73–89. https://doi.org/10.1016/j.jsp.2016.07.002

Humphrey, N., Lendrum, A. and Wigelsworth, M. 2014. Making the most out of school-based prevention: lessons from the social and emotional aspects of learning (SEAL) programme. *Emotional & Behavioural Difficulties 18*(3): 248–60. https://doi.org/10.1080/13632752.2013.819251

Iniesto, F., Charitonos, K. and Littlejohn, A. 2022. A review of research with co-design methods in health education. *Open Education Studies 4*: 273–95. www.researchgate.net/publication/362071326_A_review_of_research_with_co-design_methods_in_health_education

John, I. D. 1994. Constructing knowledge of psychological knowledge: towards an epistemology for psychological practice. *Australian Psychologist 2*: 174–7. https://psycnet.apa.org/doi/10.1080/00050069408257343

John, I. D. 1998. The scientist-practitioner model: a critical examination. *Australian Psychologist 33*: 24–30. https://doi.org/10.1080/00050069808257259

Jørring, N. T. and Jensen, K. G. 2018. Treatment efficacy of narrative family therapy for children and adolescents with diverse psychiatric symptomatology. *Scandinavian Journal of Child and Adolescent Psychiatry and Psychology 6*(2): 107–14. https://doi.org/10.21307/sjcapp-2018-012

Joyce, K. E. and Cartwright, N. 2020. Bridging the gap between research and practice: predicting what will work locally. *American Educational Research Journal 57*(3): 1045–82. https://doi.org/10.3102/0002831219866687

Kallitsoglou, A. and Mahmud, A. 2023. Teacher attitudes towards evidence-based practices for social, emotional and mental health difficulties in school and association with teacher academic research engagement. *Emotional and Behavioural Difficulties 28*(4): 263–81. https://doi.org/10.1080/13632752.2023.2276024

Kumah, E. A, McSherry, R. Bettany-Saltikov, J., van Schaik, P., Hamilton, S,. Hogg, J. and Whittaker, V. 2022. Evidence-informed practice versus evidence-based practice educational interventions for improving knowledge, attitudes, understanding, and behavior toward the application of evidence into practice: a comprehensive systematic review of undergraduate students. *Campbell Systematic Review 18*(2): e1233. https://doi.org/10.1002/cl2.1233

Leadbeater, B. and Gladstone, E. 2016. Supporting schools for the widespread implementation of evidence-based mental health promotion programs: what is needed? In R. H. Shute and P. T. Slee (eds), *Mental health and wellbeing through schools*. Abingdon: Routledge, 27–38.

Lendrum, A., Humphrey, N. and Greenberg, M. 2016. Implementing for success in school-based mental health promotion. In R. H. Shute and P. T. Slee (eds), *Mental health and wellbeing through schools*. London: Routledge, 53–63.

Lerner, R. M. and Fisher, C. 2014. Evolution, epigenetics, and application in developmental science. *Applied Developmental Science 17*(4): 169–73. https://doi.org/10.1080/10888691.2013.848677

Lerner, R. M., Fisher, C. B. and Weinberg, R. A. 2000. Toward a science for and of the people: promoting civil society through the application of developmental science. *Child Development 71*: 11–20. https://doi.org/10.1111/1467-8624.00113

Lewis, M. D. 2000. The promise of dynamic systems approaches for an integrated account of human development. *Child Development 71*: 36–43. https://psycnet.apa.org/doi/10.1111/1467-8624.00116

Massad, S., Khammash, U. and Shute, R. 2017. Political violence and mental health of Bedouin children in the West Bank, Palestine: a cross-sectional study. *Medicine, Conflict and Survival 33*(3): 188–206. https://doi.org/10.1080/13623699.2017.1368307

Masten, A. S. and Barnes, A. J. 2018. Resilience in children: developmental perspectives. *Children 5*(98): 1–16. https://doi.org/10.3390/children5070098

Miller, D. and Philo, G. 2002. Silencing dissent in academia: the commercialisation of science. *The Psychologist 15*: 44–6. www.researchgate.net/publication/44285342_Silencing_dissent_in_academia_the_commercialisation_of_science

Mucherah, W. and Mbogori, T. 2019. Examining child development from an African cultural context. *Global Journal of Transformative Education 1*: 11–17. http://dx.doi.org/10.14434/gjte.v1i1.26140

Murdock, L., Taylor & Francis, and Stephenson, R. 2024. Advancing translational research. *Journal of Translational Research 1*: 2432753. https://doi.org/10.1080/29947448.2024.2432753

Murdock, N. L. 2006. On science-practice integration in everyday life: a plea for theory. *The Counselling Psychologist 34*: 548–69. https://doi.org/10.1177/0011000006288129

Murgatroyd, S. and Morgan, C. 1993. *Total quality management and the school.* Philadelphia: Open University Press.

NAEYC. n.d. *Our work.* www.naeyc.org/our-work

Overton, W. F. 1998. Developmental psychology: philosophy, concepts, and methodology. In W. Damon and R. M. Lerner (eds), *Handbook of child psychology: theoretical models of human development.* Vol 1. Fifth edn. New York: Wiley, 107–89.

Parker, L. 2011. University corporatisation: driving redefinition. *Critical Perspectives on Accounting 22*(4): 434–50. https://doi.org/10.1016/j.cpa.2010.11.002

Parker, L. D. 2022. Public university research engagement contradictions in a commercialising higher education world. *Financial Accountability & Management 40*: 16–33. https://doi.org/10.1111/faam.12341

Pepper, S. 1942. *World hypotheses: a study of evidence*. Berkeley: University of California Press.

Phillips, L. G. and Ritchie, J. 2025. Contemporary challenges for children's rights, well-being, justice and equity: policy, community activism and pedagogy. *Global Studies of Childhood 15*. https://doi.org/10.1177/20436106241311329

Raimy, V. 1950. *Training in clinical psychology*. Englewood Cliffs: Prentice-Hall.

Sanders, K. and Farago, F. 2018. Developmentally appropriate practice in the 21st century. In M. Fleer and B. van Oers (eds), *International handbook of early childhood education.* Dordrecht: Springer, 1379–400.

*Science*Insider. 2025. Monday edition: Collins departs, societies speak out, NSF backs down. www.science.org/content/article/science-trump-latest-news

Shapiro, D. 2002. Renewing the scientist-practitioner model. *The Psychologist 15*: 232–4. www.bps.org.uk/psychologist/renewing-scientist-practitioner-model

Shipton, M. 2025. Cardiff University Vice-Chancellor 'implied poverty is caused by genetics'. *Nation Cymru*, 5 March. https://nation.cymru/news/cardiff-university-vice-chancellor-implied-poverty-is-caused-by-genetics/

Shonkoff, J. P. 2000. Science, policy, and practice: three cultures in search of a shared mission. *Child Development 71*: 181–7. https://psycnet.apa.org/doi/10.1111/1467-8624.00132

Shonkoff, J. P. and Bales, S. N. 2011. Science does not speak for itself: translating child development research for the public and its policymakers. *Child Development 82*: 17–32. https://psycnet.apa.org/doi/10.1111/j.1467-8624.2010.01538.x

Shute, R. H. 2016. 'Promotion with parents is challenging': the role of teacher communication skills and parent-teacher partnerships in school-based mental health initiatives. In R. H. Shute and P. T. Slee (eds), *Mental health and wellbeing through schools: the way forward*. Abingdon: Routledge, 64–74.

Shute, R. H. 2018. Schools, mindfulness, and metacognition: a view from developmental psychology. *International Journal of School and Educational Psychology 7 Supp. 1*: 123–36. https://doi.org/10.1080/21683603.2018.1435322

Shute, R. 2019/2024. School-based mindfulness interventions. In L. Zhang (ed.), *Oxford research encyclopedia of education*. New York: Oxford University Press, np. https://doi.org/10.1093/acrefore/9780190264093.013.979

Slee, P. T. 2023. Big talks for little people: child mental health module. In B. A. Gerrard, E. Hernandez and S. Deb (eds), *School-based family counseling for crisis and disaster: global perspectives*. New York: Routledge, Taylor & Francis, 183–95.

Slee, P. T., Lawson, M. J., Russell, A., Askell-Williams, H., Dix, K. L., Owens L. *et al*. 2009. *KidsMatter Primary evaluation final report*. Melbourne: KidsMatter and the Centre for Analysis of Educational Futures. https://www.researchgate.net/publication/280093612_The_KidsMatter_Evaluation_Final_Report

Slee, P. T. and Murray-Harvey, R. 2007. Disadvantaged children's physical, developmental and behavioural health problems in an urban environment. *Journal of Social Services Research 33*: 57–69. https://doi.org/10.1300/J079v33n04_05

Slee, P. T., Murray-Harvey, R., Dix, K. L., Skrzypiec, G., Askell-Williams, H., Lawson, M. J. and Krieg, S. 2012. *KidsMatter early childhood evaluation*. www.researchgate.net/publication/280082254_KidsMatter_Early_Childhood_Evaluation_Report

Slee, P.T., Murray-Harvey, R., Dix, K. and van Deur, P. 2011. *Kidsmatter quality assurance system for KidsMatter Primary: a scoping paper*. Adelaide: Flinders University. https://fac.flinders.edu.au/dspace/api/core/bitstreams/189469f1-eb4e-4b86-a677-ba7b9c276663/content

Slee, P., Pill, S. and Agnew, D. 2025. Big talks for little people: a pilot study of a classroom based mental health program. *Health Promotion Journal of Australia 36*(2): e70014. https://doi.org/10.1002/hpja.70014

Smith-Walter, A., Peterson, H. L., Jones, M. D. and Marshall, A. N. R. 2016. Gun stories: how evidence shapes firearm policy in the United States. *Politics and Policy 44*(6): 1053–88. https://doi.org/10.1111/polp.12187

Sonuga-Barke, E. J. S. 2024. Editorial: qualitative contributions to translational science – practical pointers towards methodological pluralism in child psychology and psychiatry. *Journal of Child Psychology and Psychiatry 65*(10): 1255–7. https://doi.org/10.1111/jcpp.14049

Stehr, N. 1994. *Knowledge societies*. London: SAGE.

Stetsenko, A. 2016. Moving beyond the relational worldview: exploring the next steps premised on agency and a commitment to social change. Commentary on Karimi-Aghdam. *Human Development 59*(5): 283–9. https://doi.org/10.1159/000452720

Suryani, A. and Fleer, M. 2024. Theory-informed beliefs in early childhood education: contradictions in child development theories and models of play. *Oxford Review of Education*. https://doi.org/10.1080/03054985.2024.2331180

Sussman, S., Valente, T. W., Rohrbach, S., Skara, S. and Pentz, M. A. 2006. Translation in the health professions: converting science into action. *Evaluation and the Health Professions 29*: 17–32. https://doi.org/10.1177/0163278705284441

Tierney, W. G. 2001. The autonomy of knowledge and the decline of the subject: postmodernism and the reformulation of the university. *Higher Education 41*: 353–72. https://doi.org/10.1023/A:1017588907541

Tiron-Tudor, A., Nistor, C. S. and Ştefănescu, C.A. 2018. The role of universities inconsolidating intellectual capital and generating new knowledge for a sustainable bioeconomy. *Amfiteatru Economic 20*(49): 599–615. https://doi.org/10.24818/EA/2018/49/599

Toffler, A. 1984. *Future shock*. London: Random House.

UK Office for Health Improvement & Disparities. 2022. *Wellbeing and mental health: applying All our Health*. www.gov.uk/government/publications/wellbeing-in-mental-health-applying-all-our-health/wellbeing-in-mental-health-applying-all-our-health

UNICEF. 2025. Two years of hellish war have devastated Gaza's children. Statement by Executive Director. UNICEF, 7 October. www.unicef.org.au/media-release/two-years-of-hellish-war-have-devastated-gaza-s-children

Wandersman, A., Duffy, J., Flaspoler, P., Noonan, R., Lubell, K., Stillman, L. *et al.* 2008. Bridging the gap between prevention research and practice: the interactive systems framework for dissemination and implementation. *American Journal of Community Psychology 41*: 171–81. https://doi.org/10.1007/s10464-008-9174-z

Wing On, L. 2014. The changing knowledge functions of university in the 21st century: implications for learning and teaching in higher education. *International Journal of Chinese Education 3*: 7–29. https://doi.org/10.1163/22125868-12340028

Student Resources

This part of the book provides an array of supplementary materials for both students and lecturers to accompany the latest edition of *Child Development: Theories and Critical Perspectives*. These include:

- A list of historical milestones relevant for developmental psychology
- Discussion questions, activities and relevant websites for each chapter.

In addition, there is a separate glossary on **p. 353**.

Some historical milestones relevant for developmental psychology

19th century

Darwin publishes *On the Origin of Species* (1859)
Wundt opens first experimental psychology laboratory (1879)
Preyer publishes first developmental study (1882)
Peirce undertakes philosophical work on pragmatism (1880s)
James' *Principles of Psychology* published (1890)
Titchener establishes 'structuralism' (1890s)
Pearson develops statistical theory of correlation (1896)
Cattell influential in development of mental tests (1896)
Thorndike performs experiments on animal learning (1898)

Early 20th century

Freud presents ideas on psychoanalysis (1900)
Spearman proposes theory of intelligence (1904)
Hall publishes *Adolescence* (1904)
Binet and Simon devise first intelligence test for children (1905)
Pavlov publishes findings on classical conditioning (1906)
Spence writes history of child care in South Australia (1907)
Dewey publishes ideas on problem-solving (1910)

Stern presents concept of IQ (1911)
Wertheimer begins Gestalt psychology (1912)
Watson publishes on behaviourism (1913)
Binet intelligence test revised as Stanford-Binet by Terman (1916)
Köhler publishes studies on problem-solving by apes (1917)
Watson and Rayner publish study on 'Little Albert' (1920)
Jones lays foundations for behaviour therapy (1920s)
Jung publishes *Psychological Types* (1921)
Gesell introduces maturation theory (1925)
Piaget publishes theory of language and thought in children (1926)
Klein influential in object relations school (1920s)
Pavlov's work on conditioned reflex published in English (1927)
Mead's *Coming of Age in Samoa* published (1928)
Tolman presents ideas on purposive behaviourism (1929)
Ethology established (1920s/1930s)
Vygotsky presents sociocultural theory (1930)
Thurstone develops factor analysis (1935)
Bridges and Bühler (independently) work on infant emotion (1930s)
G. H. Mead promotes social constructivism (1930s)
Skinner publishes on operant conditioning in *The Behavior of Organisms* (1938)
Rubinstein writes on mind–body question (1940)
Pepper writes on metaphors for worldviews (1942)
Family therapy developed (1940s)
Werner elaborates the orthogenetic principle (1948)

Later 20th century

Erikson publishes *Childhood and Society* (1950)
Scientist-practitioner model formulated (1950)
Lorenz publishes on ethology (1952)
DSM first published (1952)
Spitz studies 'maternal deprivation', using film (1952)
Bowlby publishes *Child Care and the Growth of Love* (1953)
Havighurst writes about developmental tasks (1953)
Kelly publishes personal construct theory (1955)
Gibson and Gibson establish work on infant perception and 'affordance' (1950s)
'Birth' of artificial intelligence (1956)
Ariés writes about views of childhood (1962)
Vygotsky's *Thought and Language* translated into English (1962)
Maslow publishes on self-actualization (1962)
Luria establishes field of neuropsychology (1962)
Sellars theorizes about scientific image (1962)
Kuhn publishes on scientific paradigms (1962)
Popper proposes that 'falsification' is central to science (1963)
Bandura and Walters introduce observational learning (1963)

Satir publishes on family therapy (1964)
Lakatos presents ideas on philosophy of science (metatheories) (1965)
Hold applies ethology to children (1960s)
Kohlberg applies Piaget's theory to moral development (1960s)
Bruner proposes his social cognitive theory (1966)
Neisser establishes cognitive psychology (1967)
Information processing theories instigated (1960s)
Bertalanffy applies general systems theory to biology (1968)
Bayley Scales of Infant Development first published (1969)
Mead publishes *Culture and Commitment* (1970)
Blurton Jones promotes ethological study of children (1972)
Rutter critiques notion of maternal deprivation (1972)
Bateson theorizes about family systems (1972)
Ainsworth develops the 'Strange Situation' (1970s)
Riegel develops transactional theory (1970s)
APA considers sexism in psychotherapy (1970s)
Maccoby and Jacklin publish *The Psychology of Sex Differences* (1974)
Hinde publishes on biological bases of behaviour (1974)
Humphrey provides feminist critique of family therapy (1975)
Wilson establishes sociobiology (1975)
Dawkins publishes *The Selfish Gene* (1976)
Nicolis and Prigogine write about self-organizing systems (1977)
Bandura publishes on social learning theory (1977)
Notion of child–environment 'goodness-of-fit' introduced (1977)
Biopsychosocial perspective on health introduced (1977)
Donaldson publishes *Children's Minds* (1978)
Theory of mind introduced (1978)
Bell proposes that socialization is two-way process (1978)
Bateson publishes on systems theory (1979)
The Ritchies critique western attachment theory (1979)
Bronfenbrenner founds ecological systems theory (1979)
Notion of the 'competent infant' promoted (1970s)
Maccoby adds 'social' to cognitive development (1980)
Baltes founds Centre for Lifespan Psychology in Berlin (1981)
Connectionism emerges (1980s)
Gilligan's *In a Different Voice* published (1982)
Baillargeon studies infant cognitive competence (1985)
Developmentally Appropriate Practice introduced (1987)
Maturana and colleagues publish ideas on constructivism (1988)
Adoption by United Nations of Convention on the Rights of the Child (1989)
Increasing fragmentation of developmental psychology (1990s)
Calls for theoretical integration (1990s)
Postmodern/critical/feminist perspectives on psychology offered (1990s)
Wanganeen adapts grief and loss theory for Indigenous Australian colonization (1990s)

Behaviour genetics gains currency (1990s)
Applied developmental science introduced (1991)
Dunbar proposes 'social brain hypothesis' (1992)
Thelen and Smith publish on dynamic systems (1994)
Worell and Etaugh identify feminist principles (1994)
Burman publishes *Deconstructing Developmental Psychology* (1994)
New Sociology of Childhood takes off (mid-1990s)
Critical state and complex systems theories gain momentum (1990s)
Teo provides postmodern critique on philosophy of knowledge (1997)
Perry theorizes about neurodevelopment in violence/trauma (1997)
Social networking sites begin (1997)
Evolutionary developmental psychology gains increasing prominence (1990s)
Nsamenang promotes African perspective (1990s)
Brain imaging research increases (1990s)
Medical model of mental health gains ground (1990s)
Indigenous psychologies begin to gain recognition (2000)
Arnett proposes the stage of 'emerging adulthood' (2000)
Shonkoff differentiates cultures of science, policy and practice (2000)
Universities becoming increasingly corporatized (2000)
Qualitative research becoming more accepted in psychology (2000)

21st century

Shier promotes 'listening to children' (2001)
Hedegaard proposes cultural-historical theory (2002)
Positive psychology movement established (2002)
Human genome sequence announced (2003)
Epigenetics research increases (2000s)
Cascades and trajectories are highlighted (2000s)
Increasing shift from cross-cultural to cultural psychology (2000s)
Mixed-methods research promoted in psychology (2004)
Overton highlights relationalism (2006)
Fine identifies 'neurosexism' (2010)
Sameroff proposes unified theory of development (2010)
Translational research highlighted (2012)
Greater focus on change processes and plasticity (2012)
Karmiloff-Smith theorizes about neuroconstructivism (2012)
Kağıtçıbaşı proposes universal model of family types (2012)
The nature–nurture 'interactionist consensus' is questioned (2019)
Bhatia and others argue for 'decolonizing' developmental psychology (2020)
Metamodernism applied to psychology (2020)
Large-scale genotyping studies become feasible (2020)
The 'cultural brain hypothesis' becomes more prominent (2024)
Artificial intelligence rapidly developing (2025)

Discussion questions, activities and selected websites*

*All websites cited in this section were last accessed on 2 July 2025.

Chapter 1

1. What are some reasons for studying child development?
2. What is the difference between a theory and a metatheory?

Activities

1. As a group or individually, draw up a table with three columns: 'development', 'maturation' and 'growth'. Identify the significant characteristics of the terms, distinguishing between them.
2. Draw a 'tree diagram' indicating two (or more) possible lifespan developmental pathways of an infant with severe vision impairment, one where early surgery corrects the problem and another where the impairment is not treated.

Websites

What is developmental psychology? www.youtube.com/watch?v=8O6z5-WTHt0
Child Research Net (CRN): www.childresearch.net/
Positivism, interpretivism and pragmatism video:
www.youtube.com/watch?v=GEf5sGFXmUE
Brief post-positivism video: www.youtube.com/watch?v=Wr1hkshpcTU
BPS blog about Bame Nsamenang's African view of developmental psychology:
www.bps.org.uk/blog/bame-augustine-nsamenang-extraordinary-thinker-global-psychology

Chapter 2

1. Consider the various 'views' of children in Figure 2.1; identify and discuss their distinguishing features.
2. In attempting to find out about teenagers' attitudes towards the use of artificial intelligence in their studies, how might you combine the use of interviews, focus groups and questionnaires?

Activities

1. Form small groups. Each group draws an outline of a child on a large sheet of paper approximately 90 cm x 30 cm. For 10–15 minutes, members write on the outline words that they associate with the word 'child'. Each person then explains the words they have contributed and upon what basis they hold such views.

2. Discuss in a group the knowledge and attitudes towards qualitative research that you have picked up from your studies in psychology, in other subjects, or in your general experience.

Websites

Brief explanation of ontology, epistemology and methodology:
www.youtube.com/watch?v=t3gz-PxXTjE
Philosophy of childhood: http://plato.stanford.edu/entries/childhood/
Talk about Lakatos and difference between paradigms (Kuhn) and research programs: www.youtube.com/watch?v=VExVaR8S_wQ
Erica Burman one-hour lecture on critical psychology of childhood (with Spanish subtitles):
www.youtube.com/watch?v=XkAyhz9vmtc
BPS Blog. The 'street children' of Latin America: www.bps.org.uk/psychologist/street-children-latin-america
TED talk. Debra Pepler on what we now know about how to raise happy and healthy children: www.youtube.com/watch?v=gg2a7zic_zQ

Chapter 3

1. Is evolutionary psychology just a politically correct version of sociobiology?
2. How far has Darwin influenced theorizing about children's development?

Activities

1. Find some internet articles about ADHD. How far do they reflect a biological perspective?
2. In a group, discuss whether you believe psychology has become 'too biologized'.

Websites

Brief introduction to evo-devo psychology: www.youtube.com/watch?v=B4ltEkub5og
What is a genome-wide association study? www.youtube.com/watch?v=sOP8WacfBM8
Annette Karmiloff-Smith lecture on lifespan neurocognitive development: www.youtube.com/watch?v=akxaRZFy3mo
TED talk explaining epigenetics: www.youtube.com/watch?v=JTBg6hqeuTg
Podcast: How feminism changed primatology: www.abc.net.au/listen/programs/philosopherszone/how-feminism-changed-primatology/105199142
Podcast about DSM controversy:
https://podcasts.apple.com/gb/podcast/labelling-the-world-the-power-of-dsm/id73802620?i=1000656023464

Chapter 4

1. To better understand the contemporary relevance of Watson's work, find and critically examine an article utilizing a behavioural framework in terms of the challenge that it is not really a theory of development.
2. Initially, consider your likely thoughts about what might be happening when you see a child having a tantrum in a supermarket. Then read this article about Functional Behavioural Assessment in schools and see whether you have any new thoughts about the tantrum situation: https://behaviour.education.qld.gov.au/supportingStudentBehaviour/PositiveBehaviourforLearning/Documents/functional-behaviour-assessment-schools-guide.pdf

Activities

1. Draw up a table comparing and contrasting the theories of Pavlov, Watson, Skinner and Bandura.
2. Watch this short talk about moral disengagement by Albert Bandura. Discuss how these ideas might apply to school bullying. www.youtube.com/watch?v=JjuA4Xa7uiE

Websites

B. F. Skinner Foundation: www.bfskinner.org/

Classical and operant conditioning of a needle phobia: www.youtube.com/watch?v=9EMdqPfEA18

Mary Cover Jones video: www.youtube.com/watch?v=GENBRF0rFl4

Social information processing theory video: www.youtube.com/watch?v=heDmw9zCLwk

Chapter 5

1. Identify the characteristics of the root metaphor underlying the worldview of 'organicism' and discuss.
2. Debate the usefulness or otherwise of 'stages' in describing development.

Activities

1. Find a policy document (such as a government document) related to children's health or education. Discuss how far 'stages' of development are implicitly or explicitly used as a guiding framework. Present your findings in class.
2. After watching the first video listed below, find a website and analyse how far it draws on Gestalt principles.

Websites

Introduction to Gestalt psychology:
www.youtube.com/watch?v=4VWrl98KzCE
Child Development Institute: http://childdevelopmentinfo.com/ages-stages/
Eleanor Gibson's ecological theory: www.youtube.com/watch?v=Xj6yRu20A_4

Chapter 6

1. Explain how Baillargeon's research supports the concept of 'the competent infant'.
2. Research and present the identifying features of Bruner's constructivist understanding of development.

Activities

1. Search the internet for journal reviews regarding the nature of the child as an 'active participant' in development. What evidence can you find that contemporary theories of development consider the child from this perspective?
2. Find three journal articles about theory of mind. How clearly does each specify its focus (whether on concepts, cognitive processes or individual differences)?

Websites

Introduction to Piaget: www.youtube.com/watch?v=TRF27F2bn-A
Transcript of interview with Eleanor Maccoby:
www.srcd.org/sites/default/files/documents/maccoby_eleanor_interview.pdf
Article on theory of mind in different cultures: www.hindawi.com/journals/cdr/2014/893492/
Baillargeon talks about 'the competent infant': www.youtube.com/watch?v=NtgcUYLit2A

Chapter 7

1. Is attachment theory universally relevant?
2. What are the advantages and disadvantages of the Strange Situation as a measure of attachment?

Activities

1. Explore and discuss the status afforded to Freudian theory in some standard child development textbooks.
2. After reading the below blog about attachment, and watching the video about Romanian orphans, discuss how the attitudes towards child-rearing that are

portrayed reflect the images of children discussed in Chapter 2. What are the implications for children's development and happiness?

Websites

Why do we still teach Freud? www.youtube.com/watch?v=aTd-lrnZvsQ
Beyond attachment: www.psychologytoday.com/blog/freedom-learn/201307/beyond-attachment-parents-children-need-community
Romania's orphans grow up: www.youtube.com/watch?v=JS77QOD0Mt8

Chapter 8

1. After reading Chapters 5 and 8, review the videos describing Piaget's and Vygotsky's theories and compare and contrast the views of the developing child that they provide.
2. Discuss the notion of constitutive relationalism. Explain how the 'Rubin vase', the yin/yang symbol and Overton's 'hands' drawing illustrate this (the latter is shown in numbers of Overton's articles).

Activities

1. Observe parents and children engaged in activities together. Look for examples of scaffolding.
2. Discuss how the philosophical basis of Rubinstein's theory differentiates it from Vygotsky's. Would it be useful for Rubinstein's theory to be included in developmental psychology courses?

Websites

Dory as an introduction to Vygotsky's theory: www.youtube.com/watch?v=7T6CNoI4dlI
Scaffolding: www.youtube.com/watch?v=aofSkZsy6IY
Vygotksy and teaching: www.youtube.com/watch?v=ifxQZS_QWX0
Myra Barr interviewed about her 2022 book on Vygotsky: www.youtube.com/watch?v=2uHzZ_Z4BKw

Chapter 9

1. Research and discuss the controversy about whether Margaret Mead was fooled by her young Samoan study participants.
2. What lessons does Peirce hold for education today? https://philarchive.org/archive/LEGPAE

Activities

1. Take a look at this old blog and explain 'brushing your teeth' to a friend in terms of contextualism. https://contextualscience.org/book/export/html/201
2. Examine the 'Milestones' in the previous section, identifying the main philosophical, cultural and historical changes that have influenced developmental theorizing in the 21st century.

Websites

William James: www.youtube.com/watch?v=OukjuPQR6sE
John Dewey's relevance today: https://theconversation.com/why-john-deweys-vision-for-education-and-democracy-still-resonates-today-222849
Dewey and education today: https://youtu.be/y3fm6wNzK70
Margaret Mead: www.interculturalstudies.org/Mead/biography.html
Functionalism in therapy: http://contextualscience.org/functional_contextualism_0

Chapter 10

1. Systems thinking has been informed by a long and distinguished group of philosophers, writers and scientists. Provide an overview of the various influences and their particular contributions to the metatheory of systems thinking.
2. Dynamic systems theory (DST) has emerged as a force in child development theory. Describe its particular focus and identifying features.

Activities

1. Select a relevant research paper from a child development journal or journal of family therapy and identify, critique and present in class the key elements that distinguish its basis in systems theory.
2. Divide into small groups. Each group draws a large diagram of Bronfenbrenner's ecological systems model and chooses a specific situation: an 8-year-old child diagnosed with Type 1 diabetes; a teenager offered a vape for the first time by a friend; a child who migrates with their family to a new country. Add to the diagram as many specific examples as you can of the various aspects of the subsystems relevant for the child's development.

Websites

Bronfenbrenner and *Head Start*: www.youtube.com/watch?v=Zcp1YGW6JNQ
Dynamic systems theory review article: https://pmc.ncbi.nlm.nih.gov/articles/PMC3224018/
Complex adaptive systems, cooperation and competition: www.youtube.com/watch?v=IWhkUne8T68

Chapter 11

1. Research and discuss the notion of 'cultural evolution'.
2. How might 'folk wisdom' differentially influence the development of a Chinese child and one from the United States?

Activities

1. Examine a standard textbook on child development. How far does it reflect a western perspective on children's development?
2. Watch this video on Filipino culture and suggest how it relates to Kağıtçıbaşı's theorizing about families. www.youtube.com/watch?v=8JTQjABNfgM

Websites

Mothering Japanese newborns: www.theatlantic.com/health/archive/2013/05/the-lasting-influence-of-mother-infant-attachment/275428/
TED talk: don't westernize Africa: www.youtube.com/watch?v=-yRKAekvpBM
Two-part documentary: Mumbai's slum community experienced by UK architect:

Ep. 1: www.youtube.com/watch?v=Im0tHRs9Bng
Ep. 2: www.youtube.com/watch?v=l-yjpvzGKZQ

Article on research on interventions for mental health in Indigenous children: www.sciencedirect.com/science/article/pii/S0190740922004261
Amos Wilson interview (US pioneer of Black psychology): www.youtube.com/watch?v=EhKuz7SPgGs

Chapter 12

1. Are women and girls morally underdeveloped compared with men and boys?
2. Research and discuss how feminism inspired notions of 'masculinities'.

Activities

1. Watch a children's cartoon program on television and the commercials associated with it. Observe any differences between the portrayal of boys and girls (e.g. activities, dress, values, music, toys, voice-overs).
2. What evidence of androcentrism in the history of developmental psychology did you notice in the earlier chapters of this book?

Websites

Freud and femininity: http://scandalousthoughts.wordpress.com/2010/02/18/some-notes-of-my-reading-on-freuds-femininity/
Pinkstinks: www.pinkstinks.co.uk/

One teenage girl's view of feminism: www.youtube.com/watch?v=qHzVIq-Wft4

The Manosphere: www.abc.net.au/news/2025-04-19/better-bloke-project-blokes-advice-mental-health-toxic/104975574

Video: A developmental scientist's experience of early motherhood: www.storycollider.org/stories/2017/6/2/early-childhood-development-amy-brown-cassie-soliday

Chapter 13

1. What challenges does the notion of children's 'being' (as compared with 'becoming') pose for developmental theorizing?
2. Research and discuss the hermeneutic approach for listening to children.

Activities

1. Discuss how 'Photovoice' could be used to examine the views of children (in a cultural other than your own) about children's rights.
2. Imagine you are planning to introduce a mental health prevention program into a school. How might Shier's revised *Pathways* guide you?

Websites

Scottish Golden Rules for children to ensure their voices are heard: www.cypcs.org.uk/wpcypcs/wp-content/uploads/2020/03/Golden-Rules-children.pdf

Does parenting matter? TED talk. www.youtube.com/watch?v=5g8tHEXtCXE

Children's voices: www.youtube.com/watch?v=x14_2chx3lE

www.youtube.com/watch?v=bBQkiK61DMc

Photovoice:

http://ctb.ku.edu/en/table-of-contents/assessment/assessing-community-needs-and-resources/photovoice/main

Reggio Emilia approach to early childhood education: www.youtube.com/watch?v=tnbNNZBpXi0

Chapter 14

1. Explain how Bronfenbrenner's theory might be adapted for the digital age.
2. Research and discuss the advantages and disadvantages of banning mobile phone use in schools.

Activities

1. In your group, discuss the notion of 'affordance' with respect to young people's use of information technologies.
2. If you were developing a humanoid robot, which developmental theory or theories would offer the best guide? Present your ideas to the class.

Websites

A child's TED talk about the need to connect with children in the early years: www.youtube.com/watch?v=aISXCw0Pi94
Lecture on child development in the digital age: www.youtube.com/watch?v=8rTnfCrwloY
What do children understand about the internet? www.abc.net.au/abckids/early-education/what-does-your-child-understand-about-the-internet-/103001188
A digital maturity index: https://theconversation.com/kids-and-the-internet-how-our-new-tool-assesses-childrens-digital-maturity-252825
Lecture by Alison Gopnik: What can young children teach us about AI? www.youtube.com/live/HD__ChnwH-I
Video talk on promoting healthy technology use, by Donna Cross:
www.youtube.com/watch?v=yilBnfY0Umo

Chapter 15

1. Of the various theoretical schools, which do you find most compelling, and why?
2. What holds the most promise as an integrative theory of development?

Activities

1. Do an internet search to find a study of children's development that illustrates transactionalism and explain it to the class.
2. Read this article about Mariane Hedegaard's approach to teaching. Can you suggest how this could be applied to the teaching of developmental psychology at university level? www.researchgate.net/publication/332149249_Mariane_Hedegaard's_Contribution_to_Developmental_Didactics_and_to_Pedagogical_Research_in_the_Brazilian_Context

Websites

Article on the integrative potential of evolutionary psychology: https://link.springer.com/article/10.1007/s12124-023-09783-y
Multisystemic therapy for troubled youth: http://mstservices.com/
Article: very clear description of Overton's scheme re theories and metatheories: www.researchgate.net/publication/284564323_Meta-theories_theories_and_concepts_in_the_study_of_development

Chapter 16

1. What are the implications for developmental theory of the notion that there is more than one 'type of knowledge'?
2. What are the advantages and challenges of working in a multidisciplinary team, and how might the challenges be overcome?

Activities

1. Take Shonkoff's (2000) three cultures of 'science', 'policy' and 'practice' and interview a practitioner regarding how they impact on psychological practice.
2. Imagine you are planning an observational study of children in an early childhood centre. As an individual or in a group, write a list of ethical issues that you would need to consider. Afterwards, read this article and compare its contents with your list: https://aifs.gov.au/research/family-matters/no-96/ethical-research-involving-children

Websites

Scientist-practitioner model set to music: www.youtube.com/watch?v=823ydlMwZAU

Shonkoff's Connecting Science and Community site: https://csc.developingchild.harvard.edu/?_gl=1%2Ap63bxf%2A_ga%2AMTc0MjI2MjkyOS4xNzQ1MDkzMjk1%2A_ga_79B4BMF875%2AMTc0NTA5MzI5NC4xLjEuMTc0NTA5MzQxNy4wLjAuMA

Psychology in multidisciplinary mental health care team: www.youtube.com/watch?v=JbIugUsV05A

Talk on taking a stand by Anna Stetsenko: www.youtube.com/watch?v=nboAHYo2H0c

Glossary

accommodation in Piaget's theory, the modification of mental structures to incorporate new knowledge

ACEs (adverse childhood experiences) potentially traumatic events in childhood, such as abuse, neglect and bereavement

adolescence a term for teenagers derived from the Latin *adolescere*, 'to grow to maturity'

affective processes processes regulating emotional states and elicitation of emotional reactions

affordance opportunity that the environment gives an organism for action

agency the idea that people are active in making decisions about their lives

androcentrism male-centred

applied developmental science use of science to inform developmental interventions

artificial intelligence a set of technologies primarily based on machine learning and deep learning

assimilation in Piaget's theory, the incorporation of new information into the child's existing patterns of thought and behaviour

associationism the view that all knowledge derives from associating one small item of information with another

atomism the idea that the world is made up of particles (ancient Greek and Indian traditions)

attachment the primary social bond between one individual and another

attachment behaviour behaviour that promotes contact and/or proximity of an infant to the caregiver

behaviourism a reductionist approach that focuses entirely on the overt and visible

biological determinism the idea that all human behaviour is determined by biology

biopsychosocial holistic approach to health and development

canalization the idea that there are decision points in development and that proceeding down certain 'channels' makes it difficult or impossible to 'back-track' to take alternative channels

Cartesian dualism Descartes's idea that the mind and body are separate

cascade a sequence of developmental changes with a trigger and high likelihood of reaching a particular endpoint
childism prejudice against children, or advocacy for children as a group
children's voices children's right to be listened to in matters that concern them
classical conditioning learning in which a neutral stimulus elicits a certain response by repeated association with another stimulus that already elicits the response
cofigurative a culture in which children learn from their peers (Mead)
cognition the way we know about the world through the use of thinking, reasoning, learning and remembering
cognitive processes thinking processes involved in the acquisition, organization and use of information
coincidentia oppositorum looking at things from complementary standpoints (Cusa)
coloniality hidden oppressive power structures remaining after a colonized nation's independence
competent infant, the recognition that infants have more capacities than often assumed
complex adaptive systems a way of thinking about systems in terms of dynamism, emergence and self-adjustment in response to events, rather than linear cause-and-effect
concrete operations period Piaget's stage between 7 and 11 years when children begin to understand the relationship between things in the world but still cannot think in abstract terms
conditioned reflex occurs when a previously neutral stimulus acquires the ability to produce a response through association with an unconditioned stimulus (a stimulus that evokes an unlearned response)
connectionism a view of mental structures as subject to logical and mathematical reasoning
conservation in Piagetian theory, the ability to understand that an object or substance retains certain properties, regardless of changes in shape or arrangement
constitutional present at birth
constitutive relationalism Rubinstein's theory that nervous system activity and the material world are inseparable, with the relationship primary
constructive development occurs when a child actively participates by finding personal meaning in a situation, making decisions and sharing viewpoints
constructivism a school of thought in psychology that emphasizes the subjectivity of experience and the role of individuals in actively construing their world
constructivist emphasizing the subjectivity of experience and the role of individuals in actively construing meaning in their world
contextualism the idea that an action only has meaning in relation to its context
critical psychology a movement initiated by Holtzcamp that critically interrogates psychology to promote human emancipation and agency
cultural-historical theory Hedegaard's theory that it is crucial, in education, to examine the interaction between culture/values within different societal institutions in which children participate

decentration a child's ability to look beyond their own viewpoint
decolonization addressing negative effects of western developmental psychology on former colonies
deduction drawing inference from premises by reasoning
defectology term formerly used in Russia for the study and education of those with disabilities
development increase in the functional complexity of an organism; changes that take into account the effect of experience on an individual
developmental psychology the study of the individual from conception to death, or the study of human development in context
developmental resilience science the study of children's adaptation to potentially traumatic circumstances
developmental science as developmental psychology, especially when related to quantitative research and neuropsychology
developmental tasks in Havighurst's theory, tasks that must be completed during certain periods of a person's life
developmentally appropriate practice guiding framework for education of young children, initially based on Piagetian theory
dialectical proceeding by debate between conflicting viewpoints
differentiation increasing ability to perceive different features of the environment
double-dialecticism Riegel's theory that biological, psychological, sociocultural and historical aspects related to the individual are mutually defined and in constant transaction
Dunbar's number the idea that humans can handle a maximum of about 150 stable interpersonal relationships
ego in Freudian theory, the conscious self, the realistic rational part of the personality that mediates between the instinctual demands of the id, and the superego
egocentric speech the young child's self-directed speech that has a controlling function (Vygotsky)
egocentrism the young child's inability to take another's perspective (Piaget)
Electra complex Freud's female version of the Oedipus complex
embodied cognition the idea that cognition is intimately connected with the whole body in its environment, and not just located in the brain
emergence the coming into being of an entity that is greater than the sum of its parts
emerging adulthood period of postindustrial pre-adulthood (ages 18–25)
empiricism the approach to understanding the world which assumes that only information that can be detected physically and measured should count as valid knowledge
enactive representation Bruner's first stage of cognitive development through action
entropy tending towards lower level of organization
epigenetics broadly: the interplay between genetic and ecological conditions to determine the phenotype; narrowly: environmentally induced genetic changes

that do not alter the DNA sequence and can be passed on to subsequent generations

epistemological development development of the child's knowledge base

epistemology the study of the theory of how humans acquire knowledge

ethology the study of the behaviour of animals or humans in natural contexts

evolutionary developmental psychology a school of thought that seeks to explain human development through natural selection, with a focus on mental structures

executive functioning mental processes that aid planning, problem-solving and managing emotions

experiential child refers to the concept that children develop solely as a product of their experience

feminism advocacy of women's experiences, values and contributions, aimed at achieving equality between males and females

FoMO fear of missing out

formal operations period Piaget's fourth stage of cognitive development, from about 11 years of age, when individuals acquire the ability for abstract thought

functionalism the idea that the mind functions to adapt the individual to the environment

genes biological units of heredity involving self-reproducing DNA

genetics the scientific study of heredity

genotype the genetic composition of the organism

Gestalt a school of thought in psychology suggesting that the perceived organized whole is more than the sum of its parts

goodness of fit how well a child's individual proclivities fit with their environment

grounded theory a qualitative research method whereby theory is developed from data

hermeneutics the theory and practice of interpretation

holism the idea that systems possess properties beyond the sum of their parts

iconic representation Bruner's second stage of cognitive development, when thought has become more decoupled from action

id in Freudian theory, that part of the personality containing all of the basic impulses or drives

implementation science the development and application of criteria for accurate implementation of interventions

Indigenous psychology recognition and study of an Indigenous culture in its own terms

induction drawing inferences from data

information processing the taking in, storing and using of information by humans and animals

iniquitous child Wesley's view that children are inherently sinful

integration resolving different aspects (e.g. of cognition or theories) to create deeper understanding

internal working model a temporary schema, especially of human relationships

interpenetration the relationalist view that different aspects of the world are inseparable, but that phenomena can be viewed from different standpoints
intersectionality the effects of belonging to multiple oppressed sectors of society
Lamarck French naturalist who theorized that acquired characteristics could be inherited
logical positivism a scientific philosophy that rejects metaphysical doctrines and bases knowledge on empirical observation and logic
manosphere, the an internet phenomenon that promotes masculinism
masculinism an ideology that regards certain male traits (e.g. self-sufficiency) as superior to others and to feminine traits
masculinities different ideologies of how to be a boy/man
maternal deprivation Bowlby's theory that infants deprived of maternal attention and affection develop abnormally
maturation the changes that occur in an organism as it fulfils its genetic potential
mechanism (a) a causal structure, with the whole the sum of the individual parts; (b) the idea that organisms are like complicated machines with the whole the sum of the parts
metacognition thinking about thinking
metatheory a paradigm, or group of theories with similar core assumptions
méthode clinique Piaget's method of interviewing to help him understand the child's thought processes
modern synthesis, the the unification of Mendelian genetics, population genetics and natural selection
neural network a group of biological or artificial units that transmit signals to one another
neurodiversity the acceptance of people with atypical ways of thinking and learning
neuroplasticity the ongoing ability of the brain to change in response to experience
neurosexism Fine's term for neuropsychological research that is biased in terms of sex
New Sociology of Childhood the idea that children have agency, rather than being passively 'socialized'
niche-picking the idea that a child selects their environment in accord with their own genetic propensities
object relations Klein's psychoanalytic approach to development
Oedipus complex Freudian idea that young boys are in competition with their father, and fear castration
ontogeny the development of an organism from conception
ontology issues of reality or being
operant conditioning learning as a result of reward or punishment
organicism the idea that development is significantly shaped by mutual influence and the patterning of its parts
organismic emphasizing the contribution individuals make to their own development

orthogenetic principle, the Werner's concept that the process of development involves moving from globality to differentiation and hierarchical integration
perceived self-efficacy people's beliefs about their capabilities to produce effects
perezhivanie Vygotsky's idea that the environment is not deterministic for development, but responded to by the filter of the individual's own perspective
personal constructs dynamic bi-polar mental structures that encapsulate an individual's unique perception of the world (Kelly)
phenotype the physical or behavioural traits in an individual that reflect both genetic and environmental factors
positivism a branch of philosophy advocating the methods and principles of the natural sciences in the study of human behaviour
post-feminism the backlash against second-wave feminism in the early 21st century
post-positivism a philosophy of science that aims for objective truth by recognizing and controlling for the effects of biases and values
postfigurative a culture in which children learn from their forebears (Mead)
pragmatism the application of science to solve everyday problems
praxis theory-informed practice
prefigurative a culture in which adults can learn from children (Mead)
pre-operational period Piaget's name for the stage between 2 and 7 years, when children acquire the ability to represent the world using symbols, such as language
quality assurance a system for setting and auditing practice standards
queer theory the study of gender and sexuality within a framework that rejects heterosexuality as 'normal'
reaction range the broadest possible expression of a genotype
recapitulation Haeckel's and Hall's idea that ontogeny mirrors phylogeny
reciprocalism mutual influence between variables
recuperative masculinity politics increased efforts to recover masculinist ideals in the face of feminist progress
reductionism the idea that a phenomenon can be understood in terms of lower level entities
regressive fragmentation the breaking up of developmental psychology into many mini-theories
reinforcement any stimulus that increases the likelihood of a behaviour recurring
relationalism the idea that entities only exist in relation to one another
relations of constraint characterizes the power difference in adult–child relationships
scaffolding the way in which a person skilfully encourages a learner to acquire a new skill or understand a concept, as in Vygotsky's theory
schema in Piagetian terms, a pattern of action or a mental structure (plural: schemes or schemata)
scholasticism worldview of a God-ruled static cosmos

scientism the idea that all true knowledge arises from the use of empirical scientific method
scientist-practitioner model devised in 1950 for training clinical psychologists
self-regulation exercise of influence over one's own motivation, thought processes, emotional states and patterns of behaviour
sensitivity to context the idea that infants vary in how strongly they are affected by their environment, whether positive or negative
sensori-motor period Piaget's first cognitive development stage, in which infants use their senses and motor skills to explore their environment
social brain, the the idea that humans have evolved a large neocortex in order to manage social relationships
Social Cognitive Theory Bandura's theory that emphasizes individual agency and learning by observation
social identity sense of self as a member of social groups
sociobiology a scientific movement based on explaining population-level social behaviours through natural selection, focusing on genes rather than mental structures
SOLES self-organized learning environments
stolen generations term for removal of Indigenous Australian children from their families in the 20th century
Strange Situation, the Ainsworth's protocol for assessing infant/toddler attachment to carer
structuralism Titchener's idea that the mind can be analysed into components
Sturm und Drang storm and stress; free expression of emotions in adolescence
superego in Freudian theory, that part of the personality incorporating the individual's internalized values, corresponding to the injunctions of the parent
symbolic representation Bruner's third stage of cognitive development, when there is understanding that arbitrary symbols, such as language, stand for things
system a complex group of interacting elements that constitute a whole
tabula rasa blank slate
technoference disruption of face-to-face relationships by technology
temperament behaviours that comprise relatively stable characteristics of a person's personality (generally considered constitutional)
theory of mind the ability to impute mental states to self and others
trajectory a developmental path
transactional view of development the view that development is a two-way interaction between child and environment; strictly, that the entities concerned do not exist independently
transitional object object to which young child is strongly attached
transivity in Piaget's theory, the ability to recognize relationships between things in serial order (e.g. increasing in size)
translational science making findings from basic science useful for solving real-world problems
Ubuntu the pan-African perspective that 'I am because you are'

Verstehen understanding a phenomenon from an actor's perspective
virtuous child refers to Rousseau's notion that the child is inherently good
vitalism the idea that life comes from a force that inanimate objects lack (Aristotle)
WEIRD acronym for typical samples in psychological studies: western, educated, industrialized, rich, democratic
zone of proximal development (ZPD) the 'gap' between what individuals can achieve alone and what they can achieve with the help of a more knowledgeable person (Vygotsky)

Index

For Product Safety Concerns and Information please contact our EU representative GPSR@taylorandfrancis.com Taylor & Francis Verlag GmbH, Kaufingerstraße 24, 80331 München, Germany